TROPICOPOLITANS

Post-Contemporary Interventions

Series Editors: Stanley Fish

and Fredric Jameson

TROPICOPOLITANS

Colonialism and Agency, 1688–1804

Srinivas Aravamudan

DUKE UNIVERSITY PRESS

Durham and London 1999

© 1999 Duke University Press
All rights reserved
Printed in the United States of America on acid-free paper ∞
Designed by Amy Ruth Buchanan
Typeset in Adobe Caslon by Tseng Information Systems, Inc.
Library of Congress Cataloging-in-Publication Data
appear on the last printed page of this book.

For my parents, Dorai and Srimathi

Contents

Acknowledgments ix

Introduction:
Colonialism and Eighteenth-Century Studies 1

Virtualizations

ONE Petting Oroonoko 29

TWO Piratical Accounts 71

THREE The Stoic's Voice 103

Levantinizations

FOUR Lady Mary in the *Hammam* 159

FIVE The Despotic Eye and the
Oriental Sublime 190

Nationalizations

SIX Equiano and the Politics of Literacy 233

SEVEN Tropicalizing the Enlightenment 289

Conclusion 326

Notes 333

Index 411

Acknowledgments

I incurred many intellectual and material debts over the long period of writing this book.

First, I want to thank my erstwhile teachers at Cornell University: Jonathan Culler, Laura Brown, Dominick LaCapra, Satya Mohanty, Mary Jacobus, Reeve Parker, and Rick Bogel. To Laura Brown I owe a special thanks, as she remained my preferred reader well after the termination of her institutional obligations toward me. In Paris, I learned significantly from the very different critical approaches of Roger Chartier and Jacques Derrida. I thank Charlotte Sussman and Alok Yadav for being fellow travelers on the road toward a postcolonial eighteenth century, and especially for reading several chapters at short notice and making countless suggestions for improvement. For the gift of enduring friendship that began at Ithaca, I would like to express gratitude to Anne Berger, Patty Chu, Misha Kavka, Richard Klein, Mark Scroggins, and Jim Siegel.

I will always cherish the wonderful intellectual community at the University of Utah, my first job, from 1991 to 1996. Collegiality and friendship were synonymous, especially in my exchanges with Henry Abelove, Geoff Aggeler, Gillian Brown, Robert Caserio, Bruce Haley, Brooke Hopkins, Howard Horwitz, Karen Lawrence, Jim Lehning, Dave Mickelsen, Susan Miller, Wilfred Samuels, Henry Staten, Tom Stillinger, Kathryn Stockton, Steve Tatum, Anand Yang, and Barry Weller. Especially for their friendship I thank Karen Brennan, Lee Rust Brown and Carol Koleman, Norman and Cathy Council, Karen Engle, Jackie Osherow, Ileana Porras, and Deborah Porter. Here at the University of Washington, I am deeply grateful to Marshall Brown, Tom Lockwood, David McCracken, and Priscilla Wald for much support during the finishing stages of this book. I also want to thank Rob Weller for invaluable assistance while grappling with various electronic forms of this text. I wish to thank, even though I am ignorant of their names, the anonymous readers of my manuscript for Duke University Press as well as other anonymous external reviewers who labored over my materials so that they could recommend me for reappointment and tenure. Some of their encouragements and criticisms were passed on to me, and this book has benefited greatly as a result. Reynolds Smith was a terrific editor. He knew exactly when I needed to be pressured and when I needed time. Jean Brady's production advice and Judith Hoover's copyediting were both very helpful.

In addition to staff at the libraries of my respective home institutions, I want to thank those at the British Library and the Bibliothèque Nationale. Both places served for extended periods as homes away from home in cities where I was officeless, although not footloose and fancy-free. For help with images I would like to acknowledge both the above libraries and also the Suzzallo and Allen Libraries at the University of Washington, the British Museum Department of Drawings and Prints, Sotheby's, the National Portrait Gallery, and the Earl of Harrowby. An earlier version of chapter 4 was published in *ELH* and an earlier version of chapter 7 was published in *Diacritics*. I would like to acknowledge the editors of *ELH* and the editorial board of *Diacritics* for permission to reuse these materials.

The greatest thanks, however, go to Ranji Khanna, who, as intellectual companion, spouse, and soulmate, gave me much academic, physical, and moral support. This book may have been possible without her, but it would have been vastly inferior.

Introduction:

Colonialism and Eighteenth-Century Studies

Trope, Tropus, in rhetoric, a word or expression used in
a different sense from what it properly signifies. Or, a
word changed from its proper and natural signification
to another, with some advantage. As, when we say an
ass, for a *stupid person; thunderbolt of war* for a *great captain;* to *wash the black-moor white,* for *a fruitless undertaking.*

—EPHRAIM CHAMBERS, *Cyclopaedia,* 1741

The definition of trope in Chambers's *Cyclopaedia* suggests that
tropological change can be purposeful. Because trope is transitive, it swerves from self-adequation to surplus and, while
doing so, moves from the "proper and natural" to another meaning with
"some advantage." The realization that tropes are efficient and salutary features of language—and indeed that the tenor is changed by the
vehicle—is the advantage that any such illustration of linguistic potential gives an eighteenth-century European reader. As these illustrations
exist only in order to describe how tropes work, they form a potentially open-ended series; the third illustration, with its gratuitous racial
prejudice, can always be replaced by a more neutral example. However,
the significance of the illustration may strike some twentieth-century
readers differently. Sensitized as our age is to the destructive effects of
racial ideologies, a casual metaphor concerning the fruitlessness of epidermal laundering would be seen as inappropriate by a contemporary
lexicographer. Given the restricted context of the definition, it is certain
that such illustrations would be eschewed as distracting or inflammatory

in a modern dictionary. However, coming to us from different cultural and historical moments, such illustrations of trope perform a function likely unforeseen at the time of their writing. From a contemporary critical perspective, what is striking is not so much the trope's technical sufficiency but its display of eighteenth-century European prejudices concerning Africans. To be sure, we can condemn its overt racialism, but that would be a political objection to the choice and context of the illustration rather than its undeniable tropological structure.[1]

If we let this example get under our skins—so to speak—and if we were then to assess its technical sufficiency, we would find that the third illustration, a metaphor, consists of a concrete vehicle, *wash the blackmoor white*, representing a more abstract tenor, *fruitless undertaking*. We may thus begin to interrogate the community of readers that this illustration addresses. Who would want to wash the blackamoor white, and who would be in the position of realizing that such an act was a fruitless undertaking? With its obligatory racial assumptions, the signifying structure of the third illustration involves at least two mentalities. One is the aspiration of the racially minded progressive or assimilationist, who, having assumed that in all contexts white is desirable over black, attempts to render the black skin white. This attitude, reminiscent of Michael McKeon's definition of "naïve empiricism," interprets racial debasement as corrigible through amelioration.[2] However, alongside this very attitude is the conservative one of "extreme scepticism," recognizing the attempted washing as revelatory of a *fruitless undertaking*. The trope, therefore, encapsulates an attitudinal shift. It guards a collective memory, gained through cumulative empirical experiment, that the epidermis cannot be changed through washing, only in order to process this into something of a moral lesson. In collective terms, experimental observation has led to experiential truth. However, the truth is gained from the processing of a failure that resulted from an incorrect hypothesis. To remember this failure as predictable is, in fact, to succeed in a different way, as memories of failure perform salutary work.

The evocative paradoxes generated by this illustration of trope in Chambers's *Cyclopaedia* vex us even as they teach us, in the manner of Swiftian satire. Nowadays, for literary criticism, colonial discourse —and its historical contexts—is often the reference point when the blackamoor appears in literary representations. Paradoxically, this development is also a sign that scholars would like to seize a tropologi-

cal opportunity with the hope of *some advantage*, seeking a renewed
critical purchase on literary texts and their historical contexts. Reflecting on the impact of colonialism, perhaps, could lead us to a fuller,
more accurate, and more responsible account of the eighteenth century
and its participation in origin narratives of global modernity. Alternatively, there is also the danger that such an act is equivalent to *fruitless
undertaking*. Can an investigation of colonialism transform eighteenth-
century studies, or does mentioning it merely signify and revisit a traumatic impasse or blockage?

The illustration I began with foregrounds racial typologies. If the
image of failed epidermal whitewashing were used to suggest the abstract idea of *fruitless undertaking*, it would often result in the separation
of the trope away from the process of making meaning. In ordinary
usage, differences between the tenor and vehicle are suppressed in favor
of contingent similarities. However, while metaphor is the assimilation
of two objects to each other, an expanded focus on the metaphorical vehicle may result in our asking more searching questions about residual
differences. Who exactly do these so-called blackamoors refer to, and
how were they treated? Why were they the object of these randomly
pathological perceptions in the European eighteenth century? Why are
coeval inhabitants of this era considered objects to be acted upon rather
than acting subjects? What is the significance of the illustration's reliance on a preexisting cultural knowledge of failed efforts to whiten the
black? And how does asking and answering these questions improve our
understanding of literature and culture?

The trope of "Ethiop" or blackamoor as incorrigible other goes
back to 570 B.C. Later, Erasmus's *Adagia* proverbializes Aesop's fable:
Αἰθίοπα οὐ λευκαίνεται (the Ethiopian cannot be whitened). In 1565,
an English emblem book depicts under the title "Impossible Things," a
black man being washed by two white men.[3] Bunyan glosses this image
in *The Pilgrim's Progress*: "they saw one Fool and one Want-wit washing
of an Ethiopian with intention to make him white, but the more they
washed him, the blacker he was." Richardson's Anna Howe writes to
Clarissa concerning Lovelace's Rosebud intrigue, "Mr. Lovelace comes
out with so much advantage from this inquiry, that were there the least
room for it, I should suspect the whole to be a plot set on foot to wash
a blackamoor white."

As external other that preexisted unsuccessful incorporation through whitening, the tropological blackamoor becomes the sign of *failed whitening* or *unachievable whiteness*. By way of a metalepsis the supplementary signification of "failure"—a negative outcome of an attempted action of whitening—is exuded by the signifier as if it were a primary attribute. *Blackness* begins to signify *unchangeability*, just as much as this *unchangeability* suggests, in turn, *uselessness:* hence, fruitless undertaking. By associative reduction, the blackamoor thereby lapses into the stereotype of *unchangeable uselessness*. The signifier, in this case, an empiricist desire to act upon the other, through the verb *wash*, is linked to a knowledge of the impending failure of the attempted whitewash.

This subtle dynamic of both historical and tropological *denigration* leads me to explain the neologism in my title, which activates the tropological in the tropicopolitan. According to the OED, the word tropicopolitan exists as an adjective used mainly in natural history, describing species dominant in the tropical regions; the quoted examples are from botanical discourse of the late nineteenth century. With a portmanteau etymology that combines the idea of *tropic* with that of *cosmopolitan*, tropicopolitan is a term currently languishing in its proper and natural signification and one that can be used to some advantage. Indeed, there is a need for this word, if we apply it as both noun and adjective paralleling terms such as *metropolitan* and *cosmopolitan* (indeed, language purists may take me to task for converting the adjective into a noun and proceeding toward polysyllabic infelicity). However, I would like to propose the term tropicopolitan as a name for the colonized subject who exists both as fictive construct of colonial tropology *and* actual resident of tropical space, object of representation *and* agent of resistance. In many historical instances, tropicopolitans—the residents of the tropics, the bearers of its marks, and the shadow images of more visible metropolitans—challenge the developing privilege of Enlightenment cosmopolitans.

Yet tropicopolitans are also the vehicle of the metaphor that inaugurates the self-valorization of the metropolitan subject.[4] Famously, for instance, Jean-Paul Marat's *Les chaînes de l'esclavage* (1774) discusses the metaphorical enslavement of the French at a moment that is the pinnacle of plantation slavery. In his antimonarchical tract, the term *esclavage* is used principally to refer to the condition of the French citizenry rather than that of the slaves on the colonial plantations. Of course, the etymology of *slavery* refers back to the particular servitude of Slavs rather than the later history of the commodification and enforced transportation of Africans, which in the eighteenth century, it may be suggested by some, is the proper and natural signification of slavery. In this case, the proper and natural signification is itself the result of having forgotten an earlier ethnogeography. Such tropological recursions—from ethnic-linguistic particularization (Slav), to generalized condition (slavery), to subsequent historical and geographic deduction concerning those in that condition (Africans), to metaphorical application in a different national context (Marat's French)—allow slavery to trope, or turn through various contexts. However, the negative position suggested by an unincorporated and unincorporable remainder also allows tropes to be reappropriated by resistant positions and redeployed by the agency that comes from those positions. When the abolitionist motto, "Am I not a man and a brother?" began to appear on Josiah Wedgwood's pottery as the utterance of an African-looking body, the slave in the representation was interpreted as deserving emancipation, suggesting a potentially fruitful undertaking to free the black body, rather than the fruitless one of attempting to bleach it. Such reappropriated signifiers operate as catachreses, described by Gayatri Chakravorty Spivak as "concept metaphors for which no historically adequate referent may be advanced from postcolonial space."[5] Tropicopolitans embody this tension between representational surplus and referential lack. Literary stereotypes of blackamoors vastly differ from worlded historical beings, and yet these stereotypes are made accountable by the tyranny of historical and literary tradition and their constant revisions and reinscriptions. Tropicopolitans are evidence bolstering Salman Rushdie's claim that the empire doesn't just write back, but does so "with a vengeance."[6] Tropicopolitans thus transgress their prescribed function and reanimate cultural discourses in response to different contexts and intentions.

Despite the fact that most linguistic change could be attributed to contingent and unmotivated shift sign changes certainly can also reflect individual or collective intentions. Intentionalist accounts of such change are one small part of all motivated change. I characterize motivated instances of such change within colonialist contexts as tropicalizations. By motivated, I would like to suggest a gamut of causal factors, including discursive, historical, and psychoanalytical determinations in addition to the conscious intentions of agents. Tropicalization means

Introduction

5

a tropological revision of discourses of colonial domination (something that can happen immediately and directly as well as retroactively and indirectly.) Such a revision is ultimately a contestation of European rule by tropicopolitans, inhabitants of the torrid zones that were the objects of Europe's colonial ambition. Tropicalization has been used, in a more literal sense, to describe the acclimation of flora, fauna, and even machinery to warmer habitats. The same could be said for ideas, habits, and attitudes that, in the eighteenth century, were traded back and forth as much as populations and produce. In this sense, tropicalization is similar to Mary Louise Pratt's definition of transculturation (modifying earlier uses of these concepts by Cuban Fernando Ortiz and Uruguayan Angel Rama).[7] Tropicalization and transculturation suggest acts of cultural transformation, or "going native," in various colonial "contact zones." Or, as Frances Aparicio and Susana Chávez-Silverman suggest, tropicalizations occur in "plural forms and multiple subject locations" and function as "a tool that foregrounds the transformative cultural agency of the subaltern subject."[8] Calling this subaltern a tropicopolitan in a manner that foregrounds the tropological along with the tropical and the geocultural is fitting, especially as recent theories have reified the subaltern as resisting native and radical other who is completely outside the discourses of domination. On the contrary, a search for the subaltern mostly reveals a subject who is an idealized and rediscovered metonymy of European repressions and projections, even while critics find it necessary to reaffirm this subject as the site of resistance to hegemonic practices.[9] Signaling the tropologically provisional and the actually existing, and emphasizing the catachrestical structure of colonial representations, tropicopolitans function as residents of the tropics subjected to the politics of colonial tropology, who correspondingly seize agency through contesting language, space, and the language of space that typifies justifications of colonialism. Yet, like the nymphs and reapers of the masque scene in Shakespeare's *The Tempest* that "heavily vanish" when their Neapolitan spectators try to grasp them, tropicopolitans are projections as well as beings leaving stubborn material traces even as they are discursively deconstructed (4.1.138, stage direction).

Let us consider a visual representation of blackamoors, in William Blake's etching for John Gabriel Stedman's *Narrative of a five years' expedition against the revolted Negroes of Surinam in Guiana on the wild coast of South America from the years 1772 to 1777*, published in 1796 (Fig. 1). The

Figure 1 William Blake, *Group of Negros, as imported to be sold for slaves,* from John Gabriel Stedman, *Narrative of a five years' expedition against the revolted Negroes of Surinam in Guiana* (1796). (Special Collections Division, University of Washington Libraries)

tableau shows the disembarking captives pointing and being directed to a location out to the left of the frame, on their way to a slave market to be auctioned and presumably then onward to a plantation. The slave lot is a typical one, composed of mothers, infants, children, and adolescents as well as able-bodied male slaves. The overdressed white slave driver stands between the geometrical masts of the ships still visible in port, indicating that the tortuous Middle Passage has just ended, even as the wrenching disruptions of further separations of the survivors from each other, and the brutality of life on the plantation, are still to follow for the captives. The movement of the slaves, diagonally from right to left, is also a movement in time, from past to future. The tableau is stylized, the bodies are in unison despite their casual arrangement (notice the parallel lines of the slaves' limbs), and the dog snapping at the heels of the largest male slave along with the bushes in the foreground testify to a skilled pictorial harmony that redirects the view. Although other plates in Stedman's narrative show the horrors of slave life, this particular image by Blake is something of a tropological transition. Obviously, there is more than just one audience. Knowing Blake's abolitionist sympathies, we may want to read this image as an indictment that waves the magic wand of representation even as it acknowledges tacitly that the real horrors that remain unrepresented are off to the left. Even as this freeze-frame shows the slaves moving away as directed, expressing a mixture of emotions ranging from sorrow, apprehension, disbelief, to perhaps even a positive expectation as others are also pointing to the destination, the tallest male slave, his hands tied behind his back, naked except for a loincloth, looks straight at the viewer, possibly in reproach. Yet, on the other hand, his body is the most stylized and eroticized, and his sidelong gaze rivets the viewer. The viewer is implicated in a number of ways, as the display of the bodies in the auction was also a marketing exercise. Is the viewer here in the position of an eager purchaser, rushing to the port to greet the arriving party in order to make a choice pick? From the viewpoint of a purchaser, the male slave is very desirable property, and yet his unrelenting gaze suggests that he is going to be the least tractable member of the lot. The male slave's gaze can be read as indicating valor, insolence, or rebelliousness. The herding gesture of the slave driver is ambivalent, partly indexical and partly obfuscatory. His actions and his professional role suggest that he must support slavery, but is it possible to read a hint of apology in his gesture? The slaver appears to point in the direction of the life the slaves have to lead just as much as commanding the direction they are to physically move, but it is also possible that he is hurrying them offstage away from the scene of representation and abolitionist reproach. The triangulation of gazes among the viewer, the slave driver, and the slave who returns the gaze suggests a complicity, a shared understanding of that which lies to the left of the image, and which remains unspoken, but which is the animating principle of those gazes. Inside the triangle of gazes is a young mother and infant, also looking at the viewer, and also pointing left (her right). Young, nubile, and attractive, she is a prime target for purchasers who desire a mistress and also a reproducer. Is it possible that she is pointing out the male slave who is the father of her child and with whom she hopes to remain? If so, the exchange of gazes between her, the viewer, and the male slave becomes instantly clear. What we may have liked to read as political reproach in the eyes of the male slave has collapsed into the more predictable narrative of sexual desire, jealousy, and impending tragedy. Earlier, Stedman tells the story of his passion for the mulatto slave Joanna, whom he "rescues" from ill-treatment. Whatever the complicities conjured up by this image, they would have to be decoded by purchaser and abolitionist alike.

Non-Europeans in eighteenth-century literary representations are often, although by no means always, inhabitants of the torrid zone, tropicopolitans, like the male slave whose gaze challenges the imperial presumptions of cosmopolitans. However, representations here should not be read as politics *tout court*, but as vicariously so. As colonialist representation features an unstable rhetorical mixture of geographical, historical, and literary apprehensions of the colonized, such a politics manqué works in the manner of the fantastic and the grotesque, the romance and the gothic. Reading for tropicalizations tactically allows the discussion of a wide range of representational and rhetorical techniques used by metropolitan cultures (sometimes erratically, at other moments systematically) to comprehend the colonized.

The politics of representational language, in the margins of the text as well as in the exchange of gazes, is no small consequence of the accidents of empire, and it behooves us to attend to the filiations and affiliations that crisscross the study of colonialist representations with multiple threads. English has spread to the far corners of the globe and has spawned a huge Anglophone literature in its wake, but literary history has remained a largely nationalist enterprise, identifying, celebrating, and occasionally criticizing England as a cultural origin. Literary histories have to be updated, at the very least, by *geocultural* histories of production, reception, and institutionalization. The eighteenth and nineteenth centuries, which vastly expanded literacy and the culture of print, correspondingly need a scholarship that reimagines its communities of readers rather than one that takes those communities to be already imagined. For this reason, I would especially like to emphasize the critical stakes of tropicalization as retroactive change. Motivated change includes but is not limited to those changes effected by various forms of political and cultural agency. No doubt, agency refers to the active resistance by tropicopolitans and their metropolitan allies to discourses and practices that silenced and disempowered various groups, groups who were subjected to immediate economic and political hegemony, as well as the long-term ecological, social, and cultural repercussions of colonialism and imperialism. It is much more likely that we now interpret the Blake etching with abolitionist indignation, but the mutual complicities it exposes go beyond the stability we desire from it.

We should be correspondingly wary of another form of washing the black-moor white, a rendering of the tropicopolitan as metropolitan, or even as cosmopolitan, something that is often the indirect result of the process that merely includes Britain's others as subordinates in some larger nationalist metanarrative. This is why I intend the title *Tropicopolitans* as something of a rhyming (but ironic and parodic) contrast to Linda Colley's *Britons*. Colley's book is one of the most effective metanarratives of recent times, claiming that the forging of British national identity occurred from an internal Protestant dynamic. While staying on literary terrain, *Tropicopolitans* indirectly contests Colley's parthenogenetic account of eighteenth-century British nationalism. Xenophobia, colonialism, orientalism, and racism had just as large a role to play in the constitution of national identity as the admittedly important category of religion.[10]

The self-consciousness exhibited by tropicopolitans toward the colonial contexts and uses of literacy also needs to be addressed. Reading resistance—now a familiar kind of ethical literary criticism—is supplemented here with accounts of the resistance to reading as well as to literacy itself. However, when it comes to deducing agency retroactively, tropicalization itself undergoes a shift from denotation to connotation, as well as from a proper and natural meaning to other meanings with some advantage. Agency can take other forms and is an extremely complex category to read *into* texts. When we do find agency at work, it is never simply a matter of the important postcolonial phenomenon that Salman Rushdie and others have characterized as "the empire writes back."[11] If that were my only model, this book would have had to rely entirely on tropicalizations by later eighteenth-century figures such as Olaudah Equiano or Toussaint Louverture. Those figures are indeed crucially relevant—as the last two chapters of the book attest—but agency is much more than conscious replies to colonialist ideologies, and replies to the larger economic and political exploitation that underwrote those ideologies, crafted by literary respondents and political activists. The task of recognizing agency is considerably complicated by the larger function of *genealogy* that Michel Foucault derives from Nietzsche. Rejecting "the metahistorical deployment of ideal significations and indefinite teleologies," genealogy fashions a "history of the present," demanding "relentless erudition" and "a vast accumulation of source material" along with a simultaneous abandonment of the "search for 'origins.' "[12] Such a genealogical investigation of eighteenth-century literature as *colonial archive* relies on the method of retroactive reading, through the deferred action that Freud calls *Nachträglichkeit*, as well as the surplus signification and action yielded by catachrestic structures such as the blackamoor, the tropicopolitan, or even this figure's more positivist form, the slave. Freud's definition of deferred action involves the manner in which memory reformulates trauma into the experience of agency over the past. Responding to the inherited trauma of colonialism, tropicopolitans revise their "memory-traces" and the colonial archive in a manner that reanimates the past and gives it the psychical and material rationale, and effectiveness, of agency.[13] The literary eighteenth century that this book tackles is perhaps like Chambers's accretion of random tropes, a series of memory-traces, all of which exhibit tropological (here tropicopolitan) functions. I deal here with a constellation of texts, chosen for tactical reasons, that demonstrate the tropicopolitan connotations of metropolitan denotation. With this task

Introduction

in mind, I have eschewed treating the period as a continuous tradition in need of obedient conservation, instead fragmenting the continental shelf of literature before me into manageable textual archipelagoes.

By interpreting a series of texts concerned with colonialist representation and anticolonial agency within the eighteenth-century literary corpus, this book tracks tropicopolitans as troublesome tropes that—and colonial subjects who—interrupt the monologue of nationalist literary history. Such an encounter between postcolonial theory and eighteenth-century studies is, in disciplinary terms, a continuation of earlier work on imperialism and literature in this period by scholars such as C. L. R. James, Edward Said, John Barrell, Laura Brown, Peter Hulme, Christopher Miller, Mary Louise Pratt, Moira Ferguson, and Felicity Nussbaum, to name just a few.[14] By synthesizing postcolonial criticism and literary studies on a terrain that is partly recognizable to both specialties, these scholars have nudged their peers toward a recognition of the period's discursive complicity with imperialism. A newer, more pluralized eighteenth-century studies is now possible, indeed, is becoming a critical reality.[15]

However, until a decade ago, a Whiggish teleology on the significance of the long eighteenth century prevailed. Felicity Nussbaum and Laura Brown then described this orthodoxy as follows: "The prominence of political analysis in modern historiography has continued to support the stereotype of pervasive and long-term stability in the period, a political stability linked to an image of equivalent social and cultural coherence, to a sense of an unchallenged class hierarchy represented and perpetuated in a literary culture where aesthetics, ethics, and politics perfectly mesh."[16] There is enough evidence that the earlier inertia resulted from a unique combination of a formalist-historicist approach to literature with a partisan consensus concerning its political significance.[17] The recently revisionist critical approaches to the British "new eighteenth century"—now fast becoming mainstream strategies of disciplinary renewal—focus on teasing out the implications of ideologies of empire and domesticity, authorship and aesthetics. This shift in focus is paralleled by disciplinary exposé, such as William H. Epstein's careful reconstruction of the cold war milieu of eighteenth-century studies.[18] Such work has demystified the pretended political neutrality of disciplinary practices as traditionally conceived. Meanwhile, the ready assimilation of feminist concerns (after their somewhat late arrival) has been criticized cogently by Donna Landry.[19] While attention to political forms of criticism in general, and to the dynamic between colonialism and culture in particular, is to be considered typical of both Renaissance and Victorian studies today, eighteenth-century studies is now also coming to terms with the recent growth of literary criticism written from a perspective that recognizes the constitutive role of imperialism. Though the economic, political, and cultural consequences of imperialism, modernization, and nationalism are both global and local, it can still be argued that the central cluster of historical problems that began this process finds some important sources in the European eighteenth century. As British literature and culture participated vigorously in colonialist cultural justifications in the eighteenth century, the period becomes a prime target for postcolonial interpretation.

However, until recently, the obsessions of postcolonial studies concerned the immediate implications of a *pouvoir-savoir* nexus. Edward Said's *Orientalism*, for instance, claims that its animating purpose, following Raymond Williams, is the " 'unlearning' of 'the inherent dominative mode.' " Said hoped to undo the Manichaean oppositions between "Occident" and "Orient," even as he helped Third World readers comprehend "the *strength* of Western cultural discourse, a strength too often mistaken as merely decorative or 'superstructural.' "[20] Postcolonial criticism derives its ethical sustenance from proposing an engaged scholarship—such as Said's or Spivak's—that reflects on global inequities and interconnectedness, thereby suggesting progressive alternatives to the continuing elaboration of Western political and cultural hegemony.

The discovery, documentation, and theorization of resistance to ideologies of dominance—"the unlearning of the inherent dominant mode" mentioned by Said—takes many forms other than the violent one of armed, or unarmed, physical opposition to oppression that Frantz Fanon urges on his readers in his anticolonial manifesto, *The Wretched of the Earth*.[21] Violent insurrection certainly is one justifiable form of political and cultural agency, but there are many other options for tropicopolitans to manipulate the ideological circumstances of their situation and to move from fatal histories to empowering ones. Talking back or writing back as a mode of resistance is one that literary scholars understandably privilege. However, although a focus on literary questions has its disciplinary benefits, the question of agency should not be collapsed into celebrating the acquisition of literacy. Some of the chapters in this book, especially those on Olaudah Equiano and Toussaint Louverture, analyze the distortions created when presenting literacy as cultural evolution. Postcolonial criticism ought not to reify agency from the position of *other* or *subaltern* in the manner of its precursor, decolonization discourse. Rather, in an analysis of cultural and historical texts, the postcolonial critic is inclined to find resistance through acts of reading, transculturation, and hybridity as well as from those of separation, opposition, and rejection. Culture is, after all, a constantly changing process rather than a prepackaged product swallowed whole by generations of consumers. Rather than reifying *a* voice of resistance or dissent, the act of reading makes available the differing mechanisms of agency that traverse texts, contexts, and agents themselves.

Though some critics would have us choose between hybridity and authenticity, or collaboration and opposition, the messy legacies of empire do not always afford such clear-cut choices. One manifestation of agency may look like assimilation, incremental change, or liberal reformism. Aphra Behn or Mary Wortley Montagu, women who became authors in this period, can often be dismissed as colonialists despite their sympathetic portraits of Britain's others, or naïvely celebrated as progressive even when it is clear that they share in many ruling-class assumptions that compromise and delimit their qualified sympathies for these others. Swift, notoriously misogynistic and racially prejudiced in his writings, is nonetheless an early anticolonial voice in texts such as *The Drapier's Letters*. Similarly, Olaudah Equiano, a manumitted slave who rose to some prominence in late-eighteenth-century British society, went along with various colonialist projects for the resettlement of the black poor as a productive labor force. Most famously, Toussaint Louverture, the legendary liberator of Haiti from the French, opposed the scrapping of the sugar plantation system that had propelled the colony of Saint-Domingue into its economic and political prominence for European interests. For all these reasons, none of these figures can be readily characterized as colonialist villains or anticolonial heroes. What standards of purity and which anachronistic litmus tests could determine such characterizations? Rather than use ethical criticism as a form of social therapy, where reading anachronistically leads to rhetorics of condemnation and celebration concerning the political values of texts or the attitudes expressed by their authors, we should identify the institutions and reading practices that determine these shifts of value.

As a result, tropicalization also exploits the open-ended possibilities of discursive redeployment. Such a tactic has been assigned different theoretical names by the practitioners of postcolonial criticism: colonial mimicry, readerly resistance, or catachresis. As I have already indicated, tropicalization is a reworking of colonialist discourse through revisions by postcolonial agents or tropicopolitans; the deployment of newer reading formations toward the middle of the eighteenth century and after; and the continued retroactive creation of postcolonial genealogies, including my own, that further deform the phenomena, in the manner of a Freudian Nachträglichkeit, or deferred action. If we move from examining the motives of authors to documenting the uses of texts, we find that literary representations—such as Behn's Oroonoko, Defoe's Friday, and Johnson's Rasselas, and others by authors such as Swift, Montagu, and Equiano—can speak to tropicopolitans across different continents, providing a literary lingua franca for political or cultural association. In the manner of any lingua franca, colonialist literature becomes a staging point for ideological contestation by many forces that are asynchronous and multilocal. It is through cultural and political deformation that colonialist tropologies become tropicalizations. As we know, some of the best of what is known as postcolonial literature is written in terms of explicit response to colonialist literature—whether by Chinua Achebe, Salman Rushdie, or Assia Djebar. The empire, as we also know nowadays, writes back very quickly, and not just in terms of literary repartee. The postal delivery system is being replaced by the accelerated logic of facsimile and electronic transmissions. Such a development—whether in terms of cultural politics by way of the Booker Prize or through the Internet—may, with the help of Deleuze and Guattari, be called the deterritorialization and reterritorialization of imperialist cliché by the mechanism of the book.[22]

It should therefore be the aim of literary criticism to relocate these moments of rhetorical reappropriation to multiple contexts, both present and past, even while the developments I sketched preclude the possibility of writing a unified history of reading practices. The readerly contexts of eighteenth-century colonialist tropologies are undoubtedly important but ought not to be privileged as definitive, especially when tropicalization is an open-ended process that reconfigures those contexts. As Jacques Derrida has amply shown, it is the laborious task of reading that transforms texts rather than any magical proclamation that they are always already deconstructed. An exploitable ambivalence is often present in textuality, but the seduction of semantic richness should be tempered by a knowledge of the institutional nature of reading, whether past or present. Tropicalization is intimately connected to a reading that happens not merely through the quaint mechanisms of literary history but also in the larger developments of cultural politics and the historically bounded horizon of the technology of literacy. For this reason, tropicalizations can only be elicited by renewed literary contextualization, speculative reconstruction, and critical elaboration. These acts of reading are interpretive interventions that unsettle canon formation.

My deployment of postcolonial theory is a catachrestic gesture in an era of late-capitalist and neocolonialist entrenchment. Decolonization has not been much more than a nominal process. The management of former colonies by corrupt local elites and the failure of Third World nationalisms to solve the pressing economic and social problems that these countries inherited when the colonizers departed have led in turn to the competition of emerging markets for global capital, along with the general decline of socialism and the eradication of local cultures and ecologies. To consider that we are beyond colonialism in any way is to misrecognize—dangerously—the world's current realities. However, despite its referential inaccuracy, the catachresis *postcolonial* signals an unachieved possibility or a critical space that could eventually make way for a lived economic, political, and cultural one, in the very manner that the words *liberty* and *equality* energized a host of post-Enlightenment intellectuals, and *socialism* a range of nineteenth- and twentieth-century thinkers and activists.

This plural definition of tropicalization is, no doubt, in the hope of some theoretical and disciplinary advantage. With the help of specific readings of eighteenth-century texts, I characterize three kinds of tropicalization—virtualization, levantinization, and nationalization. These three definitions possess the major features of tropicalization that I already outlined but are differentiated from each other according to the contexts of their deployment.

Although notions concerning virtuality, virtual reality, and virtualization are very topical nowadays, they are perhaps too readily associated with cyberspace and video and computer technology. Some of these postmodern technological innovations are not necessarily "new" epistemologies but rather more like uncanny and belated recognitions. The rise of hypertext has renewed our awareness that print literacy was also a technology; virtual reality machines also make us aware that nations work along similar lines. The term virtualization describes colonialist representations that acquire malleability because of a certain loss of detail, a process that enables readier identification and manipulation by readers, thus putting the trope of the tropicopolitan into motion toward an open-ended future. In his adaptation of Deleuze's philosophy for an understanding of postcolonial cinema, David Rodowick argues that "time as series"—the juxtaposition of several pasts in the present—describes how a conceptual structure that is "not yet" summons a people who are "not yet." Virtualizations work as retroactive focalizations of postcolonial "becoming-other." Virtualizations found and identified within a colonial archive reveal the narrative of a "line of flight" from colonialist representation to postcolonial revision.[23]

Virtualizations possess a high degree of discursive malleability. The virtualizations of colonialist and anticolonial representations in the first section of *Tropicopolitans* can be related to different forms of anticolonial agency. Behn's narrative's eroticized portrait of Oroonoko, Defoe's evocation of a seafaring and piratical milieu, and the diverse applications of neostoicism indicate that a number of tropicalizations and resistances were already under way in the early eighteenth century. Yet these representations are virtualized in ways that allow them to be recuperated by "histories of the present," as sources for retroactive identification and projections of counterhegemonic tradition. Such virtualizations do not simply dissolve back into their contexts as much historicist eighteenth-century criticism is wont to let them.

The first three chapters of this book deal with different examples of virtualization. The legend of Oroonoko in texts by Aphra Behn and Thomas Southerne, Defoe's depictions of accounting and piracy in *Robinson Crusoe* and *Captain Singleton,* and the vocabulary of neostoicism in writers such as Addison, Swift, and Gordon and Trenchard compose various chapters in the first section. In the manner of both Moira Ferguson's and Laura Brown's books on eighteenth-century colonialist literature, I begin with a discussion of Behn's novella, *Oroonoko, or the Royal*

Slave (1688). Ferguson argues, interestingly, that *Oroonoko* heralds "the birth of a paradigm" of colonialist representation. However, unlike Ferguson's teleological realization of this paradigm in the abolitionist writings of the later eighteenth century, it is my argument that abolitionist recuperations of *Oroonoko* represent just one feature, albeit an important one, of colonialist tropology. By way of an exposition of the intertextual dialogue between Behn's novella and its dramatic adaptation by Thomas Southerne (1695), my focus is instead on the implications of a developing incommensurability in this type of representation. Limited kinds of anticolonial identification occur in these texts through analogies with discourses of domesticity that involve pets as well as women. However, such constructions parodically undercut what they are meant to serve.

Chapter 2 investigates another colonialist paradigm through Defoe's well-known elaborations of piracy and criminal narrative, especially in his novels *Robinson Crusoe* (1719) and *Captain Singleton* (1720). Working within received, historically inflected accounts of Defoe's depiction of the upward mobility of the mercantilist and lower-middle classes, I discuss textual evidence of antimercantilist proletarian resistance and the hegemonic conversion of those resistances by Defoe's narratives. In his focus on what Mary Louise Pratt has called "the contact zone," Defoe keeps the reader aware of colonizers and colonized in the process of mutually constituting as well as deforming each other's identities.

The section on virtualization is rounded off with a chapter on neo-stoicism and anticolonialism, one that enables a fresh reading of Joseph Addison's *Cato* (1713), Swift's *Gulliver's Travels* (1726, 1735) and *The Drapier's Letters* (1725-26), and Gordon and Trenchard's *Cato's Letters* (1720-23). Moving rapidly among three regional contexts of the reception of early-eighteenth-century Cato discourse—English, Anglo-Irish, and American—allows me to focus on the colonialist and anticolonial implications of English neostoicism. Addison's *Cato* starts off a fashionable critique that provides, whether Addison intended it to or not, an idealist alternative to the dominant discourse of bourgeois mercantilism. Swift exploits a coinage crisis to generate anticolonial intellectual coin. At the same time, Gordon and Trenchard's *Cato's Letters* popularizes Cato discourse in relation to anxiety about colonialist and mercantilist expansion, focusing on economic disasters such as the South Sea Bubble in order to propagate a generalized republicanist discourse.

Virtualizations occur in very different literary contexts, yet it is the elaboration of colonialist ideologies in these various contexts that unifies them. Piracy, plantation slavery, and neostoicist discourse are mobile discursive resources for writers who depict colonialism and its consequences. These contexts yield a representational surplus with anticolonial potential. However, this surplus is not always discerned by the writers themselves, because virtualization is frequently an inference made from the reading situation, when we read with a view to uncovering, retroactively, the mechanisms of agency. Although virtualization is a feature of the earlier moment in eighteenth-century colonialist representation, when ethnic stereotypes were more readily interchangeable, its fluidity connotes something like a textual idealism. Virtualization is always, to a lesser or greater degree, an enabling feature of tropicalization. Any kind of tropicalization cannot take place without some degree of ideological fluidity, intellectual license, and cross-identification, all of which are various characteristics of virtualization. In its most debased form, virtualization could appear as *nominal* or *ideal* anticolonialism rather than a historically actualized variety, a false memory syndrome rather than real memory-traces.

Another kind of tropicalization, one that concerns the middle section of the book and its two chapters, is the category of levantinization. Levantinization is a creative response to orientalisms as a plural rather than singular category and the specifically dynamic interactions of European culture with Islamic ones that go back at least to the Crusades. Levantinization starts off as a vehicle for cultural and anthropological perceptions of the Levant: the Mediterranean, Asia Minor, and North Africa. The relativist and rivalrous definitions that overdetermine Europe's perceptions of its eastern and southern boundaries are crucial to the contextualization and further elaboration of levantinization. Focusing on travel and aesthetics, Mary Wortley Montagu's *Letters from the Levant* (better known as *The Embassy to Constantinople* or *The Turkish Letters*) demonstrates levantinization as Montagu's hybrid synthesis of feminist and orientalist impulses. Montagu's letters are based on travels conducted between 1716 and 1718, when Edward Wortley was appointed ambassador to the Ottoman Empire, but were published just after Lady Mary's death in 1763. Montagu's appreciation of Turkish aristocratic women reads female agency as occurring within an autonomous space, a construction of utopian levantinization within the social restrictions of Ottoman high culture. Montagu's praise of Turkish culture is not unlike the more benign biases of cultural relativism typical of the anthropologist's stance. She especially fixes on the arbitrariness of norms in a manner that heralds the advent of European secularism and its stronger associate phenomenon, dechristianization.

Chapter 5, on Burke's *A Philosophical Enquiry into the Sublime and the Beautiful* (1757, 1759), Samuel Johnson's *The History of Rasselas, Prince of Abissinia* (1759), and William Beckford's *Vathek* (1786), analyzes representations of the sublime and oriental despotism in the eighteenth century, documenting levantinization's extended reach. A sustained meditation on the phantasm of oriental despotism unites all three texts. The trope of abacination, or blinding, dominates orientalist discourse that foregrounds the presumed absolutist power of the monarch and the "blind" obedience of the subject. The obsession with happiness in Johnson's parable and the corresponding focus on terror in Burke's disquisition on the sublime and on bathos in Beckford's novel ensue from a tropological process of overplay or debasement in relation to orientalist figments—through managed romance in Johnson, referential cancellation in Burke, and debased spectralization in Beckford. The philosophy of the sublime, central to these texts, expresses an anxiety concerning the phantasm of oriental despotism.

This specific anxiety operates behind Burke's willful characterizations of the East India Company as orientalist in the Hastings impeachment trials, alongside his candid acknowledgment of oriental despotism as entirely false when used to describe Islamic regimes, including the Mughal rule of India. Burke, Johnson, and Beckford represent the opposing prong of an orientalist counterimpulse (sometimes called preromantic) when compared to Montagu's flirtation with a neoclassical orientalism. The non-European elements are no longer atomized into their constituent parts; they are instead decomposed into the inchoate category of the sublime. Presentation and performance, characteristic of the sublime, come perilously close to fixing upon the unchangeable and eternal verities of the Orient as pure and unmotivated signifier. Hence, the sublime as phenomenological process parallels the Orient as colonialist tropology, subsuming its contradictions and consuming its artifacts. Johnson, Burke, and Beckford commence a trend more clearly visible in the subsequent fixations of late-eighteenth- and early-nineteenth-century gothic and Romantic literature. Yet Burke, Montagu, and others occasionally tropicalize their uses of these tropologies in ways that are exploitable by subsequent readers and that are indeed indicative of their own ambivalences. Levantinization thus helps name the multiple uses—some utopian, others repressive—that orientalisms were put to in the eighteenth century. But although levantinization especially helps frame the discussion of the mid-eighteenth century, it is not confined to this chronological stage or, for that matter, to its primary locale. As a geocultural application of tropicalization, levantinization can be used to describe earlier and later orientalisms, that of the Crusades as well as the discourse of contemporary Zionism. In fact, the term thus far has been used only pejoratively to characterize Zionists who had abandoned the goals of Europeanization and gone native.

The third section of the book addresses a more generalized form of tropicalization, indeed that of the "empire writes back" variety. In the eighteenth-century context, this is a form that I call nationalization. Nationalization resembles anti-imperialist political practice most effectively. It speaks the discourse of nationality and collectivity in the manner of the later eighteenth century. This discourse most resembles our present understanding of imperialism, inflected as it is by the long nineteenth century, and the decolonization debates of the short twentieth century. The later eighteenth century furnishes us with extensive documentation, both literary and otherwise, of textual reappropriation by tropicopolitans who see themselves as targets of earlier tropologies and orientalisms. Although some of these subjects can be merited with initiating a self-motivated tropicalization of literary tropology, I argue against those who find and celebrate agency by glorifying literary activity for its own sake. By reflecting on the underpinnings of the very category of Literature in relation to unexamined and teleological notions of literacy, I suggest that a careful contextualization and activation of the multiple contexts and uses of literacy, readerships, and reading formations yield a much more complex picture of agency than hitherto imagined. The celebration of tropicopolitans as literary subjects who had been denied their subjecthood and who then empowered themselves through literacy ironically continues the meliorative trope in Chambers's *Cyclopaedia*. The fruitless undertaking is now being heralded as a fruitful one in minority discourse, but just as with the colonial trope, structural aspects of the relationship between the Eurocentric self and its other remain unchallenged. Seemingly oppositional, such perspectives recognize a subjecthood that was denied earlier to the other, but neglect the critical examination of this ideologically dubious process of subjective investiture.

Nationalization is characteristic of the discourses of black British subjecthood as well as that of the Sierra Leone resettlement project, which involved transporting poor blacks from England and manumitted slaves from the West Indies and Nova Scotia to start up a commercial colony in West Africa. The first chapter of this section demonstrates how Olaudah Equiano's *Interesting Narrative of Gustavus Vassa the African*, published coincidentally in the year of the French Revolution, 1789, hybridizes colonialist, orientalist, and anticolonial discourses under the rubric of autobiography. While Equiano speaks Crusoe's and Singleton's values with Friday's voice, writing simultaneously as fetish object and desiring subject, the autobiographer experientially investigates the nature of colonial fetishism and tropical figuration that produces him to English society. He repeats the Oroonoko legend in his continued employment of the trope of the royal slave and also the discourse of mercantilism in Defoe. However, in the process of repetition, Equiano sets off a process of colonial mimicry that reworks Behn's romance and Defoe's conversion narratives with occasional touches of Swiftian satirical brilliance. As vintage autobiography the narrative produces irony different from the self-conscious and detached effect favored by Swift. Whereas colonialism dismembered colonized bodies and disrupted so many different kinds of precapitalist communities, Equiano is concerned with the re-membering of himself as fetish, a genealogical exercise that leads back to colonialism, its discourses, practices, and institutions, from the standpoint of postcolonial identity. What occurs is a radical rehistoricization of the fetish despite, and in fact because of, its decontextualization as personal history. Equiano's case is to be understood within its historical constraints. He was a colonial projector, mercantilist entrepreneur, evangelical activist and abolitionist leader of the black poor in London and Philadelphia. His autobiography is contrasted with the black resettlement of Sierra Leone, an expedition he initially favored as potentially granting manumitted slaves a chance for political freedom as agricultural yeomen. Equiano's literacy, and indeed his literariness, are often confused by literary critics with the larger question of anticolonial agency. Literacy is a complex technology that was being redeployed by various practices in the colonial sphere. Celebrating an act of literacy by a postcolonial subject such as Equiano plays back into colonialist assumptions in a bizarre and paternalistic way.

Similarly, nationalization is present in one of the most spectacular instances of eighteenth-century political revolution. The last chapter begins by interrogating late-eighteenth-century colonialist ideology through a consideration of Abbé de Raynal's *Histoire philosophique et politique du commerce et des établissements des européens dans les deux Indes* (1780, 3d edition), which had a considerable impact on the French Revolution and perhaps on the Haitian Revolution. *Histoire des deux Indes* is obviously a massive compilation involving disparate authorial contributions; these contributions multiply into a dizzying number of diverse fragments exemplifying a plethora of voices and positionings with respect to the fact of a globally multicultural but economically homogenized world history. As a rich, encyclopedic source of both imperialist and anticolonial attitudes, the text serves as a synecdoche of colonialist representation. Fiery denunciations of Western imperialism, absolutism, and religious intolerance, both at home and abroad, subsequently identified as the writings of Diderot, are juxtaposed with careful disquisitions by lesser known authors on the problems of colonial trade and suggestions for its improvement. The 1791 slave revolt of Saint-Domingue is unique for its reworking of the French Enlightenment as well as for its surpassing of those metropolitan discourses into what has been the catastrophic trajectory of nationhood for Haiti after the country's independence in 1804. Toussaint Louverture's tropicalization of the Enlightenment is a fitting culmination to this book, but that phenomenon is in many ways an exceptional coda to the eighteenth century rather than its teleological outcome. This event, which eventually freed the black and mulatto population of the island of Saint-Domingue from French colonial rule at a terrible cost, provides a different way into the question of anticolonial agency. The reading of repressed and enigmatic resistances, such as the relative silence on gender issues in *Histoire des deux Indes,* further opens up such a text for appropriation by a postcolonial literary criticism that is attuned to feminist issues. The last section of this chapter attempts to make such an elision relevant through a reinterpretation of Diderot's description of Medea in *Histoire des deux Indes.* Lacking empirical evidence, I nonetheless ask the question of what the Medea passage would signify if read by a tropicopolitan reader who I designate as Toussaint's daughter-in-law.

My demurral at the prospect of stagist arguments, modernization narratives, and historical positivism—even as they arise in my own sequencing here—is in order to signal that colonialism and anticolonialism in the eighteenth century is not so much a prehistory of the twentieth century but a *specific* genealogy that leads us back to the present in terms of the existing conflicts of inequity between a neocolonial North and an underdeveloped South. Studying a process, tropicalization, that contests logics of political, economic, cultural, and racial superiority, reminds us that the discourses and practices of colonialism—and those who resist it—have changed but nonetheless continue to flourish around us as political neocolonialism and corporate transnationalism. Tropicalization, or practices of discursive revision and reversal like it, should be just as relevant today as in earlier historical periods. Although the three-part movement of this book—from virtualization to levantinization to nationalization—functions in the manner of a chronological sequence and literary taxonomy of the eighteenth century, I consider these differentiations provisional conveniences rather than a reified ontology of colonialist literary history. Despite its historical underpinnings, this book is a literary-critical foray that focuses on plural and fragmentary acts of reading. Though I am attentive to empirical claims concerning this period, my principal aim is to reconstitute the discursive connections between tropology and tropicalization as reversible rather than teleological. As a result, the connections among the three parts increasingly become more contingent than causal. What I have in mind is a constellation of texts, a kind of strategic canon that is eminently disposable. The omissions of this book should make clear that the traditional eighteenth-century canon was never within its sights. I offer no significant interpretations of eighteenth-century poetry nor, for that matter, do I engage in generic literary history, whether of prose fiction or drama, in any systematic way. However, I hope to show that even if I have read eccentrically, I have read widely. I hope to make available a postcolonial criticism that interrogates the ideological constraints of the national paradigm (and hence the very project of canonical literary history) but that also does justice to the accumulated archival richness of period specializations. Faced with an accretion of texts around a chronological and geocultural monolith, a continental shelf known as the European eighteenth century, what I have proposed is not so much the complete dissolution of this landmass and library, but a pluralization and fragmentation of it into multiple textual archipelagoes. Faced with a resolutely metropolitan eighteenth century replete with discursive, disciplinary, and nationalist reifications, we can instead propose several eighteenth centuries animated by the agency of their differently worlded subjects, whether they be cosmopolitans or tropicopolitans.

Virtualizations

CHAPTER ONE

Petting Oroonoko

A book on colonialism and eighteenth-century literature cannot begin without invoking Oroonoko. In fact, recent critical attention has bordered on the obsessional. Why this figure? What animates recent fixations on Behn's *Oroonoko, or The Royal Slave* (1688), especially as Southerne's play *Oroonoko* (1695) and then Hawkesworth's adaptation of that play (1759) were better known in the eighteenth century than Behn's novella? With the inclusion of *Oroonoko* in the *Norton Anthology of British Literature* and the subsequent release of a Norton critical edition in 1997 as well as several other competing editions in print, Behn's story of the transportation, resistance, and execution of the enslaved prince has truly arrived.[1]

There are good explanations for this interest. According to Janet Todd, the Behn revival demonstrates the affinity of her texts with the concerns of many contemporary readers. Recent interpretations of Behn's writings have found the dispersal of the subject, multiple voices and positionings, expressions of ideological ambivalence, and clear assertions concerning the political construction of culture and gender. Her fiction and poetry are feminist experiments in genre and theme for the time, but Behn's earlier drama also interrogates femininity, commodification, and masquerade amid Royalist contexts. We are repeatedly told by critics that Behn was a sexual radical, a generic innovator, and the first professional woman writer in English literary history. Concerned with the hypercanonicity of Behn, Todd hopes that Behn critics will refuse to indulge the obvious themes that make Behn our contemporary.[2]

But why refuse the obvious when it satisfies so many desires, especially through *Oroonoko*? Such formulations of the obvious lead to a veritable oroonokoism. British Restoration specialists and historians of prose fiction—as well as feminist literary critics and historians of slavery—are enthralled with a brief narrative about chivalric romance, colonial venture, and slave rebellion that follows its eponymous hero from Coromantien to Surinam. Laura Brown's "The Romance of Empire," an astute contextualization of Behn's colonialist ideology and Royalist sympathies, inaugurates *The New Eighteenth Century* and a critical oroonokoism with it. As *Oroonoko* combines Old World romance with New World travelogue, William Spengemann makes a compelling case for it as an early example of *American* fiction and ethnography. Heidi Hutner argues that Behn's writing "make(s) visible what puritanical ideology subsumed into language—nature, women, people of color." More generally, *Oroonoko* helps anchor readers interested in "juggling the categories of race, class, and gender," as Margaret Ferguson has put it. Moira Ferguson sees in *Oroonoko* "the birth of a paradigm" of antislavery discourse by British women writers culminating in the later abolitionist movements. Readily collocating a number of critical concerns within a historical frame, such oroonokoism reclaims *Oroonoko* from the racial clutches of Anglo-Africanist discourse.[3]

If Oroonoko is the poster boy of Behn appreciation, there is more to him than meets the eye. His character suggests an ample negative capability. Catherine Gallagher sees Oroonoko's "blackness" as a model for "nobodiness," a personhood emulated by eighteenth-century women novelists. Behn thereby indirectly explores agency in a marketplace that denigrated women writers. Gallagher's sophisticated oroonokoism singles out Oroonoko's inky sheen as signifying writerly exchange and sovereignty within a Royalist value system. Women writers confront exchange in the marketplace even as the concept of sovereignty interrogates female autonomy amidst women's social objectification. Inevitably, it is the transferential relationship between the novella's female first-person narrator (equated with the historical Behn by many readers) and its black hero that drives oroonokoism. As Robert Erickson points out, Behn was forty-eight, ailing, and shortly to die when the novella was written, whereas the unnamed character who narrates the story is around twenty-three. We need to distinguish between the diegetic character of 1663 and the nondiegetic author of 1688. The autobiographical narrator straddles the divide between the Surinam story world and the English-speaking audience's time. Rediscovering a perfectly positioned text, published in the year of the Glorious Revolution, oroonokoism dramatizes transitions from early modern to eighteenth-century literary culture and the present. A historiographical transference (or retroactive focalization) may occur from several vantage points: Moira Ferguson's search for precursors of late-eighteenth-century abolitionist writers, Gallagher's hypothesis that Oroonoko is an intriguing disembodiment of the later "nobodiness" of women novelists, and Spengemann's post-Americanist desire to undo (or aggrandize?) the nationalist boundaries of U.S. literary history.[4]

However, there are countermoves of ritual self-abnegation in this oroonokoist feeding frenzy, critical versions of the self-mutilations of the war captains in the Peeie Indian village and Oroonoko's own. More recent interpretations have challenged oroonokoism with imoindaism. Focusing on the novella's—and perforce the narrator's—marginalization of Oroonoko's lady love and common-law wife, Imoinda, who is killed by Oroonoko in a suicide pact before his recapture and execution, critics nominate Imoinda as the ideological crux. Ros Ballaster, perhaps the first imoindaist, criticizes the "new hystericism" of those who collude with white feminist herstory (Behn's celebrated "Female Pen") and the creation of black male fetish objects. We are to understand that oroonokoism has actively constructed the black woman as hysteric. Because the deputy governor of the fledgling colony, Colonel Byam, is wounded by Imoinda's arrow during the revolt but saved by his Indian mistress, who sucks the poison out of the wound, Margaret Ferguson identifies a narrative process in Behn's text that splits "'other' women into the extreme roles of dangerous rebel and erotically complicitous slave." Similarly, Stephanie Athey and Daniel Cooper Alarcón decipher Imoinda's predicament and the silence of contemporary critics as yet another instance of the presumed "rapability" of the black woman. However, all this recent discussion means that Imoinda is no longer ignored. Using the historiography of "gynecological rebellion" by female slaves, Charlotte Sussman proposes that "Imoinda's womb might be the focal point of a rebellion against slavery." Oroonoko, by cutting a piece out of his neck and disemboweling himself, acts out upon his own body what he had already done by killing the pregnant Imoinda and their unborn child. Susan Andrade's imoindaism identifies the narrator's sexual desire for Oroonoko being vicariously fulfilled by the black woman's decapitation. Imoinda's death takes place so that "the narrator may explore—literarily if not literally—new sexual territories."[5]

For critics who rely on oroonokoism to construct narratives of Behn's progressive ideology, feminism, and empathy for slaves, imoindaism is the stumbling block, revealing unrecognized complicities. If oroonoko-ism emphasizes the positive transferential value of a novella that explores the subjection of women and slaves in the contact zone, imoinda-ism points to elisions that are revealed when literature constructs, as Suvir Kaul puts it, "sentimental community [as] an antidote to the realities of slavery and colonialism." One could anticipate further developments in the criticism that so far has emphasized Anglo-Africanist discourse and the institution of African slavery. The colonial history of Surinam could be further investigated along with the orientalist antecedents of Behn's Coromantien. Whether or not these other lines of inquiry become recognizable reflexes of thought, imoindaism and its hybrid descendants continue to question the original transference at work in *Oroonoko*.[6]

In the context of oroonokoism's attempts to make *Oroonoko* exemplary and imoindaism's problematization of that exemplariness, this chapter emphasizes the logic of pethood in the transition from *Oroonoko* as personal fetish to the literary canonization of *Oroonoko*. *Oroonoko* responds to trends in new historicism, criticism of empire, and race and gender studies, and these approaches rely on it, in turn, to satisfy a checklist of political concerns. This rush to *Oroonoko* as a convergence point for criticism and coalition politics, literary history and cultural studies, oroonokoism and imoindaism is ultimately ironic. The process by which literary critics are engaged in canonizing *Oroonoko* is neither coincidence nor conspiracy. By uncovering the petting that is part of the text's inaugural dynamics, I highlight scholarship's ironic continuation of Behn's celebratory intentions. The title character's implication as personal fetish, status symbol, virtualized hero, and even domesticated animal—as well as the bathetic and tragicomic aspects of his plight alongside the heroic and tragic strains—should give readers pause. The provisional nature of Oroonoko's subjectivity needs historical testing and theoretical reflection. *Oroonoko* has become a desirable origin for postcolonial eighteenth-century studies. Unlike the *useless exemplariness* of the blackamoor in Chambers's *Cyclopaedia*, this origin becomes virtualized as useful. Reading *Oroonoko* is a fruitful undertaking even if it now promises deferred rewards rather than instant gratification. Tropology has come full circle here, from symptomatic denial, to sentimental identification, to ironic distancing.

Further circumspection is warranted. Petting Oroonoko—or Imoinda

—can result in "*mak[ing]* the heathen into a human so that he can be treated as an end in himself," enacting what Gayatri Spivak has called "the terrorism of the categorical imperative." Readers seek far too earnestly, in an ironic text, for a renewed purchase on agency. I discuss the logic of Oroonoko's humanization in three stages. First, I assess the complex juxtaposition of Oroonoko—novelistic character and interpretive figure—within contemporaneous discourses of pethood and virtual subjectivity. Second, I discuss the implications of Southerne's adaptation, especially with respect to the limited analogies it creates between the sale of slaves and the marriage market for Englishwomen. I conclude with a discussion of the varied implications that arise when representing Oroonoko, whether as sacrificial figure or parodic butt. Although the virtualization of *Oroonoko* as origin makes the trope of the royal slave available for eventual nationalization by Equiano, Toussaint, and others discussed in later chapters, a closer attention to Behn's and Southerne's generic protocols shows that redemptive readings are undercut by tragicomic, parodic, and satirical strains. *Oroonoko* is a treacherous text to place at the origin. It shows us that a decolonized eighteenth-century studies can advance only by relentlessly pitting identification and disavowal against each other.[7]

PETS

In his fascinating book, *Man and the Natural World,* Keith Thomas discusses how petkeeping became widespread in Britain in the sixteenth and seventeenth centuries. Legal and social practices accommodated this newly emergent category. Pets exist for emotional gratification, and the special dispensations increasingly granted to this class of animals challenged assumptions about the boundaries between them and human beings. Thomas documents battles around the admissibility of pets into church, the appropriateness of humanizing them with personal names, and the taboo that developed around eating them. Pets were often fed better than servants in the same household. Concluding that "by 1700 all the symptoms of obsessive pet-keeping were in evidence," Thomas also discusses various aesthetic practices that developed to commemorate the death of a pet through epitaph, elegy, and portraiture. Wills began to recognize pets through bequests for their maintenance if they survived their owners.[8]

Simultaneously, Africans seized for the slave trade were also transported to England and sold as pets and domestic servants. Several historians of slavery have documented cases of Africans as exotic possessions in addition to their more general use as a captive workforce for plantations. The ownership or service of an African represented privilege and status among the English aristocracy in the seventeenth and into the eighteenth century. A variety of cultural mechanisms collocated Africans with domestic pets in seemingly innocuous and bathetic sociocultural contexts. African children were especially prized as flesh-and-blood status symbols among those who could afford them. As *The Character of a Town Misse* recommends satirically in 1675, a fashionable young woman "hath always two necessary Implements about her, a *Blackamoor*, and a little *Dog*, for without these, she would be neither *Fair*, nor *Sweet*." By 1710, Richard Steele writes a spoof letter, purportedly sent to *The Tatler* by a black boy called Pompey, asserting that his mistress's parrot who came over with him "is as much esteemed by her as I am. Besides this, the Shock-Dog has a Collar that cost almost as much as mine." The portraiture of this period amply confirms the fashion for Africans as props. Van Dyck's portrait *Henrietta of Lorraine* (1634) and Dandridge's *Young Girl with Dog and Negro Boy* (n.d.) are good examples.[9]

Especially significant for the discussion that follows are Pierre Mignard's portrait, *Louise de Keroualle, The Duchess of Portsmouth* (Fig. 2), Benedetto Gennari's portrait, *Hortense Mancini, the Duchess of Mazarin* (Fig. 3), and the mezzotint of Anne Bracegirdle in the title role of Dryden's *The Indian Queen* (Fig. 4), all of which feature glamorous female contemporaries of Behn with black pages as props. Behn was close to Mancini and disliked Keroualle intensely. Their portraiture suggests a pervasive Restoration cliché that she must have known well. Given Behn's service to the king as a spy around the time of and perhaps during her Surinam voyage and her persistent Royalism despite disappointments over continuing patronage, it is my claim that *Oroonoko* is an authorial act of self-portraiture that transcreates the ideology animating these images into literary form.

Charles II had bought a black boy for £50 in 1682, and, according to some accounts, this slave was later presented by him to Louise Renée de Penancoet de Keroualle, the Duchess of Portsmouth. Another account identifies the slave in the portrait as originating in the present of a boy

Figure 2 Pierre Mignard, *Louise de Keroualle, The Duchess of Portsmouth* (1682). (National Portrait Gallery, London)

Figure 3 Benedetto Gennari, *Hortense Mancini, The Duchess of Mazarin*. (Sotheby's, London)

Figure 4 W. Vincent and T. Smith, *Anne Bracegirdle as The Indian Queen*. (British Museum, London)

to the king by the Moroccan ambassador in 1681, but in the Mignard image the child seems to be a girl (or is at least dressed as one). Whatever the provenance and the gender of the black child, the Mignard portrait (which was painted in France and was probably in England only briefly in the 1680s, if at all) conveys all the exoticism of colonial venture and commodity acquisition, identifying a female consumer who is herself an object of display. The child proffers some exquisite red coral and pearls to the duchess, and the window in the background suggests the overseas origins. The ground lapis lazuli that went into the striking blue paint of the robe suggests a more costly chromaticism than royal portraitist Peter Lely's more typical use of reds and browns.

Gennari's portrait of Mazarin, the niece of the famous French minister and cardinal, is a remarkable contrast to Portsmouth's. Replete with baroque fantasy and the erotics of bondage, the sitter is allegorized as Diana the huntress even as her black pages are conflated with her hounds; a parallel reading of Portsmouth's portrait sees her as Thetis, thus also alluding indirectly to her royal bastard, the Duke of Richmond, as Achilles. The gentle exoticism of Portsmouth's portrait is in contrast to the sadomasochistic eroticism of Mazarin's. These two

Petting Oroonoko

women were jealous rivals of each other in the mid-1670s, when Mancini came to England dressed as a man with a little Moorish page given her by the Duke of Savoy and promptly alienated the king's affections from Keroualle for a couple of years; but Mancini soon fell into disfavor after an affair with the Prince of Monaco. There is evidence that Mazarin was lampooned as coupling with a black man as was Charles's daughter, the Countess of Sussex. The physical ease of the juxtapositions of the pages in the two portraits of Charles's mistresses, however, suggests an erotic complicity and uneasy violence that leads transitively through the black bodies to the king himself.[10]

Bracegirdle's theatrical image also attempts to synthesize African with Amerindian in the features of the trainbearer and parasol holder. The narrator in the novella claims to have brought back from Surinam the ornamental feathers used in *The Indian Queen*, featured here in Bracegirdle's impressive headdress. *Oroonoko* responds to the coordinated logic of the aristocratic pethood of Africans suggested by these three images, if not to the images themselves. The exoticism, bondage, and theatricality of colonial acquisition, seen as sexual acquisition, is further inflected by the suggestion of proximity to the king's body and hence to political power.

William III, the reigning monarch during the first productions of Southerne's *Oroonoko,* possessed a favorite black slave, always on display in Hampton Court, complete with "carved white marble collar, with a padlock, in every respect like a dog's collar." An African impostor called Aniaba, who appeared in Paris in 1688, was adopted by Louis XIV as a godson. The visit to London of the Iroquois sachem in 1710 drew curious crowds, primarily interested in the exotic nature of foreign royalty. In the same period, there were newspaper advertisements selling "silver padlocks for blacks or dogs." Precise information on the costumes worn in performances of Southerne's *Oroonoko* is unascertainable, but it is likely that the hero would have worn an ornamental collar on stage. Though field slaves, as property, were often branded in the manner of cattle, domestic Africans wore ornamental collars made of precious metals such as gold and silver, on which were stamped the owner's name, initials, and coat of arms. In the case of Oroonoko's representation in England, the choice is between domestic pet and plantation laborer, or that of privatized fetish and public commodity. The brandings and ornamental collars became markers that exhibited the subject's special status as aristocratic property. These external markers recalled the status of these Africans not only as pets but as commodities that could, at any time, be converted to cash. As a slave argues in a text written by Behn's friend Thomas Tryon, "[we] are nothing more in many of our Masters esteem, than *their Money*."[11]

Man and the Natural World accounts for changes in subjectivity in the early modern period. Whereas one process, such as slavery, involves the dehumanization of Africans, pet keeping anthropomorphizes the animal world. Oroonoko, renamed Caesar, is forced to participate in a logic that entails the investiture as well as the divestiture of subjectivity. For the female narrator he is a human pet as well as an enslaved African prince. In light of the above discussion, the contexts of pethood in Behn's treatment of Oroonoko should be discernible. The novella participates vigorously in the process of making the eponymous character an exotic pet for the entertainment of the colonists. Several passages portray Caesar as a chivalric vassal, always "panting after more renown'd Action" (42). When he kills a tiger that chases the colonists, the prince fetches the cub as the spoils for the narrator as if he were a loyal hound and the narrator were Diana: "with an unconcern, that had nothing of the Joy or Gladness of a Victory, he came and laid the Whelp at my Feet" (45). We are reminded of Gennari's portrait of Behn's patron. As he cannot drink, Oroonoko likes the company of women much more than that of men. Speaking collectively for the women, the narrator boasts that, "obliging him to love us very well, we had all the Liberty of Speech with him, especially my self, whom he call'd his *Great Mistress; and* indeed my Word wou'd go a great way with him" (41). These instances show that perceptions of African pethood overlap the chivalric discourse around Oroonoko as Herculean hero. Slaying beasts such as marauding tigers, but not dragons or rival knights, Oroonoko again gently insinuates his pethood into his flirtation: "*What Trophies and Garlands, Ladies, will you make me, if I bring you home the Heart of this Ravenous Beast, that eats up all your Lambs and Pigs?* We all promis'd he shou'd be rewarded at all our Hands" (45). The narrator has already informed us that this tigress (Oroonoko kills two different ones) was responsible for having "born away abundance of Sheep and Oxen"; Caesar here reduces these cattle into smaller livestock, lambs and pigs, potential pets for the ladies. Oroonoko is a much more prestigious pet than a dog or lamb could be and is well aware of it. The term pet originally referred to a pet lamb; Caesar, as chivalric pet, is promised something from all the ladies' hands. Indeed, their love for him is reminiscent of the symbolic petting that dominates the narrator's early description of the indigenes in Surinam as well: "we live with [them] in perfect Amity, without daring to command 'em; but on the contrary, caress 'em with all the brotherly and friendly Affection in the World" (8). The choice of *caress* is not so odd, especially if we realize that almost immediately the passage proceeds to descriptions of the various exotic pets that can be imported:

> Marmosets, a sort of *Monkey*, as big as a Rat or Weasel, but of a marvellous and delicate shape, and has Face and Hands like an Humane Creature: and *Cousheries*, a little Beast in the form and fashion of a Lion, as big as a Kitten; but so exactly made in all parts like that noble Beast, that it is it in *Miniature*. Then for little *Parakeetoes*, great Parrots, *Muckaws*, and a thousand other Birds and Beasts of wonderful and surprizing Forms, Shapes, and Colours. For Skins of prodigious Snakes, of which there are some threescore Yards in length; as is the Skin of one that may be seen at His Majesty's *Antiquaries:* Where are also some rare Flies, of amazing Forms and Colours, presented to 'em by my self; some as big as my Fist, some less; and all of various Excellencies, such as Art cannot imitate. (8–9)

The demand for specimens to stock curio cabinets may have fueled part of the mercantilist activity during the early modern period, but the frequent fascination with brilliant colors and strange shapes also generated satirical reversals. Such features of numerous post-Renaissance travel narratives (later parodied by the formal conceits of the first two books of Swift's *Gulliver's Travels*) disclose a mixture of allegorical and realist modes and rely on aesthetic amazement alongside mercantilism. Echoing this consumerist impulse, the narrator assimilates Oroonoko's and Imoinda's scarification to statuary: "I had forgot to tell you, that those who are Nobly born of that Country, are so delicately Cut and Rac'd all over the fore-part of the Trunk of their Bodies, that it looks as if it were Japan'd; the Works being raised like high Poynt round the Edges of the Flowers: Some are only Carv'd with a little Flower, or Bird, at the Sides of the Temples, as was *Caesar;* and those who are so

Carv'd over the Body, resemble our Ancient *Picts,* that are figur'd in the Chronicles, but these Carvings are more delicate" (40). Joanna Lipking points out that there may be a factual error on Behn's part here, as Coromantees were not scarified; however, such ornamentation is relevant as a description of a potential pet and a variety of other mercantile objects, to elicit a collector's desire to possess the "curios" that adorned the mantelpieces and cabinets of the leisured classes. Jean Hecht, in one of the first monographs on this subject, asserts that Africans were "no less ideally suited to adorn the homes of the elite and their imitators than the porcelains, textiles, wall papers and lacquered pieces that were brought from the East."[12]

However, the colonists in Surinam were not necessarily the best representatives of English mores of petkeeping. Surinam's tenuous status as an English colony is emphasized by the fact that the Royalists' attempt to settle it in 1651 was already the fourteenth attempt. Willoughby of Parham, who had a twenty-one-year lease on the colony, had invested upward of £20,000 with a view to make it a sugar plantation (he published an investor's prospectus in 1655). A settler population of roughly 4,000 lived in 130 plantations. If we are to take Behn's account as factually based, it is within this context that the colonists attempt to establish rival and conflicting claims over Oroonoko and Imoinda, treating them as valued and exotic domestic properties, not just political threats to be feared. The narrator's befriending of Oroonoko could mean establishing his loyalty not only as vassal or slave, but also as pet. As the narrator's status is in some dispute with the other settlers, her access to Oroonoko increases her prestige and establishes her social superiority through his metonymic proximity to her. That she is termed his Great Mistress is obviously a point of pride. These marks of proximity are a necessary exercise, not just from the point of view of aristocratic portraiture but the power lines made visible by it. The narrator enhances her status, improving her tenuous position as daughter of the intended lieutenant governor who died en route before he could assume charge (or, as Todd points out, that is what Behn would have us believe). Just as it is noticeable that she evades responsibility for Oroonoko's behavior by absenting herself from the scene when he threatens to revolt as well as when he is brutally punished, the narrator also presents herself through the chivalric action earlier in order to make Oroonoko into *her* pet African. Perhaps she hopes to garner the credit ensuing to her from his activities, hence pursuing a fantasized social promotion just as much as she indulges her private desires.[13]

While the historical Behn may have been sent to Surinam either by the absentee Governor Willoughby or the Royal Court to spy on the activities of Byam and Willoughby's other surrogates, the novelist indulges in a retroactive self-fashioning, wilfully rearranging political identities to make her role more central. The process of the narrator's self-fashioning as aristocrat, and perhaps a fantasy identification as one more of Charles's numerous mistresses, is generalized by the symbolic function she attaches to Oroonoko's arrival in Surinam: "But if the King himself (God bless him) had come a-shore, there cou'd not have been greater Expectations by all the whole Plantation, and those neighbouring ones, than was on ours at that time; and he was receiv'd more like a Governor than a Slave. Notwithstanding, as the Custom was, they assign'd him his Portion of Land, his House, and his Business, up in the Plantation. But as it was more for Form, than any Design, to put him to his Task, he endur'd no more of the Slave but the Name, and remain'd some Days in the House, receiving all Visits that were made him, without stirring towards that part of the Plantation where the *Negroes* were" (37). Establishing Oroonoko as pet-king involves a complex balancing act. He is apprised of his slave status, including the assignments that go with it; however, the coercive force of the interdiction is immediately suspended. From the moment of disembarkation there is a recognizable gap between the general perception of Oroonoko (royal) and his legal status (slave). When the narrator says, "it was more for Form, than any Design, to put him to his Task," we may want to ask what motivates this desire to keep to the form of slavery even as its practical effects are suspended and replaced by others. Oroonoko gives audiences to people who come to see him, and the rhetorical flourish of the claim that there were king-size expectations is at least unintentionally ironic, given the ridicule Oroonoko later faces from his captors and the dispatch with which he is executed.

Behind this recuperative logic of idealization, beginning with the narrator herself, is a desire to affirm Oroonoko's agency and activate the genre of "pet romance" as restitutive. The dialectical process of pethood and ludic kingship is one that the prince, after all, temporarily seizes to his advantage. Oroonoko actively manipulates his "royal" status by overstepping the boundaries of his aesthetic and comic function. By leading a slave rebellion, Oroonoko as Caesar crosses a different Rubicon, converting his status as pet-king to a claim of actual political authority. As mock-Caesar, Oroonoko resists his captors by finding a new vocation as anti-Roman scourge when he incites the slaves to rebellion: "he told them, that he had heard of one *Hannibal* a great Captain, had Cut his Way through Mountains of solid Rocks; and shou'd a few Shrubs oppose them; which they cou'd Fire before 'em?" (53). The eventual failure of the rebellion makes the identification with Hannibal especially poignant, as does Oroonoko's defiant bravado just before his final capture: "you will find no more *Caesars* to be Whipt" (62). Oroonoko is perhaps also modeled on Spartacus, whose name does not get mentioned in either Behn's or Southerne's texts, but whose symbolic presence surfaces with the specter of slave rebellion.

Chafing at his symbolic bit in response to the experience of his treatment at the narrator's hands, as well as the more widespread treatment of Africans as domestic pets, Caesar, in his rebellious speech, rants that he and his fellow slaves "*are Bought and Sold like Apes, or Monkeys, to be the Sport of Women, Fools and Cowards; and the Support of Rogues, Runagades, that have abandon'd their own Countries, for Rapin, Murders, Thefts and Villanies*" (52). This statement clearly expresses Oroonoko's anxiety upon undergoing feminization because he is object in a logic where he ought to have pride of place as subject. Along with that of the other colonists, the narrator's attempt to appropriate Oroonoko into an aristocratic model of subordination and pethood is exposed by him as a sham. Nonetheless, Oroonoko's description of his antagonists unwittingly reveals that he holds the same assumptions concerning their class identity as does his Great Mistress. Some of the colonists, such as George Martin and Behn's associate William Scot, are themselves refugees from the English Civil War, marginal elements on the make, Parliamentarians fearing retribution as well as turncoat Royalists. The accusation Oroonoko makes concerning pethood is a specific reproach that applies to several of his minders; the narrator is clearly implicated, but also the bumbling Cornishman Trefry, who cannot obtain his release despite frequent promises, as well as the other colonists, referred to as riffraff, who cannot be trusted to rectify the ambivalent legal situation ensuing from his capture. Resenting his own pethood, a process that is continuous with that of ludic kingship, Oroonoko expresses conventional chivalric anxieties about feminization. His description of Africans as pets is an inescapable yet seriocomic assertion. Recognizing that women were themselves treated much as domestic properties belonging to men, dressed objects of conspicuous consumption and display, Oroonoko balks at seeing himself reduced to a second-order pet, a lady's fashion accessory, and conflates the evils of mercantilist reification with folk anxieties about cuckolding: *"to be the Sport of Women, Fools and Cowards."* His chivalric character cannot fully enter the white homosocial domain predicated on the exchange of women and slaves.

Oroonoko's commentary on this process of objectification that accords Africans transitory forms of subjectivity despite their commodity status nonetheless criticizes the political discourses that mask the interests of colonial property holders. Pets, once acquired and privatized, can be suspended from their earlier participation in the public sphere as objects, taking on an honorary subjectivity. The initial status of the pet subject is honorary, or virtualized, because it depends on the contingent and fetishized investment of the owner. The owner's disinvestment returns the pet to the identity of an objectified commodity in the marketplace, as the advertisements in the *Athenian Mercury* attest all too well. Although such virtualization starts out as a reversible process, it soon acquires an autonomy of its own. The beginnings of social contract discourse allowed the theorization of subjectivity on the basis of "natural" rights that rationalized the possession of property; Africans and women, variously extraneous to such ideas, begin challenging those who claim ownership of them by exerting subjective authority over themselves as objects.[14] The subject is simultaneously alienated (this body is property that belongs to someone else) and empowered (as I'm property, I can own myself). The construction of this pet-subject through interpellation, where the subject voluntarily responds to a "call" by the dominant law that then subjects "it," is not that different from the construction of the human subject. If this is a scandal, it is one that, arguably, Behn used to expose, whether intentionally or unintentionally, the process of Oroonoko's making and unmaking.[15]

As pet-king, Oroonoko resists appropriation through the very forms and visible material marks that delimit his status. To sketch this process out in literal terms is also to expose such investiture as ludicrous. In the rush to affirm Oroonoko's humanity, the narrator disavows her specific cathexis of him as pet. Her empathy flows through both anthropomorphism and identification. Both processes are delusive, as the former involves reducing human beings to animals and then paradoxically retrieving them as pets, whereas the latter is a political fantasy of aristocratic self-fashioning by secondary revision a quarter century later. By petting a royal slave, the narrator enacts the categorical imperative as colonialist practice. A violent *"making of the heathen into a human,"* to return to Spivak's phrase, is modified here in terms of a violent petting of the slave as a king. This making is followed by a gothic drama of unmaking, where the pet is disfigured in a manner that suggests the totemism and trauma of the rending of another social pet, the king himself. In his analysis of the doctrines that rationalized the king's divine right, Ernst Kantorowicz has suggested that the Restoration had no liking for Shakespeare's *Richard II* because it would have revived the traumatic memory of the violent separation of the king's two bodies in 1649. The blocked mourning evident in the account of the protagonist's death implies that *Oroonoko* is very much a text written in 1688, on the cusp of the constitutional evacuation of divine right, looking back to Charles's execution in 1649 as a violent precursor to what would soon become a bloodless coup when William and Mary replace James II. Or as Janet Todd suggests, the text could be a coded warning to James as Imoinda is a near anagram of the Queen's patronym, Modena.[16]

The king's two bodies, as Kantorowicz explains it, made for a complex *persona mixta,* whereby the investiture and divestiture of the divine agency, a *character angelicus,* could be presumed to inhabit and depart from the human body of the monarch's. With *Oroonoko,* there is an ersatz repetition of this process, where the persona mixta of the royal slave is inhabited by the character angelicus Oroonoko attains through the narrator's narrative and ownership. The Christomimetic behavior of kings under the New Covenant was a feature of Royalist accounts of Charles I's death, and it is no surprise that the execution of Oroonoko is assimilated to a similar model of martyrdom. The narration culminates with the static tableau of the pet-king's disincorporation and desacralization: "He had learn'd to take Tobaco; and when he was assur'd he should Dye, he desir'd they would give him a Pipe in his Mouth, ready Lighted, which they did; and the Executioner came, and first cut off his Members, and threw them into the Fire; after that, with an ill-favoured Knife, they cut his Ears, and his Nose, and burn'd them; he still Smoak'd on, as if nothing had touch'd him; then they hack'd off one of his Arms, and still he bore up, and held his Pipe; but at the cutting off the other Arm, his Head sunk, and his Pipe drop'd; and he gave up the Ghost, without a Groan, or a Reproach" (64).[17]

The dismemberment and mutilation of Oroonoko, though typical of the brutality with which slave insurrections were suppressed, also reveals symbolic aggression directed against the narrator herself (Todd sees a parallel with accounts of the punishment meted out to one Thomas Allin, who attempted to take the life of Governor Willoughby). The apparently indistinct profiles of the English presence in Surinam should not be misread as implying a unified plantocratic class. Various regicides, loyalists, adventurers, overseers, and functionaries in Surinam make for a volatile mixture. The execution of Oroonoko suggests a complex statement of symbolic aggression alongside its obvious significance as punishment for rebellion. Rending apart a favorite so cruelly, as the Byam faction does, combines male misogyny directed at the narrator's pretensions along with a riposte, perhaps including an element of social protest, aimed against those who wished to exempt royal slaves from the punishments meted out to ordinary ones. The entire colony is aware of Oroonoko's pethood and the special dispensation his supporters demand for him. Like the many cruel attacks on dogs, horses, and deer leading up to the Black Act of 1723, Oroonoko's especially barbaric execution is a deliberate violation of live property. In the ritual slaying of such scapegoats, their executioners also intended the manner of their killing as protests aimed at their social superiors, as Robert Darnton has demonstrated in the French context of *The Great Cat Massacre*. The history of statutes that prosecute the "malicious wounding" of animals is not just a sign that the English are animal lovers, but an indication that the legislation was intended to protect the living and breathing symbols of aristocratic privilege. If proximity to Oroonoko, therefore, indicates a wishful manipulation of status and prestige as well as curiosity and empathy, hostility to him is not simpleminded. The callousness with which he is mutilated sends a very deliberate message—to the surviving slaves, warning them against rebellion, but also to the pretensions of the narrator's opposition to Byam. If we can continue with the theory that the narrator is making a retroactive bid to refashion herself as an erstwhile erotic accessory of the king with the help of Caesar as prop, in the manner of the Duchesses of Portsmouth and Mazarin, the hostility directed against her from the beginning is both misogynist and fanta-

Figure 5 *The Execution of Breaking on the Rack,* from John Gabriel Stedman, *Narrative of a five years' expedition against the revolted Negroes of Surinam in Guiana* (1796). (Special Collections Division, University of Washington Libraries)

sized as anti-Stuart—perhaps even antimonarchist class warfare, given the presence of Cromwellian regicides in the colony.[18] It is expedient for the narrator to fantasize that opposition to her must be anti-Royalist, when in fact the record shows that Behn had much more truck with the Parliamentarians in the colony than did the resolutely Royalist Byam.

One of the visual depictions of dismemberment in Surinam, also from Stedman's much later narrative, still faintly suggests a Christomimetic possibility, as the victim is bound on the rack with one hand just severed from his body, along with a distant figure hanging on the gallows evocative of the thief at the crucifixion (Fig. 5). Is this figure a representation of the end met by the male slave featured arriving in the previous plate of Stedman's (Fig. 1)? Caesar's gruesome end throws light on the provisional nature of his assimilation as pet. These "frightful Spectacles of a mangled King," along with the exaggerated self-possession of Caesar at the execution, transvalues chivalric honor into a parable of stoical detachment from the body. Such an overwhelming degree of self-possession, granted mythically by tobacco since its Elizabethan introduction in England, constructs a disincorporated subject whose stoicism and negativity are unsurpassed. In fact, the name Orinoco itself referred to a kind of tobacco.[19] Though some historical evidence points to the incredible bravery and dignity with which Akan-speaking Coromantees such as Oroonoko bore their death, the controlled exaggeration of the report reveals a narrator desirous of sparing him pain.[20]

The narrator was not herself present at the macabre scene of execution but represented by surrogates: "my Mother and Sister were by him [Caesar] all the while, but not suffer'd to save him" (64). Her graphic description, despite her physical absence from the scene, suggests traumatic repetition and a wish fulfillment of sorts. Though she is largely sympathetic to Oroonoko, the narrator distrusts his intentions and controls his actions when he threatens the power structure of English colonial rule. At other points her empathy for him is tinged with repulsion, especially after Oroonoko's recapture following the murder of Imoinda.[21] However, the narrator's decision to leave after Oroonoko's final capture reveals a more idealized relation: "the Chirurgeon assur'd him, he cou'd not Live . . . we were all (but *Caesar*) afflicted at this News, and the Sight was gashly; his Discourse was sad; and the earthly Smell about him so strong, that I was perswaded to leave the Place for some time (being my self but Sickly, and very apt to fall into Fits of dangerous Illness upon any extraordinary Melancholy)" (63–64). Admitting to hysterical depression, the owner is concerned that the pet's illness could spark a personal trauma. By contrast, her departure enables a continuation of the memory of the pet as an idealized figure incapable of pain. Oroonoko, while dying an excruciating death, never complains: "he gave up the Ghost, without a Groan, or a Reproach" (64). Such stoicism in the face of complete disembodiment borders on a superhuman sensibility of the sublime. Faced with the disappearance of the object, the narrative relocates trauma in the owner. As bearer of the pet's trauma through a reconstructed and imagined memory, the narrator is involved with the anthropomorphic process of *humanizing*, but does not confront adequately the implications of that process as an arrested development. Oroonoko's final moments are clearly Christomimetic, where the victim's refusal to reproach his persecutors is a figure of speech that signifies his own irreproachability, making him into a sacrificial object. If the evasive approach to Oroonoko's slave status in the narrative allows him the humanization that is clearly denied to field slaves, the withdrawal of that humanization is not uniform. Byam's faction executes a rebel who poses a political threat, but is no less the Royalist for it; whereas the narrator's approach is to idealize that outcome in the form of pet romance that parodies Royalist martyrology and makes her more loyal than the king. Although she fails to appropriate the African as pet in any lasting fashion, the narrator reinvents herself as epitaphist to recuperate this object more effectively: "Thus Dy'd this Great Man; worthy of a better Fate, and a more sublime Wit than mine to write his Praise; yet, I hope, the Reputation of my Pen is considerable enough to make his Glorious Name to survive to all Ages; with that of the Brave, the Beautiful, and the Constant *Imoinda*" (65).

If *Oroonoko* initiates antislavery discourse, as Algernon Swinburne and successive readers have argued, it does so by building on the fantasized project of the aristocratic subordination of the royal slave as pet. The literature of empathy, which creates antislavery discourse, is itself a vicarious replacement for the more personalized dramas of pethood, seen here as the culture of the caress. The narrator's hand, which can no longer stroke the pet, writes his epitaph.

ENGLISHWOMEN

As Robert D. Hume has perspicaciously argued in a review essay, Thomas Southerne's career has been persistently misjudged by criteria that favor wit and comedy of manners over Southerne's true strengths, which exist in satire, generic innovation, and social commentary. A discomfiting mixture of heroic or pathetic tragedy and cynical sex comedy, the effects of the split plot in Southerne's *Oroonoko* are closely tied to the logic of pethood in Behn's novella. Although it absorbs many details from Behn's plot, Southerne's dramatic version does not depict the sexually charged relationship between the narrator and the protagonist, instead opting for an analogy between slaves and Englishwomen through two significant transformations. Imoinda becomes a *white* woman (the daughter of an English mercenary in Africa), and a comic parallel plot presents the adventures of Charlot and Lucy Welldon while husband hunting in Surinam. The first change allows implicit judgments on the risks of interracial romance along the lines of Shakespeare's *Othello*, and the subplot contrasts marital comedy against the parallel tragedy of Oroonoko's abortive rebellion.[22]

These Englishwomen in Surinam come into minimal contact with the slave population. The parallel depiction of each group's vicissitudes assumes the existence of the theatrical spectator, whose comparative assessment measures the relative success of one group alongside the failure of the other. Charlot Welldon, a female rakehell, herself utilizes a process of comparative assessment that makes slavery, and the distractions of managing it, the primary instrument for her own advancement. It has been suggested that Charlot functions as a mock-Behn, expressing Southerne's hostility and indebtedness toward Behn's influence on him. I return to this question later, but it is evident that Charlot's character is Behn-like for the manner in which various intrigues are staged around herself. Putting on masculine garb, Charlot's eventual aim is to further her sister's marital prospects and likewise her own. Charlot's success as a rakehell is not very different from that of Julia in *The Lucky Chance* and Angellica Bianca in *The Rover* or the female libertine Lucia/Sir Anthony in Southerne's own *Sir Anthony Love; or, The Rambling Lady.* If Charlot is a satirical version of Behn, through the references to disguise and colonial adventure, she is also subversive. If Charlot's dynamism aroused female desire, both heterosexual and homosexual, it might have been one of the lesser known reasons why Southerne's *Oroonoko* was especially deemed a "favorite of the ladies." Behn's self-mockery in her plays draws attention to the apparatuses of literary convention and gender subordination. Similarly, Charlot's opportunistic manipulations and impersonations while matchmaking and dowry hunting make her a libertine and a trickster. As a woman, she finds her agency through manipulating the constraints of her objectification even if she cannot fully throw off her shackles. The Welldons' husband-hunting plot is distinctive because it raises the themes of domestication and fetishization already explored in Behn's treatment of pethood, but treats them in mixed modes, suggesting bathos far more than romance. The same could be said of Behn's mocking embrace of the analogy of prostitution to female authorship in her drama.[23]

In the opening scene of Southerne's *Oroonoko,* the Welldons search for husbands as commodities in a manner that alludes to the naturalized exotica that the narrator wanted to export back to England in the novel:

Luc[y Welldon]: What will this come to? What can it end in? You have persuaded me to leave dear *England,* and dearer *London,* the place of the World most worth living in, to follow you a Husband-hunting into *America:* I thought Husbands grew in these Plantations.

[Charlot] Well[don]: Why so they do, as thick as Oranges, ripening one under another. Week after week they drop into some Woman's mouth: 'Tis but a little patience, spreading your Apron in expectation, and one of 'em will fall into your Lap at last. (I.i.1-10)

The Englishwomen act out a retaliatory fantasy of men as "oranges" (perhaps a hit at the new Dutch immigrants who had arrived with William of Orange). Attracting these men lewdly when orange-women in Covent Garden were considered harlots, a woman has to signal her sexual availability, "spreading [her] Apron in expectation." But the audience knows that the joke rebounds on the women. No one is more knowledgeable than Charlot, who facilitates Lucy's and her prospects by assuming a male identity with which she barters on the marriage market to joint advantage. Unlike Oroonoko, who uncritically accepts his status as property well into the second half of the play,[24] Charlot is not just aware of the economic system that dominates marital outcomes, but inaugurates the play with a systemic analysis of the marriage market: "they say there is a vast Stock of Beauty in the Nation, but a great part of it lies in unprofitable hands; therefore for the good of the Publick, they wou'd have a Draught made once a Quarter, send the decaying Beauties for Breeders into the Countrey, to make room for New Faces to appear, to countenance the Pleasures of the Town" (I.i.34-38). If women as movable goods cannot be put to productive use, the new mercantilist logic identified by Charlot requires more reproductive services of them. A quick turnover of inventory maximizes profits, and the rotation of goods ameliorates the inefficiency associated with a large inventory. As decaying merchandise must not be wasted (herein women figure as livestock), thrifty management requires recycling and conservation. Hence Charlot's cynical observation concerning social expectations. Women are especially perishable commodities, and Charlot defines their depreciation: "you may tumble 'em [women] over and over at their first coming up, and never disparage their Price; but they fall upon wearing immediately, lower and lower in their value, till they come to the Broker at last" (I.i.22-25). The "tumble" metaphor refers to Charlot's previous characterization of women as "Rich Silks" (I.i.19). As fabrics for sale to customers who wish for hands-on inspection, women's bodies are also, frequently, their only salable ware. But, just like clothes and most other commodities, women's bodies have their highest value at the moment of inspection before first use, then depreciate steeply—once they are "soiled" or "sold"—in relation to the marriage market.

The Welldons' successful manipulation of their commodity status is at the expense of the Widow Lackitt, who also wants a husband but is scapegoated as a result of her prominence as the only woman planter. The widow is a figure for female self-advancement without male acceptance. Her name signifies an obvious sexual lack that handicaps her biologically and socioeconomically. Especially as plantations grew also by the coerced reproduction of the female workforce, the widow cannot disregard the destiny of her anatomy—and admits as much early in the play—when she berates Captain Driver for giving her a preassigned "lot," or batch of slaves, that consists only of women and children. Exclaiming, "I am a Woman my self, and can't *get* my own Slaves, as some of my Neighbours do," Lackitt recognizes that the objective of acquisitive "getting" in a slave system is itself predicated on reproductive begetting (I.ii.10-12). One can imagine the widow as an implicit spectator of a scene like that depicted by Blake for Stedman's narrative (Fig. 1). Handicapped in an economic system where the sexual ownership and reproductivity of slave women is one of the principal motors for profit, the widow faces constant taunting from her male rivals. Though some of the other planters agree with her, the group decides that preassigned lots will not be redistributed. The widow is forced to accept her lot, in more than one sense. Humiliated by Captain Driver, who casts aspersions at Lackitt's desirability as a sexual object, the widow bemoans the lack of a husband who might protect and defend her honor in the marketplace. Charlot, however, does not go on to passively accept her lot in the way the widow succumbs here to the slave driver and later to Charlot's own manipulations. Although Charlot manipulates the market by entering as a disguised male participant, the widow's honorary status in the fraternity of male planters works against her through various forms of invidious discrimination.[25]

In her systemic analysis of the marriage market, Charlot oscillates between deploring the phenomenon and confronting its unavoidability. After hearing from Jack Stanmore, an opportunist who wishes to marry the widow, Charlot soliloquizes:

She wou'd have a Husband; and if all be, as he says, she has no reason to complain: but there's no relying on what the Men say upon these occasions: they have the benefit of their bragging, by recommending their abilities to other Women: theirs is a trading Estate, that lives upon credit, and increases by removing it out of one Bank into another. Now poor Women have not these opportunities: we must keep our stocks dead by us, at home, to be ready for a purchase, when it comes, a Husband, let him be never so dear, and be glad of him: or venture our Fortunes abroad on such rotten security, that the principal and interest, nay very often our persons are in danger. If the Women wou'd agree (which they never will) to call home their Effects, how many proper Gentlemen wou'd sneak into another way of living, for want of being responsible in this? then Husbands wou'd be cheaper. Here comes the Widow, she'll tell truth: she'll not bear false Witness against her own interest, I know. (IV.i.54–70).

Charlot regards women as stuck with frozen assets that cannot be readily transported. Women cannot speculate in marital futures, invest their capital without jeopardy (prostitution), or indulge in entrepreneurship (libertinism). Men are merchants who trade on credit, a privilege that allows them to traffic among different sorts of capital; women, however, as fixed capital themselves, must constantly guard themselves in anticipation of a purchaser, as "principal and interest, nay very often [their] persons are in danger." By principal Charlot is referring to a woman's marriageability, which is her main capital property; by interest, her reputation, which is the sole means of inflating her plummeting value; and by person, her physical health, which could be threatened by the ravages of rape, venereal disease, and death itself. "Call[ing] home their effects," however, implies that women could withhold conjugal rights. Such withholding humorously alludes to the comic situation explored in Aristophanes' *Lysistrata*. By withholding sexual services, could Charlot's peers go on strike and get what they want? However, as women can never agree on this point, Charlot prefers to be opportunistic.[26]

The refusal of sexual services is not a genuine possibility. In the action that immediately follows this passage, Charlot goes on to accept (while in male drag) a bribe from the widow for sexual services on obviously false pretenses. However, Southerne's dramatization of an ethical split in Charlot is not so much a judgment of her as it is an acknowledgment of a very restricted set of possibilities. When it comes to the slave plot, Lucy and Charlot are, in fact, mildly sympathetic to Oroonoko's plight as a piece of property, but they realize as well that the slave rebellion is a diversion that can result in masking their principal intrigue: "we fish in troubled waters: we shall have fewer Eyes upon us" (IV.i.192–93). Charlot, in male disguise, negotiates with Captain Driver as potential husband for Lucy, even as she differentiates the more private commodification of eligible Englishwomen from the public context of the sale of slaves: "this is your Market for Slaves; my Sister is a Free Woman and must not be dispos'd of in publick" (I.ii.113–14). The private-public distinction with respect to the economic disposal of women is enforced by Charlot's chiding of Driver for his category mistake. However, rather than take umbrage permanently, her very next act is to invite Driver home to negotiate terms, unaffected as she is by his humiliation of Lackitt. She advises Lucy, who found Driver's behavior repugnant, to swallow her pride, as "he's a man to thrive in the world, Sister: he'll make you the better Jointure" (I.ii.259–60). Such contradictory behavior is not a sign of incoherence, however, as Restoration comedies repeatedly dissociate social judgment from moral judgment. Indeed, it has been argued that it is this innovation that gives them far greater critical potential.[27]

Credit, as the key term for success in the period, implies financial worth as well as interpersonal trustworthiness. Whereas Oroonoko clings to the older discourse of chivalric honor that Charlot satirizes in the epilogue, it is the crucial yet elusive category of credit that Charlot learns to manipulate. Making the transition from bartered female object to bartering male subject, she remains doubled in the position of both currency and currency user, playing a sound game by adopting each identity when needed. Bartering Lucy to Lackitt's son in one transaction gets Charlot even more indebted as the eligible male that the widow has her eyes on. Then, as homosocial male, she barters her hidden female self as a long-lost cousin to her heterosexual love object, Stanmore, even as she arranges for his kinsman to take her place in the widow's mistaken affections. The dowry for Charlot is money that Lackitt has given to her as a "husband," an act Charlot interprets later as payment for the sexual services she had arranged for Lackitt through Stanmore's brother Jack.

In her reading of *The Country Wife*, Eve Kosofsky Sedgwick remarks on the way that Wycherley's play, as a typical Restoration comedy, insists on "the routing of homosocial desire through women . . . clearly presented as compulsory."[28] Southerne's play also necessitates such a logic. Revealing a society of males who treat women as currency, Charlot is not content with merely theorizing her diminished socioeconomic status. Parodying male rakes in Restoration comedy, Charlot succeeds by reversing the standard routine. She profits through her role as a pimp, procuring male services for her female customer. With the help of these substitutions she can convert credit into money (in her dealings with Lackitt) and money into credit (in her dealings with Stanmore) on the basis of male heterosexual promises (to Lackitt) and homosocial surety (to Stanmore). Stanmore helps procure Jack for Lackitt, and Charlot reappears as a woman with a dowry by making over to Stanmore the money she has received from Lackitt. Charlot's eventual acceptance of Stanmore's offer of marriage is nominally independent of her resemblance to her male identity; however, she is so confident of her ploy that she reveals her impersonation to Stanmore after accepting his marital offer (V.i). Earlier, Charlot invents a promise to a dying father to nudge Lackitt into accepting Lucy as a bride for her son (II.i.15–20) and secures Lackitt's approval to poison an imaginary wife in England in a stalling move when Lackitt's marital demands become increasingly strident and unsatisfiable (III.iii.29–36).

Whereas Charlot constantly reinvents the temporality of the homosocial promise to further her sexual and socioeconomic projects, Lackitt often demonstrates a spendthrift willingness to satisfy her lust. This parodied "feminine" desire sacrifices future economic profitability for present sexual satisfaction (II.i). Even as the widow acts out this stereotype, Charlot recasts herself as an ideal male, through the crucial devices of a male world, accepting social obligations founded on exchange. Charlot has compromised between being commodity fetish and desiring subject; she bargains herself into the hierarchy at the place convenient to her. It is her sense of owning herself, even while remaining commodifiable, that enables her success.

The mutual regard among slaves and Englishwomen recognizes a provisional agency analogous to that of pethood. Charlot's exploitation of the slave rebellion fashions an opportunity much as Oroonoko is denied it. The fetishization of femininity in relation to pethood is no trivial point here. Flying into "pets," or "taking the pet," was a legendary attribute of aristocratic female behavior in this period, in the manner of what we now call a "pet peeve." An assessment of various emotional dispositions also reveals the special subjectivity of personal subordinates and favorites (whether spouses, retainers, or children), various kinds of "domestic slaves" who in turn "enslave" their masters with unreasonable demands from appetitive disenchantment to irrational rage. Women and retainers, including the pet Africans, make demands of their social superiors that cannot be dismissed. There is a quid pro quo between the caresser and caressed, ranging from the mildly affective to the sexually charged. The affective wake of pethood retroactively reveals a surprising source of agency.

Despite their similarities to slaves in an increasingly commodified marriage market, Englishwomen inhabited a different universe. Charlot manipulates this difference to her advantage. Through masculine impersonation, she reenters a homosocial marketplace in Surinam after disappointment in London where she and her sister had lost their sexual credibility and "durst not appear in Publick Places" (I.i.46-47). Charlot refers to the lack of credit faced by single women in church as well as newer gathering places; even "the Maids at the Chocolate Houses found [them] out, and laughed at [them]: [their] *Billet-doux* lay there neglected for Waste-Paper" (I.i.66-67). The older public spaces such as theater and church included women, but those like the coffeehouse curtailed their presence. These newer establishments depended on the conspicuous consumption of once exotic but increasingly familiar colonial products (coffee, tea, chocolate, sugar, and tobacco). Coffee houses also made possible the auctioning of artworks and slaves, the elaboration of a private mailing system, and the floating of insurance schemes and shipping intelligence, such as the creation of Lloyd's of London. Lloyd's newsletter begins to appear in 1696, a few months after the first theatrical productions of *Oroonoko*. At the same time, Africans were also present in symbolic form as the exotic trademarks that advertised different commercial establishments, such as coffeehouses. As the space of egalitarian discourse, the coffeehouse allowed a hubbub of male voices expressing different political persuasions. If the coffeehouse was a nascent democratic space, as Habermas has suggested, it would have also been the arena for testing out common attitudes toward women and slaves who were excluded. Excluded from the discursive advantages of these establishments from the outset, it seems that women were also capable of creating disturbances.[29]

In the coffeehouse of today's critical methodologies, we can reassess the limits of Southerne's split-plot treatment of Englishwomen and slaves. Although the change in genre imposes a static separation in the place of the fluid relation between the narrator and Oroonoko in the novella, the play also refuses some of the identificatory impulses of oroonokoism, replacing them with a metropolitan disregard for the colonial relation altogether. The notable absence of a black woman in Southerne's text should alert us to the limits of the analogical use of slavery in the advancement of a metropolitan agenda of women's rights. Imoinda, no longer the potential Amazon of Behn's novella, is instead an object of pity and ridicule for not being able to play the system as well as Charlot managed to:

> Forgive this Indians fondness of her Spouse;
> Their law no Christian Liberty allows:
> Alas! they make a Conscience of their Vows!
> If Virtue in a Heathen be a fault;
> Then Damn the Heathen School, where she was taught.
> She might have learn'd to Cuckold, Jilt, and Sham,
> Had Covent-Garden been in Surinam. (Epil. 29–35)[30]

These concluding lines suggest that Southerne's Imoinda, though white, still possesses some "ethnic" qualities carried over from Behn's novella, making her an "Indian" and a "Heathen." Written by William Congreve and spoken in the first productions by Susannah Mountfort Verbruggen playing Charlot Welldon in the "breeches part" (Southerne's earlier role for her was as Sir Anthony), these lines assimilate Imoinda. This anti-imoindaism is a more generalized cultural interpretation of Imoinda's failure. Spoken by Mountfort when the theatrical apparatus is momentarily suspended, these lines attempt to bridge the distance from Surinam to London. The disdainful sympathy expressed here establishes a hierarchy, with metropolitan women succeeding where colonials cannot, even as racial difference is elided. Of course, the cynical treatment of Imoinda's badly done romance against the Welldon successes is one that many spectators may find reprehensible.

Whereas contemporary imoindaism exposes the romance involved in the narrator-Oroonoko identification, Southerne's anti-imoindaism leaves Oroonoko as the odd man out. Imoinda's death appeals to the sadistic fears present in romance desires and Charlot's transvestite success to the bisexual hopes fulfilled therein. Charlot's sexual transgressiveness parallels the varied object cathexes produced by widespread pet ownership and the mixed modes of tragedy and bathos that characterize pet culture.

Not pet-inclined themselves, the Welldons are only minimally interested in Oroonoko's position and exploit any contingent similarities with their own predicament that they find there. If contemporary imoindaists desire that Behn's narrator go beyond her fixation on Oroonoko and find Imoinda as radical difference, Restoration spectators may have found an Imoinda standing behind Charlot as a failed similarity. The politics of representing Imoinda appears to be a dialectical counter to that of representing Oroonoko. Southerne's adaptation is a "rightist" denial of difference, yet many contemporary readings enact "leftist" desires for difference's reassertion and reinscription. Imoindaism can be seen as a negative theology that mourns the absences created by colonialist representation, just as much as oroonokoism fetishizes the presence of the colonial object. Southerne's Oroonoko, compared to Behn's alternately honorable and horrific protagonist, commits a heroic act, killing the unjust governor even as Oroonoko himself dies—thus his ready assimilation to the model of the "noble Negro," royal and yet tragic, like Othello, who can be the "glorious Name" and narrative that Behn's final paragraph hints at. The play emphasizes the injustice of slavery but within older chivalric codes, in a way that confuses love and enslavement with the experience of being under the tyranny of willful pets. Self-promoting attitudes by representatives of each group, of Englishwomen and of African male slaves, are elaborated at the expense of others. Behn's *Oroonoko* propagates both hostility toward and fascination with the spoils of mercantilist colonialism. Southerne's play also criticizes the reification of bourgeois subjects when they encounter capital and commodity, even if it offers no practical solutions. Both texts are marked by an aristocratic nostalgia for the feudal past—whether in the fixation on kingship in Behn's text or the static heroicization of Oroonoko in Southerne's—along with an articulation and promotion of a self-fashioned ethical subject. Although an ostensible synthesis between a newly liberated bourgeois subject and anticapitalist values fails to take place in the novella—the question remains whether such a synthesis is viable or possible—the play juxtaposes the success of the English-women with the failure of the slave rebels. Hence the play moves on, it seems, from the disavowal that is characteristic of a logic of metonymy in Behn's text. With the play, a logic of metaphor operates to assert that difference, as witnessed in Imoinda's character, is a failure of identity. Bleaching Imoinda white, to go back to Chambers's trope, is rendered successful epidermally, even while it is shown to be a fruitless under-taking ultimately: "forgive this *Indians* fondness for her spouse." Oroo-noko's obsession with honor becomes a sign of his failed whiteness, whereas Charlot's celebration of credit is a sign of her successful manli-ness. Of course, Charlot's metaphors are economic, whereas Behn's are thanatoerotic, combining longing and loss. Charlot's clear-eyed cyni-cism is matched by Behn's teary-eyed heroization. Ultimately, meta-phor in Southerne assimilates difference to a logic of identity. Identity itself is supplied by a white male position that can juxtapose one brack-eted difference, that of *white* (women), against another, that of (black) *men*. The blind spot of such a logic of identity can be seen in the tex-tual elision of the category of the black woman. In contrast, Behn's novella fetishizes Oroonoko within a logic of metonymy, as the female narrator oscillates between her (white) identity and her (female) dif-ference. This oscillation disrupts the more seamless ideological closure afforded by metaphor but also ignores Imoinda as a secondary relation of contiguity.[31]

BLACKAMOORS

Oroonokoism has led to a number of interpretive blind spots. Critiques of oroonokoism have taken the route of reclaiming Imoinda, but they should not just end there. Otherwise, imoindaism too turns into a pious wish, an analogue of liberal desires for affirmative action. The logic of parodic subversion in both texts has not been adequately explored. Still, Southerne's play is assessed as derivative even as the complex perfor-mance history of the play is ignored. All tropicalizations are potentially parodic; virtualization, as an idealized form, is even more susceptible to parody. As Margaret Rose's economic definition goes, parody is "the critical refunctioning of preformed linguistic and artistic material with comic effect." Parody uses quotation marks that recontextualize through

Petting Oroonoko

deprecation and humor. Both versions of *Oroonoko* involve critical re-functionings of colonialist discourse and are therefore virtualizations replete with many tonal effects and suffused with critical potential. We have already taken note of some of these effects with respect to the rhetoric of pethood in the novella and that of the marriage market in the play, yet the presence of parody helps pose further metafictional questions concerning the representational adequacy of virtualization.[32]

Parody in Behn's novella is present in subtle but widespread fashion. Oroonoko's chivalric heroism consists of a quixotic belief in the inviolability of promises, ensuring his failure on many occasions. For instance, Oroonoko's gullible belief in Trefry's promises of amnesty comes just after a second betrayal at the hands of the slave driver. Oroonoko simplemindedly confuses honor with wit: "for it was one of his Maxims, *A Man of Wit cou'd not be a Knave or a Villain*" (35). If the narrator's tone here patronizes Oroonoko, it also criticizes, implicitly, the hypocrisy of Restoration rakes in the way that Charlot Welldon perfects in the play. Simultaneously there is bemusement concerning Oroonoko's naïveté. Similarly, what are we to make of the slaves' exaggerated veneration of Oroonoko or that they "paid him even Divine Homage" as they kiss his feet and cry out "*Long Live O King,*" especially when Oroonoko was personally responsible for having sold these individuals into slavery (37)? Either the slaves are an unthinking mob who would follow even the most cynical demagogue or they are innocent to the point of being simpletons. But the amnesia combined with the adoration leads to Oroonoko's acceptance as a credible leader. There are many such moments of parody, of inadvertent pastiche at the very least, moments that are invested with satirical potential if read imaginatively. For instance, at the high point of Oroonoko's and Imoinda's suicide pact, a telltale rhyme undercuts the moment of overkill, when Oroonoko "drew his Knife to kill this Treasure of his Soul, this Pleasure of his Eyes" (60). Does the rhyme enhance the melodrama or undercut it? Similarly, the parenthetical explanation of Imoinda's equanimity before being despatched by Oroonoko is sardonic: "while Tears trickl'd down his Cheeks, hers were Smiling with Joy she shou'd dye by so noble a Hand, and be sent in her own Country, (for that's their Notion of the next World)" (60). Has Imoinda already forgotten the gruesome treatment meted out to her in Coromantien, described at length earlier?

These various markers of stock romance formulae seem indeterminate. Behn's artistry and intentionality are not so much the issue here as our understandings of these topoi as parodic reproduction as well as retroactive focalization. The pet romance, as it is elaborated here, parodies martyrology and is therefore maudlin *and* burlesque. These random instances represent an exercise in Restoration simulation, where parodic counterfeiting can conceal as well as expose its own task of critical refunctioning. Parody in the novella follows a comedy-of-errors pattern: the African prince who is a slave trader is himself sold as slave (smirk), only to be himself resuscitated as pet-king for the English colonists (smirk), only to rebel against that very construction as feminizing him (smirk), only to be put to death as the real king himself was not so long ago (smirk). However, the more conventional interpretive sentence passed on Behn's *Oroonoko* would be formally identical to the one above, given that the pattern of sentimental melodrama prevails. If parody creates the parenthetical negative reaction (the smirk), it is in place of an affirmative one (the sigh). It is this structural, indeed structuralist, identity of sentimentalism and parody at the heart of *Oroonoko* that most clearly explains the logic of virtualization.[33]

Discourses of pethood and their implications have already been discussed as comic refunctioning—the creation of Oroonoko as pet-king—as well as critical reassertion in the face of that refunctioning—when Oroonoko balks at his domestication and rebels. Satirical implications of such rhetorical conflicts are also crucial to pursue throughout the narrator's treatment of Caesar's chivalric exploits. A miniature allegory presents itself when Caesar's defeat of the man-eating tigress is contrasted with his humbling by a different kind of beast, the Numb-Eel (46–47). The mock-epic context of this challenge and the eventual victory of the protagonist is no different from Gulliver's pathetic heroics in Brobdingnag. After nearly dying from electric shock in the episode, the resuscitated hero is cheered up by the narrator and her friends by being asked to have the eel for supper and thus reassert his mastery over that which nearly destroyed him. Figured in these contrasted "natural" exploits, perhaps, is a narrative of social evolution. The encounters with the tigresses function as mock-chivalric slayings, whereas the Numb-Eel's near victory over a chastened Oroonoko becomes a parable that teaches the subtle workings of action-at-a-distance. If the former exploits target identifiable enemies, the latter suggests a process that cannot be confronted by individual valor alone. The slave trade that ultimately destroys Oroonoko is also based on the new economic principles of action-at-a-distance. Reading with this didactic framework in mind, the electric eel's effect on Oroonoko appears to be a prolepsis of his subsequent political paralysis, and Oroonoko's execution reduces him from the honorable enemy he would like to be to the common criminal that the planters make of him. The royal slave is sacrificed to global movements that cannot be fought as chivalric monsters were in a certain age. It is impossible to pronounce with finality on the exact tonality of such juxtapositions of parody and sentimentalism, and whether they warrant "meaningful" explanations of the kind favored by satire or allegory. Yet interpretive contexts are considerably altered by attending to these indeterminacies, which are paradoxically principal determinants of Oroonoko's representation.

Similarly, the split-plot treatment in the play makes more explicit the ambivalent parody already present in the novella. If we *read* the parody into the novella, we are more inclined to *see* it in the play. As Peter Holland's trailblazing book on Restoration drama shows, both performance history and dramatic text are idealized when kept apart from each other; their mutual interference allows us to confront the dual nature of literary *reading* and theatrical *seeing*.[34] As the Oroonoko story was best known in the eighteenth century through its dramatic rather than novelistic version, it may likewise considerably alter our sense of the play if we realize that a sampling of the performance contexts—themselves representative of the performance contexts of many other plays of the period—reveals a vast number of entr'actes, afterpieces, and entertainments, involving vaulting, comic singing, horse jumping, and other buffoonery. All these olios attest to a burlesque context existing alongside tear-jerking sentimentalism.[35]

Precise information on performances in the 1690s is scanty. *The London Stage* documents one performance of July 9, 1698, as taking place "with the Italian shades" and an "Entertainment after the Carnaval at Rome . . . with several Grotesque dances." However, in the first decade of the 1700s, performances of *Oroonoko* were regularly accompanied by farcical mixtures. The performances of July 7, 1702, February 2, 1703, and April 27, 1703, included various combinations of dancing, singing, and horse vaulting as entr'actes. By the next decades, the sideshows became even more extravagant. The performance of January 9, 1717, saw a "Mimic Night Scene after the Italian Manner between a Harlequin, a Scaramouch and Dame Ragonde"; June 7, 1717, had "an Epilogue to be spoken by Spiller, riding on an Ass"; September 30, 1718, presented "the diverting Entertainment of the Dancing Dogs, newly arriv'd from France, who had been shewn at Court with much success"; October 1, 1724, had an "Afterpiece: Concluding as usual with a Grand Masque of the Heathen Deities." Dancing seems to have been by far the most common accompaniment. The performance of November 17, 1724, saw five dances, one after each act: saraband, Irish dance, Scotch dance, wooden shoe dance, and "Dame Ragonde and Her Two Sons." Those of October 25, 1725, and September 19, 1728, had, respectively, "a new dance of Slaves" and "a Tambour dance of Moors." It would seem that Congreve's parodic tone in the epilogue to Southerne's play is further buttressed by these light-hearted additions.[36]

Undoubtedly, comic interludes were collocated with sentimentalist aesthetics in the early part of the eighteenth century in a manner that cannot just be dismissed as tasteless and unfortunate. It is somewhat later, in 1759, that Hawkesworth's excisions of the comic subplot were justified by an anonymous Samuel Johnson. Even later, in 1784, John Ferriar revises *Oroonoko* yet again, retitling it *The Prince of Angola*. With abolitionist goals clearly in mind, Ferriar characterizes both Southerne's and Hawkesworth's renditions as "a grovelling apology of slaveholders."[37] Even as the entertainments in the earlier period, just as much as the subplot, could be read as challenging an easy sentimentalism, research on reception history suggests that the play's sentimentalism was correspondingly heightened. Arthur Nichols, for instance, has found that the title role in *Oroonoko* was most successfully declaimed by actors who specialized in rant. Although the small and sensitive David Garrick was acclaimed as Aboan, Oroonoko's trustworthy servant, in 1760, he had already failed as Oroonoko in 1759. Garrick's unusual failure contrasts with the relative success of minor performers such as Milward, Dexter, Delane, and Ryan in the title role. Jordan and Love emphasize that Nichols's study proves "a triumph of the ranters," and it was in fact Garrick's failure, along with the general change in taste, that broke the stranglehold that Southerne's play had on the repertory. It is no coincidence that this moment in the reception history also led to the jettisoning of the comic subplot. Just as Garrick, despite his talents, seemed unsuitable to his audiences as Oroonoko (despite the fact that he became legendary in other roles), he was also a failure as Othello because

Figure 6 William Hogarth, *The Quarrel With Her Jew Protector*, Plate II of *A Harlot's Progress* (1732). (British Museum, London)

he did not rant. Maybe there is a pattern to be discerned here, where excessive rant creates another linkage to the already existing ones between *Oroonoko* and *Othello*, strengthening Southerne's move to emphasize the theme of interracial domestic tragedy. When Garrick played Othello, he was promptly heckled by James Quin, a ranter known for his bombastic successes as both Oroonoko and Othello. The rival actor's devastating retort compared Garrick with the black page in Hogarth's *A Harlot's Progress:* "[H]ere's Pompey, where's the tea-kettle?" (see Fig. 6).[38]

Quin's retort to Garrick works to underscore the parodic doubleness of the Roman African and, indeed, that of the royal slave. Whether Caesar, Pompey, or Cato, classical names were used to personalize pets and rename slaves, fulfilling a range of comic functions for the owners. In terms of parody, one is reminded of Alexander Pope's humorous "Epigram. Engraved on the Collar of a Dog which I gave to his Royal

Highness," that satirizes the pretensions of aristocratic lackeys: "I am his Highness' Dog at Kew / Pray tell me Sir, whose Dog are you?"[39] Oroonoko's renaming domesticates epic. Even in republican Rome, Greek names indicated slave status or lineage, but in the modern period, "pompous classical names preferred by many planters were resented by most slaves, except when they were reminiscent of African names." Cattle names and slave names were similar, and "slaves were given either classical names such as Phoebe and Cyrus, or insulting nicknames . . . [such] as Beauty, Carefree, Monkey, Villain, and Strumpet." Names such as Zeno, Socrates, Scipio, and Scipio Africanus were common for slaves, but such names were also later adopted for dogs. According to one hypothesis, the practice of renaming slaves after Greeks and Romans may have been to indicate the owner's favorite neoclassical philosopher. In this regard, the renaming of Oroonoko as Caesar is an act that both Behn and Southerne merit as worthy of reflection.[40]

Although the renaming of slaves is characterized as pragmatic for the slave owners ("their native ones being likely very barbarous, and hard to pronounce"), the narrator justifies Trefry's choice of a classical name on the grounds of Oroonoko's courage. If the name *Caesar* is ironic, as Oroonoko's death is obscure compared to the Roman dictator's universal renown, the narrator asserts that his obscurity is a consequence of a paucity of "People, and Historians, that might have given him his due." Hinting at the asymmetrical and mock-epic nature of feminist herstory, Behn's narrative reverses roles. In an obscure world, devoid of chivalric heroes, the narrator performs the function of Oroonoko's biographer and memorialist (36). As pet-king and as a participant in a mock-epic, Caesar is treated by a "Female Pen" that combines romance with parody.

As an act of condescension for his or her owners, a slave's renaming had a deep-rooted ritual significance that cannot be explained only in terms of a slave owner's desires. At the same time, English poets, increasingly relishing the country's newfound quasi-imperial status, address English monarchs as versions of Roman emperors. For instance, David Hoegberg finds the appellation *Caesar* to be a complex allusion in *Oroonoko* to Plutarch's treatment of the original Caesar, with a lion-in-toils simile. When captured by the captain of the slave ship, Oroonoko "resented this Indignity . . . resembl[ing] a Lion taken in a Toil" (31). As a name, *Caesar* runs the gamut from most royal to most enslaved, and from having conservative implications to demonstrating resisting reappropriations of the same name.[41]

Orlando Patterson traces the transition to slavery through four important steps: the slave's symbolic rejection of the past and of his or her ties with former kin, the slave's change of name, the imposition of a visible mark of servitude upon the slave, and the slave's assumption of a new status in the master's household. Behn's and Southerne's texts exhibit all these liminal features of natal alienation. It is Patterson's claim that these ontological parameters of slavery paradoxically form a new politically inclined subject.[42] It is certainly the case that Oroonoko becomes the chosen leader of the slaves, yet the reworking of his earlier ties to these very people is not without skeptical undertones. If the sociopolitical context and discursive appeal of Caesar's leadership differ appreciably from the former kinship relations based on monarchical privilege, the parodic aspects of the representation interfere with any straightforward political meaning. If renaming is intimately linked with a new self-recognition and self-appropriation, the mockery implied by the use of classical names is a severe undercutting of the significance of such empowerment. Similarly, the act of renaming in Southerne's hands takes the route of emphasizing dramatic irony. Oroonoko is informed by the governor that Caesar is the most appropriate name as he too was a slave (to pirates), "a great Conqueror," and "unfortunate in his Friends," being murdered by them (I.ii.236–55). Ironically, the novella's conclusion idealizes the protagonist's name as the ultimate fetish, hoping that the author's reputation "is considerable enough to make his glorious Name to survive to all Ages" (65). The meaning of Oroonoko-as-Caesar, killer of man-eating tigers and gastronomic victor over electric eels—the chivalric hero and the domestic pet—is part of the bathetic and sentimental logic of pethood that strikes a chord with Quin's savaging of Garrick's Othello as a version of Hogarth's black Pompey. In the half-century since the portraits of Charles's mistresses were painted, the black boy as stage prop had been downwardly mobile. This can be seen in Hogarth's depiction of him as a figure of fun in *A Harlot's Progress*, in which Moll Hackabout's acquiring the boy and a pet monkey at the expense of her Jewish protector demonstrates her unbecoming and tenuous imitation of gentility (see Fig. 6). To this we should also add the existence of Francis Coventry's popular novella published in 1751, *The History of Pompey the*

Little or the Life and Adventures of a Lapdog—"the Little" in contradistinction to the Roman senator, who was often dubbed "the Great."

If Behn eventually is turned into a fervent Tryon-inspired abolitionist through the wishful thinking of a postabolitionist age, Oroonoko represents the continuation of pethood through textual canonization. As Tryon's character Sambo puts it, grisly portrayals of slave suffering would make "the Extremity of our Calamities . . . seem Romantick" (76).[43] The overblown description of an unbearable death becomes very bearable, if sensationalist, entertainment. The description oversteps direct access to the suffering body and instead draws attention to its own constructedness (through a female pen) in the final paragraph of the story. It is as if Behn's novella, as one of the multiple origins of English novelistic discourse, deconstructs in one uninterrupted movement the very history of the English novel in miniature, moving from romance convention through high realism back to postmodern self-consciousness.

Virtualization is ultimately not about sentimentalism and condescension; it concerns mimicry, counterfeiting, and parody. In this respect, the novella's treatment of mutilation is a parodic practice, replicating itself through a number of cultural contexts. Suvir Kaul has acutely remarked that there are at least three different kinds of mutilation in the novella. I have already mentioned them in passing: the ritual scarification of the Coromantee protagonists that mark them as upper class, adorned, and exotic; the competitive self-mutilation of the Amerindian generals that ennoble them at considerable personal and mutual jeopardy; and the bloody decapitation and dismemberment that both Oroonoko and Imoinda suffer at story's end. Kaul's definition of these three admittedly different body practices into continental codes is, however, the reverse of their slippery novelistic effects. Although it is heuristic to distinguish the African, American, and European forms of mutilation, Surinam, the colonial space, is where these forms are tentatively hybridized. As with Oroonoko's violent chivalric exploits, mutilation can be attached with ennobling as well as disenobling meanings, but its interpretive reification avoids facing up to its parodic repetition.[44]

In yet another suggestive interpretation, Laura Rosenthal has argued that Behn's novella is about the transition from an African gift economy to the commodity economy of the New World. Imoinda's circulation as gift in Africa is violated by her removal to Surinam, and Behn's memorialization of the royal slave is a compensatory restitution, an idealized literary gift based on nostalgia. In contrast to Behn's noblesse oblige, Southerne is decried for being comfortable with commodification. Again, a continentalist reification (the *African* gift and the *American* commodity) as well as an idealization of the gift occludes matters. Behn's narrator juggles the erotic fetishization of pethood with its status convertibility as well as its value as commodity. Southerne's *Oroonoko* is in many ways far more sentimentalized than Behn's and much less related to the commodity motivations of Behn's. Rather, Southerne contrasts Behn's fetishistic concern with exotic *commodity* by exploring an analytical logic of *commodification* through Charlot Welldon. Southerne's innovation consists of the separation of the logic of commodification from that of affect. Economic success — and colonial success — are linked to parody; colonial failure — and economic failure — are linked to sentimental loss and tragedy and the inability to separate commodification from affect.[45]

A play cannot be a novel in the way it reports events, represents its action, or reflects on its own capacity to represent. Of course, it could be a different play than itself. But rather than treat counterfactuals, we need to examine each language game in terms of its potential as well as its limits. Although Southerne is often blamed for disavowal and Behn frequently applauded for memorialization, both possible outcomes of the logic of colonial representation are coded by the remnants of a sentimentalist nostalgia. Do we always have to choose between Behn's *Oroonoko* and Southerne's, or can we see them both as differently (dis)abled when articulating the inadequacies of colonialist representation?

In all fairness, coping with an absence of Oroonoko's body is clearly Southerne's task from the beginning. In his introduction to the play, Southerne characterizes the problem as follows: "[Behn] had a great command of the stage, and I have often wondered that she would bury her favorite hero in a novel when she might have revived him in the scene. She thought either that no actor could represent him, or she could not bear him represented. And I believe the last when I remember what I have heard from a friend of hers, that she always told his story more feelingly than she writ it. Whatever happened to him at Surinam, he has mended his condition in England. He was born here under your Grace's influence, and that has carried his fortune farther into the world than all the poetic stars I could have solicited for his success" (4). Yet, why could Behn "not bear him represented"? Could Behn not bear the pain it caused her, or did she resist the inevitable appropriation of Oroonoko's representation within the split-plot contexts that Southerne worked out after her death? The novella in many ways most emphatically depicts Oroonoko as bearing the unbearable. His stoic fortitude, silently suffering mutilation at the hands of the colonists, is Behn's final depiction of Oroonoko smoking on, unperturbed as he is castrated and dismembered, a mythic evocation that we are invited to swallow wholesale. Is it possible to ask whether this most treasured and pleasured moment is a parody that invites us to *remember* dismemberment? Surely that would be in bad taste, as it would be to ask if Oroonoko was blowing a nonchalant smoke-ringed "O" as he was killed. Why this emphasis on the absence of a need to exclaim, cry out, or lose self-possession? Or is that role deliberately denied the sufferer by the logic of sentimentalism and kept aside for the empathetic reader?

Behn favors the firsthand testimonial, with its foregrounding of narrative voice as a guarantee of authenticity as well as a hermeneutic obstacle that intervenes between the reader and the historical object. Southerne favors the theatrical illusion of direct representation, which is complicated by the split-plot interferences that draw attention to the mechanisms of that representation. Indeed, Southerne revels in the fact that the real Oroonoko is truly irrecuperable. For him, the transition from reference to representation, or history to literature, is precisely that of tragedy to comedy: "whatever happened to him at Surinam, [Oroonoko] has mended his condition in England." Oroonoko the dying slave has become *Oroonoko* the successful play. Southerne is not just crudely celebrating his success at converting a story of human suffering into a commercial potboiler. He recognizes that Oroonoko's discursive effect is far in excess of the dead pet that Behn agonizes over, and his callousness toward it reveals a demystificatory impulse withheld by Behn's undecidable sentimentality concerning her function as author.

Colonialist representations do not just act out the closure of historical subtexts but also exude a necessary fiction of that history's sovereign irrecuperability. If the past is irrecuperable as a presence rather than as sorry fetish, it can be put to multiple uses as parodic text. Oroonoko, as a literary character, is a cipher echoing lost persons, subject effects, or statistical numbers, called up—rhetorically—to *represent* the Triangle trade, the birth of plantation capitalism, and the African diaspora. In that respect, he remains an exhibit, still very much a pet to our interpretive strokings, restitutive impulses, and erotic cathexes. A human pet is an amalgam, itself an *effect* of the physical and epistemic violences of colonialism. Pets cannot be set free; generally, they die when they are "liberated." Staying with the effect, as sentimentalist investment in Oroonoko does, diverts critical attention from other causes and effects. Alternately, real-world tropicopolitans—rather than virtual ones such as Oroonoko—successfully revolted through marronage (a combination of insurrection and desertion) in the Caribbean when the eighteenth century culminated, as does this book, with the Haitian Revolution.

CHAPTER TWO

Piratical Accounts

It happen'd one Day about Noon going towards my
Boat, I was exceedingly surpriz'd with the Print of a
Man's naked Foot on the Shore, which was very plain to
be seen in the Sand: I stood like one Thunder-struck, or
as if I had seen an Apparition; I listen'd, I look'd round
me, I could hear nothing, nor see any Thing; I went
up the Shore and down the Shore, but it was all one, I
could see no other Impression but that one, I went to it
again to see if there were any more, and to observe if it
might not be my Fancy.

—DANIEL DEFOE, *Robinson Crusoe*[1]

These lines, among the most memorable in English fiction,
mark an eerie moment in Robinson Crusoe's pseudo autobiography. Until that point in his island stay, the protagonist
had learned to survive without human interaction. But the footprint
augurs transactions that Crusoe dreads. Serving as a warning of alien
power, the sighting reintroduces human agency. Where the sand ought
to have been as smooth as a tabula rasa, Crusoe finds the superimposition of culture. The trauma of discovery *is* the event itself: "I was exceedingly surpriz'd with the *Print* of a Man's naked Foot on the Shore."
Events happen without warning, and produce unnerving repercussions.
Although the print is "very plain to be seen in the Sand," Crusoe can
nevertheless "hear nothing, nor see any Thing" that may have caused it.
The footprint is explicit, but its history is irretrievable. Indeed, as a signature, the footprint *initiates* the open question of its own history and
interpretation. Nothing can be deduced, as no sequence of prints exists:
"there was exactly the very Print of a Foot, Toes, Heel, and every Part

of a Foot; how it came thither I know not, nor could in the least imagine" (112). Crusoe returns home projecting a phantom agent, "looking behind [himself] at every two or three Steps, mistaking every Bush and Tree, and fancying every Stump at a Distance to be a Man." But he does not find anyone. As literal index, the footprint *indicates* a premonitory value. It points, as the printer's icon ☞ would, perhaps, to other spatio-temporal zones. Crusoe wants to read the footprint into the present, but it is a calling card that deictically hints at past and future while generating a trauma that deterritorializes the novel's protagonist, threatening his property, propriety, and very sense of self.

The footprint is illustrative in its emphases as well as its elisions. The devil is exonerated as a possible culprit because he too is subject to the laws of probability (no less than ten thousand to one) defied by this incident. Crusoe can thus comfortably eliminate the supernatural agency that he is so fond of citing on other occasions. Instead, he makes a commonsensical conjecture, saying that "the Savages of the main Land over-against [him]" must have visited the island (122). However, this realization undercuts his earlier desire for human company: "for I whose only Affliction was, that I seem'd banished from human Society, that I was alone, circumscrib'd by the boundless Ocean, cut off from Mankind, and condemn'd to what I call'd silent Life . . . I *say*, that I should now tremble at the very Apprehensions of seeing a Man, and was ready to sink into the Ground at but the Shadow or silent Appearance of a Man's having set his Foot in the Island" (113–14). Using this shoreline intrusion to shore up his own shaky sense of self, Crusoe's narration transforms it from sense impression to phenomenological event. Impinging on Crusoe's sensory horizon, the footprint becomes an "incident" to which meaning can be ascribed. Defoe places this episode at the precise center of the novel, as the hermeneutic kernel of Crusoe's subjectivity at work. Busily processing and containing these marks found in the sand, Crusoe under threat re-emerges as self-contained subject.

Such dramatic moments of subject preservation and self-apprehension in relation to an exemplary instance are typical of the challenges posed by colonial trauma perceived as an event. The above episode participates in a larger process that constructs a self-rationalizing modern subject, even as that process subordinates the "savage," either as entity or occurrence. Indeed, much Defoe criticism has been fixated on this kind of Blakean "minute particular," which constitutes narrative through a simple hermeneutic oscillation between the subject and its environment or the self and the world. This shuttling—from random external impressions and occurrences to discontinuous moments of internalized interpretation of what has happened before—produces the category of experience in these novels. Reconstructing and processing actions through reflections, and objects through subjects, the narrator can "own" his life, and his account of it, by the retroactive process of deferred psychological action, what Freud calls Nachträglichkeit. Reclaiming the past creates the fiction of subjective continuity. Rearranging and transcribing the past in his journal, Crusoe gives it psychical agency. Reading a narrative of "minute particulars" in Captain Cook's Pacific voyages, Jonathan Lamb playfully distinguishes them by five codes before their breakdown into empiricism: "the vindication of providence, the enlightenment taxonomy, the sweep of history, the sentimentalization of the loose circumstance, and the anthropological genealogy." Colonial travel narrative and its imitators, from Columbus to Crusoe to Cook, replete with singularities such as the footprint episode, would respond fruitfully to such an analysis.[2]

Colonialism is more than the brutal but simple act of imperial conquest. No mere conqueror, the colonialist subject is the accompanying historian, trader, and missionary. While Columbus the conqueror acquires territories and subjugates peoples, his historian double keeps a careful record of the significance of these happenings in his journal. Inevitably, this preliminary documentation leads to a more involved process of classification and evaluation. In the manner of double-entry bookkeeping, appropriation is balanced by enumeration in colonialist accounts. Mary Louise Pratt has suggestively described the second aspect of the imperial process as "anti-conquest."[3] The persistence of memory alongside the widespread destruction of other genealogies characterizes colonialism in the modern era. Colonialism correlates with imperial agendas, but it is not coextensive with them; as conquest evacuates living cultures from a territory or subordinates them, so anticonquest, as discourse, replenishes the gaps with information and "reductive normalization." Geography, natural history, and anthropology make up the anticonquest, with travel narrative as its preferred literary genre. The careful archival preservation fostered by the techniques of anticonquest—surveying topographies, collecting specimens, and observing customs—continues the conquest but also makes available the materials that, when marshaled together, can prove, through tracing the efficacy of anticonquest as epistemological violence, the egregiousness of conquest as physical violence. Whereas the Spanish conquest of the Americas precedes the anticonquest, the British Empire largely follows it. The student of colonial discourse is forced to proceed in both directions, prognostically as well as diagnostically.

The Crusoe story, as we know, has become mythic as an instance of modern individualism, indeed of colonialist man just as much as of *homo economicus*. Friday's role is doubly relevant as Crusoe's symbolic son and as his first political subject (his age when he enters Crusoe's life as his "New Companion" is twenty-six, which happens to be the duration of Crusoe's stay on the island). According to Crusoe, Friday "kiss'd the Ground, and laid his Head upon the Ground, and taking me by the Foot, set my Foot upon his Head; this it seems was in token of swearing to be my Slave for ever" (147). The illustration in one of the first French translations, *La vie et les avantures surprenantes de Robinson Crusoe*, published in Amsterdam in 1720, shows the significance of Friday's self-abasement, which could not have been scripted better (Fig. 7). Though Crusoe conveniently interprets Friday's gesture as one of voluntary servitude, the action provides a symbolic solution to the question posed by the footprint episode: Using Crusoe's stationary foot to stamp himself, Friday "chooses" subjection. If Crusoe's reaction to the footprint as alien impression was out of fright, by a logic of pantomime, Crusoe's propriative footwork that *impresses* Friday into servitude—as eighteenth-century naval press gangs *impressed* able-bodied vagrants—is presented as Friday's own handiwork. The scene of Friday's foot-worship is also the commencement of the cult of Crusoe. Crossing the creek and escaping his captors, Friday abandons cannibalistic carnage for the new dispensation of protective servitude and cultural deliverance. Is a slave's foot-worship of the master less hallucinatory than the impression made by a solitary footprint in the sand? The performative gesture ascribed to Crusoe's foot emanates from Friday's low-key directorial staging, naturalized as it is by Crusoe's narration. Friday's self-fashioning as Crusoe's foot soldier is a continuation of Crusoe's colonial performance fulfilled by its purported object. The footprint to foot-worship sequence is but one imagistic correspondence in the text. As Geoffrey Sill argues convincingly, the scene with the old goat in the cave is a precise mirror image of Crusoe's earlier dream of the aveng-

Figure 7 *Friday prostrating himself at Crusoe's feet,* from the French edition of *The Life, and Strange surprising adventures of Robinson Crusoe* (1720). (British Library, London)

ing angel. The presence of such indirect reworkings make *Oroonoko* and *Robinson Crusoe* into what Peter Hulme has called "concessionary narrative." Both texts, when read imaginatively rather than symptomatically, recognize subordination and criticize it, but only implicitly and indirectly. Friday enables Crusoe's subjective impressions, diaristic imprints, and the impressment of the former as unfree labor. As with Oroonoko's earlier example, Friday is also Crusoe's pet, approaching him on all fours, digging a hole in the sand with his bare hands, following him close at his heels, and even calling his own father, Friday Sr., "an Ugly Dog." After all, Friday is successor in a line of previous members of Crusoe's "family" that conflated pethood and subjecthood in his island kingdom and included cats, an old dog, and a parrot adept at mimicry.[4]

However, the relationship is far more complex beneath the surface.

As Roxann Wheeler suggests, a desire for clear boundaries generates a master-slave dichotomy in Defoe's language as well as ours.[5] The text can also be seen as indirectly acknowledging racial polymorphousness and generating a corresponding ambivalence. Friday is described as a cross between Amerindian and European, even though he is sometimes mistaken for an African. There is considerable slippage in the description of Friday's role as well, alternating as he does among the positions of slave, servant, assistant, and companion. The ambivalences represent a microcosm of rapid change in perceptions of race from the late seventeenth century to the story's publication in 1719 and subsequent reinterpretations. The novel consists of multicornered racial, political, and cultural conflicts involving Spaniards, Morescos (the descendants of the exiled Iberian Arabs), Moors (North Africans), Caribs, black Caribs, English sailors, and pirates. For these reasons, there is no simple oppositional stance to identify within the novel, even if Friday tempts us with that prospect. After he cuts the umbilical cord with his birth family, Crusoe encounters several human interlocutors including Moley and Xury, the Brazilian planters, the presumed cannibals, the piratical Will Atkins and his associates, and the Spaniards, all of whom, in addition to Friday, alternately suffer and prosper at his hands.

Defoe's other novels are also notable for rationalizing the contingencies of tropicopolitan experience into the teleological narrative of metropolitan representation. Defoe mimics the accounting procedures of travel narrative — its minute particulars and its involvement in anti-conquest — and also features virtualizations of these procedures. Liminal presences such as slaves, pirates, prostitutes, and renegades interfere and collude in differing degrees with the colonial project. *Robinson Crusoe, The Farther Adventures, Captain Singleton,* and *Colonel Jack* — as well as *Moll Flanders* and *Roxana,* despite their differently gendered protagonists and more domestic locations — make layered progressions through techniques such as anticonquest onward to virtualization, eventually returning, with varying degrees of ambiguity, to bourgeois domesticity through the trope of conversion. Defoe's last novel, *A Voyage Around the New World,* which I discuss later, interestingly eschews moral discourse altogether. Deciphering these ideological differences could lead to a more detailed picture. By looking at the wooden world, and representations of it, we can analyze the ship as a carrier not just of goods and populations but of tropicopolitan narratives and metaphors. As the most significant interface for several centuries between metropolitan and colonial spheres, shipping was the primary means of contact, trade, conquest, and, indeed, of tropicalization.

Focusing on a lesser known novel of Defoe's, *The Life, Adventures, and Pyracies of the Famous Captain Singleton,* published in 1720, this chapter analyzes the role played by piratical narratives for the elaboration of colonialist ideology, as well as the transcultural challenges that could be posed to it from within this literature. To some extent, piratical narratives are the obverse of concessionary narrative, flaunting a "no excuses" colonialism against sentimental depictions. However, this apparent hardness is a different kind of idealization that I want to explore as equally implicated in the construction of tropicopolitan agency. The first section speculates on the range of the word *account,* one of the submerged motifs in *Captain Singleton.* Notions of accounting traverse the different but related registers of representation, involving criminal, financial, seafaring, and novelistic procedures. The second section specifies Defoe's understanding of the sociopolitical as well as tropological significance of various kinds of maritime violence, including buccaneering, privateering, and piracy. Seeming to admire the egalitarianism and dynamic energies behind piratical violence on the one hand, Defoe and other mercantilist observers distrust the anarchic threat piracy posed to the extension of a generalized colonial commerce. The burden of the third section is to show how Defoe manages to assimilate the virtualizations suggested by piracy—including those of homoeroticism— by absorbing practices into representations. Piracy's "floating" threat to conceptions of international law is successfully eradicated by aggressive countermeasures, even as there remain fantasized alternatives not subject to moral or political economy, in the South Seas and South America.

ACCOUNTS AND ACCOUNTANTS

The best known—and presumably the most reliable, according to contemporaries—source for criminal lives in Defoe's time was the periodical compilation of biographical sketches by the clergymen assigned to extract repentances from the condemned at Newgate prison. The Newgate minister was known as an ordinary, and his proto-journalistic report was simply "the Account."[6] These preliminary accounts from

Newgate, often sparse and laconic, were drastically reworked by Grub Street hacks through a spate of pamphlets, ballads, and novels, thus creating the rich literature of criminality.

The word account, which proliferates throughout early-eighteenth-century literary discourse, indicates the traffic among the realms of narrative, economics, and criminality in *Captain Singleton*. The term figures prominently in a pamphlet biography published by Defoe in 1719, of the famous pirate captain John Avery or Henry Every, a narrative that provides the closest historical referent to Singleton's personality. The title takes aim at piratical mythologies: *The King of Pirates: Being an Account of the Famous Enterprises of Captain Avery, The Mock King of Madagascar. With His Rambles and Piracies; wherein all the Sham Accounts formerly publish'd of him, are detected*. The author asserts that his true account debunks other sham accounts, implying that accounts themselves occupy a marketplace where literary commodities are in cutthroat competition with each other for commercial success. The first-person narrator asserts in the preface that the story "will give the Readers how much they have been impos'd upon in the former ridiculous and extravagant Accounts" which had made "a kind of monstrous unheard of Story."[7] Continuing with this play on accountability, Defoe's 1725 pamphlet on Jonathan Wild is called *The True and Genuine Account of the Life and Actions of the Late Jonathan Wild; Not Made up of Fiction and Fable, but taken from his Own Mouth, and Collected from Papers of his Own Writing*. The disclaimers issued when attempting novelistic verisimilitude indicate that procedures of accusation and authentication, veracity and mendacity, are preliminary to all "accounts." If accounts are doctored, they draw the reader's attention to extratextual standards of accountability that obscure the transparency of particular accounts more than others. Defoe learned to defend himself from attacks that questioned his claims of verisimilitude (such as Gildon's well-known diatribe against *Robinson Crusoe*) by appealing to instrumental notions of fictional value. For instance, in the preface to *Colonel Jack*, Defoe says that it is not "of the least Moment to enquire whether the *Colonel* hath told his own Story true or not; If he has made it a *History* or a *Parable*, it will be equally useful, and capable of doing Good; and in that it recommends it self without any other *Introduction*."[8]

As it happens, the full title of *Captain Singleton* uses the word account three times while dishing out a plot summary.[9] In its first occurrence, account is narration: "an Account of his being set ashore." The second time, it refers to the quasi-anthropological descriptive information gleaned from travel narratives: "an Account of the customs and manners of the People." Finally, the third occurrence, "with an Account of his many Adventures and Pyracies with the famous Captain Avery and others," connotes an episodic listing of occurrences much like the first. Of course, the significant financial meaning of account is left out in the title (although we hear mention of "the great Riches" Singleton acquired). This financial meaning nonetheless pervades the novel, which often lists in great detail the economic transactions undertaken by its characters. The novel rehearses the possibilities and dangers of seeking financial gain. The long expedition to African interiors, in search of primitive accumulation, is followed by accounts of piratical activity at sea. The commercial sense of account is often lurking behind or alongside account as the narrative explanation of heroic exploits, much like venture capitalism's conflation with older ideologies of adventure.

Critics have sporadically seized on the nexus between adventure and commerce, an especially obvious link between conquest and anticonquest, in Defoe's fictions. As Maurice Wehrung puts it, "the historical adventurer appears as much as an administrator, an exchequer, a tally-clerk, and a lawyer as a sea-captain or villain. Much of his time is devoted to paperwork: he draws lists, keeps accounts, calculates food allowances, pens out rules and regulations, calls his men to the polls, writes formal letters to friends and enemies." Defoe was himself adept at financial balance sheets, and his father, James Foe—who twice declared bankruptcy—is said to have innovatively reorganized bookkeeping procedures. Defoe exercised these skills working full time as an accountant from 1695 to 1699.[10]

Composed of a series of adventures centered around a faceless protagonist, *Captain Singleton* rationalizes the rise of venture capitalism through adventure. The peculiarity of Singleton's story, however, is more than a compulsive conflation of the narrative with the financial account. The transactional nature and textuality of all accounts, whether those of accountants and their auditors, storytellers and their listeners, or writers and their readers, are caught up in an activity of rendering them, justifying their authenticity, and proving or pretending, through an autofoundationalism, a stable and trustworthy origin. In this light, the very first paragraph of *Captain Singleton* reminds the reader that all accounts are playing within an economy of self-justification in the eyes of others. Captain Bob (as the protagonist Singleton would like to be known) exhibits a self-conscious awareness of how accounts of remembered social origin relate to more complex processes of novelistic and historical self-justification. Indeed, the narrator is aware of how such accounts produce the subject of autobiography: "As it is usual for great Persons whose Lives have been remarkable, and whose Actions deserve Recording to Posterity, to insist much upon their Originals, give full Accounts of their Families, and the Histories of their Ancestors: So, that I may be methodical, I shall do the same" (1). Speaking as he does from an amused recognition of genealogy as an important factor in the production of bourgeois subjecthood, Captain Bob promises to "give full Accounts." English novels would also highlight full-fledged mock-genealogies, as in Henry Fielding's *Joseph Andrews* and *Jonathan Wild*. But almost immediately, Singleton perpetrates a comic substitution by parodically referring to financial transactions that, in his case, preempt any recuperable family background. The narrator reveals that the woman whom he had thought was his real mother had told him at the age of six that "she was not my Mother, but that she bought me for Twelve Shillings of another Woman" (2). Meanwhile, this "good gypsy mother, for some of her worthy actions, no doubt, happened in Process of time to be hang'd" (2). The previous owner of the child was "a Beggar-Woman that wanted a pretty little child to set out her Case" (2). Captain Bob traces his origin through the gypsy's account to a belief that he was stolen at the age of two from an affluent family as a result of the negligence of a nursemaid. Compounded by multiple transfers through sale away from the world of respectability to that of crime, Singleton's representation of this original theft of his identity establishes a dubious claim of noble birth. Singleton's account of his origins is, in fact, the story of their irreversible occultation, as a result of force and fraud, into pure financial circulation. As a reified object himself, Singleton is stolen and commodified much before he can ever speak in his own name as a desiring subject. These fictions of Defoe, like American captivity-and-redemption narratives, are important precursors to slave narratives such as Olaudah Equiano's, which I discuss in chapter 6. Through circumstantial abandonment, Singleton the child falls on the parish account for maintenance, until he can escape aboard ship and repeat his vagrancy by eventually becoming a sea rover. It is only following these successes that the adult can speak by possessing the narrative of the child that he claims he was, emphasizing a certain radical, alienated individualism with potentially tragic consequences.[11]

The ironization of identity and authority resurfaces in another disclaimer at the end of the novel, neatly framing the novel's ironic status from first to last page:

> And now, having so plainly told you, that I am come to *England,* after I have so boldly own'd what Life I have led abroad, 'tis Time to leave off, and say no more for the present, lest some should be willing to inquire too nicely after
>
>
>
> *Your Old Friend,*
> CAPTAIN BOB. (277)
>
>

This turning of a constative predicate into a performative signature, through Defoe's accounting procedures, neatly frames and suspends the novel's status as truth claim. In a typical transformation of the epistolary grammar, the direct object, by virtue of being set off as a signature, turns into an authorizing subject. The sentence becomes a parable of the novel's larger process of conversion, where the reified commodity, the child Singleton, has found a voice. There is a broader irony as the novel's realism undermines itself when it draws attention to the fabrication of all doctored accounts, even as it holds out the tantalizing possibility of a subject construction from outside the fiction of the novelistic enunciation itself. The very name Singleton evokes a fundamental alienation from society as did other criminal biographies.[12]

GOING UPON THE ACCOUNT

"[T]hey were going upon *the Account,* which by the Way was a Sea Term for a Pyrate; I say, as soon as ever they heard it, they went to work, and getting all things ready in the Night, their Chests and Clothes, and whatever else they could, they came away before it was Day" (*Singleton* 169–70). In this passage, Captain Bob explains maritime vocabulary when his men join forces with others who have turned pirate. "Going upon the account" also alludes to the private commercial activity undertaken by sailors that went on parallel to the ventures of the captain and the ship's owner. For instance, an economistic Englishman that Singleton's band met in Africa in the first half of the novel, and who spurred them on to further accumulation, is said to have illegally "traded on his own Account" in the ports before being reduced to penury when the party finds him naked in the interior (124). In a pamphlet written later, Defoe also warns that piracy may make inroads into the labor force: "the tempting Profits of going upon the Account (so our Sailors call that wicked Trade of turning Pyrates), in which horrid Employment (however scandalous) many thousands of our Seamen have engaged since the late War . . . has been a Great Cause of the Decrease in the Numbers of Seamen among us, and will continue to be so, unless some Remedy may be found out to reduce them and restore them to the Service and Interest of their Country."[13] The alarmist language of the pamphlet leads to the candid acknowledgment that sociopolitical solutions rather than penal ones had to be sought. Defoe's stated aim is to restore the pirates to "the Service and Interest of their Country." He analyzes piracy as a social problem caused by the demobilization of the Navy after the Treaty of Utrecht in 1713. This warning is actually anachronistic, as the substantial threat of piracy had dissipated when this paragraph was written in 1728.

Though legal rhetoric characterized the pirate as *hostis humani generis,* a common enemy to all humankind, piracy during the period is marked by complex moment-by-moment shifts in legal status. Paradoxically, piracy was often co-opted and exonerated as a tolerated abuse, even though, at its high point in the 1690s and 1710s, it posed a major threat to mercantile shipping on the principal British trade routes to the West Indies and India. Pirates posed crucial challenges to law enforcement by preying on merchant shipping and escaping punitive action. On the other hand, state-sponsored privateering expeditions that were issued "letters of marque" encouraged the seizure and destruction of competitive merchant shipping by other European countries. Such quasi-piratical activity was frequently sanctioned in order to protect the commercial interests of the country that organized them; needless to say, all major European countries organized such expeditions against each other's shipping. Hence, pirates were in the dangerous and profitable position of opportunistically playing various legal and political minefields to their advantage. The issuance of frequent pardons and royal proclamations, as piratical activity could not always be stopped by force, also presented unique occasions when blanket absolutions could be obtained for previous piratical acts.[14]

Defoe's thematization of piracy needs some definition. A number of illegal and violent maritime activities, such as buccaneering, privateering, and wrecking, existed alongside piracy. The social and circumstantial natures of these activities were quite distinct from each other. Yet they frequently merged in the popular imagination and also were occasionally convenient in enabling shifts of identity. Buccaneers were vigilante settlers and only occasional seafarers who acted violently on their own initiative in ways that enhanced the colonial presence of the British. Like Sir Henry Morgan, governor of Jamaica, a noted buccaneer who sacked Panama, they were frequently rewarded for their prescient services after the fact. Privateers operated against rival shipping with governmental approval through secret letters of marque that could maintain a level of deniability for the state. Of course, as in the 1701 case of the trial of Captain Kidd, a privateer turned pirate, this could embarrass the state considerably. Pirates, however, were not identified with or beholden to the national project. They formed a renegade subculture recruited from insubordinate elements of the seafaring milieu and struck out for themselves in remarkable fashion, to the extent that historians have speculated that they were remnants of the radical elements from the English Revolution. Piracy was especially significant as a virtualizing activity on the colonial periphery. Some aspects of piracy represent a proletarian, anticapitalist challenge to the bourgeois economic and political institutions that Defoe supported. It is significant that Singleton's activities in the second half of the novel are clearly piratical and distinguish themselves from the buccaneering and privateering described in Defoe's *A New Voyage Round the World* (1725), itself beholden to narratives by Dampier, Exquemeling, and Rogers.[15]

Captain Singleton, as a criminal biography, serially records the narrator's piratical heists, but the novel also flirts with alternative projects for sociopolitical advancement, written in direct response to its characters' alienation. The novel's treatment of piratical cultures should be read against the foil of the earlier *Robinson Crusoe* and its sequel, *Farther Adventures*. The theme of piracy is structurally important in all three novels, with Crusoe and Singleton taking up opposing stances with respect to it. In the first novel, Crusoe suffers from enslavement by pirates and then escapes from the Algerian rovers of Sallee. His establishment of a physical and then a political presence on the island comes into direct contestation with the piratical behavior of Will Atkins and his followers at the conclusion of the novel. In *Farther Adventures*, Crusoe's return to the island involves a protracted narrative of the rebellion staged by Will Atkins and his followers. Their refusal of the work ethic and contestation of the legitimacy of Crusoe's distribution of property is successfully exorcized by a dose of family ideology, when the restless insurgents are persuaded to marry captured native women.

Piratical discourse should be treated with some caution, as its relation to piracy as a historical practice is still somewhat unclear. Although Defoe's *General History of the Pyrates* has become an *ur*-text for studies of piracy, its imaginative power derives from a deliberate confusion of real and fictional pirates. Piratical articles often revealed a collectivist origin behind the fraternal contract. The *General History*, for instance, describes the petition by which a mutiny is authored: "it was unanimously resolved on, and the underwritten Petition drawn up and signed by the whole Company in the manner of what they call a *Round Robin*, that is, the Names were writ in a Circle, to avoid all Appearance of Preeminence, and least any person should be mark'd out by the Government, as a principal Rogue among them."[16] The round-robin testifies to a political formation that is collective at its very origin. Because it is authored and signed in a circular fashion, the round-robin, if discovered, cannot be narrativized into sorting out the troublemakers or leaders as distinct from the instigated herd; the petition highlights the equal individual responsibility alongside the collective security of numbers, in case the conspiracy is abortive. Such a round-robin is diametrically opposed to Walpole's practice of autocratic rule, dubbed Robinocracy from 1728 onward, and thus forms an interesting layer of retroactive allusion to the autogenesis of power on Robinson Crusoe's island. Both Crusoe and Singleton prefer to be called by their nicknames, Robin and Bob, which derive from Robert (Robinson is sometimes called Bob in *Robinson Crusoe*). However, the ostensible antecedent, the Christian name Robert, is one that Singleton explicitly repudiates when the protagonist learns from his "gypsy mother" that his previous guardian had informed her that "my Name was *Bob Singleton*, not *Robert*, but plain *Bob;* for it seems they never knew by what Name I was Christen'd" (2). Perhaps by the late 1720s the absent and delegitimized "Robert" Singleton can function as yet another unintended allusion to the great man himself, Walpole. In the *Beggar's Opera*, we also find Robin of Bagshot, a highwayman who preys on unwary travelers near Windsor Forest, and who bears a close resemblance to Walpole.

Despite the myth of possessive individualism that characterizes the first part of the Crusoe trilogy, it should be remembered that the eventual political legacy of Robinson Crusoe is the institution of a colonial collective on his island with the increased redundancy of his own role as paternalist arbiter, as seen in the sequels. This tussle suggests a transposition of the maritime context, with Crusoe acting like an individualist captain and Atkins and others behaving in the manner of piratical renegades. Singleton is a rendition of maritime upward mobility, with the motto that where Atkins was, there Crusoe shall be.[17]

Piracy was different from buccaneering and privateering because it generated an identifiable idealist discourse and a somewhat messier but related practice. In its most ideal form, piratical discourse puts forward clearly articulated political principles and stipulates mechanisms of collective organization. When Singleton's band of mutinous sailors unites upon being marooned on Madagascar early in the novel, it undertakes the following political compact: "the first thing we did was to give every one his Hand, that we would not separate from one another upon any Occasion whatsoever, but that we would live and die together; that we would kill no Food, but that we would distribute it in publick; and that we would be in all things guided by the Majority, and not insist upon our own Resolutions in any thing, if the Majority were against it; that we would appoint a Captain among us to be our Governour or Leader during Pleasure; that while he was in Office, we would obey him without Reserve, on Pain of Death; and that every one should take Turn, but the Captain was not to act in any particular thing without Advice of the rest, and by the Majority" (20-21). This kind of egalitarian partnership, "giving every one his Hand," is repeated as a foundational compact whenever new members join the group and throughout the piratical episodes. Many "articles" of pirate fraternity included anachronistically generous work conditions and compensation for the loss of limbs and eyes in battle. Mechanisms that recreated inequity, such as theft or gambling within the pirate groups themselves, are proscribed in *Captain Singleton* (95). Though gambling within the group is strictly prohibited under threat of dispossession and expulsion in order to prevent the emergence of inequalities, there is much rhetorical energy invested in the notion that the loot would be equally shared, much though we know this did not occur as equitably in practice or even, for that matter, in Singleton's fictional dealings.

There is some evidence that pirate groups divided their booties on a proportional and therefore much more equitable basis than the wage system would have allowed, evoking feudal forms of labor organization and the medieval share system while rejecting the more recent developments of a capitalist structure. Also, pirates restricted the captain's authority by granting him only the status of an elected primus inter pari, balancing this executive authority against the enforceable arbitration of a quartermaster who had jurisdiction over disputes and complaints. According to *A General History of the Pyrates*, whose attribution to Defoe by J. R. Moore is under dispute, "the Quarter-Master is an humble Imitation of the *Roman* Tribune of the People; he speaks for, and looks after the Interests of the Crew." Provisions for the sailors, a frequent area of maritime dispute and mercantilist efficiency measures, were abundant on pirate ships, on which sailors were allowed unlimited access to food and drink. At the same time, small but crucial incentives were said to have encouraged what we now call "productivity." As one of Captain Lowther's articles says, "he that sees a Sail first, shall have the best Pistol, or Small-Arm, on board her."[18]

The pirate ship was the inverted response to the merchant ship, which, as some historians have remarked, along with the plantation was the closest precapitalist workplace that approximated a factory. Smaller ships were still run on paternalistic lines, but larger ones were increasingly "total institutions" that gave captains unrestricted executive and judicial power. In the capitalist ships, the captain was not chosen by the sailors he commanded but foisted upon them by an owner with strict instructions to maximize profit. These merchant ships, according to Rediker, applied "industrial" disciplinary techniques involving large capital outlays, marked division of labor, regimentation and repetition of specific tasks under close supervision, and collective labor away from home. Seamen were the first collective laborers without traditional craft skills, and they "occupied a pivotal position in the movement from paternalistic forms of labor control to the contested negotiation of waged work." Feudal expectations concerning the customs and usages of the sea and the fulfillment of mariners' "necessaries" were being replaced by stringent accounting and rationing of provisions.[19]

In addition to the hints of political rebellion, Defoe's depictions of the actual conditions that foster piracy suggest that his sympathies were engaged. Sailors resisted mercantilist impositions of stringent regulations by their employers; employers attempted to increase profitability by restricting provisions, while sailors defended their living standards by general and petty pilferage, and the dereliction of duty for personal gain and enjoyment. Captain Bob talks about a ship on which "happen'd a most desperate Mutiny among the Men, upon Account of some Deficiency in their Allowance" (10). When Bob and his companions are themselves put ashore for mutiny, they excuse their arming themselves on the grounds that, "as there were considerable Sums due to them for Wages, they hoped [the captain] would allow the Arms and Ammunition upon their Accounts" (18).

These examples confirm, as does other evidence, that seamen were also the most militant of all workers, often defying their employers by going on strike. In fact, the origin of the word strike as a work stoppage is a maritime phenomenon, when sailors struck or lowered the sails on ship to air their grievances (the OED identifies the first published occurrence of this new usage as late as 1768). However, there are several inferential moments of such behavior in *Captain Singleton* and many of the piratical narratives in the *General History*, where the old meaning of strike is an indication from the ship (usually the merchant victim) that gives up a fight by lowering sails, or is associated with sailors deserting one ship for a pirateer because of poor working conditions. Atlantic maritime culture, according to Peter Linebaugh, appears as "the oceanic generalization of the theory and practice of antinomian democracy." There are a number of accounts of pirate political democracy insisted upon in the *General History*. The communal contracts and democratic experiments that the compilation represents have been identified by historians of the English working class as involving groups of "revolutionary traditionalists" and "masterless men." The uniqueness of the discourse of piratical democracy is its focus on a collectively inspired subject, an interesting contrast to the notion of an autonomous self-conceived subject as typified by Crusoe. Though Singleton is an individualist more like Crusoe than his piratical brethren, his associations suggest an intriguing alternative. All seamen were exceptionally mobile, and this mobility was their best weapon for ensuring better working and living conditions and evading the ship's restructuring as plantation or factory. This restive, disconcerting mobility is the most enduring feature of Singleton's milieu. As liminal, criminal, and even subliminal democrats, pirates strongly challenged the legitimation of trade, and with it the ideology of possessive individualism, not out of any high-flown ethics of passions and interests, but at the violent level of practice. As Marcus Rediker puts it, "the sea *was* 'a wet-nurse to democracy.' " Much of Defoe's fascination with pirate fraternities is tempered by an indirect acknowledgment of the anarchic possibilities of too much democracy. Most of these ideal republics are bound to fail. The notorious instability of actual seventeenth-century republics, whether attributed to Polybian cycles or to the historical precedents of earlier Greek and Roman experiments, was never far from citation in political thought.[20]

Defoe's depiction of the Madagascar interludes in *Captain Singleton* attempts various narrative formulations of a progression from a proto-Hobbesian state of nature to the state as social organization. Singleton's character extends the legendary derring-do of pirate captains such as Avery, Bartho Roberts, Bellamy, Bonnet, Teach (or Blackbeard), Kidd, and others, who as famous criminals embodied different qualities such as boisterousness, chivalry, fair play, and wit, or cruelty, treachery, and exceptional rapacity, thus constituting different types in popular oral mythology. When we look to Abbé de Raynal's colonial encyclopedia, *Histoire philosophique et politique des deux Indes,* discussed extensively in chapter 7, we find that pirates (*flibustiers*) are described as heroic "coastal fraternities" (*frères de la côte*), whose debauchery, expenditure, and wanderlust is inassimilable to aims of colonial settlement.[21]

As a model for Singleton, Captain Avery occupies a special place as an "arch-Pyrat." Most renowned for his daring heist of a ship transporting the Mughal emperor Aurangzeb's retinue (see Fig. 8), Avery was celebrated for his forcible abduction of the Mughal princess aboard this ship and his presumed establishment of a pirate kingdom on Madagascar (179). Other English adventurers such as John Plantain and Adam Baldridge were also said to have established a virtual kingdom on Madagascar, as was Abraham Samuels, a Jamaican mulatto. Avery's notoriety for these acts was in large part a result of the considerable embarrassment that they caused the East India Company at the time. Aurangzeb held the company accountable for the outrage and threatened serious punitive action against its trade, causing much trepidation in British mercantilist circles. Piracy was having a structural impact on the con-

Figure 8 W. Pritchard and W. Tett, *CAP. AVERY and his Crew taking one of the GREAT MOGUL'S Ships* (1734). (British Museum, London)

duct of trade far in excess of the individual depredations committed, especially as legitimate trade and robbery were becoming indistinct. In this context, the celebration of Avery is connected to antimercantilist attitudes. The mezzotint (Fig. 8) combines portrait with maritime action scene, rendering Avery as a proud organizer of the violent event he has engineered. The viewer can admire Avery's derring-do and approve of him. As showman he is safely separated from the action he presents, packing pistols with cutlass in hand. Joel Baer suggests that the story's resilience testifies to its functioning as an inspiration to eighteenth-century seamen and as "protest lore."[22]

In *Captain Singleton*, Avery's pirates want "to maintain themselves on Shore and yet carry on their cruising Trade too" (183). Again we see a slippage in the text from piracy to freebooting and privateering. Piracy's artificial states, however, are regulated more by social contract than by the power of a monarch. The *General History* emphatically appropriates Avery's utopian value in the narrative entitled "Of Captain Misson," the most obviously fictitious account in the book. Misson is an astonishingly generous and politically astute French pirate captain, who, along with a renegade Italian priest called Carracioli, founds an idealistic antislavery pirate settlement called Libertalia on Madagascar. Upon settling, Carraciolo "objected, that they were no Pyrates, but Men who were resolved to assert that Liberty which God and Nature gave them, and own no subjection to any, farther than was for the common Good of all" (392). The colony's subjects are called Liberi to appeal equally to the French, English, Dutch, and even African citizens. The Liberi (also meaning "children" in Latin) are an interesting creation of Misson's democratic paternalism. When the colony becomes too large to run by collective plebiscite, Misson's experiment outlines, in detail, an ideal multiracial, egalitarian, and democratic commonwealth with a Lord Conservator—in this case, Misson himself—subject to election every three years. The author of the *General History* says that Misson then "chose a Council of the ablest among them, without Distinction of Nation or Colour; and the different Languages began to be incorporated, and one made out of the many" (433). Misson's narrative displays the vestiges of seventeenth-century idealist civic humanism and republicanism, along with its utopian project of constructing a universal language. The experiment ends with a fitting lesson of the dangers that threaten such idealistic attempts. Such a state cannot but found itself through an act of colonization on expropriated land. Libertalia is suddenly and inexplicably wiped out by an army of local tribes whom Misson had managed to outwit earlier by divide-and-conquer methods. Singleton's crew, on the other hand, is never as utopian as Misson's, once even selling a cargo of slaves they find aboard a slave ship where an uprising had resulted in the deaths of all the European crew. However, the rebellion is described with detailed sympathy and a reversal of expectations about the blood that was spilled; the cause of the rebellion was the general ill-treatment of the slaves and the rape of one of them (156–65).[23] The encounter with Avery in *Captain Singleton* is rendered with a faint whiff of all this utopianism. Demonstrating an almost obsessive concern with a Protean story, Avery's cameo appearance in *Captain Singleton* is to suggest the plausibility of a pirate commonwealth, one that Singleton rejects: "*Captain Avery* to give him his due, proposed our building a little City here, establishing our selves on Shore, with a good Fortification, and Works proper to defend our selves; and that, as we had Wealth enough, and could encrease it to what Degree we pleased, we should content our selves to retire here, and bid Defiance to the World" (182).

What is the value of these various piratical attempts to signify utopian state formation? Misson's state is certainly critical of a limited chauvinist and culturalist nationalism. However, it is just as likely that such a cosmopolitanism is similar to that legislated in *The True-Born Englishman*. In that masterful poem by Defoe, the mongrel origins of "Englishness" get reworked into subtle dreams of imperialist mastery through transcultural subordination of Angles, Saxons, Normans, Scots, Picts, Welsh, and a host of others. All this talk of pirate commonwealth appears to be a highly idealized account of the organization of various lumpen groups into piratical colonies and settlements, especially in the West Indies. Alongside these specific connections, piratical accounts are also textual displacements of larger social conflicts, absorbing practices into representations. Avery perhaps represented social rebellion in more ways than have been acknowledged, especially as the name of the ship on which he organizes a successful mutiny is the *Charles II*. As Defoe participated in the abortive Monmouth rebellion in 1685, characterized by many historians as the last popular peasant uprising in British history, his ideological slipperiness is again in evidence through such interpretive instances.[24]

As we saw earlier, many of the Avery myths make the persistent claim that Avery had established, or was in the process of establishing, a political entity on Madagascar and had audaciously offered to buy the royal pardon, something that Defoe had in fact recommended as a solution. The "conservative" implications of a discourse that favored landed property was at odds with the "progressive" mercantilist aims of increasing prosperity through the circulation of money. The print of Avery in Figure 8 dresses him up as a bewigged if violent man of substance, who is in the process of making himself respectable. If theft destabilized the safe acquisition of freeholds as permanent fixed assets, circulation favored a form of grand larceny, encouraging dispossession, speculation, and bankruptcy. In his journalism, Defoe expresses this problem forcefully, extending a notion of piracy to include all forms of commercial activity:

> it would make a sad Chasm on the *Exchange of London*, if all the Pyrates should be taken away from among the Merchants there, whether we be understood to speak of your Litteral or Allegorical Pyrates; whether I should mean the Clandestine Trade Pyrates, who pyrate upon fair Trade at home; the Custom-stealing Pyrates,

who pyrate upon the Government; the Owling Pyrates who rob the Manufacturers; the privateering Pyrates who rob by Law; and because *A* the *French* Man of St. *Maloes* rob'd them, rob *B* of *Marsellies*, that never did them any Hurt; whether we mean the cheating Pyrate, that robs a home, or the Factory Pyrate, that robs abroad, of all Sorts, from the *Madagascar* Man to the *Buchaneer*— If all these should be taken off of the *Exchange*, and rendezvous'd, might we not say of them, as once of the Coward Captains of the Fleet. *Bless us. What Crowding ther'd be when they meet!*

Piracy at its worst is the carnage of conquest. As the character Boreal says scathingly in Charles Johnson's *The Successful Pyrate*, "I laugh to see a Scepter'd Robber at the Head of a Hundred Thousand, truss up a poor Caitiff as an Example to the rest of his Brother-Theives, for stealing two eggs out of Form, while he is burning Cities, ravaging Countries, and depopulating Nations."[25]

Defoe's glib conflation of all of the activity on the Royal Exchange with piracy is reinforced by another standard literary topos, present in the *General History*, which imputed piracy as instrumental in the creation of Rome: "Rome, the Mistress of the World, was no more at first than a Refuge for Thieves and Outlaws; and if the Progress of our Pyrates had been equal to their Beginning, had they all united and settled in some of those Islands, they might, by this Time, have been honoured with the Name of a Commonwealth, and no Power in those Parts of the World could have been able to dispute with them." Originary theft, which defined Captain Bob's existence as an individual, is offered up in these multiple examples as the basis of civic and social organization as well as national and cultural identity. Such a narrative criticizes the genealogy and the legitimacy of accounts that deal with the origins of property. To call theft originary is to obfuscate origins entirely, although subsequent exercises in social contractualism legitimate through consent what has already been won through coercion. As Hobbes had already indicated in *Leviathan*, "amongst men, till there were instituted great Common-Wealths; it was thought no dishonour to be a Pyrate, or a High-way Theefe; but rather a lawful Trade." The extensive comparison that Defoe launches in this passage has an undercurrent of irony, hinting that the very facile charge of piracy—rendered as a form of business as usual—is the most leveling of all distinctions among trades. If all trade is allegorized by piracy, Defoe's economic writings are scattered with acknowledgments that there is a vast difference between honest men and tradesmen because "Trade is almost universally founded upon Crime." The appeal for a certain mercantilist ethics, then, is similar to necessitating honor among thieves. Consistency of outcome and regularity of procedure might ensure that all participants play the system by manipulating its terms of "credit" to their advantage, but the early capitalist game shows the centrifugality of one-upmanship as inherently transgressive of its own purported rules.[26]

At its most utopian, however, piracy is the circumstantial birth of "coastal fraternity" that displaces laterally what would otherwise turn into a chain of colonial command. Of course, pirates as historical entities were likely to be just as implicated with conquering agendas as the commercial masters they overthrew. But Defoe's fictional pirates are thought experiments. Historical pirates were radical malcontents found within colonial ventures, and their "turning to account" is testimony that their activities became virtualizations of colonialist accounting. Admittedly, this reading could be criticized, because European pirates bore, at best, a family resemblance to the indigenous groups more directly affected by the depredations of colonial conquest even while bearing considerable hostility toward those groups. However, it is important to pursue these connections even if they are tangential to the eventual outcome of links between pirates and anticolonialism. Though piracy is an expression of a conflict internal to the practices of colonialism rather than a direct instance of tropicopolitan resistance, the fact that pirates trafficked opportunistically on the margins of colonial venture makes their liminality into a transitional and contingent subculture and one that could, at least potentially, mediate between reified oppositions of colonizer and colonized. Will Atkins does not band together with Friday against Crusoe and is instead disciplined by Crusoe in both the original novel and the sequel; however, his band poses repeated resistance to the work ethic that Crusoe wants to impose. Atkins and characters like him suggest unrealized possibilities that are worth exploring further, given that the fantasies of piratical discourse lead to virtualizations above and beyond the hints of utopianism found in the documentation of practices. The historical reconstruction of these practices is being further pursued by students of maritime culture.

Piratical Accounts

When conversion surfaces at the end of Captain Bob's account, he asks his spiritual and political guide, William Walters the Quaker, whether "there is a God above, as you have so long been telling me there is [and] . . . must we give an Account to him?" (266). If God is the ultimate auditor with whom all accounts have to be settled, a good accountant—indistinguishable from a crooked one—makes sure that perceptions of irregularity are subsumed. This is something Bob barely manages to do. He has to go through the despair of suicidal thoughts when he cannot convert a criminal and sin-laden account into a spiritual one. Singleton fears that "Repentance could not be sincere without Restitution" (267). This blockage between the economic and the spiritual is dissolved by William, who teaches Bob how to "vert" his personal accounts. Restitution is unfeasible; therefore, William casuistically recommends that the ill-gotten gains should be kept in case a future opportunity for restitution may arise. In fact, it is supposed to have arisen, according to Bob, even if there is no room in the narrative for its retelling (270).

Casuistical reasoning on William's part convinces Bob that religious *conversion* and economic *exchange* are conceptual equivalents. Trading a freight of sin and shiploads of goods for ready money and a clear conscience, the partners in crime become gentlemen merchants: "We were perfectly secured at *Bassaro*, by having frighted away the Rogues, our Comrades, and we had nothing to do but to consider how to vert our Treasure in Things proper to make us look like Merchants, as we were now to be, and not like Free-booters, as we really had been" (263). *Verting* here is a turning backward, whereby a complex process of money laundering can get the misappropriated wealth back into England. Bob looks to "turn our spices and *European* good into ready Money" and "resolved . . . that [he and William] should leave off being Pyrates, and turn Merchants" (198-99). By the time both Bob and William reach Venice disguised as Armenians, they have "converted all [their] effects into Money" (272). The process of the laundering of Bob's soul and his money are coterminous; he has perhaps achieved, through his twin voyages overland and overseas, the condition that Moll Flanders scathingly refers to as an "amphibious creature, this *Land-water-thing* call'd a *Gentleman-Tradesman*."[27]

This process might appear to our modern eyes as indeed a laughable justification of present plunder in terms of potentially charitable acts in the future. However, conversion, or a "turning with" the account, is presented in opposition to the unregenerate criminal's tendency of having "turned to" account; in piratical terms, conversion, as exegetized by William, is a "coming to" account for prior actions after having succumbed to the initial temptation of "going on the account." Conversion is also a re-turn from a tropical voyage. Singleton, as he turns goods into money, has also turned himself from pirate to merchant and, as we shall now see, perhaps exchanged identities from crypto-homosexual to heterosexual. This sexual aspect of conversion—though it may appear tangential to the economic and political aspects of piracy as an activity on the colonial margin—is a crucial part of the libidinal energies invested in the "cruising" voyage.

Nancy Armstrong and Leonard Tennenhouse's study of changes in early modern subjective consciousness asserts that "Defoe's narrator . . . is still not consciousness . . . not yet a self within a gendered body whose identity depends on the sexual uses to which that body is put." The slipperiness of the sexual identities of Defoe's characters still remains important as a corrective exercise to those tradition-minded critics who automatically assume that heterosexuality in the period was not just normative but overwhelming. The marriages undertaken by Defoe's characters are implausible from the standpoint of interiority and bourgeois subjectivity. Novels of piracy and privateering describe a colonial liminality, only to look back, at the last possible moment, as does *Robinson Crusoe*, to revalidation and transvaluation by bourgeois domesticity. This is the return of value and the reaggregation and consolidation after critical distance—whether sexual, economic, or geographical—that characterizes one outcome of virtualization. However, Hans Turley has suggestively described Defoe's piratical novels as involving the dual elaboration of a *homo eroticus* alongside the more recognizable *homo economicus*. Adopting a Greimasian analysis of this dichotomy, Turley sees the piratical subject as "a masculine alternative to the deviant sodomitical subject." As neither heterosexual hero nor feminized sodomite, the pirate—both "real" and "fictional"—doubly inverts eighteenth-century expectations concerning gender as well as sexuality.[28]

The sexual conversion in the novel is by no means effortless and can be indicated by analyzing the novel's treatment of "unmentionable" practices. Pirate articles often hint at unstated agreements and fraternal bondings over and above the explicit clauses in them. After a full listing of Bartho Roberts's articles, the *General History* adds that the pirates "had taken Care to throw over-board the Original they had signed and sworn to, [and] there is a great deal of Room to suspect [that] the Remainder contained something too horrid to be disclosed to any, except such as were willing to be sharers in the Iniquity of them" (213). The existence of boys, or "powder monkeys," aboard ships leads to the reason behind the sixth clause of Bartho Roberts's articles of faith, that "no boy or woman" should be brought on board by any of the men, in order "to prevent ill Consequences from so dangerous an Instrument of Division and Quarrel" (213). The specific privilege of possessive heterosexuality or pederasty might conflict with the generalized group situation. According to B. R. Burg's provocative if occasionally fanciful account of piratical sexuality, the Caribbean, which, along with Madagascar was renowned as a refuge for pirates, was especially known as a licentious zone in the late seventeenth century. "They be all a company of sodomists," says a female letter writer of the time, characterizing Antigua's colonists with piratical pasts.[29]

Although there is no overt mention of homosexuality in the novel (perhaps Defoe understandably felt that once at the pillory was sufficient), its coded situational elaboration throughout is easily discernible. Bob runs away to sea at twelve, when "a Master of a ship . . . took a Fancy to me" (3). Upon being captured by the Portuguese, his first master dies and Bob becomes the property of a Portuguese pilot; in the meantime, "the Captain took a particular Liking to me . . . in Recompence for my officious Diligence, I received several Particular favours from him" (5–6). Bob is made ship's understeward. Various hints persist of sexual services being rendered. Later Bob complains euphemistically of rape, of having been "used like a Slave, and in the worst Manner of a Slave, by my cruel Master the Pilot" (20). In fact, the pilot who owns Bob also exacted payment from the captain for his chattel's labor. Bob, in turn, demands a wage, resenting this kind of pliant "use," wanting to be paid back for "what the Captain allowed him for my particular Service to him" (12). Bob's resentment makes him side with other mutinous sailors; their plot is discovered, resulting in their being marooned on Madagascar (despite the master's special pleas for Bob's exemption). Sodomy, as an unstated piratical practice, is often hinted at, although never explicitly named; as Bob says about his first ship's countercultural milieu, "Thieving, Lying, Forswearing, joined to the most abominable Lewdness, was the stated Practice of the Ship's Crew" (6). Defoe's *Serious Reflections,* acknowledging this association of transgressive speech with sexuality, characterizes bawdy language as "the sodomy of the tongue."[30]

When Singleton reaches maturity, he meets Harris, with whom he "began an intimate Confidence . . . so that [they] called one another Brothers, and communicated all [their] circumstances to one another" (138). Most important of all, though, is Bob's lasting homoerotic bond, in the second half of *Captain Singleton,* with William Walters, who becomes Bob's "Privy-Counsellour and Companion upon all occasions," such that he "could not be without him" (168). The resoundingly homoerotic basis of this bond is described in the following manner: "William and I maintained an inviolable Friendship and Fidelity to one another, lived like two Brothers; we neither had or sought any separate Interest; we convers'd seriously and gravely, and upon the Subject of our Repentance continuously; we never changed, that is to say, so as to leave off our *Armenian* Garbs, and were called at *Venice* the two *Grecians*" (272).

When they do actually get back to England, Bob and his Quaker companion remain in disguise, ostensibly for fear of discovery by confederates. The return of Bob and William is enabled by William's sister, whom Bob marries in the penultimate sentence of the novel, a fact that is interestingly preceded by a verbalized quasi-contractual undertaking between Bob and William to remain together in fraternity and perpetual disguise. The second clause of this short contract amusingly maintains their commitment to each other in mustachioed masquerade as "*Grecians* and Foreigners" (277). It is possible to see this conclusion as continuing the typing of homosexuality as both Greek and foreign in Georgian England. Such an undertaking in *Captain Singleton,* which imposes a contractual discourse onto a romantic friendship, foreshadows the elaborate negotiations that take place later in Richardson's *Pamela.* Singleton's marriage, like Crusoe's or Will Atkins's, corresponds to the manner in which the Avery figure, Arviragus, in Charles Johnson's play, *The Successful Pyrate* (1713), attempts to impose marital ideology in his island kingdom on his unmarried, perhaps sodomitical, subjects.[31]

With the benefit of hindsight given us by recent developments in queer theory, the illustration accompanying Crusoe's *A Vision of the An-*

Figure 9 *Vision of the Angelic World*, appended to the French edition of *Serious Reflections during the life and surprising adventures of Robinson Crusoe* (1720). (British Library, London)

gelic World that is appended to the 1720 French translation of *Serious Reflections* is also suggestive of a parodic sexual indeterminacy (Fig. 9). Crusoe floats with gay abandon in the plasma of outer space, surrounded by stars, astrological icons identifying the planets, and various cherubim, devils, and angels. The sun looks askance at him as he looks upward, unsure of where he is floating. Crusoe's narcissism here, as in the scene just after acquiring Friday when he describes the sleeping Friday's handsome features while he is milking his goat, has much potential for contextualizing his queerness, combining hints of alternative sexualities with parodic representations of them.

As I have already suggested with respect to *Oroonoko*, there is more of a parodic undercurrent in early sentimental discourse than has hitherto been acknowledged. Bob and William's sentimentalized understanding looks hilarious when contractualized. Perhaps this is Defoe's sly hit at the apocryphal status of articles of pirate fraternity. Legal discourse, as eighteenth-century observers knew all too well, could occult when it was meant to clarify and confine what it aimed to liberate. Like Defoe's parody of the pirates on the Royal Exchange, merchants are pirates in disguise and pirates are aspiring merchants. As we have seen, the cant for piracy, "going upon the account," alludes to the paramount accounting motif, itself setting up the activity as an ironic euphemism. Pirates were occasionally said to have issued parodic receipts when ransoming merchants, signing with facetious names such as Aaron Whisslingham and Simon Tugmutton. Similarly, in the section entitled "Of Captain Anstis" in Defoe's *General History,* there is a hilarious send-up of the kangaroo courts that tried pirates. The episode entails the creation of "a Mock-Court of Judicature to try one another for Pyracy, and he that was a Criminal one Day was made Judge another" (292). However, parody cuts both ways, and these parodic performances may also be seen in terms of what E. P. Thompson has called "counter-theater." Parodying juridical procedures was typical of various kinds of social banditry at the time. The metaphorization of Oroonoko, which in the previous chapter was seen to energize the marital intrigues of Englishwomen, in fact made a tantalizing parodic appearance among social criminals as well. One of the fraternities of the Waltham deer poachers was led by "Prince Oroonoko, King of the Blacks."[32]

It is not surprising that Defoe's last novel, *A New Voyage Round the World* (1725), approaches the same seafaring circumstances of the second half of *Captain Singleton* but from the viewpoint of a resolutely privateering captain. Glyndwr Williams has discussed how this version of a furtive cruising voyage criticizes earlier voyages such as John Narborough's in 1670 even as it imitates William Dampier's *A New Voyage Round the World* (1697) and *A Voyage to New Holland* (1703). By 1726, Swift's first version of *Gulliver's Travels,* rendered as *Travels Through Several Remote Nations of the World,* satirizes these various accounts of mercantile cruising. The unnamed protagonist of Defoe's fiction proclaims that he and his men are traders who can have it both ways. Their secret letters of marque allow these itinerant merchants to attack Spanish ships when necessary, even as a convenient front man on board, Captain Mirlotte, allows the ship's crew to "change faces," allowing them to trade under French colors where English shipping was proscribed. The unnamed Englishman—who is the real captain—deals with a mutiny by persuading the recalcitrants to give up their cause and punishing only two of them. In an intriguing interpretation of this novel, Robert Markley calls its fantasy of infinite riches and upper-class identification, along with its erasure of maritime labor and moral consciousness, capitalism's "positive unconscious."[33] *New Voyage* is a plausible depiction of infinite economic value that mimes the incipient novel form as an inexhaustible fountain of narrative, but it is certainly untypical of Defoe's novels in its erasure of moral consciousness.

There are enough indications in Defoe's work to help us regard his fictions as marking several stages in a longer process of several experimental "projects" that bridge economic actions with spiritual reflections, and indeed speculation with peculation. Defoe's sense of any project involved concrete plans as well as imaginative thinking, technical blueprints as well as phantasmatic projections. In this respect, the tropology of piracy takes a particularly significant swerve in Defoe's discourse. One rhetorical conversion that helps both reify and convert Defoe's earlier observations on piracy's floating threat to maritime property is his association of the activity with a theft of literary property. The kind of piracy that was steadily increasing from the early 1700s, also of great concern to Defoe, was print piracy. Appropriately, given the context of the eighteenth-century debates about fixed and mobile property, Defoe is the first writer who coined the common usage of piracy to mean the theft of that kind of especially mobile property that we have come to understand as copyright. The OED attributes to Defoe the first published usage of the verb *to pirate*, meaning "to appropriate or reproduce (the work or invention of another) without authority, for one's own profit." The trope of "going upon the account" comes full circle here, as it becomes a description of literary protocols and narrational credibility just as much as it is a coded term for the misappropriation of economic property. To go upon the accounts rendered in Defoe's texts is to realize, as Sandra Sherman has done, that he "links the market, the public sphere, and processes of fiction into a single dynamic."[34]

The novel as an illegitimate discourse that eventually legitimated itself is fundamentally and repeatedly associated with criminality in this period. Yet the emphasis we have placed on accounts underscores the felt need to rationalize criminality, whether through bookselling or bookkeeping. Telling stories and telling money, accounts are narrative and financial, conflating credit with credibility. These strong structural implications of the homologies between commodified writing and economic value also make us interrogate a more specific relation, that between the triumph of capitalism and the successes of colonialism. Indeed, as discussed earlier with respect to conquest and anticonquest, the circulation of narrative as well as that of the commodity form appear to correlate capitalism with colonialism as both these forms present themselves in the eighteenth century. There may be a colonialism before capitalism, as practiced by the Spanish in the Americas, as well as a capitalism at least *nominally* after colonialism (yet to be realized) as some may characterize the future trajectory of globalization and the pax americana. For these reasons, to choose between a causal and a homological history at *this* chronological moment is a matter of faith rather than proof.[35]

James Thompson similarly eschews the choice between homological and causal history in his ambitious reading of value theory into eighteenth-century narrative economies, characterizing Defoe's novels as marking the transition from "primitive accumulation (crime) to fully capitalized trade."[36] Paper money, promissory banknotes, and all related commercial practices were fabricated by those wishing to capitalize on these new forms of financial creditworthiness. Such fabrication underwent violent suppression by the British state in the eighteenth century when judged as counterfeiting, a transgression of an activity jealously guarded by the state. While the forging of money was ruthlessly extirpated at a time when credit threatened to replace money, the sham accounts that are the counterfeiting of history—the novel—rose, and were erected, as a monument to value. Would the novel have gained social credibility if the fiction of money had been rejected systematically rather than just erratically? Value, law, and narrative all collude in fulfilling a new reality principle constructed in the early eighteenth century. These discourses, at that point in time, subtend the spheres of socioeconomics, juridicopolitics, and literature-culture, indeed constituting the three apexes of what has been called, for want of a better name, the subject. Yet behind this three-cornered subject of value, law, and narrative (all major aspects of piratical subjectivity) is yet another historical development in process: the ongoing task of colonial exploration, interaction, and acquisition.

Defoe understood piracy in several ways: as a sociopolitical *practice* that challenged mercantilism, as a *parodic representation* of the transgressiveness of mercantilism, even as a *reflex* of the commodification of intellectual property. There is an unaccountable slippage between practice and representation. Singleton's upward mobility requires effacing a past that may prove dangerous to his future survival. Defoe's texts transform their restive protagonists, co-opting those aspects of piratical resistance that threaten trade into the lesser transgression of privateering, converting actual pirates on the Spanish Main into the pretended ones on the Royal Exchange. Defoe's fictions are often credited with the conversion of religious motifs into secular and materialist ones (or vice versa). Here we also see how effectively he converts pirates into privateers and exchanges renegades for venture capitalists. The various transformations of practices into representations in *Captain Singleton,* by verting accounts, paves the way toward a modern slippage from one ideological register to another. The conversion of a pirate into a merchant, as represented in Singleton's case, evacuates the ontological essence of pirate (hostis humani generis), replacing it with a contingent and relative persona. Claiming his riches surreptitiously, the narrator treats the identity of Singleton as not much more than a dispensable subject position, legally awkward to reclaim. Silently substituting exchange for conversion, Singleton virtualizes piracy into privacy. His colonial revels ended, the narrator vanishes into thin air, indeed into a rarefied "Air-Money," Defoe's favorite alchemical trope for finances or accounts that escape the cognitive grasp of moving fingers and outstretched hands.

CHAPTER THREE

The Stoic's Voice

This chapter's investigation into the Stoical contexts of cultural and economic crisis rounds off my account of early-eighteenth-century virtualization. If piratical discourse's utopian aspects are humble in their origins and transformative reach, the figure of Cato leaves an ambitious legacy. The Stoical signature reduces anticolonialism to anticorruption discourse. Loosely *Stoical* rather than precisely *Stoic* discourse reveals retroactive virtualizations similar to Oronooko-related sentimentalism and piracy-related utopianism. Deriving authority from civic humanism, the Stoical voice reacts to the bewildering challenges posed by the Glorious Revolution and the Hanoverian succession following it, the South Sea Bubble of 1720, and the coinage crises of 1696 and 1725. The presence of racialized and colonial contexts gives the neostoic—or his most ideal rendition as Cato—an anticolonial face that is significant for our purposes. Cato's dissenting statements oppose a static figurehead of republican virtue to debased coin, speculative bubble, or arbitrary tyrant. When applied effectively, the Stoical voice articulates the need for reform by parodying economic activity and political maneuvering. Mildly republican rhetoric makes Cato Whiggish, but this rhetoric can also express Country and Patriot sentiments. Cato is a transitional voice reacting to the changes sweeping through a recently capitalist and colonialist polity. But he is by no means against trade. Rather, he is a figure who mediates between still uncertain political structures developing alongside capitalism and the remnants of Renaissance civic humanism. A more effective application of Cato's voice occurs during the American Revolution, but there are qualifications to be made concerning its anticolonial garb.

Several key texts concern the argument here, and I examine them in five sections. The free-floating eighteenth-century clichés concerning freedom and slavery generated by Joseph Addison's play, *Cato* (1713), created a neostoicist vogue that lasted long enough to be used by the American Revolutionaries. However, the parallel between the Punic

Wars in Roman times and the more recent English Revolutions of 1642 and 1688 brings a second set of comparisons concerning the role of North Africa in the allegory. Cultural difference in Addison's play is represented by Cato's protégé Juba and his political dilemma—which is also a colonial one—concerning the extent of Numidia's fealty to Rome. Political sentiment, as it was generated and managed around the performance of Juba's racialized identity in Addison's play, is put forward as a consensual rhetoric of virtue acceptable to all but the most entrenched Jacobites. Nonetheless, Juba's reach encounters little resistance by 1748, when a sympathetic biography of the Young Pretender can ingeniously refer to Charles Edward Stuart throughout as Young Juba and to Jacobites as Jubeans without having to explain this political crosswiring.[1] Juba's and Cato's images eventually generate a convenient consensus around Cato's virtue. As Cato takes a different turn with Thomas Gordon and John Trenchard's journalistic writings, collected as *Cato's Letters* (1720-23), I consider their response to the national crisis of the South Sea Bubble in the third section. This instance of Cato as ombudsman is politically tenacious. The volatility of the impersonation in *Cato's Letters* suggests that economic crisis transforms the scope of reformist rhetoric. Later, Commonwealthmen, Classical Republicans, and Dissenters come together to articulate the rationale of the American Revolutionaries through Cato's voice. After considering Gordon and Trenchard's intervention and its American afterlife, I turn to an analysis of Swift's forays into Irish politics, also based on his self-fashioning as Cato and the reclamation of Caesar's assassin, Brutus, as a political icon. My reading of Swift's famous satire, *Gulliver's Travels* (1726, 1735), demonstrates his complicated stance as anticolonial sage and insane neostoicist through Gulliver. I conclude with Swift's pamphleteering against the new Irish coinage in *The Drapier's Letters* that adapts the traditional Stoic's voice to a commercial milieu. In its neostoicist and commercial contexts, this partisan intervention reveals virtualization as an actual, albeit qualified, instance of anticolonial resistance.

As a personification of public sacrifice, Addison's *Cato* represents the last gasp of the earlier, more comprehensive Renaissance interest in Stoicism. The demand for political regulation that Cato generally represented was reactive but also innovative, flowing from a recognition that commerce was increasingly influencing politics. Posed against the imagery of corruption and that of Credit as fickle and hysterical female, eighteenth-century political discourse, according to J. G. A. Pocock, generates "a gallery of countertypes." These opponents of corruption are "self-mastered, stoic, public, and agrarian," and Cato becomes "in all his manifestations the arch figure." Although Pocock's paradigm-shifting intervention into eighteenth-century political history is not my primary concern here, it is important to state that my reading of republican rhetoric departs from his standard interpretation. Simply put, Pocock argues for a coherence in political rhetoric that is hard to find in the historical archive. As a result, he is forced to resort to a structuralist idealization of a civic humanist worldview, a *langue* itself instantiated through the *parole* of "constant adaptation, translation, and reperformance." A monolithic account of ideology allows Pocock to dissolve the vexed question of power relations over a period of time into a history of *one* political mentality. When this admittedly significant political language is writ large, all other responses become those of collaboration or opposition, coherent countermoves to the initiating rules of civic humanism. As a result, the extensive retooling of the citizen as consumer throughout the post-Restoration period poses no challenge to Pocock's reinterpretation of the eighteenth century as a continuation of Machiavellianism through English epigones such as Harrington and Hobbes. Locke's early social contractualism is correspondingly downgraded as brilliant but inapplicable because of its ahistorical appeal in a history-obsessed age. As Joyce Appleby has accurately observed, the problem here is not so much the dethroning of Locke, but the systematic reduction of eighteenth-century political debates to a single struggle between the rational outcomes of Renaissance virtue and a sphere of commerce that is presumed irrational. Pocock's confinement of commercial discourse and activity to "a zone of secular irrationality" avoids accounting for the nascent political challenges of capitalism. By recognizing the plurality of political languages at the time, we can put to active use the prehistory of criticisms of colonial venture by revisionary genealogy. Pocock's analyses, therefore, are important but not definitive. As Appleby puts it trenchantly, Pocock has come to the field as a scholar but remains in it as a partisan, dissolving the reality of power relations, like the proverbial Cheshire cat, into the smile of civic humanism as constitutive of political culture.[2]

Though Pocock in excess distorts the picture, he can be ignored only at peril. The eighteenth-century instances of Cato discourse were the coda to a long and more knowledgeable encounter with Stoicism during the early modern period. Mary Thomas Crane, in a fascinating article on the widespread pedagogical use of Cato's *Distiches* during the English Renaissance, suggests that the *Distiches* were used in grammar schools and universally required to teach the pupil the construction of the second person and the first person in Latin. The *Distiches* were good for grammar exercises in the imperative and the indicative, as they expressed Stoical admonitions and aphorisms in the voice of the sage. These locutions were widely imitated by sixteenth-century poets. Such serendipitous facts reveal the unique role of the Stoical voice in the ideological interpellation of early modern Englishmen, even as these forms adapt themselves to new content. Later in the American colonies, editorials were signed "Cato" in newspapers, even as journals capitalized on the name on both sides of the Atlantic: *British Cato, English Cato, Cato Junior's*. Continuing a longstanding use of Cato as pedagogical tool, Noah Webster included huge extracts from *Cato's Letters* in his educational reader, and Benjamin Franklin, in *The Education of the Youth in Pennsylvania* (1749), recommended it as one of several sources for the teaching of English grammar. The endurance of the Stoical voice signals its contextual adaptability.

Such evidence of neostoicism as a lingua franca also shows its limits as virtualization. The colonial elite liberate themselves from a metaphorical slavery to English hegemony using neostoicist vocabulary, even while willfully ignoring the contradictions entailed in their own practice of chattel slavery on Africans.[3] Marat's republican rhetoric in his famous work, *Les chaînes de l'esclavage* (1774), is also constructed on a similar obliviousness to racial exclusion at a moment known to be the peak of plantation slavery. As we have seen, Oroonoko, Charlot Welldon, and Captain Singleton decry their own commodification, even as they are oblivious to and sometimes actively encourage the commodification of proximate others. Virtualizations are evidence of the prehistory of anticolonial agency in colonialist discourses, sometimes taking individualist and sometimes communitarian form. However, this task of reconstruction is futile if we wrench it entirely from its historical context and celebrate it as edifying. We are in a space of nuanced interplay among practices, representations, and retroactive focalizations.

Addison's *Cato* is a bland medium that anchors early-eighteenth-century versions of republicanism, constitutionalism, absolutist monarchy, and imperial rule within biblical, Saxon, and Greco-Roman antecedents. A political mythology is created afresh for the "empty time" of secular history and modern nationalism. Whether or not a republican tradition existed continuously from classical times, the process of the "invention of tradition" created the ancient constitution and the transhistorical relevance of Cato's voice.[4] The old conflict between the royal prerogative and Parliament returned within the constitutional confines of the Revolution Settlement of 1689. The Whiggish nature of that settlement led to the defensive posture of reconstructed Tories who abjured Jacobitism through the first half of the eighteenth century. However, the precarious political supremacy of the Whig family alliances in a context of widespread economic change put these ruling oligarchies on the defensive. The subversion of moral authority meant a bitter and continuous battle for legitimacy. British society endured a multipronged ideological conflict between Court and Country, Anglican and Dissenter, consumer and citizen.

The defenders of royal prerogative, when they were Tories under Queen Anne, ran the danger of vilification as Jacobites; when they were Whigs under the Hanoverians, they were exposed as corrupt courtiers colluding with avaricious stockjobbers. British society was faced with sapping contradictions. The unresolved consequences of the Glorious Revolution meant that several parts of the realm and all sections of society were periodically prone to significant Jacobite sympathies, while at the same time, the triumphant Whig oligarchies colluded with the newfound English appetite for mercantilist venture and colonial acquisition. Writers across the spectrum—Dryden, Locke, Defoe, Shaftesbury, Mandeville, Bolingbroke, and, of course, Addison and Swift—attempted to contextualize, rationalize, and mutually negotiate these problems. This ideological task was a strategy of consolidation in a Britain that was still an ancien régime even as social and economic upheaval outstripped the elaborate fictions of continuity and tradition created to contain these changes. Mild republicanism coexisted with royalism, and monopolistic oligarchies disputed free-traders and projectors on the make. The platitudes present in *Cato* can be attributed to the play's gingerly negotiation of—some would say its inability to negotiate—these multiple conflicts.[5]

Cato was drafted perhaps as early as the 1690s and revised several times in response to critical suggestions after circulation in manuscript. Roman history presented two famous Catos: Marcus Porcius Cato, known as Cato the Censor, famous for his reactionary anti-Hellenism and animosity toward Carthage, and his great-grandson Marcus Porcius Cato Uticensis, known as Cato the Younger, who sided with Pompey the Great against Julius Caesar in the civil wars. The popularity of Cato the Younger as a republican icon began, even in Roman times, as a counterfoil to the perception of Caesar as a despot. Addison's source for the patriotism and radical republicanism of Cato the Younger derives from the Renaissance revival of Lucan, Livy, Cicero, Plutarch, and Seneca. The ten books of Lucan's poetical account of the civil wars between Caesar and Pompey, known as the *Pharsalia* after the battlefield where Pompey was decisively defeated, had already been translated into English several times in the seventeenth century. Probably the best-known version was in rhymed couplets by Thomas May. Lucan, as the chronicler most favorable to Cato, was likely one of Addison's most important sources. The vogue for Addison's *Cato*, which had encouraged Lewis Theobald to publish a quick prose version of *The Life and Character of Marcus Porcius Cato* (1713), probably played a role in Nicholas Rowe's handsome folio versification of Lucan, the best-known eighteenth-century version, dedicated posthumously by Rowe's wife to George I in 1718. Many influential members of the aristocracy and Parliament are in the list of subscribers, including literary figures such as Addison (four books), Steele, Congreve, Pope, and Mary Wortley Montagu.[6]

Cato's importance increased by his placement in a pantheon of Stoic sages. Stoicism was studied by both Addison and Swift in their youth. Justus Lipsius's *De Constantia* (1584) was the single most important text of the neostoic revival, and Epictetus's *Enchiridion* was a close second. Translations of Stoical literature found a receptive market well into the seventeenth century. Most important among them were Charles Cotton's translation of Du Vair's *The Morall Philosophy of the Stoicks* (1664, 1671), Nathaniel Wanley's rendition of Justus Lipsius, entitled *War and Peace Ridiculed, or, a Discourse of Constancy in Inconstant Times* (1668),

George Stanhope's *Epictetus His Morals with Simplicius His Comment* (1694), and Ellis Walker's *Epicteti Enchiridion Made English in a Poetical Paraphrase* (1695).

Stoicism was also increasingly under attack. The most frequent objection made against the philosophy was its presumed celebration of hyperrationalistic (hence anti-Christian) apathy toward politics. While R. S. Crane argues that divines of the Latitudinarian school favored the push toward anti-Stoic thought because of Stoicism's pagan and rationalist offshoots, Henry Sams identifies the real target as the Stoic doctrine favoring the suppression of passions, something that neostoics such as Addison and Bolingbroke also criticized. In *The Spectator*, Addison argues implicitly against extreme neostoicism by suggesting that compassion refines and civilizes human nature, and Steele favorably contrasts "the impartial SPECTATOR" with "a Pedantick Stoick, who thinks all Crimes alike." The belief that the ideal of self-sufficiency leads to pride and irreligion was actually a misunderstanding of classical Stoic doctrine. Imputations that Stoicism meant cold-blooded asceticism were made in ignorance of its original Roman contexts. For instance, in *A Christian Hero* (1701), Richard Steele complained that Christianity was unfairly dismissed by its detractors as primitivistic even as Stoicism was celebrated despite an inhuman apathy to suffering. Steele later backtracked on his criticisms, probably as a result of Addison's success with the topic. George Lillo's *The London Merchant* (1726) was venerated as a middle-class Christian tragedy and in many respects represented the opposing doctrine to the aristocratic altruism of Addison's *Cato*. Bernard Mandeville's defense of luxury in the *The Fable of the Bees* (1714, 1723, 1728) was intended as a manifesto against the moral rationalism of Renaissance philosophies of humanist temperance, and especially Shaftesbury's neostoicism. The misunderstanding—that Stoicism and public life are incompatible—persisted despite the large number of examples that demonstrated the coexistence of philosophical attitude and political action in Roman history. Much like Lady Mary Wortley Montagu and Lady Mary Chudleigh, Addison preferred to explore Stoicism in a moderate version. *Cato*, in particular, reflects a synthesis of mercantilism and Stoicism in Addison's defense of the Whiggish liberties enshrined in the Revolution Settlement. For these various reasons, it would be accurate to consider Addison, like most English neostoics, as loosely *Stoical* rather than precisely *Stoic*.[7]

Cato was successful as Whig propaganda, putting its audiences on guard, at a delicate moment very close to the Hanoverian succession, against Jacobite resistance to the Revolution Settlement of 1689 and the Act of Settlement finalized in 1704. The play was first performed with great success in April 1713 and achieved the pinnacle of popularity with 226 performances by 1776. Pope, who wrote the prologue—in which there are hints of his satire of Addison as Atticus in the "Epistle to Arbuthnot"—sardonically told Caryll that "Cato was not so much the wonder of Rome itself in his days as he is of Britain in ours." The occasion marked what Johnson would later describe as "the grand climacterick of Addison's reputation." Much like Southerne's *Oroonoko*, Addison's play featured the bombastic cadences of speeches on liberty. Cato was played by ranters such as Barton Booth and James Quin.[8]

On the first night of the play, despite interpretive grandstanding from Bolingbroke and others who pursued Tory interpretations, a vaguely Whiggish interpretation of Cato prevailed. Steele had packed the audience with Whigs to ensure Addison's success, resulting in frenetic applause for the passages declaiming liberty. Apocryphal accounts have it that the Tories in the audience clapped even louder in a desperate attempt to make the play their own. An anonymous Tory critic subsequently flays Addison's blandness, saying that the play "can be call'd *Whiggish* upon no other Account but upon the frequent Repetition of the Word *Liberty*, and the Catastrophe that attended the Heroe of it." Caustic about the Whigs' success with the political allegory, the pamphleteer hopes that Cato's eventual suicide will influence Whigs to do the same, "for this is a Time for the Gentlemen of that Species to execute themselves."[9]

The first night was also notable for Bolingbroke's rearguard action, commending Booth for representing English liberty through Cato and thrusting a purse of 50 guineas at him. Bolingbroke's gesture was taken as a hit at the Duke of Marlborough, the Tories' pet candidate for "Caesar," who had broken with the Court in 1711 after Queen Anne repudiated his wife earlier in the year and relieved the captain-general and his Whig allies of their duties some months later. Rival interpretations of the allegory were in abundance. The overcautious Addison had hedged his bets by seeking Tory approval beforehand, dining with Bolingbroke and Swift a fortnight before the play was first produced. Swift followed up by attending a rehearsal. According to Pope, Addison had asked both Oxford and Bolingbroke to approve the play before production. By not dedicating the play either to the Marlboroughs or to Queen Anne, or to anyone else, Addison kept it ostensibly above partisan politics.[10]

Having already written a celebrated panegyric on Marlborough and his famous Whig victories in *The Campaign* (1704), Addison attempted to placate both Tory and radical Whig anxieties about a newer state despotism, soothing anxieties that had persisted since the controversy generated in 1697–99, after the Treaty of Ryswick, around William's decision not to demobilize the army. For instance, the standing army controversy comes to mind when Cato rebukes Caesar's envoy:

> *Cato.* Bid him disband his legions,
>   Restore the common-wealth to liberty,
>   Submit his actions to the publick censure,
>   And stand the judgment of a Roman Senate. (2.2.28–31)

While these lines would have struck a chord in 1713, such references remained relevant throughout the century for the Country opposition as well as the American colonists. The play's sweeping generalizations could be applied without requiring great ingenuity. Cato's son Marcus anaphorically links "guilt, rebellion, fraud, and *Caesar*," even while the other son, Portius, associates his father with "honour, virtue, liberty, and *Rome*" (1.1.13, 32).[11]

If "Cato" was seen by many as representing Whig "liberties," "Caesar" suggested the "arbitrary tyranny" of royal prerogative. Since the mid-seventeenth century, Caesar had been a positive epithet for English monarchs, but had steadily undergone debasement. Royalist writers such as Dryden and Behn unabashedly celebrated Charles II as Caesar and referred to his father likewise. On the other hand, Waller addresses the Lord Protector as Caesar in the Horatian ode of 1654. Charles II is Caesar in Dryden's panegyrical *Astraea Redux*, William III is Caesar in Addison's *Pax Gulielmi Auspiciis Europae Reditta* of 1697, and Anne is Caesar for Matthew Prior in 1706. However, with the ejection of the Stuarts, the term begins to be associated with the Pretender. By the time Swift's *Drapier's Letters* equates George I with Caesar, the reference is an obviously odious one. The imperial monarch eventually receives rhetorical comeuppance as tyrannical usurper.[12]

On the lookout for a historical consensus above the conflicts of faction, Addison argues in *The Spectator* that "we can now allow *Caesar* to be a great Man, without derogating from *Pompey;* and celebrate the Virtues of *Cato,* without detracting from those of *Caesar.*"[13] Cato's voice, taking aim at the Pretender and his allies, taught the virtues of a moderate polemic against opponents of the Revolution Settlement. The Whigs treated a shaky dynastic succession as if it were enshrined consensus. Addison's recasting of that dubious consensus in Stoical terms may have felt strange. The same play at an earlier moment would have appealed to radical republicans and dissenters (whose politics Addison would have consciously repudiated). It so happened that Calvinism was sometimes called "baptized Stoicism" and was notorious among royalists for being especially antagonistic to the religious claims of monarchy. Stoicism was therefore seen by some as a natural ally for radical republican articulations of virtue, certainly more than Addison could have intended. For instance, Milton's defense of tyrannicide in *The Tenure of Kings and Magistrates* (1649) quotes approvingly from Seneca's *Hercules Furens,* another play that celebrates the most famous of Stoic heroes: "There can be slaine / No sacrifice to God more acceptable / Then an unjust and wicked King."[14] But it has to be said that there was little danger of a regicidal reading, for much had changed in the political and religious context since the mid-seventeenth century. It is the quick descent to political cliché that makes for Samuel Johnson's judgment—characteristically crushing—that "those who affected to think liberty in danger, affected likewise to think that a stage-play might preserve it." Addison's blandness tempers his rhetoric, leading Johnson to say, "nothing here *excites or assuages emotion;* here is *no magical power of raising phantastick terror or wild anxiety.*"[15] The *apatheia,* or Stoic detachment so deliberately constructed by Addison, is deemed aesthetically inconsequential.

Following on from Johnson's judgment, *Cato* is often dismissed by earlier historians of English theater as a closet drama that wrongheadedly followed French neoclassical formulae. John Dennis's early criticism of *Cato* also faults it for Addison's idiosyncratic observance of neoclassicism. Addison sticks to these rules when they are most illogical, according to Dennis, and ignores them when they could have helped his play considerably. Unlike several English poets who wished to identify neoclassical rules with French tyranny and celebrate the liberties allowed in English verse, Dennis favors sound classical compositions alongside Whiggish politics.[16] He bitterly criticizes the packing of plays' audiences in the manner of juries, leading to "Party, Passion, Prejudice, and Prepossession" (41–42).

It is more fruitful to consider *Cato* an innovative example of early sentimentalism. Addison's subplot imitates the intrigue in Otway's *The Orphan*, as both of Cato's sons are in love with the same woman, Lucia, and one of them even woos her on the other's behalf. Although critics are almost unanimous in condemning this dramatization of fatal sibling rivalry as unnecessarily digressive, it reflects the efficacy of a romantic subplot in a previous defense of the Whiggish doctrine of mixed government, Nathaniel Lee's *Lucius Junius Brutus* (1680). Lee's Brutus patriotically sentences his own son to death for a romantic distraction even as he defeats the Tarquins and makes Rome a republic.[17] Addison's subplot participates in the moral purposes of Lee, Otway, and Rowe, but is neither wholly tragic as they are, nor at all comic in the manner of Wycherley's comedies or the subplot in Southerne's *Oroonoko*. Promoting masculine sentimentalism, the play concludes with the sacrifice of Cato unlike that of female figures such as Lucrece in *Lucius Junius Brutus* or Monimia in *The Orphan*. Surviving the war and learning the political and moral lesson, Cato's protégé Juba is also honored by winning the hand of Cato's daughter Marcia. As a result, the subplot does not flirt with gendered satire or farce, as do Wycherley and Southerne, or melodrama, as do the former tragedians. Clearly influenced by Dryden's heroic plays in which the political and the erotic symbolize each other amid familial sacrifice, Addison's sentimental tragedy dovetails "female" love and "male" honor.[18]

JUBA, OR AFRICAN VIRTUALIZATION

Reading Addison's *Cato* and Thomson's *Sophonisba*, Julie Ellison insightfully argues that "ambivalent Africans serve the Whig desire to be politically central." Seeing a dynamic of apologia behind Whig ideology in these plays, Ellison suggests that the racialization of the North African republican hero enables the expression of masculine sensibility. "Cato's tears," as her essay aptly titles the phenomenon, are theatrical excesses that reconfirm British masculine subjectivity—in the twin categories of disinterestedness and sentiment—through a plot of black surrogacy, eliciting *"Roman* drops from *British* eyes," as the prologue

The Stoic's Voice

spoken by Juba (and written by Pope) asserts. Eventually, for Ellison, sentiment occludes race in these representations because race serves as a trope for emotion. Here Ellison applies—too boldly for my comfort —Toni Morrison's notion of "black surrogacy" in American literature to the problem of early-eighteenth-century British nationalism, seeing analogies between literary representations of the North African in late Stuart high culture and the mulatto in antebellum novels. As privileged mediators between whites and blacks, mulattos and Moors serve as sentimental objects (as Oroonoko does as royal slave). With the lachrymose blurring of vision their literary presence produces, these racial objects eventually dissolve. Though it is reasonable to suggest that various cultural others are necessary scapegoats for the creation of national selves, a number of historical differences remain to be explored. Both "Moors" and "mulattos" are literary constructs; the former category is notoriously slippery and Americanists also argue whether the literary reification of mulatto overstates its historical relevance. However, Ellison's essay is a significant breakthrough, especially for the insights that " 'the classical republican' is not a figure but a plot, not a position but a relation . . . republican ideologies and affiliated strands of Cato discourse comprise, not a discrete set of beliefs or attitudes, but a recurring arrangement of positions defined by the interdependent presence and absence of masculine sentiment." To this we can add that, in its early-eighteenth-century context, Cato expresses the ambivalent relation between politics and commerce, in addition to the Whig ideology of sacrifice through homosociability, oedipal mimesis, and imperial filiopiety.[19]

It may be more useful to analyze race in the early-eighteenth-century context of *Cato* as a metonymic rather than metaphorical principle, itself dependent on a newly acquired conception of national culture. When it comes to the elaboration of Whig national allegory in theater, *Cato* and *Sophonisba* are only two instances. In this respect, Moors have no weeping privileges when it comes to Whiggish tears; sentimental objects and models of liberty from almost anywhere do just as well if not as famously as the Roman senator from Utica. John Dennis, whose criticism of *Cato* I discuss shortly, garnered moderate success with *Liberty Asserted* (1704), celebrating an Iroquois prince, Ulamar, in the French and Indian Wars. A number of plays exploring patriotic themes in "archaic" national contexts follow *Cato*. Especially notable are those, such as Edward Young's *Busiris* (1719), featuring ancient Egypt;

William Philips's *Hibernia Freed* (1722), about old Ireland; and Ambrose Philips's *The Briton* (1722), which celebrates political freedom in Roman Britain. Philip Frowde's *The Fall of Saguntum* (1727) deals with Hannibal's wars in classical Spain, and the tragedy of the Amazon queen Candace and the Roman hero Fabius resemble Sophonisba's. Nationalism, an entirely modern ideology, exists alongside an insatiable desire for its legitimation through mythic roots. Narratives of national birth spring from the overthrow of a foreign yoke. Conveniently putting aside its hybrid presence in Britain, writers used race as a multilayered feature. Whigs saw themselves as Saxons throwing off Latin rule in the light of Tacitus's *Germania*. France — or, alternatively, Catholicism — fulfilled the idea of the "Roman" yoke, and England's Anglo-Saxon roots could be identified as the same as Germany's. Indeed, Thomson's long poem *Liberty* indulges such an imaginative exercise, inventing a naturalized English democracy with full-blown Saxon roots.[20] Paul de Rapin-Thoyras, in his *History of England* (1732–47), translated by Nicholas Tindal, made a well-known case for English constitutionalism deriving from originary Germanic liberty. This invented tradition was applied by Thomson's friend William Paterson in his *Arminius. A Tragedy* (1740), where the eponymous hero decries Roman tyranny and its vices while praising the Germans:

> Give me, ye Gods! the plain unconquer'd *German*,
> Rich in hard Toil, and opulent in Freedom;
> Unpolish'd into Vice, and void of Guile,
> Of rough, but kind and hospitable Heart,
> This is the Man, the Friend I would prefer
> To *Rome*'s proud Lord, array'd in Spoil and Ruin (19).

Arminius was banned just after Thomson's historical play *Edward and Eleonora* met the same fate, and so was Henry Brooke's *Gustavus Vasa* (1740), which celebrated the liberator who united Sweden against its Danish rulers. Also, as the legal name of Equiano, Vasa could suggest without incongruity a partly emancipationist meaning later in the century (see chapter 6). Also relevant was yet another recently performed political play, David Mallet's *Mustapha* (1739), critical of the government through the vehicle of a Turkish harem intrigue. Mustapha's evil queen, Roxolana, plots to ensure the succession of her son, but her scheme goes badly wrong, resulting in the death of both princes who are contenders for the throne. All these plays using national allegory appear to occlude the specificity of the metaphorical vehicle for the political payoff in the tenor. However, the tenor in literary representation is affected even as the vehicle begins to acquire a life of its own. The juxtaposition of a variety of vehicles implies a mutual polyvalence and circulation under the Whiggish umbrella of national freedom. The contiguity of these vehicles suggests cultural curiosity despite the obvious inaccuracies in the representations.

In light of these multiple models of experimentation—featuring analogies for British freedom as far afield as Egypt as well as among the Iroquois, and throughout the extent of Europe from Scandinavia to Spain—Numidia's and Juba's identity become transitive staging points. George Washington's later identification with Juba, as well as the styling of the Young Pretender as Juba, are less about Juba's blackness and more about his political transitivity. Race here is more than emotional impasse but not yet racial essentialism. The "portability" of race—unlike its "fixity" in Chambers's *Cyclopaedia*—is suggested intriguingly in *Cato* when the villain Sempronius "passes" as Juba through the palace guard to attempt an abduction of Cato's daughter Marcia (4.2). When the real Juba challenges and kills his impersonator, race is "disguise" as well as "revelation," dangerously portable as well as culturally corrigible. Slaying his own treacherous double, the real Juba wins even while recognizing his racial and cultural exchangeability, thus reclaiming his identity from impropriety.[21] But what is the meaning of Juba-nature? This question is answered in the long discussion between Juba and his old counselor, Syphax, at the beginning of the play, when the issue of loyalty to Cato is moot. In league with Sempronius, a disaffected associate of Cato's, the Numidian general Syphax is entrusted with winning Juba over to Caesar's camp. Juba defends the superior virtue of the Roman character but confuses virtue with might:

> *Juba.* Why do'st thou cast out such ungenerous terms
> Against the Lords and Sov'reigns of the world?
> Dost thou not see mankind fall down before them,
> And own the force of their superior virtue?
> Is there a nation in the wilds of *Africk,*
> Amidst our barren rocks, and burning sands,
> That does not tremble at the *Roman* name? (1.4.11–17)

In response to this sign of vassalage, Syphax's rejoinder is couched in a comparative assessment reminiscent of Shylock's self-humanization in *The Merchant of Venice*:

> *Syphax.* Gods! where's the worth that sets this people up
>   Above your own *Numidia*'s tawny sons!
>   Do they with tougher sinews bend the bow?
>   Or flies the javelin swifter to its mark,
>   Launch'd from the vigour of a *Roman* arm?
>   Who like our active *African* instructs
>   The fiery steed, and trains him to his hand?
>   Or guides in troops th'embattled Elephant,
>   Loaden with war? these, these are arts, my Prince,
>   In which your *Zama* does not stoop to *Rome*. (1.4.18–27)

Syphax's argument concerning Numidian martial prowess and Zama as rival to Rome is sophistical given his secret disloyalty. If Syphax is reminiscent of Shakespearean predecessors such as Aaron and Shylock, Juba's relationship with Syphax echoes that between Othello and Iago. In his response to the play, Steele links Syphax with Iago, but also adds to the list other Shakespearean characters such as Richard III, the Gloucester of *King Lear*, Cardinal Woolsey in *Henry VIII*, and the Duke of Gloucester in Rowe's *Jane Shore*.[22] Syphax's "Machiavellian" advice founders on its own contradictions; yet, like Iago, Syphax occasionally renders insight that is disqualified within the moral rubric of the play as a result of his personal malignity. Juba's response to Syphax takes the form of devaluing African character. Through the clichés of African nature and Roman culture, Juba juxtaposes the superiority of Roman mind to African body. Syphax argues back that Juba is capitulating to dissimulation and urban sophistry, quintessentially Roman arts. Juba replies:

> These all are virtues of a meaner rank,
> Perfections that are placed in bones and nerves.
> A *Roman* soul is bent on higher views:
> To civilize the rude unpolish'd world,
> And lay it under the restraint of laws;
> To make Man mild, and sociable to Man;
> To cultivate the wild licentious Savage

With wisdom, discipline, and liberal arts;
Th' embellishments of life: Virtues like these,
Make human nature shine, reform the soul,
And break our fierce barbarians into men.

Syphax. Patience kind Heavens!—excuse an old man's warmth.
What are these wond'rous civilizing arts,
This *Roman* polish, and this smooth behaviour,
That render man thus tractable and tame?
Are they not only to disguise our passions,
To set our looks at variance with our thoughts,
To check the starts and sallies of the soul,
And break off all its commerce with the tongue;
In short, to change us into other creatures,
Than what our nature and the Gods design'd us? (1.4.28–48)

If Juba is guilty of undervaluing the "native" sources of his virtue, identifying his countryman as "the wild licentious Savage" in need of Roman discipline, commercial culture, and *artes liberales*, Syphax is caught in a rhetorical trap of greater proportions. Syphax's denunciation of "wond'rous civilizing arts" and "*Roman* polish" corresponds rather too well with his own behavior in this scene, itself illustrating the dissimulation he decries. Syphax suggests that Juba might be the agent of an anticolonial rebellion, but this possibility is wholly tainted by Syphax's predetermined motive of deserting to Caesar, the greatest imperialist of them all. Both Syphax and Juba are Romanized through and through; hence Syphax's denunciation of Rome is a greater delusion than the naïveté that may be involved in Juba's celebration of it. As a result, Juba's republicanism occupies a middle position that renders dubious both Syphax's Caesarianism and his coconspirator Sempronius's Machiavellianism. Cato's uncompromising position, admirable if inimitable, is all about politics as the devolution of ideal principles rather than as ex post facto rationalization of existing facts. In a Stoical reading, the Caesarian position stands for the passions and their arbitrariness, a kind of boundless and unlimited energy that suggests the movement of capital as much as it does the politics of arbitrary rule, whereas the Catonic position suggests the repudiation of unbridled passion—in Sempronius and Marcus—as well as cowardly fear and defeatism—in Lucius. Cato is ultimately in favor of heroic adherence to principle alongside the task of rational reflection. What better justification of Whiggish trimming between virtue and commerce? This Whiggish position blithely reduces the question of cultural conflict to national-cultural transitivity and translatability, emphasizing the priority of moderate temperament over that of either sentimental monarchism—Jacobitism—or anticolonial nationalism—radical republicanism.

After the conspiracy of Syphax and Sempronius leads to the revolt of the Numidian army, Juba humiliates himself for the guilt by association of being Numidian. Cato comforts him with the fact that "Falshood and Fraud shoot up in every soil / The product of all climes—*Rome* has its *Caesars*" (4.4.45-46). To this consolation, Juba responds that Cato's praise is worth more "than *Numidia's* empire" (4.4.53-54). Juba wants Numidians to progress through "the restraint of laws." In the manner of Juba, and Oroonoko before him, Cato earlier rejected Juba's presentation of a Hannibal option as inconsistent with his honor, unwilling to be "Reduced like *Hannibal*, to seek relief / From court to court, and wander up and down, / A vagabond in *Africk!*" (2.4.42-44). Moderate Stoical freedom means freedom "through" rather than freedom "from" the constraints that the world imposes. By imbibing good "Catonic" virtues—and this means not being Cato, but learning the lesson of Cato without emulating his suicide—Numidians can be free even within formally Roman domains. Commercial civilization's Roman character has to be tempered by Rome's republican aspect. Rome's imperial aspect has to be eschewed just as much as Rome's fall into decadence. For Juba, independence from Rome, whether nominal or actual, does not guarantee that Numidians benefit. Virtue, on the other hand, by domesticating the unruly stallions that are his soldiers, will "break [Juba's] fierce barbarians into men" (1.4.38). As Syphax's brief in this scene is to make Juba defect to Caesar's camp, it is he who has inherited the worst of the Roman attributes, even as his prince selectively celebrates the best of them by eulogizing Cato as the conclusion to the argument. When Juba resists political temptation in the first act, the play's moral action is essentially over.[23]

The cultural and nationalist implications of Roman imperialism arose in the minds of at least some of Addison's contemporaries and predecessors. Thomas May's versified Lucan describes how Numidia, following Juba's capitulation "from a Kingdomes state is now become, / A subject province to Imperiall Rome." Nathaniel Wanley's translation of Justus Lipsius discusses the establishment of colonies as the supreme example of state-sponsored "Exactions and Rapines." No other invention contributed more to a country's strength, "and nothing could be devised more grievous to the subject" (270).[24]

Amid the plethora of curmudgeonly criticisms he heaped on Addison's play, John Dennis observes tellingly that Addison's exploration of anti-Roman nationalism is blatantly inconsistent. Dennis realizes the anticolonial significance of Syphax's remonstrances:

> For the most shining Qualities in *Cato*'s Character were the Love of his Country, and the Command which he had of his Passions.
>
> Now, Sir, for the first of these Qualities give me leave to observe, that *Cato* was a Lover of his own Country, and not of *Numidia;* and he and his *Romans* design'd to subdue *Numidia* to *Rome*, and not *Rome* to *Numidia*. If *Syphax* had been a loyal Subject and a true Friend to his Prince, and not a false Traitor and a Friend to *Rome*, he would have advis'd his Prince to have defied both *Caesar* and *Cato*, and the *Romans* in general, and taking this Advantage of their civil Dissensions to have retreated into his own *Numidia*, and to have rows'd up all the Nations between the Tropicks against those accursed Plagues of the Human Race, who design'd to sacrifice the Happiness and the Virtue of Mankind to their insatiable Avarice, and their detestable Ambition. And *Juba* had follow'd that Advice, if he had been wise or magnanimous enough to have had any Regard for his own Royalty and his Independency, or had been a true Patriot enough to have had half so much concern for the Liberty and Happiness of *Numidia* as *Cato* had for that of *Rome*. (2:92)

Dennis's objections present a credible alternative even if they are posed in literal-minded terms that are deaf to the play's allegorical resonances. Reading against the grain, he concentrates on the play's lack of psychological realism. Juba has not recognized the potential worth of Syphax's advice despite its compromised nature, and his choices in the play are reduced from being a king's to a vassal's choice between Caesar and Cato. Juba ultimately maintains his virtue by choosing the republican liberty offered by Cato over the monarchical tyranny represented by the ambitions of Caesar—although it is not clear what his real political options are after Cato's suicide.

Juba wins Marcia's hand in marriage from a dying Cato and also inherits the legacy of Catonic virtue. The historical Cato's daughter Portia was married to his own nephew Marcus Brutus, Julius Caesar's famous assassin (Brutus himself had always been traditionally identified as not a Stoic but a Platonist). Juba, like Oroonoko or Chapman's Bussy d'Ambois, is a Herculean hero, both king substitute and potential tyrannicide, also resembling characters from Dryden's chivalric "Indian" plays, such as Montezuma, Morat, and Aurung-Zebe. The doubled position of the royal African as both proto-monarch and archrebel undoubtedly reminds us of Oroonoko, called Caesar by both Behn and Southerne. Thus, the gamut of allegiances from royalism to republicanism can be at least symbolically included; as a result, imperial and anticolonial sentiment can coexist, as in Dryden's plays, without contradiction.[25] Such a transfer of qualities may have been further suggested by a circumstantial irony. The first run of *Cato* had to be stopped in May 1713 because Anne Oldfield, who played Marcia, was in an advanced state of pregnancy. This accidental feature may have alluded to the pregnant Imoinda's character (or could for us), even as Juba's status as African prince suggests that of Oroonoko. A double metamorphosis is at work: if Juba has taken on Cato's mind to carry his political principles further, Cato acquires the "mute" African body. While Juba conveniently crosses over to Roman virtue, he leaves Cato to pay the price. Even as Juba acquires Cato's moral values, republican rhetoric, and the hand of his daughter Marcia, the Roman senator correspondingly turns into an abject victim of circumstance. Cato's stabbing of himself, even though it does not take place on stage, is reported in a manner reminiscent of the gruesome self-disembowelment of Behn's Oroonoko. An earlier Cato, Chapman's, falls upon his sword and proceeds to pluck out his entrails on stage. Some accounts of the classical Cato suggest yet another parallel with Oroonoko, whose bowels were put back into his body after self-disembowelment. However, Chapman's Cato manages to rend his bowels yet again. On the other hand, there is no simple parallel to slave rebellion here, as Cato was a willing volunteer under Lucius Gellius, the consul and praetor who was instrumental in putting down the revolt led by Spartacus.

All these representational uncertainties indicate that Cato's morally ambiguous suicide sits uneasily in cultural translation. In fact, a smug Whiggish superiority to Cato's Stoicism remains in Addison's play as Portius brings the news—too late, as Cato has already stabbed himself—of a promise of support "From Pompey's son, who through the realms of Spain / Calls out for vengeance on his father's death, / And rouses the whole nation up to arms" (5.4.55–57). Are we to think that if Cato had stayed his hand, he may have profited from last-minute Whiggish ingenuity, not to be confused with expediency? Of course, there is no simple way to incorporate Roman conventions of honorable suicide into Christian ethics. According to one Tory critic, it was "done in Violation of the Law of Nature and *Pagan* Morality." For that matter, with respect to the larger intellectual frame of the play, another Tory scribe sneers that "*Stoicism* was a Corruption of the *Roman* Morals, and came in with the *Eastern* Fashions, after the Expedition into *Macedonia.*" The writer points out that there was debate about the doctrine of just suicide even in classical times, with Virgil, Cicero, and Macrobius attacking it even as Tacitus, Paterculus, Lucan, Valerius Maximus, and especially Seneca systematically defended it as a fundamental personal liberty. For this critic, the English were too squeamish to countenance the gruesome disembowelment that Cato historically attempted upon himself.[26]

Suicide is the favored manner of death for classical African queens such as Cleopatra, Dido, and Sophonisba. The Second Punic War between Rome and Carthage featured the joint suicide of the Numidian Massinissa and the Carthaginian queen, Sophonisba. Syphax, in this history that comes from Livy, is actually Sophonisba's husband and the king of West Numidia; Massinissa, the king of East Numidia, sides with the Roman consul Scipio Africanus and opportunistically capitalizes on his rival Syphax's defeat to woo Sophonisba (her marriage conveniently annulled upon political defeat). Sophonisba remains a zealous Carthaginian patriot interested only in the furtherance of her political ambitions by any means necessary. Her affair with Massinissa is one more gambit toward that end. Sophonisba's virulent anti-Roman patriotism is frustrated by Scipio, who rules that Sophonisba has to be part of the Roman triumph with no exceptions made to accommodate Massinissa's erotic desires. The Carthaginian queen chooses rather to kill herself, railing against Massinissa's impotence and Roman treachery. The suicide is assisted by Massinissa, who also kills himself (not in all versions) while Scipio's change of heart comes too late.[27]

James Thomson's *Sophonisba* (1729) was the most successful English attempt to represent the title character as a female Cato. This play, like *Cato,* positions liberty against the historical example of ancient Roman imperialism deliberately confused with Jacobite monarchism, while ancient republican virtues are rendered as Whig ideals, if not quite policy:

> The Romans are the scourge
> Of the vext world, destroyers of mankind,
> And all beneath the smooth dissembling mask
> Of justice, and compassion; as if slave
> Was but another name for civiliz'd.
> Against her tyrant power, each gen'rous sword
> Of every nation should be drawn. While Carthage
> Unblemish'd rises on the base of commerce,
> Founds her fair empire on that common good,
> And asks of heaven nought but the winds and tides
> To carry plenty, letters, science, wealth,
> Civility, and grandeur, round the world. (3.3.70–80)

The audience is encouraged to think of Carthage as Britain in *Sophonisba,* and in his preface and prologue the Scottish Thomson recommends Whiggish political virtues anchored within general patriotism. For Thomson, Britain is the target of external attempts, by the Pretender and others, to subordinate it. However, he and the meaning of his play move into Opposition circles later.[28]

Such a plot—associatively Stoical, although technically not Stoic at all—produced an intersection of chivalric romance and tragedy that is reminiscent of older political romances in North African settings, the most prominent being those of Aeneas and Dido and Anthony and Cleopatra. Dido, Sophonisba, and Cleopatra are all *queens* of African kingdoms in danger of supersession by masculine Roman power. The superimposition of the Roman dispensation is seen as an inevitably tragic outcome (even though this does not happen immediately in Dido's case). The African prince—Massinissa or Juba—stands at the crossroads and is an admirer of Roman virtue, as embodied in Cato, Scipio, and Caesar. Oroonoko's depiction by Behn as a Herculean hero is beholden to this tradition as well. The African prince's role is that of an ideological shifter, a virtual subject who can be the vehicle for cultural transference and apology, that harks back to the anticolonial tradition of the Spanish *leyenda negra*. On the other hand, the royal women, such as Dido, Imoinda, Cleopatra, and Sophonisba, die in these narratives, with no symbolic resolution that can accommodate them. As Ellison puts it, "Sophonisba stands precisely for the absence of ambivalence."[29]

Commerce and virtue are interrelated in this story as well, although most visually suggestive perhaps in an earlier depiction of Sophonisba, David Murray's 1611 version. Murray's play, in Spenserian stanzas, presents the African queen as a synecdochic receptacle for the spoils of mercantilism, foreshadowing many descriptions of Trade as a bedecked female in the early eighteenth century, such as Addison's in *The Tatler* and *The Spectator*. Sophonisba's beauty shone "like a polisht Diamond of Ind,"

> Her teeth like rankes of orientall pearle,
> With corrall died lips were compas'd round,
> From whence farre sweeter then the well tun'd merle:
> Her heart-bereauing tongue did softly sound:
> Words of such force the flintiest heart to wound.
> Her baulmy breath, in worth, in taste, in smell,
> Did ciuet, muske, and amber-greaze excell. (n.p.)

In *Cato,* however, Addison leaves mercantile metaphors implicit, opting instead for its indirect expression through the trope of immoderate lust, as is Sempronius's for Marcia, or its more respectable equivalent, the passion of Marcus's for Lucia and Juba's for Marcia. Cato's tearlessness at the death of Marcus—passion-free in the face of the death of a son who represented unbridled passion—is consistent, if tautologically so. In a scene that inevitably raised many objections, Addison portrays Cato's stern patriotism as one in which he cries for country but not over the battle-scarred body of Marcus (4.4.77–106). Historically, it was Portius who was killed at the battle of Philippi. Crying only for country but not for a dead son, along with almost every detail of the play, was ridiculed by Dennis as "wretched Affectation."[30]

However, while the dying Cato dispatches his surviving son Portius back to his country seat with the admonition to imitate the agrarian virtues of his ancestor Cato the Censor, he approves of an alliance between Juba and Marcia. Cato's blessings are issued with an ambiguous recognition:

> A senator of *Rome,* while *Rome* surviv'd
> Would not have match'd his Daughter with a King,
> But *Caesar*'s arms have thrown down all distinction;
> Whoe'er is Brave and Virtuous, is a *Roman.* (5.4.88–91)

Addison has significantly changed the orthodox meaning of Cato's death by placing this acknowledgment in Cato's mouth. Cato's approval of Juba, along with a sense of his own obsolescence, ushers in the new dispensation. The presence of the African as domestic pet in England, as we have seen, signified the culture of colonial commerce, and Juba is like Oroonoko, royal but incongruous, looking for a politics. Portius's dispatch to the country results in the reduction of Roman Stoic to country gentleman, even as Juba likely turns into some version of a Court Whig, probably Addison himself. Juba is a more balanced composite of virtue and passion, whereas Portius is a residue of the older dispensation, somewhat passionless as he was in his dealings with Lucia. It is no surprise that the legacy is not an equal one, as it is likely that the country gentleman is more prone to Jacobitism, perhaps rendered here as structurally equivalent to its polar opposite, seventeenth-century radical republicanism. Cato's legacy, different from Cato's own politics, places his political heirs, Juba, at the Addisonian center, and Portius at a moderate Tory right. "Caesar's arms have thrown down all distinction," suggests the collapse of Stoical virtue because of military despotism, yet it also describes commerce's leveling of social ranks. Cato's associates in the Senate at Utica are Roman patriarchs and repeatedly addressed by him as "fathers" throughout the play, whereas his successor sons are more likely (despite the strenuous objections that Pocock may raise) Lockean contractualists. A moderate dialectic of Country and Court is favored, even as this middle path marginalizes the two ends of extreme leveling and autocracy, or radical republicanism and Jacobitism. Whig ideology is a play for a hegemonic center from which the margins are denigrated as violating its consensus. Through the collapse of romantic passion with commerce, Addison also subordinates the traditional complication of romantic rivalry between Massinissa and Syphax in the Sophonisba plays to the generalized conflict between Caesar and Cato. Syphax, as we saw, is an old general who is Juba's Machiavellian

The Stoic's Voice

counselor. Addison's source for the other Machiavel was probably from a Roman coin that had Caesar's portrait minted on one side and that of an associate, Tiberius Sempronius Gracchus, on the other.[31]

Addison opts for abstract principles mixed with sentimental identities and hence finesses the excesses of mercantilist ideology by mixing it with a palatable amount of neostoicism. Although Addison was certainly not an amoral anti-Stoic such as Mandeville, he was also not Shaftesbury. No opponent of the commercial benefits of colonial trade, he remarks in *The Spectator* that "Trade, without enlarging the *British* Territories, has given us a kind of additional Empire."[32] Correspondingly, as secretary of state, Addison was instrumental in enacting the royal proclamation that suppressed piracy and set up a commission to try colonial pirates. He dispatched extra ships to Jamaica to ensure the safety of the colonial trade. In a callow "Poem to His Majesty" written in 1695, the young Addison praises the economic consequences of William's sea war that will make the English "Secure from wars, / New lands explore, and sail by Other stars; / Fetch Uncontroll'd each labour of the Sun, / And make the product of the World our own."[33]

By going back a generation and reading Addison's father's writings on North Africa, a biographical source for Addison's nationalism is revealed in the face of competition over trade rights. The senior Addison, an Anglican clergyman who eventually became dean of Lichfield, had written several tracts on the political situation of Tangier, where he had lived as garrison chaplain in the 1660s. The writings emphasized a standard Christian hostility toward Arab and Turkish rule, characterizing them as despotic and absolutist, whereas ancient Roman imperialism in the area is lauded even as the recent curtailment of the liberties of Europeans is decried. Speaking of the Jews in Morocco under Arab rule, Lancelot Addison says how they "with a Stoical patience support all the Injuries and Contumelies to which they are Dayly exposed." The Jew as a metaphor for the long-suffering Englishman is a Restoration commonplace famous in Dryden's defense of Charles II in *Absalom and Achitophel* (1681). However, for Addison the Jews' stoicism "cannot be imputed to any Heroick Temper in this People, but rather to their customary suffering, being born and Educated in this kind of slavery." Swift too described the stoicism of the Irish as being the result of unfortunate political circumstances rather than any intrinsic heroism. Although Lancelot Addison's North African tracts are obviously intended to contribute to diplomacy rather than political philosophy, we can see that the son derived a strain of libertarian allegory alongside polemical anti-Turkish history from the father's writings on North Africa. In the fifth and last *Whig Examiner,* the son writes that the Anglican doctrines of "Passive-Obedience and Non-Resistance are the Duties of *Turks* and *Indians,* who have no laws above the will of a Grand Signior or a Mogul."[34]

When we move forward from Lancelot's colonial connections to Joseph's, we see a greater sense of reassurance concerning mercantile activities. Joseph's brother Gulston was appointed by the East India Company to serve at Fort St. George (Madras) in the 1690s. Gulston rose to being a member of the Presidential Council and eventually was appointed governor of the colony after the downfall of "Diamond" Pitt. He died soon after, in 1710, leaving his colonial fortune in gems to Joseph, who pursued futile hopes of recovering the considerable inheritance from the trustees. Addison eventually got about £600 worth of diamonds from the estate, which was estimated at some point to be worth anywhere from £14,000 (his own estimate) to £18,000 (by others). The capital had been advanced to a local merchant and was mostly unrecoverable. However, Addison benefited more from public colonialist opportunities than private ones. He persistently attempted to receive an Irish pension after serving as secretary when Wharton was lord lieutenant of Ireland. Eventually successful at deriving this benefice from the Irish colonial establishment, Addison added to the burden of the Irish financing of English place-seekers. All these biographical details are indirectly relevant to the dual aspects of the figure of Cato, showing neither hypocrisy nor contradiction but rather a ready compatibility between neostoicism and colonial commerce in Addison's synthesis.[35]

CATO'S LETTERS, OR SOUTH SEA CRITICISM

Following the spectacular success of Addison's *Cato,* the Whig pamphleteers John Trenchard and Thomas Gordon authored weekly letters signed "Cato," which were serialized in *The London Journal* and subsequently in *The British Journal* from 1720 to 1723. Collected and widely distributed as *Cato's Letters,* these writings articulated Whiggish ideas of liberty and property that reconciled neostoicism and mercan-

The Stoic's Voice

tilism. Marie McMahon persuasively argues that Pocock's reading of Trenchard and Gordon as a neo-Harringtonian Country opposition in *The Machiavellian Moment* misrecognizes their critique of Whig rule from within the fold. Indeed, some material made its way from *Cato's Letters* to *The Craftsman,* but the former work is just as Lockean as neo-Harringtonian. Virtue and commerce cannot be harmoniously reconciled by recourse to Machiavellian rhetoric. Country ideologues could subsequently appropriate Gordon and Trenchard as a conservative anti-corruption discourse while muting its Whig ideals, but the original intention and journalistic context derive from the challenge posed by the South Sea Bubble to the Whiggish left.[36]

The first volume of *Cato's Letters* began as a journalistic exposé of the Bubble. The South Sea Company had been started in 1711 by Harley as a rival financial operation to the Whig-dominated Bank of England and East India Company, and the directors convinced the Ministry into a public flotation of the war-related national debt. Because the payment of interest on government bonds was a major drain on the exchequer, there was considerable enthusiasm for, along with some trepidation at, the conversion of long-term government annuities into company shares. Capital was raised several times without reference to the company's (non-existent) assets, which consisted of vague trading rights in South America. The company's pyramid scheme paid old investors with capital from new ones eager to cash in. The inevitable crash occurred after huge fortunes had been made and lost in the rampant share speculation. South Sea shares fluctuated wildly from £130 in January 1720 to giddy peaks of £1,050 in June, and £1,100 in August, but crashed irreversibly to £190 by September. Ironically, the collapse occurred as a result of the company's crackdown on smaller Bubble companies that had sprung up in imitation of its success.

Crashes in Paris and Amsterdam, despite their superficial similarities, demonstrate the divergence of causes behind these events. John Law's reorganization of French state finances in 1719 was based on sounder economic assumptions and genuine assets, but entrenched political interests reasserting themselves following market volatility led to his spectacular failure. The shenanigans on Exchange Alley, unlike those on Rue Quincampoix, were the result of greater irresponsibility and unscrupulousness than were ever involved in Law's experiment. More recently, Larry Neal has suggested that there was rational behavior in the speculation as participants may have been practicing a "discounted martingale," or a series of raised bets after each loss in the hope of an eventual win. Whatever the psychology of the actors, Cato's voice stridently demanded the punishment of the company directors and their backers, aiming to reform the irregularities that led to the collapse. The cover-up had involved the shielding of participants such as the king himself, who had speculated through his mistress, the Duchess of Kendal. The cashier of the company, Robert Knight, fled to Brabant. Fearing exposure of the entire Whig oligarchy, the Ministry chose not to pursue his extradition and obstructed the parliamentary investigations. Rumors circulated identifying Walpole as the principal architect of the "Brabant Skreen." The successful manipulations behind the scenes eventually earned Walpole the prime ministerial post, with the eclipse of Sunderland's and Stanhope's careers.[37]

Of course, there was a considerable body of older antivenality satire that could be drawn upon to criticize this unseemly pursuit of stocks. Replete with religious imagery, Hogarth's satirical print, *The South Sea Scheme* (1721) shows foxes chasing each other under the London Fire Monument, even as a Roman Catholic priest, a Jew, and a Puritan leave "their strife Religious bustle" to play a gambling game of "pitch & Hussle," as mentioned in the appended verses (Fig. 10). The devil is present with a scythe, as is a statue of Gog. Allegorical figures of Honour and Honesty are being punished by Self-Interest and Villainy, even as a crowd of women rush into a building that advertises "Raffleing for Husbands with Lottery Fortunes in Here" over the door. However, Hogarth's print does not make much of the geographical associations of the South Seas, instead opting for a carnival atmosphere that foregrounds the degenerate distractions and entertainments of commodity culture.

All the same, Britain's first full-blown financial scandal was a grandiose colonial venture. Domestic confidence in colonial trade was shaken as never before at a time when it was reaching center stage. Addison's Spectator had taken pride as an Englishman that his metropolis had become "a kind of *Emporium* for the whole Earth." As a Citizen of the World, the Spectator comments on the specialized haunts of global businessmen, "distinguished by their different Walks and different Languages."[38] The Spectator is referring to the architecture of the Royal Exchange, itself reflecting the new sense of a global trade. Proximate

Figure 10 William Hogarth, *An Emblematic Print of The South Sea Scheme* (1721). (British Museum, London)

as well as distant trade was represented in terms of "walks" that included Spanish Walk, Virginia Walk, East-India Walk, and Jamaica Walk. Stockjobbers and projectors, not bona fide merchants and therefore disallowed from the Royal Exchange, had set up shop in nearby Exchange Alley. Full-time merchants as well as the new class of Bubble speculators were drawn by the imagining of the "inexhaustible Riches" of the South Seas. The collapse of the Bubble was, like all financial collapses, a blow to the utopian aspects of the capitalist imagination. Many speculators were ruined, and the inflationary upheaval followed by a sudden deflation immiserated even the laboring poor who had not participated in the boom. Anxieties about gender also played a role in representations of the stockmarket frenzy that was likened to hysterical disorder, enthusiasm, and riot. It was confirmed that Lady Credit, described by Addison earlier as "a beautiful Virgin, seated on a Throne of Gold," was a most fickle mistress, as following distempers she could decay into a skeleton.[39]

Even though the authors of *Cato's Letters* are self-confessed Whigs, they refuse to support the government blindly. A blind defender performs "the base Office of a Slave, and he who sustains it, breathes improperly *English* Air: That of the *Tuilleries* or the *Divan* would suit him better."[40] "Publick Spirit" means "slaughter or be slaughtered" at the prince's will in "arbitrary" countries; in "Protestant Free" ones, this sentiment "is to combat Force and Delusion," "expose Impostors, and to resist Oppressors," and "to maintain the People in Liberty, Plenty, Ease, and Security" (1:280). "Tyranny" is depicted as Turkish, French, or Caesarian, whereas "liberty" is consistently Protestant, English, and Catonic. The level of vituperation directed against the South Sea interest and its powerful backers was unprecedented. Described as "Ravens," "Monsters," "Vermin," "Money-Leaches," and "Horse-Leeches," the wrongdoers would be alternately beneath contempt and dangerous beyond belief (1:11, 12, 17, 19, 40). As "Harpies and Public Robbers and small Sharpers," the culprits are also likened to "Crocodiles and Cannibals, who feed, for Hunger, on human bodies" (1:15, 12). The mixed metaphors of mock-epic vocabulary would lead to the excoriation of "*British* Lions crouch[ing] to a Nest of Owls" (1:28). One letter that abuses the company interest as "Bloodsuckers" signs off as the public hangman, John Ketch, Esq. (1:147-56). However, suspicions concerning the cover-up led to the rhetorical shift of warning political manipulators to limit their foul play: "The Conspirators against Mankind ought to know, that no Subterfuges, or Tergiversations; no knavish Subtilties, or pedantick Quirks of Lawyers; no Evasions, no Skulkings behind known Statutes; no Combinations, or pretended Commissions, shall be able to skreen or protect [the Murtherers of our Credit] from public Justice" (1:77). Such fearless rhetoric led to widespread popularity. John Carteret's spies had written to him that Cato's journalism was found in every alehouse for forty miles around Birmingham, had corrupted the population, and was accepted as gospel. For quite some time, the Old Whig Viscount Molesworth was rumored to be the identity behind Cato, as one of the uncompromising voices in Parliament swearing revenge against the culprits. He declaimed hyperbolically that the directors were guilty of parricide and ought to be subjected to the ancient Roman punishment of being sewn up in a sack with a monkey and a snake and then drowned. As a result, a print of Molesworth styled as Cato sold very well in 1721.

However, things came to a head when *The London Journal,* dated August 12, 1721, breached parliamentary privilege and published an account of the depositions taken by the Committee of Secrecy in its examination of the Bubble culprits. The paper breathlessly reports that an examination of the company's various ledgers shows that "false and fictitious Entries were made: In others, Entries with Blanks; in others, Entries with Rasures and Alterations; and in others, Leaves were torn out. They found further that some Books had been destroyed, and others taken away or secreted."[41] Ten thousand copies of the newspaper were seized and destroyed and charges of seditious libel hung over the publisher, Benjamin Norton Defoe. Even though Gordon as MP had voted for the Septennial Act of 1717 that extended Parliament to a seven-year from a three-year term, Cato was beginning to see a demagogic opportunity, according to the junior Defoe, of "deprecating some great men, and of disposing the people to petition for a new parliament." However, Walpole adopted his favorite tactics of determining the opposition's price and buying people out piecemeal. With Benjamin Defoe's cooperation and the buying out of *The London Journal* by the government, the paper became a government organ, and Cato in the meantime shifted activities to *The British Journal.*

The key to the ready reception of unwelcome Whig dissent by disaffected Tories may lie here. Certainly, there was government-sponsored opposition to Cato's rhetoric. The anonymous *The Censor censur'd: or, Cato turn'd Catiline* (1722) accuses Cato of falling into the arms of Jacobites. Defending the job of the Ministry as a thankless one, the pamphlet astutely uncovers the generalized rhetoric behind Cato's ostensibly specific accusations. Cato had set up his rhetorical game so that he always won: "If a Man prosecutes the Guilty, he's a *Persecutor:* If he defends the Innocent, he is a *Screen.* And thus by asserting boldly, arguing sophistically, demanding every thing, and granting nothing, by malicious Turns and invidious Allegories, he has put forth a Bundle of Letters, which, leaving out *South-Sea* and shifting Names, wou'd serve as well for any Government and any Age, from the Time of the true *Cato* to that of the feigned one.[42] Cato was going after a real problem, but the specific accusations based on investigative journalism and the immediate outrage were being replaced by a generalized anticorruption discourse. *Cato's Letters* itself acknowledges the variety of abuses leveled at its eidolon, which included the choice epithets *"abandon'd Atheist,"* *"bigotted Presbyterian," "flaming Jacobite,"* and *"arrant Republican."* Cato lays claim to none of these identities, professing the middle-of-the-road credo of tolerant Anglicanism and constitutional monarchy.

As one survey of South Sea literature points out, rhetoric around the South Sea Bubble consists both of polemic and metapolemic. It appears that *Cato's Letters* started as journalistic polemic, reacting to the crisis posed to Whig ideology by the event, but retreated to the abstractions of metapolemic when actual revelations dried up following the "Brabant Skreen" and the political crackdown.[43] *Cato's Letters* continued to make arguments for limited monarchy and public accountability, but the topical wind had been knocked out of its sails, especially with the threat of proceeding against the pseudonymous authors. More abstract reflection on political principles would be the norm. Even as the phase of investigative journalist and public ombudsman had come to an end, the lesson learned was that threats to political life were just as much internal as external: "a Nation has but two Sorts of Usurpation to fear, one from their Neighbours, and another from their own Magistrates" (3:70). While the usual remarks against uncircumscribed monarchy prevail, they are tempered with others that repudiate commonwealths as equally oppressive. In Holland, commercial monopolies such as the East India Company are said to have the state by the throat, whereas in France the royal prerogative poaches on individual and entrepreneurial freedoms (3:177–84). The typical rhetorical collapse is made concerning the criminal origins of a polity: *"Alexander,* who robbed Kingdoms and States, was a greater Felon than the Pyrate whom he put to Death, though no One was strong enough to inflict the same Punishment upon him . . . for unless we are determined by the Justice of the Action, there can be no Criterion, Boundary, or fixed Mark, to know where the Thief ends and the Hero begins" (1:134). Unsurprisingly, the idealized version of the British mixed polity, involving free trade and state regulation, king and Parliament, is the best system imaginable. Whereas the concerns of the initial letters are to correct the greatest crime of all, which is *"Peculatus,* or Robbing the *Publick,"* the later ones expound more abstract theories of political liberty, with some polemical passages favoring tyrannicide (1:136). One letter celebrates Brutus's assassination of Julius Caesar, and another defends Cato against his defamers (1:167–81,

The Stoic's Voice

1:216–23). In the manner of Mercier's famous Spartacus passage, which I discuss in relation to Toussaint Louverture and the Haitian Revolution in chapter 7, the letters formulate an early version of an Enlightenment political catechism: "Tell me, O ye unlimited Slaves, ye Beasts of law-less Power, ye loyal Levellers of Right and Wrong! how came *Caesar* by a better Title to Dominion than *Spartacus* had, whose Sword was as good, tho' not quite so prosperous and destructive, as *Caesar's*?" (2:24). It is only a *neo*classical mentality that could link Cato with Spartacus, as Cato Uticensis served under Lucius Gellius to put down the most famous slave revolt of antiquity.

However, after the writers' fury is vented on the South Sea Bubble, they theorize in a more removed fashion, giving both encouraging and admonitory advice. When it comes to colonies in "Of Plantations," Cato distinguishes between colonies for conquest and those for trade. One kind of colony is "to keep conquered Countries in Subjection, and to prevent the Necessity of constant Standing-Armies." This is de-scribed as the policy of the ancient Romans and that of the English in Ireland, whereas "the other Sort of Colonies are for Trade" (3:283–84). Trenchard sees it both ways, counting the benefits but decrying the abuses. As colonies eventually want to shake free of the mother country, it is deemed to be in the interest of metropolitans to keep tropicopolitans contented. Men contribute to public welfare by quit-ting their country, whether they are ambassadors, merchants, or sol-diers. Travelers especially "teach us the Customs, Manners, and Poli-cies of distant Countries." Later letters scapegoat Jacobites, Catholics, and economically "unproductive" occupations performed by tradesmen and servants. With the prose of the conduct book the tract discusses the abuse of words, the failure of charity schools, the advisability of disbelieving superstitions, and the meaning of God (4:3–12, 4:238–49, 4:251–57, 4:280–87). After the death of Trenchard in 1723, Gordon mar-ried Trenchard's widow and made his peace with Walpole by the end of the decade. The threat to the "Screenmaster-General" was, for the mo-ment, over.

However, well after Addison's and Gordon and Trenchard's fash-ioning of Cato as an eidolon, the American colonists exploited this readymade apotheosis of virtue to frame the cause for independence. By this point, Cato could be just as Whig as Tory, just as Machia-vellian as Lockean. Pocock quotes, conveniently for his purpose to be sure, Alexander Hamilton, who turns Addison's allegory upside down in the way that Bolingbroke's Tories had tried to but failed: "Cato was the Tory, Caesar the Whig of his day . . . the former perished with the republic, the latter destroyed it."[44] The fact of the matter is that by the 1760s, Addison's play had become a general symbol of American colonial resistance to British tyranny, whatever the ideological stripe of the opposition. *Cato* ran the gamut of public and private performances as well as school productions. For instance, the play was performed in Charleston and in Virginia in 1735 and 1736 and as the opening production of the Murray-Kean company theater in Philadelphia in 1749. Students at the College of William and Mary planned a production in 1751. The most historically significant performance was probably that at Valley Forge in front of George Washington and the troops of the Continental Army on May 11, 1778, just before battle. The play deeply influenced Washington, who quoted its Stoical platitudes at length to justify his retirement. Perhaps most fascinating of all was the general's admission on several occasions that he greatly liked the character Juba, expressing a desire to play the role.[45] Several important studies of the American Revolution, such as Caroline Robbins's and Bernard Bailyn's, have made much of the fact that *Cato's Letters* was one of the significant ideological resources for the Revolutionaries. According to Bailyn, Addison, reinforced by Gordon and Trenchard, "gave rise to what might be called a 'Catonic' image, central to the political theory of the time, in which the career of the half-mythological Roman and the words of the two London journalists merged indistinguishably."[46]

GULLIVER, OR DEBASED NEOSTOICISM

The Stoic tradition provides Swift with a lingua franca as well as a satirical object. Drafted in the early 1720s, *Gulliver's Travels*, like *Cato's Letters,* is partly a response to the South Sea Bubble. This has been sporadically acknowledged. The satire on the Academy at Lagado, for instance, is aimed just as much at the projectors and stock-jobbers of Exchange Alley as at the experimental scientists in Gresham College. All four of the imaginary voyages are mapped in relation to the South Seas, and Australia ("New Holland") and Tasmania ("Van Diemen's Land") figure prominently. New Holland is the nearest known point to Lilliput, Blefuscu, and Houyhnhnmland. While Brobdingnag in book 2 is

farther away from Australia, and so are Balnibarbi, Luggnagg, Maldonada, and Japan (the various points visited in book 3), New Holland is
still a reference point. All these locations are in the Pacific, an area generally included in the vague term South Seas. Furthermore, like other
contemporary travelers, Gulliver is aware of the commercial significance
of his voyages, bringing back commodities for sale such as the sheep
from Lilliput and the curios fashioned in Brobdingnag. The activity is
economic and the geography suggests South Sea locales, but the reflections in the work, as in *Cato's Letters*, are political ones.[47]

As F. P. Lock suggests, when reading *Travels Through Several Remote
Nations of the World* (Swift's preferred title for *Gulliver's Travels*) it is
better to look for allusions rather than allegories and general paradigms
rather than specific portraits. Challenging the allegorical school of interpretation begun by Charles Firth and continued by Arthur Case,
Lock shows that a systematic political allegory was not Swift's intention. *Gulliver's Travels*, which operates through the circuit of allegory
but with an especially aberrant referentiality, works by counterallegori-
cal suggestion, keeping the glimmer of allegory on the horizon even as
direct allegorical correspondence is subverted. However, Lock hastily
assumes Swift's "objectivity" and "detachment from politics." To assume that Swift's general target and reference was humanity as a whole
is to eschew tracking specific historical parallels altogether, which would
be a mistake. I agree with Edward Said, who despite his own humanist inclinations, suggests that we should think less about Swift's final
views of human nature and more about him "as a kind of local activist,
a columnist, a pamphleteer, a caricaturist." Said identifies the discrep-
ancy between Swift's cynicism and idealism that is found when "the
written language of Irish protestation exacerbated the discontinuity between the intolerability of what was (Ireland) and the improbability of
what could be (English colonialist plans for it)."[48]

Rather than reiterate the South Sea contexts of *Gulliver's Travels*
that have been identified by Arthur Case, Pat Rogers, and Claude Rawson, my aim is to demonstrate that the reflections on anticolonialism
in the satire are a prelude to *The Drapier's Letters* and Swift's self-
fashioning as Stoic in that work. Swift's Tory politics, unlike Addison's
alignment with the new Whigs, make him far more suspicious of colonialism than Addison could ever have been. Much has already been said
by others about the anthropological allusions in Swift's description of

the Yahoos. Charles Firth was one of the first twentieth-century critics to suggest that Yahoos represented the "savage old Irish." Several subsequent critics have concurred, supplementing these allusions with those to colonialist discourse about Africans.[49] While Yahoo and Houyhnhnm together represent a society that depends on an unbridgeable opposition between an ideal self and a bestial other, Gulliver himself dramatizes the split subjectivity of an unclassifiable observer. There is no neutral ground. The Houyhnhnms segregate according to clearly demarcated racial criteria, and their laws brook no transgression. Focusing periodically on the viability of the total extermination of the Yahoos, the Houyhnhnms' potential aim is far more execrable than that of the randomly violent pirates of the satire's last chapter, which I discuss shortly. Underneath the bucolic appearance of this society is a set of statist assumptions, in relation to which Gulliver is calibrated and found wanting. The unregenerate baseness of the Yahoos, when contrasted with the general nobility of the Houyhnhnms, appears as a relational effect of colonial domination. Neither group is what it seems; the Houyhnhnms, contextualized in relation to anthropological discourse on Amerindians by some critics, are physical beings who eat, fornicate, and defecate despite their self-restraint concerning these activities; the Yahoos, whether involved in lust, avarice, excrementality, or hierarchical dispossession of each other, also aspire to a principle of social ordering among themselves that is not unlike the Houyhnhnms' relegation of them as beasts of burden. The structure of republican decision-making in Houyhnhnmland—at odds with the undemocratic treatment of the Yahoos, who do not merit representation—lays several traps for Gulliver, whose insanity develops because he identifies with both groups. In the manner of all Manichaean oppositions, each term cannot exist without its polar opposite. Legend has it that there was a time before Yahoos, but such claims are apocryphal, especially when the Houyhnhnms are revealed to be incapable of writing. The rulers' consideration of genocide is proof of a self-destructive blindness on the part of these primitive republicans. The elimination of Yahoos could mean that Houyhnhnms would lose their relational nobility which comes from comparison with their designated other.

As a creature capable of Houyhnhnm-like rationality and yet cursed with a Yahoo-like body, Gulliver is an unviable monster. Like Behn's Oroonoko, Gulliver resembles that chiasmic amalgam, a royal slave. His mock-heroic behavior, killing the giant wasps when himself a domestic pet among the Brobdingnagians, reminds us of Oroonoko's exploits in Surinam. Gulliver's eventual expulsion is because he can lead a rebellion of Yahoos. In a transparent analogy to slave insurrections and marronage, other Houyhnhnms make the following objection to Gulliver's master: "they alledged, That because I had some rudiments of Reason, added to the natural Pravity of those Animals [the Yahoos], it was to be feared, I might be able to seduce them into the woody and mountainous Parts of the Country, and bring them in Troops by Night to destroy the *Houyhnhnms* Cattle, as being naturally of the ravenous Kind, and averse from Labour" (11:279).[50] Perceived as a potential Oroonoko, Gulliver is a quasi-royal Yahoo who could incite a revolt. He is expelled without a formal hearing.

Confronted by Houyhnhnms, Gulliver acknowledges his family resemblance to Yahoos; upon meeting Yahoos, he condescends like a Houyhnyhnm. Alternating between self-loathing and repulsion toward Yahoos, he cannot reconcile his identity. Enacting and disavowing both identities, Gulliver's dysfunctional response, after his expulsion by the Houyhnhnms, is to live among the British, whom he detests. Representing a self-induced humiliation and megalomania, Gulliver is Cato turned upside down. He speaks the Catonic language of aristocratic superiority but lives in a stable. His context parodies his pretensions. Accused of posing a rebellious threat to the Houyhnhnms, he possesses "some rudiments of Reason" along with the "natural Pravity" of the Yahoos, representing at best an insane version of Oroonoko or Juba.

With its neostoicist vocabulary, the fourth voyage explores an impasse. The binary opposition between Houyhnhnm virtue and Yahoo passion is ineffective as a political model. As with Addison's *Cato*, there has to be a third option, which is neither ascetic virtue (the Houyhnhnms are agrarian and contented, without desire for further civilization) nor passionate commerce (the Yahoos are misers who like to hoard and quarrel over their spoils). Exploring the rhetorical implications of this third option, Claude Rawson's essays make a useful set of distinctions concerning anticolonialism in *Gulliver's Travels*. According to Rawson, Swift's criticism—of Big-Endians and Little-Endians, big people and little people, Houyhnhnms and Yahoos—works according to a tripartite rather than a binary schematicism, where there are two "them" groups and one "us" group. After implying the superiority of one "them" group

Figure 11 Francis Bindon,
Jonathan Swift. (National
Portrait Gallery, London)

to the other (for instance, the Houyhnhnms over the Yahoos) and then that of the "us" group to both "them" groups, Swift proceeds to demolish the basis of the "us" group's superiority. If the "us" group consists of those discerning readers who see the flaws in Houyhnhnm self-conceptions as well as the more obvious limitations of the Yahoos, Swift then proceeds to subject "us" to a damaging universalist critique. Such a three-part scheme is also suggested by Francis Bindon's portrait of Swift, which shows an unsmiling dean pointing to the text of the fourth voyage even as we can see some horses, presumably Houyhnhnms, in the background (Fig. 11). Where do we look to comprehend the status of these creatures—to Swift, to the text, or to the horses they resemble? The unstable relationships among authorial intent, textual representations, and physical objects produce the satire.[51]

Although Rawson's tripartite scheme may be formally exact, it also suggests the drift from polemic to metapolemic in Cato's voice that takes us away from topical specificity. When they surface at the end of the fourth voyage, the particular topoi of anticolonial critique are damaged. Gulliver has lost credibility by the time he articulates his criticisms of European colonialism:

The Stoic's Voice

For Instance, A Crew of Pyrates are driven by a Storm they know not whither; at length a Boy discovers Land from the Top-Mast; they go on Shore to rob and plunder; they see an harmless People, are entertained with Kindness, they give the Country a new Name, they take formal Possession of it for the King, they set up a rotton Plank or a Stone for a Memorial, they murder two or three Dozen of the Natives, bring away a Couple more by Force for a Sample, return home, and get their Pardon. Here commences a new Dominion acquired with a Title by *Divine Right*. Ships are sent with the first Opportunity; the Natives driven out or destroyed, their Princes tortured to discover their Gold; a free Licence given to all Acts of Inhumanity and Lust; the Earth reeking with the Blood of its Inhabitants: And this execrable Crew of Butchers employed in so pious an Expedition, is a *modern Colony* sent to convert and civilize an idolatrous and barbarous People. (11:294)

The passage contrasts the contingent nature of colonial discovery, and its excessive criminal violence, with eventual appropriation in the name of the colonizing power. Swift, through Gulliver, unerringly focuses on the spurious nominalism of the exercise, where dominion begins "with a Title by *Divine Right*" even as the unnamed territory performatively becomes a "*modern colony*." The two italicized phrases in the passage connect a traditional and a modern mode of political authority, mimicking the logic of early modern "inventions of tradition." Previously kept apart from each other through the false opposition of virtue and commerce, the doctrine of "*Divine Right*" in fact provides the sophistical justification for the creation of a "*modern Colony*," in a process that cynically exposes the compatibility of traditional and modern statehood, indeed Renaissance and Enlightenment. This compatibility of neostoicist politics and commercial venture demonstrates at the same time the "piratical" origins of law. After the vituperative rhetoric, Gulliver goes on to exhibit blind nationalism, claiming that his criticism "doth by no means affect the *British* Nation, who may be an Example to the whole World for their Wisdom, Care, and Justice in planting Colonies" (11:294). Such a Swiftian undercutting demonstrates the *positionality* of all critique and the pointlessness of its universalism, having revealed a flaw in its articulation. Gulliver proceeds to qualify—somewhat incoherently—the general "truth" he states.[52]

We have already seen that piratical practices cannot be assimilated to some grand theory of anticolonial agency, even if piratical discourses partly resisted the new civic religion of mercantile venture. Alternatively, Gulliver's antipiratical rhetoric characterizes piracy as colonialism at its most rapacious—too convenient an accusation—as this merchant-identified ship's surgeon fails to indicate that very few colonies were "founded" by pirates. Of course, most colonists arrived by ship—whether conquistadors, pilgrims, or merchants—during the expansion of European maritime hegemony. The indeterminacy of piratical practices suggests that piracy cannot be definitively colonialist or anticolonial even if Gulliver equates piracy with colonialism itself. Not to be confused with the relativism of perspective—itself an important aspect of all four voyages—the subject position of anticolonial critique involves the purchase of a critique on its context, and its capacity for agency, irrespective of its other function of miming general truths indistinguishable from platitude. In this respect, Gulliver's anticolonialism is compromised by his nationalism and his scapegoating of piracy. Placing piracy at the origin of colonization universalizes both in a critique that is ultimately ineffective.[53]

Gulliver is a living example to his readers that freedom from colonialism requires something more than self-serving neostoicist detachment. Whose colonialism, and whose oppression? Gulliver's retirement from the world at the conclusion suggests a mental incapacity to cope with imperialist fact. His neostoicism is elaborated to acknowledge that seeing means going mad. Gulliver cannot successfully tropicalize his representation into a new form of action. He cannot desert to the woods, lead a rebellion, or shake off the ideological yoke of the Houyhnhnm hipparchy. Instead, he is condemned to reliving fetishistically, in the form of a repetition compulsion, the worst psychic distortions of a colonialist ideology. His withdrawal from the world is a parodic form of the classical Stoic's apatheia, or sublime indifference to the world's ability to injure him. However, resignation and withdrawal is a mistaken neostoicist interpretation of apatheia. Gulliver has not achieved the tranquillity of the Stoic sage nor his reputed capacity for public and political action. Instead, Gulliver privatizes himself and rages on at the undeserving nature of his compatriots. Lacking the Stoic's pietas, Gulliver is obviously no sapiens, even though he sets up for one. Swift's satire of neostoicism in the figure of the Houyhnhnms shows that the governing principle of the Stoic soul, the hegemonikon, which ought to assure the position of the impartial spectator, instead perpetrates colonialist hegemony.

Unsatisfied with the desire for equine beauty, Gulliver wants equine dung and odor around him as well. He transgresses the rules of abstract metaphor by insisting on materialist metamorphosis. The vehicle of the metaphor is just as important as the tenor; Gulliver would take literally Iago's taunt to Brabantio that reduces Othello to a horse, and actually want "coursers for cousins and gennets for germans." Though passions are unruly in the manner of horses, they are also indications of self-love. Gulliver's final narcissistic identification with horses, which might be called pathological hippophilia, is already suggested in a late-seventeenth-century poetical translation of the Stoic Epictetus.[54]

However, there is a model in the satire for right Stoic practice that opposes the neostoicist insanity visited on Gulliver by Houyhnhnm ideology. Swift, like Addison, considered Cato a moral paragon. Swift's writings make several complimentary references to this most principled of Julius Caesar's opponents, and biographical material confirms his lifelong reverence of this mythistorical hero. In an essay for *The Tatler* that he wrote in 1709, Swift gives Cato pride of place over Alexander, Augustus, Julius Caesar, Cicero, Hannibal, and Socrates. He consciously imitated, through his personal habits, what he understood as the Roman senator's frugality, fortitude, and simplicity; perhaps as a result, he was highly susceptible to flattering comparisons with his idol.[55] In *Gulliver's Travels,* while reliving a classical history pageant through the illusionist techniques of the magicians of Maldonada, Gulliver converses with Caesar's assassin, Brutus, who unselfconsciously assures Gulliver that "his Ancestor *Junius, Socrates, Epaminondas, Cato* the Younger, Sir *Thomas More* and himself, were perpetually together: A *Sextumvirate* to which all the Ages of the World cannot add a Seventh" (11:196). Uttered on an island by an *apparition,* this statement acquires a different status from the rest of the satire. Could the pure nature of this vision reveal a stark truth, even as the mixed nature of the rest signals fantastic realism? If the last two voyages are read in the order of their composition (Bk. 3 after Bk. 4), the satire moves from neostoicist universals to Stoic particulars. The conundrums of book 4 are best dealt with (as they cannot be resolved) as a metafiction concerning the contradictions of colonialist ideology and anticolonial critique, related to Stoicist and mercantilist understandings of them.

Swift's fiction models the Anglo-Irish acceptance of English values. However, not always going the way of the damaging universalism, it reveals the "middle" position sought out, if in a somewhat different way, by Addison. The settlers of English and Scottish origin in Ireland derived their flattering self-image from the continued debasement of the indigenous population. Yet their ire at the English arose from feelings of abandonment and resentment at being lumped with the native Irish. Gulliver personifies the intermediary class who ideologically surrenders to both facets of a binary opposition, as the result of an unreflective neostoicism. M. B., the Drapier, however, represents a simultaneous Swiftian alternative, that of successful Stoic resistance by the intermediary class through informed and self-conscious interest in the place of fantasized identification. Gulliver, it seems, stands for a static neostoicist who might be something like a parodic inversion of the sapiens, whereas M. B. is a modernized Stoic, a man of the world who successfully intervenes in public life, thus living up to his mythistorical Catonic counterpart. Gulliver models the abject victim who glorifies his own suffering through neostoicist platitudes, identifies with his oppressors, and detests his peers by projecting all his own failings onto them. If this is a mockery of neostoicist paranoia, the Houyhnhnms are at the other end of that neostoicist complex, masking their apartheid as benign rationalism. Alternatively, the Stoic M. B., who, we should not forget, is a shopkeeper, owes his provisional literary existence to a Swiftian interlude between the composition of the fourth and the third voyages. The Drapier presents readers with the suppressed intertextual reference—in the most interstitial sense—that provides the key to the interruption *and* the interpretation of *Gulliver's Travels* by way of *The Drapier's Letters*. Our reading can follow Swift's own compositional break, when Irish events made him temporarily put aside Gulliver for the direct political intervention by the Drapier.

Colonialism is not the simple unfolding of piratical violence, even if Gulliver's selective memory makes it look like that. Rather than a lightning raid by pirates aiming to colonize an island, the inversion of that image, a flying island that colonizes people, makes for a more persuasive metaphor of a *"modern colony."* This technique of ideological inversion links *Gulliver's Travels* with *Robinson Crusoe*. Although the parody of voyages of discovery and conquest is Swift's most explicit attack on the contingent beginnings of British imperialism and the complacencies of travel narrative, the oppression engendered by state structures is the more substantial counterpart of that process. The Flying Island in the third voyage fits the bill, especially when we consider the well-known suppressed paragraphs related to it. Laputa's relationship to the kingdom of Balnibarbi suggests the modern form of state surveillance and oppression, which, if not yet Benthamite in its conception, is nonetheless a suggestive prototype. Gulliver informs his readers that on the way to the capital city, his Majesty ordered that the Island "should stop over certain Towns and Villages, from whence he might receive the Petitions of his Subjects. And to this Purpose, several Packthreads were let down with small Weights at the Bottom. On these Packthreads the People strung their Petitions, which mounted up directly like the Scraps of Paper fastned by School-Boys at the End of the String that holds their Kite. Sometimes we received Wine and Victuals from below, which were drawn up by Pullies" (11:163). The state structure, kept alive by the food and drink from below, is also the recipient of unspecified petitions from its subjects. Yet the nonchalance implied by the transmitting mechanism renders the petitions into playful confetti. The state floats high as a kite, drunk on its own altitude, hovering unreachably above its supplicants. This passive neglect can very soon become violent reprisal "if any Town should engage in Rebellion or Mutiny, fall into violent Factions, or refuse to pay the usual Tribute" (11:171). The king's options range from impeding the rebellious inhabitants' access to the sun and the rain, to pelting them with stones, to "the last Remedy, letting the Island drop directly upon their Heads, which makes a universal Destruction both of Houses and Men" (11:171).

Gulliver also explains that this "last Remedy" has been rarely used, as cities could defend themselves with tall rocks that would break the adamantine bottom of the island. Five paragraphs that were suppressed from all contemporary editions and only reincluded in the text at the end of the nineteenth century expound the anecdote of Lindalino, a rebellious town that successfully held out against the threat of extermination by devising a defensive system that would have destroyed the island if it had come too near the city. This interpolation alludes transparently to the Irish defiance of the patent for Wood's halfpence, orchestrated from Dublin ("Lindalino"), an action greatly aided by Swift's composition of *The Drapier's Letters* in 1724–25.[56]

The next section focuses on that more explicit occasion responded to by *The Drapier's Letters*, one that allowed Swift to act out the role of Roman tribune. Swift plays the role of M. B. in the manner of Epictetus's doctrine that likened the Stoic sapiens to an actor. Epictetus recommended that the wise man was not the same as an actor, even though he ought to play—but not identify with—his self-conscious role. Gulliver, in contrast, is so completely identified with his didactic role that he violates the rules of classical Stoic practice. My reading of these two works shows that Swift implicitly separated debased neostoicism from right Stoic practice, allowing for differences to emerge between a neostoicist Gulliver and the Stoic Drapier, differences that result in a distinction between the success of one kind of anticolonial rhetoric and the failure of another.

DRAPIER, OR IRISH COINAGE

The Drapier's Letters attacks the patentee of the Irish halfpence as a Caesarian "mock-Monarch" whom M. B. would like to shoot, flay, hang, burn, and catapult out of existence. A Wolverhampton ironmaster, William Wood, had obtained a lucrative patent for coining £100,800 of brass halfpence, having paid a huge bribe of £10,000 to the Duchess of Kendal, George I's mistress. Fear of debasement was paramount. The patent had been opposed by both Houses of the Anglo-Irish Parliament and other influential petitioners, but it appeared that the project would go ahead regardless. The concern of *The Drapier's Letters* was a moderately bullionist one: that the citizen should always be able to translate, at an acceptable discount, the face value of coinage into bullion. Swift's alarmist rhetoric alleged that the bullion value of Wood's coinage would only be the Lilliputian ratio of one-tenth to one-twelfth of face value. The result would have been the eventual dispossession of all gold and silver and the pauperization of the fragile Irish economy.[57] Though brass coinage did not dissociate commodity from symbol as radically as paper money did, Irish anxieties increased at the prospect of debasement. Along with the needless floating of more than £100,000 of small change (estimates put the actual need closer to £25,000 worth) came the specter of counterfeiting, and unauthorized overproduction by Wood himself. Swift entered the fray, probably at the suggestion of Archbishop William King, at a seemingly hopeless moment in early 1724 when Irish representations to the English authorities drew a blank. Swift's pamphlets helped maintain public discontent at fever pitch.

There had been previous recoinage crises in both England and Ireland, and the debate between John Locke and William Lowndes in 1696 had been notable. English silver currency had been debased as a result of widespread "clipping" in the early 1690s, and monetarists had suggested replacing the existing coinage at face value with milled coin that would have had less silver in it, thus discouraging melting and "clipping." However, bullionists had always argued that real specie provided the much needed hedge against inflation and fraudulence, basing their assumptions on Gresham's law. Because "bad money drove out good money," bullionists thought that ensuring the purity of coin was best. Locke, an extreme bullionist, ferociously opposed a coin with less silver and had written in *Further Considerations concerning Raising the Value of Money* (1695) that the value of money was rooted in nature; his opponents had argued that exchange was decided by social convention and backed by monetarist discipline. Irish coinage had been abused previously by the debasement of specie under Elizabeth and James II. Unfortunately for the populace in 1696, Locke won the day, and approximately £4.7 million of currency was exchanged at bullion value, reducing its worth to £2.5 million. There was a run on the new coin as well, because of its higher bullion value. The poor had to pay a terrific price, while those who had substantial frozen assets, such as landowners, were only marginally affected.[58]

Swift's pen takes up the question of coinage and subjects it to a variety of metaphorical applications and symbolic reversals. Wood's halfpence presents Swift with an occasion to gesture skillfully toward larger and more systematic injustices in the colonial relationship between England and Ireland. The readers are warned that the introduction of Wood's coin was prelude to the destruction of Ireland, that the debased halfpence was a detestable symbol of English exploitation, and that the threatened devaluation instigated a crisis of colonial legitimacy. Suggesting that the coinage itself would be the instrument of torture, Swift conducts an incendiary analysis of Walpole's rumored threat to *"cram his Brass down our Throats,"* lambasting the Great Man who *"hath sworn to make us swallow his Coin in Fireballs*" (10:67). Making ludicrous arithmetical calculations, the Drapier divides the weight of the total coinage by the population to ascertain the number of swallowable shares of molten brass that needed to be administered to each Irish citizen. The response to the threatened debasement of the currency takes the form of a wild rhetorical inflation of possible consequences: coinage, the means of economic exchange, is to be forced down unwilling throats in the form of molten lead. Torture by force-feeding can exterminate the populace. It is through such images that Swift effectively casts, molds, and pours molten rhetoric back into Walpole's ears.[59]

Swift had already faced the threat of prosecution for his pamphlet recommending the boycott of English goods in 1720, entitled *A Proposal for the Universal Use of Irish Manufacture . . . Utterly Rejecting and Renouncing Every Thing wearable that comes from England.* Irish commerce had suffered extensively from blatantly restrictive monopolies that favored the English woolen trade to the detriment of the Irish. Favored by tax laws that discouraged agriculture for pasturage, absentee English landlords had plunged Ireland into renewed depths of dependency on English produce. Swift decried the attitude of English administrators who "from their *high* Elevation . . . look *down* upon this Kingdom, as if it had been one of their *Colonies* of *Out-casts* in *America*" (9:21). The pamphlet suggests that the Anglo-Irish Parliament should opt for economic nationalism. A resolution should ban foreign goods and force consumers to use only locally manufactured textiles, for "*Ireland* would never be happy 'till a Law were made for *burning* every Thing that came from *England,* except their *People* and their *Coals*" (9:17). Swift felt that an imitative fashion for English goods exacerbated the suppression of the Irish economy.

Using a farmer's voice, as Crèvecoeur would later in the American context, preserves the natural-law connection of land with liberty and the myth of an unbroken lineage from classicism to neoclassicism through feudal aristocratic values. The shopkeeper's voice in *The Drapier's Letters,* however, is grafted onto a neoclassical political tradition that highlighted farmer republicans such as Cincinnatus, and Cato the Censor. To make tradesmen into political spokesmen is to follow the more recent innovation by Defoe and Mandeville. Dependent on a money economy, a tradesman cannot survive on his own produce. Whereas earlier political discourse addressed a landed elite, Swift's is

The Stoic's Voice

an issue-specific adaptation. According to Carol Fabricant, Swift could sympathetically identify with humble craftsmen such as "Thatcher, Ditcher, Gard'ner [and] Baily" during his travels in the Irish country-side.[60] In contrast to the direct political pamphleteering of *The Drapier's Letters* and the first volumes of *Cato's Letters*, Addison's consensus-seeking *Cato* seems tame. Addison is working from a different Renaissance tradition, probably that of Erasmus, who in the *Apothegmata* teaches the reader to crystallize history into character by constructing "a brief, episodic chronicle of the heroic life."[61] Rather than rely on the limited effectivity of static hero worship, Swift satirizes and legislates through the Drapier's active persona. Satire about venality in high places was not new, and Swift's homespun metaphors and biblical allusions successfully fabricated the voice of the market and the street.[62] By speaking in pithy populist aphorisms, Swift forged a new anticolonial vocabulary—albeit in a limited Anglo-Irish context—out of the debased coinage of Roman republicanist rhetoric and venality satire. Producing something like a prototype of boycott—a word coined later in Irish history—Swift translated Stoicism into local politics.

A boycott of English coin encourages local autonomy while laying bare the colonial relationship.[63] Refusing goods and services in the modern Irish context involved a "violence inflicted upon the self" as an alternative mode of protest to the classic form of rebellion that involves "violence inflicted upon others."[64] Several passive strategies can be employed to highlight the asymmetrical power relationship between rulers and ruled. Boycotts could also be one of several forms of peasant resistance, including work slowdowns, cheating, and pretended ignorance.[65] As a political "action," a boycott is especially successful when coupled with an efficient information system and a leadership that can coordinate strategies of response. Effective when there are large numbers of relatively anonymous transactions that take place daily, boycotts accord consumers the agency to refuse the purchasing of goods and services. Refusing the proposed medium of exchange in a tactical manner, a boycott administers short-term pain to the participating individuals in the hope of achieving long-term gain for the social whole. Though the Stoic analogy is not made explicit, the parallel is clear.

For instance, an engraving printed in Dublin in 1724 called *Wood's Halfpence* demonstrates the penury to which the Irish would be driven if the scheme were to succeed (Fig. 12). The cart laden with sacks of

Figure 12 *Wood's Halfpence* (1724). (British Museum, London)

coins is being drawn by a group of devils, and Poverty is weeping, attached to the cart, a small child in tow. Hibernia weeps, sitting on the side of a hill, even as she is petitioned by opponents to the coinage, as well as other supplicants and place-seekers. A crowd is walking to the sea with chests full of money, indicating that the dross would, by Gresham's law, be the bad money that would drive out the good overseas toward England. Money is also being offered to a wealthy-looking couple in one corner of the print, possibly an absentee English landlord and his wife. The appended verses attack the projectors who are supporting the scheme in the hope of making a profit, even though it also praises George I as the country's savior, probably to avoid its otherwise seditious appearance. Nonetheless, the verses culminate with a description of the ship at anchor in the bay as the vessel "that first brought o'er the Brazen Cargo," but "the bold Irish resolutely now, / Resolve th'Infernal Scheme to overthrow, / Bear back the Dross, return it to the Sea, / And from the heavy Curse their Country free."

The Stoic's Voice

Wood's Halfpence is one more illustration of commodity culture in an increasingly literate age. The printed pamphlet, a prime instrument for the dissemination of political tactics to divergent groups with a common interest, delivers its message through discourse in the market and the street, as well as other venues. Various forms of oral culture multiply the effects of the pamphlet from the pulpit to the privy. Sermons, rumors, gossip, and even folktales and jokes are among the ephemeral activities that get the word out.[66] Therefore, the printed pamphlet is but one crucial motor of an extensive process of social and political rhetoric. By studying these processes that were unleashed by Swift (or, conversely, studying Swift as an illustration of this larger process), we can see how resisting Wood's English coinage led to a critical (although not revolutionary) revaluation of the colonial relationship.

M. B. ventriloquizes his milieu, that of "the Liberties" of Dublin within the Anglo-Irish Pale, into a single oppositional voice. The letters proceed serially from immediate to larger constituencies, culminating in the hyperbolic address to "the whole People of Ireland" in letter 4. The Drapier, however, starts by addressing the middling and bottom tiers of the Pale in the first letter, "To the Shop-Keepers, Tradesmen, Farmers, and Country-People in General of the Kingdom of Ireland." Thus he distinguishes among various groups even as he argues for their converging interests on the single issue of the patent concerning Wood's halfpence. Beginning with this awareness of several constituencies, the Drapier attempts a synthesis toward a collective Anglo-Irish will. This appeal to a common interest, an "imagined community," takes the form of exchanging particular interests for a general one: "I do most earnestly exhort you as *Men,* as *Christians,* as *Parents,* and as *Lovers of your Country*" (10:3).

Swift appeals to the bullionist idea of a pure and untarnished currency, which he associates with an egalitarian and uncorrupt commerce. The problem of sedition is finessed cleverly, as subjects can reject brass based on a legal loophole. The statutory specification concerning coinage stated that the royal prerogative existed for coinage in gold and silver; the Irish establishment could hide behind this hedge, as brass coinage was, strictly speaking, not legal tender, but could be accepted for convenience. Thus, Swift finds legalistic cover for an action that was clearly defying the government. Operating within the law, Swift challenges the legitimacy of its performative function and renders its aims egregious. The Crown cannot force its subjects to take just any money, "For then by the same Reason we might be bound to take *Pebble-Stones,* or *Cockle-shells,* or *stamped Leather* for *Current Coin;* if ever we should happen to live under an ill *Prince;* who might likewise by the same Power make a *Guinea* pass for Ten Pounds, a *Shilling* for Twenty Shillings, and so on; by which he would in a short Time get all the *Silver* and *Gold* into his own Hands, and leave us nothing but *Brass* or *Leather,* or what he pleased" (8). Swift shows that he is well aware of the monetarist argument that social convention determined the medium of exchange, especially as some of his alternative examples—cockleshells, stamped leather—had been known to function as money. However, gold and silver are ascribed a special value and power. Political confusion arose from recognizing that an oversupply of brass coinage could flush out existing bullion, inflate prices, and debase coin. The brass money patent becomes a license for the grand larceny of Ireland with the approval of the British monarch and his government. Such fraudulence had to be detected and resisted by public boycott of this fool's gold. As the Drapier puts it in the second letter that attacks the dangerous compromise proposed by Wood, "if a Physician prescribe to a Patient a *Dram* of Physick, shall a Rascal Apothecary cram him with a *Pound,* and mix it up with *Poyson?*" (10:16). The Irish are put into the position of the ignorant but disempowered Esau selling his birthright for a mess of pottage, whereas the mock-heroic Drapier describes himself as a David who can single-handedly defeat the brass-covered Goliath. Reversing the trope of highway robbery, the Drapier threatens to "shoot Mr. *Wood* and his Deputies through the Head, like *High-Way Men* or *House-Breakers,* if they dare to force one Farthing of their Coin on me in the Payment of an Hundred Pounds" (10:20).

During the course of this unrelenting attack, Wood becomes a satirical butt for the English king. In a transparent hit at George I, Wood is called "this little Arbitrary *Mock-Monarch,*" whose "Proposals conclude with perfect *High-Treason*" (10:19). The Irish establishment may think that "it is no Loss of Honour to submit to the *Lion,*" but the Drapier shames them with the question, "who, with the Figure of a *Man,* can think with Patience of being devoured alive by a *Rat?*" (10:20). Wood is a personification of "this Publick Enemy of ours" even as the Drapier styles himself as a fairy-tale tailor turned hero, who snatches his country from the jaws of devouring fate (10:15).

The Stoic's Voice

The event was a synecdoche for exploitation by Britain. Ireland's political and economic circumstances had been severely damaged in the period roughly equivalent to Swift's lifetime. Beginning with the Navigation Act of 1663, the Irish shipping, livestock, and woolen trades had been systematically destroyed by English legislation. These humiliating conditions worsened after the insurrection against the Glorious Revolution that William defeated at the Battle of the Boyne. Swift's analysis of the Irish economy, *A Short View of the State of Ireland* (1728), would conclude that Ireland had been made deficient by her colonial masters in twelve out of the fourteen natural conditions that could make a nation prosperous. The Declaratory Act of 1720 had stated that Ireland was "a Dependent Kingdom" and this would not be repealed until 1782. Swift's hatred of this law followed in the libertarian tradition of William Molyneux, who wrote the *ur*-text of Anglo-Irish nationalism, *The Case of Ireland's Being Bound by Acts of Parliament in England* (1698). Old Whigs like Molyneux and Swift aimed to defy the legislative formalization of such inequality, which had begun with Poyning's Law in the reign of Henry VII, decreeing that Irish legislative business could be enacted in England. The Drapier declares Irish autonomy self-evident in a manner that inevitably courted charges of sedition, questioning the characterization of Ireland as a "*depending Kingdom.*" Claiming allegiance only to his sovereign but not to England, the Drapier is "ready at the first Command from his Majesty to take Arms against [the English]" (10:61–62). Again, the satire makes the Drapier ironically more loyal than the king, when in fact the pamphlets communicate dangerously seditious thoughts. Expressing pro forma pledges of allegiance to the king creates space for disavowals, allusions, and innuendo concerning the incompetence, venality, and repugnance of George I.

The Drapier's aspersions work according to a screen of metonymic substitutions. It is as if Swift learned a lesson from the South Sea Bubble and converted a financial pyramid scheme into a rhetorical one. The initial enemy, William Wood, is derided as "*a mean ordinary Man, a Hard-Ware Dealer*" and, in a paragraph Swift wrote for the *Dublin News Letter*, as an "*Obscure, Inconsiderable, Insignificant, Ill-Designing Mechanick*" (10:4, 10:154). A humorous dustup, involving interprofessional rivalry between a tailor and a tinker, turns into a burlesque of the king himself. The unflattering portrait of George I consequently becomes a screen for the venal manipulations of Walpole, whose threatened punishments are ridiculed as unenforceable. If Walpole as the most powerful man in England cannot enforce his will, can the English nation? The screen method works according to the method of satirical inoculation. Garish villains are first painted as omnipotent; after the initial scare, the same figures are debunked as paper tigers, only to reveal real tigers behind them that are progressively belittled like the previous ones. This satirical pyramid scheme of Swift's, starting from a small target, manages to interrogate—if not dethrone—the most powerful of political assumptions. The slide toward general insurrection in the rhetoric enables Swift to construct a virtualization. Though economic boycotts have often been the raw material of anticolonial actions, and military action its culmination into armed rebellion, a numismatic boycott is a Stoic innovation that rejects coin as *corruption itself*. Readily conflating colonialism and corruption, anticolonial discourse and Stoic virtue are rendered formally equivalent. However, the context and the temporality of this action is so locally determined that this interventionist gesture works efficaciously. By suggesting the impossible at that point—the absolute separation of Irish virtue and British colonial and commercial exploitation—Swift enables the overturning of the patent through political pressure. Stoic virtualization here is not anticolonial generalization across contexts, just as Gulliver's neostoicist universals have little local purchase.

In the fifth letter, addressed to the Old Whig Viscount Molesworth, the Drapier reveals his allegorical method, one that makes the shopkeeper's commerce in various textiles stand in for specific textual interventions by Swift (10:82-83).[67] Revealing this traffic between virtue and commerce, or politics and economics, the Drapier lays bare the idealizations behind both categories. The letter ends with the following incongruous image: "Since your last Residence in *Ireland*, I frequently have taken my Nag to ride about your Grounds; where I fancied my self to feel an Air of *Freedom* breathing round me . . . but I have lately sold my Nag, and honestly told his greatest Fault, which was that of snuffing up the Air about *Brackdenstown;* whereby he became such a Lover of *Liberty*, that I could scarce hold him in. I have likewise buried, at the Bottom of a strong Chest, your Lordship's Writings, under a Heap of others that treat of *Liberty;* and spread over a *Layer* or two of *Hobbs, Filmer, Bodin,* and many more Authors of that Stamp, to be readiest at Hand, whenever I shall be disposed to take up a *new Set* of Principles in Government" (10:93-94). The reappearance of an equine metaphor should alert us to the Drapier as re-enacting a later phase of Gulliver's fixation. The Drapier rides what is now his nag—something the horse-worshipping Gulliver would not have dared—but eventually releases the utopian liberty that it represents. The Drapier claims to have gone underground, hiding his Whiggish principles under a layer of absolutist political theory: Hobbes, Filmer, Bodin. In typical Swiftian manner, this works as double irony: decrying political hypocrisy even while backhandedly reaffirming its inevitability. The Drapier hopes for retirement on Molesworth's estate, if he can "feed on plain homely Fare, and live and die a FREE honest *English* Farmer: But not without Regret, for leaving my Countrymen under the Dread of the brazen Talons of Mr. *Wood*" (94). In what can only be a deliberate self-deception, the Drapier succumbs to petty Anglo-Irish fantasies of retiring to landed liberty in England. The anticolonial interlude of Wood's coinage being over, the Drapier reaffirms an ironic return to the beginning that underscores the binary circumstance of Irish slavery under Wood's talons and English liberty under Molesworth's benevolent patronage. In his guise as shopkeeper, the Drapier aspires incongruously to landed identity, finally caught in the throes of the ideology of neoclassical rural retreat. Speaking from the Pale, and only by implication for and to the dispossessed Irish, the Drapier remains a shopkeeper of the Dublin Liberties. His desire to retire parallels the role that the equivalent hankering had in Swift's life.[68]

Despite Swift's brilliance in this episode, his resistance is carefully circumscribed by ironic self-exposure in the Drapier's address. Before we make too much of Swift's success in fighting off the imposition of Wood's halfpence, it should also be remembered that Walpole paid Wood an enormous compensation of £24,000, secretly charged to the Irish establishment under the fictitious name of Thomas Uvedale. Pope praises his friend in *The Dunciad* as unbinding his "griev'd Country's copper chains" but as still unable to prevent the hatching of "a new Saturnian age of Lead." The brilliance of Swift's literary performance should not blind us into sentimental celebrations of his transcendental position as "Irish Patriot," as earlier critics such as Middleton Murry (sometimes even Irish nationalists such as Yeats) were wont to do.[69] The Drapier is, like Defoe's characters, a lower-middle-class construct. The character suggests hard-headed moral rationalism even as he eschews sympathetic identification. The Catholic population cannot represent themselves; and therefore, they must be represented. Swift's feelings toward the Irish Catholic majority underwent some change as his English ties vanished into the oblivion of disappointed expectations. Although some evidence suggests they were similar to Gulliver's feelings toward the Yahoos—racial loathing, blaming the victim, and despair at their unregenerateness—Swift's sympathy for indigenes also takes the form of a negative appraisal out of alienation and horror, as it does in the most famous satirical pamphlet, *A Modest Proposal* (1729). Not masking his contempt for the natives, as "Hewers of Wood and Drawers of Water," Swift uses their debasement as evidence for the depredations of colonialism rather than an intrinsic inhumanity (2:120).[70]

The Drapier does not mystify his implication within the colonial system, but makes the tactical move of siding with the colonized even as he realizes that his own position is that of intermediary. As a shopkeeper, he expresses an unusual level of altruism in order to sound the most effective of anticolonial warnings: caveat emptor. Hybridizing the idealism of the Stoics with the mercantilist realism of the British Yahoos, the Drapier avoids the colonialist implications of identification with either position in the binary. In doing so, he is nonetheless clearing the way— or appears to be doing so from a virtualized perspective—for a different kind of colonial subject, such as Olaudah Equiano or Toussaint Louverture, one who speaks the master's voice with a self-emancipatory purpose and combines the drawbacks of (self)-commodification with the subjective idealism of political agency.

By century's end, Irish radical Arthur O'Connor deplores the misery of his compatriots in *The State of Ireland* (1798). British domination is excoriated as that of "Nations which dignify Usurpation and Robbery with the title of Empire." The French Revolution had transformed earlier Jacobite remedies for the Irish problem into Jacobin ones. O'Connor offers the capitalized credo of "CATHOLIC EMANCIPATION" and "POPULAR REPRESENTATION" as the only viable solution.[71] In his most famous republican tirade, castigating Edmund Burke, O'Connor defends the French Revolution against the British reaction and excoriates the conservative reliance on monarchy, aristocracy, and concentrations of landed property that made British representative democracy so feeble. O'Connor bemoans the defeat of the French fleet even as he predicts that the huge national debt incurred by Britain in fighting the French Revolution will eventually result in the very revolution that the establishment feared. Entitled *The Measures of Ministry to Prevent a Revolution are the Most Certain Means of Bringing it On,* O'Connor's pseudonymous pamphlet of 1794 is signed, "A Stoic." The figure of the Stoic, having gone through Addison's bland idealism, Gordon and Trenchard's volatile impersonation, Swift's negative criticism through Gulliver and positive application through the Drapier, as well as the appropriation of the American Revolutionaries, resurfaces here in O'Connor's Jacobin pamphlet recommending democratic reform—with little effect, by no fault of his. Britain's hold in Ireland, brazen as well as ironclad, would not be pried loose until the twentieth century.

Levantinizations

CHAPTER FOUR

Lady Mary in the Hammam

Forth rush the Levant and the Ponent Windes.

—JOHN MILTON, *Paradise Lost* (10.704)

B ased on a journey to the Ottoman Empire undertaken during the years 1716–18, Lady Mary Wortley Montagu's travel letters were first published in 1763. The author had died the previous year. Montagu's stay at Constantinople with her husband, Edward Wortley, who had been appointed ambassador to the Sublime Porte, provides the central focus of the letters. But as her reflections range widely across the culture and geography of the eastern Mediterranean, a more inclusive title seems appropriate. Among various titles given to this collection by editors over the ages, J. A. St. John's choice in 1838, *Letters from the Levant, During the Embassy to Constantinople, 1716–18*, is more suggestive than *The Turkish Embassy Letters*.[1]

Levant broadly signifies the Orient (more precisely the eastern Mediterranean) and its exotic appeal for Europeans as the land of the rising sun. On the other hand, *levantinization* is the term Islamophobes have sometimes used for the contamination of European values by supposedly degenerate Levantines. However, as I define it, levantinization is both an investigative tool and a utopian projection of Montagu's that anticipates a positive outcome; in chapter 5, on despotism and the sublime, its more familiar negative aspect is revealed along with a utopian underside. This fashioning of a new term, levantinization, is a strategic wager in its own right. Reading against the grain of the monolithic interpretation of orientalism, critical revisions of the discourse can be explored within its boundaries even as their limits are defined. Lisa Lowe's pluralization of orientalism into *orientalisms* and Billie Melman's specification of *women's* orients have already familiarized us to the importance of making national and gendered differentiations when analyzing the orientalist network of power/knowledge.[2] With tropicopolitans in mind, I describe levantinization as a strategic deformation of orientalism's representational mechanisms. Leading from general discourses into specific practices, levantinizations enable subjects to fashion their agency from unpromising materials. With a gamut of linguistic and psychic consequences that accompany such self-fashionings—whether repression, sublimation, or projection—levantinizations indicate that agency can be found in a number of guises and forms, sometimes even within orientalism itself. For instance, *Letters from the Levant* inaugurates a phantasmatic identification with Turkish aristocratic womanhood. A specific *fantasy,* according to Laplanche and Pontalis, is not so much the activity of an already existing subject as the performative dispersion of the subject into several identificatory positions. For our purposes, the subject inhabits the position of both desiring subject and object, thereby reconfiguring itself into the agency granted to Turkish aristocratic women. While Montagu's levantinization occurs from a privileged context, it demonstrates the ambivalence and the malleability of orientalist tropologies while challenging orientalism's quest for national-cultural essences. Where orientalism's goals were culture-bound by producing a logic of self and other, Montagu's levantinization is class-bound but cross-cultural.[3]

Additionally, a title such as *Letters from the Levant* enables a reading of intellectual wagers made through the subject's dispersal. Montagu places and then hedges her cultural bets in a manner reminiscent of eighteenth-century gamesters who "ran a levant" or "threw a levant"—that is, made a bet with the intention of absconding if it was lost. In similar fashion, the aristocratic Montagu uses her ample intellectual "credit" for a utopian levantinization. Cross-cultural apprehension is the objective of Montagu's speculative intellectual wagers in her Levantine writings. Featuring intellectual wagering without accountability, levantinization makes visible the dynamic interaction between orientalist and anti-orientalist figuration.[4]

Montagu's embellished letters, written on several occasions to individuals such as Lady Mar, Alexander Pope, the Abbé Conti, and others, synthesize the writer's interests with the appeal of commentary. The empiricist epistemology of the traveler interacts with the revisionary and relativist "feminism" of the woman scholar; the neoclassical antiquarianism of the humanist intersects with remarks on early eighteenth-century fashion from a society lady. One of the primary experiences of the Levant for Montagu came through sustained interactions with the aristocratic women of the Ottoman Empire within their sexually segregated milieu. These women's pleasing alterity and seemingly unfettered agency are inferred as deriving from their spatial autonomy. Montagu interprets the aristocratic women she meets as already free rather than waiting for emancipation like their European counterparts. Therefore, her epistemological veracity is complicated by risky rhetorical wagering and generic hybridization. As Cynthia Lowenthal points out, Montagu drew her epistolary models of female experience from the performance-oriented context of the theater rather than from the bourgeois domesticity newly legitimated by the novel.[5]

This chapter concentrates on three interlocking stages that structure the interaction between the epistemological and the rhetorical modes in *Letters from the Levant*. In the first and most easily identifiable step, Montagu visualizes a secular anthropologizing stance toward cultures, similar to many other post-Renaissance appreciations of the arbitrary norms that undergird cultural identity. Such a perception replaces the existing bias—of a simple ethnocentrism in favor of the observer's culture—with an eclectic relativism. This phenomenon corresponds to the observer's experience of cultural separation or alienation. Montagu's heuristic levantinizations occasionally unsettle the norms of travel narrative, as her perceptions often problematize the positional fixities of the supererogatory ethnographer and the grounded native. The second stage concerns the observer's idealization of putatively desirable characteristics from the observed cultural phenomena. The move from idealization to actualization threatens to transform the observer irreversibly, giving rise to the experience of liminality. The eclectic relativism of the first stage is abandoned for that of (a fantasy of) assimilation to the other, a process of "going native" or "passing"—different names for the transformation of identity when an individual from one culture is absorbed into another. The phantasmatic and partial nature of identification should itself suggest that *levantinization* is a function of related psychological intensities rather than any single qualitative factor that can determine identificatory effectivity.[6]

This stage of liminal identification, developed from an interrogative first phase, proves transitory for Montagu, as a full-fledged passing does not take place and especially not in the famous bathhouse scene that I discuss in the second section. The honorary subjectivity in the guest culture is temporally circumscribed, and there are implicit anxieties and criticisms that do not disappear as a result of this partial identification. Consequently, the observer undergoes a third phase that can be described as a postliminal mode of reaggregation, a romance manqué that synthesizes a banal return home rather than a romance metamorphosis. Antiquarian classicism comes to Montagu's rescue as a compromise, shifting the focus from current identities to past ones and displacing politics back into history.

Montagu's ambivalence about the masquerade of feminine identification is strikingly reminiscent of Joan Rivière's assertion that "womanliness . . . could be assumed and worn as a mask, both to hide the possession of masculinity and to avert the reprisals expected if she [the analysand] was found to possess it." Montagu's self-positioning as a female author competing with male predecessors resembles Rivière's concept of womanliness as masquerade. Derived from a bisexuality complex, this Kleinian formulation has been generalized in a free-floating fashion by post-Lacanian psychoanalytical feminists, who partly overlook the involvement of atavistic racist fantasies with more modern professionalist contexts in the psychic structure of Rivière's original analysand. Rivière characterizes her analysand's masquerade as "the 'double-action' of an obsessive act" involving aggression and deference to two kinds of threats: academic father figures in the real world and phantasmatic "negro" attackers in an imagined one. Montagu's racial typing of the North African women she meets, juxtaposed with the quasiprofessionalized rivalries with travel writers that inflect her views on Turkish women that I discuss, similarly bring out the "double action" of her authorial masquerade. Rivière compares the disingenuousness of the masquerading woman to "a thief who will turn out his pockets and ask to be searched to prove that he has not the stolen goods." Montagu polices herself scrupulously in the *hammam* (Turkish bathhouse), even as she titillates her readers, suggesting a like disavowal. In what follows, I concentrate on Montagu's cultural relativism, her levantinization of Ottoman aristocratic womanhood, and her classicist recuperation, which I interpret as symbolic inoculation.[7]

Montagu's remarks amalgamate long-standing traditions in Western travel narrative. Her travel letters are affiliated to earlier generic precursors that initiated the imaginative geography of orientalism and defined the religious and political challenge represented by Islam. Hybridizing the prose genres of ethnography, aesthetic criticism, and personal memoir, Montagu reflects on various cultural topics and geographical locations. *Letters from the Levant* can be appreciated as an abbreviated sample of English and French ruminations concerning proximate regions such as the Balkans, Asia Minor, and North Africa.[8]

As Montagu builds up to her arrival in Turkey following a stately progress across the Continent, her eclectic perceptions evolve into a pattern as her itinerary unfolds. Montagu commences *Letters from the Levant* with the familiar moral didacticism of some travel narratives, remarking on the cleanliness and industriousness of Dutch maids and the general affluence and civic orderliness of Rotterdam, the Hague, and Nimeguen (248-52). Such salutary lessons for the English are tempered by the skepticism with which she treats the Catholic relics she sees in Cologne and Vienna, where nuns believe that a wooden head of Christ speaks and claim that a crucifix spoke to the emperor (276, 279). Catholicism encourages "the grosse superstition of the common people," and its reliance on ritual pageantry makes it "as offensive and apparently contradictory to all common sense as the Pagods of China" (277). In keeping with her Whiggish sympathies, she extols the advantages of republican principalities in Germany over those run by absolutist monarchs (254-55). Montagu remarks upon cultural differences, as all travelers do; at the same time, she contests the normative masculine vision of her predecessors, noticing different phenomena and correcting previous misrepresentations from a woman's perspective. Thus, Montagu reshapes travel narrative as a vehicle that simultaneously signals "romance," "science," and "satire"; aspects of "Behn," "Defoe," and "Swift" adhere to the epistemological positions she takes. Her account presents us with a dialogical relationship between the categories of "romance idealism," "naive empiricism," and "extreme skepticism" suggested by Michael McKeon as formative of novelistic discourse.[9]

A self-conscious and skeptical practitioner of travelogue, Montagu deplores the biased and inconsistent expectations of her readership: "We

Travellers are in very hard circumstances. If we say nothing but what has been said before us, we are dull and we have observ'd nothing. If we tell any thing new, we are laugh'd at as fabulous and Romantic, not allowing for the difference of ranks, which afford difference of company, more Curiosity, or the changes of customs that happen every 20 year in every Country. But people judge of Travellers exactly with the same Candour, good Nature, and impartiallity, they judge of their Neighbours upon all Occasions" (385). Travel writing is obliged to produce novelty but also expected to fulfill preexisting stereotypes. Just as people interpret anything done by their neighbors with cynical and stubborn prejudices, travel writing is often compelled to produce the *same* difference. Complaining in this way to her sister Lady Mar, Montagu is exasperated at the calcified expectations of readers who refuse to acknowledge historical change elsewhere and delude themselves that knee-jerk reactions are signs of sensitivity.

Such a critical edge is typical of Montagu's discourse. The empiricist impetus behind her worldview is accompanied by a strong skeptical commitment to demystification. Furthermore, she carefully circumscribes her empiricism within subjectivist and gendered limits, foregrounding those limitations as a badge of honor that enhances her credibility. The willing adoption of a female voice emphasizes her empirical reliability against a masculine norm; her analysis rises "out of a true female spirit of Contradiction, to tell you the falsehood of a great part of what you find in authors" (405). Montagu lays claim to superior skills of anthropological decipherment.

In this confident vein, Montagu casually reveals an excellent grasp of extant travel writing in French and English on Turkey. She could, if she wanted, "with little trouble, turn over Knolles and Sir Paul Rycaut to give you a list of Turkish Emperours" (405).[10] However, she prefers demystifying others' errors. Montagu sneers at descriptions of Turkey that come from ignorant merchants and travelers who "pick up some confus'd informations which are generally false, and they can give no better an Account of the ways here than a French refugee lodging in a Garret in Greek street, could write of the Court of England" (316). She is sarcastic about the unmerited success of Aaron Hill's book on Turkey, whose contents were "reveal'd to him in Vision during his wonderfull stay in the Egyptian Catacombs" (406).[11] In the same vein, Montagu later uses her high-placed informant, Hafise Kadinefendi, to refute the fabulous assertion perpetuated by travelers that the sultan selected an odalisque for the night by throwing a handkerchief at her (383). Similarly, Montagu deplores the ignorance of Jean Dumont, a state-sponsored Frenchman who mistakenly described the Greeks as chattel slaves rather than as political subjects of Ottoman rule (368).[12] The incompetence of previous writers on Turkey—all of them male—is a result of their retailing of uncorroborated information from unreliable informants. Montagu's criticisms are intended to demonstrate her superior erudition, contemporaneity, and novelty. A healthy tone of one-upwomanship permeates her firsthand account.[13]

Montagu's early erudition—translating the Stoic philosophy of Epictetus's *Enchiridion* from the Latin version for Bishop Burnet of Salisbury and, at Wortley's request, writing a trenchant critique of Joseph Addison's *Cato* before its completion—already gave her a significant profile as an unpublished female wit. Montagu speaks later of the Stoical qualities of women that reveal that "Greatness of Mind may be shewn in Submission as in Command." Some of her sex "have suffered a Life of Hardships with as much Philosophy as *Cato* traversed the Desarts of *Africa,* and without that Support the View of Glory offered him."[14] As Lisa Lowe suggests, Montagu's self-conscious protofeminism ought to be contextualized by the aristocratic signature that underwrote her intellectual credentials. In an autograph preface to *Letters from the Levant,* Mary Astell writes, "Let the *Male-Authors* with an envious eye / Praise coldly, that they may the more decry."[15] Montagu was a prominent member of a social class familiar with authorship, but even more so with patronage. By avoiding publication of the letters until her death, Montagu escaped some of the notoriety suffered by many female authors in her time.[16] In *The Nonsense of Common Sense,* she commences her defense of women with the recognition, "I expect to be told, this is downright *Quixotism,* and that I am venturing to engage the strongest part of Mankind with a Paper Helmet upon my Head."[17] Writing this two decades before the publication of Charlotte Lennox's novel, Montagu is herself a candidate for the eighteenth-century figure of the female Quixote, whose rebellious unpredictability alarms those who wish to uphold gender norms, and yet amuses them by acting out the incongruity brought by gender subversion of their bodies and identities.

Women are underprivileged in a variety of cultures but often in very different ways; *Letters from the Levant* demonstrates the specialized codes by which women achieve agency in the face of subjection. Montagu's comments on the topics of dress, masking, carnival, and private language (such as the language of flowers) explore several cross-cultural constructions of femininity. While womanhood is always the topic, the peregrinations of the ambassadorial retinue en route to Constantinople allow for a subtle methodological confrontation between objective realism and subjective impressionism. This central problem, frequently aired in the quasi-anthropological mode of travel writing, develops incrementally as Montagu proceeds to the moment of greatest levantinization in the hammam.[18]

Montagu's arrival at Vienna leads to the first of several complex responses on female attire. Though she is impressed with the magnificence of the imperial court, and critical of the drama, she is scandalized by the ridiculous attire and the ugliness of the aristocratic women. Moreover, these women's aesthetic infelicities are compounded by their libertinism. Allegedly, aristocratic Viennese women manage to retain both a husband and a publicly acknowledged lover amidst the persistence of archaic ideas of honor and genealogy (273–74). Proceeding to Hanover, Montagu finds its German beauties "ressemble one another as much as Mrs. Salmon's court of Great Brittain, and are in as much danger of melting away by too near approaching the Fire" (288). This criticism of the artifice of Hanover's painted beauties evokes London waxworks mentioned in *The Spectator*.[19] Artifice impels Montagu's comment on the arbitrary norms of female beauty as she moves from Vienna to Prague: "I have allready been visited by some of the most considerable Ladys whose Relations I knew at Vienna. They are dress'd after the Fashions there, as people at Exeter imitate those of London. That is, their Imitation is more excessive than the Original, and 'tis not easy to describe what extrodinary figures they make. The person is so much lost between Head dress and Petticoat, they have as much occassion to write upon their backs, This is a Woman, for the information of Travellers, as ever sign post painter had to write, This is a bear" (280–81). Conventions of female beauty undergo bizarre transmogrification when imitated at a distance. Translating across cultural codes and mapping Prague onto Exeter and Vienna onto London, Lady Mary also alludes to a celebrated anecdote from *The Tatler* and to yet another by Addison in *The Spectator* about the "daily Absurdities" resulting from the unstandardized arbitrariness of London shop signs.[20] Even sympathetic imitation, when conducted from a distance, collapses into irresponsible and incongruous mimicry.[21] However, though Montagu's remark appears to chide these women, she never clarifies what alternative they might have. In her rush to condemnation, the narrator has herself resorted to caricature, thus momentarily transgressing the realist code she otherwise favors. Her mildly excessive response dramatizes the transgression of her own expectations concerning femininity. If we take her phrase at face value, the women she met were almost unrecognizable as women without denotative placards of designation, especially as she finds that "'tis not easy to describe what extrodinary [sic] figures they make" (281). Her grammatical construction suspends the imaginary umbrella of a potentially excessive fictionality above the women's strange attire, much like a deictic signpost. Montagu's rhetoric signals that more complicated feints—concerning the excessive fictionality and potential veracity of gender construction—develop as she proceeds.

The discovery of inimitability forms part of the self-authenticating logic behind much travel writing. Montagu bears personal witness to a shifting and transcendental cultural reality. The discourse of the eyewitness is nevertheless wedded to a radical skepticism for Montagu; she intends to elicit the reader's approval of her more sophisticated and self-doubting reliability. Chiding an unnamed lady for her uninformed skepticism (unlike her own informed interrogation of the local culture), Montagu writes from Vienna about the temporary prohibition of masquerade in Viennese carnival: "You may tell all the World in my Name that they are never so well inform'd of my affairs as I am my selfe, and that I am very positive I am at this time at Vienna, where the Carnival is begun and all sort of diversions in perpetual practise except that of masqueing, which is never permitted during a War with the Turks" (291). In this epistolary tiff with an unnamed lady, Montagu insists on her self-consistent veracity as a categorical fact, flaunting its unverifiability by others. Even as Montagu celebrates the performative nature of the act of writing, drawing attention to her authorial powers, there is a wry implication that female travel writing is not very different from the context of carnival, encouraging "all sorts of diversions in perpetual practise." From the viewpoint of her female identity, Montagu wittily dismisses the suspicions of English high society, suspicions that she invites in order to vanquish.

The metafictional twist suggests a larger question by implicitly re-

Lady Mary in the Hammam

167

versing terms. If there can still be a carnival without masquerade, there can also be masquerade without the formal contexts of carnival. In other words, can the proscription of masquerade matter very much, especially when women are the chosen objects of a travel narrative written by a female author? Montagu's focus on the artifice of femininity suggests that antirealist practices can function quite freely whether or not masking has been banned. A pessimistic reader may conclude that the proscription of masquerade in wartime has gutted carnival behavior of its essential attribute, but a more careful one might pick up on the suggestion that masquerade exists in many forms. At moments such as these Montagu is hinting that empiricism is too blunt a tool to describe and analyze cultural constructions of femininity. The ground is being prepared for the subtler instrument of levantinization.

Montagu searches for the semantic building blocks that can describe women, and their desires, within the cultures they inhabit. One of the letters she writes from Turkey celebrates her discovery of "the language of flowers," a means of secret communication between lovers.[22] In this private language, "There is no colour, no flower, no weed, no fruit, herb, pebble, or feather, that has not a verse belonging to it, and you may quarrel, reproach, or send Letters of passion, freindship, or Civillity, or even of news, without ever inking your fingers" (389). One can detect an orientalism at work here, a sense that there is a cultural mystery to be unlocked. Montagu's intellectual fascination with this technique, known as the *selam,* again suggests the problem of artifice. An object-related system of signification that pivots around free association as the primary mode of grammatical composition indicates arbitrariness and subjectivism.[23] Such a private system of communication cannot be comprehended through a naturalistic logic, as the deciphering techniques are hit or miss when the code is based on a rhyming free association that motivates grammar, not by reference to a rule-bound lexicon, but according to the desires and moods of the participants. Though the code coincidentally resembles Cockney slang, its objectives are romantically rather than commercially oriented.[24]

Secret language is the linguistic form of masquerade. This erotic practice of using psychic mechanisms such as rebuses (perhaps the rudiments of a proto-psychoanalysis centered on the genre of romance) has a rich tradition in Turkish erotic poetry. Its supposedly unmarked gender status could also function, according to Anne-Marie Moulin and Pierre

Chuvin, as a crypto-lesbian mode of communication when circulating in the harem or the bathhouse. Montagu's quotation of the selam combines with a poetic form known as *mâna* used only between women.[25]

When indulging in the citation of these erotic norms and conventions, Montagu addresses the same unnamed lady to whom she describes the famous scene at the hammam. This unidentified correspondent appears as a fictive device of self-reflexivity on the letter writer's part: "I have got for you, as you desire, a Turkish Love-letter, which I have put in a little Box" (388). Written ostensibly as a reply to a request for erotic secrets, the letter functions ironically. A more fanciful reader may hear the rumblings of aggression toward an unidentified rival, lesbian desire, autoeroticism, or even professional caution. This obvious mystification of the letter's performative status means that the citation of the letter within the letter connotes more than it denotes. It involves an epistolary mask that takes the very trope of concealment as unmasked meaning. In the context of a series of letters addressed to identifiable correspondents "in the world," the single unidentified and mysterious addressee becomes a metafictional referent collapsing author, reader, and mode. The subject, Montagu, addresses her object, womanliness, through a *mise en abîme* that reduces womanliness to masquerade. As in Fanny Burney's diaries addressed to Nobody, anonymity, fictionality, and realism concerning female interiority coincide.[26]

Masquerade comes to be the "perpetual practise" that suggests a model of female agency for Montagu, one that is structurally related to a freedom that suspends truth. It is this paradoxical truth, the permanent possibility of fiction, that Lady Mary envisages identifying and possessing. The interplay between nudity and masking fascinates her, especially because it provides aristocratic Turkish women—and ought, she thinks, to provide all women—with an escape from social ties by means of negativity and anonymity.

FROM LIMINAL TO LIMINOID: WRITING THE *HAMMAM*

Victor Turner speaks of the early modern transition from the "ludergic liminal" to the "ergic liminoid."[27] According to Turner, liminality and the experience of defamiliarization it brings is more properly an attribute of communitarian societies and those special sections of industrial societies (such as universities) that maintain initiation structures and rites of passage. In contrast, the modern structure of the liminoid is "experimental, idiosyncratic, quirky, subversive, utopian." Whereas the liminal is premodern and correspondingly anonymous or divine in origin, the liminoid is a feature of modern social disorder, connected with symbolic inversions but no longer part of communal ritual. The liminoid is present in packaged experiences, such as literature or tourism, which constitute autonomous genres or commodities in modernity. The liminoid is open, optative, and not conceptualized, whereas the liminal is a predetermined midstage of the process of religious ritual. Turner's theoretical distinction helps separate Montagu's *experience* of Turkish women's freedom, one of playful liminality, from her *description* of it in *Letters from the Levant*, which fits into the liminoid work performed by touristic travelogue and the vicarious consumption it promotes. Although Montagu did not publish immediately because of family pressures (despite Mary Astell's strong recommendation to do so), the commodity status of the letters is deferred rather than altogether denied.

Montagu is unconcerned in her letters with the multiple constructions of masculinity or with the long descriptions of Turkish street culture that other authors provide. Her desire for liminality leads to the public bathhouse and its "secrets."[28] In the course of this levantinization, she reiterates, "Upon the Whole, I look upon the Turkish Women as the only free people in the Empire" (329). She throws a levant here, refuting masculine predecessors such as Aaron Hill, whom she attacks for mouthing conventional European condemnations of harem slavery. Western observers considered the Sultan's seraglio—not to be confused with the harem as a social institution—as a state-within-a-state, with special laws as well as freedoms. However, Montagu's view is remarkably different from the typical Christian propaganda that Islam denies women souls.[29] Hill and "all his Brethren voyage-writers lament the miserable confinement of the Turkish Ladys, who are (perhaps) freer than any Ladys in the universe" (406). In her own opinion, these are "the only women in the world that lead a life of unintterupted [*sic*] pleasure, exempt from cares, their whole time being spent in visiting, bathing, or the agreable Amusement of spending Money and inventing new fashions" (406). These women's liberties arise from the "perpetual Masquerade" of the veil, which "gives them entire Liberty of following their Inclinations without danger of Discovery" (328). The idea of emancipatory female subjectivity commences with Montagu's celebrated letter on the nudity of women in the bathhouses at Sophia and is sustained throughout her stay in Turkey by the impressions she receives when making courtesy calls to aristocratic residences. The use of the veil in public enables a radical sexual freedom: " 'Tis impossible for the most jealous Husband to know his Wife when he meets her, and no Man dare either touch or follow a Woman in the Street" (328). In this levantinization, women are magically exempt from the gradations of class within female identity: "You may guess how effectually this disguises them, that there is no distinguishing the great Lady from her Slave" (328). Tenuous though this fantasy may be, Montagu invents a female subjectivity existing without subjection, a sexual agency without concomitant object status, and generalized public privileges abiding with few corresponding obligations. This position structurally reverses the condemnation of the German beauties' empty artificiality. The compulsory "disguise" that women wear in public, a restriction that keeps their social participation to an unindividuated minimum, paradoxically enhances their unfettered agency.

The passage celebrating "perpetual Masquerade" is in a letter to Lady Mar that reveals intimate details of Montagu's Turkish outfit and the honorary status it confers on her. Turkish women's clothing obsesses Montagu. Her portrait, often in lavish Turkish costume, was painted by accomplished portraitists including Charles Jervas, Godfrey Kneller, Charles Philips, Jonathan Richardson, Carolus de Rusca, Jean-Baptiste Vanmour, Christian Frederick Zincke, and others. Looking at these portraits, we recognize that the "Turkishness" of Montagu's clothing ranges from the use of authentic costumes to the sartorial syncretism of masquerade. Two of these portraits show the range of Montagu's improvisational exhibitionism. A well-known painting in the National Portrait Gallery, attributed to Jean-Baptiste Vanmour, emphasizes the exotic ambassadorial venue (Fig. 13). Montagu stands on a dais decorated with a beautiful carpet in a large hall, herself richly attired with a blue ermine-edged coat over a gold dress. A female musician plays a lute in the palatial setting, giving some light local entertainment, while from the other side, a steward is offering Montagu a letter. Presumably it has just arrived from a correspondent in England, no doubt anxious to hear the latest gossip and needing to be reassured of her welfare. Through the open foyer we can see a landscape with the distant minarets of the Constantinople skyline. Though her husband is absent, Lady Mary has her

Figure 13 Jean-Baptiste Vanmour, *Lady Mary Wortley Montagu, with Her Son Edward* (1717). (National Portrait Gallery, London)

hand on the shoulder of her young son, Edward Wortley Montagu, who is in a long white dress. The painting suggests a cultural conundrum. The woman's music may take her more toward Turkish female interiors, even as the correspondence draws her back to the tight circle of English aristocratic society. The architecture outside the foyer is a third, more conventional touristic attraction. Yet, faced with these three choices, she poses for a fourth entity, the undisclosed viewer, who assesses these three clearly different directions of her inclinations. Or is the absent husband the implied viewer? The other portrait, a half-length likeness of Montagu's also attributed to the circle of Jean-Baptiste Vanmour, is intriguingly unflattering (Fig. 14). The feathered turban and the jewelry seem incongruous, too big for her head and misplaced. Though she is handsomely attired, a few wisps of Montagu's hair have nonetheless escaped and the veil attached to her turban trails behind her head as testimony to a slightly hasty appearance. There is something a little pathetic, pretentious, and quite lost about this figure, in contrast to the controlled staging of the former occasion. It seems that the portraitist is

Figure 14 Circle of Jean-Baptiste Vanmour, *Lady Mary Wortley Montagu.* (Sotheby's, London)

presenting Montagu with compassion, but nonetheless, there are hints of the dishevelled eccentric with delusions of grandeur.

Felicity Nussbaum has discussed sexual self-fashioning through Turkish clothing as an important feature of Defoe's *Roxana,* and clearly several of Montagu's portraits suggest some important emotional investments in the same direction. By her clothing, Montagu acquires a fantasy of the beauty she felt she had lost when she was infected with smallpox: "I am now in my Turkish habit, thô I beleive you would be of my opinion that 'tis admirably becoming. I intend to send you my Picture; in the mean time accept of it here" (326). Montagu paints a pen portrait of herself in this new costume. However, her Western gaze that fetishizes Levantine clothing does not automatically occupy the position of the orientalist subject. As Joan Copjec suggests provocatively in her interpretation of the thousands of photographs of veiled women taken by G. G. de Clérambault, the photographer sometimes disavowed lack by positioning himself as the gaze of the Moroccan other. Montagu's levantinization of Turkish clothing creates similarly heterogeneous effects.[30]

Herself wearing Turkish clothes, she is full of praise for the elaborate costumes of the Turkish aristocratic women she encounters. She visits Hafise Kadinefendi, the widow of the previous grand vizier, and is even

Lady Mary in the Hammam

more rapturous about the beauty of Fatima, the *kahya*'s, or royal steward's, wife (349). Fatima may well be a composite fiction of the best of Turkish femininity, created with the explicit purpose of seducing the reader with idealized accounts of Turkish womanhood and the costumes that fascinated Montagu. Despite her sequestration from male society, Fatima is at peace within a world of fountains and gardens, surrounded all the same by impeccable female company. Meeting both these women on separate occasions, Montagu is impressed by the dignity of Hafise's mourning and the reciprocal warmth of Fatima's friendship (380–86). Idealized descriptions of meetings with beautiful people are fairly typical of eighteenth-century letters, often written with an eye to posthumous publication. However, the gossip such letters relay may suggest, if not explicitly contain, the sexual flavor of diarists such as Pepys and Boswell. Cynthia Lowenthal suggests that the agency attributed by Montagu to women such as Hafise arises from the performative effects of sexual segregation rather than from the psychological interiority imagined through literary representations of novelistic "characters." Lowenthal's nuanced reading of Montagu's epistolarity within the contexts of eighteenth-century genres interprets Montagu as aestheticizing Turkish women through the interlocking, purportedly antifeminist genres of pictorial representation and seventeenth-century romance. According to this reading, Montagu's "stopped-action" scenes arrest the feminine at the moment of reemergence into self and transcendence. Even though Lowenthal is correct in insisting that Montagu's account is distorted for seeing only the agency and not the subjection, it is necessary to look for more appropriate background. For instance, Fanny Davis argues that women sultans (daughters of sultans who were also addressed by the same title), unlike typical Turkish women of the period, went out, shopped, walked around, and had their own palaces. A faulty extrapolation from the personal freedoms that women of this milieu possessed may partly account for Montagu's assertions concerning all Turkish women.[31]

With the help of one remarkable scene, Montagu negotiates the ambivalent significance of "revealing" women's interiors. The bathhouse letter to an unnamed lady, a minor prose classic that inspired painters such as Ingres, comes to us riddled with feints concerning anonymity. In it, Montagu articulates a central paradox: aristocratic Turkish Muslim women are naked but not immodest, free but not licentious, languid but not unproductive. If her portraitist "Gervase" (Jervas) could look upon the bath, "it would have very much improv'd his art to see so many fine Women naked in different postures, some in conversation, some working, others drinking Coffee or sherbet, and many negligently lying on their Cushions while their slaves (generally pritty Girls of 17 or 18) were employ'd in braiding their hair in several pritty manners. In short, 'tis the Women's coffée house, where all the news of the Town is told, Scandal invented, etc." (314). One can discern a fine balance in this passage between the containment of Jervas's masculine gaze and the subversion of the ongoing autonomous female activity, even if this activity is as seemingly innocuous as the relay of news and the invention of scandal. Montagu's language mimics the traditional masculine gesture of voyeuristic penetration with the gaze, as does Ingres's famous *tondo* from the perspective of a keyhole voyeur, *Le bain turc* (1862), influenced as it may be by Montagu's account of the hammam. Ruth Yeazell points out that Ingres's return to the fantasy of the harem distorts Montagu's shift of emphasis to bathhouse as public space.[32] Chodowiecki's illustration (Fig. 15), published in 1781 in an edition of the letters printed in Berlin and also discussed by Yeazell, is probably a much more accurate rendition of Montagu's letter than Ingres's. The hammam is, for Montagu, the Turkish woman's riposte to the Englishman's coffeehouse. Englishwomen could not themselves come up with an alternative to the coffeehouse's resolutely masculine monopoly of sociopolitical space. The exclusively male preserve of the coffeehouses has been identified by historians of modernity as a vital innovation that created a public sphere of free political discussion, leading to the invention of liberal democracy. In this precise sense, the bathhouse simulates the Habermasian sphere of communicative freedom. The alternative Turkish women's public sphere possesses a hedonistic atmosphere within which slaves enable their mistresses' desultory enjoyment of quasi-erotic pleasures: "Braiding their [ladies'] hair in several pritty manners." Montagu visualizes an inclusive women's sphere at the bath, a gynaecium of unselfconscious but interactive female nudity that contrasts with the exclusionary masculine preserve of the Greek gymnasium, whose participants were also naked while demonstrating their athletic prowess. However, this women's world is not devoted to the efficiency-oriented

Figure 15 D. Chodowiecki, *Lady Mary Visiting the* Hammam (1780), in Letters of Lady M—— W—— M—— (Berlin, 1780). (British Library, London)

syntax of muscular masculinity but to the expanded time of productive leisure (witness the parataxis of the simultaneous activities: conversing, working, drinking, lying down, braiding).

Montagu suggests that the nudity of the women displaces the signs of their psychic readability from the face down to the entire body: "I was here convinc'd of the Truth of a Refflexion that I had often made, that if twas the fashion to go naked, the face would be hardly observ'd" (314). The claim of widespread nudity may have been an exaggeration, empirically speaking, as evidence suggests that women wore linen wraps in the bathhouse.[33] Montagu validates the reasons for nakedness, however, observing that the heat had been bothering her, making it "impossible to stay there with one's Cloths on." Lady Mary remains doubly unreadable, demure in her "travelling Habit, which is a rideing dress"

(313). At this point, she has not yet reached Constantinople and acquired the new Turkish costume that she speaks of delightedly to Lady Mar. Her demure behavior in the riding dress appears bizarre to her hosts, and her overdressing does not easily undo the social conventions of hospitality already in force. No one is surprised at her deviance from the expected protocols: "there was not one of 'em that shew'd the least surprize or impertinent Curiosity, but receiv'd me with all the obliging civillity possible" (313). This curiosity soon takes the form of solicitude.

In this letter, Montagu is aware of her anomalous position even before she vicariously adopts Jervas's male gaze, an irony that many readers have missed. By desisting from participation, Lady Mary also maintains modesty for her English audience. At least she claims she did not strip, as such activity would compromise her identity as *Lady* Mary, who kept her title and maiden name, Montagu. It is at this moment, perhaps, when the English lady "decides" not to submit her own nakedness to double scrutiny, that masquerade begins. A fictional parenthesis has opened, as Lady Mary maintains having entered Turkey, and the bathhouse itself, unchanged and fully dressed. The hammam visit at Sophia that formally marks her entry into Turkish utopian female space is followed by a second visit to a bathhouse at Istanbul just before she leaves, making for an eventual closure of the parenthesis. It is from this part of the Levant that Montagu composes her most assertive levantinization.

The bathhouse passage provides the reader with an interpretive option between the naïveté of Montagu's English punctilio and the false modesty it signifies in Turkish surroundings. A superficial and a subcutaneous reading of social convention diverge from one another. The narrator cannot think of any "European Court where the Ladys would have behav'd them selves in so polite a manner to a stranger" (313). The inversion of the voyeuristic position becomes part of the tableau she sketches, and Montagu is immediately called to account by the objects of her gaze through an embarrassing reverse fetishization: "The Lady that seem'd the most considerable amongst them entreated me to sit by her and would fain have undress'd me for the bath. I excus'd my selfe with some difficulty, they being all so earnest in perswading me. I was at last forc'd to open my skirt and shew them my stays, which satisfy'd 'em very well, for I saw they beleiv'd I was so lock'd up in that machine that it was not in my own power to open it, which contrivance they attributed to my Husband" (314).[34] There are several contrivances in this passage other than the one the bathhouse acquaintances attribute to Wortley. Lady Mary contrives not to be undressed for her English audience; in continuing to maintain herself in full dress, she appears both dignified and ridiculous, imprisoned by her own culture. She has pulled off a brilliant improvisation, successfully negotiating the Scylla of offending her Turkish hosts and the Charybdis of scandalizing her English readers. By banking on Turkish cultural misapprehension, she narrowly escapes the sacrifice of her English virtue. However, doubly bound as her body is by her lingerie, she is also in a fictional double bind as she is masquerading in the same costume for two audiences simultaneously. For the Turkish women, her English stays are an infernal machine, a straitjacket imposed upon her by a jealous husband. She does not dispute the perception of this theatricalized cruelty, and accepts the commiseration she receives from her hosts. Yet she has exposed herself, ever so slightly, to the English gaze by granting the women a glimpse of her underwear. The tantalizing unavailability of her straitjacketed body to the Turkish ladies is all too readable within this passage, providing a further contrast with the enigmatic and wide-open unreadability of the characters amidst their exultant freedom in the hammam. The focus shifts to her, as she is the fetish for the female gaze at the bath and for the mixed gaze back in England. Having represented the voyeuristic aspects of the scopophiliac complex, Montagu now takes a quick turn toward exhibitionism. Both the viewing Turks and the reading English are led on to fantasize medieval chastity belts on Montagu, if not quite whips, chains, and handcuffs. Suddenly, it is Montagu who is the object of pity as well as of a phantasmagorical bondage scenario; her constraining clothing is misapprehended as her husband's handiwork. By extension, this constriction restricts access to her clothesbound body. However, the subtle effects of this masquerade rebound upon those who are taken in by it. For the English readers, the bondage scene probably suggests itself as a fictional by-product of the steamy bathhouse atmosphere and can then be readily associated with European pornographic fantasies that confuse harem with hammam. In this sexual traffic, the traveler invents a script, plays a role, and peddles an effect, all the while silently disclaiming her moral liability. Montagu flaunts her virtue as the truth behind the imaginary mask of her chastity belt. Perhaps it is not so remarkable a coincidence that at the same time, Alexander Pope's erotic focus on Montagu involves his imagining various long-distance liberties with underwear: "Let us be like modest people, who when they are close together keep all decorums, but if they step a little aside, or get to the other end of a room, can untie garters or take off Shifts without scruple."[35] Could the bathhouse letter—published much later—also be a complex response to the initial erotic attentions of Pope and his subsequent vilifications? Many of the misogynistic smears by Pope and Horace Walpole concerning the purported lack of physical cleanliness observed by Montagu could be coded attacks on her chastity following this minor Turkish escapade.[36]

In her obsession with women's interiors, Montagu is not just opposing a domestic perspective to that of the Grand Tour, as Clare Brant points out, but countering the calculated masculine hedonism of the exercise with a female alternative that may, underneath it all, be more satisfying for women. Addison and her husband, Edward Wortley, were very close friends who went on the Grand Tour together for three years. By implicitly opposing the exclusionary nature of this type of male bonding with a female alternative, there may well be a concealed rejoinder that Montagu is issuing to her marital partner.[37] A naked Montagu would be subjected as no ordinary woman to the strident charge of indecent exposure. Such a charge would in any case be leveled if she published anything, as Pope does in his polemic against her as Sappho.[38] In this description of naked interiors, Sapphism suggests itself, but in a very different way from the salacious discussion by previous male writers with overheated imaginations.[39] Even as Montagu squelches the specter of lesbian eroticism—"there was not the least wanton smile or immodest gesture amongst them"—some believe that her equanimity sounds more like ladylike disavowal. Montagu's quotation of the selam technique that combines with a poetic form known as mâna used only between women, discussed in the previous section, is nonetheless suggestive of lesbian possibilities.

The bathhouse letter conceals a challenge to its addresses even as it delivers it. Montagu's strategy consists of exposing a little in order not to expose too much. By maintaining the several senses of constriction that uphold her identity, the European aristocratic woman is momentarily rendered the slave, while the object of her reflection, Turkish ladies of quality, are seen as completely unfettered. Female subjectivity is divided down the middle, revealing agency all on one side and subjection all on the other. It first seems that agency is all on the side of those who can remove their clothes and the subjection on the side of she who cannot take them off. But the sexual trick makes the bound-over into the binder. Montagu has depicted herself in imaginary chains, having willingly chosen, at least at that point, subjection over agency. She allows the Turkish women to interpret her cultural limitations, about which she may not want to complain directly. Montagu's belief that Turkish women have agency is a levantinization, just as much as her choice to perform her own subjection is conscious masquerade.

Levantinization and masquerade go hand in glove. The richer women lounge on sofas and their slaves sit behind them. However, the women are "without any distinction of rank by their dress, all being in the state of nature, that is, in plain English, stark naked, without any Beauty or deffect conceal'd" (313). This ambiguous state of nature cannot be the Hobbesian one that Montagu highlights when discussing the wartime devastations of the Austrians and the Ottomans.[40] Rather, it appears prelapsarian. The starkness of the object demands a plain English, wedded to a heavy-duty biblical and epic forebear: "They Walk'd and mov'd with the same majestic Grace which Milton describes of our General Mother" (313-14).[41] The exact proportions of these latter-day Eves remind Lady Mary of naked goddesses "drawn by the pencil of Guido or Titian" or, even more conventionally for her eighteenth-century eye, the well-coiffed "figures of the Graces." Despite the overlay of Christian iconography, this is not European court society. Montagu finds "none of those disdainfull smiles or satyric whispers that never fail in our assemblys when any body appears that is not dress'd exactly in fashion" (313). Of course, nudity in a hammam is tenuously related to the ephemeral notion of fashion, as the concern is rather with an eternal undress, the perdurableness of the classical female body rather than the historical variability of clothing. Montagu relies in a subsequent letter on the relativism of a character in an Aphra Behn play who forces others to modify their perceptions to explain all this unfamiliarity: "As to their [Turkish women's] Morality or good Conduct, I can say like Arlequin, 'tis just as 'tis with you, and the Turkish Ladys don't commit one sin the less for not being Christians. Now I am a little acquainted with their ways, I cannot forbear admiring either the exemplary discretion or extreme Stupidity of all the writers that have given accounts of 'em. 'Tis very easy to see they have more Liberty than we have" (327-28).[42]

There is a dreamlike quality to perceptions of the hammam as the originary state and indeed source of such freedom, one that is repeated when, before she leaves, Montagu attends a ceremony in the bathhouse at Constantinople. The women epithalamize a young bride in their midst and give her rich gifts while they are naked. Though strictly sexually segregated, the Turkish baths also allowed women to bring with them preadolescent children of both sexes, who could thus participate in the general nudity and exchange of gazes. In a suggestive if somewhat idealized anthropological analysis of the history of Levantine Muslim sexuality, Abdelwahab Bouhdiba has argued that the baths provided a liminal space where the demarcation between public and private spheres was ritually suspended.[43] Bouhdiba demonstrates the structural interplay of oppositions in the activity of the hammam, between hot and cold water, soft towels and hard scrubs, male and female schedules, dirt and cleanliness, purity and impurity, interiority and exteriority, self and other, angels and demons. In his analysis, the hammam becomes the privileged locus for the release of social and political tensions, as well as the site where a certain Levantine unconscious is constructed. In addition to the inevitable developmental role the hammam would have played in answering childhood curiosity about the body, it also performed the quotidian function of ritual purification, as a propaedeutic as well as a conclusion, to the business of love. The hammam was an antechamber to the mosque, thus becoming the transitional site between the carnal and the spiritual; it thereby represents a parasexual space for the unfolding of sexuality, one that helped fix the meaning of sex more than sexual acts themselves. Architecturally labyrinthine, the enclosed hammam, unlike the open Roman *balneae*, served as a complex site for the staging and regulation of sexual desire, as well as became a more generalized allegory for psychosexual interiors. The dreamscape of the bathhouse may suggest a uterine memory of the mother—or the figure of "our General Mother," as Montagu formally states it. However, Montagu's own gesture converts the liminal communitarianism of the hammam into what Victor Turner characterizes as the liminoid genre of free tropological appropriation typical of commodity culture. This conversion signals the advent of modernity and cross-cultural levantinization, the decline of ritual symbolic space, and the rise of a neoclassical synthesis.

There is a further tease in this overdetermined masquerade at the bathhouse for informed readers, even if very few of Montagu's English contemporaries would have apprehended the sexual provocation of the entire episode. Bouhdiba informs us that in Turkish and Arabic, "going to the hammam" is a popular euphemism for sexual intercourse.[44] Montagu sometimes refers to the bathhouse by the libertine Italianate term, bagnio. Consequently, the letter from the bathhouse turns into an immense metaphor for the very thing it was trying to skirt around: sexual impropriety. In shifting the masculine focus from the Turkish harem to the rather different hammam, Montagu emphasizes that it is not the sexual possession of women that interests her (as it invariably interests male observers) but something we might anachronistically call women's sexual self-expression. The hammam, as one of the sites that allegorizes the unconscious, imbricates the public with the private, underwriting both. As the only quasi-public space where the Qu'ran cannot be recited because of the ritual impurity of the bathers and their surroundings, the hammam is already a liminal space for Levantine cultures. For Montagu, this space serves as liminal too, but also has the additional function of a liminoid institution such as the coffeehouse to which she compares it or, for that matter, to the developing domain of Literature. The scene ends with the following paragraph: "Adeiu, Madam. I am sure I have now entertaind you with an Account of such a sight as you never saw in your Life and what no book of travells could inform you of. 'Tis no less than Death for a Man to be found in one of these places" (315). The narrator is instrumentalizing the encounter, marketing it aggressively for vicarious consumption. These are novelties that only a woman can sell: here we have phantasmagorical desires titillated in the face of death and natural beauty hawked in lieu of artifice. As a transitional figure, and as a cultural translator, Montagu claims to have observed without participation, even as she tempts her readers with the taste of forbidden fruit. She has crossed and recrossed a ritual threshold, flirted with a liminal situation but has returned to tell the tale. Yet, the power of her narrative is that of liminoid extrapolation for herself and her readers.

Montagu enforces the closure of the fictional parenthesis that opened with her insistence on her English femininity being kept apart. Ultimately, the lady in Montagu cannot justify a crossover that involves undress. She has nonetheless created an opening for the fantasy projections and partial identifications of levantinization. If this was not quite a room of her own when she entered the bathhouse, Montagu at least makes sure to emphasize that she went literally where "no Man" had gone before. She entered women's space as an honorary Turkish lady, while maintaining her Englishness. Montagu has shown that by enforcing sexual segregation the masculine desire for exclusive possession has dispossessed itself. More importantly, the passages on various female interiors are often written to the unnamed lady, a blank addressee, or a social equal, the Countess of Bristol, both of whom are mirror images of Montagu. If the descriptions are interpreted as memoranda to herself, they indicate an autoeroticism that is made fully public just after her death. Rather than deny it altogether Montagu defers her self-exposure; she can perish and then publish. Trying to keep her clothes on in the sweltering atmosphere, Lady Mary runs out of steam while still trying to undo her stays.

Some readers think that Montagu is locked in that infernal machine called orientalism; as I suggested earlier, however, she has run or thrown a levant as an eighteenth-century gamester would. Montagu writes her travels from a place with no fixed address and makes sure to indicate that she is a visitor, ready to bolt or steal away. She may also be doing the equivalent of the Spanish *levantar la casa*, breaking up housekeeping. Not a regular herself, Montagu need not be, to continue the pun with a legalistic eighteenth-century phrase, *levant and couchant* there. Unlike Colley Cibber's daughter Charlotte Charke, who dressed in male drag and fell afoul of her scandalized male peers, Montagu succeeds at an understated self-exposure by masquerading *as herself*. She has collapsed her self-exposure with that of the Turkish women, yet the exposure she feared in 1718 came about favorably. After the letters were published following her death in 1763, she received a complimentary review from Smollett, having already received grudging admiration from an enemy, Horace Walpole.[45] Several decades after her trip, the lucidity of her stylistic masquerade won the day, just as much as the substance of her assertions or the female authorship she vindicated.

INOCULATIONS: MEDICAL, CLASSICAL, CRITICAL

While the bathhouse provides the backdrop for Montagu's description of aristocratic women, the same female environment is most likely where Montagu learned the technique of smallpox inoculation. The bathhouse was a site for hygienic, aesthetic, and therapeutic practices; hence, it was common in that environment to find herbalists, magicians, and medical practitioners.[46] Montagu reports in one of the letters that smallpox is rendered "entirely harmless by the invention of engrafting . . . a set of old Women . . . make it their business to perform the Operation" (338). After describing the process in detail, she claims to be "Patriot enough to take pains to bring this usefull invention into fashion in England" (339). Montagu's own face had been scarred after a life-threatening attack of smallpox in 1715, the year before leaving for Turkey. Her pioneering dissemination of inoculation occurred at considerable personal risk. Montagu inoculated her son and subsequently her daughter, even while she was the object of antifeminist polemic resulting from her sponsorship of the idea. According to some reports, she convinced Caroline, then Princess of Wales, to inoculate her daughters. At the initiative of the princess, resistance to this technique was countered by a public experiment in 1721, whereby six condemned prisoners at Newgate were induced to undergo the inoculation by promising them a reprieve if they survived, which they did.[47]

As the obvious practical benefit of the travels, inoculation seems an anomalous by-product of *Letters from the Levant.* The technique was still dangerous, as the inoculation was performed with a live culture (rather than by using a vaccine which contains dead bacteria, popularized later by Edward Jenner in 1798). However, the travels themselves serve a cultural function resembling the homeopathic act of inoculation that stalls a disease by subjecting the body to a weaker version of it. Travel narrative, after flirting with cultural crossover, acknowledges the superiority of the return home. Montagu's return with the actual technique of inoculation is a masterstroke, because it coincidentally provides a model for English cultural retrenchment. Roland Barthes defines symbolic inoculation as a process by which "one immunizes the contents of the collective imagination by means of a small inoculation of acknowledged evil; one thus protects it against the risk of a generalized subversion."[48] Montagu's deliberate self-blinkering following a disorienting experience denotes her reaggregation to the cultural and social matrices of Englishness. The three stages of the process represent Montagu's version of an "ordered antistructure" to the developing ideology of modernity.[49] She symbolically inoculates herself against the temptation of cultural passing. Witness the following comment in her penultimate letter of the series, addressed to the Abbé Conti, which shuts down the search for betterment by conscious reidentification with Englishness, despite the obvious deficiencies of such reaggregation: "And, after having seen part of Asia and Africa, and allmost made the tour of Europe, I think the honest English Squire more happy who verily beleives the Greek wines less delicious than March beer, that the African fruits have not so fine a flavour as golden Pipins, and the Becáfiguas of Italy are not so well tasted as a rump of Beef, and that, in short, there is no perfect Enjoyment of this Life out of Old England. I pray God I may think so for the rest of my Life; and since I must be contented with our scanty allowance of Daylight, that I may forget the enlivening Sun of Constantinople" (444). This symbolic inoculation against the temptation of an elsewhere is not wholly relevant to Montagu, who ended up spending a large part of her later years in Italy, returning to England just before she died. However, it is one more instance of the sophisticated textual outcome of Montagu's levantinizations. A systematic practice of cultural perception through these stages—of relativism, liminality, and reaggregation—operates behind the desultory façade of Montagu's epistolary production. Such a move, invested in the historiographical re-turn that Michel de Certeau has astutely analyzed as the reinvention of the past, circumscribes the very real limits of Montagu's attempt to reach, comprehend, and assimilate the other.[50]

Jonathan Richardson's portrait illustrates this point well (Fig. 16). The painting has Montagu standing in a regal manner attended by a black page, in that respect resembling the seventeenth-century aristocratic portraits I discussed earlier, or even the portrait by Vanmour, where she uses her own son as a prop (Fig. 13). However, there are significant differences too. There is not so much emphasis on exotic commodity or allegory, even though it is clear that Montagu is richly dressed; the black boy is still a foil, assisting, looking, and directing attention back to her, but the setting is solitary, outdoors, and most likely in something like an English country estate even though the buildings in the distance still suggest the skyline of Constantinople. It seems that there is much in the portrait that reaggregates Montagu back to Englishness, even though the Turkishness is acknowledged but now kept at bay. The black boy is a metonym for the tropicopolitan space that Montagu experienced but left behind.[51]

Such retrenchment was already at work after the teasing letter to the unnamed lady describing the secret selam techniques. The narrator steps back to reflect philosophically on the advantages and perils of linguis-

Figure 16 Jonathan
Richardson, *Lady
Mary Wortley Mon-
tagu* (ca. 1717–18).
(Earl of Harrowby)

tic multiplicity. By means of a territorial metaphor, Montagu expresses
her anxiety about losing the mother tongue: "I am allmost falln into the
misfortune so common to the Ambitious while they are employ'd on
distant, insignificant conquests abroad, a Rebellion starts up at home. I
am in great danger of loseing my English" (390). In Constantinople, she
"live[s] in a place that very well represents the Tower of Babel." Listing
a bewildering multiplicity of the languages spoken around her (spoken
languages in addition to private ones, such as the code of flowers, masking, and so on) and the multifarious ethnicities of her servants and ambassadorial retinue, Montagu fears that the natives of Constantinople
while multilingual and cosmopolitan, are woefully illiterate "in the perpetual hearing of this medley of Sounds" (390). She oscillates between a
scathing dismissal of the monolingual and parochial uniformity of English society, where "Ladys set up for such extrodinary Geniuses upon

the credit of some superficial knowledge of French and Italian," and the equally worrisome prospect of the loss of that very identity: "as I prefer English to all the rest, I am extremely mortify'd at the daily decay of it in my head, where I'll assure you (with greife of heart) it is reduce'd to such a small number of Words" (390-91).[52]

Linguistic alienation as a matter of course is one of the first signs of the culture shock from which Montagu wishes to cushion herself, even as she exacerbates the shock to increase its heuristic value for a jaded, provincial, and complacent English society. Her cautious celebration of heterogeneity is tempered by a fear of the loss of an Englishness that she still prioritizes as prima inter pares. At the end of her travels, Montagu turns to an archaeological stance, promoting classicism and cultural antiquarianism as a lingua franca after encountering an Ottoman Empire that tolerated the social mixture of multinational, multiethnic, and multireligious populations in a manner that would have bewildered the still provincial English.

Despite criticism concerning Christian beliefs and practices, Montagu insists in a letter to Princess Caroline that her journey "has not been undertaken by any Christian since the Time of the Greek Emperours" (310). Writing to Pope, she scales down the same claim as a journey not made by a Christian for a century (330). These pointers help anchor some of the religious discussions and friendly disputes she had with an Islamic scholar, whose outcome she relays to the Abbé Conti. She reserves high praise for the effendi's moderation and intellect and attempts to assimilate Islam to "plain Deism" even as she dismisses the controversies about Islamic theology's recognition of women's souls (318, 376). A sect of Arnounts who respect Islam and Christianity equally are endorsed for their relativist humility (319).[53]

Attempts at contemporaneous syncretism of this sort—that Islam is not all that unfamiliar theologically—are matched by nudging the reader toward her idea of a stable antiquarian "Levant." Montagu's return to England is by way of various archaeological sites containing ruins of classical civilizations, including a misidentified Troy and an actual Carthage. Pastoral poetry and Greek myth help contextualize these yet-to-be tourist attractions for her audience. Humorous self-deprecation comes in handy, as she tours the battlements of the misidentified Troy by hiring an ass, "the only voiture to be had there" (420). Ida, Lesbos, Knossos, Etna: the list proceeds as if from a geographical touring dic-

tionary. Ruins are idealized in her accounts. Temples are silently reconstructed from empty shells and mutilated statues are rendered whole.
Classical inscriptions are painstakingly recopied. The last third of her
letters increasingly highlights this wistful step backward into a mythic
past that may reunify the Mediterranean under the cultural rubric of a
dead Roman and Greek civilization rather than the immediate justifications of a burgeoning one under the British. Shocked by the fact that
the classical monuments in Carthage are being used by the locals as
granaries, Montagu suffers something of an ideological breakdown with
respect to the women of the Maghreb: "Their posture in siting, the
colour of their skin, their lank black Hair falling on each side their faces,
their features and the shape of their Limbs, differ so little from their
own country people, the Baboons, tis hard to fancy them a distinct race,
and I could not help thinking there had been some ancient alliances
between them" (427).[54] Faced with this racist speculation, the modern
reader would be impelled to think likewise of some ancient alliances between the clans of the Montagus and the Monboddos. The teratological
side of orientalist discourse is not entirely absent in Montagu's reflections. The Maghrebians are "not quite black, but all mullattos, and the
most frightfull Creatures that can appear in a Human figure" (412). So,
does this mean that Montagu's comparison of the Maghrebian women
to baboons neutralizes the intellectual wager of syncretism? Not necessarily. She is similarly uncircumspect earlier about the dwarves in the
Austrian court or the "odd and monstrous" Armenian acceptance of
physical deformities by the practice of bridegrooms agreeing to marry
veiled brides, "be she deaf, be she blind" (411). In search for classical
reassurance at the point she reaches Carthage, Montagu's reality cannot stand very much of humankind. In retrospect, it would be too easy
to either accuse Montagu of an avoidance mechanism or overstate the
case in favor of her radical brilliance by ignoring the racial ephemera.
But from the vantage of her own historical moment, her travels appear
as a tentative ideological step that, for the most part, levies "positive"
orientalist empiricism against the gothic extravagances more typical of
eighteenth-century English orientalisms.

Montagu's critically engaging levantinization projects the unfreedom
of English women toward the different agency that Turkish upper-
class women may have possessed. To appreciate the nuanced nature of
Montagu's contemporaneity we need to interrogate her writings with-

out pigeonholing her as either a symptom of her class and nationality or as an unthinking practitioner of oppressive aestheticization. Rather than belabor Montagu's writings with the blunt accusation of orientalism, or naïvely celebrate it as the twentieth-century feminism that it is not, I have attempted to reinterpret her levantinization as produced by an unsteady mixture of Whiggism and neoclassicism, which in turn can be read as proto-feminist or proto-orientalist by different readers.[55] Montagu's archaeological classicism ultimately foregrounds a joint Euro-Islamic Levantine heritage. This tactic mostly disavows the Manichaean dialectic of self and other characteristic of high orientalism for the wager that the benign play of differences in syncretic neoclassicism could lead to transcultural understanding.[56] This humanist dream of transcultural understanding on an equal footing did not subsequently actualize itself, but that should not blind us to the validity of critical appropriations such as Montagu's. Having thrown her levant, Montagu eventually absconds to the Continent and is finally published after her death in a manner ensuring literary success. However, her levantinizations ought to reconfigure critical approaches to orientalist humanisms whose legacies are more complex and malleable than had previously been supposed.

CHAPTER FIVE

The Despotic Eye

and the Oriental Sublime

> Hence the two great mythical experiences on which
> the philosophy of the eighteenth century had wished to
> base its beginning: the foreign spectator in an unknown
> country, and the man born blind restored to light.
>
> —MICHEL FOUCAULT, *The Birth of the Clinic*

Reassessments of eighteenth-century English aesthetics have suggested that the sublime is a bourgeois masculine category celebrated in opposition to the beautiful, which is coded feminine. In addition to the gendering of aesthetics and its implications, evaluations of British Francophobia at midcentury also enable a clearer understanding of how aesthetics participated in the chauvinistic imagination. British "freedom" is often rendered as a confused medley of political *and* aesthetic liberties, favorably contrasted with the "tyranny" of absolutist politics *and* French neoclassicism. Some of these criticisms began in France even before their cross-channel popularization. For instance, absolutist monarchy was satirized as oriental despotism by Montesquieu's *Persian Letters* as early as 1721, spawning many imitators who also drew attention, as Montesquieu did, to the aesthetics of political power.[1]

Edmund Burke's influential *Philosophical Enquiry into the Origin of Our Ideas of the Sublime and the Beautiful* (1757, 1759) and *Reflections on the Revolution in France* (1790) explore the new aesthetics of power with a radical methodology. Deriving the sublime from terror and coercion, Burke's thematization of it through examples of darkness, blindness, and political cannibalism emphasizes the underside of rational Enlightenment. Perceptions of terror and monstrosity vitiate the aesthetic subject's capacity for self-aggrandizement. Constructed and constrained in relation to a despotic eye, the aesthetic subject is coerced into a predetermined itinerary. The despotic eye is present in the *Enquiry* as well as in two eighteenth-century prose romances that explore oriental sublimity: Samuel Johnson's *Rasselas* (1759) and William Beckford's *Vathek* (1786). By creating oriental gothic, these texts explore abstract allegories of subject formation even as they parody the universalistic claims of novelistic realism and Enlightenment rationality.

Johnson's and Beckford's orientalia problematize *vision* in order to emphasize what Jean-François Lyotard calls "the unpresentable in presentation itself." Lyotard sees progress from a modern sublime that distinguishes between an unpresentable content and a pleasing form to a postmodern sublime that collapses form and content by searching "for new presentations, not in order to enjoy them but in order to impart a stronger sense of the unpresentable," yet the artifacts of the oriental sublime indicate both modern and postmodern aspects. Burke's relentless search for origins and principles collapses form and content, whereas Johnson and Beckford balance the unpresentable against pleasurable detours and interruptions. As the sublime stages aesthetic crisis around vision to reveal larger questions of unpresentability, it is an Enlightenment precursor to the antiocularcentrism that Martin Jay identifies in much twentieth-century French thought.[2] As with Turner's seascapes or Piranesi's carceral visions, the sublime presents the limits of the eye along with a maelstrom of powerful feelings produced as the viewing subject teeters on the brink of perspectival and epistemic collapse. When presented as discursive or visual sublime, the "Orient" is a limit case of the despotic extreme, a carceral terminus with an imaginative potential rather than a historical referent. Obsessed with the imagination of suffering and the suffering of imagination, sublime speculations generate, as it were, a "writhing" degree zero.

Ocularcentric crisis also pits the static subject of despotism against the sublime agency of the despot. As Alain Grosrichard puts it economically in his study of Montesquieu, "in a despotic régime, where orders are 'blindly' obeyed, the blind man [*l'aveugle*] is the emblematic figure of the subject."[3] The political subject also submits, irrespective of the question of whether anything else could have been done, indeed an academic question given that submission precedes inquiry. The orientalist—and sometimes colonialist—sublime frequently relies on the radical unfreedom of an abjected tropicopolitan as a constitutive trope of "Occidental" or metropolitan aesthetics. Orientalism is here also levantinization, but with a minus sign and a greater geographical and cultural generalizability. Oriental despotism as a *disposition* is universalized by the end of the century, applicable just as much to British colonial functionaries as to stereotypical Turkish emperors. Using the same tropology, French, Ethiopian, Persian, and Arab despots are paraded through the texts I examine. Whether as Jacobin demagogues or colonial monopolists, various usurpers receive admiration and invective for the power with which they blind the ethical observer. As opposed to Montagu's construction of a "perpetual masquerade" of utopian and liminal freedom across a Levantine boundary and in a specific location, the fictions of oriental despotism investigate the ethics of subject constitution in the face of a blinding—and therefore unpresentable—tyrannical power. Blinding, mutilation, and sensory deprivation of all sorts are the fearful pleasures of the aesthetic subject's political prehistory. In contrast to the limited agency promised by utopian levantinization, the oriental sublime paints with a broader and more negative brush. Carceral humiliation and dystopian subjection typify the unpresentability at the heart of these dystopic levantinizations. However, the subject gains a precarious knowledge—with both political and aesthetic consequences—concerning the binary opposition of agency and subjection. Power can be seized or withheld, cloaked or exhibited, with frightful repercussions. It is only with the fullest awareness of these repercussions that subjects become agents. Any claim of agency, in this context, is tantamount to seizure of power where oppressed become oppressors. In Burke, Johnson, and Beckford, submission to political society as a braided continuity accedes to the polite trappings of power, while severing with the past indicates usurpation and hubris. The oriental sublime empowers its discoverers, who are also its practitioners, but at the price of converting its tropicopolitan antecedents into mere pretexts. Laying bare these pretexts, our criticism can consider the ends—goals as well as limits—of the sublime as a project of nationalist aesthetics.

REVERSING BLINDNESS

In part 4 of the *Enquiry*, Burke hypothesizes that the sight of darkness naturally produced pain in the observer. He illustrates his claim with an intriguing anecdote derived from the *Philosophical Transactions of the Royal Society:* "Mr. Cheselden has given us a very curious story of a boy, who had been born blind, and continued so until he was thirteen or fourteen years old; he was then couched for a cataract, by which operation he received his sight. Among many remarkable particulars that attended his first perceptions, and judgments on visual objects, Cheselden tells us, that the first time the boy saw a black object, it gave him great uneasiness; and that some time after, upon accidentally seeing a negro woman, he was struck with great horror at the sight" (144).[4] The technique for the couching of cataracts that cured some congenitally blind persons was a favorite for philosophical speculation, and takes an aesthetic and racial turn here. The origins of this philosophical question lie in Locke's relaying of an empiricist question, published in the *Essay on Human Understanding,* following a correspondence with William Molyneux, whether a blind person seeing a cube and a sphere together for the first time could tell them apart without touching them. Molyneux, Locke, Berkeley, and Cheselden (following his experiments) had concluded in the negative for different reasons; Leibniz and Condillac (after reversing himself) had hypothesized in the affirmative. Cheselden's discovery was that the newly sighted experimental subject had no sense of perspective, scale, or even of figure and object boundary. His conclusions were also discussed at length by Diderot in *Lettre sur les aveugles à l'usage de ceux qui voient* (1749). Burke's interpretive wager that fear and obscurity—the origin of the sublime—could be readily recognized in the body of the black woman was an idiosyncratic response to a long-standing philosophical conundrum. The boy's reaction typified the sublime as aesthetic shock. Additionally, the occasion presented the unpresentable months after the moment of visual initiation.[5]

In an article on racial stereotyping in Burke's and Kant's theories of the sublime, Meg Armstrong has argued that this "accidental" sighting of an African woman reveals the anomalous difficulties in Burke's attempt to prove cultural attitudes as "natural" and physiological. Alleging that Burke's "imagined subject of aesthetic experience necessarily remains a *reactionary* agent," Armstrong traces the unfolding of a deleterious racial logic in Kant's reflections on national stereotype as well.[6] However, it is not so clear that Burke's aim is to naturalize or domesticate familiar ideas of racial hierarchy even if his example does indeed have that effect. The radical nature of the interrogation of aesthetics in the *Enquiry* reveals unpalatable truths about the linkage between aesthetics and power, truths that ultimately defamiliarize and alienate the observer. Although the ideology critique is plausible, the anecdote's intrinsic function is to present defamiliarization effects created by physical shock. To be sure, the choice of the example cannot be put down to mere coincidence, but its ideological function is duplicitous. In keeping with the physiological empiricism derived from Locke, Burke insists that the boy's terror was not based on any prior association of ideas. Though it is evident to modern readers that empirical darkness is not the same idea as either the colorist or the racial category of blackness that mobilizes interpretations of pigmentation, physiognomy, and consequently cultural identity, for Burke's purposes the concepts of blackness and darkness "are much the same," except that "blackness is a more confined idea" (144). Effectively, the early focus on physiology in the *Enquiry* is later matched by a radical anti-epistemology. The boy is literally blindsided. If we are to take Burke at his word, the boy's response is precisely *not* the learned racism that comes from hearing negative stereotypes about Africans. Of course, this is hard to believe, but if we take this denial of association at face value, the racial nature of the response is relegated to metaphysics even as it is reaffirmed by optics. Learned racism is replaced by a priori horror. If we can call this racism, it is of a metaphysical kind, one that puzzlingly would have—or ought to have—elicited the same response if the viewed object had been a black Madonna from medieval France or a badly burned fire victim.

While the example of Cheselden's boy—Foucault's "man born blind restored to light"—is fundamental to Burke's anti-epistemology, it is one of several revealing illustrations concerning the concealment of cultural terror at the sublime's very origin. A little earlier, there is the claim that "those despotic governments, which are founded on the passion of men, and principally upon the passion of fear, keep their chief as much as may be from the public eye" (59). This reference to the unviewable source of despotic power suggests Montesquieu's influence.[7] Both Persia and Turkey were candidates for Montesquieu's orientalist construction of despotism, and as Alain Grosrichard's book shows, many popular seventeenth- and eighteenth-century discussions of political despotism were based on popular travel narratives such as Sir John Chardin's *Voyages in Persia*. Accounts of despotic terror as revealed through the practice of abacination, or punitive blinding, in Persia surface in Chardin's text.[8] Chardin provides a compelling example of the association of power with vision and terror with the catastrophic denial of vision. Burke may have been aware of Chardin, but lacking such evidence, it is best to consider the relevance of the example on its own terms.[9] The implications of the scene of blinding described by Chardin are crucial to Grosrichard's analysis of Montesquieu and likewise to the focus of Burke's aesthetic manifesto:

> The King issues a written command to blind a particular child, and this command is delegated to the first comer (as in Persia there is no official executioner). The officer goes to the gate of the Seraglio where this child can be found, and proclaiming his arrival on behalf of the King, demands to meet with the particular young prince in question and ensure his well-being. The command is soon broadcasted throughout the Seraglio, provoking sobs and cries. However, soon enough, the child has to be handed over. The Eunuchs bring him to the cruel messenger who throws them the writ, or the *lettre de cachet*. Getting on the ground, the officer seizes the child and stretches him out lengthwise on his lap, face upwards, holding his head down with the left hand. Then with one hand he opens the child's eyelids, while with the other he takes his dagger by its tip and extracts the pupils one by one in their entirety, taking care not to disfigure them, in the manner that one might shell a walnut. He puts them in his handkerchief and carries them to the King.[10]

In this example of surveillance the despot is himself deemed unviewable (as asserted in *Vathek*) but omniscient. Grosrichard rightly suggests that in this paradigmatic example we encounter a despotic regime "where orders are 'blindly' obeyed, and the blind man is the emblematic figure of the subject."[11] While Chardin makes the blinding an emblem of the perpetual obedience of the subject, Burke's anecdote of Cheselden's boy suggests its chiasmic opposite. The newly sighted boy does not suffer the blinding gaze of the despot of natural causes. Instead, by being granted sight, he undergoes the reverse of abacination. With his cataracts surgically couched, the boy emerges from the proverbial black box a resolutely empiricist subject. Entering the domain of sight, he later expresses great horror when gazing at a "negro woman," perhaps because she is visible as the despot's trace, even as the despot—who can here stand for slavery or obscurity or blindness—remains hidden from sight. The complementary effect makes the African servant, or more likely slave, function as an impotent antitype to the omnipotent oriental despot, and thus as a catalyst for "occidental" subject construction. The subject is caught between the oriental despot and the African slave, experiencing them as aesthetic equivalents, extremes of power and abjection, respectively.

The example of Cheselden's boy reaffirms Frances Ferguson's characterization of Burke's empiricism and subjectivism as a combination that is "caught between a completely nonsubjective (nonidealist) scientism on the one hand and a completely subjective irrationalism on the other."[12] On the search for other examples of anti-epistemology, or vision *despite* abacination, Burke borrows from Joseph Spence's account of the Scottish poet (appropriately named Blacklock) who was blinded by contracting smallpox as an infant. Thomas Blacklock demonstrates against all expectations how "few men blessed with the most perfect sight [could] describe visual objects with more spirit and justness than this blind man" (168–69).[13] Yet another example is provided by the celebrated blind Lucasian Professor of Mathematics at Cambridge University, Nicholas Saunderson, who could lecture on optics. Blinded anti-epistemology, whether produced by natural causes or despotic governments, reinforces the normalization of the pathological in the case of Cheselden's boy as a physiological a priori rather than as a weak culturalist afterthought.[14]

There are many such formal repetitions of type and antitype in the fictions of levantinization, where agency and subjection are mutually opposed. In the substantial section on "Power," added to the second edition of 1759, Burke claims to know of "nothing sublime which is not some modification of power . . . pain is always inflicted by a power in some way superior, because we never submit to pain willingly" (64–65).[15] He illustrates these remarks with a long discussion of the sublimity of Job's blind submission to that most oriental archtyrant, God.[16] Burke explains that terror and "*natural* power" are allied in the respect commanded by political and military leaders. For this reason "sovereigns are frequently addressed with the title of *dread majesty*" (67). The sublime is a relation between despotic power and blind abjection. Being a tyrant can make one sublime in others' eyes, but that cannot prevent the tyrant's submission to an even superior force.

Before Burke, the relationship of despotism to the sublime was described by resort to examples from either the battlefield or monumental architecture. In the celebrated essays on the pleasures of the imagination, Addison marvels at Semiramis, who "could accomplish so great works, with such a prodigious multitude of labourers." Discussing Semiramis going to battle, the Babylonian hanging gardens, the Tower of Babel, the Egyptian pyramids, and the Great Wall of China, Addison says, "everything that is majestic, imprints an awfulness and reverence on the mind of the beholder, and strikes in with the natural greatness of the soul." Shaftesbury too had suggested that colossal size was the primary attribute of a sublime monument. Again, number, measure, and intensity overcome qualitative distinctions, suggesting the simple infinity of what Kant later calls "the mathematical sublime."[17]

According to Andrew Ashfield and Peter de Bolla, the discourse of the sublime is "a technical discourse of the subject that bridges the gap between aesthetic pleasure and ethical action."[18] As an anti-epistemology revealing the mechanisms of subjective coercion rather than those of rational choice, the sublime is a precursor to the psychoanalytical interpretation of politics. By demonstrating the pathological within the normative, theories of sublimity unite experience and ontology. Emerging from darkness into the bright light of vision, the boy experiences terror at an uncomfortable proximity but, according to Burke's theory, could have experienced "delight" at a greater remove. Delight is Burke's technical term for the relief from pain that is not the same as positive pleasure. In the oscillation between newly found vision and its possible collapse back into an originary abacination, it is therefore possible for the boy to experience the aesthetic remnant of terror as a normalizing ethical process. The combination of the viewing subject and the terrifying object creates two related psychotropic phenomena: the perceptible sublime and the barely perceptible abject. The contingent black body, as the barely perceptible residue of horror, is a "subliminal" and abjected figure of repression within the subject, even as the "supraliminal" process of the perceptible sublime results in the provisional erection of the subject-ego. Rather than exaggerate the agency of the black slave woman in the text and read her psychoanalytically as a maternal trace, her abjection by an unrevealed source—slavery perhaps—shows her lack of political agency.[19]

Recognizing the impact of oedipal as well as preoedipal readings, W. J. T. Mitchell has argued that the *Enquiry* finishes with two mutually contestatory notions. A metaphorical sublime of obscurity and darkness dominates the first part, whereas a metonymical sublime of feeling and verbal excess return in the final sections. The metaphorical sublime is characterized as false and French through Burke's accusatory theatricalization; the metonymical sublime, according to Mitchell, represents an exposition of Longinus as true and English.[20] However, it is uncertain if the true/false contrast is one that ultimately matters for Burke, as sublime value is ascertained by the effectiveness of the performance. Similarly, the contextual goals create the appropriate Burkean polemic that could just as easily be reversed, as happens so often, both in the *Reflections* and the speeches on the Hastings trial. Articulating abysmal terror and semantic excess, the oriental figurations in the *Enquiry* encompass both types of sublimity. Limning his favored trope of obscurity, Burke alleges: "Almost all the heathen temples were dark. Even in the barbarous temples of the Americans at this day, they keep their idol in a dark part of the hut, which is consecrated to his worship. For this purpose too the druids performed all their ceremonies in the bosom of the darkest woods, and in the shade of the oldest and most spreading oaks" (59). All religion has some component of fear, and "false" religion that of fear only (70). In fact, at moments such as these, Burke's metaphorical definition of the sublime is indistinguishable from his account of false religion. The handsomely illustrated seven-volume encyclopedia of world religion by Bernard Picart entitled *The Ceremonies and Religious Customs of the Idolatrous Nations* (translated 1733–41) comes to mind as one of Burke's likely sources of information on religious anthropology. One of the plates in the volume that seems especially representative of Burke's insistence on the conjunction of physical darkness and idolatrous religions is a fantastic rendition of Hindu worship (see Fig. 17). Collocating idols in dark altars with numerous "fakirs" in postures of mortification and penance under the acreage of a large banyan tree, the image brings up the same generalized obscurity that Burke finds in a variety of "heathen" religions. Later, in the *Reflections*, Burke accuses the Revolutionaries of idolatry despite iconoclasm, as they sacrifice "to the idol of public credit" (8:90).[21] Forced to give some quarter to the Revolutionaries, he acknowledges that heredity is "too much idolized by creeping sycophants and the blind, abject admirers of power" (8:103). He implies, therefore, that the correct approach to politics lies somewhere between blind idolatry and drastic iconoclasm.

Figure 17 Bernard Picart, *Various Pagodas, or Penitence of the Fakirs*, in Bernard Picart, *Cérémonies et coûtumes religieuses de tous les peuples du monde* (1728). (British Library, London)

If the figures of darkness and the threat of the despotic eye suggest the metaphorical sublime, the metonymical sublime is introduced to the reader by way of the notion of "oriental" languages. In his concluding remarks in part 5, Burke reiterates the link between the passions and the oriental attributes of the sublime by commenting on the deficient strength of the "polished" languages in relation to the "great force and energy of expression" contained in "the oriental tongues, and in general the languages of most unpolished people" (176). Epic also suggests imprecise passions and oriental terror, leading to the identification of Homer as an oriental writer (18). According to this view, "orientals" feel more even if they cannot express themselves as precisely. Locke's *Essay* too speaks of the oriental tongues, with their supposed profusion of figures, as passionately imprecise in the manner of the sublime.[22]

Burke's preoccupation is with obscurity, and blinding is a specific manner of creating that distancing effect. At its most banal, the sublime is an unwanted physical shock, a denial of expectations. Seeing black-ness as a "partial darkness," Burke sees "black bodies as so many *va-cant spaces* dispersed among the objects we view" (147; emphasis mine). By this definition, the black woman is sheer absence and therefore re-inforces the discovery of the sublime as anti-epistemology. The hy-pothesis concerning blackness is backed up by physiologism, with ex-amples of ocular reaction: "when the eye lights on one of these vacuities [vacant spaces], after having been kept in some degree of tension by the play of adjacent colours upon it, it suddenly falls into a relaxation; out of which it suddenly recovers by a convulsive spring" (147). There are other illustrations of the subject's self-recovery after false reassurance, including the experience of trying to sit on a chair that is lower than ex-pected and that of inadvertently taking an extra step when descending a flight of stairs (147).[23] The blinded subject is a puny opponent when placed in relation to the unviewable despot, who is obscure in person as well as by principle. But safe from the despot's clutches, the English aesthetician can experience a frisson of "delight" precisely through con-templating the despot's *dread majesty* and the subject's near effacement. By this token, "heathens," "barbarous Americans," "druids," and sub-jects of "despotic governments," including the blind, are deemed able to experience the sublime more naturally. But when political terror comes too close to home, it can no longer be countenanced with aesthetic equanimity. Instead, it arouses horror and revulsion. An older and more conservative Burke repudiates his youthful enthusiasm for terror when he hears of the French royal family being forcibly brought back to Paris from Versailles during the October days. In this world turned upside down, one of several graphic comparisons, the spectacle resembled "a procession of American savages, entering into Onondaga after some of their murders called victories and leading into hovels hung round with scalps their captives" (8:117).

However, the pain upon seeing blackness is the shock of absence in relation to the surfeit experienced from seeing too many colors. Pain as an effect of oriental visual stimuli was already suggested earlier in the century. When Pope sent Galland's *Arabian Nights* to Bishop Atter-bury, he received a caustic response criticizing its extravagant stylistic machinery and absurd contrivances. Atterbury too talks about the eye as a hypersensitive sphincter that can register pain upon viewing ori-ental visions: "They are to me like odd paintings on Indian Screens, which at first glance may surprise and please a little; when you fix your eyes intently upon them, they appear so extravagant, disproportionate, and monstrous, that they give a judicious eye pain, and make him seek for relief from some other object." Here the bishop already seems to have had Burke's empiricist eye, except that he was arguing for a temperate Britishness in the face of an excessive Orient rather than ambivalently embracing its implications as Burke would. Darkness is the antitype to oriental aesthetic excess, just as the African woman seems in a strange structural equivalence to the despot. Darkness was concomitantly a favored trope of oriental tales. According to one supporter of this kind of fiction, when hearing about the characters in oriental tales, readers "naturally tremble for their fate, with the same anxious concern, as [they] should for a friend wandering, in a dark night, amidst torrents and precipices." [24]

Given this logic of pleasurable bondage and physiological shock in the oriental tale and the aesthetics of the sublime, the implications of decapitation as a topos are spectacular but unsurprising. A story that was treated as laughable by Voltaire and Gibbon serves Burke's purposes as well. [25] In the introductory essay on taste, a monarch's direct knowledge of death impinges on sublime aesthetics. When the Turkish emperor, Muhammad II, was shown "a fine piece of a decollated head of St. John the Baptist" by the Venetian painter Gentile Bellini, he was dissatisfied because "the skin did not shrink from the wounded part of the neck" (20). Burke does not provide the conclusion to this episode from the Quattrocento, where the prince orders a slave beheaded so that the copy can be compared with a freshly produced original. Both copy and original—false sublime and sublime—are attempts to present the unpresentable. Success is determined by performance and, correspondingly, falsity by failure to perform. The logic of unpresentability demonstrates the irrelevance of *mimesis* or *representation* as a category of assessment. The decapitation—subliminally present even if unrepresented for those who know the story—reveals the sublime as a transportation system that begins in empiricist comparison of copy and original but ends in gothic abandonment. In the act of referring to an earlier beheading, the painter was representing unsuccessfully; on the other hand, the emperor in the act of reference eschews representation and instead redoubles the referent, with success. The bifurcated *logic* of *representation*—suggesting what Lyotard calls "the world *of* which one tells"—

has been replaced by the monist *practice* of *presentation,* concerning just "the world *in* which one tells," a world that cancels out all others.[26] In an act of sublime cancellation, the despot makes mimesis irrelevant even as his power dissolves aesthetics into the performance of absolute terror. Bellini, traumatized and fearful for his own life after witnessing the emperor's maniacal decapitation of the slave, asked after an appropriate interval if he could return home to Venice. The despot stayed where he was, redoubling the referent, at home, in the Orient.[27]

VISIONS OF FLIGHT

Like Bellini, Samuel Johnson also failed to represent adequately the sublime aspect of execution, although he encountered audience parody rather than despotic actualization. Johnson's only dramatic composition, *Irene,* features the same Turkish emperor, Muhammad II, and Irene, the fair Greek, who becomes his mistress at the fall of Constantinople and eventually suffers the beheading one comes to expect for this sultan's victims.[28] Irene's execution, originally represented by Johnson as an impending strangulation, misfired when the actress appeared with a bowstring round her neck and the audience merrily responded with "Murder! Murder!" Johnson struck out the passage, but it was the only performance of the play in his lifetime. In subsequent productions Irene went to her execution offstage.[29] This failed moment yet again shows the difficulty of *representing* the sublime, especially when it is associated with the raw power of the despot.[30]

Both orientalism and the sublime present genre difficulties. They are styles of presentation backed up by self-authorization and tautology. Paradoxically, both styles enabled a hitherto unprecedented democratization of taste. Jonathan Lamb summarizes this radical potential of the sublime well, describing its availability to "anyone capable of responding to its intensities, internalizing them, and then expressing them as one's own."[31] The oriental *tale*—as opposed to some monolithic version of orientalism as ideology—possesses similar possibilities. Discussing the generic status of *Rasselas,* Gwin Kolb finds that a bewildering multiplicity of options presented themselves to early classifiers. *Rasselas* was deemed to be "a 'moral tale,' a 'novel' (but not conforming to the ordinary pattern), a 'romance' (whose contents belie the connotations of its title), a 'satire,' and an 'eastern story' (or 'fable' or 'tale'). Later writers added such phrases as 'philosophical discourse,' 'philosophical romance,' 'classical romance,' 'oriental apologue,' and 'philosophic tale' to the list."[32] Indeed, in the manner of satirical or utopian fiction, the Ethiopian locale allows a moral fable about agency amongst an exotic but familiar people (the Monophysite Abyssinian Patriarchate was still Christian even though it had separated from the early Church upon rejecting the Council of Chalcedon in 451). It is likely that in this parable about agency, Johnson was playing with the etymology of Abyssinia as meaning "free and independent people."[33] Garbled rumors of an African Christian emperor on the other side of the traditional Muslim enemies of Europe provided romance material from medieval times. Depicted as a chivalric European king but colored black, the Ethiopian emperor known as the "Prester John" of legend is not all that different from Oroonoko. The pagan Oroonoko is more noble than his Christian enslavers. The Christian Rasselas in Johnson's fable, as a self-conscious moral agent, also resists the despotic injunction and liberates himself from imprisonment in a mountain palace. He then proceeds to live an anonymous daily life in cosmopolitan Cairo and Alexandria.

The lack of novelistic realism in Johnson's version of Abyssinia and Egypt has, in the past, led to fruitless debate about the story's fraught universalism amid insufficient particularities.[34] Although the author's awareness of Ethiopian history was extensive—early in his career he translated the Portuguese Jesuit Jeronimo Lobo's *Voyage to Abyssinia* from the French—he could not, or chose not, to render the particularities of East and North Africa, instead crossing Turks with Arabs. Rather, the Cham's levantinization involves romance periphrasis to set the scene: "On one part were flocks and herds feeding in the pastures, on another all the beasts of chase frisking in the lawns; the spritely kid was bounding on the rocks, the subtle monkey frolicking in the trees, and the solemn elephant reposing in the shade. All the diversities of the world were brought together, the blessings of nature were collected, and its evils extracted and excluded" (9). Compared to the realism he promotes in the introduction to *Voyage to Abyssinia*, Johnson opts for clichés that resemble the "Romantick Absurdities and Incredible Fictions" he rejects in the earlier work. Though there is nothing absurd in periphrasis, its simulation of received wisdom bypasses the open-ended empirical representations favored by novels. Clearly deliberate, the narrator is signaling that readers ought to put aside realist expectations for a moral vision. The tale involves a thought experiment and a different kind of prose from novel or travel narrative.[35]

As novelistic particularity is lacking in *Rasselas,* many interpreters criticize or uphold its purported universalist humanism.[36] As one of the most interpreted eighteenth-century literary works, the tale has served the agenda of neoclassicists as well as those who wish to unmask that agenda. Was Johnson dressing a moral tale in oriental garb, or does the locale have a more substantial function? Burke, who reviewed *Rasselas* for *The Annual Register* in 1759, does not pick up on the tale's nuanced interaction with his own obsessions concerning despotism and the sublime, instead asserting that, "in this novel the moral is the principal object, and the story is a mere vehicle to convey the instruction."[37] Efforts that focus on the purported universality of *Rasselas*—whether in support or criticism of that claim—mistakenly assume that the tale's orientalism is superficial. Commentators routinely fail to recognize that as with the sublime, the garb radically enables the function. Dismissing the oriental as fancy dress would mean leaving the tale's emperor with no clothes. The philosophizing or allegorizing function in *Rasselas* derives from levantinization. Demonstrating the negation of particularities into an orientalist syncretism, *Rasselas* reconfirms agency (and its inverse, despotism) as *presentational* categories whose validity is determined by the adequacy of performance, in the manner of the sublime.[38]

The prince's escape is an inconclusive act of rebellious self-assertion. The moral doubt that drove Rasselas to leave is unresolved at story's end even as the transgressive implications of the escape are never addressed. However, the escapees have made a choice of death even as they pursue the bloodless intrigue of an appropriate "choice of life." Francisco Alvares's travel narrative, *The Prester John of the Indies* (1520), mentions that the punishment for princes who escaped mountain confinement was either death or blinding. Tropes of blinding are used by Alvares to describe the process of royal succession, the darkness near the confinement of the princes, and the punishment for those who attempted to enter the mountain gates where they were held.[39] Ellis Cornelia Knight's sequel to the tale, *Dinarbas,* builds on the punitive consequences of escaping the royal confinement in Abyssinia that narratives such as Alvares's emphasize. In Knight's sequel, Rasselas, who is after all "the fourth son of the mighty Emperor," eventually inherits the throne after the fratricidal wars between his older brothers Zengis, Sarza, and Menas. But before this eventuality, Knight has the emperor condemn Rasselas's danger-ous disobedience as having set a bad example to his more malevolent brothers. However, recognizing Rasselas's moral superiority, the em-peror pardons him in his letter inviting him back to Abyssinia.[40]

These contexts, from both before and after, enable a clearer discus-sion of the submerged presence of blinding in *Rasselas*. Monarchical surveillance and authority are expressed through the trope of visual-ization. No stranger to idle reverie, Rasselas's unmitigated leisure is matched by grandiose plans of philanthropy. Rasselas is a living parody of the enlightened despot, the Enlightenment's benevolent counterpart to the Oriental antitype: "His chief amusement was to picture to him-self that world which he had never seen; to place himself in various conditions; to be entangled in imaginary difficulties, and to be engaged in wild adventures: but his benevolence always terminated his project in the relief of distress, the detection of fraud, the defeat of oppression, and the diffusion of happiness" (17-18). Rasselas visualizes problems as well as their solutions; his actions, if they can be deemed that, consist of imagining adequate responses to situations that themselves arise from either a deficit or a surfeit of visualization. Detached spectation prom-ises power and yet fails to deliver the goods. Before Rasselas leaves the Happy Valley with Imlac's help, he explores the possibility of Daedalian flight with the help of a resident artist. The prince's curiosity is piqued at possibly being "a philosopher furnished with wings," one who would know the intricacies of the world as it rolls beneath him. The plate from Francis Godwin's utopian fiction concerning a lunar voyage is an appropriate visual accompaniment for these early modern fantasies of flight (Fig. 18). A bird-assisted flight machine is also featured in Samuel Brunt's *A Voyage to Cacklogallinia* (1727). Johnson's fable satirizes these fantasies of domination. Rasselas is a doublet of curiosity and credulity. Tempted by the prospect of viewing and knowing as "pendent specta-tor," the Abyssinian prince listens avidly to the inventor's promise that he could "survey with equal security the marts of trade, and the fields of battle" (25-26). As D'Alembert says in his introduction to the *Encyclo-pédie*, "the encyclopedic arrangement of knowledge places the philoso-pher at a vantage point . . . whence he can perceive the principal arts and sciences simultaneously. From there he can see at a glance the objects of their speculations and the operations which can be made on these ob-jects. . . . It is a kind of world map which shows the principal countries,

Figure 18 Bird-Assisted Aerial Flight, in Francis Godwin, *The Man in the Moone: Or, a Discourse of the Voyage Thither* (1638). (British Library, London)

their position and their mutual dependence, and the road that leads directly from one to another." This stratospheric subject-position, of the cosmopolitan philosopher floating above the cares of the world is subsequently repeated by the introduction of Abbé de Raynal's *Histoire des deux Indes*.[41] As a scientist's desire for knowledge—like Foucault's "foreign spectator in an unknown country"—the prince's curiosity is that of the scholar's disinterested equanimity or the enlightened despot's urge to use his absolute power to do good.

However, credulity follows curiosity. Rasselas's naïve and mimetic desire is for this new technology to be universally accessible. Such plans are criticized by the artist as dangerous: " 'If men were all virtuous,' returned the artist, 'I should with great alacrity teach them all to fly. But what would be the security of the good, if the bad could at pleasure invade them from the sky? Against an army sailing through the clouds neither walls, nor mountains, nor seas, could afford any security. A flight of northern savages might hover in the wind, and light at once with irresistible violence upon the capital of a fruitful region that was rolling under them'" (27–28). This famous reversal is often taken as Johnson's little parable about the inherent dangers of technology or the primacy of moral philosophy over the amoral manipulability of science. The failed flight attempt may superficially favor such a reading, especially as the inventor is fished out by Rasselas, who finds him "half dead with terrour and vexation" after he falls into the lake (28).[42] According to that hermeneutic separation, the artist would have thought about the merits and demerits of the new technology even though he has not, or at least not yet, made the engineering breakthrough; Rasselas, alternately possessed with the twin attributes of credulity and curiosity, wants open access to the technology even as he is naïve about the sociopolitical implications of the innovation. But is vision separable from projection? Visualization unites the physiological aspect of sight with the speculative aspect. The projector's subsequent application could result in realization or failure, and on that outcome depends the projector's moral probity. To accept this episode as moral instruction, the reader has to adopt an insight already communicated to us as the artist's. Though the artist has apparently gauged the philosophical meaning of his invention, assuming its success, his credibility soon takes a literal and symbolic ducking. The ethicist who convincingly argues for the potential dangers and necessary secrecy of the technology he has yet to perfect is ridiculed for his inadequate craftsmanship. Johnson's text does not so clearly— despite attempts to read it that way—allow for the separability of the moral from the fable.

At this point in the tale, Rasselas looks for various escapes from the Happy Valley. The technique of flight is promised him on the condition of secrecy, but not delivered because of the aspiring aviator's incompetence. Written when the technology of flight is pure projection, the fable reflects ironically on the projection of science as an objective correlative of humanism. The aviator is no different from the mad astronomer at the end of the story, who thought he could control the elements but was eventually disabused of the notion. Therefore, when we look forward to the unfolding of the narrative, the performative failure of the "Dissertation on Flying" undercuts the "Dissertation on Poetry" that follows it. Indeed, why is it that if both episodes are this similar, they are often both interpreted so differently? Imlac's status as the enunciator of the *speculum principi*—and as the party's travel agent—makes his pronouncements more serious, of course, than that of the failed aviator's. But the suspended resolution of the tale suggests that Imlac's role is open-ended and could very well end in the manner of the aviator's.

We might say that the aviator's projection is oriented toward a symbolic abacination. He stands like Burke's sublime spectator, on the edge of the yawning precipice, projecting imprecise passions; as a result, he falls and is found abjected at the bottom, "half dead with terrour and vexation." Yet the aviator is also Rasselas's instrument, his human telescope. Rasselas as benign despot is meant to be served by all his employees; therefore, the aviator is also a projection of Rasselas's visualization of princely power. The fantasy of flight is, by extension, Rasselas's dream. The lesson, then, is not just the aphoristic one of the ethics of technology, but also that of the subjective schism produced by the oriental sublime. Surveillance and abacination go hand in hand, as do potential power and actual abjection; the subject's attempt at freedom is itself revelatory of the "slavery" of the subject to the sublime. We are sublime to those who submit to us, and we submit to that which can destroy us, thereby respecting it as sublime.

This is the logic of Johnson's well-known tale in *The Rambler* that features Seged, the emperor of Ethiopia. The emperor begins the tale in absolute mastery, issuing a despotic injunction to his craven subjects: "Seged, lord of Ethiopia, to the inhabitants of the world: To the sons of presumption, humility and fear; and to the daughters of sorrow, content and acquiescence." The supreme monarch, who commands all his armies to the trepidation of the world, declares ten days of uninterrupted happiness at the pleasure palace of Dambea. After suffering various countereffects to his injunction to happiness—from witnessing the fawning and hypocrisy of various courtiers to dreams of "inundation" and "imaginary irruption into his kingdom"—Seged realizes that "discontent and melancholy were not to be frighted away by the threats of authority, and that pleasure would only reside where she was exempted from controul." Unexpectedly, this lesson is to be followed by a far more bitter one. Seged suffers the illness and death of his daughter. The tale ends with the moral that "no man hereafter may presume to say, 'This day shall be a day of happiness.'" Seged the despot, himself sublime to his subjects, is humbled by an even greater force, the cruel fate that snatches away his daughter.[43]

While the aviator's episode brings us to the structure of the oriental sublime by logical paradox, Imlac's dissertation on poetry states this fixation in the baldest possible terms. Imlac says, "To a poet nothing can be useless. Whatever is beautiful, and whatever is dreadful, must be familiar to his imagination: he must be conversant with all that is awfully vast or elegantly little" (42). This passage echoes Burke's *Enquiry*, as do some comments that follow concerning the awful beauty of nature. However, the tenor of Imlac's reflections on the nature of the poet proceeds upward to the disconnected and omnivoyant spectatorial position, just as the aviator's or D'Alembert's: "He must divest himself of the prejudices of his age or country; he must consider right and wrong in their abstracted and invariable state; he must disregard present laws and opinions, and rise to general and transcendental truths, which will always be the same . . . he must write as the interpreter of nature, and the legislator of mankind, and consider himself as presiding over the thoughts and manners of future generations; as a being superiour to time and place" (44-45). The verbs in the passage—divest, disregard, rise, preside—along with the tag of the poet as "a being superiour to time and place," are projections of an impossible hovering, potentially satirical, coming as it does on the heels of the aviator's plunge into the lake. It requires a special kind of critical self-abacination to take this passage at face value and ignore the aviator, reading Imlac as Johnson's literal mouthpiece or even as an ironical sage, at the same time accepting the ducking of the aviator as a kind of rough justice. Imlac and the aviator are both in structurally identical positions, as servants of Rasselas's benign will. Both of them provide chimerical fantasies under the mock-scholarly label of dissertation. Both goals of flight generalize and universalize in literal or symbolic fashion—in the manner of Rasselas wanting to "picture to himself that world which he had never seen." The fantasy of flight remains projection for quite some time to come. Its more immediate index is the omnivoyance exercised by the oriental despot. The central theme in *Rasselas* can be glossed, therefore, as the fusion of both contrasted meanings of Daedalian "flight": the creative power of invention, aerial travel, and the surveillance that goes along with it—the despot's—and the sense of escape from an undesirable or dangerous situation—the fugitive's. The royal party is always fleeing its presentness, even as it constantly projects universal power over the world that it presumes to master. Flight *from* melds into flight *over*, and escapable conditions are fantasized into masterly domains as inactive drones try to become meaningful agents through oversight. To be an agent here is to be benevolent despot; the final chapter again parodies this outcome with reference to Pekuah's goal of being prioress at St. Anthony's, Nekayah's desire to "found a college of learned women," and Rasselas's wish for "a little kingdom, in which he might administer justice in his own person, and *see all the parts of government with his own eyes*" (175–76; my emphasis). However, as the narrator laconically adds, the prince "could never fix the limits of his dominion, and was always adding to the number of his subjects" (176).

In keeping with the constraints of the oriental sublime, *Rasselas* and its analogues reiterate the mutual imbrication of bondage fantasies with escape fantasies, fear of death with love of life, indeed the coimplication of blindness and insight. Freedom and slavery are false universals, themselves extrapolated from an imaginary scene involving the oriental monarch who can blind, or the would-be monarch, the prince, who could be blinded in turn. As Imlac earlier tells the story of his life, Rasselas, as African prince, naïvely asks Imlac the reason for European power: " 'By what means,' said the prince, 'are the Europeans thus powerful? or why, since they can so easily visit Asia and Africa for trade or conquest, cannot the Asiaticks and Africans invade their coasts, plant colonies in their ports, and give laws to their natural princes? The same wind that carries them back would bring us thither' " (46–47). Rasselas's question is similar to the one of technology that he posed to the artist. Imlac's answer is unsatisfyingly brief. He asserts that Europeans are wiser and that knowledge will always dominate over ignorance (and, if the aviator's projection is to be followed, evil over good). Stressing the possibility of inherent reversibility, Imlac worries that what the Occident is doing to the Orient can, in a flash, be done by the Orient to the Occident. Visions of flight by the late eighteenth century were also just as much satirized as they were fantastically imagined. For instance, a print in the extensive balloon literature of the late eighteenth century, *Montgolfier in the Clouds: Constructing of Air Balloons for the Grand Monarque* (1784), inflects flight with colonial mastery even more explicitly than in the manner discussed by the aviator (Fig. 19). A caricatured Frenchman expresses his dreams of making England and the rest of the world a colony

Figure 19
Montgolfier in the Clouds: Constructing of Air Balloons for the Grand Monarque (1784). (British Library, London)

of France: "O by gar! dis be de grande invention—Dis will immortalize my King, my Country, and myself; We will declare de War against our ennemi; we will make des English quake, by gar: We will inspect their camp, we will intercept their Fleet, and we will set fire to their Dockyards: And by gar, we will take de Gibraltar in de air balloon, and when we have Conquered d'English, den we conquer d'other countrie, and make them all colonie to de Grand Monarque." This extreme Francophobia is allied with a fear of French imperial designs on English sovereignty. Or, as discussed shortly, during Burke's impeachment proceedings against Warren Hastings, the Occident strangely becomes the best historical example of what was until then deemed oriental despotism.[44]

Johnson's fixation on despotism also concerns the fantasy of internment as it relates to interment. J. C. D. Clark, the dean of eighteenth-century Jacobite studies, has suggested provocatively that Johnson felt himself to be "an internal exile" in Britain because of hidden Jacobite sympathies. (Witness here the conundrum of "internal exile" as it was coined and experienced in various despotic regimes.) Alan Liu asserts that "the embalmed signifier" is key to the tale. If so, the central absent signifier in the story is the emperor himself, whose injunction Rasselas is fleeing even as he attempts to replicate that state of power.[45] It is for the safety of the emperor that Rasselas has been interned in the Happy Valley, and it is the emperor who has the power and the knowledge to reveal the location of the interred treasures in the palace's pillars and columns. Burial remains Johnson's hidden focus, even though it is necessary to be suspicious of Boswell's assertion that the tale was written in a single week to make enough money to pay for Johnson's mother's funeral. The palace in the Happy Valley anticipates this gothic theme of "private galleries," "subterranean passages," and "unsuspected cavities" (11). The royals have indeed been buried alive in the Happy Valley, and their escape is a flight from death itself—inside the tomb—to life— the world outside. However, if their thoughts inside were focused outside, once they do get out their reflections turn back. If the royal party lived their inter(n)ment in the womb of the Happy Valley, they have to confront its meaning only once they leave it. The theme of entombment—yet another enactment of madness or blindness that was one of Johnson's phobias—recurs in the center of the narrative with the episode of Pekuah's abduction outside the Pyramids which the others have entered, and as the tale draws to a close, the royal party enters the catacombs and "roved with wonder through the labyrinth of subterranean passages, where the bodies were laid in rows on either side" (168). This episode leads to a philosophical disquisition on the nature of the soul, and Nekayah decides to abandon the quest for the choice of life in order to "think only on the choice of eternity" (175). Beginning with Ethiopia and ending with Egypt, the story flows along the course of the Nile— the Father of the Waters and Father Time himself—from its fantasized source to its conclusion. The absent emperor looms large in the moral parable but can never be accessed by the royal party. This endless search for a meaning is because access to the master signifier is not possible. Just as the vizier becomes a placeholder for the despot in the malevolent aspect, moral agency in its benign form shifts inexorably from Rasselas to Imlac and perhaps to the astronomer by the conclusion, just as much as it also shifts from Nekayah to Pekuah.[46] Meaning has to be deferred, as the emperor is the end of time for the royals—the reason why they live pointlessly, as a choice of life was imposed upon them before they could make one for themselves. The more they avoid the question of their preassigned and enforced inter(n)ment in the valley, the more the emperor's power, which is the power to blind, is proven beyond doubt. Returning home is to deliver oneself up to charges of treason. It is tantamount to suicide or at least voluntary self-abacination. Yet the fantasized, indeed tantalizing nature of the impending return (the party may go home after the inundation recedes, we are led to believe) suggests an impossible outcome: that Rasselas may look the emperor in the eye.

Choosing, the paradigmatic function in language, commits choosers to one of several options, hence canceling the totality of choices that were hitherto present. However, each moment of choosing gets linked syntagmatically to the next one, creating a symbolic "sentence" of entailed choices plotting the meaningful trajectory of a life. If the effect of the tale is to transcend choice toward choicelessness, it creates a version of the oriental and the sublime. Despite their vague inaccuracies, Abyssinia and Egypt become a presentational mechanism for "moral truth." The impending choice at the end of the tale makes for a blockage, a sublime impasse. Here is the anti-epistemology of the royal party. Are they potential despots, or are they about to be blinded when they return to Abyssinia? This deferment of authority reaffirms the fantasy of oriental despotism.

Perhaps the answer to the deferment of authority is found at the end of Johnson's *Journey to the Western Islands*, where Johnson remarks on the realization of the seemingly impossible: "after having seen the deaf taught arithmetick, who would be afraid to cultivate the Hebrides?"[47] This strangely optimistic conclusion to the *Journey* connects the miraculousness of teaching language to the deaf at Braidwood College, where "they hear with the eye," with the possible repopulation of the Highlands. Symbolically, this is reverse abacination, empiricism as negation. Through antiepistemology, like that of Cheselden's boy, the sublime despotism of history and circumstance can be converted into quotidian well-being. The counter to deafness is alphabetization and enumeration, the very act of reading performed by the deaf subject at the end of the tour of Scotland. Johnson's girl (the analogue to Cheselden's boy) quivers her fingers but doesn't write where the sum total shall stand. Language compensates for the blinding—or deafening—stroke of the despotic sublime. Burke's and Johnson's metonymical sublime generates a phase of continuity in relation to the severance created by the meta-phorical one; cultural literacy, visual or aural, follows the injunction of silence.

Beckford's uninhibited celebration of despotism concludes a logic begun by Burke and continued by Johnson's fable. The tropes of blinding, omnivoyance, and entombment also figure prominently in *Vathek*. The first paragraph of the tale features the caliph's baleful eye: "His figure was pleasing, and majestick; but when he was angry, one of his eyes became so terrible, that no person could bear to behold it; and the wretch upon whom it was fixed, instantly fell backward; and sometimes, expired. For fear, however, of depopulating his dominions, and making his palace desolate; he, but rarely, gave way to his anger."[48] The adjectival trajectory of the sentence ascends from the beautiful to the sublime: "pleasing . . . majestick . . . angry . . . terrible." The ascent of the modifiers, however, reaches ultimate unpresentability. As "no person could bear to behold" the monarch's gaze, it stands for the unviewable and indescribable sublime. The victims of the caliph's anger suffer dreadful effects. The gaze falls on a "wretch" who feels the literal volte-face and falls backward. From unviewability, the monarch can propel the chosen subject into unconsciousness or even death itself. However, this possibility is acted upon infrequently. In the manner of the nuclear sublime, the caliph's power is too great to exercise on his subjects. Power in abeyance is that much more sublime. The monarch, aware of his own power over others, refrains from depopulating his dominions and losing his minions, without whose subjection he is no monarch at all. The sublime energy of the caliph's eye is another version of Burke's "dread majesty."

Beckford got the "terrible eye" straight from Barthélémy D'Herbelot's description of the historical Vathek in the *Bibliothèque Orientale*. D'Herbelot's description emphasizes blinding: "the Caliph Vathek had such a baleful eye that even on his deathbed he directed an angry glare at one of his attendants who had failed him in some way. The man lost consciousness and collapsed on another attendant near him. By an extraordinary coincidence, it so happened that when [Vathek] expired, and when his face had been covered by a shroud, a weasel crept up from underneath, and tore out the very eye whose glance had been so unsustainable."[49] The caliph's baleful stare is reversed by natural causes after his death, when the very eye that had the power to kill is gouged out by an animal. D'Herbelot describes a blinding of a body that can no longer feel the experience it had inflicted on many others. The source of abjection abjected, the caliph's body is further dispossessed of the eye that once expressed his malevolent agency. The ready dispossession of eye by weasel resembles the theme of the reversibility of power mused on by Rasselas. The eye is the fetish and the conduit of power, a master trope that Beckford elaborates after this initial suggestion from D'Herbelot. Similarly, Clara Reeve's Charoba, after her feminist triumph over Gebirus the Metaphequian, is blinded by a serpent bite, whereupon she dies, acknowledging the same process of the slayer slain that Gebirus had already predicted.[50]

However, the visual is not automatically powerful. An impotent aesthetics of the beautiful parallels vision's more potent politics of the sublime. For instance, the visual faculties, in Vathek's hedonistic establishment at Samarah, constitute the third of five palaces devoted to the senses and are presented as devoid of the implications of power. The palace of vision is called "THE DELIGHT OF THE EYES, or THE SUPPORT OF MEMORY." "Rarities collected from every corner of the earth were there found in such profusion, as to dazzle and confound, but for the order in which they were arranged" (3). Within the hedonistic realm vision is beautiful, balancing perspectivism, naturalism, and "the magick of opticks." Running the gamut from realism to trompe l'œil, Vathek's palace of sight serves the function of "gratify[ing] the curiosity of those who resorted to it, although he was not able to satisfy his own" (4). He shuts down the palaces of the senses when mourning the disappearance of the giaour. Dissatisfied with hedonism, Vathek reaches for the experience beyond sensory adequation and, more precisely, beyond exhibition.

Vathek, the despot, is in search of the sublime, an experience perforce unavailable in a museum. Hence his project of the insolent tower, one that earns the disapproval of heavenly observers. Vathek's antics are condemned by none other than "the great prophet Mahomet, whose Vicars the Caliphs are" (6). The prophet suspects Vathek of "the insolent curiosity of penetrating the secrets of heaven" (7). Correspondingly, in a sting operation authorized by the prophet, genii hasten the construction of the tower, adding two cubits overnight to every one cubit the caliph's workmen construct during the day. When built, the skyscraper activates another sublime reversal: "His pride arrived at its height, when having ascended, for the first time, the eleven thousand stairs of his tower, he cast his eyes below, and beheld men not larger than pismires; mountains, than shells; and cities, than bee-hives. The idea, which such an elevation inspired, of his own grandeur, completely bewildered him; he was almost ready, to adore himself; till, lifting his eyes upward, he saw the stars, as high above him, as they appeared, when he stood on the surface of the earth" (7–8). Through this diminution, the small is simply the loathsome. Men, who look small from a great height, are contemptible "pismires."[51] This miniaturization of the world—cities are beehives and even mountains are shells—momentarily erects the viewer as omnipotent because he is omnivoyant. However, the self-adoration is cut short when the despot reverses his gaze to the stars and devalues himself. In a moment of bewilderment, Vathek is humbled by the thought that there is a vantage point still just as far above his reach, implicitly that of the prophet in the seventh heaven who has been looking down on him without his knowledge. This sudden deflation after exaltation leads to self-consolation: "he consoled himself, however, for *this transient perception of his littleness*, with *the thought of being great in the eyes of others; and flattered himself, *that the light of his mind would extend, beyond the reach of his sight; and transfer to the stars the decrees of his destiny*" (8; emphases mine). A postsublime stability returns the megalomaniac to his own limited significance. The consolation prize, of being sublime to others, arrives on the heels of a traumatic encounter with a sublimity even greater than the despot's.

The ascent of the tower turns the despot into a subject with seigneurial rights. From the position of being the creator and consumer of desire, Vathek regresses to a precarious disequilibrium between pleasure and danger. The humbling of the experience at the tower top is repeated when the giaour sustains with no adverse consequences "one of the Caliph's angry and perilous glances" even though "his eyes were fixed on the terrible eye of the Prince" (11). First, the undecipherable sabers, furnished by the giaour, prick Vathek's desire for the Halls of Eblis. In keeping with the sublime's visual tropology, the writing on the sabers herald a future experience of acquisitive viewership: "we are the least of the wonders of a place, where all is wonderful; and deserving the *sight* of the first Potentate on earth" (19; my emphasis). These magical characters later transmogrify into the warning "Woe to the rash mortal," a warning that Vathek will not take kindly (20).

The Faustian contract with the giaour also resonates with some fustian. The Faustian narrative—or its exoticized equivalent entered into with genii that possess magical powers—is one of the hackneyed devices for the standard English and French oriental tale.[52] Vathek's deal with the giaour enables several twists of the plot. Beckford is satirizing the incompatibility of two worldviews, a medieval and a capitalist one. The sublime cannot be delivered through a contract, as that would imply the adequation and containment of the sublime, the equivalent of confining the ocean to a teacup. In any case, infantilized despots such as Vathek make for very poor contract keepers. Consistency, coherence, and even chivalric honor are strikingly absent from the monarch's dealings. Vathek, arbitrary, forgetful, and hedonistic, finds Protestant dogma, such as the triumph of principle and the deferral of reward, foreign to his nature. The despot pursues the immediate desire at the expense of its ultimate sentence. Hence, the giaour's agency increases as Vathek's influence diminishes. Correspondingly, the greater the giaour's insolence, and the more he flouts the protocols of deference toward the despot, the more injudiciously Vathek sacrifices long-term goals for current status.

The most bizarre image in the tale is that of the grand kicking scene, where the caliph and all his subjects are drawn inexorably into one vast movement of chasing the body of the giaour transformed into a ball (32–36). Some intriguing similarities link the giaour-kicking episode to the death of Beckford's great-grandfather, governor of Jamaica, who rolled down the stairs to his death after a long physical scuffle with other parliamentarians in the colonial assembly. By violating the esoteric contract between despot and magician, Vathek and his subjects choose the wrong scapegoat. This image, of a frenzied kickathon, reduces the sublime from referent to trope and from person to object. The author converts an ancestral trauma into a fictional joke. If Vathek, like Rasselas, is the figure of identification for the Western reader with the trappings of moral choice, the giaour is radically anti-identificatory, a figure of inadequation and a form of delirium. The giaour enables the dissolution of boundaries in violence and ecstatic possession. The disappearing ball is a paean to the radical expenditure of energy, and the giaour's boundlessness is the presentational inadequacy of the sublime itself.

The incident ends when Vathek cannot continue the chase into the abyss because "an *invisible agency* arrested his progress" and the crowd too returns to Samarah "without ever reflecting, that they had been impelled, by an *invisible power*, into the extravagance, for which they reproached themselves" (36; my emphasis). At this point, Vathek is confronted with the contractual stipulation that is the sublime's ridiculous antithesis: he sacrifices fifty boys into the abyss to placate the giaour, but the ebony portals of the Hall of Eblis disappear nonetheless, as a result of the giaour's perfidy. The encryption of a contractual plot within a sublime narrative leads from impasse to abyss in interpretive terms as well. The narrative engine sputters again for the hecatomb organized by Vathek's mother, Carathis, who as a Greek is a practitioner of judiciary astrology. The reader is given the frisson of amoral delight at the resulting carnage when the citizenry attempt to put out the fire. Vathek leaves Samarah, embarking on his expedition toward his architectural doom. Having begun with the stratospherically oriented tower, he ends eventually in the cavernous space of the infernal hall. Architectural motifs, as several critics have suggested, initiate a shift from inner character to the spatialization of subjectivity in the gothic imaginary. The Hall of Eblis points to the somber lines of Piranesi's *Carceri d'Invenzione* (1761), or the geometric repetition—characterized as "artificial infinity" by Burke's treatise—that is a feature of Islamic religious architecture.[53] We thereby witness in Beckford's orientalist gothic a transition from early modern despotism, as seen in Vathek's and Carathis's grotesque menagerie of one-eyed Africans, deaf-mutes, eunuchs, and cripples, to the bureaucratic fantasy of the disciplined body, underground but in a vast space, where all prisoners are formally indecipherable because all are morally equivalent. The court's surfeit of signification, through a combination of the beautiful and the metonymic sublime, is swept away by the metaphorical sublime of the Hall of Eblis.

However, the punishment at the ending cannot remove the impression of hedonistic excess described with an ironical tone that dominates most of the story. As Vijay Mishra argues, the sublime surfaces as discursive excess in *Vathek* because "the Other lacks any adequation in the existing discourses . . . were such an 'adequation' available, the program of orientalism itself would have collapsed."[54] The presentation of "lack of 'adequation'" in *Vathek* happens repeatedly. Carathis's consolatory advice shows this point in a minor way when she suggests to Vathek that the feat of deciphering the secret writing on the sabers is simply infra dig rather than beyond Vathek's power. The royal menagerie frequently exhibits debased versions of inadequation in the form of sensory and linguistic deprivation. Linguistic inadequacy is signaled as the enigma of gesture and mien, indeed the grotesquerie of face as rhetorical *figure*. The eunuch enables these shifts and alienation effects as a result of his traditional role of monstrous exceptionality. For instance, Bababalouk's name in the tale, which alludes to Voltaire's oriental characters, Balbec and Bababec, also parodies a stuttering impotence.[55] Faced with the prospect of the antigastronomic banquet in the desert, "Vathek made *wry faces* at so savage a repast; and Bababalouk answered them with *shrugs and contortions*" (88; my emphasis). The story eventually leads, of course, to the single affect of resentful rage expressed by the faces of all denizens of the infernal regions. Meanwhile, Carathis's practice of keeping her ghoulish treasures "under the guard of fifty female Negroes, mute, and blind of the right eye," is one more example of monstrous inadequation. The grotesque "Negresses" "squinted in the most amiable manner, from the only eye they had; and leered with exquisite delight, at the skulls and skeletons, which Carathis had drawn forth from her cabinets; whose key, she intrusted to no one: all of them making contortions, and uttering a frightful jargon, but very amusing to the Princess; till, at last, being stunned by their gibbering, and suffocated by the potency of their exhalations, she was forced to quit" (55). Monstrosity and repulsion are generated by problems of scale and sensory distortion. However, Beckford is prone to the absurd effect. Vathek, who has developed a voracious appetite following the visions of grandeur, asks the deaf-mutes for food. When they do not oblige, "he began to cuff, pinch, and push them, till Carathis arrived to terminate a scene so indecent, to the great content of these miserable creatures" (56). As with the encounter between Vathek and the giaour, the monarch's infantile subject position interpellates the European reader, whereas the position of the negresses, analogical to that of the black woman to Burke's visionary boy, is radically anti-identificatory. The *monstrous* object of contemplation, produced to the subject by a narrator in each instance, offers presentational hyperreality. As with the Latin pun, the monster demonstrates the failure of realism. The deaf-mutes cannot respond to Vathek's forgetful appetite. His creation of "a scene so indecent" is more than an outrage on propriety, it is an outrage on the sublime itself.

The deaf cannot hear but can indeed be beaten; their corporeality is the monstrous reality that Vathek cannot confront. As they do not talk back, they are, because of what they cannot be.

As placeholders for the subject in the manner that the blinded prince was in Chardin's narrative, there are still other sensorily deprived monsters who pursue the caliph along his progress-in-state to the underworld, where he too eventually turns into a despairing captive:

> Wherever the Caliph directed his course, objects of pity were sure to swarm round him: the blind; the purblind; smarts, without noses; damsels, without ears; each to extoll the munificence of Fakreddin; who, as well as his attendant Grey-beards, dealt about, gratis, plasters and cataplasms, to all that applied. At noon, a superb corps of cripples made its appearance; and, soon after, advanced, by platoons, on the plain, the completest association of invalids, that had ever been embodied, till then. The blind went groping, with the blind; the lame limped on, together; and the maimed made gestures to each other, with the only arm that remained. The sides of a considerable water-fall were crowded by the deaf; amongst whom were some from Pegû, with ears uncommonly handsome and large, but [who] were still less able to hear, than the rest. Nor were there wanting others in abundance, with hump-backs; wenny necks; and, even, horns of an exquisite polish. (109–10)

The maddening punctuation of the passage, for which Samuel Henley is responsible, creates some presentational brilliance—inadvertently perhaps—through syntactic fits and starts.[56] The useless but "uncommonly handsome and large" ears of the deaf next to a waterfall signals a sublime inability to appreciate the sublime. This chiasmic image of the subject's imperviousness suggests a sensory deprivation beyond sublimity, like that of abacinated anti-epistemology. Themselves found at the sublime site that later earns the Wordsworthian tag of "the stationary blast of waterfalls," how would the deaf be asked about the experience of a deafening blast anyway? The deaf are not merely a sign of the ridiculous, as that can only be a function of the familiar; instead, the inadequation they present suggests the absurd. It is the collapse of the sublime into the absurd that can be seen in the subtle intrusion of the adjective "the *superb* corps of cripples," a phrase about the pleasing limblessness of the platoon that is a sardonic commentary on the eventual mutilation to which all soldiers' bodies are headed. This surprise-prone aesthetics of dismemberment and sensory deprivation dominates, as in the sly pun "smarts, without noses; damsels, without ears." Bababalouk, the eunuch who feels the stirrings of desire as he is humiliated by Nouronihar and her epigones, gives a slapstick rendition of sexual desire that connects sublime, ridiculous, and absurd.[57] Defined as a man without a "working" penis, the eunuch is alternately a figure of horror and absurdity, an inverted version of the deaf with uncommonly handsome ears. Sensory deprivation reduces the status of all the characters in the tale to the point that the only category of relevance is the oriental sublime that Vathek is pursuing.[58]

Vathek teaches its readers that the despot is surrounded by multifarious victims of sensory deprivation, physical debility, and mutilation, all doleful reminders of the process of subjection. While Grosrichard points out that monsters—such as the *diltsis* or the mutilated mutes (*muets mutilés*) who are the subject of an article in the *Encyclopédie*—are phantasmatic counterpoints to the presumed masterful plenitude of the despot, Vathek's acting out makes him a privileged participant, at the top of his social pyramid, but in the same domain as his subjects.[59] Beckford was a reader of Nicolas Boulanger's treatise on oriental despotism that attempted to modify Montesquieu's theory toward the analysis of its religious origins. Boulanger's hypothesis concerning the "strict and fatal alliance . . . between idolatry and Despotism" was favored by Voltaire, and his identification of "the false sublime of superstition and gloomy-minded savage stoicism" suggests Burke's attitude toward "oriental" religion and language discussed earlier. All these theorizations suggest that despotic structures imprint subjects with masochistic needs.[60]

Amid this masochism, parodic orientalism, as practiced by Beckford, is an ambivalent performance. It revels in all the favorite tropisms and unmasks them at the same time. As various kinds of presentational inadequacy are performed, the sameness of their referential function is revealed. The youthful Beckford's satire of art criticism reveals this well. In *Biographical Memoirs of Extraordinary Painters*, Aldovrandus Magnus's warehouse of paintings are destroyed by fire, appropriately at the moment when he is working on the subject of "Prince Drahomire who in the year 921 was swallowed up by an earthquake on the spot of the palace of Radzen." Fittingly, the painter, exclaiming, "Drahomire! Canvas! St. Luke!," expires on the spot. Aldovrandus's disciple, Og of Basan, whose imagination "delighted in solitude and gloom," paints a metaphorical sublime, the St. Denis who beheads himself as a present for the king of France, and a metonymic sublime of St. Anthony with shoals of every imaginable fish. Concerning the St. Denis, the narrator drily observes that "the astonishment in the head at finding itself off its shoulders was expressed to admiration." In the manner of Burke's anecdote concerning the beheading of the slave by Muhammad II discussed earlier, Beckford reproduced the head of St. Denis looking at his beheaded trunk as a frontispiece for a much later edition (Fig. 20).[61] Comparing this example to Burke's, we might say that the fictitious Muhammad II, or his surrogate Vathek, would have approved heartily if Gentile Bellini had given up painting and following the example of St. Denis, decapitated himself. However, Burke's reference to beheading, following his political shift by the time of the *Reflections*, is a disapproving rather than enthusiastic one, comparing Richard Price of the Revolution Society to Hugh Peters's oration in 1648 that called upon the people to turn executioner, with "a *two*-edged sword in their hands . . . to bind their *kings* with chains, and their *nobles* with fetters of iron" (8:62).

While the sublime is derived out of otherworldly terror for the earlier Burke, Beckford defers terror to the culmination of *Vathek* even as its early intimations are savored, cultivated, and pursued. To reformulate a cliché, Burke brings the mountain to Muhammad, whereas Beckford takes his despot to the cavern. Laughter, witticism, and irony are present in good measure in Beckford, but oriented toward an inexorable outcome that is punitive and carceral; Burke takes the sublime in all seriousness, but prefers to measure its intensities and plot the subject's escape from its unforgiving violence. Burke is a modernizer, and Beckford rejects progress. St. Denis, Beckford's example of the self-decapitating subject, appears as the ultimate sick joke, a forward-looking indictment of modernity and the subject's ready interpellation by the state. Beckford has shown us that Foucault is the continuation of the oriental sublime by other means, magically transformed into the dialectic of Enlightenment. After all, the gruesome *écartèlement* of the failed regicide, Damiens, in 1757, has pride of place as Foucault's first example in *Discipline and Punish* and is discussed in Burke's second edition of the *Enquiry* (39–40). For Foucault, Damiens's treatment shows the ancien

Figure 20 Beheaded St. Denis Extending His Decapitated Head, in William Beckford, *Biographical Memoirs of Extraordinary Painters* (1834). (British Library, London)

régime's focus on the body rather than the subjectivity of the criminal; for Burke, the execution demonstrates that pain is more painful because allied to death, "an emissary of this king of terrors." Pain cannot be discounted. For Beckford, the image of terrible culmination in the Hall of Eblis collapses despot and regicide into a wish fulfillment of the sublime-obsessed subject's itinerary. Burke aspires to Enlightenment in its positive form, whereas Beckford anticipates Foucault. The despot inflicts death, whereas the blind, the mutilated, and the otherwise sensorily deprived are emblematic of the sublime's disciplinary futures.

OCCIDENTAL DESPOTISM

Ronald Paulson and Tom Furniss have demonstrated the contrapuntal relationship between Burke's *Enquiry* and the much later *Reflections on the Revolution in France,* analyzing the relevance of Burke's early aesthetic treatise with his famous Francophobic response of the 1790s. Images of despotism and blinding are also present in much of Burke's later writings. However, changed political circumstances led to Burke's backtracking on radical aspects of the sublime, a category that initially favored the world of "men of ability" over interests of "men of property," much as the French Revolution would later (8:102). A reversal of tropes also occurs in Burke's opposition to extraparliamentary rule in India by the British agents of the East India Company. As Kate Teltscher puts it, Burke rejects the historical charge of oriental despotism even as he "opportunistically makes use of its negative associations." The political management of the East India Company represented something like "the vigorous and active principle" of ability, one that he feared would also dominate France if unchecked. By reversing the charge of oriental despotism onto its British administrators and accusing the French antimonarchists of a cruel sublime, Burke returns the trope from an imaginary Orient to European practitioners.[62]

Burke's long regulatory involvement, from the 1770s to the 1790s, with parliamentary proceedings against the East India Company, resulted in the impeachment of Warren Hastings, who had been governor-general of Bengal.[63] In the *Reflections,* Burke asserts that the British Parliament can maintain its greatness only "as long as it can keep the breakers of law in India from becoming the makers of law for England" (8:96). Even as Burke rejects orientalism's referential function vis-à-vis the Orient, his parliamentary oratory makes for an oriental gothic.[64] As a result, an "Indian sublime," as Sara Suleri calls it, is produced, with the East India Company as the despotic villain and Indians as the abject victims.[65] To begin with, India certainly indicates the obscurity that marks Burke's sublime; in fact, he acknowledges, as is his wont, that it is hard to feel "sympathy for the unfortunate natives . . . whilst we look at this very remote object through a very false and cloudy medium."[66] Johnson, remarking on the charges against his friend Warren Hastings in the 1770s, concurs: "there is a cloud between, which cannot be penetrated: therefore all distant power is bad."[67] However, as his researches continue, Burke becomes one of a growing number of voices that rejects the idea that Islamic rule in India corresponded to oriental despotism. Analyses of Company rule, such as William Bolts's and Alexander Dow's, were already critical of Robert Clive and other officials as "European bashaws," even though this development was explained circumstantially as a result of the native influence.[68] Despotism in India is no longer the perceived tyranny of the Orient over its subjects. Rather, it is the principle of British political tyranny, bred at home in England, honed abroad on convenient victims in the colonies, and capable of returning home, as the corrupt nabob who enters Parliament by his newfound money and influence.

As Hastings's defense tactics were initially a clumsy exoneration of himself on the grounds that he was operating in a locale where all politics was despotic and "arbitrary," Burke conducted lengthy expositions of local laws proving the contrary. In the face of this onslaught, Hastings later glossed his reference to the arbitrary nature of power as meaning nothing more ominous than "discretionary." Contending that corrupt British administrators were justifying their own arbitrary actions by depicting a highly diverse and law-bound society as despotic, Burke validates Islamic law—whether in Turkey or in India—as "a law interwoven into a system of the wisest, the most learned, the most enlightened jurisprudence that perhaps ever existed in the world" (6:21). While the treatise on the sublime promulgates a bourgeois aesthetics along with a fascination for despotism, the Hastings trial and the French Revolution generate in Burke a deep suspicion of the "men of ability" that the treatise appeared to favor. Whatever the motives behind Burke's lifelong obsession with Indian government, his speeches during the Hastings impeachment trial indulge in a complicated positive levantinization, with Indians alternating between playing the roles of rational actors in an advanced legal system and of pathetic victims when they fall into the clutches of the East India Company and their surrogates.[69] Burke's research allows him to characterize Indians as civilized social beings governed by Mughal jurisprudence: "the idea of arbitrary power has arisen from a gross confusion and perversion of ideas . . . I am to speak of Oriental Governments, and I do insist upon it that Oriental Governments know nothing of this arbitrary power. I have taken as much pains as I can to examine into the constitutions of them. I have been endeavouring to inform myself at all times to a certain degree; of late my duty has led me to a more minute inspection of them, and I do challenge the whole race of man to show me any of the Oriental Governors claiming to themselves a right to act by arbitrary will" (6:351–53). In contrast, the pathos-ridden speech at the Hastings trial, condemning the atrocities on the Indian peasants at Rangpur and Dinajpur in Bengal, emphasized the torture and rape of native women causing much horror in the audience. As Richard Brinsley Sheridan was also, along with Burke, a comanager of the impeachment, his wife, seated in the Ladies Gallery, fainted in response to Burke's speech. Burke was himself taken ill toward the end of this speech in Parliament, on February 18, 1788, leading to the session's adjournment, and giving a melodramatic culmination to the "horrid scenes" just painted.

Just as the sublime aesthetic effect was produced by the undisclosed and incomprehensible master referent of power, Burke's rejection of despotism continues to be a fascination with its mechanisms and representations. The earlier promoter of the sublime is scandalized by the application of its dramatic power in the political sphere in France: "considerate people . . . will observe the use which is made of *power*, and particularly of so trying a thing as *new* power in *new* persons" (8:59). In a famous phrase, the Revolutionaries' "new conquering empire of light and reason" results in "all the decent drapery of life [being] rudely torn off." By understanding the frightening effects of the sublime and applying it to politics, the "superadded ideas from the wardrobe of a moral imagination" that were needed to "cover the defects of our naked, shivering nature" are instead "exploded as a ridiculous, absurd, and antiquated fashion" (8:128). There is no admiration for the power to make the subject yield, one that the young Burke justified unabashedly in the *Enquiry*. Instead, he is concerned that the antimonarchists not "break prison to burst like a *Levanter*," as otherwise he and other viewers may be overwhelmed by this attempt "to sweep the earth with their hurricane and break up the fountains of the great deep" (8:109). The metaphor is not apt, as hurricanes hardly happen in the Home Counties, but Burke continues with others. The terrific power of the Revolutionaries has not yet managed to disembowel the English. In contrast, Burke implies that the French have been "filled, like stuffed birds in a museum, with chaff and rags and paltry blurred shreds of paper about the rights of men" (8:137). Image upon image emphasizes the greater ambivalence Burke feels toward the expression of sublime power in the realm of French politics. Although the sublime is what threatens to hurt but is kept at a distance, Burke is obliged to defend politics as the realm of the beautiful but necessary art of maintaining appearances and softening the effects of power through custom and tradition. The French, greedy for liberty, are inclined to abuse it in the manner of "a gang of Maroon slaves suddenly broke loose from the house of bondage" (8:87). With this striking prolepsis, Burke paints Jacobins as black slaves just before Haitians become, in history, black Jacobins.

Similar to his repugnance at the events in France, Burke's closing speeches on the lengthy impeachment proceedings, which culminated in Hastings's acquittal in 1794, reveal a conflation of sublime aesthetics and unfettered tyranny in the figure of Hastings ruling over a fantasy space of tyranny and servitude that he had made happen: "Your Lordships will find it a fairy land, in which there is a perpetual masquerade, where no one thing appears as it really is, while the person who seems to have the authority is a slave, while the person who seems to be the slave has the authority. In that ambiguous government everything favours fraud; everything favours peculation; everything favours violence; everything favours concealment."[70] The phrase "perpetual masquerade" is reminiscent of Montagu's speculations concerning Turkish aristocratic women. However, Burke transforms the canard of despotism from another direction. The Company servants, like the agents of the Jacobin Terror, practice the masquerade negatively, in order to perpetrate fraud, peculation, and violence. In a satirical print that Gillray also repeats later in his *Camera Obscura*, Burke is satirized as a showman during the impeachment trials, exhibiting political curiosities with a magic lantern that suggests their artificial, indeed theatrical, existence (see Fig. 21). As orchestrator of a "Galante Show," Burke displays microscopic monstrosities, including "a Benares Flea," "an Ouzle" (a whale spouting, presumably in unison with the deluge of tears shed), "a Begums Wart," and "Begums Tears," with four large floating eyeballs staring back at the viewer, images of torture and sentiment. A picture of an oriental figure sitting cross-legged and smoking is also visible outside the camera obscura. The extravagant machinery of despotism (normally disliked as the Orient's primary attribute, for instance in Bishop Atterbury's letter to Pope, discussed earlier) is shown here as a theatrical ploy, magnifying minute abuses to elicit sentimental tears. Of course, if this attack is likely from Hastings's supporters, Burke's aim is to characterize Hastings himself as the operatic puppetmaster: "You now see by what secret movement the master of the mechanism has conducted the great Indian opera, an opera of fraud, deception and harlequin tricks . . . all the strutting signors and the soft signoras are gone; and instead of a brilliant spectacle of descending chariots, gods, goddesses, sun, moon, and stars, you have nothing to gaze on but sticks, wire, ropes, and machinery."[71] The great Indian opera, reduced to its brute mechanisms of production, no longer creates the pleasing masquerade. The radical constructivism of the architect of the sublime concludes with a conser-

Figure 21 *Galante Show "redeunt Spectacula mane"* (1788). (National Portrait Gallery, London)

vative deconstruction of politics as debased rhetoric. Nostalgia for the opera of royalism later reminds Burke of Marie-Antoinette, not just as "soft signora" but as goddess, or indeed "glittering like the morning star, full of life and splendor and joy." With a delicate pun that conflates earth and eye, Burke avers, "surely never lighted on this orb, which she hardly seemed to touch, a more delightful vision" (8:126).[72] Word for word, this image is a reversal of the horror felt by Cheselden's boy at the sight of the African woman. Continuing with the rich ambiguity of the phrase "Oh what a revolution!," Burke suggests sidereal, political, and ocular motion all at once. The queen's rise and fall is registered on his eye, on the earth, and in the political sphere, as a tragic event. For the older Burke, the sublime has destroyed the beautiful.

The aesthetics of terror continues its grip on Burke. As power distinguishes the sublime from the beautiful, the difference between the two, as he acknowledges in the *Enquiry,* is that between admiration and love, although this is acknowledged to be a wide one. Simply put, "we submit to what we admire, but we love what submits to us; in one case we are forced, in the other we are flattered into compliance" (113). Despotic governments are sublime because they coerce their subjects, but is this submission based on admiration or fear? The sympathy for the dying age of chivalry following the passage on the stripped queen shows a paradoxical pity for that which is destroyed because no longer feared. Thus, the initiators of the Revolution are, as heartless "men of ability," similar to the vilified functionaries of the East India Company, oppressing populace and fallen monarch alike. Adjudicating the rival claims of "old fanatics of single arbitrary power" and "new fanatics of popular arbitrary power," Burke is worried about the absence in France of the middle ground that he sees enshrined in Britain's constitution (8:76–77). If the old absolutism had found its best expression through the fantasy of Oriental despotism, the new populism of the French Revolution is its modern replacement. Quoting from Addison's *Cato*, he fears that France "may be obliged to pass . . . 'through great varieties of untried being,' and in all its transmigrations to be purified by fire and blood" (8:293).[73] Forced into choosing the monarchy as the lesser of two evils, and reactionary because of his ambivalence toward the "untried being" of arbitrary power despite his conscious protestations against all forms of it, Burke ends the *Reflections* with a word that motivates but ultimately eludes him during the course of his levantinizations: "equipoise" (8:293).

Nationalizations

CHAPTER SIX

Equiano and the Politics of Literacy

The British nation, in the literary-critical sense, was constituted by canonizing authors and texts in the late eighteenth century. The momentous *Donaldson* v. *Beckett* ruling in the House of Lords in 1774, allowing copyright to lapse into the public domain, meant that publishers could reprint older literature without fear of litigation. Thomas Warton's *History of English Poetry* (1774–81), John Bell's *Poets of Great Britain Complete from Chaucer to Churchill* (1776–92), and Samuel Johnson's *Lives of the Poets* (1779–81) institutionalized English literature. Texts circulated within a system that reified nation, language, and culture, conferring the sphere of print with the representative powers of the "daily plebiscites" that, according to Ernest Renan, perpetuate nationalism. Along with the publication of poets, there was the ready availability of drama as text as well as performance, for instance, with John Bell's *British Theatre* (1776–78). The most significant generic development of the century was, of course, the elevation of the novel from a scandalous to a moral genre. These literary activities enabled the serialization and differentiation of a collective national oeuvre, written increasingly by authors whose ties to aristocratic patronage were attenuated even as they began to enjoy the benefits of individual copyright. The great popularity of graphic satires, as well as the explosion of nonfiction, ranging from travel narratives to sermons, almanacs to periodicals, and collected history to technical manuals, suggests that publishers successfully targeted diversified audiences in need of stimulation, and perhaps pacification, by the culture of print. Gerald Newman, who has analyzed the cultural nationalism of the period exhaustively, confirms that "Eng. Lit., as a critical discipline, grew out of passionate nationalistic claims," nourished as it was by a bourgeois resentment of aristocracy and by popular Francophobia. Print capitalism enabled this assertion of Britain's vernacular roots and rejection of French fashion and purported political perfidy.[1]

Predicated on the triple scheme of nation, language, and culture, Eng. Lit. invents a "Britain" as a collective subject who authors *a* literature, proceeding diachronically with authorial highlights, from Spenser to Shakespeare to Milton, as Richard Hurd's essay *Letters on Chivalry and Romance* argued in 1762. Cynics may allege that this process has grandfathered itself into a discipline that is tone-deaf to its own millennial pretensions, parodically chiming from Beowulf to Virginia Woolf and well beyond. The nation is the *subject* of literary history, a bildungsroman whose moves are plotted over a millennium from Old English epic to a postcolonial Anglophone literature. Second, the nation is also a *fetish*, an object of displaced libidinal investment accompanied by a quasi-religious practice, yielding as its outcome the national narcissism of literary criticism and cultural history. Finally, the nation is also the *universe* that appears to anchor literature—and literacy—within sociological, aesthetic, and political parameters that are resolutely Anglocentric. Collective subject, fetish object, and discursive universe, the nation cannot be pinpointed in Eng. Lit., for it is everywhere. Hardly a benign receptacle of cultural activity, the nation enforces norms and narratives that create continuity and mediate shared conflicts among its disciplinary residents—whether authors, readers, or texts—even as it relegates others to its margins. Rather than accord the nation the preeminence that Eng. Lit. has granted it since the late eighteenth century, criticism of this period ought to exhibit greater suspicion toward the correlation between the rise of literacy and that of nationalism and thereby investigate the function of literary canonicity as a rationalizing process.

Especially since the late eighteenth century, Eng. Lit. is an aesthetic project of texts and authors sequenced in a manner that respects principles of diachrony and synchrony but that also devalues filiations straying out of national-cultural boundaries. This canonicity is challenged by voices previously *heard* but not (disciplinarily) included. Even as national literature is forced to include those who were left out, such benevolent eclecticism grows the nation into *imperium*. In the manner of cutting the Hydra's head, contestation of the internal romance of nation-building is countered by the monster's exponential growth into the responsibilities of empire, a geocultural transformation of vernacular into lingua franca. Alternative nationalisms and transnational imaginings are thereby imbricated with the earlier, more insular imaginings of Eng. Lit. However, a sharper focus on the appeal to nation, national culture, and even imperial residue—whether as a historical referent or as a disciplinary power move—brings other alternatives to the fore. Nationalization—the public and political recasting of older traffic between literary representations of colonialism and the agency of tropicopolitans as it traverses those discourses—could lead to assimilation as well as separatism. As we shall see in this and the subsequent chapter, nationalization can enable an Equiano to work with the British Parliament as well as a Sierra Leone that challenges the writ of Company rule; in the French context, a Toussaint Louverture who works with the Directorate as well as a Haiti that irrevocably breaks with France and tropicalizes the Enlightenment.

Keeping these complications in mind, I read the eighteenth century from the vantage point of an Olaudah Equiano who looks backward in 1789 and implicitly recognizes preceding literary production as rationalizing the nation. Equiano situates himself at the culmination of a national culture, reworking a range of English literary figures, including Milton, Bunyan, Defoe, and Cowper. Along with its literary debts, his narrative also interrogates, at varying levels of explicitness, the nation as repository of colonialist thought. Anthropological, economic, religious, and political discourse jostle with each other even as they cohere around the personal dramas foregrounded by the choice of autobiography as the dominant form of address. Stemming from the genre of Indian captivity narrative that inaugurates emancipatory tropes also used by subsequent slave narratives, Equiano's work suggests both religious and secular consequences and, like slave narrative, refers back to a picaresque origin.[2]

Situated in the long wake of nationalization, the renewed popularity of Equiano today is related, no doubt, to the contemporary search for postcolonial and minority literature that instantiates the multicultural moment. However, Equiano's ready availability to literary history poses other problems. By viewing Equiano through the optic of minority literature or making him represent an African American or black British slot in an ever-expanding canon, the modern reader also edifies nation into imperium. Entitled *The Interesting Narrative of the Life of Olaudah Equiano, or Gustavus Vassa, the African. Written By Himself,* the autobiography's credibility is anchored within an identitarian literary history, except that Equiano's readers also witness his difference prior to acculturation. Using an ideology of progress and the tools of comparative anthropology, Equiano demands fair treatment of Britain's residents — and its literature's practitioners — according to a *jus soli* as well as a *jus sanguinis*.[3] Defoe had already paved the way earlier in the century by his satirical acknowledgment that a "true-born Englishman" was a creature of political and ethnic contingencies rather than genealogies and bloodlines; Equiano initiates a practice that derives Englishness from African otherness and weds the national identity to abolitionist ideals. As conversion narrative and autoethnography situated at the historical confluence of British, West Indian, North American, and even West African interests, *Interesting Narrative* proposes that the ravages of slavery, when rectified, can result in mercantilist profit alongside slave emancipation and repatriation. The thematization of "fetishism" and its displacements — through tropes such as the famous ones of "the talking book" or that of white cannibalism — is a significant pointer. Olaudah Equiano's trajectory toward Gustavus Vassa seems both transitive and intransitive. His conversion *of* his West African roots *into* a working British identity — a reciprocal transfer — contrasts with his baptismal conversion *to* a charismatic form of evangelical Christianity — a complete assimilation — that knows no conscious compromise with earlier religious allegiances. However, Vassa's reclaiming of the name Equiano transfigures anthropological attitudes. Equiano converts the fetish, learned about by travelers in the West African context, into the forms of worship acceptable to the British nation. Displaying his complicated cultural difference alongside the achievement of his Anglophone identity, Equiano participates in a religious and political commingling — of differences and identities — that makes him meritorious in the eyes of his readers. Subtle layerings in the narrative nonetheless complicate its function as a conversion tale. Christianity is highlighted in the autobiography, even as its clearly stated intention to intervene in politics cannot be ignored.

Though *Interesting Narrative* speaks for black minorities within a British sphere of influence, it also suggests other possibilities, including the potential national separatism of the Sierra Leone Resettlement Project and the still unfolding abolitionist movement. The immediate aspirations for abolishing the slave trade are entailed with a further consequence, less directly articulated, of the end of slavery as an institution. Much of the entrepreneurial capitalism Equiano engages in over his travels was yet to be formally sanctioned by the British state. The commercial ideology of Equiano's African ventures resembles the earlier form that we have already encountered, that of Defoe's progressive Protestant mercantilism. The colonialist milieu of Equiano's thought led to his espousal of the twin projects of political restitution for Africans inside and outside Britain, and a general economic expansion into Africa. Assuming the position of commissary of the black poor in November 1786, Equiano initially collaborated with plans to resettle the floating black population, of emancipated slaves, demobilized sailors, and urban indigents, who eked a living in London and other English ports. Dismissed by his paymasters a few months later for supporting his constituency's complaints about the corruption of the agent Joseph Irwin, Equiano was disappointed in his hope of immediately creating a lucrative African free market in lieu of the slave trade. In his discussion of the commercial advantages of the African trade, Equiano nonetheless continued to echo several of his contemporaries who were colonial projectors. From a position that implied a trenchant critique of slavery, Equiano turned the opposition of British master and African slave into its dialectical synthesis of manumitted black British entrepreneur, or in his case, adviser, lobbying for investment in the continent of his origin and occasionally collaborating with the slave trade itself.

This paradox has led to differing interpretations: many readings of Equiano celebrate his triumph over slavery, but others cautiously condemn his continued collaboration with colonialist commerce. For instance, Susan Warren argues for Equiano's fashioning of a "'transgressive' narrative self" that deliberately undoes the binary oppositions of racial essentialism, whereas Joseph Fichtelberg refracts Equiano through the lenses of Immanuel Wallerstein, seeing him as an accommodationist relying on imperial commerce to transform "the liminal condition of the slave into the peripheral relation of an economic client."[4] Rather than pigeonholing Equiano as revolutionary or collaborator, this chapter aims to exploit some of the resonances of nationalization retroactively. While *Interesting Narrative* played a significant role in arguing for the eventual abolition of the slave trade that took place in 1807, colonial projects such as the one in Sierra Leone testify to the neocolonial ethos of the abolitionist debates in the 1790s and 1800s. Examining the writings of the black settlers in Sierra Leone alongside

Equiano's, we can appreciate the advantages and the limits of creating a newfangled black British minority literature or celebrating a blandly homogenized version of black Atlantic culture. Anna Maria Falconbridge's *Two Voyages to Sierra Leone During the Years 1791-2-3* also sheds interesting light on the same milieu. An implicit intertextual dialogue develops when the writings of Falconbridge, a white woman with a commercial stake in the colonial establishment, and Equiano, a black British freedman, are compared with the records left by the settlers about their harsh experience.[5]

I examine Equiano's simultaneous use and implicit criticism of Puritan spiritual autobiography *and* secular nationalist narrative in the three sections that follow. The first section investigates how Equiano, through a self-authorizing tropical baptism, writes himself centrally into the narrative of British nationalism. The second section contextualizes the experimental settlement in Sierra Leone also alluded to in *Interesting Narrative*. Despite their best intentions, the tropicopolitan settlers in Sierra Leone cannot write themselves into the center of the British nation, nor can they successfully secede from it. Focusing the first two sections on parallel narratives, the inclusion and imminent canonization of Equiano into literature and the exclusion and continuing marginalization of the barely literate Sierra Leoneans, the third section returns to the central problem posed by the politics of literacy as raised in literary studies. Faced with two narratives of tropicopolitan agency, what is revealed by literature's favoring of its own? Both interventions, Equiano's and that of his Sierra Leonean compatriots, involve literacy. Yet, while the former makes the transition from literacy to literature, the latter instance of literacy remains functional, local, and ephemeral. Both interventions have shown that literacy is a political weapon in its trajectory toward nationalization. Using literacy, Equiano achieves his goal of securing a voice for himself and other free blacks within hostile political institutions, by interanimating the concepts of nation and state. Equiano can be reappropriated as a fetish, in the manner of a domesticated but resistant voice. Alternately, the agency of the Sierra Leoneans dissolves back into its context, which is one of practice. The facts of their existence generate a critique of literacy as precondition for the institution of literature, and the irony of selective humanization, whether it be of metropolitans or tropicopolitans.

As Defoe's fiction showed us, maritime culture was a secret sharer in the fluid identity formations of the eighteenth century. Seafaring vessels mobilized goods and populations, also serving as ships of passage that enabled syncretic practices and shifting identities. Sailors, merchant mariners, pirates, and naval conscripts lived in an especially volatile environment aboard ship. In addition to experiencing—and perpetrating—battle, coastal plunder, and the generalized violence of slaveholders and press gangs, mariners also faced the natural terrors of the sea and an onslaught of pathogens. As a result, alongside human depredation, vast numbers were also lost at sea and devastated by epidemics.[6] Murderous social divisions could assert themselves on board ship alongside potentially creative cultural interactions. The intense social laboratory of shipboard culture comes to the fore when reading texts by Defoe, Smollett, and Equiano.

Religious sentiment varied from the contemplative to the curious. For instance, new sailors were frequently subjected to ritual ablutions when ships crossed important nautical lines. The English version of François Froger's African travel narrative refers to this process as "the Ceremonies of the *Tropical Baptism* or Ducking." Emphasizing the shipboard sense of unbelonging and placelessness, these liminal rites governed the shedding of older group identities and the acquisition of others. Speaking of the "Eccentric Humour of Ducking and Shaving on board British Ships when Crossing the Line" a century later, *Fairburn's Naval Songster* describes a ceremony, "grotesque in the extreme," in which "one of the rummest old Tars is chosen to represent Neptune." The seagod and his retinue "appear handsome as Sea Devils, and as queer tog'd as your London Masqueraders." While Neptune received customary tributes of money from those who wished to evade rough treatment, the typical younger sailor was initiated into his new identity in the following manner: "a speaking trumpet is put into his hand; whilst one of the attendants besmears [his face] with a composition of tar and grease, and another who acts as a barber, scrapes it with a bent piece of an iron hoop (instead of a razor). He is then told to speak through the Trumpet to Neptune for mercy, when a bucket of mixture not the most pleasant, is poured into the trumpet." After subjecting novices to near suffocation on waste matter, "the remainder of the after-noon is devoted to singing, dancing, blacking each other's faces, and all manners of tricks."[7]

This well-documented comic ceremony shows the playfulness of shipboard culture. As rite of passage, it both undercuts and reinforces religion through syncretic parody. Witnessing a variety of horrors aboard ship makes Equiano humorously allege that he "soon grew a stranger to terror of every kind" and therefore "in that respect at least almost an Englishman" (1:132). The provisional mastery of religious sentiment in maritime contexts should not be homogenized. As practitioner of religion in an abolitionist setting, Equiano's maritime background inflects his evangelical performance. It makes for a curious distortion when Adam Potkay and Sandra Burr excise the maritime aspects of Equiano's *Interesting Narrative* for their edition of *Black Atlantic Writers of the Eighteenth Century* while emphasizing "in full what [they] perceive as the central unifying theme of his autobiography: his account of his spiritual and intellectual development."[8] The sheer fact of survival after a few years at sea was no mean feat. Despite and perhaps because of their frequent lack of moorings, sailors were especially subject to a gamut of religious beliefs, from whole-hearted evangelical conversion to folkloric superstition. The harsh environment in which, or in fear of which, con-version occurred gives the mixture of doctrine, devotion, and supersti-tion a different meaning from terrestrially produced belief. Even though Equiano's qualified Methodism—along with a nominal adherence to the articles of the Church of England—is not a contingent happening aboard ship, it is intimately connected to his maritime experiences, his entrepreneurial vicissitudes, and his physical survival. Omitting signifi-cant material aspects of his life decontextualizes radically what remains of it to be told.[9]

Evangelism is a sincere calling for Equiano. Having survived a major fall unscathed on ship when others assumed he had fallen to his death, the narrator interjects that he could "plainly trace the hand of God without whose permission a sparrow cannot fall" (1:160). Nonetheless, the evangelical outpourings of many eighteenth-century black writers are intimately related to the uprootings they encountered, as well as the syncretic outcomes of these traumas. Though converts felt the physical hardship of the evangelists they emulated, such as Bunyan and White-field, their baptisms cannot be entirely divorced from the pathos, irony, and the carnivalesque nature of maritime religious sentiment. Equiano describes with humor an episode in which he and his captain were disappointed in their expectations from serving an ailing silversmith on board ship, who dies without leaving the money they both expected. (2:8–11). Conversion, or Christian behavior, like the tropical baptisms mentioned above, is a response to liminal rootlessness but is also occasionally shown up as knowingly self-interested and complicitous. Equiano's conversion enables an inclusive narrative of the rediscovered cultural *simultaneity* of African and Euro-American contexts, one that replaces the initial sense of exclusionary spiritual *development* from one to the other. Evangelism, as it was for the verting accounts of the fictitious Captain Singleton, becomes a bridge between personal loss and a new public identity.

Even though Christianity is often presented as triumphant culmination to such narratives, their stock conclusions legitimate much in the life trajectory that can be scandalous, unsavory, or otherwise uninteresting. Reading along with Christianity in such narratives is useful but also limiting if religious claims are taken only at face value. Assessing their schismatic variances in their historical contexts is revealing. In her survey of eighteenth-century English religious thought, Isabel Rivers discusses the irregular practices and structures of the Evangelical Revival, which involved lay preaching, open-air and itinerant meeting places, and various unconventional "connexions" that make documentation of its innovations difficult. Equiano appears to straddle the major schismatic divide that separated the Calvinists from the Arminians during the Revival (with the Calvinists stressing faith and the Arminians holiness). Anglo-Africans such as Equiano were generally under the patronage of the Countess of Huntingdon and more influenced by the Calvinist doctrines of George Whitefield than the Arminian doctrines of John Wesley (who nonetheless kept cordial relations with Whitefield). Wesley's Arminianism, which goes along with the doctrine of universal rather than just personal redemption, is also a useful reference point for Equiano's later political Christianity.[10]

Potkay and Burr propose to divide Equiano's life into three broad stages suggested by evangelism. The first stage, Equiano's youth, is "the patriarchal stage of Igbo/Hebrew culture." The second stage, the period of enslavement, corresponds "to the captivity of Israel in Egypt, the bondage of the house of Jacob among a people of a strange language." The final stage conflates emancipation with Christian conversion, "a literal freedom that serves as well to anticipate and to allegorize spiritual deliverance from innate depravity." Hence, they interpret the frontispiece engraving of *Interesting Narrative,* a portrait of the author pointing to a Bible open at Acts 4:12, as showing that "[Equiano] writes from the perspective of Christianity; and from this vantage, he reads and renders his own life—and perhaps, by extension, the life of the black race—as mirroring the movement of biblical history from the Old Testament to the New. Having been born among the patriarchs, Equiano ends up among the apostles."[11] Allegorical interpretation is rendered plausible by minimizing the material aspects of Equiano's life and refusing to recognize the nationalization of the narrative. However, the convert's use of evangelism in his self-emancipating teleology is multivalent. The Igbo/Hebrew analogy is an autoethnographic gesture stimulated by comparative anthropology just as much as it is a religious justification. Similarly, though the metaphor of Egyptian captivity is a powerful reference for many black writers—including the barely literate Sierra Leone settlers—Equiano's life does not dwell very long on this parallelism. What Potkay and Burr call the third stage, spiritual conversion, occurs much later in the narrative, highlighted by a sense of *private* transformation and consequence. "I was determined to work out my own salvation," says Equiano, "and in so doing procure a title to heaven" (2:116). This private calling is different from the biblical analogy of Egyptian captivity that would require interpreting the African slaves as the chosen people. Equiano has split religion into two parts: private significance, or use, and its public exchange, suggesting a different set of assumptions from the collapse of ethnicity and religion required by the metaphor of Egyptian captivity. Furthermore, this important moment of evangelical conversion is but one of several structurally necessary features of the book's address. The preface and the conclusion to the book address a nationalist and a colonialist audience, rather than the somewhat different universe of the Christian faithful. For this reason, Equiano's political Christianity should be contrasted with the more quiescent example of Philip Quaque, who was appointed Missionary, School Master, and Catechist to the Negroes of the Gold Coast in 1766.[12] Equiano exposes his allegiance to charismatic Methodism at the same time as he advertises his Anglicanism. Like several emancipated Anglo-Africans, he affiliated himself to the evangelical circle around

Figure 22 W. Denton and D. Orme, *Olaudah Equiano*, in *Interesting Narrative* (1789). (British Library, London)

Olaudah Equiano;

or

GUSTAVUS VASSA,

the African?

Publish'd March 1 1789 by G. Vassa

Selina Hastings, the Countess of Huntingdon, and George Whitefield, mentioning the impact of hearing him preach (2:5).

Furthermore, biblical "tropology" is part of a fourfold process of biblical hermeneutics. Moving from the literal (Old Testament) event, through the typological (Christomimetic) meaning, to the tropological (evangelical) level, Potkay asserts that the third stage "interests us [*sic?*]" and "relates the historical event to an occurrence in our [*sic?*] own spiritual lives." Assuming only an audience of the Christian faithful, this reading arrests Equiano at the penultimate stage of the hermeneutic.[13] As Fredric Jameson has shown in *The Political Unconscious*, creatively deploying the fourth, anagogical level of biblical hermeneutics could lead the reader in a collective historical direction. "In a terminological shift," says Jameson, Northrop Frye ideologically recontains medieval typology through a process "in which political and collective imagery is transformed into a mere relay in some ultimately privatizing celebration of the category of individual experience." Potkay's interpretation of Equiano appears to have done much the same. Equiano's different deployment of the anagogical fourth stage, the Arminian one of universal redemption, is much closer to medieval *applications* than it is to the presumptive category of bourgeois individualism. The framing devices of the autobiography magically transform religion into politics. The shell of spiritual autobiography crumbles to reveal a political manifesto within the generic structure. Paradoxically, the medieval application leads dialectically to nationalization as a modern outcome, whereas the modern application, of individual experience, is stuck in a privative, more Calvinist cul-de-sac, from which the subject cannot confront the implications of his or her position within the ideology of the nation.[14]

The religious garb Equiano wears in the portrait (Fig. 22), thus exemplifying his own life and spiritual conversion, serves a political function alongside its spiritual one. His thumb on the letter of the canon law, Equiano is dressed not as an exclusively religious man, but as an evangelical lay preacher, mediating between religion and its potential adherents. The ruffled collar and button-studded coat suggest modest gentility. The structure of the caption under the frontispiece in the 1789 edition is especially significant:

Olaudah Equiano,

or

GUSTAVUS VASSA,

the African.

Published March 1 1789 by G. Vassa[15]

Within the cursive, italicized name, "*Olaudah Equiano, the African,*" is placed the capitalized alternate name of "GUSTAVUS VASSA," a reference to the Swedish hero credited with delivering his country from Danish rule.[16] Vassa was a slave name that the young boy initially resisted, receiving "many a cuff," but at length he submitted "and was obliged to bear the present name," which also explains why "G. Vassa" takes legal responsibility as publisher (1:96). Interestingly, the author adopts his pre-Christian Igbo appellation as his postevangelical spiritual name. This choice confirms that most eighteenth-century New World slave religions were highly syncretic. Religious practices remained strongly African and, according to Walter Pitts, underwent much deeper Christianization only after the second wave of evangelical revival that began in 1799. Equiano's early enslavement makes for a more thorough cultural deracination in his case and reveals his conversion as atypical when compared to that of Africans who were enslaved in adulthood.[17] It is difficult to generalize from Equiano's case, even though his own nationalization encourages it. However, simple incidents—such as the one on the Isle of Wight, where an unknown black boy of his own size ran to meet him "with the utmost haste" and "caught hold of [him] in his arms as if [he] had been his brother"—demonstrate an unstated bond among black Britons (1:152–53). Vassa, the European name imposed through slavery, and first hated, also paradoxically establishes public legal identity as freedman. Thus, nominal and charismatic Christianity supplement each other through the device of the name itself. The italicized external name, "*Olaudah Equiano, the African*," typographically contains the capitalized internal name, "GUSTAVUS VASSA."[18]

Equiano wears his pre- and post-Vassa ethnic spirituality ("Equiano" as exemplum of Igbo Christianity) on the outside, in the manner of a fetish, pointing to biblical injunction in the portrait. Or is this a rebus that reveals a progression when deciphered? The movement of the names suggest that of the life itself, from the particular to the general, and from Igbo Equiano to British slave Vassa to manumitted African (the objective of the exercise being general abolition). The secular European name is both inside (as the capitalized contents of the italicized frame) *and* outside, underwriting the publication as legal entity and temporal signature, plain and unemphasized. In this typographical play, the author, wearing his heart upon his sleeve, has inverted the traditional location of the spiritual within or above the carceral. This ludic reversal of inner and outer reality, more than the typical evangelical preacher's portrait prefacing a book of sermons, enables a manumitted slave, named after a Swedish patriot-king who led his people out of Danish rule, to perform the admonitory and prophetic action of looking the reader straight in the eye while pointing to the evangelical sentence of Acts 4:12, Bible in hand.[19] Though the verse speaks of Christ's conversion of the "Ethiopian" eunuch, the caption also suggests that "GUSTAVUS VASSA" is the secular kernel of "*Olaudah Equiano, the African*," the spiritual shell.

The finger, pointing to chapter and verse, evokes a parallel with the preface's address "To the Lords Spiritual and Temporal, and the Commons of the Parliament of Great Britain" (iii). Evoking the tag of God, King, and Country, the preface's formulation acquires additional institutional significance through the use of the plural "Lords." The signatory, "Olaudah Equiano, or Gustavus Vassa," coincidentally addresses himself to Church, Nobility, and Gentry—the three estates—in the watershed year of 1789. Mildly rebuking these three social categories, Equiano earlier characterizes his life as "the history of neither a saint, a hero, nor a tyrant" (1:2). Phrases such as these demonstrate that Equiano has mastered the cadences of accusatory false modesty in polite society: "I am sensible I ought to entreat your pardon for addressing to you a work so wholly devoid of literary merit; but, as the production of an unlettered African, who is actuated by the hope of becoming an instrument towards the relief of his suffering countrymen, I trust that *such a man,* pleading in *such a cause,* will be acquitted of boldness and presumption" (1:iv). The locution here suggests its exact opposite. It is most likely that the author wishes to reveal himself as not just a literate but a literary African and is proud to represent "his suffering countrymen" rather than excusing himself for presumption. Evangelical Christianity is certainly not the *"cause"* in question, and only arguably the principal "instrument." The primary cause is "the inhuman traffic of slavery," not the ignorance of Christianity. The means of extinguishing this human trade, suggested at the end of the text, are also by way of establishing "a system of commerce" in Africa. Evangelism is only as good as evangelism does.

The espousal of commercial progress comes as a later alternative to Equiano's earlier failed attempt to be a missionary. Perhaps consciously emulating Philip Quaque, who was, according to C. F. Pascoe, "first of any non-European race since the Reformation to receive Anglican ordination." In 1779 Equiano wrote to the bishop of London requesting ordination as an Anglican clergyman.[20] Acting upon the suggestion of his good friend and patron Governor Macnamara, who gave him a testimonial, as did another associate, Dr. Thomas Wallace, Equiano includes the full text of this application in the autobiography. Macnamara mentions the case of Quaque in his recommendation in the hope of eliciting a favorable response. Equiano was received by Bishop Robert "with much condescension and politeness," but the official declined to ordain him "from some certain scruples of delicacy" (2:222). Although there is no overt attempt to interpret the reasons for this refusal, the euphemistic "scruples of delicacy" and the inclusion of the entire application while eschewing commentary speak volumes, indicating disapproval of Anglican bigotry. Slightly on the defensive for "dwelling on this transaction or inserting these papers," Equiano defers to the opinion of "gentlemen of sense and education" concerning the evangelical potential of Africa. Evangelization cannot successfully happen unless "the attempt were countenanced by the legislature" (2:222–23).

In the meantime, Equiano was actively involved in ameliorating the conditions of the black laboring poor in several locations by collaborating with a number of religious groups. He commends the Quakers of Philadelphia for "freeing and easing the burthens of many of [his] oppressed African brethren" through setting up free schools for blacks. He throws down this example as a gauntlet to slave society: "Does not the success of this practice say loudly to the planters in the language of scripture—'Go ye and do likewise?'" (2:226). In appreciation of the Quakers during his stay in Philadelphia, Equiano led a delegation of Africans to the Quaker Church at Lombard Street to present a petition thanking the group. Christianity, therefore, is a catchphrase for a range of social and political activity envisaged by its practitioners. The need to establish Equiano as representative toward a larger audience is shown, just as forcibly, by the very different cast to Equiano's portrait in the unauthorized New York edition of 1791 (Fig. 23). Working off the earlier plate engraved by Daniel Orme from William Denton's painting, the engraver Cornelius Tiebout lightens Equiano's coloring and styles his hair to make him appear typically African American. Equiano's features in the American edition seem to have been altered with the goal to make him seem more multiracial and thereby less alien to a differently racist audience from that addressed by the British editions.[21]

Whatever use was made of Equiano in the American colonies, including his rediscovered importance as a precursor for nineteenth-century slave narratives including Frederick Douglass's, his political focus following the publication of the narrative remained within the British Isles. Equiano recommends the practical solution of global commerce and African consumption of British goods after narrating a previous attempt in which his missionary offers were refused by the Church of England, and another in which he expressed gratitude to the Quakers.

Equiano and the Politics of Literacy

Figure 23 C. Tiebout, *Olaudah Equiano*, in *Interesting Narrative* (1791). (British Library, London)

Economic solutions conclude the narrative, after retailing a more limited success with religious solutions. Certainly, there may be no conflict, perhaps even a relative conflation in Equiano's mind, between the categories of consumer and Christian. However, Equiano's text cannot be assimilated to the earlier disdain of filthy lucre in Bunyanesque spiritual autobiography. In the manner of many mercantilist writers of the eighteenth century, from Defoe to Adam Smith, who saw global betterment through free commerce and the demand for European goods, Equiano's hope is that after the abolition of the slave trade, "the demand for manufactures would most rapidly augment as the native inhabitants [of Africa] . . . insensibly adopt the British fashions, manners, customs, etc." (2:249–50).

Equiano's most important precursor was the Defoe who synthesized Christianity, capitalism, and colonialism. A general affiliation to Defoe was noticed as early as 1808 by Abbé Grégoire in his fascinating tract, *De la littérature des nègres*.[22] Reinflecting in racial terms a picaresque trope from *Robinson Crusoe*, Equiano says, "my life and fortune have been extremely checkered, and my adventures various" (2:254). Equiano echoes Crusoe's solitary penitence: "How strange a Chequer-Work of Providence is the Life of Man! and by what secret differing Springs are the Affections hurry'd about as differing Circumstances present! . . . for I whose only Affliction was, that I seem'd banished from human Society, that I was alone, circumscrib'd by the boundless Ocean, cut off from Mankind, and condemn'd to what I call'd silent Life."[23] The peculiar "Chequer-Work of Providence" seems actively to "banish," "circumscribe," "cut off," and "condemn" Crusoe to perpetual loneliness. In keeping with the carceral metaphor, it is apt that Crusoe is marooned wearing "a Chequer'd Shirt."[24] Indeed, the metaphor of checker-work, with its additional racial implications, appears several times in early Anglo-Africanist discourse. John Marrant also speaks of being "much chequered with wants and supplies, with dangers and deliverances" (18). Meanwhile, Ukawsaw Gronniosaw was bought by a Dutch captain "for *two yards of check*," explaining that this material "is of more value *there* [Africa], than in England." Mary Prince allows herself to be inspected by scandalized abolitionist women who stated that "the whole of the back part of her body . . . is distinctly scarred, and as it were, *chequered*, with the vestiges of severe floggings."[25] Perhaps Anna Maria Falconbridge, a traveler to Sierra Leone, foreshadows this submerged trope when she speaks of her own stay in Sierra Leone as being "chequered throughout with such a complication of disasters." However, more colorful than that example is her description of King Naimbanna's costume: "he was dressed in a purple embroidered coat, white satin waistcoat and breeches, *thread stockings*, and his left side emblazoned with a flaming star; his legs to be sure were *harliquined*, by a number of holes in the stockings, through which his black skin appeared."[26] Here the epidermal contrast brought out by Falconbridge—of a black man wearing a white satin waistcoat and breeches, and the checkered appearance of his black skin through holes in the stockings—is employed for comic effect. Equiano's life is discontinuously rather than uniformly checkered, indeed cobbled together from disparate episodes, forming a patchwork quilt of different life experiences. It is remarkable that the last six chapters of the autobiography each end with Equiano fulfilling different shape-shifting fantasies: as a naval captain, a parson, an Arctic explorer, an evangelical poet, a colonizing missionary, and as a colonial projector. These additions to Equiano's curriculum vitae jostle with a list of other qualifications, including shipboard powder monkey, domestic servant, trader, accountant, barber, labor organizer, abolitionist activist, and Parliamentary lobbyist.

Equiano's conscious imitation of Defoe is clear enough, even as he slyly complicates the racial metaphor by averring that his life "was written by one who was as unwilling as unable to adorn the plainness of truth by the colouring of the imagination" (2:254). Equiano would like to be counted among the white narrators, plain, colorless, and perhaps insipid, even as he suggests that imagination is a "colouring" he eschews. Early reviewers often took this plainness at face value. As one of them said, "the narrative wears an honest face." The Reverend James Aldridge similarly characterizes John Marrant's narrative as being "as plain and artless as it is surprising and extraordinary."[27] Writing from Friday's subject position, as it were, Equiano's reworking—and that by other black writers—of the "plain" character of Robinson Crusoe is richly ironical. In the manner of the sociological and commercial bent of Defoe's writings, Equiano's text is a first-person testimony of the checkered circumstances of the multiracial laboring classes in the Western hemisphere, their transnational mobility and agency.[28]

Although Equiano chose Defoe—bourgeois radical and commercial apologist—as his precursor, his African identity was immediately and unthinkingly linked to literary figures such as Othello. In his useful listing of the conventions of slave narrative, James Olney points out that an allusion to a "plain, unvarnished tale" was one of the most enduring critical reflexes when slave narratives were reviewed or introduced by amanuenses, even if Othello was not alluded to by the teller. Correspondingly, one of the first reviews of Equiano highlights the double origin of Shakespeare and Defoe, true life and picaresque: "this is 'a round unvarnished tale' of the chequered adventures of an African."[29]

In the manner of Oroonoko, and Othello before him, the voiced African's royal antecedents come to the forefront alongside the narrative of Christianization. It is this aspect, of voicing African royalty, that makes up the other half of a peculiar bourgeois-aristocratic composite. Othello took his "life and being from men of royal siege," and Oroonoko was an anomalous royal slave. The cliché of the royal black captive recurs incessantly in British literary representation from *Oroonoko* to *Rasselas*. Thomas Bluett's account of the devout Muslim, "Job ben Solomon" (Ayuba bin Suleiman Diallo of Bondu), suggests that Ayuba, who appeared "lean and weakly" because of "religious Abstinence," was a king who killed lions with poisoned arrows in Africa. Noble status reveals itself through physical deportment in Ayuba's case. "By his affable Carriage, and the easy Composure of his Countenance," the narrator says, "we could perceive he was no common slave." William Ansah Sessarakoo, "sold at Barbadoes in 1744, brought to England 1748," was similarly celebrated in William Dodd's poem, *The African Prince*. Dodd explores the well-worn ground of royal pathos, describing the lost prince as "a naked captive on a barb'rous coast." However, in the manner of all romance disasters, the outcome is for the greater good of Africa. While Bluett argues that Job's redemption should provide a boost to English trade, Dodd's prince rhapsodizes on the evangelical fruits of his travails in the following fashion:

Be calm my bosom since th'unmeasured main,
And hostile barks, and storms, are God's domain:
He rules resistless, and his pow'r shall guide
My life in safety o'er the roaring tide;
Shall bless the love, that's built on virtue's base,
And spare me to evangelize my race.[30]

The mistaken captivity and eventual return of African kings is a sign of divine providence that Africans can reap the benefits of British commerce and Christian "civilization." There are records of several such princes being voluntarily sent to Europe for their education, evangelization, and eventual return.[31] One such instance was that of Naimbanna of the Temne grouping in Sierra Leone, whose visit to Britain and abolitionist impact was well-known. An idealized portrait of the evangelized young prince was published in Hannah More's *Cheap Repository Tracts;* like Dodd's poem, this work was also entitled *The Black Prince*.[32]

As a result of this funneling effect from sentimentalist desires that conflated the pathos of abjection with royal dignity, it appears that when individualized, Africans in British literary discourse were oftentimes blue-blooded. It is not surprising, therefore, that Ukawsaw Gronniosaw, born in Bournou, also lets slip that his mother was the eldest daughter of the reigning king of Zaara. Similarly, Equiano's friend Quobna Ottobah Cugoano, speaking of the time he left Ajumako, in present-day Ghana, lets readers know that his "father and relations were then chief men in the kingdom of Agimaque and Assinee." Ignatius Sancho, whose letters were cited by abolitionists as proof of the mental capacity of Africans, showed his desire for aristocratic connections differently, wishing to play the noble African parts of Othello and Oroonoko on stage. However, according to Abbé Grégoire, "a bad articulation prevented him from succeeding in a situation which he considered as a resource against adversity."[33]

These multiple examples of aspired royalty by African visitors precede Equiano's assertion concerning his own relative social privilege in Igbo society. The first chapter of the autobiography speaks in idyllic terms of the village of Essaka, where Equiano was the son of a tribal elder designated as Embrenche. This social distinction is confused by Equiano with the decorative ritual of scarification that does not itself signify social authority. According to Adiele Afigbo, Equiano confuses Igbo scarification, *igbu ichi*, with the designation for elders, *Ndichie*.[34] According to Equiano's recollection, however, elders are designated Embrenche by "cutting the skin across the top of the forehead, and drawing it down to the eye-brows . . . until it shrinks up into a thick *weal* across the lower part of the forehead" (1:6). This mistake functions as a usefully misplaced signifier. Equiano feels *destined* to this tribal title from his parents, except that he is kidnapped and sold into slavery before he can be so honored. Highlighting this missed avocation early in the narrative makes his subsequent conversion an evangelical fulfillment of a Calvinist sign of election. The adult Equiano eventually regains, in a different form, that to which he was destined, although after much tribulation. These various literary antecedents—which we can characterize broadly as bourgeois empiricism and royalist romance, history and fiction, discovery and projection—continue a dialectic in English colonialist literature from *Oroonoko* onward. "Vassa," "Crusoe," and "Othello," if thought of as more generalized literary principles rather than just characters, mediate for Equiano as myth, symbol, and precursor.

However, Equiano's first impressions aboard ship are terrified thoughts, anticipating that he and his fellow captives "were [not] to be eaten by those white men with horrible looks, red faces, and loose hair" (1:72). Following this reversal of cannibalistic expectations for his audience, the narrative shows the young boy being made to gulp some liquor after which he was forced down the hold, where he sickens and loses his appetite as a result of the stench and shock whereupon he is severely flogged for refusing to eat (1:72–74). However, the ironic narrator watches over the naïve youth about to embark on the horrific Middle Passage. Ducking himself under the waters of English religious and literary tradition and surviving the punishments of slavery, Equiano surfaces with an *Interesting Life,* which he bequeaths to his readers. Indeed, we can imagine Equiano as the maritime novice, undergoing tropical baptism by English literary history and emerging as sailor *and* writer. Like the novice's attempt to speak to Neptune for mercy, the youthful Equiano opens his mouth only to be flooded with the fecal matter of English literary allusion from Milton to Cowper by many a well-meaning critic, first among whom is none other than the older Equiano. Yet, contained within the baptismal structure that separates the Igbo youth from the Christian adult are disparate political as well as religious elements, from evangelism to fetishism. These knowledges and practices mediate between the youthful sufferer of slavery, naval wars, and human betrayal, and the narrator, triumphant veteran of these experiences.

SIERRA LEONE: LITERACY DEGREE ZERO

As a form of radical conservatism, abolitionism mobilized political boycott by combining sentimentalist philanthropy and xenophobic insularism. When reformers confronted the sociopolitical consequences of imperial and commercial ventures, they preferred segregationist solutions to the problem of slavery, even that of emancipation. The Revolutionary War resulted in the heightened visibility of free blacks in London and Canada after 1783, which was promptly decried as a social problem in need of a solution (the increased visibility was sometimes falsely attributed to the Somerset decision of 1774 that had not led to any influx of refugee slaves). In the meantime, the humanitarianism of James Ramsay's *An Essay on the Treatment and Conversion of African Slaves in the Sugar Colonies* (1784) was championed by abolitionist circles even as it provoked the wrath of the pro-slavery forces. Arguing that French slaveowners were more humane than British planters, who acted like absentee landlords, Ramsay suggested that emancipation combined with religious instruction would lead to slaves making a greater contribution to society. Against such hopeful rhetoric, James Tobin launched a bitter invective in *Cursory Remarks Upon the Rev. Mr. Ramsay's Essay* (1785), in which Ramsay's detailed solutions were rebutted point-by-point even as the claimed benevolence of French planters was hotly disputed and British national honor defended. Ramsay was accused of being the equivalent of a Negro rebel, in the manner of a "negro *Calvin,* a sable *Knox,*" an "artful conjurer," and "merry nose-piper."[35] The controversy continued over several rounds even as others substituted for the initial controversialists. Much of the debate was framed around whether Africans were "children" in need of paternalistic care or "beasts" that responded only to the lash. Equiano's friend Quobna Ottobah Cugoano entered the fray as a black Briton in 1787, with *Thoughts and Sentiments on the Evil and Wicked Traffic of the Slavery and Commerce of the Human Species.* The preceding year had also seen Thomas Clarkson's *An Essay on the Slavery and Commerce of the Human Species, Particularly the African.* Echoing the jingoistic strains of earlier apologists such as Malachy Postlethwayt, Tobin was reduced to a "Short Rejoinder" against Ramsay's reply and others who had risen in his defense. Meanwhile, Equiano attacked Tobin, "the Cursory Remarker," in several letters to newspapers and also in the *Interesting Narrative* (1:219).[36]

Amid these debates concerning long-term solutions to slavery, the "blackbirds of St. Giles"—around 10,000 to 20,000 in London by the end of the century—were the favored target of social experiments by philanthropists and projectors. Figures such as Granville Sharp, William Wilberforce, Hannah More, the Clarkson brothers, Cugoano, and Equiano were intellectual activists and social managers concerning themselves with emancipist futures. Ironically, returning black freedmen to an idealized Africa also suited those who wanted to purify Britain racially. In contrast, Equiano himself, from much earlier in his life, desired to "return to Old England," to "see Old England once more" (1:250, 2:20). The Sierra Leone Resettlement, however, exposed the harsh realities of West African colonization. Celebrated through a literary humanism that fetishizes his book, the personal success of an Equiano is recast by the collective experience of the Sierra Leonean settlers whose cause he advocated. Sierra Leone provides an alternative scene of reading, just as Haiti does in the next chapter, of the ironical undoing of Enlightenment discourse.

There was an African Association, begun by Joseph Banks, that anticipated the scientific discovery of Africa; an African Committee that recommended the commercial exploitation of the continent; and an African Institution that promoted humanitarian aid and evangelical conversion of the heathen. Granville Sharp's utopian plan to transport the black poor to "a province of freedom" was part of this general background of discovery, exploitation, and evangelism. Utopians such as Sharp thought that the maladjusted and unwanted black minority could be relocated to a colony where blacks would largely govern themselves. Since 1672, ships of the Royal African Company had stopped at Sierra Leone, also a rendezvous point for pirates such as Bartholomew Roberts. A botanist adventurer, Henry Smeathman, had already formulated a money-making scheme for the settlement of this West African enclave but had died before realizing how chimerical the financial opportunities indeed were. Just in 1785, Burke had criticized a plan to send convicts to Gambia on the grounds that the climate made it effectively a death sentence after a mock display of clemency. The convicts were sent instead to Botany Bay, resulting in the first major settlement of what would become the colony of Australia. Sierra Leone was far closer than Australia, however, and offered the lure of commercial profit to many others. Saying that "every one feels a sort of Political and Œconomical Slavery," Charles Wadstrom concocted a plan based on Swedenborgian numerology. Swedenborgian theory had, in fact, predicted that the celestial fifth church would be found in Africa.[37]

Building on Smeathman's plan which claimed to guarantee "both civil and religious liberty as in Great Britain," Sharp wrote up *A Short Sketch of Temporary Regulations (until better shall be proposed) for the intended settlement* that gave the earlier proposal an elaborate and idealistic structure. Modeling his ideal Sierra Leone on the myth of Saxon democracy, Sharp's organization of political life according to decimal units showed a Roman aspect as well. Modern equivalents of decurions and centurions were found in Sharp's agricultural society composed of "tythingmen" and "hundredors." Relying on republicanist notions of mutual frankpledge, Sharp envisaged a self-policing community with a built-in flexibility that, once it got going, needed no authorizing reference to British customs and laws. Though the plan, according to one historian, was "a curious mixture of communism and Anglo-Saxon customs"—the unit of exchange in the colony was to be a day's labor—there was no doubt in Sharp's mind that this was to be a Christian settlement that promoted Western civilization, with agrarian laws and a tax on pride and indolence. In Sharp's mind, Anglo-Saxon common law was "closely connected" to the Established Church. Like Burke, he attacked pro-slavery arguments as "English Gentooism" fostering "wicked Braminical doctrines [that] are equally perverse and obviously refutable."[38] Like Equiano, Sharp also referred to the baptism of the black eunuch in *Acts*. As a devout Christian, Sharp nonetheless hoped to reconcile the different goals of philanthropy, profit, and Protestantism.

Opposed to those who understood the project as simply yet another colonial venture, Sharp was keen to characterize the venture as "*a free settlement*" based on "the glorious Patriarchal system" of frankpledge. This system was to him "the only effectual antidote to unlimited or illegal government of any kind, whether under monarchical, aristocratical, or democratic forms." According to Sharp, "in all *national colonies* . . . the first care must be to *plant* and *cultivate Justice* and *Common Right*."[39] Sharp's radical democracy also corresponded to perceptions of the consensual nature of local customs. The slave trader John Matthews observes that the prevailing form in Sierra Leone is "a kind of mixed monarchy, elective, and extremely limited both in external and internal power . . . very much resembl[ing] the authority of the mayor of a corporation town in England."[40] Several investors were persuaded to defray the costs of Sharp's venture in the hope of commercial benefit from the success of a free black agricultural and commercial enclave. Meanwhile, the first black settlers of Sierra Leone demonstrated that governance by tythingmen was never the company's intention, no matter what Sharp had said.

The grand scheme, of collecting the black poor from London and settling them in Sierra Leone, dominated the year 1787. As a projector who envisaged the yet unrealized mercantilism that some hoped would follow abolition, Equiano expresses his initial reaction as being filled with prayers and rejoicing (2:230–31). However, this wishful thinking was soon undone by the corruption of those involved. As commissary, Equiano was based in Plymouth, from where the ship was to sail; Cugoano was one of nine black leaders elected to act as liaisons during the first week of June 1786. Equiano's prescient and principled objections to the financial mismanagement of the project by the agent Joseph Irwin led to his dismissal, with even Sharp initially characterizing him as a troublemaker.[41] Equiano vindicated himself in *Interesting Narrative*, as his role had been "made the subject of partial animadversion." The catastrophic failure of the project later justified Equiano's stand, although only after the sorry toll of many wasted lives. Equiano's charitable but sober assessment judges the expedition "humane and politic in its design" but attributes its failure to "sufficient mismanagement attending the conduct and execution of it." He is, however, pleased to have been reimbursed £50 by the Treasury for his expenses and labor during the four months of his involvement (2:238, 2:243).

The economic and humanitarian failure of the Sierra Leone venture is a fascinating one to study, both for Equiano's initial involvement and later disapproval and for the lesson it teaches concerning the constraints which anticolonial agency faced in the age of abolition.[42] One of the false assumptions of greatest consequence was the belief in tropical exuberance and invigoration. Equiano is not himself exempt from the ludicrous claim that "cotton and indigo grow spontaneously in most parts of Africa" (2:253). Quoting Ogilby's earlier tract, Granville Sharp waxes eloquent on the consensus between "ancient Writers, as well as Modern Travellers of Respectability" concerning Sierra Leone's "very extraordinary Temperature and Salubrity of the Air, for European Constitutions." John Wesley also describes the Guinea coast in rapturous terms.[43] Given this prevailing assumption of natural bounty, and the wild hope of West Africa becoming a second West Indies, the very real devastation from disease and the failure of agriculture were unfairly interpreted as evidence of the laziness and debauchery of the settlers and the local population. Sharp laid the blame for the failed 1787 expedition on the "intemperance of the people themselves . . . (both Whites and Blacks) became so besotted during the voyage, that they were totally unfit for business when they landed."[44] Although Sharp thought that "the allowance of rum, granted to them by the Government with the most benevolent intention, really proved their greatest bane," as did the Sierra Leone Company in its deliberations that faulted "excessive drinking and other debaucheries," the truth lies beyond the reach of human agency and in the sobering statistics of epidemiology. Known for centuries to the Portuguese as *sepulcro dos Européos*, or the Europeans' graveyard, West Africa was a fatal destination. As copious documentation and subsequent medical anthropology prove, it was not personal intemperance but the lack of immunity to pathogens that led to the extinction of the 1787 expedition.[45] Of 411 settlers who sailed from Plymouth in April 1787, only 276 were left alive when HMS *Nautilus* left Sierra Leone in September. The Reverend Fraser, chaplain of the settlement, informed the alarmed Sharp that only 130 persons remained by March 1788, although some part of the diminution is attributed to the desertion of some settlers to nearby trading posts. In the short-lived period of Company rule from 1791 to 1807, at which point Sierra Leone was formally absorbed as a Crown colony, the project met with one disaster after another. The Company's stated aims were to obtain raw materials through "mutual interchange of commodities," scout out "a continually increasing market for the sale of the produce of British industry," and provide Africa with "the light of religious and moral truth, and all the comforts of civilized society."[46] The whole of the Company's subscribed capital of £240,000 was lost before the settlement of 1807. Writing in 1808, Abbé Grégoire laments the failure of the Sierra Leone project by comparing it to the Portuguese destruction of the great and little Palmares republics in the 1620s.[47]

Galloping mortality rates bedeviled the expedition at the beginning for the reasons already discussed.[48] The considerable depletion of the 1787 expeditionary force by epidemic (with roughly 50 percent mortality in the first year) led to a fresh attempt to bring more people. John Clarkson, brother of the famous abolitionist Thomas Clarkson, convinced a group of more than 1,200 blacks from Nova Scotia to hazard the voyage. Resettled as freedmen in the cold climate of eastern Canada by the British for having helped them fight the United States in the Revolutionary War, many of the Nova Scotian blacks were indigent and desperately unhappy. Nova Scotian whites, who profited from the cheap labor provided by the blacks, attempted to prevent their departure by concocting false debts and generating rumors that the project was going to reenslave the freedmen. Under the leadership of John Clarkson and the black preacher Thomas Peters, the Nova Scotians arrived in Sierra Leone in January 1792 to face new yet equally disastrous circumstances.[49] Of the 119 Company employees, 57 died in the first year alone. With respect to the fresh batch, Anna Maria Falconbridge reports that of the 1,200 settlers, 700 were suffering from fever, and with 5 to 7 dying daily, they were "buried with as little ceremony as so many dogs and cats . . . it is quite customary to ask, 'how many died last night?'" (140). To compound matters, a devastating attack by a rogue French fleet in 1794 razed the colony to the ground a second time. The colony had already suffered the loss of the first Granville Town (later rebuilt as Freetown) to a retaliatory attack from a local chieftain, King Jimmy, whose village had been firebombed by Captain Savage of the HMS *Pomona*. Sharp's infant democracy nominally survived only the first four years of the colony's history; with the Sierra Leone Company wresting control of the management from a dejected Sharp and formalizing its hold in 1791, some of the civil structure drawn up by Sharp remained alive to create considerable tension between the democratic aspirations of the new Nova Scotian settlers and the managerial aims of the company. For instance, under Sharp's system, women without husbands had voted until 1797, when they were excluded, a little-known fact for the history of suffrage.

Falconbridge's narrative, dedicated to the inhabitants of Bristol, speaks of her vicissitudes on "the inhospitable Coast of Africa" after a hasty marriage and elopement. In the manner of previous women travelers such as Mary Wortley Montagu, Falconbridge is keen to foreground her womanhood as an advantage for the understanding of cultural difference: "it is an unusual enterprize for an English woman to visit the coast of Africa" (3). From a more modest class background than Montagu, Falconbridge was the wife of Alexander Falconbridge, an abolitionist ship's surgeon who had been employed by the Sierra Leone Company as their factor. The Falconbridges undertook two voyages there on company business, with Alexander dying there during the second trip. His widow returned to England after having remarried Isaac Dubois, a pro-slavery loyalist, two weeks after her husband's death. Anna Maria Falconbridge aimed to publicize a messy financial dispute with the Company, which had not fully paid her first husband's salary and other expenses. This personal grievance takes the predictable form of exposing the Company's general mismanagement of the colony. As a result, Falconbridge's narrative presents detailed descriptions of harsh life, daily shifts of colonial policy, and unsettled relations with the local chieftains from whom the lands around the colony had been "bought."[50]

Falconbridge describes in lurid detail the wanton drowning, by one Captain Tittle, of the son of a native chief called Signor Domingo. When Tittle's hat blows overboard, he insists that the boy, who could not swim, jump into the water and retrieve it. The father is willing to consider the death accidental, but Tittle further insults him by sending a cask of "emptyings from the *tubs* of his slaves" instead of the rum for the ritual lamentation. Tittle is captured and tortured to death by Domingo, "to the great joy and satisfaction of a multitude of spectators" (21). There are many such abuses of the natives, and retaliatory violence by them, and Falconbridge also accuses the Company's transportation of London prostitutes. These women were "intoxicated with liquor, then inveigled on board of ship, and married to *black men,* whom they had never seen before" (57). Falconbridge fulminates at the British government's countenancing of "such a Gothic infringement on human Liberty at this advanced and enlightened age, envied and admired as it [the government] is by the universe" (58). Her general assessment of the project is equally scathing: "It was surely a premature, hare-brained, and ill digested scheme, to think of sending such a number of people all at once, to a rude, barbarous and unhealthy country, before they were certain of possessing an acre of land; and I very much fear will terminate in disappointment, if not disgrace to the authors; though at the same time, I am persuaded the motives sprung from minds unsullied with evil meaning" (117). In a voice alternately sensible and compassionate, bitter and angry, Falconbridge decries the futility and suffering of the colonists. Though she does not fault the Company's aims conceived in London during the first voyage, by the second voyage she lambastes the directors as "sporting with the lives of such numbers of their fellow creatures" and the local functionaries as "a pack of designing, puritanical parasites" (142). The Company is blamed for its lack of planning and provision. Meanwhile, Falconbridge suspects that the benign treatment she and her husband experienced in London between the two voyages "was only a complication of hypocritical snares" (160). When the anniversary of the ship's arrival is celebrated in February 1793, the appropriate response would have been "to have fasted and mourned on the occasion" (199). Perhaps a better-planned venture would have also succumbed because of the lack of immunity and medical treatment that all newcomers faced. However, the settlers' morale suffers greatly as a result of their abandonment. Falconbridge fears that the colony may soon be "dwindled into a *common* slave factory" (218).

Falconbridge's vivid narrative dramatizes the subtle power dynamics among the settlers, the locals, and the Company officials. Although initially the black settlers are most hostile to the local Africans, who they see as encroaching on the territory and threatening their land rights, the broken promises and mismanagement of the Company start creating alliances between very different sets of "Africans." Falconbridge reports several altercations between the settlers and the Company. Asked to relinquish their current lots, the settlers are quoted as replying:

> When placed on the lots we at present occupy, we were informed, they were merely for our temporary accommodation, and we promised, when the plan of the town was fixed upon and surveyed we would remove, but we were assured no public or other buildings would be erected between our lots and the sea; now, in place of this, the sea shore is lined with buildings, therefore, your promise being broken, we consider ours cancelled, and will not remove unless the new lots are run from the water's edge, and we indiscriminately, partake of them. Mr. Clarkson promised in Nova Scotia that no distinction should be made here between us and white men: we now claim this promise, we are free British subjects, and expect to be treated as such; we will not tamely submit to be trampled on any longer. (198)

Falconbridge claims to have the speech "nearly in the same language from more than a dozen people who were at the meeting" (198). This claim of being "free British subjects," along with the notion of formal equality to whites, was obviously explosive. Seeing themselves as part of the British expedition rather than as colonized natives, the settlers asked for redress in novel ways.

Falconbridge's policy-oriented complaints are accompanied by some comic prattle about local chieftains and the warm reception by King Naimbanna of the Koya Temne. The petty diplomacy that Alexander Falconbridge conducts on the Company's behalf allows his wife the modest pleasure of being received as an ambassador's wife. With humorous detachment, Anna Maria describes the nominal king's "*harliquined*" attire and his insistence on changing before dinner, and contrasts the queen's "dignified stile" with the absence of shoes and stockings on her feet (26, 37). She decides not to offer her services as a seamstress who could darn the holes in the king's stockings, because she was "fearful least [her] needle might blunder into his *Majesty*'s leg, and start the blood, for drawing the blood of an African King . . . whether occasioned by accident or otherwise, is punished with death" (31–32). After the facetious description of the encounter, she "awoke the next morning without the slightest remains of fancied importance." On another occasion, she "swooned into hystericks" upon being subjected to a meeting that involved lengthy palavers (37, 47). On the second trip, Falconbridge gives King Naimbanna a portrait of his son then being educated in England. She takes pride in noting that this represented "the first of his family transfered on canvas" (128). The gift of the portrait may have been a delicate turning point in the negotiations about the territory. Moved deeply by the likeness of his son, Naimbanna decided to forgo demands for further payment. When the king dies, his coffin was "the first in all probability his family ever had" (199). These supercilious comments, like those by other observers, indicate that Falconbridge perceived these syncretic coastal cultures through the incongruousness of their clothes. Native men in coastal West Africa wore coats and trousers for some time, while chiefs sat on chairs and dressed in ornate footman's liveries bought from Europeans. John Matthews too describes Naimbanna as sitting in an armchair, "dressed in a suit of blue silk, trimmed with silver lace, with a lace hat and ruffled shirt, and shoes and stockings."[51] Naimbanna visits Clarkson dressed in English attire with a gentleman's wig. Because there are so few examples of female-authored travel narrative by the end of the eighteenth century, it may be argued that Falconbridge is consciously modeling herself on Montagu, who also analyzes culture through clothing and prides herself on privileged access to the social elites of the observed culture as a result of her derivative ambassadorial status. Whatever fantastic identification Falconbridge might have felt with the by then celebrated Montagu, her class position was humbler and the stakes of her husband's diplomacy smaller.

Despite her liminal sympathies for the settlers that reveal themselves on site, a more reflective Falconbridge writes a philosophical conclusion supporting an enlightened slave trade, changing sides from what she considers her earlier, uninformed opinions that were "*bigoted for the abolition.*" To her mind, the trade ought to continue "while those innate prejudices, ignorance, superstition, and savageness, overspread Africa" (230–31). She charges that three-quarters of Africa are being treated like hogs and sheep "to be rob'd of their lives by the other fourth." In this apologia, typical for the 1780s and 1790s, the slave trade is rendered salutary by "pacifying the murderous, despotic chieftains of that country" (227). Falconbridge assumes that self-interest prevents masters from misusing their acquired property, the slaves. Positing gradualist evolution rather than the extreme proslavery argument of Africans as unregenerate, Falconbridge advocates the establishment of seminaries that can fulfill the Africans' "thirst for literature." The long passage is worth quoting as her culminating pro-slavery views concede much ground to the abolitionists:

> Pray do not misinterpret my arguments, and suppose me a friend to slavery, or wholly an enemy to abolishing the Slave Trade; least you should, I must explain myself,—by declaring from my heart I wish freedom to every creature formed by God who knows its value,—which cannot be the case to those who have not tasted its sweets; therefore, most assuredly, I must think favourably of the Slave Trade, while those innate prejudices, ignorance, superstition, and savageness, overspread Africa; and while the Africans feel no conviction by continuing it, but remove those errors of nature, teach them the purposes for which they were created, the ignominy of trafficing in their own flesh, and learn them to hold the lives of their fellow mortals in higher estimation, or even let me see a foundation laid, whereupon hopes itself may be built of their becoming proselytes to the doctrine of Abolition; then, no person on earth will rejoice more earnestly to see that trade suppressed in every shape; nor do I apprehend it would be impracticable, or even difficult to effect it, for I still admit what I said upwards of two years ago, to be strictly just.—"That Nature has not endowed the Africans with capacities less susceptible of improvement and cultivation, than any other part of the human race,"—and I am sure they thirst for literature; therefore, if seminaries were established on different parts of the coast, and due attention paid to the morals and manners of the rising generation, I do not question but their geniusses would ripen into ideas congenial with our own; and that posterity would behold them, emerged from that vortex of disgrace, in which they have been overwhelmed since time immemorial, establishing social, political, and commercial connections throughout the globe, and even see them *blazing* among the *literati* of their age. (230-31)

Falconbridge must have been thinking of Equiano and perhaps others such as Ignatius Sancho, Phillis Wheatley, and Francis Williams. As models for the literate African, competent political and social voices, these black writers were already "*blazing* among the *literati* of their age." Equiano knew very well the above vocabulary of cultural assimilation even as he contemplated the separatist protonationalism of Sierra Leone as potential outcome. As a workingman at ease among middle-class British abolitionists after having risen from slavery, Equiano is a rare example of class mobility in eighteenth-century British society. Expecting the Africans to emulate Equiano's literariness, Falconbridge ignores the egregious conditions of slavery that actively prevented this acquisition of letters.

Examining the brief writings of the literate Sierra Leoneans forces us to confront the aesthetics of literariness with the pragmatics of literacy, and indeed demonstrates the minimal access to cultural capital in this colonial situation. Sharp receives a long letter from "the Old Settlers at Sira Leone" dated March 3, 1788. It speaks of the managers as "diabolical spirits" and "instigators of all [their] confusions [and] many miseries." The letter asserts that "the rascality of the captains" results in the interception of all but two or three of the one hundred letters of complaint that were sent to England. Despite clearing the land, the irrigation arrangements remain "in a state of *anorky*"; building materials are unavailable; slave merchants ("Liverpool traders") interfere with the settlement "by sending repeated challenges to our *senit*" and stirring trouble with the locals.[52]

Prince Hoare reproduces this letter in a manner that silently normalizes spelling but draws deliberate attention to the misspellings of "senate" and "anarchy" that remain italicized. Here is a moment of complicity between anti-abolitionists such as Falconbridge and Hoare's qualified defense of Sharp's abolitionism. The comic incongruity of the settlers' misspellings leads to a paternalistic ideological effect. Readers are encouraged to think that if the settlers cannot spell these political words, they are probably still undeserving of the substantive content to which the words refer. The parodic misspellings are similar to Falconbridge's ridicule of West African sartorial syncretism. As critics of Eurocentric models of literacy such as Brian Street would argue, the ideological version of literacy that gets communicated here is a question of "schooling" rather than the culturally specific efficaciousness of "literacies." As Olivia Smith shows in great detail, language at this moment was itself a battleground between metropolitan sophisticates and provincial proletarians: "the basic vocabulary of language study—such terms as 'elegant,' 'refined,' 'pure,' 'proper,' and 'vulgar'—conveyed the assumption that correct usage belonged to the upper classes and that a developed sensibility and an understanding of moral virtue accompanied it."[53]

Misspellings aside, the letter indicates a clear political demand. The settlers' report culminates in an appeal for some artillery and materials for fortification and self-defense. By November 1789, Sharp writes to the settlers expressing regret that some of the managers "have deserted the Province of Freedom in order to enter into the Slave Trade."[54] He asks the settlers to redouble their efforts as a militia and a watch and ward service so that they "may be able to arrest and punish *every refractory member*" of the community.[55] Decrying the actions of the renegades who joined the slave trade, Sharp says that "the practices of *oppressors* were actually compared to the cruel rage of cannibals."[56] Quoting from Micah 3, Sharp's inversion is reminiscent of the youthful Equiano's fear of being devoured by his own master (1:99). At the same time, Sharp warns the settlers that if slave dealers arrive, they are to be treated courteously as long as the community's laws are not broken. The precarious existence of the community depends on non-interference outside its limited territorial jurisdiction.

When some visiting sailors did violate the laws, the settlement's legal jurisdiction was disputed. Falconbridge describes this incident with the laconic humor that also reveals her prejudice: "three thoughtless sons of Neptune . . . wantonly killed a duck belonging to one of the settlers." Taken before the chief magistrate, "they were tried, not by their Peers, but by *Judge* McAuley, and a *Jury of twelve blacks*" (214). Upon being found guilty, one was sentenced to thirty-nine lashes and the other two were fined and confined in irons. In this world of slavery turned upside down, "poor Jack was dreadfully mortified at being whipped by a black man" (214–15). The captain of the ship came ashore and wrangled with the Company officials, asking "by what authority they tried white men, the subjects of Great Britain, by a *Jury of Blacks;* it was so novel a circumstance, that it struck him with astonishment" (215). The Company's constitution, upon examination, made no mention of court procedures and the imprisoned men were released. Such a seemingly trivial episode connotes the implications of legal "counter-theater," as E. P. Thompson has called it, showing that promises of equality were still unfulfilled.[57]

Christopher Fyfe's collection of some of the manuscript letters from the settlers allows for a critical interpretation of the social and cultural milieu of the settlement.[58] The settlers' epistolary skills, according to Charles Jones, manifest many features of late-eighteenth-century American and British English. Through his linguistic research, Jones characterizes their language as equivalent to that of native speakers of nonstandard English.[59] What is most poignantly present in the settlers' letters is a barely expressed wish for nation and its utopian promise of freedom alongside a recognition of the harshness of colonial realities.

John Clarkson, who accompanied the Nova Scotian blacks to Sierra Leone and replaced the drunken Alexander Falconbridge as project leader, was a much-loved paternalistic figure in the settlement. Inclined to enact the more utopian and democratic aspects of Sharp's regulations, Clarkson had exceeded his jurisdiction by promising more than the Company was actually willing to grant. Subject to hysterical weeping and loss of memory after falling ill in the tropical environment, Clarkson's powers over the settlers were still formidable. Falconbridge notes his "winning manners, and mild, benign treatment . . . he can, by lifting up his finger (as he expresses it) do what he pleases with them" (131). Writing to Clarkson, who had returned to England and had been sidelined from the venture, James Hutcherson and Moses Murray refer to their condition as resembling Clarkson's own evangelical comparisons to "the Oppression that King Pharoh Where With Oppressed the Egyptians."[60] Importuning Clarkson's aid, the writers look up to him as a prophetic figure: "leave us Not in the Wilderness to the Oppressing Masters—but be Amongst us. As you have took that Great undertaking As Mosis & Joshua did—be with us Until the End."[61] Prince Hoare's adulatory biography of Granville Sharp likens him to "the inspired deliverer of the Hebrews [having] brought the captives out of the house of bondage, and given them to taste the milk and honey that flowed in a land of freedom."[62] Nathaniel Snowball and James Hutcherson also warn Clarkson of an impending plan to desert: "I [*sic*] am Chosin out the head of A Number of people to take my Departure as the Ezerlites did. When we may be no longer in bondage to this tyranious Crew."[63] Though these religious metaphors persist (there were several sectarian allegiances including Huntingdonian, Baptist, and Methodist), the settlers were just as ready to use secular metaphors. Reminded by some "of the recent melancholy fate of Louis XVI," Falconbridge reports that Governor Dawes faced settlers "threatning something similar to him" (193, 217).

Isaac Anderson and Cato Perkins were delegated to meet Company officials in London, where they petitioned that they were treated in Sierra Leone just in the manner of slaves. The most serious attempted revolt by the "turbulent and refractory spirit" animating the Nova Scotian blacks—as Sharp characterized it—began on September 25, 1800, when settlers drew up a new constitution defying the Company's demand for quitrents. The short-lived rebellion was put down in October with the fortuitous arrival of a ship containing 550 Jamaican maroons from Nova Scotia. These soldiers had been unhappy with their resettlement in Canada, much like the earlier Nova Scotian blacks; tricked into surrendering by a British truce, the Trelawny Town maroons disliked Canada and wished to return to a tropical environment. Under the superintendence of a Scot, George Ross, the maroons intervened as fiercely loyal company troops. Writing in 1803, R. C. Dallas describes this event: "On their arrival, their principles were immediately put to the test. An insurrection had taken place among the Nova Scotians, who understanding that means were about to be used for establishing the company's authority, had endeavoured to possess themselves of the government. Had the Maroons been the disciples of revolutionary emissaries, or the abettors of anarchy and equality, they would in all probability have joined the people of their own complexion to extirpate the white tyrant: on the contrary, they joined with alacrity in quelling the insurrection. Some of the insurgents were killed, many taken and tried, a few executed, and several banished."[64] Actually, though only two were hanged, thirty-one rebels were banished, including one Henry Washington, former slave to the first President of the United States. The system of the hundredors and tythingmen was abolished. George Ross kept a journal, recently published, revealing the unique mind-set of the maroons and their motives for throwing their lot in with the Company.[65] The maroons also helped defeat opposition by some native chiefs. Their absorption neutralized the demographic dominance of the Nova Scotians and ensured Company rule, soon to be replaced by Sierra Leone's incorporation as a British Crown Colony. The shared location of the Jamaican Maroons and the Nova Scotian blacks did not overcome either the political antagonism they felt toward each other or the sense of superiority both groups felt toward "Recaptives" settled there from impounded slave ships after the abolition of slave trading in 1807.[66] By absorption back into the British Empire, the colony lost any hopes that may have remained concerning the fledgling collectivist experiment. However, this utopian sense, especially of the all-too-brief 1787–91 period, remains in the history. According to one scholar, "the early constitution of Sierra Leone was the first instance in modern history of a self-governing community of non-Europeans where Negro freemen were allowed the political and civil rights of Europeans."[67] Wilberforce writes to Dundas about the Nova Scotians having "made the worst possible subjects . . . as thorough Jacobins as if they had been trained and educated in Paris."[68] The first currency issued by the Sierra Leone Company showed black and white hands joined in amity; unfortunately, as with the abolitionist mottoes on Wedgwood's pottery, there was a long way to go from antiracist symbol to real political equality. The Sierra Leone experience shows the limitations of studying anticolonial agency within a largely literary corpus.

Though Equiano died in 1797, his flirtation with English radicalism can also be compared with the insurrectionary nature of the black settlers in Sierra Leone. As a casual member of the London Corresponding Society and as a friend of its founder, Thomas Hardy, and a lodger in his house, Equiano can be located physically—if not ideologically—at the nerve center of the radical milieu of 1790s London. He had arrived in London after the Gordon Riots, and knew firsthand the oppressive conditions of the urban laboring poor. Within this context, liberationist ideas ranged from religious millenarianism to constitutional reformism. After preparing his fourth edition for publication in Thomas Hardy's home in Berkshire in 1791, Equiano went to Ireland to promote the book, where he was welcomed by several Irish radicals including Samuel Neilson "the Jacobin," Thomas McCabe, and Thomas Digges. Under the terrific repression unleashed by Pitt and the anti-Jacobin reaction, Equiano's last years saw the radicalization of the urban proletariat into more violent and seditious groups, such as those that Iain McCalman has reconstructed in *Radical Underworld*. After the arrest of Thomas Hardy, Equiano's blistering responses to the newspapers ceased, probably out of fear of arrest. The London

Corresponding Society opted for armed revolution in 1797, the year of Equiano's death. The muted challenge of Equiano's political vocabulary in an era of potential restitution soon turned into an angry and violent protest in the vision of a plebeian prophet such as Robert Wedderburn. Methodism always contained the possibility of an orthodox establishment attitude (as represented by Equiano's willingness to petition and work within the system) and also an anarchic chiliasm (as suggested by the heterodox reaction of Wedderburn a few decades later). "Reading Christians will be knowing Christians," recommended John Wesley, and according to one estimate, there were 56,000 lower-class Wesleyan readers by 1789.[69] Hence the typical context of a reader such as Wedderburn, who "derived much ghostly consolation" from a black autobiography given him in jail by William Wilberforce. It is tempting to ask if this unidentified text was Equiano's.[70]

THE FACTISH OF LITERACY

Are literary studies of colonialism overinvested in the book as cultural and aesthetic category? Should we investigate other forms of political and technological domination to rectify the imbalances generated by literary perspectives? Of course, agency is textualized, and the book is an especially convenient entry point into the role of ideology and the structures of hegemony in the modern era. However, literary studies cannot stop with the teaching that the world is textualized. The symbolic implications of colonial conflict often make us circle back to the book as a symptomatic displacement, but the historical and ethnological underpinnings of literature are sometimes more relevant than its contents. The writings of the Sierra Leonean settlers demonstrated that literary and aesthetic criteria are insufficient on their own for grasping the texture of agency. Literary study can lead to further analysis of models of reading, and cultural production and their interpretive matrices, but only with the help of greater circumspection.[71]

In a powerful analysis of the centrality of the book and its role in the colonial relation, Henry Louis Gates Jr. showcases Equiano as exemplary of revisionary "signifying" practices conducted by writers of African heritage on Western discourses they inherit and transform. Tracing the "Trope of the Talking Book" through the writings of Gronniosaw, Marrant, Cugoano, Equiano, Jackson, and Jea, Gates argues that black writers achieve full-blown subjectivity by appropriating the high cultural value assigned to literacy. Skillfully manipulating the colonialist uses of Bible and breviary which justified the subjugation of African slaves and American indigenes, Anglo-Africans reclaimed their agency by talking back in the master's voice, literate and learned as this voice was deemed to be. According to Gates, the cultural connotation of blackness as the sign of absence contrasts with these first literate attempts to speak it into presence, and hence, into subjecthood. These early writers cite and revise each other's attempts to represent scenes that highlight the illiterate African's confrontation of literacy. Gronniosaw, Marrant, and Jea recount the transition from the oral to the written in their own life as an element of plot, demonstrating the "miracle" of literacy; Cugoano and Equiano treat the Talking Book in a more sophisticated manner, as rhetorical figure. Through deliberate irony, these writers emphasize the racial and cultural hybridity of New World Africans and refute the racist stereotype of black as bestial. According to Gates, "in the black tradition, writing became the visible sign, the commodity of exchange, the text and technology of reason."[72]

Describing the uphill task faced by early black writers wishing to achieve recognition, Gates's reading is an impressive conflation of the category of subjecthood with the agency that comes from the complex technology of literacy. Such a reading pays the price of reiterating the evolutionary narrative so dear to early abolitionists, that of humanizing the African, even as it inevitably ignores the role of workaday literacy. Resistance to slavery took many forms, ranging from marronage and civil insubordination to contestation through music and fable. It is true that eighteenth-century racialists deemed slaves irrational by pointing to their illiteracy, yet why should the act of literate—idealized as literary—persuasion be privileged as *an end in itself* (to the extent that it is conflated with the a priori definition of humanity) if not for the fact that we believe, perhaps too much as literary critics, in the transformative power of literature and are all too willing to demonstrate literature *as* the sign of humanity?

Convincing the master of the slave's humanity through the power of writing was but one of several possibilities. Certainly, Equiano was actively discouraged from literate pursuits, but the acquisition of literacy did not magically lead to the appreciation of his humanity by many of the racialist characters he encountered over his life. Freedom for a few blacks when most were enslaved paradoxically meant greater vigilance for the free: Equiano suggests that "the state of a free negro" appeared "in some respects worse" than that of slaves because freedmen "lived in constant alarm for their liberty," which was often only nominal (1:249). In Georgia he was beaten and left for dead by white ruffians for "talking with some negroes in their master's yard" (1:268-69). Common sense would grant that slaves were already political and psychological subjects of the human community despite their masters' treatment of them as chattel and commodity and continued to be subjects both before and after they were coerced into the Middle Passage and the work of the plantation. Should we always assume that the master's definition of humanity was not just dominant but preemptive? Did the slave learn writing only reactively, to appear reasonable and refute the charge of inhumanity? More likely, the *humanist* focus on literacy has a narrative agenda, because literacy reconfigures, so effectively, the relationship between subjecthood and objectification. As a result, literacy illustrates its own transitive role—agency rendered self-reflexive— more than it proves subjecthood or its lack. Humanism seizes on literacy as self-exposure and makes it a foundational act on which it builds an aesthetic edifice. However, literacy can also represent a cynical ploy for mastery, the tyranny of the Mandarins, or the *trahison des clercs*. Equiano also generates a counter to the "talking book," demonstrating the pacification and subordination of the Miskito Indians and their neighbors by himself as a literate "Englishman." This standard colonial anecdote, concerning the power of almanacs to manipulate natives by predicting an eclipse, derives from Columbus's diaries and continues all the way to late Victorian fiction and Hollywood melodrama. Pointing to the Bible, Equiano frightens the Indians by threatening to read "and *tell* God to make them dead" (2:187). Such self-consciousness around scenes of reading can be interpreted as a veritable metaliteracy, where the subject's entry into the technology of print is understood as ironic and instrumental, self-empowering and ultimately self-critical. Gates has also shown how this African American trope of literacy effectively displaces the significance of cultural difference and ignorance onto a third group, such as the Incas or the Cherokees. Much like the ambivalence toward writing since Plato, literacy is shown as manipulative of others' fears even as it appears to enlighten the ignorant through book learning.[73]

Analyzing the book as colonial fetish could shed some light on this problem. The widespread instances of bibliophilic fetishism—dramas of the book and around its use—in the colonial record suggest that literacy further justifies the political and economic coercion already in place. A fetishization of technology is often produced—through the stagist narratives of eighteenth- and nineteenth-century political economy and comparative historiography from Montesquieu to Millar to Marx—to argue for European cultural and moral superiority. By no means a uniquely European invention, literacy, when allied with the Gutenberg revolution of moveable type, led to print capitalism, a formidable innovation with colonial consequences, among others. Printed books, along with guns and shipping, aided European dominance more than anything else.[74] Coming to literacy, therefore, as a coming to technology, expands the sphere of agency, even if this entry is falsely depicted as into the "West." As Brian Street puts it, literacy "is a social process in which particularly socially constructed technologies are used within particular institutional frameworks for specific social purposes."[75] Even if it sounds repetitive in this quotation, the mantra of social relevance and particular use is necessary so that historians can pose renewed questions: Whose literacy? For which purposes? And to what ends? Different from coming to literacy, coming to subjecthood implies entering the social sphere through language and occurs in all human cultures irrespective of the mastery of the technology of literacy. Relating subjecthood to objectification, autobiography creates the illusion of manipulating that relationship in a dialectical fashion through the subject. However, the agent "who" performs that manipulation is the subject who appropriates himself or herself as stable entity at the moment when he or she is in a fleeting transitivity of meaningful action. In the colonial context, the discovery of the book functions in the manner of a fetish whose origin and power are not fully comprehended. The Bible, for instance, is interpreted in the colonial sphere as metonym rather than transparent metaphor because the rules of recognition concerning its function are occluded. As Homi Bhabha puts it suggestively, "the book retains its presence, but [it] is no longer a representation of an essence; it is now a partial presence, a (strategic) device in a specific colonial engagement, an appurtenance of authority."[76] Applying this insight to abolitionist discourse, we can see this choice presented in the cover of the popular tract, *The African Prince*, which shows the model convert, Prince Naimbanna, spurning a licentious book even as the story emphasizes his deep adherence to Christianity as imbibed through contact with an approved book, the Bible. So, rather than argue Equiano's importance for literature along the lines that literacy allowed blacks to become full-blown subjects, let us return this humanist appropriation as a gift to its context: What does literature do, as fetish, for Equiano, and what are its repercussions in the context of his nationalization? By tracking metaliteracy, we can assess the more ironical implications of this process for Equiano, and for the larger romance narrative of "Eng. Lit." within which he is exhibited as a newly rediscovered text.

The history of the fetish as anthropological event clearly situates Equiano's multiple depictions of fetishism as a process, and analyzing the recent critical debates around the fetish can help recontextualize the fetishistic role of the book and Equiano's innovation. By way of a series of articles on the origins of the fetish, William Pietz has argued that what Europeans understood and described as fetishism arose in a mercantilist intercultural space, through a set of mutual contacts, perceptions, and misunderstandings between Portuguese and other European traders and the various peoples they traded with off the coasts of West Africa. Pietz's sustained meditation on the word "fetish" in its religious and ethnological contexts is tempered by his attestation of the term's "conceptual doubtfulness and referential uncertainty."[77] Fetishes, principally understood by Europeans as functioning within a religious context, came to comprise at least six kinds of objects that Pietz identifies: (1) sacramental objects, (2) aesthetic or erotic objects, (3) economically commodifiable objects, (4) medical and talismanic objects, (5) oath vehicles, and (6) European technological objects such as ships, instruments of navigation, and firearms. It could easily be shown that an object as culturally significant as the book participates in all six of these categories for Equiano. The part of fetishism that was compatible with economics was eventually absorbed by global trade, and those African practices that were seen as superstitious and obscurantist—because they were not end-oriented and commercial—were deemed confused concerning causality and hence "fetishistic" in a pejorative sense.[78]

In *A Natural History of Religion*, David Hume sees the rise of religion, and especially polytheism, as the inability to explain causality, leading to the objectification of the fetish. This explanation—of the lack of explanation—can be redirected to the similarly murky origins of the nation as subject. Like his French counterpart, Charles De Brosses, who actually coined the term fetishism, Hume took fetishism to represent a more radical contingency of object choice than earlier comparative ethnologists such as Lafitau, who had wanted to see fetishism as a degeneration from monotheism. For De Brosses, fetishism was the direct deification of objects; for Hume, the deification of objects and phenomena served to represent invisible beings, humanizing and substituting for that which was beyond explanation. The entry of philosophical method into comparative anthropology also led to reflections by Adam Smith, Denis Diderot, and others along the lines of Hume. This line of fetishism as false religion and misplaced causality stretches through a range of applications by nineteenth-century thinkers including Kant, Hegel, Tylor, and Comte, to Marx, and eventually to Freud.[79]

Bruno Latour, in his recent intervention into the fetishism debates, suggests that this conversion of religion into a causal problem for epistemological demystification ultimately leads nowhere. Rather than worry about its epistemology we ought to acknowledge the role of fetish as pragmatic application. Freud accuses the sexual fetishist of inversion, dissimulation, and displacement of desire onto an object, and Marx attributes the same kinds of effects to general phenomena—such as the commodity—that are impacted by a multitude of actors and social processes. Modernity, as we know it, is a perspective that distinguishes fact from fetish and truth from error, leading to the claims of the social sciences—even if at another level, the same perspective is forced to acknowledge the artificial construction of fact and the production of truth as a discursive effect—the discoveries of poststructuralist theory. Latour recommends an agnostic abandonment of epistemologies that rely on the critical *denunciation* of structures of *belief*—whether psychoanalytic or socioeconomic—in favor of a perspective from *a*modernity, one that refuses the primitive-modern distinction. Analysis, then, tracks the subject's capacity to *make do* (*fait faire*) with the fetish, a process that dispenses with questions concerning belief and instead concentrates on those oriented around practice. Dubbing this new recognition of the identity of fact and fetish a *factish* (*faitiche*), Latour characterizes this factish as "the robust certainty which allows action without having to believe in the difference between constructivism and empiricism, immanence and transcendence." In other words, the factish reunites, under the sign of practice, the contradictions created by a rationalist critical analysis that evaluates *other* unenlightened beliefs, even as this analysis fails when applied to the analyst's own subjective performance. This factish promises to go beyond the rationality-belief opposition always at stake in both Marx's and Freud's very different applications of the fetish.[80]

We can see that the Sierra Leonean settlers treat literacy as a factish, practicing Enlightenment to the degree that it solves their pressing situation and abandoning it for armed resistance (that also turns out to be an equally abortive means). Equiano's own literacy is a factish in terms of its political efficaciousness, but we should also notice his ready reabsorption into literature as fetish, a delayed result stemming from his narrative of nationalization. For these reasons, I propose a brief detour through Equiano's precursor text, *Robinson Crusoe*, which illustrates the fetish-factish distinction and makes clear its eventual outcome for literacy when revised by Equiano.

In the second part of the narrative, *Farther Adventures of Robinson Crusoe*, Crusoe tells proudly how he destroyed a local deity, thus denouncing the natives' belief in a god called Cham-Chi-Thaungu, worshipped in a remote region of Central Asia. Crusoe magnanimously rejects the proposal by a Scottish fellow traveler to massacre the entire local populace, but instead decides to humiliate the diabolists by destroying the "senseless log of an idol" in their presence even as they are prevented from doing harm to themselves (see Fig. 24). The crude illustration, also from the 1720 French edition, represents the apotropaic and irrational nature of this gesture of "Christian" Enlightenment, which has to establish the true religion on the basis of a violent destruction of the deity shown as bogeyman. In the culminating volume, *Serious Reflections*, Crusoe confirms his actions in the *Farther Adventures* by insisting that "no quarter should be given to Satan's administration; no part of the devil's economy should have any favor, but all the idols should be immediately destroyed and publicly burnt, all the pagodas and temples burnt, and the very face and form of paganism, and the worship attending it, be utterly defeated and destroyed." Even as Crusoe charges the savages of America and Africa with diabolism, in "A Vision of the Angelic World," appended to *Serious Reflections*, he begins to suspect that his encounters with the devil on the island were "all hypochondriac delusion." Denouncing and violently persecuting others' beliefs, Crusoe as modern ends with doubts concerning incidents that earlier were lived certainties.[81]

Figure 24 *The Destruction of the Idol Cham-Chi-Thaungu,* from the French edition of *The farther adventures of Robinson Crusoe* (1720). (British Library, London)

If we turn from Crusoe's fetishistic epistemology to his practice, his behavior on the island is just as much the primitive's tactic of "making do" with the factish. Subsequent to his shipwreck Crusoe plunders the ship of all its ironwork—razors, scissors, knives, and forks—indeed, the very goods that would have been bartered for slaves on the West African coast. Tools and weapons were the equivalent of ready money as well as the instruments with which to extract surplus. Even as Crusoe rediscovers the use value of objects that were present on the ship for exchange purposes precisely when their exchange potential is rendered irrelevant, the ready money that Crusoe finds is bereft of immediate use. Recognizing the agency of the tools is linked in Crusoe's mind to the inutility of their exchange counterpart, money itself. Crusoe addresses money in the animated apostrophe early on in the narrative as "O Drug!" and as a "Creature whose Life is not worth saving."[82] This animation of money occurs alongside the discovery of its lack of agency on a desert island and a brief contemplation of its "murder" by neglect. While the prudent Crusoe does not jettison the money and instead hoards it, the tools are commodity fetishes that turn into factishes, active agents of Crusoe's plantation capital as well as objects of sacramental use that mediate more directly between him and his island environment.

Crusoe is the only human subject on his island for a long time, and the lack of society makes him ascribe agency to several nonhuman sources. He peoples his domain with virtual subjects, for instance, jokingly speaking of his family of pets, and literally worries himself sick about phantom agents that are never quite understood as subjects. The devil, neither wholly present nor absent, is held responsible for the footprint episode. In Crusoe's world, commodities are especially significant agents, dissolving in themselves the agent-object distinction. Tobacco, for instance, highly commodifiable, is the lucrative crop in Crusoe's Brazilian plantation but also of great medical and talismanic significance to him on the island. Crusoe's heterodox Brazilian cure for moral and physical "Distemper" attempts a drug overdose (when Crusoe calls money a "drug," it is in the older sense of a useless commodity, posset, or "drug on the market").[83] Crusoe reads the Bible, chews tobacco, dissolves it in rum and drinks it, and finally, in the same sitting, inhales its smoke on a pan of hot coals. While "doing" tobacco in these three different ways—solid, liquid, and gaseous—Crusoe resorts to a Puritan bibliomancy to enact the mysterious workings of agency. Impressing Friday with the mysteries of agency also happens through repeating a set piece of European travel narrative that began with Alvise da Cadamosto: Crusoe claims superiority through the technological mastery of his gun (147, 153).[84]

These factishes are created by Crusoe's improvisational practices. The didactic element of the novel has always produced critics, from Rousseau to the Edgeworths to Marx, who marveled at Crusoe's role as bricoleur, good housewife, or *homo economicus*, strangely conflating these very different social positions into the flexible positionality of his functional improvisation and survival. Crusoe's objects are seized opportunistically from his environment. If Crusoe did not have the tobacco to smoke, he might have thought about scraping dried banana peels if he had found them. Factishes are fabricated out of existing resources.

Later, these factishes are redistributed as "objects," introduced into a network by "a" "subject," who organizes their relational meaning. This organizational activity itself involves a Freudian narrational fetishism that is *retroactive,* resulting from Crusoe's stay on the island, most clearly represented in the sequence of action and reflection that occurs in the footprint passage discussed earlier.

If late-seventeenth-century England treated domestic slaves as pets, or as personalized fetishes, the booming slave economy by the end of the eighteenth century treated slaves as commodities or transactional fetishes. Lieutenant John Matthews writes, for instance, that in West Africa "slaves are the medium, instead of coin, for the purchase of every necessary, and the supplying of every want; and every article is estimated, by its proportion, to the value of a slave."[85] However, Crusoe's island interlude involves the unselfconscious discovery of the factish even as its textual *representation* is a confusing mixture of the discourse of pets and the discourse of commodity, and thereby, the modern Janus-like composite of personal fetish and transactional fetish, two faces that together make up the world of affect and economics. Equiano, writing seventy years later, appropriates Crusoe's double discourse from Friday's subject position, speaking from the psychoanalytic sense of himself as personal fetish when describing his youth, and the economic sense of himself as commodity when he arrives at adulthood. There are a number of intriguing moments that stage these perceptions in Equiano's text. Through an agile use of narrative technique, the early portions of the autobiography ventriloquize the feeling of initial cultural encounter through the voice of a naïve adolescent, creating uncanny effects of objectival animation and supernatural wish-fulfillment. For instance, a fellow sailor who swore in vain immediately faces the literal consequences of his oath, losing an eye that he had damned (1:117). A captain who refuses to allow him to trade on his own account is butted by bullocks being brought on board. He makes amends by allowing Equiano to bring aboard turkeys, but is still punished by losing his cattle by flooding in the hold even while the birds survive (2:29–30).

Equiano perceives factishes early in the narrative (just as Crusoe does early in his). These factishes are later, retroactively and narratively, converted into fetishes. Upon being sold to Captain Pascal in Virginia, the young boy sees unfamiliar objects as undifferentiated factishes. Seeing "a watch which hung on the chimney," the lad "was quite surprised at the noise it made, and was afraid it would tell the gentleman any thing I might do amiss." Similarly, in a much discussed passage, Equiano "observed a picture hanging in the room, which appeared constantly to look at me" (1:92). After first thinking "it was something relative to magic," the youth assumes, quite rightly, the portrait's function as a way "the whites had to keep their great men when they died, and offer them libation as we used to do to our friendly spirits" (1:93). Both these examples are well chosen. Though they are "mistakes" of agency from a realist perspective, they identify the fear of surveillance that dominates the life of a slave. Gates, for instance, has argued that the watch and the portrait represent abstractions of the commodification of the slave's time and the master's assertion of ownership over his body.[86] This reading, however, translates the diegetic nature of the factish into the non-diegetic interpretation of it as commodity fetish, ascribing the agency perceived in the object to its putative subjective owner. But the frontispiece had already suggested the complex involvement of the portrait in narratives of agency. The reader is encouraged to distinguish between diegetically reading along with the youth who sees the master as tyrant, and reading extradiegetically from the perspective of the older narrator's analysis of slave society. The agency of the portrait or the watch "belongs" properly neither to diegetic master and slave nor to the emancipated, extradiegetic narrator. It exists, rather, as the sign of plenitude and the transition from one to the other. The literary fetish is the residue of the factish after its efficacy, and agency disappears even as we appreciate literature as the leavings of this earlier human activity.

Agency flows through the portrait as a transitional energy (tyranny) between master (subject) over youthful slave (object), or in reverse form (emancipation) from the narrator (subject) to the reported earlier incident of master's tyranny (object). Agency can be seen in the immediate power of the master as well as the retroactive power (Nachträglichkeit) of the narrator, and yet it is not a unique possession of one or the other. It is a naïve reading that would claim that the slave (object) becomes emancipated (subject), whereas this reading is overlaid by another, that of slave (already subject) who recognizes his own oppression as not just the immediate one by the physical master but, by a more complex agent, that of slave society. As oppressive interdictions, the injunctions of slave society stand behind the master as the law. It is this law that Equiano cannot access as a youth, even as he sees it accessed by a special tool presented as a metonym of power: "I had often seen my master and Dick employed in reading; and I had a great curiousity to talk to the books, as I thought they did; and so to learn how all things had a beginning: for that purpose I have often taken up a book, and have talked to it, and then put my ears to it, when alone, in hopes it would answer me; and I have been very much concerned when I found it remained silent" (1:106-7). This famous episode is yet another reworking of *Robinson Crusoe*. Equiano demonstrates and readapts Crusoe's bibliomancy to inaugurate his entry into literacy.

Yet, the passage also reflects the failure that Crusoe experiences with the footprint. Despite all his bricolage, Crusoe is flummoxed when he encounters an undecipherable sign in his environment, a sign that suggests other powers and dangers even as it withholds its meaning. The agents who act upon Crusoe are frequently metaphorical abstractions perceived as metonymic absences and presences: "God," "Providence," or "Devil." Crusoe's deliverance occurs after he experiences captivity, shipwreck, and familial alienation. Such is also the case with Equiano. Deploying a fetishistic logic of subject construction, the older Equiano looks back toward factishes felt by the boy, such as watch, portrait, and book, and separates magic from market and fetish from commodity. Captain Pascal, the tyrannical former master, demystifies the nature of the miraculous within the youth's psychology. Meeting Equiano by chance in Greenwich Park, Pascal asks how he came back. Equiano's surly reply, "in a ship," is responded to with "I suppose you did not walk back to London on the water" (2:82). Indeed, these three memorable factishes from the autobiography are brought together as a mise en abîme with the frontispiece portrait, of Equiano, rather than the master, manipulating his own Bible rather than observing the ostensible miraculousness of others' reading. The element of time returns through the appropriation of the traditional Christian gesture of the admonitory glance. Equiano is, as subject, pointing to the book in his hand, an indexical rather than an iconic gesture that resituates the Bible as factish rather than transparent revelation. The curious shift of tense in the above passage demonstrates the ongoing power of the book as factish, pragmatic *and* mystifying. Whereas the youth *had* seen the miracle of reading demonstrated, the subject reports his perplexity in a past tense suggesting a continuation into the present: "I *have* often taken up a book . . . *have* talked to it . . . *have* been very much concerned when I found it remained silent."

Defoe's and Equiano's representations of the book are responses to a crisis of intercultural representation. Their respective fetishisms of the book are symptomatic misapprehensions that do not properly "belong" to either subject or ethos. As a semantic event with historical and epistemic repercussions, fetishism involves what Gayatri Chakravorty Spivak has called, in the context of subaltern history, "a functional change in a sign-system."[87] Equiano is applying an intercultural concept to his situation even as he is transiting from one condition to another, allowing a new kind of agency to traverse his being. The factish for him and for Crusoe is the Bible, a catachresis for agency arising at a felt moment of disculturation. In the manner of catachresis, the book is a concept-metaphor without an adequate referent. It stands for the workings of culture, the ultimately secreted and untraceable origin of change. The more readily the "factitious universal" of the book makes itself available to Equiano, the more it represents a utopian escape from subjection through the acquisition of literacy. It is through such catachrestical reappropriation that Equiano tropicalizes colonialist representation. The appeal to a culture of bibliolatry makes for a symbolic transition that Equiano fashions between an Igbo mode of knowing and a British literacy: the book is embraced as a prerequisite for becoming a representative "voice" in British culture. It is not literacy per se that makes the difference but the agent's, Equiano's, operation and deployment of that specific "technology" which just like the West African "fetish," or *grisgris*, or Crusoe's gun, obtains a performative power on its wearer and creates action-at-a-distance. Literacy, as technology, redistributes Equiano (subject or object) to a different location vis-à-vis his master and slave culture (also subject or object). Equiano's story is not just about the development from slave object to desiring subject through literacy, as narrated by Gates, but also about how literacy, as a reconfiguration of agency, gives the subject the catachrestical sense of "owning" himself or herself, something articulating these historical property dynamics through metaliteracy.

Activating catachresis, metaliteracy performs a *re-membering* of the fetish as factish. Putting economic commodity and personal fetish back together results in a genealogical exercise that leads back to colonialism, its discourses, practices, and institutions, from the standpoint of Equiano's subaltern identity, an identity relinquished as soon as he finds voice. The memory of dismemberment or alienation suggests a lapsarian narrative of fetishism where both gods and men become mute material objects that are then ventriloquized in relation to an absent cause. The performance of rememoration, or the factish, makes the book much more than a "trope"; it is an object (to be pointed to), a fetish (on the wearer's body), a commodity (to be sold on endless book promotion tours until Equiano's death), a factish (that performs without the previous analytical distinction between fetish and commodity), and a generic vocabulary (of autobiography, slave narrative, biblical typology). Imaging the withheld magic of translation, the famous setpiece of the talking book presents cultural incommensurability. The book offers the autobiographer in Equiano a paradoxical freedom, despite his marginal status in the past that he subsequently describes. One of the principal motivations of Equiano's text, as we discussed, is to make the case for the abolition of the slave trade. In this respect, Equiano represents his naïve and youthful self as a necessary didactic fiction of his rise to the world of letters that refuted racialst dismissals of African intellect. Equiano has to euhemerize himself as a warrior-hero, suggesting that his Igbo name Olaudah means "vicissitude or fortunate," also "one favoured, and having a loud voice, and well spoken."[88] Preferring the biblical name Jacob, he initially resists the ironical slave name Gustavus Vassa, the king who was the liberator of Sweden. Euhemerism—making gods out of men—is necessary for heroicization, but it has to be understood that it is related to its reverse. Dehumanization, caused through chattel slavery, inflicts fetishistic dismemberment. Equiano's cultural nationalism—through his idealized account of Essaka in Benin—produces a mythistorical re-membering. His evocation of *his* people uses the trope of catachrestical synecdoche as a politically effective beginning. While the subject was always subject, the postcolonial fetish-turned-agent, the combination of author and book in the frontispiece portrait, through *making do* with the fetish, performs the factish. Therein lies the paradox of *finding agency* in the dead matter of books.

Equiano narrates the magical agency of his own birth, perhaps like Athena's, fully armed, into a national literature. His writing is overwhelming testimony to the newfound persistence of the context of nationalization. Equiano represents himself to the nation; in answer to the charge that enslaved Africans cannot represent themselves (fostered as much by the abolitionists as by the apologists), literacy helps Equiano represent his class in the plural. However, his nationalization comes from a full-fledged understanding of the rhetorical basis of national literature in the notion of imagined community. Showing the triumph of an eighteenth-century literature qua English literature, Equiano performs a process, animating the tropicopolitan as factish—through agency—into the category of the postcolonial subject. A simple narrative of *before* and *after,* object to subject, is transposed into a performance. The agency that we assume led from *before* to *after,* is in fact Nachträglichkeit, a deferred action, emerging from the past that can, in the future, rationalize itself into the present.

The complex representation of writing, culture, and nationality in Equiano's text therefore has merited this long examination, especially as literature impinges on the relationship between *a* nation and *the* state and Equiano's imagining of an "*African* community" in relation to the hegemony of the *British* state. At different moments in his career, Equiano's nationalization presents both the faces of civic nationalism and ethnic nationalism, demanding to be treated on equal terms without prejudice as well as exploring the separatist possibility of repatriation for emancipated slaves. The imbrications of literacy with modern nationalisms is doubly relevant for the central narrative of personal emancipation from slavery that Equiano wants to tell. Literacy represents access to political discourse and socioeconomic privilege, indeed access to the British state itself. But this access, claimed by the particular subject (Equiano), transitively evokes a postemancipatory nation of "my oppressed countrymen." Equiano addresses his autobiography to "the Lords Spiritual and Temporal, and the Commons of the Parliament of Great Britain," identifying himself as "an unlettered African, who is actuated by the hope of becoming an instrument towards the relief of his suffering countrymen" (iii–iv). Political representation is at the forefront here; Equiano says his "chief design . . . is to excite in your august assemblies a sense of compassion for the miseries which the Slave-Trade has entailed on my unfortunate countrymen" (iii). However, this quasi-nationalist interlocution—*your* political leaders need to empathize with what has been done to *my* people—gives way to the rhetoric of minoritarian inclusion. Equiano says that the experience of slavery has been, paradoxically, "infinitely more than compensated by the introduction I have thence obtained to the knowledge of the Christian religion, and of a nation which, by its liberal sentiments, its humanity, the glorious freedom of its government, and its proficiency in arts and sciences, has exalted the dignity of nature" (iv).

Notions such as "the dignity of nature" also stood in for concerns about slavery's brutality to women. Equiano's apostrophe to his sister, whom he momentarily encounters after his kidnapping, though to his chagrin he is torn away from her again, as well as his indignant descriptions of the "violent depredations on the chastity of female slaves" brought renewed attention (1:59–61, 205). Toward the end of the autobiography, Equiano begins to lay the ground for his marriage to a white woman, Susanna Cullen, by discussing other successful interracial marriages (2:216–17). Whereas it is the slave trade as dehumanizing principle that Equiano deplores, the twin cultural entities of Christian religion and British nation are what he recognizes as emancipatory. The theme of coming to consciousness to the imagined community, or reawakening, is central to the articulation of nationalist ideology and makes its appearance in Equiano's text, which went to nine editions in his lifetime and thirty-six editions from 1789 to 1850.[89] In this sense, acquisition of literacy is a protonationalist moment par excellence. The renaming of Equiano as Vassa (after dry runs through Jacob and Michael) mocks the slave. Vassa's reclaiming of a euhemeristic Equiano transforms mock-heroic into heroic through performance, much as the fictional Oroonoko did. The petition to Queen Charlotte on March 21, 1788, is included in the first edition of the autobiography. Subsequent editions are bolder, supplementing the original list of subscribers with Scottish and Irish ones and implicating the subscribers as Equiano's co-petitioners, as Vincent Carretta has copiously demonstrated in the apparatus to his Penguin edition of the 1794 text.[90] Not included in any of Equiano's editions are all the other parliamentary petitions he wrote (at least a hundred, and the very practicum of political literacy). Equiano frequently led delegations of black leaders to Parliament, held individual consultations with members, and was on at least two separate occasions received by the prime minister and the speaker of the House.[91]

Autobiography is a genre that can be placed somewhere between novels and newspapers: Equiano has to, as a writer, think through his position on "nation" even as he situates himself as a national subject. By nation Equiano sometimes means tribe and at other moments perhaps a more generalized *ethnie*. When he narrates his childhood memories of life in West Africa, his description benefits from a modular transposition of quasinationalist rhetoric. The description of the Embrenche as judges and senators culturally translates Essaka into an oligarchic Roman Republic, while the Igbos are described as similar to Jews and most likely descended from those people of the book (both groups circumcise males and engage in many acts of ritual purification). Equiano translates cultural difference into something recognizable to an English audience. The anthropological manners-and-customs discourse is transformed into a repeatable modular form, suggesting the credible rationality of such a protonationalist and ethnocomparatist method.

Equiano choreographs his origins in a manner that combines the real importance of danced ritual in Igbo society with the tenets of early Romantic communitarianism: "[W]e are almost a nation of dancers, musicians, and poets" (1:10). Group dancing for him becomes a form of collective national self-representation. "Each [dance] represents some interesting scene of real life, such as a great achievement, domestic employment, a pathetic story, or some rural sport; and as the subject is generally founded on some recent event, it is therefore ever new" (1:11). Later, he describes how "each different nation of Africa meet and dance after the manner of their own country" among the black population of Jamaica (2:101). In *The Analytical Review*, Mary Wollstonecraft picks up on these communitarian aspects of dance in the narrative, as does the reviewer in *The Gentleman's Magazine*. Equiano concludes his nostalgic account of benign and exotic origins with a flourish from the Bible harnessed to combat color prejudice, from Acts (1:43).[92]

This sententiousness suggests a preacher's conventional ability to combat the ideology of slavery. However, Equiano passes, not just discursively but sometimes ethnically. Once he impersonates a white man in order to liberate a former slave who was kidnapped and about to be forcibly returned on ship to St. Kitt's (2:121). Cleverly placing compliments about himself in other people's mouths, Equiano resists conversion to Catholicism even though a priest tempts him with the crass bait that he "might in time become even pope; and that Pope Benedict was a black man" (2:165). His sounding of the rhetoric of Christian universalism as imperative resembles Homi Bhabha's characterization of the contentless hybridity of the colonial moment. What begins as a cultural challenge, leveling the European with the African, is quickly silenced with the prospect of the European's exultation being tempered by benevolence and gratitude. For example, Thomas Thompson, the English missionary off the Guinea coast, says that he "really was dissatisfied with their [the natives'] passive and easy behaviour, as *they never started any argument at all*. This seemed to indicate that they were the most resolved against persuasion and conviction." Thompson, who had fruitlessly attempted to convince several West African natives to convert to Christianity, "*white man's fashion*," is confused by the pliant behavior of the potential converts. Saying that "*white man knows best*," the West Africans adamantly continue with certain fetishistic practices, arguing that "black man follow black man's fashion."[93] This "sly civility" in Equiano's deference to the Bible or Thompson's complaint of the lack of resistance might seem like loss of courage. However, witness Bhabha's account of the wily mimicry of the colonial barber (one of Equiano's multiple professional personae) who, as he picks his client's pocket, cries out, "How the master's face shines!" and then whispers, "But he's lost his mettle."[94]

Equiano's autobiography leads us to the "emptiness" of a historical content that characterizes the colonial realism within narratives of nationalization. But this "emptiness" can also be interpreted by drawing attention to the suppressed trace of the factish. In this regard, the framing devices of the portrait, the dedication, the opening and closing chapters, as well as the thematization of the Bible as factish, lead the reader to an appreciation of the limitations of nationalization. A Britannocentric cultural studies can readily lay claim to Equiano as a black British voice, much in the manner of his ongoing relevance for African American literature. However, it is the historical context of the Sierra Leone expedition that wrests Equiano from being a fetish for national literatures. Despite its very real intervention in the British abolitionist debates, *Interesting Narrative* is located within the plural processes and many factishes of tropicopolitan agency. The important but ignored context of Sierra Leone suggests that there is more to Equiano's act of literacy than the specific nationalization that is favored by either black British or African Americanist literary humanist agendas.

Does literary criticism need proof of anticolonial agency in writing? If so, what kind of writing is acceptable? Is it possible to go beyond the self-rationalizing gesture of criticism that confuses agency with literacy and ultimately literacy with literature? Perhaps, but only if criticism pays greater attention to the multiple ideological significations of the culturally variable technology of literacy and the historically different constructions of the institution of "Literature." Literature, when it is investigated in relation to the diversity of readers and reading formations, reveals its own relation to various literacies. Within the specifically tropicopolitan focus of this study, the multiple acts of reading and writing generate a very different picture from the binary opposition of an assumed colonial literacy and literature to its other, a colonized orality. If, as Renée Balibar has pointed out, the institutional function of literature consists of the magical act of "making a literary text appear in its context," we need to be much more aware of how certain contexts are naturalized and aestheticized in the discipline and how the literary ideals we pursue efface more unaccustomed contexts.[95]

By resuscitating a context such as the curious history of the Sierra Leone project, reading Equiano's text brings the politics of literacy—still a burning question—to the fore. Literacy has advanced to another dimension in today's computerized world, one that is beset with problems of access to technology, schooling, and greater socioeconomic and environmental discrepancies between industrialized North and underdeveloped South. Using Equiano's text as a springboard into the problems of literacy and technology may appear an unnecessary enhancement of background noise by this sudden acceleration to problems of the present. However, as Wai Chee Dimock suggests, it may be time to forgo the "poetics of wonder" fostered by literary aesthetics and instead recontextualize literature according to "a theory of resonance."[96] The resonances of Equiano's literacy, and all its implications, as they have arisen in relation to his contexts have led to several outcomes. A contemplation of the open-endedness of literacy suggests an interminable, unfolding conversation. Equiano's tale, of the book that refused to talk to him or, for that matter, the contemporary woes of the computer illiterate who cannot afford or access this new literacy, appear on the surface to be a naïve lament of the uninitiated. However, we have found in our investigation that underneath the sign of inadequacy there lies a complex set of questions concerning the nature of literacy, the fetish of technology, and the continuation, through subterranean echoes, of the buzz, murmur, and crackle of multiple resonances. Vocal, alphabetical, visual, and electronic, the force field of multiple literacies traverse human activity in myriad directions. Within these lexical nexuses, and supported by a network of readers, Literature crystallizes as a thing apart in the long wake of rhetoric, Enlightenment, and nationalism. Like Crusoe's violence toward the heathen god and the idolatrous people, Literature drags multiple literacies into a coercive acknowledgment of its superiority, mastery, and greater humanity. Yet, Literature is ultimately not different from the idolatry it wishes to destroy. As the book confronts the computer screen and libraries unravel into the electronic archive, Literature spontaneously combusts and sublimates into the multidimensional futures of literacies. The dystopian nightmare, as exemplified by the manipulation of the Miskito Indians, envisions computer literacy leading to greater social divisions and hierarchies. The utopian dream takes the form of the Talking Book, that literacies, no longer fetishized, perform themselves as factishes within a chaosmos of ordered uncertainties. The neocolonial politics of the electronic archive, like those of the print library, remain open-ended.

CHAPTER SEVEN

Tropicalizing the Enlightenment

Saint Domingue is the first country in modern times to have posed in reality, and to also have posed for human reflection, the great problem that the twentieth century has not yet succeeded in resolving [*s'essouffle à résoudre*] in all its social, economic, and racial complexity: the colonial problem.

—AIMÉ CÉSAIRE, *Toussaint Louverture*[1]

Nationalization, which collectivizes the entry of the tropico-politan into literature, begins incrementally but revises tradition retroactively. Literacy in Equiano's life develops from the episode of the talking book, proceeds to the pacification of the Miskito Indians, and ends with the petitioning of Queen Charlotte. From dazzling miracle to strategy of survival, literacy eventually enables a legislative proposal. Proceeding from passive to active, from the unlettered to the schooled to the scholar, Equiano's rise theatricalizes—and ironizes—literacy's cumulative force. The idealized figure of reading motivates and thwarts empirical readers such as the Sierra Leone settlers or the young, still illiterate Equiano. *Reading* is replete with potential and plenitude: a fluid imagining of apprehension, understanding, and action, a pure literacy as wish-fulfillment, a dream of talking books; whereas *readers* stutter their way through books imperfectly: realizing few possibilities, imposing too many circumstantial desires, and suffering the use of the book as confidence trick. Scenes of reading are mobile dramatizations of the abstract process of literacy. In response to colonialist arguments that foreground, fetishize, and falsify the relationship between literacy and civilization, scenes of reading generate a kind of *metaliteracy*, enabling the reconceptualization and tropicalization of that purported relationship. In the late eighteenth century, when universal cosmopolitanism followed European practices, leading to the globalization of commerce *as* civilization and literacy *as* culture, metaliteracy reminds readers of the violence of the word upon the world.

The biography and the novel edify the individual life in modern literary form while the history and the encyclopedia anchor those lives within concrete social practices, historical pasts, and natural environments. The great literary projects of the British and French eighteenth century include Boswell's *Life of Johnson* and Johnson's *Dictionary;* Diderot and D'Alembert's *Encyclopédie* and Voltaire's *Le siècle de Louis XIV.* Global histories, including Montesquieu's, Hume's, Gibbon's, and Robertson's, satisfy the desire for minute particulars within a hierarchical synthesis even as the biography or the novel aims to capture a life as much as the age. In this regard, as both colonial encyclopedia and global history, Abbé Guillaume-Thomas Raynal's *Histoire philosophique et politique du commerce et des établissements des Européens dans les deux Indes* has undergone a remarkable revival in recent years. The text's uneven literary value and inordinate length (more than 2,500 quarto pages and 4,800 octavo ones by the 1780 third edition) had consigned it to relative obscurity in the nineteenth century when the heritage of Enlightenment philosophy was being assessed and its principal authors were being canonized.[2]

A glance at the division of the *Histoire des deux Indes* reveals the spatial reorganization of history and anthropology by way of a commercial rationale. The work is divided geographically into nineteen books, each subdivided into numerous chapters. Books 1–5 deal with European expansion in Asia—the "Indes Orientales." Following the actions of individual European powers in different regions, the history also describes the local cultures and histories that these powers had to confront. Major colonial establishments, such as those run by the Portuguese, Dutch, English, and French in Asia, get a book each, while book 5 summarizes the commercial activities of minor European powers in Asia, such as the Danes, Belgians, Swedes, Prussians, Spaniards, and Russians. Books 6–9 concern themselves with the other continental extremity from Europe, South America, where Spanish depredations in different parts of that continent and the Portuguese domination of Brazil figure prominently. Las Casas influenced Raynal and Diderot considerably, providing the work with a springboard from which to launch anticolonial invective aimed at Spain. Books 10–14 approach the policy implications of the work as they deal with the sugar islands of the West Indies, then the most profitable European colonial possessions. The political and economic implications of the institution of slavery in the plantations are analyzed at great length, and the constraints posed by intra-European competition form an undercurrent that compromises the various reforms that the text advocates. Book 11 deals uniquely with the history and practice of the slave trade. The final quarter, books 15–18, deals with British and French possessions in North America and was significantly rewritten with a radical edge for the third edition following the American Revolution of 1776. The nineteenth book becomes an omnibus compilation by topic of important intellectual forays made in the previous books. The division of the world into spheres of influence by competing mercantilist powers reveals that trade is paramount, and the accompanying world history correspondingly features Europeans as actors among non-Europeans rendered as contexts. Agency resides with the philosopher who floats above the globe, a detached, omnivoyant spectator registering human activity as commercial, even as the political and cultural aspects of the dominated regions are rendered as a plethora of exotic and subordinate detail. However, despite these Eurocentric references, the heterogeneous cultures of the globe, documented in their diversity, animate what later proves to be the radical emancipationist underside to a mercantilist encyclopedia.[3]

Interrogating colonial commerce with the help of philosophical and political principles, the *Histoire des deux Indes* becomes a secular alternative to Equiano's Bible, a prize exhibit for the unfolding of metaliteracy. Staying with the effects of metaliteracy, this chapter is structured around scenes of reading. Talking books inevitably lead to discourses marching in the streets. The first scene involves the Jacobin-French radicalization of Raynal's compendium under the conditions of censorship, a radicalization that plays out the incendiary consequences of Diderot's interpolations. This scene splits into several related parts: the reading of Raynal as visionary by the Jacobin clubs, Raynal's refusal to claim responsibility for a text that had outrun his editorial intentions, and his more recent reception in a plurality of contexts both national and philosophical. The second scene of reading features the metaliteracy suggested by accounts associating the Haitian leader Toussaint Louverture with the black Spartacus passage in the *Histoire des deux Indes*. This speech foreshadows Toussaint's leadership of the Haitian Revolution of 1791–1804. The heroization of Toussaint through agonistic metaliteracy—a largely retroactive process—involves elegiac sonnets by Wordsworth as well as the Trotskyist reading made famous by C. L. R. James in *The Black Jacobins*. James's historiography initiated a reversal of the Eurocentric histories of slavery, emancipation, and decolonization, as well as those of the French Revolution that have tended to depict democratic ideals as spreading outward from Europe and America to liberate the rest of the world. Texts such as James's *The Black Jacobins* and Aimé Césaire's *Toussaint Louverture* have credited the last quarter of the eighteenth century with a fourth major, if often forgotten, revolution with global implications, namely the Haitian Revolution (in addition to the Industrial, American, and French Revolutions). In the light of this decolonized vision a different set of scholarly questions could be posed upon reading *Histoire des deux Indes*.[4]

The third scene of reading moves from apocrypha to thought experiment, imagining, as nationalization, a reading of the trope of Medea by Toussaint's virtual daughter-in-law, a scene that could function as a textual analogue of the voodoo ceremony at Bois-Caïman that began the cycle of slave insurrections. Themes of regeneration intermix with apprehensions of female sacrifice and sorcery in the *Histoire,* as well as in Saint Domingue, revealing female agency in the narration-that-was and also, equally, in the nation-to-be. Catachrestically revivifying myth, postcolonial genealogies tropicalize the Enlightenment. Burke's misplaced lament for the bygone age of chivalry and his resentment of œconomists and calculators in the *Reflections* could be addressed by the postcolonial recognition that in this new Viconian age of mere men (even if their heroism is suspect and their reading skills are exaggerated) readers are heroes, and writers are gods.

TROPING THE COLONIES IN FRANCE

Histoire des deux Indes is now recognized as the most widely distributed of global histories in the half century following its publication. Especially in France, it functioned as a journalistic intertext that mediated political philosophy for less intellectual readers and spoke for the political aspirations of middle- and working-class subjects outside the tight circle of institutional patronage.[5] Spearheaded by cultural historians of the French Revolution such as Roger Chartier, Robert Darnton, Daniel Roche, and Keith Baker, a larger interest in the materialist history of the book has brought Raynal's text back to center stage. Recent commentators, such as those included in Hans-Jürgen Lüsebrink and Manfred Tietz's anthology, *Lectures de Raynal,* concentrate on the book's dissemination of various political attitudes among a vast readership. As Yves Benot also argues in *Diderot: De l'athéisme à l'anticolonialisme,* Diderot's encyclopedic materialism makes *Histoire des deux Indes* highly critical of the ancien régime, which constrained but did not neutralize its political effectivity. Published in 1780, the influential third edition was under Diderot's secret editorship and served as a vehicle for the expression of his increasingly radicalized anticlerical, antimonarchical, and anticolonial perspectives. Amid the entries on colonial geography, history, agriculture, and anthropology presented in *Histoire des deux Indes,* Diderot inserted a large number of rhetorical interludes that denounced monarchical absolutism and ecclesiastical intolerance. In the pre-Revolutionary context, these stirring passages, known as political catechisms (*catéchismes politiques*), which I have analyzed more extensively elsewhere, were transmitted to the semiliterate and even the illiterate by collective reading practices.[6]

The Parlement of Paris banned the third edition of *Histoire des deux Indes* by public edict on May 25, 1781. It must be remembered that only a small number of books, an average of four to five a year, were banned in the liberal years of the ancien régime, 1770–89. It was judged that *Histoire des deux Indes* ought to be "shredded and burned in the Palace Square as impious, blasphemous, seditious, and as inciting the masses to rebel against sovereign authority and to overturn the fundamental principles of civic order." Despite his high-level ministerial contacts, Raynal, as nominal author claiming to be "Defender of Humanity" (*Défenseur de l'Humanité*), was forced to flee France until the furor died down (see Fig. 25). The proscription enhanced the notoriety of the book and the sale of a large number of copies printed through as many as fifty different pirated editions. Raynal, essentially a moderate monarchist, was mistakenly lionized by Jacobins as having encouraged revolutionary upheaval. Ironically, and much to the consternation of the legislators, an aged Raynal backtracked on the book's perceived sympathy for antimonarchism and wrote a much vilified *Adresse à l'Assemblée Nationale*

Figure 25 N. De Launay and C. N. Cochin, *Guillaume Thomas Raynal* in *Histoire politique et philosophique des deux Indes* (1780). Special Collections Division, University of Washington Libraries

that was read in absentia in the legislature on May 31, 1791. The pamphlet condemned the emasculation of the king's authority and advised the legislators to restore monarchical executive power, abolish the political clubs, and crack down on popular violence. Forestalling retribution against Raynal, Robespierre argued that the philosopher was suffering from senility. Raynal's major contribution to the onset of the Revolution was acknowledged, and the National Assembly chastised the old man only mildly. Raynal's reputation nonetheless plummeted: on June 9, 1791, his bust was removed from its exalted place in the conference hall of the Jacobin Club of Marseilles and, after a carnivalesque procession, was deposited at Saint-Lazare, the lunatic asylum of the province.

The reasons for the misidentification of Raynal's politics by the Jacobins and their surprise at his disavowal of those who claimed to follow his text's precepts have been outlined by Hans-Jürgen Lüsebrink along a tripartite sociological separation of an author's role, self-presentation, and social identity. The transformation of Raynal's sociopolitical role, according to Lüsebrink, occurred not as a result of his age, as Robespierre would have had it, but in terms of a restructuration of the intellectual field. The unfettered reception of *Histoire des deux Indes* by the commercial bourgeoisie and the Jacobin factions had reimposed a radical social identity on an exiled author; Raynal was not prepared to assume this identity in 1791 and chose to reassert his social position, which derived from being a liberal intellectual in the salons. Therefore, Raynal was not directly the agent of a liberating act, but was constructed as such a posteriori through the mechanisms of authorship.[7]

The reception history of this text, however, is a more recent development. Michèle Duchet's erudite work on Raynal, *Anthropologie et histoire au siècle des lumières,* written in the heyday of structuralism, showcases *Histoire des deux Indes* as evidence that colonialist ideology was seamless. Documenting the impact of post-Renaissance travel narratives on the anthropology of Buffon, Voltaire, Rousseau, Helvétius, and Diderot, Duchet looks to the *Histoire des deux Indes* as a proof text of an Enlightenment will-to-power culminating in the high imperialism of the nineteenth century. Raynal's text is "a turn-table where the tangled skeins of individual relationships and interests can be disentangled, and where the diverse 'contributions' to Raynal's work reveal themselves as the materials for a colonialist policy."[8] The developing break between history and anthropology denied non-Western cultures historicity, even as *Histoire des deux Indes* became a discursive microcosm, a reading lesson on how rules of syntax generate particular ideological positions in Enlightenment anthropology:

> The reality of the savage world remains constricted by a network of negations that, by the play of combinations, allows the construction of antithetical models. Sometimes, they [Enlightenment writers] talk of people without history, without writing, without religion, without manners, without a police, and in this first type of discourse, the negations combine with positively marked characteristics to signify the lack, the immense emptiness of savagery when opposed to the full world of the civilized. At other times, they envy these same cultures who live without masters, without priests, without laws, without vices, without *meum* and *tuum,* and the negations, combined here with negatively marked character-

istics, speak of the disenchantment of social man and the infinite happiness of natural man. In the first case, the parallelism turns out to the advantage of civilized man; in the second, the difference is entirely to the disadvantage of social man. It follows that a simple change of sign suffices to invert the entire logical direction [*sens*] of the discourse: from Voltaire to Rousseau or Diderot, the elements hardly vary as much as their distribution in a system where they assume sometimes a plus sign, and sometimes a minus sign.[9]

In a subsequent book, *L'écriture fragmentaire*, identifying most of the diverse "contributions" and plagiarisms that constitute the text over three major editions allows Duchet to decompose the chimerical unity of the *Histoire des deux Indes* back into its disparate sources. Texts were solicited or plagiarized by Raynal, and then by Diderot, from those who had contributed to the *Encyclopédie*, such as Pechméja, Deleyre, Buffon, Mercier, Saint-Lambert, and d'Holbach. The discovery by Herbert Dieckmann of the Fonds de Vandeul, a cache of Diderot manuscripts, helped prove that the scale of Diderot's collaboration with Raynal was much larger than had previously been assumed. As ghostwriter and editor for the massive third edition, Diderot can be assigned with the authorship of dozens of interpolations. The text's multiple authorship made the editor's task a stitching together of polyphonic fragments. Culling from a variety of quasi-anthropological, commercial, bureaucratic, and literary sources, the editor unites these fragments through the discourse of "philosophical and political history."[10]

However, though the careful collection of texts and their organization creates the sense of encyclopedic wholeness at the level of literary production, reception history is forced to confront the fact that multiple metropolitan audiences responded to truncated sections, made available through the excerption and republication of key passages. One of the celebrated political catechisms was the "Call to the Hottentots" (*Appel aux Hottentots*), written by Diderot, who defended the Khoi group's culture and mode of life. The anticolonial stance solicits sympathy from ethical French citizens for colonized peoples through the sentimental construction of the "Hottentots" as victims exhorted in the imperative voice to resist the depredations of the Dutch. In similar passages, specific oppressions of Africans, Indians, and Batavians are rendered formally equivalent to each other, resulting in the repeated articulation of a subject of oppression who serves as a nodal point of identification for the incipient French republican. Political catechisms reveal two antagonistic enunciatory positions with immediate consequences, that of the adviser to executive authority alongside that of the agitator of oppressed peoples. The construction of a democratic subject position requires an analytical understanding of exploitative sociopolitical and economic structures alongside a rhetoric of vindication that redresses grievances through self-empowerment. The resultant synthesis of the two enunciatory positions—the farseeing, reformist administrator and the impatient, mass-mobilizing revolutionary—clears a space from which the modern democratic subject can speak and act.

Diderot's technique of sympathetic apostroph generalizes techniques of aesthetic appreciation, such as those used in the analysis of art or literature, into the discourse of speculative moral philosophy. Drawing attention to metropolitan *political representation* (what Marx called *vertreten* in *The Eighteenth Brumaire*) through the help of a colonialist *aesthetic representation* (Marx's *darstellen*), *Histoire des deux Indes* conducts a "literarization of politics" and "politicization of literature" typical of the Enlightenment. According to Tocqueville, literature in France directly becomes repressed politics, unlike in England, where intellectuals managed to find niches for themselves within the establishment. While Tocqueville assumed a socioprofessional marginality of the *philosophes* that has been refuted by Chartier's analysis of print culture and Roche's work on the provincial academies, the reasons behind the erroneous hypothesis still ring true. Enlightenment criticism brought forward alternative political desires, posited ideal social practices, and sought to will existing worlds out of existence (*la déréalisation du monde social*).[11]

Although *Histoire des deux Indes* was not formally as well organized as the *Encyclopédie*, it effectively fulfilled the subversive political aims envisaged by Diderot for that earlier compilation. In the *Encyclopédie*, Diderot had intended that the technique of the *renvoi*, or the cross-reference, would give readers the power to link topics using personal priorities and motivations. As he puts it in the entry "Encyclopédie," cross-references "will oppose ideas to each other; they will attack, shake, secretly overturn ridiculous opinions that one would not dare insult openly. If the author is impartial, they will always have the double function of confirming and refuting; of troubling and reconciling." Diderot claims that just as the encyclopedist dismembers other books to compose the body of his article, readers dismember and recompose their way to empowerment by cross-reference. By deciphering encyclopedic collage, the reader recognizes the need for both decomposition and recomposition. Though *Histoire des deux Indes* eschewed a system of cross-references, many editions had detailed chapter headings and a comprehensive index which enabled some reference of topics. A combination of anthropology, history, philosophy, journalism, and demagoguery multiplies the ideological possibilities made available to readers through a large number of unauthorized and partial editions. In fact, the physical mixing of pages of proscribed books with innocuous ones was prevalent for purposes of secrecy. Books were transported unbound. This practice in the bookselling trade was jokingly referred to as the clandestine "marriage" of contraband books with licensed ones. Cannibalized, detachable, and reproducible fragments could cajole readers into antinomian subject positions in varied contexts. Some parts of *Histoire des deux Indes* galvanized republicans into political action through a complex use of cross-identification in political harangue, and other, more technical and information-oriented parts, sedimentations from the earlier editions, conducted a crash course for budding ministerial functionaries interested in equipping themselves with the necessary skills for colonial government. After all, Napoleon, who took the book with him on his Egyptian campaign in 1798, professed a great youthful admiration for Raynal and the "pragmatic" relevance of the work, and Franz Karsten culled an early business management primer out of the text.[12]

The numerous depictions of colonial oppression in *Histoire des deux Indes* served two distinct versions of metropolitan politics. One function of anticolonial rhetoric was to metaphorize wrongs abroad in order to radicalize democratic aspirations in France even while escaping censorship. A parallel trajectory of the text presented these wrongs to errant colonial administrators as warning bells that might help save the colonies. These alternatives still processed the colonies as raw material that was consumed by Europeans, whether as (literal) raw material for economic advantage or (metaphorical) experiment for political evolution. The exemplum of colonial rule served as a supplement that was assimilated and discarded in the course of conducting that material and moral edification of Europe, the Enlightenment.

Lüsebrink and Tietz's *Lectures de Raynal* testifies to the far-flung impact of *Histoire des deux Indes* on post-Enlightenment readers in Spain, Germany, Denmark, Italy, England, Hungary, Poland, the Balkans, the United States, and Latin America. These readings are built on a more comprehensive understanding of the reactions of French readers, but unfortunately the collection mostly bypasses Raynal's impact on the French colonies.[13] French colonial issues are represented by Yves Benot, who argues that Raynal's text furnished radical metropolitan abolitionists, such as Garran-Coulon and Sonthonax, and moderate ones, such as Garat, Brissot, and Grégoire, with a vocabulary. If, as the editors acknowledge in a passing comment, "among Third World writers the impact of *Histoire des deux Indes* has sustained an echo of contemporaneity and a certain freshness far from the air of a museum-piece," there must be a different way to continue actualizing the interpretive potentials of this text as an origin for a tropicalized Enlightenment.[14] Shying away from unverifiable stories of the Haitian Revolution's apotheosis of Raynal, the editors have chosen to dismiss the influence of the *Histoire des deux Indes* on Toussaint Louverture as apocryphal. However, in the manner of Michel Delon's essay, which extends the notion of fragmentation to the diversification of audiences and contexts, a close analysis of the text's effective use of apostrophe can embolden us to make occasional intellectual leaps. The impact that *Histoire des deux Indes* had on the French colonies can be reconstructed, if somewhat imaginatively, by a literary-critical urge to rush in where historians fear to tread. A history of reading is always full of gaps, characterized by tactics and improvisations rather than clearly delineated strategies.

In a remarkable exposition of the economy of subject positions in Diderot's *Le Neveu de Rameau*, Julia Kristeva draws attention to the complex dialogical tension between the unified voice of a rationalist speaking subject and the pluralization of semiosis occurring through a proliferation of subject-positions. The dialectical exchange between the philosopher "I" and the musician Rameau's outcast nephew, "Him," says Kristeva, represents a more general instance of Diderot's radical political experimentation with linguistic, semiotic, and musical techniques that disrupt subjective mastery over the voice of the other in all discursive domains. Similar subversive indeterminacy, in Diderot's harangues for *Histoire des deux Indes,* enables the text's reappropriation by those in eccentric subject-positions. Likewise, the ambivalence of colonial discourse, theorized by Homi Bhabha, has been sometimes criticized for falling short of a comprehensive analysis of resistance by the colonized. Mimicry and parody can indeed help us describe the subaltern's answer to the dominant discourse, especially if we discover mimicry to be a lived practice rather than only a subjectless and virtual discursive effect.[15]

Tropicopolitan experience does not always follow the "intellectual-diffusionist" fantasy of the benign impact of the ideas of the French Revolution. On the contrary, as Lüsebrink has effectively demonstrated, official celebrations of Bastille Day in the French colonies in the nineteenth century, planned as hegemonic exercises of imperial military pageantry, often subverted the colonial regime by inadvertently voicing aspirations for self-determination by the colonized. The celebration of Bastille Day—banned even in France from Napoleon's time until the creation of the Third Republic in 1871—was recognized as a dangerous outlet for discourses of political liberation. All such instances of mimicry and resistance communicate what ought to be more obvious than it sometimes seems in scholarship: that texts and symbols are subject to what Tony Bennett calls "productive reactivations" through unpredictable "reading formations." Is it so surprising, then, that unverifiable but heroic narratives of reading often accompany modern nationalism? According to Haitian legend, Toussaint read Raynal's encyclopedia. An investigation of this scene of reading—whether as fiction, fact, fetish, or factish—can strengthen the purchase that Equiano's talking book has given us on the drama of nationalization. Tropicopolitan metaliteracy gives an ironic turn to the heroic narrative of metropolitan literacy, and the symbolic relevance of Toussaint's reading lesson supplements the merely empirical question of whether it actually took place or if nationalists and hagiographers have imagined it.[16]

TROPICALIZING THE ENLIGHTENMENT
IN SAINT DOMINGUE

Eh bien, si l'intérêt a seul des droits sur votre âme, nations de l'Europe, écoutez-moi encore. Vos esclaves n'ont besoin ni de votre générosité ni de vos conseils pour briser le joug sacrilège qui les opprime. La nature parle plus haut que la philosophie et que l'intérêt. Déjà se sont établies deux colonies de nègres fugitifs que les traités et la force mettent à l'abri de vos attentats. Ces éclairs annoncent la foudre, et il ne manque aux nègres qu'un chef assez courageux pour les conduire à la vengeance et au carnage.

Où est-il, ce grand homme, que la nature doit à ses enfants vexés, opprimés, tourmentés? Où est-il? Il paraîtra, n'en doutons point, il se montrera, il lèvera l'étendard sacré de la liberté. Ce signal vénérable rassemblera autour de lui les compagnons de son infortune. Plus impétueux que les torrents, ils laisseront partout les traces ineffaçables de leur juste ressentiment. Espagnols, Portugais, Anglais, Français, Hollandais, tous leurs tyrans deviendront la proie du fer et de la flamme. Les champs américains s'enivreront avec transport d'un sang qu'ils attendaient depuis si longtemps, et les ossements de tant d'infortunés entassés depuis trois siècles tressailliront de joie. L'Ancien Monde joindra ses applaudissements au Nouveau. Partout on bénira le nom du héros qui aura rétabli les droits de l'espèce humaine, partout on érigera des trophées à sa gloire. Alors disparaîtra le *code noir*, et que le *code blanc* sera terrible si le vainqueur ne consulte que le droit de représailles!

Ah well, if it is only self-interest that motivates your soul, countries of Europe, listen to me again. Your slaves don't need either your generosity or your advice to break the sacrilegious yoke that oppresses them. Nature speaks more powerfully than philosophy or self-interest. Already, two colonies of black fugitives [maroons] have established themselves, safe from your assaults, through treaties and force. These streaks of lightning announce the oncoming thunderbolts, and the blacks only need a leader courageous enough to lead them towards vengeance and carnage.

Where is this great man that Nature owes to her vexed, oppressed, and tormented children? Where is he? He will appear, never fear, he will show himself and raise the sacred flag of liberty. This venerable signal will allow the companions of his misfortune to rally around him. More violent than waterfalls, they will leave indelible traces of their justifiable resentment everywhere. Spaniards, Portuguese, English, French, and Hollanders, indeed all their tyrannical masters will fall prey to fire and brimstone. The American fields will get ecstatically drunk [*s'enivreront avec transport*] with the bloodshed they have awaited for ages, and the bones of so many unfortunates, piled up for three centuries, will quiver with joy. The Old World will applaud the New World. Everywhere will be exalted the name of the hero who would have reestablished the rights of the human race; memorials will be erected to celebrate his glory everywhere! Then the Black Slave Code [*Code noir*] will disappear, and the "White Slave Code" will indeed be terrible if the victor merely follows the law of revenge [*le droit de représailles*]! (*Histoire des deux Indes* 6:206–8; my translation)

Following the rise of Toussaint Louverture as governor after the end of the British invasion in 1798, busts and portraits of Raynal, hailed as an emancipationist hero, were put up around the island. While Raynal was celebrated as a prophet of Toussaint's (and Sonthonax's) emancipation proclamation, the above catechism from the *Histoire des deux Indes* was itself plagiarized from one of the better-known utopian novels, Louis-Sébastien Mercier's *L'an deux mille quatre cent quarante* (The Year 2440), first published in 1771.[17] The adulation of Raynal ostensibly arose from Toussaint's having frequently reread, in his manumitted days as plantation overseer, a copy of *Histoire des deux Indes* at his birthplace, Bréda. According to nineteenth-century Haitian nationalists, Toussaint felt destined to emancipate the slaves, convincing himself that he was the modern black Spartacus heralded by the text. Toussaint has been associated with this call for black slave rebellion even though there is scanty historical evidence that he actually read it. Faced with an unverifiable reception of Raynal, we nonetheless can comprehend the desire for narratives of agency that foreground metaliteracy. Whereas in myth the national hero leads his people out of bondage according to a preconceived plan communicated by divine revelation (evident in the abortive rebellions of the Sierra Leone settlers, whose rhetoric harked back to the Exodus), the narrative of the secular nation-state prefers the revolutionary pamphlet as the more acceptable call to arms. Such rhetoric, therefore, moves forward in history, as does the Trotskyist argument of C. L. R. James in *The Black Jacobins*, showing the emergence of the masses as makers of history but with the revolutionary leader at the helm; in James's application, literacy is the technology of transmission as well as self-recognition, mobilization, and revelation.[18]

Haitian national memory and historiography has persistently relied on Toussaint's apocryphal self-recognition through the black Spartacus catechism. In the manner of Diderot's theory of the cross-reference, intended to both confirm and undermine established truths, the passage's exposition of a world turned upside down, merely alarmist in a metropolitan French context, becomes a rallying cry in a colonial location. If Toussaint never really read the black Spartacus passage, Haitian historiography would have needed to invent an equivalent incident. This primal scene of anticolonial reading or metaliteracy generates the nation as *ethnos*. The catechism's call to violence works through identificatory catachresis. Toussaint recognizes himself as a royal slave — as did a fictional Oroonoko or a historical Equiano. A quasi-monarchical agent much like Rousseau's legislator, the royal slave ushers in a future utopia through an act of will. The famous equestrian portrait of Toussaint (Fig. 26), probably printed after Haitian independence, imitates and revises the traditional equestrian statues in Europe, whether Tacca's statue of Philip III of Spain (1640), Girardon's statue of Louis XIV (1694), or Falconet's celebration of Peter the Great as the Bronze Horseman (1782). The rider-prince is in the saddle, holding the reins of state with one hand and uplifted sword in the other, husbanding the horse as he does his people, and crushing sedition and treason with the horse's hooves and his martial valor. Such iconography of Toussaint, frequently in full French military regalia (Fig. 27), emphasizes the manner in which resistance is primarily conceived as an armed tropicopolitan response to French rule, but resoundingly stated in vocabulary that the colonial power can understand, admire, and regret.[19]

Whether or not Toussaint read the black Spartacus catechism is a technicality, important though this question may be for scholars of *Histoire des deux Indes*. The larger consequence is that of the retroactive attribution of *revolutionary consciousness*, favored by nationalism according to recognizable narratives of influence. In contrast, Robin Blackburn's sobering assessment of the black slave rebels of the 1790s compares them to trade union leaders, negotiating for better terms under slavery rather than for full emancipation. Subsequent hagiographers of Toussaint have frequently forgotten that "just as Raynal's work reflected the aspirations of enlightened planters as well as championing slave emancipation so there was a double quality to Toussaint's new regime." Even while replacing bondage with paid labor, Toussaint was against the destruction of the sugar industry and wanted to maintain the draconian plantation

Figure 26 Equestrian Portrait of Toussaint Louverture (n.d.). (Bibliothèque
Nationale, Paris)

Figure 27 Delpeck and Maurin, *Toussaint L'Ouverture* (n.d.). (Bibliothèque Nationale, Paris)

system and its backbreaking toil. Toussaint anticipated accommodation with Napoleonic aims, a posture that led to his betrayal in 1802. Adopting Blackburn's interpretation may overcompensate in the other direction, making the question of revolutionary consciousness moot. Is it at all possible to attend to metaliteracy without adopting the standpoint of either cynical spectation or naïve identification?[20] The metropolitan discussion of *Histoire des deux Indes* offers two disparate but related outcomes to readers interested in its political fate: the French Revolution (the expression of metropolitan democratic aspirations) and Napoleonic expansionism (the eventual triumph of a ruling class). Though external imperialism and internal democracy coexist well into the twentieth century, the French contradiction was untenable for the Haitian polity. The slave insurrection opportunistically tropicalized the French Revolution into a Haitian Revolution. In this collective effort, Toussaint's arguable use of Raynal was, after all, an incidental detail which may never be historically resolved.

The deliberate evasions of metropolitan discourse on the colonies are visible through a kind of shadow-puppetry. Published in 1774, the same year as the appearance of the second edition of *Histoire des deux Indes*, Jean-Paul Marat's bestseller, *Les chaînes de l'esclavage*, furthered republican aspirations in France. Yet the reputedly radical treatise is remarkable for the ease with which it uses the word *esclavage* to discuss metropolitan politics—while being completely oblivious to the colonial referent of the word—at a moment close to the pinnacle of plantation slavery and the slave trade. *Esclaves* was an extremely volatile word that the deputies had appropriated for themselves; when colonial issues were discussed in the assembly, it was replaced by the euphemistic formula that Robespierre and other deputies favored: "unfree persons." A squirming Robespierre, embarrassedly aware of the Jacobins' rise to power through the metaphorization of slavery, felt compromised enough to retort, "Let the colonies perish! [*Périsse les colonies!*]" when yet another pro-slavery resolution aggressively reaffirmed the property in "slaves"—a volatile word—rather than the euphemistic formula of "unfree persons." In the metropolitan context, *Histoire des deux Indes* provides depictions of slavery through political catechisms that are seized upon by radicalized metropolitan subjects even though the complete text intersperses these sections amid advice concerning colonialist management. When the colonial situation that obtained in Saint Domingue is added to the other uses of the text in Europe, we find that words are wrung from their earlier discursive contexts into mythistorical reappropriation by a self-selected leader who shows the masses the way out of bondage. The virtual subject position offered in the *Histoire des deux Indes* rhetoric, "*Où est-il ce grand homme,*" heralds Toussaint Bréda to his calling as revolutionary leader, *Louverture* (Opening). Toussaint's *nominal* capacity to "open up" colonialist discourse—in many senses—reveals that this discourse is not a seamless web, especially from the position of the tropicopolitan. The reappropriation involved in Toussaint's (and Haitian anticolonial nationalism's) reading of the call to violence is different from the metaphorical displacement it carried out in the minds of its European readership. While identifying sentimentally with colonial oppression functions as a way to generate sympathy for others and redirect it toward a self-pitying radicalization, political catechisms that purport to combat slavery and colonization, written in French and addressed principally to those who would never experience plantation slavery, can also become the proximate origin of Toussaint's understanding of his own "royalist" actions, later reinterpreted in an anticolonial and revolutionary light.[21]

Rather than accepting accounts of colonialist ideology that consign *Histoire des deux Indes* to the status of false consciousness masking the interests of French imperialism, an awareness of metaliteracy contextualizes the text's apostrophes as also speaking to a context outside its European purview, to tropicopolitans who are accidental, unintended, and indirect addressees. The actions of tropicopolitans parody the overdetermined ideological terrain of the text by refuting and extending Western Enlightenment assumptions. Forced to account for their actions, we scramble for words, influences, traditions, and contingencies that may have caused them. The historian's scrambling reveals the ironic Nachträglichkeit, or deferred action, that surrounds narratives of anticolonial agency, which are often forced to deal with gaps, silences, and elisions.

Histoire des deux Indes includes long sections about the resistance to European colonization by slave revolts and marronage. These fears are especially acute with respect to Jamaica, as insurrection had been an endemic problem on that British-ruled island (7:422–32). However, by association, Saint Domingue, "the pearl of the Antilles," must have been uppermost in the thoughts of Raynal's contacts in the ministry, the officials who formulated French colonial policy and subsidized the earlier editions of the book. Saint Domingue produced two-fifths of the sugar and more than half of the coffee traded globally; more than three-quarters of this colonial produce was reexported from France. *Histoire des deux Indes* looks forward with trepidation to the troubles the colony might face, with the discussion of Saint Domingue taking up about a third of the book on the French West Indies (7:147-244). Unlike the rest of the Caribbean, Saint Domingue had been free of any major insurrections until 1791.[22]

The storming of the Bastille in 1789 was an immediate catalyst to political ferment in the colony. Whether or not Toussaint read the black Spartacus passage, it is clear that the power of print was much feared by the authorities. As early as September 1789, the alarmed *intendant* wrote to Paris: "All those who write about and concern themselves with the emancipation of the blacks are making inroads into the colony . . . these blacks agree with everything said . . . that the white slaves have killed their masters, and being liberated from now on, they will govern themselves and claim possession of all the earth's assets." If the jitteriness of the colonial officials is to believed, the metropolitan French populace had revolted after being harangued with revolutionary catechisms, many of which were included in catchall texts such as *Histoire des deux Indes,* and the blacks, slaves themselves, realized that if metaphorical slaves could revolt, literal ones ought not to be left behind.[23]

In Saint Domingue, the opposing groups were not just the rich minority of white planters and the large majority of black slaves. There were also roughly as many *mulâtres* (mixed-race residents) as whites, and both groups included slave proprietors, a skilled middle class, working-class artisans, and free laborers. Competing alongside the more privileged mulâtres, the envious poor whites (*petits blancs*) thought they had the most to gain from the Third Estate's assertion of its privileges. Much to the discomfiture of the deputies in the French National Assembly, after 1789 these tensions put various colonial interests at loggerheads. The three main political issues were: civil rights for mixed-race descendants of significant landowners, the termination of the slave trade, and the general abolition of slavery. Emancipation occurred in 1793-94 as an emergency measure to repel the British invasion of the island. Earlier attempts by the mulâtres to seek political representation, aided by Brissot's emancipationist Société des Amis des Noirs, were opposed by a planters' lobby, the Club Massiac. The royalist colonial bureaucracy increasingly favored the mulâtres and was at odds with the republican-inspired petits blancs. Whenever reform legislation was suggested by the National Assembly, the white planters alternately threatened the Assembly with secession or with the specter of a full-scale slave rebellion. Eventually, the internecine squabbles among the poor whites, the planters, and the mulâtres caught these groups unprepared when the black slaves of Bois-Caïman rose on August 14, 1791.

A multipronged civil war developed over the following decade. Most of the leaders of the blacks, self-styled military officers such as Biassou, Jean-François, and Toussaint, chose to justify their actions as royalist and negotiated secretly with the Spanish and the French. They were rightly suspicious of the agenda of the petits blancs, who favored accommodation with slavery in order not to lose the economic profits that France derived from the colony. Toussaint was a Spanish general for five years and rose to prominence only after the mid-1790s, when the French negotiated for his alliance against the British invasion. The French legislators' attempts to address demands of colonial autonomy and emancipation oscillated between semantics and crisis control. The Gironde faction, beholden as they were to ports important to colonial trading, such as Nantes, Marseilles, and Bordeaux, had earlier tried to put a lid on the seething cauldron of colonial representation by going along with the enfranchisement of the propertied mulâtres as a nominal solution. The Convention was finally forced to outlaw slavery on February 4, 1794. Victor Hugues, the Jacobin commissioner, set out for Guadeloupe from Brest in April 1794 armed with this emancipation proclamation; significantly, the other instruments of political power aboard ship were a guillotine and a printing press. The proclamation, in any case, was a mere ratification of Civil Commissioner Sonthonax's unilateral appeal on August 29, 1793, in Saint Domingue itself, issued in Kréyole unlike previous colonial decrees. The contending new elites were black military officers like Toussaint and a previously emancipated class of mulâtres, the *anciens libres*, including leaders such as Rigaud, and even white officials such as Sonthonax who could legislate proactively. The capacity to mobilize emancipated black slaves as soldiers was the key to power, and the emancipation proclamation a means to it. Literacy and metaliteracy were attempting to preempt each other amid all this maneuvering, rationalizing slave rebellion into national revolution.[24]

However, let us not forget Toussaint's historical limitations. James is aware of the mythmaking of Toussaint as hero, but rationalizes it nonetheless: "Today by a natural reaction we tend to a personification of the social forces, great men being merely or nearly instruments in the hands of economic destiny. As so often the truth does not lie in between. Great men make history, but only such history as it is possible for them to make. Their freedom of achievement is limited by the necessities of their environment. To portray the limits of those necessities, and the realisation, complete or partial, of all possibilities, that is the true business of the historian."[25] James's reading celebrates the hero in his limitations but stays within a Trotskyist agenda, reading leader and masses as mutually constitutive, performing different functions but in unison concerning their general political goals. The internal conflicts swirling around Saint Domingue at the time of Toussaint's capture by Leclerc were more complex, as subsequent historical research has demonstrated. Toussaint's favoring of proletarianization and the continuation of a coercive plantation structure was at odds with the aspirations of the former slaves to turn themselves into a landowning peasantry. As Alex Dupuy argues convincingly, the conflict was between a nonracially based bourgeois nationalist solution, favored by Toussaint, who wanted to turn the planter class into postslavery agrarian capitalists, and a racially based black bourgeois solution by Dessalines, who took the path of expropriating rather than reforming the white planters, a path that led to national independence. Toussaint's hand was revealed in his ruthless suppression of the rebellion by Moïse, who represented the countervailing desire for a decentralized economy and for subsistence farming by a landowning peasantry, a desire thus at odds with both Toussaint's and Dessalines's centralized and statist solutions.[26]

All these careful historical assessments, nonetheless, cannot dislodge a continuing euhemeristic belief in Toussaint, promoted in Romantic assessments immediately following events even before recuperations by Haitian historiography. Some of this heroization is no doubt circumstantial. In 1802, Leclerc's forces captured, through a ruse, an aging Toussaint and sent him on Napoleon's instructions to a prison in the Jura mountains in France. Toussaint died of starvation and exposure a few months later. Following the news of Toussaint's capture, William Wordsworth wrote a sonnet, "To Toussaint L'Ouverture," in August 1802. Wordsworth does away with the scene of reading and its possi-

bilities for mimicry and discursive doublespeak. In the absence of metaliteracy, a Romantic metaphorization fills the gap:

> Toussaint, the most unhappy Man of Men!
> Whether the rural Milk-Maid by her Cow
> Sing in thy hearing, or thou liest now
> Alone in some deep dungeon's earless den,
> O miserable Chieftain! where and when
> Wilt thou find patience? Yet die not; do thou
> Wear rather in thy bonds a chearful brow:
> Though fallen Thyself never to rise again,
> Live, and take comfort.

After identifying Toussaint as an exceptional sufferer, "the most unhappy Man of Men," the sonnet hypothesizes contrasting alternatives:
either Toussaint is in some rural retreat within earshot of bucolic bliss,
or he is confined below ground, away from the delights of pastoral
sociability. The first alternative presents a fanciful situation (especially
ironic given Toussaint's suppression of Moïse's rebellion). In the Jura,
Toussaint was captive in appalling conditions much closer to the death
knell of "some deep dungeon's earless den," conditions that largely contributed to the old man's death. In either case, the poem celebrates
Toussaint with a touch of triumphalist stoicism, even if he is fallen and
"never to rise again." But why is Toussaint advised to "Wear rather in
[his] bonds a chearful brow . . . [to] Live, and take comfort"? Is it that,
following a secularized gloss on Christian martyrdom, Toussaint moves
from undergoing exceptional suffering to becoming the world's moral
representative? The end of the poem builds on the soteriological alternative:

> Thou has left behind
> Powers that will work for thee; air, earth, and skies;
> There's not a breathing of the common wind
> That will forget thee; thou hast great allies;
> Thy friends are exultations, agonies,
> And love, and Man's unconquerable mind.

As the poem enacts the scattering of Toussaint's remains to the elements—"air, earth, and skies"—it is still in the process of learning from
Toussaint's political lesson. But such a quick transition leaves a whiff

of poetic embarrassment. Toussaint had not yet died when the sonnet was first published in *The Morning Post* on February 2, 1803; his death was announced only in April. However, the poem suggests the tortures still being undergone by Toussaint's body after first occluding them: "Thy friends are exultations, agonies." The mute body of Toussaint speaks via the poet, offering a reading lesson on the indomitable human spirit with the poem's final echo from Gray's "Progress of Poesy" concerning "Man's unconquerable mind." Wordsworth attempts to "turn" Toussaint into Nature but apotropaically acknowledges the realities of a "tropical" oppression both poetic and historical. Disillusioned with Napoleon by 1802, Coleridge too describes Toussaint as a "hero as much [Napoleon's] superior in genius as in goodness." Toussaint's bonds, like Prometheus's, are a powerful metaphor of Romantic empowerment, showing that the royal slave's abjection proves the domination of Romantic "mind" over others' attempts to confine slaves' bodies. Mary Jacobus's pointed rhetorical question about Wordsworth's "Ode to Duty" is pertinent here: "Could it be that with the increasing strength of the Abolition movement and the eventual outlawing of the slave trade, slavery became capable of functioning as its opposite, a metaphor for freedom?" Toussaint's imprisonment constitutes, in this poem, English Romantic freedom.[27]

Whereas the sonnet to Toussaint expounds the masculine sublime, describing a poetic conquest in the face of *someone else's* physical adversity, the companion sonnet to it, "September 1st, 1802," provides a sentimentalized portrait of the female outcast. The sonnet outlines a "Negro woman like a lady gay, / Yet silent as a woman fearing blame" who flees France after the decree that reinstated slavery and expelled free blacks was promulgated by Napoleon in July 1802. The woman, who accompanied the poet to England from Calais, elicits pathos by means of an uncomplaining muteness: "dejected, meek, yea pitiably tame . . . silent, motionless in eyes and face." Stoic sufferer that she is, the woman almost takes Wordsworth's advice to Toussaint in the previous sonnet, wearing her bonds as cheerfully as possible in the circumstances: "rejected like all others of that race / Not one of whom may now find footing there; This the poor Out-cast did to us declare, / Nor murmur'd at the unfeeling Ordinance."[28]

Unfreedom and responsibility is exemplified in a later literary representation of Toussaint by Bernard Dadié's 1973 play, *Îles de tempête.*

Dadié's play juxtaposes two euhemeristic giants, both of whom were produced out of the maw of the French Revolution. As their historical trajectories overlapped without their ever having met, Napoleon and Toussaint, as the principal characters, appear in rival scenes and justify their respective political stances and actions. Both end their lives in exile and isolation. Passages from Raynal's *Histoire des deux Indes* are heard offstage, inspiring both to their historical calling. Raynal, in Dadié's hands, becomes the common source for a dramatic reflection on the failure of political representation and on the continuation of democratic aspiration. The Enlightenment book is instrument of power and harbinger of utopia. *Histoire des deux Indes* allows various reading lessons, through tableaux of literacy and metaliteracy, mirroring power and resistance. In fact, James had also produced a play on Toussaint Louverture before he wrote *The Black Jacobins*. Through their interventions that are literary *and* historiographical, James and Dadié criticize stereotypes of the tropicopolitan as mere pawn in the game of colonial power. This problem is replicated by the epistemology of "master theories" being sustained by "native informants": the tropicopolitan is never just a stand-in object for the exercise of dominant practices of power/knowledge. However, heroes belong properly to tragedy or epic, and such analyses—whether in literary or historiographical form—move us inexorably to more poetic registers. Kara Rabbitt, for instance, discusses acutely James's heroization of Toussaint, a heroization enabled by James's willingness to compare him with Lincoln, Pericles, Paine, Marx, Engels, Roland, and, of course, the black Spartacus.[29] Are such dramatic narratives of anticolonial heroism, whether collectivist or individualist, to substitute for critical reconstruction?

Revolutionary consciousness, if we can attribute it to Toussaint, must have been generated from available discourses and practices, whether these be the locutions of the metropolitan encyclopedia or the rites of voodoo. Toussaint's metaliteracy as nationalist origin myth alternates with the sacrifice in the woods at Bois-Caïman that prefaced the uprising of August 14, 1791. The sacrifice involved the *houngan* Boukman and others, kneeling around a voodoo priestess, and examining the entrails of a wild boar. Did these entrails augur the nation to be born? Even the esoteric sacrifice is accompanied by a reading lesson of sorts. How does self-recognition occur in relation to cultural sources? How do subsequent nationalist interpretations mythologize these epistemic acts as a coming-to-consciousness? Both national origins are technically external—the spirit religions of West Africa syncretized under slavery or the newfound popular literacy of Western Europe imported to the colony with the encyclopedia. The sacrifice in the woods outside Bois-Caïman was also a reading lesson—just as much as the rituals of the talking book, for the young Toussaint, was a kind of sacrifice.

The problem of self-representation has been succinctly posed by Gayatri Chakravorty Spivak's question, "Can the subaltern speak?" But the answer to this question is highly mediated and often duplicitous. Critics of *Histoire des deux Indes,* such as Mira Kamdar, take Spivak's provisional negative answer to the question of self-representation to argue for the seamlessness of colonialist ideology. According to Kamdar, Diderot as ventriloquist embraces the impropriety inherent in speaking mimetically for someone else in his harangues and apostrophes, leading to a colonization of all other subject positions: "the Subaltern cannot speak on the stage of European world history . . . her enunciation is already colonized by the Enlightenment project of assimilation that seeks to benevolently represent her voice and thus mutes it." The account of epistemic colonization provided by Kamdar underestimates the ability of a monolithic underdog, the subaltern, to tropicalize metropolitan discourse, overstating radical alterity in the process. As we have seen, *Histoire des deux Indes* is much more than its dominant authorial appropriations. At moments like these we need to ask whether agency can be retroactively discovered in the silences and elisions of the colonialist text. The ironic critique of the fetishization of speech, writing, and representation by scenes of colonial reading, or metaliteracy, comes to the fore as an indirect challenge to assertions that colonialist ideology overwhelmed all opposition.

Metaliteracy sometimes takes the form of mimicry, even a reversal of cause and effect when postcolonial politics anticipates metropolitan meanings. For instance, as Joan Dayan shows, Dessalines, the first leader of independent Haiti, preceded Napoléon in declaring himself an emperor; Soulouque declared himself Emperor Faustin I of Haiti in 1849, before Louis Napoleon did the equivalent in France in 1851. The Parisian press dubbed the nephew's monarchical extravagance *Soulouquerie,* resulting in a French decree banning the use of the term. We may modify Marx's assertion that historical repetition shows the degeneration of tragedy into farce. Farce and tragedy are coimplicated with each other at the colonialist origin, reminding us of another black Spartacus, Oroonoko. However, virtual metaliteracy provides a different advantage, of miming anticolonial subversions in the literary text even as these subversions are not always empirically recuperable from the historical archive. Literature's anticipatory anticolonialisms are seized upon retroactively by nationalization.[30]

If Toussaint Louverture had been a woman, which passage in *Histoire des deux Indes* might she have chosen as a point of departure? Is this counterfactual question a futile and empirically perverse daydream that can generate only implausible answers? By speculating about a virtual metaliteracy, however, the postcolonial critic interrogates textual exclusions in the *Histoire des deux Indes* with cultural, anthropological, and feminist concerns. Asking such questions may allow us to measure the elisions in received histories of colonialism and its artifacts even while we continue to use *Histoire des deux Indes* as a sounding board. Grafting encyclopedic techniques and literary allusions onto each other, Diderot interpolated an intriguing passage in the book about the conditions for national regeneration. This interpolation also paradoxically reveals the existence of colonial phantasms on the edges of historiographical discourse. It may help to imagine a virtual reader of this passage in Saint Domingue whom we can designate as Toussaint's "daughter-in-law." As we shall see, however, such a tactical artifice cannot be taken literally or positivistically. Thinking of Toussaint's "daughter-in-law" amidst a reading lesson, we can expose gaps in the recuperation of reading practices.

When non-European women—for the most part marginal to the text's concerns—appear as speaking subjects in *Histoire des deux Indes,* they are sentimentalized victims on the banks of the River Orinoco in a passage plagiarized from the travel narrative of the Jesuit Joseph Gumilla, *El Orinoco ilustrado.* In contrast with the abjection of the women of Orinoco, Diderot's passage favorably depicts a singular woman as symbol of unbounded revolutionary violence. After praising those masculine nation-builders who could successfully legislate justice and the social contract, thus becoming heroes for deification by posterity, the narrator discusses why restoration of a corrupt nation is harder:

La condition du restaurateur d'une nation corrompue est bien dif-
férente. C'est un architecte qui se propose de bâtir sur une aire
couverte de ruines. C'est un médecin qui tente la guérison d'un ca-
davre gangrené. C'est un sage qui prêche la réforme à des endurcis.
Il n'a que de la haine et des persécutions à obtenir de la génération
présente. Il ne verra pas la génération future. Il produira peu de
fruit, avec beaucoup de peine, pendant sa vie; et n'obtiendra que
de stériles regrets après sa mort. Une nation ne se régénère que
dans un bain de sang. C'est l'image du vieil Æson, à qui Médée ne
rendit la jeunesse qu'en le dépeçant et en le faisant bouillir. Quand
elle est déchue, il n'appartient pas à un homme de la relever. Il
semble que ce soit l'ouvrage d'une longue suite de révolutions.
L'homme de génie passe trop vite, et ne laisse point de postérité.

The conditions faced by the restorer of a corrupt nation are quite
different [from those faced by the founder of a new nation]. He
is an architect proposing to build on a ruin-filled site; a doctor
attempting to cure a gangrenous corpse; a sage preaching reform
to hardened sinners. The restorer can only hope to receive the
hatred and the persecution of the present generation, and will
not see future ones. He will bear little fruit with much labor during his life, eliciting only sterile regret after his death. A nation
can regenerate itself only through a bloodbath, much like the old
Aeson, whom Medea could rejuvenate only by flaying and boiling
him. When the nation declines [Quand elle est déchue], no man
can set it right [relever]. That will be the outcome of a long series
of revolutions. The man of genius disappears quickly, leaving no
legacy behind. (6:22; my translation)

Diderot's national allegory unfolds a series of paradoxes, distinguishing
the foundation of the state from the near-impossible task of its restoration. In contrast with the ancient leader who sets an example of civic
virtue by fiat, and in the interests of justice and reason (or for that
matter the black Spartacus–identified Toussaint who changes the world
through a transparent act of will), the restorers of a corrupt nation face
difficulties in the manner of professionalized technicians (architects,
doctors, social reformers) grappling with perverse realities (ruin-filled
landscapes, gangrenous corpses, hardened delinquents). These modern

technocrats cannot expect rewards, results, or lasting fame, as regeneration is no longer the outcome of individual agents, however dedicated they might be. Rather, organic metaphors of reproduction are overturned for cataclysmic ones. Captivated by this image of degeneration, Diderot figures the near-impossible restoration of a nation by evoking Medea. Could we fantasize that Toussaint's "daughter-in-law," let us say a domestic servant at the same plantation in Bréda, now reads attentively?

Diderot's reference is a complex distortion of the story recounted in book 7 of Ovid's *Metamorphoses,* where Medea rejuvenates her father-in-law, Aeson, by cutting his throat, removing his blood, and giving him a transfusion of sheep's blood, milk, wine, and other ingredients. Bernard Picart's handsome French edition of Ovid illustrates this operation well (Fig. 28). Following this miracle, Medea tricks the daughters of Aeson's enemy and brother, Pelias, women who also wish to extend their father's life, by goading them into dismembering and boiling his body, which kills him. The Ovidian version describes Medea as revitalizing Jason's father even as she wreaks revenge on his brother, yet Diderot radically complicates this image by conflating the two episodes— the revitalization of Aeson and the dismemberment of Pelias—into one instance that alleges that Medea rejuvenated Aeson after flaying and boiling him, but eventually failed, in terms of her overall objectives of keeping Jason's loyalty. Medea's actions remind the writer of radical surgery on a gangrenous and moribund body politic. As Medea ultimately failed, an individual agent—man or woman—cannot succeed in restoring the nation, whether by sorcery or surgery; agency has passed into the sphere of collective sociocultural transformations (*une longue suite de révolutions*).[31]

Mona Ozouf has identified regeneration as a central obsession of French political discourse in the 1780s and 1790s and finds that for many, *régénération* and *révolution* are associated with a desire to resuscitate a moribund body politic. Louis XVI was officially dubbed *régénérateur de France* in the Estates General. In his "Premier Discours," Mirabeau attributes regenerative power to the Committee of Public Instruction, saying, "You have breathed life into these ostensibly inanimate remains . . . the corpse animated by liberty wakes up and receives a new life." Or, as the revolutionary rhetoric of Urbain Domergue at the Convention indicates in its drift toward censorship: "let us carry a revolutionary

Figure 28 Medea Rejuvenating Aeson, from Bernard Picart, *Les Métamorphoses d'Ovide* (1732). (Bibliothèque Nationale, Paris)

scalpel into the vast stores of books and let us cut off all the gangrenous members of the bibliographical body. Let us remove from our libraries the swelling [*la bouffissure*] that presages death, and only leave there the plumpness [*d'embonpoint*] that signifies good health."[32] The body politic and national library converge as allegorical personifications. The specific context of Diderot's allusion to gangrene, made a couple of decades earlier, needs some clarification. Diderot may have wished to invert the technically correct but politically conservative Hobbesian appropriation of the Medea allusion in *De Cive*, where the daughters of Pelias are furnished as examples of those who seek to reform the patriarchal state. Burke's *Reflections* alludes to Pélias's daughters as well, in the negative Hobbesian fashion. A reformer approaches "the faults of the state as to the wounds of a father, with pious awe and trembling sollicitude [*sic*]." Burke is horrified at children who "hack that aged parent in pieces, and put him into the kettle of magicians," in the futile hope of national regeneration (8:146). These reformers fall prey to the dangerous eloquence of revolutionary rhetoric and inadvertently destroy what they want to save. Diderot, on the contrary, deliberately superimposes two images of regeneration, one successful and the other failed, with a view to validate symbolic parricide even if its benefits are deferred into the future.

Unlike many other *positive* representations of parricide in Enlightenment literature, which remain oedipal in their implications, Diderot's political metaphor is cross-gendered and not within what René Girard has called "a topology of imitative desire." Medea, as a protofeminist classical figure, challenges patriarchy not from the position of a genetic descendant but as a legalized relation (Aeson's daughter-*in-law*). In origin and culture, Medea was a "barbarian," extraneous to the authority and tradition she challenges (having eloped with Jason from Colchis). Furthermore, her actions consistently challenge genetic descent: killing her brother Absyrtes; slaughtering her children to get back at Jason's appropriation of them; and attempting to murder Theseus, son of her host, Aegeus, in Athens, following her flight from Corinth.[33]

Of course, in Euripides' play, and even more in Seneca's version, Medea's eloquence is marked as false and demagogic, a classical version of special pleading. Is Medea a monster for having killed her own children, or are her actions mitigated as a betrayed wife and dispossessed mother? Medea's demand for justice [δικέ] in Euripides' play rests on a long protofeminist denunciation of women's oppression by men, just as much as the female infanticide committed by the women of Orinoco is justified by them as an act of solidarity, a euthanasia that liberates female babies from future slavery to men. It is intriguing that the two most powerful of the rare portraits of women in *Histoire des deux Indes*, those of the women of Orinoco and Medea, are of women who are socially alienated and therefore commit infanticides, women whose self-justifications are just as horrific as their circumstances. The Orinoco women are abject, favoring the total elimination of women, as their fate is worse than death; the image of Medea is monstrous, of a woman too powerful and violent to contain, who commences a regenerative bloodbath by unleashing a cathartic violence. The opposing instances of monstrosity and abjection converge, converting masculine history into feminine tragedy. Both instances foreground women as abnormal and perverse.[34]

Especially as a result of the paucity of material on women outside Europe in *Histoire des deux Indes* (even though the anecdote of Polly Baker's sexual revolution in New England receives some attention), the figures of Medea and the women of Orinoco serve as pressure points yielding insights about gender, slavery, and self-possession to this virtual reader, named Toussaint's "daughter-in-law," for reasons that should now be clear. Other descriptions in the text, of cruelty practiced by slave rebels, seem positively Medea-like:

> Instruits dès l'enfance dans l'art des poisons, qui naissent pour ainsi dire sous leurs mains, ils les emploient à faire périr les boeufs, les chevaux, les mulets, les compagnons de leur esclavage, tous les êtres qui servent à l'exploitation des terres de leur oppresseur. Pour écarter loin d'eux tous les soupçons, ils essaient leurs cruautés sur leurs femmes, leurs enfants, leurs maîtresses; sur tout ce qu'ils ont de plus cher. Ils goûtent dans ce projet affreux de désespoir, le double plaisir de délivrer leur espèce d'un joug plus horrible que la mort et de laisser leur tyran dans un état de misère qui le rapproche de leur état.

> Educated from infancy in the art of poisoning, that is, so to speak, at their very fingertips, they employ it to kill cows, horses, mules, their fellow slaves, and all beings who aid the agriculture of their oppressor. To distance suspicion from themselves, they try out their cruelties on their wives, children, and mistresses, indeed on all who are dear to them. In this frightful and despairing project they taste the double pleasure of delivering their race from a yoke that is more horrible than death itself and leaving their oppressor in a miserable condition that comes close to their own. (6:155; my translation)

The prominence given in *Histoire des deux Indes* to other celebrated instances of slave altruism work to domesticate a threat. Anecdotes that fit this model are the sublime sacrifices made by loyal male slaves, one of whom agrees to be executed in lieu of his master and another who, having purchased his own freedom, finds out that his former master lost his fortune in Parisian dissipation and therefore settles an annuity on him (6:151–54). These moments point to what Gayatri Spivak has in another context analyzed as "an allegory of the general epistemic violence of imperialism, [and] the construction of a self-immolating colonial subject for the glorification of the social mission of the colonizer." For all its sociological erudition, *Histoire des deux Indes* errs when it identifies these self-inflicted wounds as being perpetrated by male slaves (although its own acknowledgment of infanticide among the Orinoco women may be a displaced acknowledgment). There is an obverse truth behind this perceived "barbarism." Female Caribbean slaves poisoned their masters and their own children, combining motives of revenge, self-defense, and euthanasia.[35]

In yet another passage, the description of poisoning in *Histoire des deux Indes* suggests a further mythical echo of Medea-like revenge. A slave, we are told, climbed out onto the roof of his master's house with three of his master's children. When the master returned home, the slave slaughtered the children, one by one, in front of the master's eyes, and threw their bodies at their father before killing himself (6:156). Self-destructive though her actions are, Medea cannot kill her children onstage in Greek tragedy and does not give up their bodies to Jason; nonetheless, the episode is visually reminiscent of the final scene, where Medea is also on the roof, about to ascend the solar chariot along with her children's bodies, when Jason accosts her from below and discovers the deaths. These rhetorical conjunctures of images of sorcery, ritual self-sacrifice, and female resistance to slavery—along with their classical antecedents—can be juxtaposed with a description from another contemporary document that hints at their political and cultural significance, Stedman's *Narrative of a Five-Years' Expedition to Surinam:* "[The slaves] also have amongst them a kind of Sybils, who deal in oracles; these sage matrons [are found] dancing and whirling round in the middle of an assembly with amazing rapidity until they foam at the mouth and drop down convulsed. Whatever the prophetess orders to be done during this paroxysm is most sacredly performed by the surrounding multitude which renders these meetings extremely dangerous, as she frequently enjoins them to murder their masters, or desert to the woods."[36] In the context of Diderot's passage on Medea, such slave "Sybils" combat patriarchal institutions with the help of women-centered cultural resources. Throughout the eighteenth century, female slaves in the Caribbean were adept at resistance through the religious practices of *obeah, myal,* and *vôdun,* known generally as voodoo. From a feminist angle, Toussaint's emphatic rejection of voodoo for Christianity is yet another uninvestigated consequence of the male reappropriation of women's traditional political authority, as Christianity played a considerable role in co-opting the Caribbean slave elites, whereas female political leadership was much more prominent in both marronage and resistance based on voodoo. The creolized practices of voodoo were, and continue to be, a politico-religious phenomenon in Haiti. The first major insurrection before 1791 was the quickly suppressed insurrection by the voodoo *houngan* Makandal in 1758 (the term "makandal" in Haitian Kréyole became synonymous with "poison packets" and "poisoner"). The meeting at Bois-Caïman, on the night of August 14, 1791, which started the revolt, was sanctified by a voodoo ceremony involving both an animal sacrifice and a political sermon by the houngan Boukman. Of course, some oral histories also claim that Toussaint secretly practiced voodoo, worshipping Ogoun Ferraille, his *lwa* (personal deity or spirit) but officially embraced Christianity for tactical reasons. Perhaps Toussaint too could ride two horses, as cavalier and voodoo practitioner, respecting colonial law and local religious injunction. The French law (*loi*) is a Kréyole homophone for the personal deity (*lwa*), and the term for the human as the religious vehicle for the manifestation of the deity is *chwal*, analogical to a horse being mounted by its rider. A more knowing interpretation of Toussaint's equestrian portrait (Fig. 26) may now come to mind.[37]

As Joan Dayan provocatively suggests, "vodou practices must be viewed as ritual reenactments of Haiti's colonial past even more than as retentions from Africa." Political interpretations of colonial discourse can also link mythical allusions to popular practices. Duarte Mimoso-Ruiz's myth criticism has shown that, even in its original classical context, the perceived barbarism of Medea was a scapegoated and systematically recursive repression of the imperialist and patriarchal structure of the suzerain Athenian polis in its domination over nearby islands and Asian colonies. As a classical instance of the explosion and dispersal of unity (diasparagmos), the trope of Medea represents a dismembering and disorienting metonymic violence against a metaphorical and organic body politic. Such a repressed "revolutionary" content suggests that the image of Medea is a rebus that, if deciphered, can retroactively speak for the gaps and elisions in *Histoire des deux Indes*. As a technical agent, indeed a trope (woman/sorceress) for a procedure (bloodbath) that sets in motion a metamorphosis (regeneration), Medea, for Diderot, initiates a series of revolutionary displacements (*une suite de révolutions*) in response to a scene of reading embarked upon to ascertain the cure for national degeneration. The violent metaphorical condensation of images of monstrosity into slaves makes Medea akin to the Derridean *pharmakon, pharmakeus,* and *pharmakos.* Medea is a female agent who can be restorative drug and unbearable poison, the sorcerer and ultimately the sacrificial scapegoat for the rejuvenation of the body politic. The "Amazonian" source of violence, enacted upon the body politic by the violent foreign woman, remains a traumatized perception of an outside that appears on the margin, as a monstrous, excluded, dangerous, and yet necessary female "other." This agent can dismember but cannot (or will not) rejuvenate the patriarch. As self-mutilating scapegoats who mimic imperialist violence on their own bodies, images of Medean slaves contain the twin possibilities of successful liberation and violent oppression, metonymic revolutionary displacement and metaphorical sacrificial scapegoating, reminiscent of the barbaric execution scenes represented in later slave narratives. Recognizing this mythical association is not meant, however, as a substitute for historiographical research on female resistance to slavery. Pursuing the untested limits of Medea as counter to the black Spartacus passage helps plot other mythopoetic potentials embedded in the *Histoire des deux Indes.*[38]

By this point, Toussaint's "daughter-in-law" might have shut the book alluding to Medea and Aeson and instead gone to witness her father-in-law's departure. When seized, Toussaint reportedly said, "Upon arresting me, you have only laid low the trunk of the tree of black freedom at Saint Domingue. It will spring forth again, as its roots are both numerous and profound." Toussaint's famous last words uncannily bring together encyclopedic form with psychoanalytic theme, Medusa and Medea. Toussaint sounds the naïve hope that has animated many a revolution: If trunks were separated from heads, a thousand flowers might bloom. The claim sounds confident, in fact, supremely arrogant. At this most monarchical moment, a royal Toussaint reimagines his own dismemberment in a Medean conflation of victor with victim. The wheel has triumphantly come full circle. The sacrifice at Bois-Caïman that prefaced the uprising of August 14, 1791, featured Boukman and others kneeling around a priestess and examining the entrails of a wild boar. In June 1802, Toussaint looks into his own arboreal entrails—about to board the ship named *Le Héros* (The Hero), bound for France, and predicts a rhizomatic regeneration that reverses entropy. Could this symbolic moment have been scripted better? Césaire appropriately names his chapter on Toussaint's arrest "The Sacrifice": Toussaint, recognizing that he had outlived his usefulness, may have deliberately walked into a trap as his last and most mystifying political act.[39]

As the body of Toussaint the restorer drops out of the nation-building project, Dessalines takes over, massacring and being himself massacred. Who is Aeson here, and who Pelias? Dayan's interpretation of Dessalines is exemplary. He, of all the black Jacobins, was the only leader made into a lwa after his death, a kind of hanged god, both powerful (*demanbre*) and dismembered (*démembré*). It is perhaps not surprising that Dessalines's approach to the colonial problem was more bloodthirsty, evoking both Spartacus and Medea. Dessalines is said to have used a shibboleth to separate the Haitian loyalists from the Francophiles (much like the original shibboleth, those who answered a French interrogation in French rather than Kréyole were said to have been killed on the spot). If Dessalines harbored murderous intentions toward the very existence of the French language, his stated goal for "regeneration" was an avenging of the Code Noir with a Code Blanc as threatened in the black Spartacus catechism, orchestrating an unprecedented massacre of the whites after promising them protection in the spring of 1804. Renaming Saint Domingue after the Amerindian name, Ayti, Dessalines also claims to have "rendered to these true cannibals, war for war, crime for crime, outrage for outrage; yes, I have saved my country; I have avenged America." Dessalines's reign of terror, like Robespierre's, was shortlived, and he was, like his predecessor, cannibalized by the voracious Revolution he spearheaded.[40]

Activating metaliteracy is a kind of sortie for the scholar, perhaps, as we foray deliberately out of the safer confines of archival history. Toussaint's nom de guerre, Louverture, was given him for the ability to create military and political openings despite insurmountable odds (although there exists the more prosaic explanation that he was gap-toothed). As retroactively imagined in these readings, Toussaint and his hypothetical "daughter-in-law" heard, reacted to, and transformed the materials of metropolitan discourses, opening up paths toward other histories that followed them. Despite Toussaint's personal defeat and capture, Haiti declared itself independent in 1804, thus making for the first successful anticolonial nationalist revolution against European colonizers fought mostly by a population of former slaves of non-European origin.

The illustriousness of this history gives Haiti's problems no advantage whatsoever. Sometimes the *"comedy of color,"* as Dayan calls it, contrived by the mid-nineteenth century an internal "politics of the understudy" (*la politique de la doublure*), whereby the mulatto elites maintained power through a black surrogate.[41] The paradoxical success of early formal decolonization resulted in decades of punitive European and American commercial blockades and subsequent cycles of U.S.-enforced military intervention and occupation. Political isolation within the larger Caribbean context, the sorry legacy of militarist rule, and, more recently, Duvalierism, would make the population pay a terrible price. Haiti holds the unenviable position of being the poorest country in the Western hemisphere today. Nonetheless, in the social chaos of today's Haiti, could we perhaps find Toussaint's heirs, "daughters-in-law" and "sons-in-law," today's tropicopolitans who perform the modern tasks of regeneration and restoration? Haiti enters the twenty-first century still suffering the consequences of a long neocolonial afterlife.

Conclusion

The body of history does not determine a single one of my actions.

I am my own foundation.

And it is by going beyond the historical, instrumental hypothesis that I will initiate the cycle of my freedom.

—FRANTZ FANON, *Black Skin, White Masks*[1]

The critical ontology of ourselves has to be considered not, certainly, as a theory, a doctrine, nor even as a permanent body of knowledge that is accumulating; it has to be conceived as an attitude, an ethos, a philosophical life in which the critique of what we are is at one and the same time the historical analysis of the limits that are imposed on us and an experiment with the possibility of going beyond them . . . I do not know whether it must be said today that the critical task still entails faith in Enlightenment; I continue to think that this task requires work on our limits, that is, a patient labor giving form to our impatience for liberty.

—MICHEL FOUCAULT, "What Is Enlightenment?"[2]

Frantz Fanon's rallying cry represents a forgotten impulse of postcolonial studies. Taken from the conclusion of *Black Skin, White Masks,* his psychoanalytical study of racial complexes under colonialism, this passage locates freedom beyond the "instrumental hypothesis" equated with history itself. But why does Fanon refuse the determining role of history? And is the claim concerning self-liberation that follows a solipsism? Under the instrumental hypothesis, history constructs subjects who receive its determinations. The subject, it is alleged, will break free of history's deleterious influence. Sartrean existentialism is very much in the background, even as Fanon authorizes himself by citing Marx, that most historical of thinkers, in his epigraph; however, it is the apocalyptic voice in *The Eighteenth Brumaire:* "[T]he social revolution . . . cannot draw its poetry from the past, but only from the future. It cannot begin with itself before it has stripped itself of all its superstitions concerning the past. Earlier revolutions relied on memories out of world history in order to drug themselves against their own content. In order to find their own content, the revolutions of the nineteenth century have to let the dead bury the dead. Before, the expression exceeded the content; now, the content exceeds the expression."[3] Marx communicates a profound sense of history as stifling tradition and as an increasingly nostalgic drug that prevents revolutions from recognizing their own status as event. A settling of accounts with history may free social revolution from its thrall. Nineteenth-century revolutions ought to disavow history as memory; by cutting the umbilical cord with the past, "let[ting] the dead bury the dead," contemporaneous revolutions "find their own content." According to Marx, therefore, history can truly be *made* only when its agents are finally unburdened of it as deadweight.

In terms similar to Fanon's but writing before him, Walter Benjamin asserts that the historical materialist "leaves it to others to be drained by the whore called 'Once upon a time' in historicism's bordello." If the implications of this trope of emasculation were not abundantly clear, Benjamin adds, with some irony, that the historical materialist should be *"man enough* to blast open the continuum of history" (my emphasis). Seized upon in a moment of danger, history evinces metaphors of rape as liberation. For Benjamin, history negotiates between hitherto incommensurate particularities and larger collective phenomena by way of its constellated relevance rather than its referential metanarratives. Even as Marx and Fanon reject "historicism" as a compensatory mechanism that distracts the individual seeker of freedom and the collective subject of social revolution, Benjamin interprets the "turn" to history as a strategic calculation whose outcomes cannot be fully determined amidst a largely tragic record. Hence, the futile heroism of being "man enough to blast open" the process that hitherto drained the historicists dry.[4] As an ethical response, the "turn to history" reassures the subject in a similar manner to "the consolation of philosophy." Or, as Jacques Derrida has recently argued through a reading of Freud's philosophy of history, the archive commands the responsibility of the subject just as much as it enshrines narrative origins.[5] So, though Fanon claims to reject "the body of history," his self-liberation reaffirms this archive if only as a point of departure. Fanon too, like Benjamin, rewrites the old body-spirit dichotomy in terms of agency and passivity, actively arguing against the predetermined passivity of a historicism that drains the subject dry. These theorists of liberation are obsessed with history-in-the-making, or life-in-action. Like Yeats's "Leda and the Swan," Benjamin's trope revisits, at another remove, the barbarism that needs to be escaped. As a masculine "seizing" or "blasting open" of inert, feminized history or a dead archive, these romanticized self-definitions are themselves the outcome of an Enlightenment heritage that in turn harks back to a classical one.

The possibility of a different approach to the heritage of Enlightenment critique is suggested in the second epigraph, from Foucault's absorbing reflections on Kant's 1784 essay, "What Is Enlightenment?" Foucault defines the work of critique as, perforce, an open-ended analysis of the significance of historical constraints. Whereas Kant sees humanity emerging from immaturity into Enlightenment through the motto *aude sapere,* or "dare to know," Foucault's twist on this *Wahlspruch,* or heraldic device of Kant's, is something like "learn to act." He suggests that his aim is "to transform the critique conducted in the form of necessary limitation [by Kant] into a practical critique that takes the form of a possible transgression."[6] Eschewing the transcendental gesture of Kantian critique, reasoning founded on the imperative of obedience to its dictates, Foucault nonetheless hopes for a pragmatics—rather than an epistemology—of liberation. With his genealogical objectives, Foucault's reversal of critical ontology makes much of archaeological excavations, disciplinary subterfuges, and indirect method. As we are ourselves creatures of the Enlightenment, we cannot be forced into the blackmail of being "for" it or "against" it; instead, we have to test the limits of the massive series of social transformations created by the Enlightenment. Through attitudinal shifts, we are now more skeptical of the *methods* of the sciences that seek truth but are still loyal to the *desires* of Enlightenment philosophy that seek to liberate humanity from historical constraints.

How do these reflections enable an eighteenth-century studies from a postcolonial perspective? Although we cannot escape the principle of selection that creates a canon, however provisional and inclusive that may be, there is another step we need to make, with canonicity as with history, from content to expression. A postcolonial eighteenth century becomes disciplinarily relevant and critically meaningful if we shift our focus from texts to the reading formations through which those texts are perceived and institutionalized. By becoming more conscious of colonialist tropologies in relation to real and virtual tropicopolitans, the literary critic can reframe the assumed quiddity of the text toward different kinds of receptions. Rather than solipsistically affirm what eighteenth-century texts mean in relation to traditional questions, the introduction of tropicopolitan contexts diverts the otherwise frictionless circulation of the eighteenth century to itself as Eurocentric romance. Paying attention to tropicopolitans, we discover Oroonoko, a slave rebel, amid discourses of pethood and commodification, and Equiano, a colonial projector, within a fetishistic celebration of the book; we witness Montagu, in symbolic chains, surrounded by Turkish aristocratic women whom she envies as liberated, and inversely, Burke's and Johnson's sublime spectators, wresting freedom from the historical canard of oriental despotism; we judge Addison's, Defoe's, and Swift's ambivalent interrogations of colonialism at the beginning of the century, even as we question the amplitude of the Haitian response to colonialism in the form of a nationalist revolution at century's end. The gridding of tropicopolitan readers onto eighteenth-century texts situates the virtual, the real, and the reified side by side, expanding the historicity of the epoch rather than diminishing it. Such a defamiliarizing move, gestic though it may be, makes visible the contours of the conventional reading formation of eighteenth-century studies even as it experiments with others that could eventually modify, or even overturn, convention.

It is perpetual revolution that could result here, through a changing course catalogue, novel reading assignments, and fresh approaches that satisfy all those involved. Tony Bennett's exposition of the consequences of reading formations is worth emulating: "criticism's concern is to intervene within such processes [of the making of meaning], to make texts mean differently by modifying the determinations which bear in upon them." The agenda here is the pragmatic one of a *disciplinary* activism, as we "should seek to detach texts from socially dominant reading formations and to install them in new ones."[7] Bennett's description of this approach sounds similar to Foucault's call for many little acts of liberation rather than theologies translated into grand plans. Micropolitics is not necessarily a capitulation to anarchistic nihilism and hedonistic libertarianism; it is to act locally along with the injunction to think globally, conduct eccentric readings as well as mount bureaucratic arguments that inscribe the margin into the center.

In this genealogical, pragmatic, and local spirit, I do not believe that my postcolonial approach to the historical, transcendental, and global enterprise of the eighteenth century has created new doctrine. Rather, I anticipate that these sketched readings of my disciplinary object explore a variety of ways to dislodge texts from familiar reading formations and situate them in another set of historical and theoretical contexts. As an unfinished task, this postcolonial eighteenth century may go beyond the pale for some *dix-huitièmistes* and remain insufficiently transgressive for some postcolonialists. Pluralization, mobilization, and tropicalization are always open-ended goals. The gain from such strategies is the freer exchange and, in fact, the undoing of the artificial boundary that separates text from context. Literary criticism, if it takes certain set contexts for granted—class privilege, cultural literacy, historical continuity—functions as tradition, reproducing certain reading formations as natural outcomes. By making literature more accessible to a diversity of readers and interpreters and more resonant to texts, theories, or tropicopolitan readers, scholarship contends with its social mission alongside its professional self-justification. Inflexible or sedimented contexts have to be remobilized (whether they be race, class, and gender, or author, genre, and historical background), leading to the multiplication of Literature into literatures, and a pluralization of prerequisite literacies.[8]

We should seek to make visible the limitations imposed by nationalist boundaries of scholarship by different pedagogical innovations that perpetrate an alienation effect (like Brecht's *Verfremdungseffekt*) rather than accept these borders silently as the lay of the literary landscape. It is the conjuncture between *literary* institution (sedimented reading formation that masquerades as the "text") and *readerly* interpretation (a fresh gambit from a hitherto unexamined "context") that becomes the productive terrain for committed scholarship. Those who seek, wittingly or unwittingly, to argue for the institutional merits of literature as a reified category (whether that be old criticism, new criticism, or for that matter, postcolonial criticism) become obstacles to the plural purchase on texts and contexts supplied by a number of interpretive literacies. If the study of literature is an ideological symptom of something else, those of us who are implicated in it should use our critical scholarship to lead to a transformative practice concerning literature as it is studied, taught, and naturalized through reading formations. More attention to reading formations would result in an awareness of the malleability of tropologies and their multiple tropicalizations. Before we bemoan our inability to change the world, we might want to see if we can productively change our contexts. The Enlightenment concentrated its energies on transcendental critique, and its revision has taken the form of retroactively deducing, constructing, and performing the agency of those subjected to its historical constraints. The search for new reading formations is a modest version of the "patient labor giving form to our impatience for liberty" that Foucault speaks of, one that pluralizes global history into the multihistoricality of simultaneous local emergences. In this new Enlightenment, global theorists give way to local intellectuals, metropolitan readers are trumped by their colonial cousins, and cosmopolitans yield to tropicopolitans.

Notes

Introduction: Colonialism and Eighteenth-Century Studies

1 "Racism," according to various scholars, is a modern phenomenon that relies on science and pseudoscience to categorize peoples through a statist and a nationalist ideology. Full-fledged racism is a nineteenth- and twentieth-century construction. As this example is antiquarian (see n. 3), it reveals prejudices that are more loosely "racialist" rather than strictly "racist." See Nancy Stepan, *The Idea of Race in Science: Great Britain, 1800–1960* (London: Macmillan, 1982), and Etienne Balibar and Immanuel Wallerstein, *Race, Nation, Class: Ambiguous Identities* (London: Verso, 1991).

2 See Michael McKeon, *Origins of the English Novel 1600–1740* (Baltimore: Johns Hopkins UP, 1987), 103–13.

3 See Desiderius Erasmus, *Adages*, trans. Margaret Phillips (Toronto: U of Toronto P, 1982), 356–57; Thomas Palmer, *The Emblems of Thomas Palmer: Two Hundred Posies*, ed. J. Manning (New York: AMS Press), 56; John Bunyan, *The Pilgrim's Progress*, ed. James Blanton Wharey (Oxford: Clarendon P, 1960), 286; Samuel Richardson, *Clarissa, or the History of a Young Lady*, ed. Angus Ross (New York: Penguin, 1985), 287.

4 We find a homology here with what Marx calls self-valorization (*Selbstverwertung*) in the context of the erection of the money form as ultimate arbiter of value: "Value . . . is constantly changing from one form into the other, without becoming lost in this movement; it thus becomes transformed into an automatic subject . . . its valorization is therefore self-valorization" (Karl Marx, *Capital: A Critique of Political Economy*, trans. Ben Fowkes [New York: Vintage, 1977], 1: 255). I suggest reading this account as a teasing allusion by Marx to the conjunction between the rise of the bourgeois subject and that of the capitalist mode of production. The further implications of this conjoint value production concern its reliance on the elision of the tropicopolitan, in both symbolic and nonsymbolic terms.

5 Gayatri Spivak, *Outside in the Teaching Machine* (New York: Routledge, 1993), 281.

6 Salman Rushdie, "The Empire Writes Back with a Vengeance," *The Times* (July 3, 1982): 8.

7   See Mary Louise Pratt, *Imperial Eyes: Travel Writing and Transculturation* (New York: Routledge, 1992), 6; Fernando Ortiz, *Cuban Counterpoint: Tobacco and Sugar* (New York: Knopf, 1947), 102–3.

8   Frances R. Aparicio and Susana Chávez-Silverman, "Introduction," *Tropicalizations: Transcultural Representations of Latinidad*, ed. Frances R. Aparicio and Susana Chávez-Silverman (Dartmouth, NH: UP of New England, 1997), 2.

9   Such is the case, for instance, with the work of the Subaltern Studies Collective, and also with the political discussion between Deleuze and Foucault, "Intellectuals and Power," critiqued by Gayatri Chakravorty Spivak in "Can the Subaltern Speak?", in *Marxism and the Interpretation of Culture*, ed. Cary Nelson and Lawrence Grossberg (Urbana: U of Illinois P, 1988), 271–313; and in "Subaltern Studies: Deconstructing Historiography," *In Other Worlds: Essays in Cultural Politics* (New York: Methuen, 1987).

10 See Linda Colley, *Britons: Forging the Nation, 1707–1837* (New Haven: Yale UP, 1992). Colley freely acknowledges the construction of Britishness in relation to otherness and bellicose attitudes, but concerns herself with the center rather than the margins. For an account that is far more sensitive to the constitutive role of Francophobia in the making of English nationalism, see Gerald Newman, *The Rise of English Nationalism: A Cultural History, 1740–1830* (New York: St. Martin's, 1987).

11 See Salman Rushdie, *Imaginary Homelands: Essays and Criticism, 1981–1991* (New York: Viking, 1991); Bill Ashcroft, Gareth Griffiths, and Helen Tiffin, *The Empire Writes Back: Theory and Practice in Post-Colonial Literature* (London: Routledge, 1989); and Centre for Contemporary Cultural Studies, *The Empire Strikes Back: Race and Racism in 70's Britain* (London: Hutchinson, 1982).

12 Michel Foucault, "Nietzsche, Genealogy, History," in *The Foucault Reader*, ed. Paul Rabinow (New York: Pantheon Books, 1984), 76–77.

13 See J. Laplanche and J. B. Pontalis, *The Language of Psycho-Analysis*, trans. Donald Nicholson (New York: Norton, 1973), 111–14.

14 See C. L. R. James, *The Black Jacobins: Toussaint Louverture and the San Domingo Revolution*, rev. ed. (New York: Vintage, 1963); Edward W. Said, *Orientalism* (New York: Routledge, 1978), *The World, the Text, and the Critic* (Cambridge, MA: Harvard UP, 1983), and *Culture and Imperialism* (London: Chatto and Windus, 1993); John Barrell, *English Literature in History, 1730–80: An Equal, Wide Survey* (London: Hutchinson, 1983); Laura Brown, *Alexander Pope* (Oxford: Basil Blackwell, 1985), and *Ends of Empire: Women and Ideology in Early Eighteenth-Century English Literature* (Ithaca, NY: Cornell UP, 1993); Peter Hulme, *Colonial Encounters: Europe and the Native Caribbean, 1492–1797* (New York: Methuen, 1986); Christopher Miller, *Theories of Africans: Francophone Literature and Anthropology in Africa* (Chicago: U of Chicago P, 1990); Pratt, *Imperial Eyes;* Moira Ferguson, *Subject to Others: British Women Writers*

and Colonial Slavery, 1670–1834 (New York: Routledge, 1992); and Felicity Nussbaum, *Torrid Zones* (Baltimore: Johns Hopkins UP, 1995).

15 Witness Lawrence Lipking, "Inventing the Eighteenth Centuries: A Long View," in *The Profession of Eighteenth-Century Literature: Reflections on an Institution,* ed. Leo Damrosch (Madison: U of Wisconsin P, 1992), 7–25; Michael McKeon, "The Origins of Interdisciplinary Studies," *Eighteenth-Century Studies* 28.1 (fall 1994): 17–28; and Clifford Siskin, "Gender, Sublimity, Culture: Retheorizing Disciplinary Desire," *Eighteenth-Century Studies* 28.1 (fall 1994): 37–50.

16 Felicity Nussbaum and Laura Brown, "Revising Critical Practices: An Introductory Essay," in *The New Eighteenth Century: Theory, Politics, English Literature,* ed. Felicity Nussbaum and Laura Brown (New York: Methuen, 1987), 5.

17 As Brown and Nussbaum point out, much of the historicist impetus behind eighteenth-century studies was instituted as a resistance to New Criticism, and the challenge posed by deconstruction was assimilated by many to this older battle. The challenge posed by postcolonial theory, however, involves several political and theoretical paradigms: Marxism, Foucauldianism, feminism, and psychoanalysis, all of which are harnessed to expose the imperialist pretensions of British national literature and culture. The institutional machinery of eighteenth-century studies works too well if somewhat slowly. It shakes off attacks and absorbs new challenges at its own pace.

18 See William H. Epstein, "Counter-Intelligence: Cold War Criticism and Eighteenth-Century Studies," *ELH* 57 (1990): 63–99.

19 See Donna Landry, "Commodity Feminism," in *The Profession of Eighteenth-Century Literature: Reflections on an Institution,* ed. Leo Damrosch (Madison: U of Wisconsin P, 1992), 170. I find that Landry somewhat overstates the case concerning the commodification of intellectual work and, for that matter, understates the effectivity of political criticism. As she puts it, "feminist critique as political criticism . . . can be our means of resisting that complicity [with professionalization]," although she has to qualify that immediately with "no critique can hope to escape in a totalizing way some complicity with its structural context" (170). There is a question begged here. If commodification of feminist intellectual work is as relentless and irresistible as she argues, why should it be that "some critical reflection upon our self-representations in the marketplace may help us resist the commodification we cannot elude"? In the spirit of collective collaboration, I would suggest that Landry's article has collapsed, in a certain Bourdieuvian fashion, the *positioning* of the intellectual (who is doubtless caught up in the circuit of capital) with the *content* of the critique. Therefore, in a bizarre way, *self-criticism* becomes the *only* authentic form of criticism. For similar reasons, I am uncomfortable with Bill Epstein's collapse of the categories of "profession" and "discipline" in the same volume.

See William H. Epstein, "Professing Gray: The Resumption of Authority in Eighteenth-Century Studies," 86.

20 Said, *Orientalism* 28, 25. The phrase about unlearning is from Raymond Williams, *Culture and Society, 1780–1950* (London: Chatto and Windus, 1958), 376.

21 Frantz Fanon, *The Wretched of the Earth*, trans. Constance Farrington (1961; Harmondsworth: Penguin, 1967).

22 See Gilles Deleuze and Félix Guattari, *A Thousand Plateaus*, trans. Brian Massumi (Minneapolis: U of Minnesota P, 1987), 126–27.

23 See D. N. Rodowick, *Gilles Deleuze's Time Machine* (Durham, NC: Duke UP, 1997), 139–69.

ONE *Petting Oroonoko*

1 See Joanna Lipking, ed., *Oroonoko, or The Royal Slave* (New York: Norton, 1997). Page numbers to this edition are cited in parentheses. Investigation of the Oroonoko legend in this century started with Wylie Sypher, *Guinea's Captive Kings: British Anti-Slavery Literature of the XVIIIth Century* (Chapel Hill: U of North Carolina P, 1942). For an account of related literature in France, see Leila Sebbar-Pignon, "Le mythe du bon nègre, ou l'idéologie coloniale dans la production romanesque du XVIIIe siècle," *Temps Moderne* 336/337-38 (July 1974): 2349–75, 2588–613. Behn's novella was relatively obscure in England during the eighteenth century, although a version of it was one of the nine most widely read English novels in translation during the period in France. Edward Seeber, relying on Daniel Mornet's classic study of eighteenth-century French libraries, tells us that Behn's *Oroonoko* was more widely read in France than *Zadig, Manon Lescaut, La Princesse de Clèves*, or *Don Quixote*. However, the 1745 rendering of Behn's novella by Antoine de Laplace (the best known French *Oroonoko* that Seeber talks about) changes the resolution from a tragic to a comic one. See Edward D. Seeber, "*Oroonoko* in France in the XVIIIth Century," *PMLA* 51.4 (December 1936): 953–59.

2 See Janet Todd, introduction to *Aphra Behn Studies*, ed. Janet Todd (Cambridge: Cambridge UP, 1996), 3–4. See also Todd's superb biography, *The Secret Life of Aphra Behn* (New Brunswick, NJ: Rutgers UP, 1996), 37–52, 417–21. For earlier biographical treatment, see Angeline Goreau, *Reconstructing Aphra: A Social Biography of Aphra Behn* (New York: Dial, 1980); Maureen Duffy, *The Passionate Shepherdess: Aphra Behn 1640–89* (London: Cape, 1977); William J. Cameron, *New Light on Aphra Behn: An Investigation into the Facts and Fictions Surrounding Her Journey to Surinam in 1663 and Her Activities as a Spy in Flanders in 1666* (Auckland: U of Auckland P, 1961); B. Dhuicq, "Further Evidence on Aphra Behn's Stay in Surinam," *Notes and Queries* 26 (1979): 524–26; and Jane Jones, "New Light on the Background and Early Life of Aphra Behn," in *Aphra Behn Studies*, ed. Janet Todd, 310-20.

3 See Laura Brown, "The Romance of Empire: *Oroonoko* and the Trade in Slaves," in *The New Eighteenth Century: Theory, Politics, English Literature,* ed. Felicity Nussbaum and Laura Brown (New York: Methuen, 1987), 41–61; William C. Spengemann, "The Earliest American Novel: Aphra Behn's *Oroonoko,*" *Nineteenth-Century Fiction* 38 (1984): 384-414; Heidi Hutner, ed., *Rereading Aphra Behn* (Charlottesville: UP of Virginia, 1993), 118; Margaret W. Ferguson, "Juggling the Categories of Race, Class and Gender: Aphra Behn's *Oroonoko,*" *Women's Studies* 19 (1991): 159-81; and Moira Ferguson, "*Oroonoko:* Birth of a Paradigm," in *Subject to Others: British Women Writers and Colonial Slavery, 1670-1834* (New York: Routledge, 1992), 27-49. For discussions of Oroonoko's significance for the prehistory of the novel, see Michael McKeon, *The Origins of the English Novel 1600-1740* (Baltimore: Johns Hopkins UP, 1987), 111-113; Lennard Davis, *Factual Fictions: The Origins of the English Novel* (New York: Columbia UP, 1983), 106-10; and Robert L. Chibka, " 'Oh! Do Not Fear a Woman's Invention': Truth, Falsehood, and Fiction in Aphra Behn's *Oroonoko,*" *Texas Studies in Literature and Language* 30.4 (winter 1988): 510-37.

4 See Catherine Gallagher, *Nobody's Story: The Vanishing Acts of Women Writers in the Marketplace, 1670-1820* (Berkeley: U of California P, 1994), 49-87; Robert Erickson, "Mrs. A. Behn and the Myth of Oroonoko-Imoinda," *Eighteenth-Century Fiction* 5.3 (April 1993): 201-16.

5 Ros Ballaster, "New Hystericism: Aphra Behn's *Oroonoko:* The Body, the Text, and the Feminist Critic," in *New Feminist Discourses: Critical Essays on Theories and Texts,* ed. Isobel Armstrong (London: Routledge, 1992), 283-95; Margaret W. Ferguson, "Transmuting *Othello:* Aphra Behn's *Oroonoko,*" in *Cross-Cultural Performances: Differences in Women's Re-Visions of Shakespeare,* ed. Marianne Novy (Urbana: U of Illinois P, 1993), 35; Stephanie Athey and Daniel Cooper Alarcón, "*Oroonoko*'s Gendered Economies of Honor/Horror: Reframing Colonial Discourse Studies in the Americas," *American Literature* 65.3 (September 1993): 415-44; Charlotte Sussman, "The Other Problem with Women: Reproduction and Slave Culture in Behn's *Oroonoko,*" in *Rereading Aphra Behn,* ed. Heidi Hutner, 215; Susan Z. Andrade, "White Skin, Black Masks: Colonialism and the Sexual Politics of *Oroonoko,*" *Cultural Critique* 27 (spring 1994): 206. In another hallmark imoindaist reading that follows the symptomatic transformations of the *Oroonoko* texts over the eighteenth century, Suvir Kaul accounts for the changing face of colonialism from a royalist ideology to a bureaucratic rationalization. See Suvir Kaul, "Reading Literary Symptoms: Colonial Pathologies and the *Oroonoko* Fictions of Behn, Southerne, and Hawkesworth," in *The South Pacific in the Eighteenth Century: Narratives and Myths,* ed. Jonathan Lamb, special issue of *Eighteenth-Century Life* 18.3 (November 1994): 80-96.

6 Kaul, "Reading Literary Symptoms," 93. For the arguments against colonial discourse analysis and in favor of area studies of colonialist micropolitics, see

Nicholas Thomas, *Colonialism's Culture: Anthropology, Travel, and Government* (Cambridge: Polity Press, 1994). For discussion of the Coromantien episode as orientalist, see Lynne Meloccaro, "Orientalism and the Oriental Tale: Gender, Genre, and Cultural Identity in Eighteenth-Century England" (Ph.D. diss., Rutgers University, 1992), and for a more realist interpretation, Joanna Lipking, "Confusing Matters: Searching the Backgrounds of *Oroonoko*," in *Aphra Behn Studies*, ed. Janet Todd, 259-81.

7 See Gayatri Chakravorty Spivak, "Three Women's Texts and a Critique of Imperialism," *Critical Inquiry* 12 (autumn 1985): 248; and Barry Weller, "The Royal Slave and the Prestige of Origins," *Kenyon Review* 14.3 (summer 1992): 65-78.

8 See Keith Thomas, *Man and the Natural World: Changing Attitudes in England 1500-1800* (New York: Oxford UP, 1983), 117.

9 See *The Character of a Town Misse* (London, 1675) 7; *The Tatler* 245 (31 October-2 November, 1710). For the vast documentation of Africans as pets, see David Dabydeen, *Hogarth's Blacks: Images of Blacks in Eighteenth-Century English Art* (Kingston-upon-Thames, Surrey: Dangaroo Press, 1985); David Brion Davis, *The Problem of Slavery in Western Culture* (Ithaca, NY: Cornell UP, 1966); Peter Fryer, *Staying Power: The History of Black People in Britain* (London: Pluto, 1984); Orlando Patterson, *Slavery and Social Death: A Comparative Study* (Cambridge, MA: Harvard UP, 1982); and Folarin Shyllon, *Black People in Britain 1555-1833* (New York: Oxford UP, 1977). As early as 1662, Pepys records in his journal that the Earl of Sandwich brought on ship (while escorting Catherine of Braganza and her dowry to Charles II) "a little Turke and a negro" besides "many other birdes and other pretty noveltys" as presents for his daughters (Shyllon 10-11). In 1665, Pepys visited Robert Vyner, who displayed the shriveled corpse of a black boy as a curio (Fryer 25). For other anecdotal evidence, see Shyllon 41-44; Fryer 32. "Hue and Cry" newspaper advertisements in *The London Gazette, Mercurius Politicus,* and *The Athenian Mercury* announced rewards for runaway blacks alongside notices about runaway dogs and about horses and canaries for sale; often the rewards offered for the missing animals were more than those for the blacks (Fryer 22; Shyllon 10-12). Scientific discourse did not lag far behind. By 1684, the *Journal des Savants* had declared Africans as belonging to a different species (Davis 454).

10 A satirist describes a "loathsome filthy Black. / Which you (Mazarin) & Sussex in your arms did take." See Janet Todd, *The Secret Life,* 444-45, note 11. See also Bryan Bevan, *Charles II's French Mistress* (London: R. Hale, 1972); Hector McDonnell, *The Wild Geese of the Antrim MacDonnells* (Dublin: Irish Academic Press, 1996), 53-55, 64-67. The Duchess of Portsmouth returned to France in disgrace following Charles's death in 1685, and the painting in the National Portrait Gallery was acquired from France only in the nineteenth century. For an excellent discussion of the performative aspect of Bracegirdle's feathers and the Mignard portrait within a context of anxieties concerning colonialism,

superabundance, and political surrogation, see Joseph Roach, *Cities of the Dead: Circum-Atlantic Performance* (New York: Columbia UP, 1996), 119–31. Roach also speculates that the Bracegirdle mezzotint could be taken to depict Semernia in Behn's play, *The Widdow Ranter, or the History of Bacon in Virginia* (1688).

11 See Fryer, *Staying Power* 23; Thomas Tryon, *Friendly Advice to the Gentlemen-Planters in the West Indies . . .* (London, 1684), 105; and Richmond P. Bond, *Queen Anne's American Kings* (Oxford: Clarendon, 1952). The background of eroticized male bondage implicated with the history and iconography of the black male body in the West is relevant here, especially as William III was accused of homosexuality, perhaps complicating the interest he expressed in his slave. This is a speculative aside, but the homophobic denials in two major biographies are symptomatic. Stephen B. Baxter, *William III* (London: Longmans, 1966), 352, rejects allegations of homosexuality "on the ground that the King's tremendous burden of work left no time for it." Nesca A. Robb, *William of Orange: A Personal Portrait,* 2 vols. (London: Heinemann, 1966), 2:448, dismisses the charges as "damnable." The frequently mentioned English monetary unit, the guinea, was a new gold coin struck in 1663 to inaugurate the Royal Adventurers in Africa, a venture sponsored by "the king and queen, the queen mother, a prince, three dukes, seven earls, a countess, six lords and twenty-five knights" (Fryer, *Staying Power* 21). Although the company failed—to be replaced by the more successful Royal African Company—the guinea, as one of the most commonly mentioned units of currency throughout the literature of the period, carried with it a historical association of slaves also serving as a form of ready money.

12 See J. Jean Hecht, *Continental and Colonial Servants in Eighteenth-Century England* (Northampton, MA: Department of History, Smith College, 1954), 36. James H. Bunn, in "The Aesthetics of British Mercantilism," *New Literary History* 11.2 (winter 1980): 303, says that "the polyglot effects of randomly purchasing knickknacks and recomposing them pointlessly in a curio cabinet" formed the peculiar aesthetics of mercantilist culture. For a more general discussion concerning the play of colonial demand and supply for early consumerism, see Neil McKendrick, John Brewer, and J. H. Plumb, *The Birth of a Consumer Society: The Commercialization of Eighteenth-Century England* (London: Hutchinson, 1983).

13 See Todd, *The Secret Life,* 35–36. Colonial servants were petted, whereas continental servants were resented in England during the eighteenth century (Hecht, *Servants* 56). Perhaps colonial servants were treated with indulgence because they were still exotic and did not threaten the class structure in the manner European servants might have done. However, learned racism grows even as the exotic becomes increasingly familiarized through the period.

14 The writings of seventeenth-century writers with protofeminist sympathies critically deploy the natural as an inclusive rather than exclusive term. Thomas

Tryon and Margaret Cavendish, contemporaries of Behn and Southerne, demonstrated a keen sensibility toward the well-being of animals, anchored within a nonanthropocentric species-based humanism. See Kathleen Jones, *A Glorious Fame: The Life of Margaret Cavendish, Duchess of Newcastle 1623–1673* (London: Bloomsbury, 1988). Furthermore, animals could be granted agency according to medieval law and, just like human beings, be imputed with rights as well as responsibilities. A celebrated case involving an animal's psychological agency occurred in 1679, when a woman and a dog were hanged in Tyburn for alleged bestiality. See Harriet Ritvo, *The Animal Estate: The English and Other Creatures in the Victorian Age* (Cambridge, MA: Harvard UP, 1987), 1.

15 Louis Althusser, "Idéologie et appareils idéologiques d'État," in *Positions* (Paris: Éditions Sociales, 1976), 79–137.

16 See Todd, *The Secret Life,* 419. Ernst H. Kantorowicz, *The King's Two Bodies: A Study in Mediaeval Political Theology* (Princeton, NJ: Princeton UP, 1957), 41.

17 For an extended reading along these lines, see Brown, "Romance of Empire," 58–60. One critic reads Behn's account as related to the spectacular accounts of Christomimetic martyrology in Foxe's sixteenth-century text, *Acts and Monuments*. See Paul J. Korshin, *Typologies in England 1650–1820* (Princeton, NJ: Princeton UP, 1982), 213.

18 See Todd, *The Secret Life,* 54–55. Janet Todd's biography, as well as Brown's "Romance of Empire" and Ferguson's "Juggling of the Categories" discuss in depth the factionalism of the English in Surinam during the time of the novella. Brown's energies are devoted to proving that Oroonoko's execution could serve as a symbol of Charles I's; the same evidence also points to the hostilities circulating among the colonists even as they use these symbols to maneuver themselves into positions of advantage in relation to each other. In like fashion, the narrator's empathy for Oroonoko could be following a more precise agenda than mere solidarity. Witness Richard French's uncharitable attack on the antivivisectionist Francis Power Cobbe in the nineteenth century: "her dog and her cat are a great deal to her; and it is the idea of their suffering which excites her . . . she is not defending a right inherent in sentient things as such; she is doing special pleading for some of them for which she has a special liking" (in Thomas, *Man and the Natural World,* 120). The possibility of a misogynistic attack on the narrator, where animals are substituted for women, is suggested by Robert Darnton's treatment of symbolic violence in *The Great Cat Massacre and Other Episodes in French Cultural History* (New York: Vintage, 1984).

19 See Athey and Alarcón, "*Oroonoko's* Gendered Economies," 425. In "Elizabethan Tobacco," *Representations* 21 (winter 1988): 27–66, Jeffrey Knapp emphasizes the way Walter Raleigh's introduction of tobacco to England was conflated with his own stature as self-fashioned Renaissance man whose aloofness was widely disparaged (38). Raleigh smoked defiantly before his own execution and was reputed to have done so haughtily before Essex's execution for trea-

son. Knapp says that "the primary value of tobacco for [Elizabethan writers] is its negativity, its ability to mediate between normally opposed terms—between purging and feeding, high and low, superstition and religion, home and away, heaven and earth—by displacing both terms and substituting its own neither material nor spiritual 'essence' instead" (51).

20 In *Testing the Chains: Resistance to Slavery in the British West Indies* (Ithaca, NY: Cornell UP, 1982), 57, Michael Craton says, "Akan-speaking Coromantees were the most feared and admired of the early slave rebels, and in the melting pot of a hundred African ethnicities, aspects of the Akan culture became a focus and symbol of resistance, almost normative."

21 As one study on West Indian plantations documents, "[I]n this atmosphere of repression and constraint it was possible only in the exercise of their racial su- periority that white women were able to obtain some psychological satisfaction through the physical and mental domination of blacks, men in particular. In the use of their 'peculiar power,' they were reportedly as cruel as their men- folk. The whipping of negro servants was a mere 'amusement' to them and they were liable to contract 'harsh and domineering' ideas towards slaves, al- legedly enjoying seeing them stripped bare and punished in the most disgust- ing manner" (Barbara Bush, "White 'Ladies,' Coloured 'Favourites' and Black 'Wenches': Some Considerations on Sex, Race and Class Factors in Social Re- lations in White Creole Society in the British Caribbean," *Slavery and Abolition* 2.3 [December 1981]: 256). At the same time, Bush points out that interracial concubinage was accepted.

22 All references to Southerne's *Oroonoko* are from Robert Jordan and Harold Love, eds., *The Works of Thomas Southerne*, 2 vols. (Oxford: Clarendon, 1988). See Robert D. Hume, "The Importance of Thomas Southerne," *Modern Phi- lology* 87.3 (February 1990): 275–90. For earlier discussions of the implications of split plot in this play, see Julia A. Rich, "Heroic Tragedy in Southerne's *Oroo- noko* (1695): An Approach to a Split-plot Tragicomedy," *Philological Quarterly* 62.2 (spring 1983): 187–200; and Michael M. Cohen, " 'Mirth and Grief To- gether': Plot Unity in Southerne's *Oroonoko*," *Xavier University Studies* 11 (win- ter 1972): 13–17. See also John Wendell Dodds, *Thomas Southerne* (New Haven: Yale UP, 1933); and Robert L. Root Jr., *Thomas Southerne* (Boston: Twayne, 1981). Southerne's treatment of the tragedy resembles the colonial themes ex- plored by Dryden in the 1660s and 1670s, which involve a nostalgia for a chi- valric ideology. *The Indian Queen, The Indian Emperour, Aurungzebe*, and *All for Love* are all plays that construct homologies between romantic love and mili- tary conquest. The edifying aspects of characters in these plays are protestations of chastity, love, and honor, and the negative emotions expressed are jealousy, rage, and revenge. Oroonoko himself is a good example of a Herculean foil and continues this motif from Dryden's various dramatic representations. For a description of this stereotype in English literature, see Eugene M. Waith,

The Herculean Hero in Marlowe, Chapman, Shakespeare and Dryden (New York: Columbia UP, 1962).

23 For a suggestive reading of Behn's deliberate conflation of prostitution and authorship, see Catherine Gallagher, "Who Was That Masked Woman? The Prostitute and the Playwright in the Works of Aphra Behn," in *Nobody's Story* 1–48. The subversive effects of tricksters such as Sir Anthony have been trenchantly analyzed by J. Douglas Canfield, *Tricksters and Estates: On the Ideology of Restoration Comedy* (Lexington: UP of Kentucky, 1997); see also Harold Weber, "The Female Libertine in Southerne's *Sir Anthony Love* and *The Wives Excuse*," *Essays in Theatre* 2.2 (May 1984): 125–39. Southerne's ambivalence toward Behn is complex. Mary Vermillion reads the presence of parody in Southerne's play as an antifeminist devaluation of Behn. As my discussion of the bathetic logic of pethood in the first and third sections shows, the complexity of parody and pastiche in the multiple contexts of *Oroonoko* makes for a more positive interpretation of Southerne's adaptation than recent assessments. See "Buried Heroism: Critiques of Female Authorship in Southerne's Adaptation of Behn's *Oroonoko*," *Restoration: Studies in English Literary Culture 1660–1700* 16.1 (spring 1992): 28–37. This is also where I part from the otherwise superb reading by Suvir Kaul, cited above.

24   If we are Slaves, they did not make us Slaves;
    But bought us in an honest way of trade:
    As we have done before 'em, bought and sold
    Many a wretch, and never thought it wrong.
    They paid our Price for us, and we are now
    Their Property, a part of their Estate,
    To manage as they please. Mistake me not,
    I do not tamely say, that we should bear
    All they could lay upon us: but we find
    The load so light, so little to be felt,
    (Considering they have us in their power,
    And may inflict what grievances they please)
    We ought not to complain. (3.2.108–19)

25 Lackitt is reminiscent of Widow Blackacre in Wycherley's *The Plain Dealer* and Behn's own Widow Ranter (a failed play of November 1689 that was dedicated to a Mrs. Welldon). See William Wycherley, *The Plain Dealer* (1677), ed. Leo Hughes (Lincoln: U of Nebraska P, 1967), and Aphra Behn, *The Widow Ranter, or, The History of Bacon in Virginia*, in *The Works of Aphra Behn*, ed. Montague Summers (New York: Blom, 1967), 4:215–310. *The Widow Ranter* resembles Southerne's *Oroonoko* in several respects, featuring the slavery and murder of an Indian king amidst marital comedy. For an interesting comparison of the two plays, see Margaret W. Ferguson, "News from the New World: Miscegenous Romance in Aphra Behn's *Oroonoko* and *The Widow Ranter*," in

The Production of English Renaissance Culture, ed. Sharon O'Dair and Harold Weber (Ithaca, NY: Cornell UP, 1994), 151–89.

26 A banking metaphor is of course very topical, with the important event of the creation of the Bank of England in 1694 and other institutions such as the Bourse at Lyon and the Exchange at Amsterdam. In fact, we see a curious similarity between Charlot's speculations and the standard Marxist analysis of the commodity that describes the manipulation of capital through commodity value: "Value, therefore, does not have its description branded on its forehead; it rather transforms every product of labour into a social hieroglyphic. Later on, men try to decipher the hieroglyphic, to get behind the secret of their own social product: for the characteristic which objects of utility have of being values is as much men's social product as is their language" (Marx, *Capital: A Critique of Political Economy,* trans. Ben Fowkes [New York: Vintage, 1977], 1:167). See also P. G. M. Dickson, *The Financial Revolution in England: A Study in the Development of Public Credit 1688–1756* (New York: St. Martin's, 1967).

27 Southerne himself was actively courting Christopher Codrington, a prominent slave owner from the plantations, as a potential patron (Jordan and Love, *The Works of Thomas Southerne* 2:95). For an interpretation around the crux of Horner's role that speaks to the dissociation of social from moral judgment in *The Country Wife,* see Laura Brown, *English Dramatic Form 1660–1760* (New Haven: Yale UP, 1981), 50.

28 Eve Kosofsky Sedgwick, "*The Country Wife:* Anatomies of Male Homosocial Desire," in *Between Men: English Literature and Male Homosocial Desire* (New York: Columbia UP, 1985), 49.

29 See Jürgen Habermas, *The Structural Transformation of the Public Sphere: An Inquiry into a Category of Bourgeois Society,* trans. Thomas Burger (Cambridge, MA: MIT P, 1989). Also, "Many dealers in 'black Masters' were also dealers in black slaves . . . both commodities were sorted out into 'lots' to be inspected by prospective purchasers with the minuteness of a connoisseur; in England both commodities were auctioned off in coffee-houses" (Dabydeen, *Hogarth's Blacks* 87). See also Bryant Lillywhite, *London Coffee Houses* (London: Allen and Unwin, 1963). Peter Fryer locates as many as sixty-one commercial establishments known as "Black Boy" and at least fifty-one known as "Blackamoor's Head" in England between the seventeenth and the nineteenth centuries. Fryer says that "possession of a black slave was such an emblem of riches, rank, and fashion in England, and had such desirably exotic overtones, it is not surprising that innkeepers and tobacconists should have cashed in on the vogue by using portraits or caricatures of black people as commercial signs" (*Staying Power* 31). For a catalogue of coffeehouse names, see Jacob Larwood and John Camden Hotten, *The History of Signboards* (London, 1867), and Ambrose Heal, "London Shop Signs," *Notes and Queries* (January 14, 1939, and passim).

30 Southerne's play competed against the only other contemporary rival perfor-

Notes to Chapter One

mance, Thomas D'Urfey's *Third Part of the Comical History of Don Quixote*, which failed despite the success of the earlier parts (William Van Lennep et al., eds., *The London Stage 1660–1800*, 8 vols. [Carbondale: Southern Illinois UP, 1960–65], 1:453). The epilogue written by Congreve polemicizes indirectly against D'Urfey's burlesque of chivalric romance as well as the Duke of Buckingham's creation, Volscius, from the hit play, *The Rehearsal*. See George Villiers, Duke of Buckingham, *The Rehearsal*, ed. D. E. L. Crane (Durham, UK: U of Durham P, 1976).

31 David Lloyd has analyzed the relevance of metaphor and metonymy to the history of colonial and racial ideologies. Lloyd schematizes a general shift from metonymy to metaphor in the representation of race, suggesting that a differential logic, involving the spatial and geographical contiguity of a nonuniversalizable collection of races understood through metonymy, is jettisoned by Western cultural discourse over the eighteenth century for an identitarian logic of the temporal development of the races through metaphorical continuity. This fiction, according to Lloyd, legislates a Western account of a universal humanity achieved by metropolitan acculturation. See Lloyd, "Race under Representation," *Oxford Literary Review* 13.1–2 (1991): 62–94.

32 See Margaret A. Rose, *Parody//Metafiction* (London: Croom Helm, 1979), 35. I prefer this earlier definition, which describes the overlap of the critical and the comic in parody, to Rose's subsequent modification, one that subsumes parody entirely to comedy by calling it "the comic refunctioning of preformed linguistic and artistic material"; see Margaret A. Rose, *Parody: Ancient, Modern, and Post-Modern* (Cambridge: Cambridge UP, 1993), 52. I am also impressed by Linda Hutcheon's more expansive inter-art treatment of parody as a repetition with a difference and as the quintessential twentieth-century genre; see *A Theory of Parody: The Teachings of Twentieth-Century Art Forms* (New York: Methuen, 1985). Hutcheon's definition, however, threatens to make parody a postmodernist supergenre almost in the way that Bakhtin treated the modern form of the novel. Satire is inassimilable to Hutcheon's definition, and she is forced to distinguish parody as "intramural" compared to an "extramural" satire. For these reasons, Hutcheon characterizes parody as "conservative," but in saying so she partly confuses its dependence on an earlier model, and its bitextuality, with its supposed politics. My own use of the term is to see it as a retroactive focalization. Oroonoko as pet is parodic of Charles I as well as a hudibrastic venture; as a Hannibal in his own terms, or as Equiano's implicit model later in the century, Oroonoko becomes an imitative original. He thereby implies a critical parody that is transmural and bidirectional.

33 I am impressed by Robert Phiddian's dazzling interpretation of a *Restoration* rather than an *eighteenth-century* Swift, highlighting Swift's role as a destabilizing deconstructive parodist rather than as a conservative classical satirist. It is possible to see Behn's slippage into parody in *Oroonoko* as less self-conscious

than Swift's but similarly ambivalent concerning the status of culture as construction and artifice. More self-consciously parodic, to be sure, are Behn's concerted forays into metatheatrical discovery scenes in her comedies. See Phiddian, *Swift's Parody* (Cambridge: Cambridge UP, 1995).

34 Peter Holland, *The Ornament of Action: Text and Performance in Restoration Comedy* (Cambridge: Cambridge UP, 1979). See also Robert D. Hume, *The Development of English Drama in the Seventeenth Century* (Oxford: Clarendon, 1976); Judith Milhous and Robert D. Hume, *Producible Interpretation: Eight English Plays, 1675-1707* (Carbondale: Southern Illinois UP, 1985); and J. L. Styan, *Restoration Comedy in Performance* (New York: Cambridge UP, 1986).

35 The novella was serialized in *Oxford Magazine* and *Ladies Magazine*, but Behn's plummeting reputation in the eighteenth century ensured less exposure, as Walter Scott's well-known anecdote concerning his great-aunt attests. The play, by contrast, was performed at least 315 times, and at least once every year from 1695 for an unbroken period of 130 years. See John Gibson Lockhart, *Memoirs of the Life of Sir Walter Scott* (New York, 1910), 3: 596-97, and for a discussion of this anecdote, see also Gallagher, *Nobody's Story* 1.

36 For other discussions of performance contexts and reception history, see Thomas Southerne, *Oroonoko,* ed. Maximillian E. Novak and David S. Rodes (Lincoln: U of Nebraska P, 1976), and Arthur Richard Nichols, "A History of the Staging of Thomas Southerne's *The Fatal Marriage* and *Oroonoko* on the London Stage from 1694 to 1851" (Ph.D. diss., University of Washington, 1971). The performance estimates are from Novak and Rodes (xvi, n.16), who rely on Van Lennep et al., eds., *The London Stage 1660-1800.*

37 John Ferriar, *The Prince of Angola* (London, 1784), i.

38 Jordan and Love, *Works of Thomas Southerne,* 2:91-92. According to Jean Hecht, "Pompey" became in the period, "almost a generic sobriquet for black servants both young and old" (*Servants* 40). By this point in time, the flimsy evidence that sets off Othello's jealousy was especially under attack in farces such as John Gay's *What D'ye Call It.* For the anecdote, see Ruth Cowhig, "Blacks in English Renaissance Drama and Shakespeare's *Othello,*" in *The Black Presence in English Literature,* ed. David Dabydeen (Manchester: Manchester UP, 1985), 14-15. For an appraisal of the range of racial representations in English drama from *Othello* to *Oroonoko,* see Anthony Gerard Barthelemy, *Black Face, Maligned Race: The Representation of Blacks in English Drama from Shakespeare to Southerne* (Baton Rouge: Louisiana State UP, 1987).

39 John Butt, ed., *The Poems of Alexander Pope: A One-Volume Edition of the Twickenham Text* (London: Methuen, 1963), 826.

40 Patterson, *Slavery and Social Death* 56-57; Fryer, *Staying Power* 24. Consider this uncanny advertisement about a runaway domestic named Caesar, which appears a few weeks after the first production of *Oroonoko,* in the *London Gazette* of January 21-25, 1696: "Run away on Tuesday the 19th instant, from

Mr. Thomas Weedon, Merchant in Fenchurch-Street, London, a Negro Boy, named Caesar, aged about 15, the Wooll off the right side of his Head about the breadth of a Crown piece, he had a Silver Collar about his Neck, wears blue Cloth Coat lined with blue with flat Pewie-Buttons" (Shyllon, *Black People* 77). See also K. L. Little, *Negroes in Britain: A Study of Racial Relations in English Society* (London: Paul, Trench, Trubner, 1948), 168. More than a century later, the slave protagonist of Maria Edgeworth's "The Grateful Negro" (*Popular Tales,* 1804) was also a Caesar.

41 Brown's article, "Romance of Empire," reads the given name, Caesar, as a "violent yoking" of Oroonoko with Charles I (57–60). Stuart monarchs were often referred to by poets as Caesar (59). For examples of such poems, see George de Forest Lord, ed., *Poems on Affairs of State* (New Haven: Yale UP, 1963–75), vol. 6. Using the same information, George Guffey reads the novella as a coded reaction to the Glorious Revolution, as James II was also referred to as Caesar. See Guffey, "Aphra Behn's *Oroonoko:* Occasion and Accomplishment," in *Two English Novelists: Aphra Behn and Anthony Trollope,* George Guffey and Andrew Wright (Los Angeles: William Andrews Clark Memorial Library, 1975), 1–41. For the Plutarch allusion, see David E. Hoegberg, "Caesar's Toils: Allusion and Rebellion in *Oroonoko,*" *Eighteenth-Century Fiction* 7.3 (April 1995): 239–58. Depictions of Caesar in early modern visual iconography have been unusually open for ideological appropriation. According to José Rabasa in "Allegories of the Atlas," in *Europe and Its Others,* 2 vols. ed. Francis Barker et al. (Colchester: U of Essex P, 1985), 2:11, "Caesar, a symbol of imperialism, stands open to national determination . . . Caesar functions as an empty slot where different leaders may inscribe themselves. The merging of geography and history, of knowledge and power, have Caesar as a prototypical incarnation of world domination." One full-length study of eighteenth-century English literature's recasting of the Caesarian motif is disappointing in the absence of an engagement with the multiple colonialist connotations of such a transformation; see Howard Weinbrot, *Augustus Caesar in "Augustan" England: The Decline of a Classical Norm* (Princeton, NJ: Princeton UP, 1978).

42 Patterson, *Slavery and Social Death* 35–76. Gerda Lerner's critique of Patterson's androcentric bias should be taken into account; see "Women and Slavery," *Slavery and Abolition* 4.3 (December 1983): 173–98. Lerner argues that institutions of slavery were modeled on the oppression of women, which Patterson does not adequately acknowledge: "subordination of women by men provided the conceptual model for the creation of slavery as an institution, so the patriarchal family provided the structural model" (184). Patterson says, "before slavery people could not have conceived of the thing we call freedom. Men and women in premodern, nonslaveholding societies did not, could not, value the removal of restraint as an ideal" (*Slavery and Social Death,* 340). Also, "the first men and women to struggle for freedom, the first to think of themselves as free in the

only meaningful sense of the term, were freedmen. And without slavery there would have been no freedmen" (342).

43 Behn wrote a laudatory poem on a book by Tryon that advocated vegetarianism out of a doctrine of compassion toward animals, revealing her interest in his philosophy's liberationist potential. The poem, "On the Author of that Excellent Book, Intituled The Way to Health, Long Life and Happiness, By Mrs. A. B.," was appended to Tryon's *Health's Grand Preservative; or, The Women's Best Doctor.* See Montague Summers, ed., *The Works of Aphra Behn* (New York: Blom, 1967), 6:379–81. Along with its gnostic mysticism and animistic celebration of West Indian flora and fauna, Tryon's *Friendly Advice to the Gentlemen-Planters of the West-Indies . . .* (London, 1684) is especially pertinent. A passage from Tryon's text, which is one of the most sympathetic to slaves in the seventeenth century, is highly aware of the hyperbole involved in the representation of sufferings that are not visible. The slave who represents himself is conscious of his status as comic butt and sentimental victim. In the ongoing dialogue between a generic Sambo and his master, entitled "The Negro's Complaint of Their Hard Servitude, and the Cruelties Practised Upon them by divers of their Masters professing Christianity in the West-Indian Plantations," Sambo says that because of incredulity, outsiders "will scarce be able to credit us when we set forth nothing but *certain Truths* and *woful experiences;* such *Superlative Inhumanity* amongst *Nominal Christians* will surpass all Belief, and the extremity of our *Calamities* making them seem *Romantick,* debarrs us even of *Pity* and *Commiseration,* those general Slaves of helpless Misery: Shall we then fling ourselves at our Masters feet, and with Universal cries importune them to Compassion and Charity? Alas! those Vertues are Plants that scarce grow in these Islands; nothing thrives here so fast as *poysonous Tobacco* and *furious pride, sweet sugar* and most *bitter ill Nature!*" (76–77). Tryon's Sambo realizes that even firsthand testimony lacks authenticity when the victims of suffering are culturally exotic. The victim's calamity is easily converted into the sympathizer's secondhand sentimentality, creating a fictitious distancing that prevents even humanitarian intervention. Elaine Scarry too emphasizes that to have pain, a certainty for the sufferer, is a rhetorical claim treated with incredulity and skepticism by others; see "The Structure of Torture," in *The Body in Pain: The Making and Unmaking of the World* (New York: Oxford UP, 1985), 51–60. See also Ruth T. Sheffey, "Some Evidence for a New Source for Aphra Behn's *Oroonoko,*" *Studies in Philology* 59 (1962): 52–63.

44 Kaul, "Reading Literary Symptoms," 88.

45 See Laura J. Rosenthal, "Owning Oroonoko: Behn, Southerne, and the Contingencies of Property," in *Renaissance Drama* n.s. 23 (Evanston: Northwestern UP, 1992), 25–58.

1 Daniel Defoe, *Robinson Crusoe*, ed. Michael Shinagel (New York: Norton, 1994), 112. Parenthetical references in the text are to this edition.

2 See Jonathan Lamb, "Minute Particulars and the Representation of South Pacific Discovery," *Eighteenth-Century Studies* 28.3 (spring 1995): 287; J. Laplanche and J. B. Pontalis, "Deferred Action," in *The Language of Psycho-Analysis* (New York: Norton, 1973), 111–14.

3 See Mary Louise Pratt, *Imperial Eyes: Travel Writing and Transculturation* (New York: Routledge, 1992).

4 As David Blewett says, the 1720 French edition provides "the first true set of illustrations, outlining in six pictures a story with a definite moral and spiritual development." See David Blewett, *The Illustrations of Robinson Crusoe* (Gerrards Cross: Colin Smythe, 1995), 32. For the discussion of "concessionary narrative," see Peter Hulme, *Colonial Encounters: Europe and the Native Caribbean, 1492–1797* (New York: Methuen, 1986), 253. For the connection between the angel and the goat, see Geoffrey M. Sill, "Crusoe in the Cave: Defoe and the Semiotics of Desire," *Eighteenth-Century Fiction* 6.3 (April 1994): 215–32. For the canine metaphors, see Timothy C. Blackburn, "Friday's Religion: Its Nature and Importance in *Robinson Crusoe*," *Eighteenth-Century Studies* 18.3 (spring 1985): 363, and for the parrot, see Eric Jager, "The Parrot's Voice: Language and the Self in Robinson Crusoe," *Eighteenth-Century Studies* 21.3 (spring 1988), 316–33.

5 See Roxann Wheeler, " 'My Savage,' 'My Man': Racial Multiplicity in *Robinson Crusoe*," *ELH* 62.4 (winter 1995): 821–61.

6 I will not rehearse here the extensive literature on criminal biography and Defoe's involvement with that genre. The full title of this serial publication was *The Ordinary of Newgate, His Account of the Behaviour, Confession, and Dying Words of the Malefactors who were Executed at Tyburn*. It was a folio broadsheet until 1712, then increased to six folio pages; by 1734 it had become a pamphlet of sixteen or twenty-eight quarto pages. Paul Lorrain was the best known chaplain-in-ordinary at Newgate for having established this periodical as a semiofficial publication. For a detailed analysis of the importance of this publication, see Peter Linebaugh, "The Ordinary of Newgate and His *Account*," in *Crime in England 1550–1800*, ed. J. S. Cockburn (Princeton, NJ: Princeton UP, 1977), 246–69; Lincoln B. Faller, *Turned to Account: The Forms and Functions of Criminal Biography in Late Seventeenth- and Early Eighteenth-Century England* (New York: Cambridge UP, 1987), and his subsequent *Crime and Defoe* (New York: Cambridge UP, 1993); Michael Harris, "Trials and Criminal Biographies," in *Sale and Distribution of Books from 1700*, ed. Robin Myers and Michael Harris (Oxford: Oxford Polytechnic Press, 1982), 1–36; J. A. Sharpe, " 'Last Dying Speeches': Religion, Ideology and Public Execution in Seventeenth-Century England," *Past and Present* 107 (1985): 144–

67; Alexander Smith's two-volume compendium, *The History of the Lives of the most Noted Highway-Men, Foot-Pads, House-Breakers, Shop-Lifts and Cheats . . .* (London, 1714); John Brewer and John Styles, eds., *An Ungovernable People: The English and Their Law in the Seventeenth and Eighteenth Centuries* (New Brunswick, NJ: Rutgers UP, 1980); Frank McLynn, *Crime and Punishment in 18th-Century England* (New York: Routledge, 1989); and Douglas Hay, Peter Linebaugh, and E. P. Thompson, eds., *Albion's Fatal Tree: Crime and Society in Eighteenth-Century England* (New York: Pantheon, 1975).

7 Daniel Defoe, *The King of Pirates* (London, 1719), iii.

8 Daniel Defoe, *Colonel Jack*, ed. Samuel Holt Monk (New York: Oxford UP, 1989), 2. Michael McKeon has demonstrated how polysemous words create both the economic and the religious registers that compete for the attention of Defoe's critics. See Michael McKeon, "Parables of the Younger Son (I): Defoe and the Naturalization of Desire," in *The Origins of the English Novel, 1600–1740* (Baltimore: Johns Hopkins UP, 1987), 315–37. Martin Gliserman, for instance, also shows the close parallels between the economic and the psycho-analytical aspects of Defoe's rendition of cannibalism and capitalism through a Kleinian reading of tropes such as eating and encirclement in the novel, in "*Robinson Crusoe:* The Vicissitudes of Greed: Cannibalism and Capitalism," *American Imago* 47.3–4 (fall–winter 1990): 197–231.

9 *The Life, Adventures, and Pyracies of the famous Captain Singleton, Containing an Account of being set on Shore in the Island of Madagascar, his Settlement there, with a Description of the Place and Inhabitants: Of his Passage from thence in a Paraguay [a canoe], to the main Land of Africa, with an Account of the Customs and Manners of the People: His great Deliverances from the barbarous Natives and wild Beasts: Of his meeting with an Englishman, a Citizen of London, among the Indians, the great Riches he acquired, and his Voyage Home to England: As also Captain Single-ton's Return to Sea, with an Account of his many Adventures and Pyracies with the famous Captain Avery and others.* All references are to Daniel Defoe, *Captain Singleton*, ed. Shiv K. Kumar (New York: Oxford UP, 1990).

10 See Maurice Wehrung, "The Literature of Privateering and Piracy as a Source for the Defoean Hero's Personality," in *Tradition et Innovation, Littérature et Paralittérature: Actes du Congrès de Nancy (1972)* (Paris: Marcel Didier, 1975), 165; and Paula Backscheider, *Daniel Defoe: His Life* (Baltimore: Johns Hopkins UP, 1989), 27, 63. For a substantial discussion of the connections between adventure and capitalism, see Michael Nerlich, *Ideology of Adventure: Studies in Modern Consciousness 1100–1750*, 2 vols. (Minneapolis: U of Minnesota P, 1987). Martin Green emphasizes the total experience of British imperialism by contrasting the theory of mercantilist ideology with the practice of global militarist hege-mony in *Dreams of Adventure, Deeds of Empire* (New York: Basic Books, 1979).

11 Colonel Jack does not know his true name either (*Colonel Jack* 122–23). John Richetti speculates on the existence of a daemonic basis for Defoe's depictions

of an "individualist dilemma." See *Defoe's Narratives: Situations and Structures* (Oxford: Clarendon, 1975), 17, 64–65. Richetti builds on his previous insights that the "criminal's sin is individualism"; the criminal drives "towards a self-determination which is economic—but inescapably spiritual and ideological as well"; see *Popular Fiction before Richardson: Narrative Patterns 1700–1739* (Oxford: Clarendon, 1969), 31, 53.

12 Robert Singleton was a criminal hanged at Tyburn. One Singleton also ran a dissenting academy much like Morton's academy that shaped many of Defoe's religious and political attitudes. See A[rthur] W[ellesley] Secord, *Studies in the Narrative Method of Defoe* (Urbana: U of Illinois P, 1924), 117.

13 *Some Considerations on the Reasonableness and Necessity of Encreasing and Encouraging the Seamen* (London, 1728), 7–8. Historians have disputed the extent of piracy because of the inherent difficulty in ascertaining the degree to which archival records exaggerate or discount the threat. One highly researched account, of the period 1716–26, shows 5,000 Anglo-American pirates alone, with the breakdown (1716–18: 1,800–2,400; 1719–22: 1,500–2,000; 1723–26: 1,000–1,500) sharply declining to about 200 by the end of 1726. See Marcus Rediker, *Between the Devil and the Deep Blue Sea: Merchant Seamen, Pirates, and the Anglo-American Maritime World, 1700–1750* (New York: Cambridge UP, 1987), 254–58; on the differences between the privilege and venture systems of private trade by seamen, see 131–33. The premise of Rediker's impressive study is to restore agency to the subaltern classes; as he puts it in his guiding question, "not what was done to these working people . . . but what did these working people do for themselves and how did they do it?" (6). Opposing Rediker's approach, and adopting a much more conservative view of eighteenth-century maritime culture as one of "disordered cohesion," is N. A. M. Rodger, *The Wooden World: An Anatomy of the Georgian Navy* (London: Fontana, 1988), 345. See also Robert Ritchie, "Pirates and Buccaneers," in *The Age of William III and Mary II: Power, Politics and Patronage, 1688–1702*, ed. Robert P. Maccubbin and Martha Hamilton-Phillips (Washington, DC: Folger Shakespeare Library, 1989), 133–39. Paula Backscheider suggests that Defoe's readers would have identified the character Singleton found in Africa as John Freeman, the agent of the Royal African Company stationed at Sherbro, who had been dismissed and had become an independent and illegal trader (*Daniel Defoe, His Life* 475).

14 Joel Baer's article, "'The Complicated Plot of Piracy': Aspects of English Criminal Law and the Image of the Pirate in Defoe," *The Eighteenth Century: Theory and Interpretation* 23 (1982): 3–26, is an excellent source for the religious, legal, and emotional contexts behind Defoe's depictions of piracy. For a full-length treatment of Defoe's deployment of piracy, see also Joel Baer, "Piracy Examined: A Study of Daniel Defoe's *General History of the Pirates* and Its Milieu" (Ph.D. diss., Princeton University, 1970). Baer's research reveals much contemporary material, but underplays the proletarian sociopolitical implica-

tions which are my focus, tending to read and accept upper-class descriptions of piracy somewhat literally. A contemporary Dutch account of piracy, which candidly explored all these aspects, has been an important source for historians; see John Esquemeling [Alexander Olivier Exquemelin], *The Bucaniers of America* (London, 1684-85; rpt. London: Routledge, 1924). I include here other relevant histories of piracy that give useful background information: James Burney, *History of the Buccaneers of America* (London: Allen, 1912); Philip Gosse, *The History of Piracy* (New York: Tudor, 1946); C. H. Haring, *The Buccaneers in the West Indies in the XVIIth Century* (New York: Dutton, 1910); Robert C. Ritchie, *Captain Kidd and the War against the Pirates* (Cambridge, MA: Harvard UP, 1986); and Marcus Rediker, "'Under the Banner of King Death': The Social World of Anglo-American Pirates, 1716-1726," *William and Mary Quarterly* 38.2 (1981): 203-27.

15 See William Dampier, *A New Voyage Around the World* (London, 1697); Exquemeling, *The Bucaniers of America;* and Woodes Rogers, *A Cruising Voyage Round the World* (London, 1712). For an analysis of wrecking, see John G. Rule, "Wrecking and Coastal Plunder," in Hay, Linebaugh, and Thompson, eds., *Albion's Fatal Tree* 167-88; and for details of Kidd's trial, see Ritchie, *Captain Kidd*.

16 See Daniel Defoe, *A General History of the Pyrates,* ed. Manuel Schonhorn (Columbia: U of South Carolina P, 1972), 290. Page numbers to this edition are cited parenthetically in the text. Melville's *Omoo* (1847) presents an exemplary round-robin, by means of which a group of seamen affix their signatures to a statement of grievances. (Interestingly enough, this statement is written on the flyleaf of "A History of the Most Atrocious and Bloody Piracies.") See *Typee, Omoo, Mardi* (New York: Literary Classics of the United States, 1982), 402-3.

17 Crusoe can be interpreted as either for "land," or for "money," depending on which parts of his activities one chooses to highlight. He does become rich as a result of proto-bourgeois accumulation, but he derives political and psychological power from the ownership of land. In this respect, Walpole's critics often misinterpreted him as completely representing the "moneyed" interest; indications are that Walpole was simultaneously identified with the landed gentry, even if he leaned in the other direction. See Isaac Kramnick, *Bolingbroke and His Circle: The Politics of Nostalgia in the Age of Walpole* (Cambridge, MA: Harvard UP, 1968), 49. For a longer analysis of the political allegory in *Robinson Crusoe,* see Maximillian E. Novak, "Crusoe the King and the Political Evolution of His Island," *Studies in English Literature 1500-1900* 2.3 (summer 1962): 337-50.

18 Defoe, *General History of the Pyrates* 308, 423. The attribution of the *General History* to Defoe by J. R. Moore has aroused some controversy, especially as it became the attribution that helped generate many others, culminating in Moore's *A Checklist of the Writings of Daniel Defoe* (Hamden, CT: Archon, 1960). In their recent discussion of Moore's intentions and method-

ology, P. N. Furbank and W. R. Owens cast doubt on the technical procedures that led Moore to the positive identification of the work as Defoe's; see *The Canonisation of Daniel Defoe* (New Haven: Yale UP, 1988), 100–121.

19 See Rediker, *Devil and the Deep Blue Sea* 114. The ship, "whose milieu of action made it both universal and *sui generis,* provided the place where the articulation of disciplinary rules and the ratio of variable to constant capital (men to equipment) forbode the factory of the future." See Peter Linebaugh, "All the Atlantic Mountains Shook," *Labour/Le Travailleur* 10 (1982): 108. Maritime language "was constructed to serve as a precise set of relays for authority, to link captain and crew with a machinelike efficiency" (Rediker, *Devil and the Deep Blue Sea* 163). However, Ronald Schultz sees indentured service and African slavery, rather than an industrial workforce, as the better analogy for maritime drudgery; see "Pirates and Proletarians: Authority, Labor, and Capital Accumulation in the First British Empire," *Radical History Review* 44 (1989): 173.

20 Linebaugh, "All the Atlantic Mountains," 119; Rediker, *Devil and the Deep Blue Sea* 298. The idea of democracy, especially in such exotic contexts, was closely associated with an older Anglo-Machiavellian tradition's understanding of the distribution and alternation of the three forms of government (autarky, oligarchy, democracy). For this background, see J. G. A. Pocock, "Historical Introduction," in *The Political Works of James Harrington,* ed. J. G. A. Pocock (New York: Cambridge UP, 1977), 1–152. See also Christopher Hill, "Masterless Men," in *The World Turned Upside Down: Radical Ideas during the English Revolution* (New York: Viking Press, 1972), 32–45. Hill says, "beneath the surface stability of rural England, then, the vast placid open fields which catch the eye, was the seething mobility of forest squatters, itinerant craftsmen and building labourers, unemployed men and women seeking work, strolling players and jugglers, pedlars and quack doctors, vagabonds, tramps . . . it was from this underworld that armies and ships' crews were recruited" (39). However, I strongly disagree with Eric Hobsbawm's ethnocentric errors in characterizing all popular rebellion as "primitive," "prepolitical," or simply "archaic." Peasant revolts of different sorts exhibited awareness of political and economic oppression and mobilized courageous opposition against formidable forces, yet Hobsbawm characterizes peasants as always resorting to forms of communal collectivity that predated feudal structures. As piratical experiments show, political experimentation, innovation, and construction of an irreducibly modern kind was their most prominent feature. See E. J. Hobsbawm, *Primitive Rebels: Studies in Archaic Forms of Social Movement in the 19th and 20th Centuries* (Manchester: Manchester UP, 1959).

21 See Guillaume-Thomas Raynal, *Histoire philosophique et politique des deux Indes* (Paris, 1781), 5:269. Raynal too distinguishes the "barbaric" actions of the buccaneers, described in a shorter section, from the more idealistic experimentations of the pirates or flibustiers (5:247–53, 5:260–301). See also Peter Kemp

and Christopher Lloyd, *Brethren of the Coast: Buccaneers of the South Seas* (New York: St. Martin's, 1961).

22 See the collected historical documents pertaining to the Avery piracies and Aurangzeb's reactions in "Case of Henry Every," in *Privateering and Piracy in the Colonial Period: Illustrative Documents,* ed. John Franklin Jameson (New York: Macmillan, 1923), 153–87. The Avery background materials are also discussed by Secord, *Studies in the Narrative Method of Defoe.* For a subsequent investigation of the Avery contexts, see John Richetti, "*Captain Avery* and *Captain Singleton:* Revisions of Popular Legend," in *Defoe's Narratives* 63–93. For fascinating detail concerning Avery's motivations, see Joel H. Baer, " 'Captain John Avery' and the Anatomy of a Mutiny," *Eighteenth-Century Life* 18.1 (February 1994): 20.

23 This chapter of the *General History* has been reprinted as Daniel Defoe, *Of Captain Misson,* ed. Maximillian E. Novak (Los Angeles: William Andrews Clark Memorial Library, University of California, Augustan Reprint Society, 1961). See Christopher Hill, "Radical Pirates?," in *The Origins of Anglo-American Radicalism,* ed. Margaret Jacob and James Jacob (London: Allen, 1984), 17–32; and J. G. A. Pocock, *The Machiavellian Moment: Florentine Political Thought and the Atlantic Republican Tradition* (Princeton, NJ: Princeton UP, 1975). Novak enthusiastically compares Misson and Carracioli with Lenin and Trotsky; see *Economics and the Fiction of Daniel Defoe* (Berkeley: U of California P, 1962), 109. For the impact of seamen on the American Revolution, see Jesse Lemisch, "Jack Tar in the Streets: Merchant Seamen in the Politics of Revolutionary America," *William and Mary Quarterly* (3rd series) 25 (July 1968): 371–407. The sympathetic slave uprising in *Captain Singleton* brings to mind Peter Linebaugh's utopian reading of the slave trade, in "All the Atlantic Mountains Shook," as creating internationalist solidarity. However, the sale of the slaves suggests that the episode is an early version of sentimentalist compatibility with commerce. See also *Colonel Jack* 127–53.

24 See Hill, "Radical Pirates?"; B. R. Burg, *Sodomy and the Pirate Tradition: English Sea Rovers in the Seventeenth-Century Caribbean* (New York: New York UP, 1984); and J. S. Bromley, "Outlaws at Sea, 1660–1720: Liberty, Equality, and Fraternity among the Caribbean Freebooters," in *History from Below: Studies in Popular Protest and Popular Ideology,* ed. Frederick Krantz (Oxford: Basil Blackwell, 1988), 293–318. The Monmouth rebellion was one more instance of the failure in articulating a "language" of seventeenth-century left-wing democratic aspirations, shown so well by the work of Christopher Hill on the English Revolution. Defoe's participation in the disastrous Monmouth rebellion in 1685 has not been sufficiently acknowledged in interpretations of his fictions. For some appreciation of this event, see Robin Clifton, "Lessons and Consequences of the Monmouth Rebellion," in *The Monmouth Rising,* ed. Ivan Roots (Exeter, UK: Devon Books, 1986), 50–66, and *The Last Popular Rebellion: The Western Rising of 1685* (New York: St. Martin's, 1984); also Peter Earle, *Monmouth's*

Rebels: The Road to Sedgemoor (New York: St. Martin's, 1977). Of course, I am not trying to suggest that Defoe had even the remotest Jacobite sympathies, especially given his immense capacity, in most instances, to rationalize the de facto as the de jure. However, his participation at Sedgmoor suggests, likewise, a capacity to empathize with those who could stake their life on lost causes. See Manuel Schonhorn, "Defoe and the Limits of Jacobite Rhetoric," *ELH* 64.4 (Winter 1997): 871–86. Arthur Secord has remarked that Leslie Stephen misidentified the historical model for Singleton as Captain Kidd (qtd. in Secord, *Studies in the Narrative Method of Defoe* 113). But there is nevertheless a teasing coincidence that Kidd might have also occurred to Defoe's memory in the 1710s: the only person that the ill-fated Monmouth knighted in anticipation of success was also a Kid, former gamekeeper of Longleat. Of course, Kidd, as a privateer, was very much a "capitalist" pirate for whom Defoe had very little sympathy. On one occasion, Defoe writes, "the crews of Jamaican privateers ought to be hang'd just as much as the Pyrates of Madagascar, or as much as Captain Kid, and his Crew deserved it" (*Mercator* 172 [June 29, 1714]).

25 For Defoe's recommendations, see *The Review*, ed. Arthur W. Secord (New York: Columbia UP, 1938), 10:425–28. For Boreal's words, see Charles Johnson, *The Successful Pyrate*, Augustan Reprint Society no. 204 (UP of California at Los Angeles: William Andrews Clark Memorial Library, 1980), 2.

26 Defoe, *General History of the Pyrates* 7. Curiously enough, the reference to the origination of Rome by "a Company of public Robbers" or "a Gang of Rovers" is heavily relied upon by J. R. Moore in his attribution of this work to Defoe. The same reference comes up in several works that are more definitely Defoe's, such as *The Review*, *A True Account of the South Sea Trade*, and *The King of Pirates*. However, Furbank and Owens, Moore's critics, point out that the allusion to Rome's criminal origins is very old, going back to Augustine and Cicero, and not Defoe's hallmark, as Moore had erroneously assumed. See Thomas Hobbes, *Leviathan*, ed. C. B. Macpherson (Baltimore: Penguin, 1968), 156–57. It might seem that Hobbes is begging the question here, but in fact he is polemically asserting that the word *lawful* has a "natural" meaning before the legislation of the state, which outlaws certain activities. The impact of a Hobbesian problematic, and the few steps it takes to reconfigure such a problematic into a Lockean one, is one that has been consistently underemphasized in Defoe criticism. Thus, if we take Carol Kay's cue, Defoe's fictions ought to be read as "political constructions" rather than through the false dichotomy of socioeconomic realist mimesis or allegorical religious reflection; see Kay, *Political Constructions: Defoe, Richardson, and Sterne in Relation to Hobbes, Hume, and Burke* (Ithaca, NY: Cornell UP, 1988). Of previous Defoe critics, there are few who read Hobbes with or against Defoe. A notable exception was Maximillian E. Novak, *Defoe and the Nature of Man* (New York: Oxford UP, 1963), 18–20, 25–26, 34–35. Novak says that although Defoe's ideas of nature con-

sist of "a hodge-podge of traditional Puritanism, the rationalism of the Boyle Lectures, and the ideas of Thomas Burnet," the famous reference in *Robinson Crusoe* of "being reduced to a State of Nature" indicates Defoe's wish to experiment with (rather than just accept) Hobbesian hypotheses. For the trade = theft equation, see *The Compleat English Tradesman* 2 (1727), 108. Lincoln Faller, in *Crime and Defoe*, makes a defensive case for this confusion, saying that "bringing the considerable resources of literary discourse to bear on the equation trade = theft, he wrote — not to obscure or confuse it, as, say, Alexander Smith did — but to disarm it, recontextualizing certain of its more vexing implications so these might be dissolved, attenuated, or at least contained" (141). Insofar as this equation is a relativizing move on Defoe's part, I would agree that he wants to qualify his relativization rather than revel in a crude version of it. However, it is hard to argue against the fact that Defoe accepts the charge prima facie and works its implications out through casuistical justification, as for instance in the passage that a tradesman's promises are conditional in their very nature, rather than absolute (*Compleat English Tradesman* 1:231–34).

27 Daniel Defoe, *Moll Flanders*, ed. Edward Kelly (New York: Norton, 1973), 48.

28 Nancy Armstrong and Leonard Tennenhouse, "The Interior Difference: A Brief Genealogy of Dreams 1650–1717," *Eighteenth-Century Studies* 23 (1990): 460; Hans Turley, "The Homosocial Subject: Piracy, Sexuality, and Identity in the Novels of Daniel Defoe" (Ph.D. diss., University of Washington, 1994), 3, 86.

29 Hill, "Radical Pirates?" 22. Indications are that Bartho Roberts was a relatively conservative captain, especially as he explicitly (and, it should be pointed out, unsuccessfully) attempted to outlaw the excessive consumption of alcohol, the favorite pastime of pirates. Generally, pirate articles stipulate the equal sharing of loot and resources, power and danger; it is unusual for pleasure to be codified or restricted. In a somewhat ahistorical study of sodomitical pirates, B. R. Burg argues that homosexuality was regarded with far less opprobrium in the period than commonly assumed and that both pirates and male urban vagabonds lived in homosexual and egalitarian circumstances (here the early milieu of Defoe's Colonel Jack certainly comes to mind); see Burg, *Sodomy and the Pirate Tradition*, 48. Burg's study synthesizes the discourse concerning rampant fornication in the West Indies with demographic evidence that shows hardly any European women in those regions in the seventeenth century, and claims speculatively that male homosexuality was the primary form of sexual behavior. Burg's claim that seventeenth-century English society was highly tolerant of homosexuality is occasionally misleading, especially when he optimistically explains away every prosecution of sodomy as not a punishment of the act sui generis at all: "where severe penalties were imposed or when public figures were accused of buggery, motives other than the desire to extirpate proscribed sexual practices were consistently present" (40). If all prosecution of sodomy was but a ploy based

on ulterior motives involving the settlement of property disputes or personal scores, such an argument begs the question of why imputations of sodomy were so easily used to smear, discredit, and destroy individuals; obviously, even if it was socially tolerated or ignored, sodomy was a major symbolic crime. Another historian, pointing to the attempts made by Societies for the Reformation of Manners between 1690 and 1730 to erase the interlinked sodomitical, criminal, and libertine cultures, says that homosexuality occurred extensively among the middle and lower classes as well (and was not just an aristocratic phenomenon, as it has been portrayed); see Randolph Trumbach, "London's Sodomites: Homosexual Behaviour and Western Culture in the Eighteenth Century," *Journal of Social History* 11.1 (fall 1977): 1–33.

30 *Serious Reflections* 105; discussed acutely by Turley, "Homosocial Subject," 108. This passage can also be usefully glossed by Marcus Rediker's reminder that since the English Revolution, "blasphemy, cursing, and swearing had implied defiance of middle-class society and its ideals of gentility, moderation, refinement, and industry. Rough speech was thus essentially transgressive" (*Devil and the Deep Blue Sea* 166). A certain amount of circumstantial evidence suggests homosexual behavior in Defoe's piratical narratives. Defoe's Avery jokingly hints at his priorities in the *King of Pirates:* "the Queen . . . was, in a Manner, cover'd with Diamonds, and I, like a true Pirate, soon let her see that I had more Mind to the Jewels than to the Lady" (58). Previously, Avery jokingly describes the Quaker captain of a merchant ship captured by his men as unafraid of "using the Carnal Weapon of Offence, *viz.* the Cannon-ball" (9). In his complaints of abuse, it does not, I think, strain credulity to consider that Bob might be referring to anal intercourse at such moments. Maximillian E. Novak discusses a similar instance suggesting anal intercourse and "use" in *Roxana;* see "The Unmentionable and the Ineffable in Defoe's Fiction," *Studies in the Literary Imagination* 15.2 (fall 1982): 85–102.

31 Arviragus's argument exposes the necessity of marriage for the ruling ideology of the State:

> We hold our self indebted to each Man
> Who gives the Common-Wealth a Legal Heir,
> For Marriage is the Bond of Government,
> That Cement fixes us by Natural Ties,
> By joining our Affections to our Interest.
> Each Monarch Husband in his Private Realm
> While he with virtuous Order rules his House,
> Pursues the general Good—obedient Children
> Make faithful subjects—therefore we ordain'd
> This Lottery of Love you all must win. (18)

For a discussion of eighteenth-century homosexuality, see Louis Crompton, "Georgian Homophobia," in *Byron and Greek Love: Homophobia in 19th-*

Century England (Berkeley: U of California P, 1985), 12–62. These coded hints to Bob's Greciannness in this final compact add up to more than just rationalizations about homosexuality's situational occurrence as practices of buggery and sodomy in maritime milieus. Another critic makes a preposterous pseudo-phenomenological claim that the sodomite had to be killed because his association with the dark color of excrement reminded men of mortality; see Arthur N. Gilbert, "Buggery and the British Navy," *Journal of Social History* 10.1 (fall 1976): 72–98. This sounds like an especially ridiculous suggestion, given a highly multiracial eighteenth-century maritime culture. How did black sailors feel about their excrement? Gilbert needs to realize that in the sexual *combinatoire*, there is a marked difference between the umbrella term homosexuality and specific fetishisms such as coprophilia or coprolagnia (or his own projection of coprophobia onto a maritime subculture that, by all empirical accounts, wallowed in excrement and offal because of the practice of keeping livestock aboard ship).

32   E. P. Thompson rebuts the acceptance of upper-class characterizations of all criminals as "gangs" in cases such as that of the Waltham Blacks: According to him, if such acts emanated from "a criminal subculture" then the whole of plebeian England falls within the category ("Patrician Society, Plebeian Culture," *Journal of Social History* 7.4 [1974]: 400). For the reference to parodic signatures, see Frank Sherry, *Raiders and Rebels: The Golden Age of Piracy* (New York: Hearst Marine Books, 1986), 139. The phrase "going upon the account" evokes the specialized slang of criminal activity, a vocabulary that occasionally crops up in other criminal biographies by Defoe. Also see John L. McMullan, *The Canting Crew: London's Criminal Underworld 1500–1700* (New Brunswick, NJ: Rutgers UP, 1984). The origins of criminal cant can be traced back to gypsy lore and language, and Singleton's gypsy foster parent is of relevance here. Despite some attempts to reinterpret eighteenth-century crime within earlier religious matrices, post-Victorian pathological and moral categories, or even ill-fitting twentieth-century sociologistic anachronisms such as subcultures, the most impressive case study that interprets the significance of changes in law and society is E. P. Thompson, *Whigs and Hunters: The Origin of the Black Act* (New York: Pantheon, 1975), 194. For a broad survey of the shift in notions of property, see C. B. Macpherson, *The Political Theory of Possessive Individualism: Hobbes to Locke* (Oxford: Oxford UP, 1962). One criminal narrative talks about the initiation rites of the Waltham Blacks; see anon., *Remarkable Criminals* (London, 1735), 171–74.

33   See Daniel Defoe, *A New Voyage Around the World* (New York: Dial, 1935), 201; Glyndwr Williams, "Buccaneers, Castaways, and Satirists: The South Seas in the English Consciousness Before 1750," *Eighteenth-Century Life* 18. 3 (November 1994): 114–28; Robert Markley, " 'So Inexhaustible a Treasure of Gold': Defoe, Capitalism, and the Romance of the South Seas," *Eighteenth-Century Life* 18. 3 (November 1994): 164, 148–67.

34 See Sandra Sherman, *Finance and Fictionality in the Early Eighteenth Century: Accounting for Defoe* (New York: Cambridge UP, 1996), 10. The neologism concerning piracy occurs in the preface to *Jure Divino* (London, 1706), 42: "Gentlemen-Booksellers, that threatned to Pyrate it, as they call it, viz. Reprint it, and Sell it for half a Crown." Defoe is also credited with the second published reference to "pirate" as the noun with the same meaning. An early instance of Defoe's fascination with imaginative as well as imaginary social schemes is his *An Essay Upon Projects* (London, 1697). The text includes proposals as varied as the registering of seamen, the educating of women, and the institutionalizing of the insane. A vast number of friendly society schemes are floated, combining elements of insurance, lottery, and social security for particular professions. Many of the period's lotteries were called "adventures," and Defoe himself ventured in their commercial organization; see Backscheider, *Daniel Defoe: His Life* 63.

35 For a persuasive account of the criminality of novels as a genre, see Lennard Davis, *Factual Fictions* (New York: Columbia UP, 1983), 123–37. Davis analyzes this occurrence as a result of the emphasis on criminality in news/novels discourse, which smears novels themselves as generically guilty by association with the criminal subjects they tended to focus on.

36 James Thompson, *Models of Value: Eighteenth-Century Political Economy and the Novel* (Durham, NC: Duke UP, 1996), 131.

THREE *The Stoic's Voice*

1 See M. Michell, *Young Juba: or, the History of the Young Chevalier* (London, 1748).

2 See J. G. A. Pocock, *The Machiavellian Moment* (Princeton, NJ: Princeton UP, 1975), and *Virtue, Commerce, and History: Essays on Political Thought and History, Chiefly in the Eighteenth Century* (New York: Cambridge UP, 1985), 21, 235; Joyce Appleby, *Liberalism and Republicanism in the Historical Imagination* (Cambridge, MA: Harvard UP, 1992), 126, 135.

3 See Mary Thomas Crane, "*Intret Cato:* Authority and the Epigram in 16th-Century England," *Renaissance Genres: Essays on Theory, History, and Interpretation,* ed. Barbara Kiefer Lewalski (Cambridge, MA: Harvard UP, 1986), 158–86; T. W. Baldwin, *William Shakespere's Small Latine and Lesse Greeke* (Urbana: U of Illinois P, 1944), 1:595–96.

4 I refer to Walter Benjamin's notion of modern "empty time" versus sacred "messianic time" that has been creatively applied by Benedict Anderson, *Imagined Communities: Reflections on the Origin and Spread of Nationalism.* (1983; rev., New York: Verso, 1991). The invention of tradition as a more general political reflex can itself be traced back to the rediscovery of ancient Greece and Rome during the Renaissance. However, for the currency of the phrase, see Eric

Hobsbawm and Terence Ranger, eds., *The Invention of Tradition* (Cambridge: Cambridge UP, 1983). This volume addresses itself to the historical context of imperial ideologies at work in the invented political traditions of Scotland, Wales, Britain, Africa, India, and Europe in the nineteenth and twentieth centuries.

5 For competing historical accounts, see J. C. D. Clark, *English Society 1688–1832: Ideology, Social Structure, and Political Practice during the Ancien Régime* (New York: Cambridge UP, 1985); P. G. M. Dickson, *The Financial Revolution in England: A Study in the Development of Public Credit 1688–1756* (New York: St. Martins, 1967); Isaac Kramnick, *Bolingbroke and His Circle: The Politics of Nostalgia in the Age of Walpole* (Cambridge, MA: Harvard UP, 1968); Neil McKendrick, *The Birth of a Consumer Society: The Commercialization of Eighteenth-Century England* (Bloomington: Indiana UP, 1982); J. H. Plumb, *The Origins of Political Stability, England: 1675–1825* (Boston: Houghton Mifflin, 1967); and W. A. Speck, *Stability and Strife: England, 1714–1760* (London: Edward Arnold, 1977).

6 See Thomas May, *Lucan's* Pharsalia *or the Civil Warres of Rome Between Pompey the Great and Iulius Caesar,* 3d ed. (1635); and Nicholas Rowe, *Pharsalia* (London, 1718).

7 I take this distinction from Gilles D. Montsarrat's *Light from the Porch: Stoicism and English Renaissance Literature* (Paris: Didier-Érudition, 1984). There were always unresolved tensions between Stoicism and Christianity throughout all the texts of the neostoic revival. See R. S. Crane, "Suggestions Towards a Genealogy of the 'Man of Feeling'," *ELH* 1.3 (December 1934): 205–30; and Henry W. Sams, "Anti-Stoicism in Seventeenth- and Early Eighteenth-Century England," *Studies in Philology* 41 (1944): 65–78. Sams is persuasive when he suggests that "the rejection of egoistic Stoicism was implicit in the rise of national economies" (72). For Addison's and Steele's qualifications, see Donald C. Bond, ed., *The Spectator* (New York: Oxford UP, 1965), no. 397, 3:486, and no. 274, 2:568. For other anti-Stoic tracts, see Steele's friend Captain Ayloffe's adaptation of Senault, *The Government of the Passions According to the Rules of Reason and Religion* (1700), and Henry, Earl of Monmouth's earlier translation, *The Use of Passions* (1649); Timothy Nourse, *A Discourse upon the Nature and Faculties of Men* (1686); John Locke, *The Reasonableness of Christianity* (1695); and Pierre Boher, *The Art of Knowing Ones Self: Or, a Diligent Search after the Springs of Morality* (1696). See also Richard Steele, *The Englishman* 25 (November 26, 1713) and 34 (December 19, 1713).

8 All references to *Cato* are hereafter parenthetical, by act, scene, and line numbers, as presented in A. C. Guthkelch, ed., *The Miscellaneous Works of Joseph Addison* (London: G. Bell, 1914), 1:330–420. See Emmett L. Avery, ed., *The London Stage, Part 2: 1700–1729* (Carbondale: Southern Illinois UP, 1979); and Lincoln B. Faller, *The Popularity of Addison's* Cato *and Lillo's* The London Mer-

chant 1700–1776 (New York: Garland, 1988). See also Pope's letter to Caryll on April 30, 1714, in *Correspondence* (Oxford: Clarendon, 1956), 2:174. Pope also exalted Cato in *The Temple of Fame* (1715); Des Champs promptly came out with a French version called *Caton d'Utique* (Paris, 1716). For some contemporary responses, see George Sewell's *Observations upon Cato;* [Charles Gildon?], *Cato Examin'd;* and anonymous pieces such as *The Life and Character of Cato, Mr. Addison Turn'd Tory,* and *Flying Post* no. 3369. See also Addison's own essays on Cato, Socrates, and Augustus (*The Spectator* nos. 349, 183, 317). For a collection of some of these pieces on *Cato,* see Edward A. Bloom and Lillian D. Bloom, eds., *Addison and Steele: The Critical Heritage* (London: Routledge, 1980). For Johnson's comment, see *Lives of the English Poets* (New York: Oxford UP, 1906), 426.

9 See *Mr. Addison Turn'd Tory or, the Scene Inverted . . .* (London, 1714), 21.

10 See John Loftis, *The Politics of Drama in Augustan England* (Oxford: Clarendon Press, 1963), 59. See also Irvin Ehrenpreis, *Swift: The Man, His Works, and the Age,* 3 vols. (Cambridge, MA: Harvard UP, 1962–83), 2:595, and Peter Smithers, *The Life of Joseph Addison* (Oxford: Clarendon, 1968), 264.

11 John Trenchard wrote a popular attack, *A Short History of Standing Armies in England* (1698), and Defoe wrote several defenses of the governmental policy, such as *An Argument Shewing, That a Standing Army, with Consent of Parliament, Is Not Inconsistent with a Free Government* (1698) and *A Brief Reply to the History of Standing Armies* (1698). For a political history of these ideas, see Lois G. Schwoerer, *"No Standing Armies!": The Antiarmy Ideology in Seventeenth-Century England* (Baltimore: Johns Hopkins UP, 1974).

12 For general source studies that delineate the literary contexts of Augustan classicism, see M. M. Kelsall, "The Meaning of Addison's *Cato,*" *Review of English Studies* 17 (May 1966): 149–62; James William Johnson, *The Formation of English Neo-Classical Thought* (Princeton, NJ: Princeton UP, 1967); and Howard Weinbrot, *Augustus Caesar in "Augustan" England: The Decline of a Classical Norm* (Princeton, NJ: Princeton UP, 1978), and *Britannia's Issue: The Rise of British Literature from Dryden to Ossian* (New York: Cambridge UP, 1993). Johnson's earlier study provides valuable references despite its dated thesis that Augustanism was a positive norm. Although Weinbrot is more aware of the controversial nature of Augustus for the eighteenth century, he is generally silent about the dialectic of imperialist reinvention and disavowal that went alongside celebrations and repudiations of Augustanism.

13 *The Spectator,* no. 101, 1:423.

14 John Milton, *Political Writings,* ed. Martin Dzelzainis (Cambridge: Cambridge UP, 1991), 17.

15 Samuel Johnson, *Lives of the English Poets* 427, 449.

16 See Allardyce Nicoll, *A History of Early 18th-Century Drama, 1700–1750* (Cam-

bridge: Cambridge UP, 1929), and Bonamy Dobrée, *English Literature in the Early Eighteenth Century* (Oxford: Clarendon, 1959). See John Dennis, "Remarks Upon Cato, A Tragedy" (1713), and "Letters Upon the Sentiments of the two First Acts of Cato" (1713-18, 1721) in *The Critical Works of John Dennis*, ed. Edward Niles Hooker (Baltimore: Johns Hopkins UP, 1943), 41-80, 81-102, cited parenthetically hereafter.

17 See Nathaniel Lee, *Lucius Junius Brutus* (1680), ed. John Loftis (Lincoln: U of Nebraska P, 1967), and Thomas Otway, *The History and Fall of Caius Marius* (1679). It is useful to remark on the heavily Stoical rhetoric of Cato in earlier plays such as Chapman's *Caesar and Pompey* (1612-13, published 1631).

18 Dryden had seen an early draft of *Cato* in the 1690s and had recommended that it not be put on stage (Smithers, *Life of Joseph Addison* 27). However, anecdotal evidence does indicate that the subplot was thrown in by Addison at the last minute, and it was also severely criticized by Lady Mary Wortley Montagu before the first performance and by John Dennis after it. *Cato* was published without the subplot, like Hawkesworth's *Oroonoko*, in 1764. See Mary Wortley Montagu, "[Critique of *Cato* (1713)]," in *Essays and Poems and* Simplicity, A Comedy, ed. Robert Halsband and Isobel Grundy (Oxford: Clarendon, 1977), 62-68.

19 See Julie Ellison, "Cato's Tears," *ELH* 63.2 (spring 1996): 571-601, 572, 581, 584, 597.

20 See Alan D. McKillop, *The Background of Thomson's* Liberty (Rice Institute pamphlet 38.2, July 1951); Bonamy Dobrée, *The Theme of Patriotism in the Poetry of the Early Eighteenth Century* (London: British Academy, 1949); and Loftis, *Politics of Drama*.

21 See also Ellison, "Cato's Tears," 584.

22 See John Loftis, ed., *Richard Steele's* The Theatre *(1720)* (Oxford: Clarendon Press, 1962), 28-29.

23 Syphax attempts to rebut Juba's hero worship of Cato with a bucolic portrait of a Numidian soldier's endurance as more genuinely praiseworthy than Cato's much-vaunted virtue: " 'Tis pride, rank pride, and haughtiness of soul: / I think the *Romans* call it *Stoicism*" (1.4.83-84). Syphax also continues the conventional admonition that Juba's much-admired Rome was founded on a rape: "[Y]our *Scipio's, Caesar's, Pompey's,* and your *Cato's* / (These Gods on earth) are all the spurious brood / Of violated maids, of ravish'd *Sabines*" (2.5.47-49). Similar remarks, alluding to the impurity of bloodlines, had paradoxically served to celebrate the dynamism of English cultural mixture and a defense of the Dutch king by Defoe in *The True-Born Englishman* (1701). In a roundabout way, English worries concerning a German succession very soon after the advent of a Dutchman onto the English throne are being aired and then dismissed as irrelevant except to demagogues. Juba's reply is to regret that Syphax's hoary head

"abounds too much in Numidian wiles" (2.5.51). Dryden's *Absalom and Achitophel* (1681) reversed earlier traditions of the *speculum principi* by showing the effect of evil advisers on princes. Addison too demonstrates the importance of right advice. Juba has to reject the Machiavellian and embrace the Stoic *sapiens*.

24 May, Lucan's *Pharsalia* 77; Nathaniel Wanley, *War and Peace Ridiculed* (London, 1668), 270.

25 The practice of renaming African slaves, discussed at length in the first chapter, could have been a way of emphasizing the owner's favorite neoclassical philosopher, according to K. L. Little, *Negroes in Britain: A Study of Racial Relations in English Society* (London: Paul, Trench, Trubner, 1948), 168.

26 See *The Examiner* (27 April–1 May 1713); Bloom and Bloom, *Addison and Steele* 267. For an account of Stoic arguments concerning just suicide, see J. M. Rist, *Stoic Philosophy* (Cambridge: Cambridge UP, 1969), 233–55. According to Plutarch, Cato defended the paradox of just suicide to a Peripatetic the evening before his death; Chapman's Cato does the same. Chapman's last two acts, it must be noted, make Platonic rather than Stoic arguments.

27 For *Sophonisba*, see Percy G. Adams, ed., *The Plays of James Thomson* (New York: Garland, 1979), 2–103; hereafter, references are parenthetical by act, scene, and line numbers. Sophonisba was a very popular theme in European literature. She features prominently in Petrarch's epic poem *Africa*, and the theme had been treated by Trissino, Mairet, Corneille, and Racine and would also be dramatized by Voltaire. See Charles Ricci, *Sophonisbe dans la tragédie classique italienne et française* (Turin, 1904; rpt., Geneva: Slatkine Reprints, 1970). Ricci estimates that there were at least fifteen different operas in Italian on Sophonisba. Addison had seen an Italian production of *Cato Uticense* by Nori and Pollaro while in Venice on the Grand Tour with Edward Wortley and was reportedly shocked at the travesty of Cato's character (Smithers, *Life of Joseph Addison* 63). Voltaire's later play is a rant that features Massinissa as a dutiful African patriot. In the English literary tradition, Sir David Murray, John Marston, and Nathaniel Lee had already attempted dramatic renditions of Sophonisba in the seventeenth century. See Sir David Murray, *The Tragicall Death of Sophonisba* (London, 1611); John Marston, *The Wonder of Women, or The Tragedy of Sophonisba* (1606); Nathaniel Lee, *Sophonisba* (1676); and Charles Beckingham, *Scipio Africanus* (1718).

28 In the epilogue, Mrs. Cibber says,

> Ladies, he bid me say, behold your Cato.
> What tho' no Stoic she, nor read in Plato?
> Yet sure she offer'd for her country's sake,
> A sacrifice which Cato could not make. (Epil. 9–12)

Thomson imitated *Cato*, including its rant, that led to the famous line that Fielding and others parodied, "O Sophonisba, Sophonisba, O!" (III.ii.19). See also James Thomson, *Liberty, The Castle of Indolence, and Other Poems*, ed. James

Sambrook (Oxford: Clarendon, 1986). For a brief account of the Teutonic roots of Cato, see Michael M. Cohen, "The Imagery of Addison's *Cato* and the Whig Sublime," *CEA Critic* 38.3 (March 1976): 23-25. See also the anonymous paean, *The Loss of Liberty, or The Fall or Rome. A Poem* (1733). For a treatment of the vogue for Roman tragedy in the period, see Richard Morton, "*Roman* Drops from *British* Eyes": Latin History on the Restoration Stage," in *The Stage in the Eighteenth Century*, ed. J. D. Browning (New York: Garland, 1981), 108-32.

29 Ellison, "Cato's Tears," 585. For an exceptional treatment of interpretations of Cleopatra, see Mary Hamer, *Signs of Cleopatra: History, Politics, Representation* (London: Routledge, 1993).

30 Addison had already acknowledged in *The Spectator* that Sallust's description of Cato's death was "awful rather than amiable" and also that Stoicism, in its search for consistency, became something like "The Pedantry of Virtue." *The Spectator*, no. 169, 2:166; and no. 243, 2:444.

31 See Luis René Gámez, "'And Art Reflected Images to Art': Addison's Use of Numismatics in *Cato*," *Modern Philology* 85.3 (February 1988): 260. Gámez identifies the source for the coin in Jean-Foi Vaillant's *Nummi antiqui familiarum Romanum* (Amsterdam, 1703). Recently there has been considerable historical debate on the extent of the Jacobite underground in Britain during the period. If some recent work has argued in the vein that scratching any eighteenth-century Tory would reveal a Jacobite underneath, there has also been substantial resistance to such revisionism. While the historians of the Jacobite cause rely heavily on conspiracy theory and indirect evidence to make their case, critics of their views have asked for positive and incontrovertible evidence, which is, of course, hard to come by given the extremely seditious and indeed capital nature of Jacobite opinions. Whether or not important figures in this period, such as Swift and Johnson, were "serious" Jacobites, crypto-Jacobites, or "liquid" Jacobites (those who toasted to the Pretender), the emotional charge of having to take a position concerning Jacobitism permeates this literature. For some of the recent scholarship causing the debate, see especially J. C. D. Clark, *English Society, 1688-1732*; J. C. D. Clark, *Samuel Johnson: Literature, Religion, and English Cultural Politics from the Restoration to Romanticism* (Cambridge: Cambridge UP, 1994); and Paul Monod, *Jacobitism and the English People, 1688-1788* (Cambridge: Cambridge UP, 1989). See also the excellent *ELH* special issue on Jacobitism with articles assessing the impact of this historiography on our understanding of various authors including Defoe, Swift, Johnson, and Burke, in *ELH* 64.4 (winter 1997).

32 *The Spectator*, no. 69, 1:296.

33 Guthkelch, ed., *The Miscellaneous Works of Joseph Addison* 1:36-47, 44.

34 Ibid., 2:267. The slavery alluded to by Lancelot Addison is that of the Jews under Turkish suzerainty. This typical English cavil concerning Turkish absolutism was also a standard reference to the France of Louis XIV. See Lancelot

Addison, *West Barbary, or a Short Narrative of the Revolutions of the King-doms of Fez and Morocco* (London, 1671); *The Present State of the Jews* (London, 1675), 8; *The First State of Mahumedism or, An Account of the Author and Doctrines of that Imposture* (London, 1678); and *The Moores Baffled: Being a Discourse concerning Tanger* (London, 1681). Joseph Addison himself quotes Denham on Turkish fratricide during moments of royal succession, something used against him effectively by Pope in the "Atticus" passage in *Epistle to Arbuthnot* (Smithers, *Life of Joseph Addison* 239). Ellison's reading of Tangier in the origins of the standing army controversy is most astute. The garrison was an expensive but convenient excuse for Charles II's desire to maintain a military presence ("Cato's Tears," 572–75). See also E. M. G. Routh, *Tangier: England's Lost Atlantic Outpost, 1661–1684* (London: John Murray, 1912).

35 See Smithers, *Life of Joseph Addison* 234–37.

36 See Marie P. McMahon, *The Radical Whigs, John Trenchard and Thomas Gordon: Libertarian Loyalists to the New House of Hanover* (New York: UP of America, 1990). For an opposing view that sees the compatibility of libertarian Whig-gism and opposition ideology in *Cato's Letters,* see Richard Buel Jr., "Free-dom of the Press in Revolutionary America: The Evolution of Libertarianism, 1760–1820," in *The Press and the American Revolution,* ed. Bernard Bailyn and John B. Hench (Worcester, MA: American Antiquarian Society, 1980), 59–97. Adherents to Pocock's thesis argue the difference backwards. As one descrip-tion of the confluence of political discourses in this period puts it, "although neo-Harringtonianism is a Whig language, it drew heavily on a vocabulary of country politics which was far from exclusively Whig"; see Nicholas Phillipson, "Politeness and Politics in the Reigns of Anne and the Early Hanoverians," in *The Varieties of British Political Thought,* ed. J. G. A. Pocock (New York: Cam-bridge UP, 1993), 214. Needless to say, the title of the collection in which this article appears is unintentionally ironical, given that Pocock and his adherents see Machiavellianism as the only significant political master discourse of the early modern to the Enlightenment period. Despite his opposition to Namier-ism, Pocock maintains the assumption that power and principle are mutu-ally exclusive. For this reason, it is especially necessary to distinguish between Bolingbroke's critique of Whig government and *Cato's Letters.* The problem with the quote from Philippson is its collapse of old Whig—associated with Shaftesbury and the Exclusion Crisis—and new Whig—post-Hanoverian and at least partly Lockean. However, Phillipson acknowledges that Cato, unlike Bolingbroke, was not exclusively concerned with civic virtue attached to landed property (228).

37 See John Carswell, *The South Sea Bubble* (1960; London: Alan Sutton, 1993); Lewis Melville, *The South Sea Bubble* (London: Daniel O'Connor, 1921); and Larry Neal, *The Rise of Financial Capitalism: International Capital Markets in the Age of Reason* (New York: Cambridge UP, 1990).

38 *The Spectator,* no. 69, 1:293, 294.

39 *The Spectator,* no. 3, 1:15. See also Catherine Ingrassia, "The Pleasure of Business and the Business of Pleasure: Gender, Credit, and the South Sea Bubble," *Studies in Eighteenth-Century Culture* 24 (1995): 191–210.

40 See [Thomas Gordon and John Trenchard], *Cato's Letters,* 4 vols. (London, 1723–24), 1:v; all further quotations are parenthetically cited by volume and page number. For disquisitions on the terrors of despotism and arbitrary rule, see 1:181–99; 2:72–85; 2:106–33; 2:189–230.

41 *London Journal,* August 12, 1721 (Burney Collection, British Library).

42 See Michael Harris, *London Newspapers in the Age of Walpole: A Study of the Origins of the Modern English Press* (London: Associated University Presses, 1987); Laurence Hanson, *Government and the Press, 1695–1763* (London: Oxford UP, 1936), 5, 106; Charles Bechdolt Healey, *The London Journal and Its Authors, 1720–23* (Lawrence: U of Kansas P, 1935), 10, 26; and William Thomas Laprade, *Public Opinion and Politics in 18th-Century England to the Fall of Walpole* (New York: Macmillan, 1936). *The Censor censur'd* (London, 1722), 18.

43 See Silke Stratmann, *"South Sea's at best a mighty* BUBBLE*": The literization of a National Trauma* (Trier: Wissenschaftlicher Verlag Trier, 1996).

44 Pocock, *Machiavellian Moment* 488.

45 In a youthful letter to Sally Fairfax, the first American president says that he wished he could play Juba; see John C. Fitzpatrick, ed., *Writings of George Washington* (Washington, DC: U.S. Govt. Printing Office, 1931), 2:293. Patrick Henry's aphorism was probably fashioned from similar lines in *Cato,* and Nathan Hale alluded to it on the gallows; the play probably had a significant post-Revolutionary impact until 1835. See Fredric M. Litto, "Addison's *Cato* in the Colonies," *William and Mary Quarterly* (3rd ser.) 23.3 (July 1966): 431–49; John Loftis, "The Uses of Tragedy in Georgian England," in *The Stage in the Eighteenth Century,* ed. J. D. Browning (New York: Garland, 1981), 10–22; and Albert Furtwangler, "Cato at Valley Forge," *Modern Language Quarterly* 41.1 (March 1980): 38–53.

46 Bernard Bailyn, *The Ideological Origins of the American Revolution* (Cambridge, MA: Belknap Press of Harvard UP, 1967), 44; see also Caroline Robbins, *The Eighteenth-Century Commonwealthman: Studies in the Transmission, Development, and Circumstance of English Liberal Thought from the Restoration of Charles II until the War with the Thirteen Colonies* (Cambridge, MA: Harvard UP, 1959); H. Trevor Colbourn, *The Lamp of Experience: Whig History and the Intellectual Origins of the American Revolution* (Chapel Hill: U of North Carolina P, 1965); and Elizabeth Christine Cook, *Literary Influences in Colonial Newspapers, 1704–1750* (New York: Columbia UP, 1912). However, J. C. D. Clark gives a dissenting opinion that religious denominationalism was more important for the articulation of American libertarianism than the secular polemic of *Cato's Letters;* see *The Language of Liberty, 1660–1832: Political Discourse*

and Social Dynamics in the Anglo-American World (Cambridge: Cambridge UP, 1994), 27.

47 For an excellent historical interpretation of the economic significance of the objects Gulliver acquires and instrumentalizes, such as the sheep, the body parts, and the Yahoo skins, see Charlotte Sussman, "From Curiosity to Commodity: Swift's Writings of the 1720's," in *Consuming Anxieties* (Stanford: Stanford UP, 1999). For discussion of this geography and the South Sea contexts in relation to the satire, see Arthur E. Case, *Four Essays on* Gulliver's Travels (Princeton, NJ: Princeton UP, 1945); Pat Rogers, *Eighteenth-Century Encounters: Studies in Literature and Society in the Age of Walpole* (Totowa, NJ: Barnes and Noble, 1985), 11-28, 151-67; and Claude Rawson, "Savages Noble and Ignoble: Natives, Cannibals, Third Parties, and Others in South Pacific Narratives by Gulliver, Bougainville, and Diderot, with Notes on the *Encyclopédie* and on Voltaire," in *The South Pacific in the Eighteenth Century: Narratives and Myths,* ed. Jonathan Lamb, special edition of *Eighteenth-Century Life* 18.3 (November 1994): 168-97.

48 See Edward W. Said, *The World, the Text, and the Critic* (Cambridge, MA: Harvard UP, 1983), 77, 63; Case, *Four Essays on* Gulliver's Travels; and F. P. Lock, *The Politics of* Gulliver's Travels (Oxford: Clarendon, 1980). For a recent "analogical" reading that splits the difference between the allegorical and the antiallegorical, see Simon Varey, "Exemplary History and the Political Satire of *Gulliver's Travels,*" in *The Genres of* Gulliver's Travels, ed. Frederik N. Smith (Newark: U of Delaware P, 1990), 39-55.

49 Sir Charles Firth, *The Political Significance of* Gulliver's Travels (Oxford: Oxford UP, 1919). The specificity of the Irish and African references have been very well documented. See Oliver W. Ferguson, *Jonathan Swift and Ireland* (Urbana: U of Illinois P, 1962); Richard Ashe King, *Swift in Ireland* (1895; Folcroft, PA: Folcroft Press, 1969); Donald T. Torchiana, "Jonathan Swift, the Irish, and the Yahoos: The Case Reconsidered," *Philological Quarterly* 54.1 (winter 1975): 195-212; Ann Cline Kelly, "Swift's Explorations of Slavery in Houyhnhnmland and Ireland," *PMLA* 91.5 (October 1976): 846-55; Carol Fabricant, *Swift's Landscape* (Baltimore: Johns Hopkins UP, 1982); Clement Hawes, "Three Times Round the Globe: Gulliver and Colonial Discourse," *Cultural Critique* 18 (1991): 187-214; and Laura Brown, "Imperial Disclosures: Jonathan Swift," in *Ends of Empire* (Ithaca: Cornell UP, 1993), 170-200. Brown's exemplary interpretation explores Swift's double contextualization of Yahoos and females through the figure of Gulliver and allusions to eighteenth-century colonialist discourse and travel narrative about Africa within the context of mercantile economics.

50 All citations, unless otherwise specified, are by volume and page number to *The Prose Works of Jonathan Swift*, 14 vols., ed. Herbert Davis et al. (Oxford: Blackwell, 1939-68).

51 See Claude Rawson, "Savages Noble and Ignoble," 181; *Order from Confusion Sprung* (London: Allen and Unwin, 1985); and " 'Indians' and Irish: Montaigne,

Swift, and the Cannibal Question," *Modern Language Quarterly* 53 (1992): 344–54.

52 For a contextualization of this passage amid debates on conquest, see Warren Montag, *The Unthinkable Swift: The Spontaneous Philosophy of a Church of England Man* (London: Verso, 1994), 129–36.

53 Samuel Brunt's *A Voyage to Cacklogallinia* (1728) contains hints, as does *Gulliver's Travels*, of freebooting contexts, slave rebellion, and the South Sea Bubble. Brunt's slave-trading narrator escapes death during a slave rebellion in Jamaica when recognized by Cuffey, a former slave. Following retaliations between the English and the maroons, the group escapes by sea, whereupon they meet "a Freebooter, whose Crew was of all Nations and Colours." Eventually, the arrival in Cacklogallinia leads to inflated proposals for a moon voyage using oversized birds for transport, one that results inevitably in rampant speculation and disappointment. Several transparent references to the Bubble arise in the episodes among the Cacklogallinians and the Selenites, revealing the mercenary motivations behind all human activity. The Selenites are Brobdingnagian in size but can also be protean and apparitional. The contingent attributes of colonialism in both these satires are found to be speculative commerce and slave trading, and piracy and marronage are related forms of resistance to this model. Commerce and colonialism raise problems for which there are no obvious solutions despite the attempt to generate wisdom through political platitudes of various persuasions, including Stoical ones. No obviously harmonious relationship between politics and economics preexists the attempt to impose civic humanism. Samuel Brunt, *A Voyage to Cacklogallinia* (London, 1728), 17, 112, 119, 129.

54 William Shakespeare, *Othello*, 1.1.109–10. In 1695, Ellis Walker's rendition of Epictetus is replete with equine imagery—and suggestive of Gulliver. Horses represent passion and narcissism. The poem was written when Walker fled to his patron "at the breaking out of the present Troubles in Ireland." In another tantalizing prolepsis of Gulliver, the poem uses the image of a sailor who lingers on shore with "Shelfish or Roots of palatable kind" that he finds there when commanded to fetch water. The man has to hasten and catch his ship before it departs to fulfill his errand for his master, and this becomes a metaphor of the necessity of abandoning his wife and son as "worthless lumber" when the divine master beckons. See Walker, *Epicteti Enchiridion Made English in a Poetical Paraphrase* (London, 1695), 14–15.

55 See *The Tatler* 81 (October 15, 1709). Despite a long friendship and political affinity with Bolingbroke, Swift testily disagreed with the former's iconoclastic dismissal of Cato's virtues (Ehrenpreis, *Swift: The Man* 3:472). See also Addison's lighthearted proposal for a censor in *The Tatler* 162 (April 1710). For a full account of Cato's influence on Swift, see J. W. Johnson, *English Neo-Classical Thought* 101–3, 279. See also M. M. Kelsall, "*Iterum* Houyhnhnm: Swift's Sextumvirate and the Horses," *Essays in Criticism* 19 (1969): 35–45.

56 Yet Swift—or more likely, both his publishers—decided to suppress these paragraphs in the Motte (1726) and the Faulkner (1735) editions. In any case, with the battle won, there was no efficient purpose to court charges of seditious libel.

57 To appreciate the larger context of monetary anxieties in the Western world since the Middle Ages, see Marc Shell, *Money, Language, and Thought: Literary and Philosophical Economies from the Medieval to the Modern Era* (Berkeley: U of California P, 1982), and *The Economy of Literature* (Baltimore: Johns Hopkins UP, 1978); M. Beer, *Early British Economics from the XIIIth to the Middle of the XVIIIth Century* (1938; rpt. New York: Augustus M. Kelly, 1967). For a superb analysis of the interpenetration of economics and literature in the Renaissance, see Richard Halpern, *The Poetics of Primitive Accumulation: English Renaissance Culture and the Genealogy of Capital* (Ithaca, NY: Cornell UP, 1991).

58 Locke's insistence on a gold-standard policy continued in many countries, as we know, well into the twentieth century. See Joyce Oldham Appleby, *Economic Thought and Ideology in Seventeenth-Century England* (Princeton, NJ: Princeton UP, 1978); and Peter Laslett, "John Locke, the Great Recoinage, and the Origins of the Board of Trade, 1695–1698," *William and Mary Quarterly* 14 (1957): 378–85.

59 While reading Swift's pamphlets, it is important to acknowledge the way in which the text revivifies dead metaphors and allusions of monetary and economic transactions. For a useful reference tool to enable this process—short of looking up every word in the OED—see Sandra K. Fischer, *Econolingua: A Glossary of Coins and Economic Language in Renaissance Drama* (Newark: U of Delaware P, 1985).

60 Swift, *A Panegyrick on the D———n, in the Person of a Lady in the North* 156, ctd. in Fabricant, *Swift's Landscape* 253.

61 See Richard S. Ide, "Chapman's *Caesar and Pompey* and the Uses of History," *Modern Philology* 82.3 (February 1985): 255–68. As Luis René Gámez persuasively argues in " 'And Art Reflected,' " Addison favors a "numismatic aesthetics," where his Roman hero resembles the idealized and static visual images that are portrayed on coins and medallions. Another critic finds that Addison's use of Cato is not meant to be exemplary, but this is based on scanty evidence; see J. M. Armistead, "Drama of Renewal: *Cato* and Moral Empiricism," *Papers on Language and Literature* 17.3 (summer 1981): 271–83.

62 Virgil, Horace, Ovid, and Persius had exploited the venality theme, and it was richly worked in medieval times as well. See, for example, John A. Yunck, *The Lineage of Lady Meed: The Development of Mediaeval Venality Satire* (South Bend, IN: Notre Dame UP, 1963).

63 My use of the term boycott in what follows is deliberately anachronistic, as the term itself came into use at the high point of Irish nationalism during the Irish nationalist "land war" of 1879–82, fought under the leadership of Charles Stewart Parnell. Charles Cunningham Boycott was an English estate manager

who was the target of one of the peasant actions; his name became synonymous with the form of protest initiated against him.

64 See H. A. Taatgen, "The Boycott in the Irish Civilizing Process," *Anthropological Quarterly* 65.4 (October 1992): 163–76. Taatgen argues along these Eliasian lines for the sociogenesis of Irish boycotts from the late nineteenth century to the angling boycott of 1989. Although the conventional history locates the use of this boycotting process to the post-Fenian nationalist politics of the land war of 1879–82, it is easy to see the occasion of Wood's coinage as a much earlier scenario that involves using these strategies of "nonviolent" resistance. See C. H. E. Philpin, ed., *Nationalism and Popular Protest in Ireland* (Cambridge: Cambridge UP, 1987). For a comprehensive history of eighteenth-century Ireland that includes useful surveys of English and Gaelic cultural production, see T. W. Moody and W. E. Vaughan, eds., *A New History of Ireland: Vol. 4, Eighteenth-Century Ireland, 1691–1800* (Oxford: Clarendon Press, 1986).

65 See Eric Hobsbawm, "Peasants and Politics," *Journal of Peasant Studies* 1.1 (1987): 3–22.

66 A very interesting article investigates an Irish oral tradition of folktales and practical jokes—Jack and the Dane—that had developed around Swift's personality and his combative relationship with servants. The survival of such a tradition suggests that other, more ephemeral, mechanisms of cultural transmission that communicate Swift's message to the illiterate might be investigated. See Mackie L. Jarrell, " 'Jack and the Dane': Swift Traditions in Ireland," in *Fair Liberty Was All His Cry: A Tercentenary Tribute to Jonathan Swift, 1667–1745,* ed. Norman A. Jeffares (New York: St. Martin's, 1967), 311–41. For other references linking Swift to Gaelic folklore, see Vivian Mercier, "Swift and the Gaelic Tradition," in *Fair Liberty* 279–89. The function of rumor in the Indian colonial situation is also highly suggestive for Irish contexts; see Ranajit Guha, *Elementary Aspects of Peasant Insurgency* (Delhi: Oxford UP, 1983).

67 For an exposition of the allegory, see Fabricant, *Swift's Landscape* 251.

68 As the mode of the fifth letter strongly encourages allegorical parallels between Swift and the Drapier, it is conceivable that the Whig Molesworth might stand for Swift's early Whig patron William Temple, who ultimately disappointed his protégé's expectations for preferment; it is therefore possible to read the aspiration of settling on Molesworth's estate as nothing more than a send-up of an Anglo-Irish fantasy. This letter is one more indication that it is extremely difficult to read Swift as a Jacobite even though some recent attempts have been made. For one such attempt, see Ian Higgins, *Swift's Politics: A Study in Disaffection* (Cambridge: Cambridge UP, 1994), and for a critique of such attempts, see J. A. Downie, "Swift and Jacobitism," *ELH* 64.4 (winter 1997): 887–901.

69 See Alexander Pope, *The Dunciad* (book 1, ll. 20–28). For instance, Yeats claims that Swift's exposition of the doctrine of Irish independence in *The Drapier's*

Letters "passed from the talk of study and parlour to that of road and market, and created the political nationality of Ireland." Yeats's suggestion to study the transmissions from formal to popular culture is helpful; what is debatable is the ascription of the agency of the social processes entirely to the biographical entity of Swift. See W. B. Yeats, "Introduction to *The Words Upon the Window-Pane,*" qtd. in Jeffares, ed., *Fair Liberty,* 188; and John Middleton Murry, *Jonathan Swift: A Critical Biography* (New York: Farrar, Straus and Giroux, 1955).

70 For an exemplary reading of the economic contexts of the Irish tracts as influenced by "the Muse of Political Arithmetic," see Charlotte Sussman's *Consuming Anxieties.*

71 Arthur O'Connor, *The State of Ireland* (London, 1798), 30, 42. See also J. C. D. Clark, "Religious Affiliation and Dynastic Allegiance in Eighteenth-Century England: Edmund Burke, Thomas Paine and Samuel Johnson," *ELH* 64.4 (winter 1997): 1029-1067.

FOUR *Lady Mary in the* Hammam

1 For a facsimile reprint of the St. John edition, see the Eastern Europe Collection series (Arno Press and the New York Times, 1971). Fifty-two letters form the corpus of *Letters from the Levant,* and these have been deemed an autonomous literary piece within the larger context of Montagu's complete letters (as they were kept separately in albums commemorating her Levantine travels). The finished letters are most likely pseudo-letters recomposed from earlier heads of letters that Montagu had also kept. For the most detailed account of the manuscript sources and the anecdotal history of the eventual publication of the work, see Robert Halsband, *The Life of Mary Wortley Montagu* (New York: Oxford UP, 1960). For earlier biographies, see George Paston, *Lady Mary Wortley Montagu and Her Times* (New York: Putnam, 1907); Lewis Melville, *Lady Mary Wortley Montagu: Her Life and Letters* (London: Hutchinson, 1925); and Iris Barry, *Portrait of Lady Mary Wortley Montagu* (London: Ernest Benn, 1928). The most reliable scholarly edition of the letters is that by Robert Halsband, ed., *The Complete Letters of Lady Mary Wortley Montagu,* 3 vols. (Oxford: Clarendon, 1965). Unless otherwise specified, all citations follow the first volume of the Halsband edition of *The Complete Letters.* See also Robert Halsband, ed., *Selected Letters of Lady Mary Wortley Montagu* (Harmondsworth: Penguin, 1986), Clare Brant, ed., *Letters* (London: Everyman, 1992), and Isobel Grundy, ed., *Selected Letters* (New York: Penguin, 1997). The Penguin editions unfortunately do not contain all the Turkish letters, whereas the more complete reprint of the 1906 Everyman edition occasionally contains some spurious text from corrupt editions. For a recent lavishly illustrated edition, see Christopher Pick, ed., *Embassy to Constantinople: The Travels of Lady Mary Wortley Mon-*

tagu (London: Century Hutchinson, 1988). For the remainder of Montagu's collected writings, see Robert Halsband and Isobel Grundy, eds., *Essays and Poems and* Simplicity A Comedy (Oxford: Clarendon, 1977).

2 See Lisa Lowe, *Critical Terrains: French and British Orientalisms* (Ithaca, NY: Cornell UP, 1991), and Billie Melman, *Women's Orients: English Women and the Middle East, 1718–1918* (Ann Arbor: U of Michigan P, 1992).

3 I take my definition of fantasy from Jean Laplanche and Jean-Baptiste Pontalis, "Fantasy and the Origins of Sexuality," in *Formations of Fantasy*, ed. Victor Burgin, James Donald, and Cora Kaplan (New York: Methuen, 1986), 5–34. For a lucid discussion of this definition, see Judith Butler, *Bodies That Matter: On the Discursive Limits of "Sex"* (New York: Routledge, 1993), 267–68.

4 The OED's examples of this usage come from Vanbrugh and Cibber's *The Provincial Husband* and Fielding's *The Lottery* and *Tom Jones*.

5 See Cynthia Lowenthal, *Lady Mary Wortley Montagu and the Eighteenth-Century Familiar Letter* (Athens: U of Georgia P, 1994), 80–113.

6 I use the terminology initiated by Arnold Van Gennep in "The Classification of Rites," in *The Rites of Passage,* trans. Monika B. Vizedom and Gabrielle L. Caffee (London: Routledge, 1960), 1–13. For the best-known contemporary usage of this terminology, see Victor Turner, *Dramas, Fields, and Metaphors: Symbolic Action in Human Society* (Ithaca, NY: Cornell UP, 1974); and Victor Turner and Edith Turner, *Image and Pilgrimage in Christian Culture: Anthropological Perspectives* (New York: Columbia UP, 1978).

7 See Joan Rivière, "Womanliness as Masquerade," in *The Inner World and Joan Rivière, Collected Papers: 1920–1958* (New York: Karnac Books, 1991), 94; Stephen Heath, "Joan Rivière and the Masquerade," in *Formations of Fantasy*, ed. Burgin, Donald, and Kaplan, 45–61; Judith Butler, *Gender Trouble: Feminism and the Subversion of Identity* (New York: Routledge, 1990), 50–54. Butler addresses race substantially in *Bodies That Matter,* with readings of Nella Larsen's *Passing* and Jenny Livingston's *Paris Is Burning.* However, attending to the racial complication at the heart of Rivière's article could make its proposed theory of gender more than just an application to contexts of race.

8 Those who read eighteenth-century travel narratives without reference to the generic experimentation in travel writing since antiquity do so at the peril of massive simplification. A longer literary-historical perspective to travel narrative in the Western tradition has been provided by Mary B. Campbell, *The Witness and the Other World: Exotic European Travel Writing, 400–1600* (Ithaca, NY: Cornell UP, 1988). Campbell demonstrates that early travel writing is a fluid and all-inclusive origin for the developments that led to the genres of historiography, spiritual autobiography, and the novel. For more exhaustive treatments of the quantity of travel writing, especially in the eighteenth century, see Percy G. Adams, *Travelers and Travel Liars, 1660–1800* (Berkeley: U of Cali-

fornia P, 1962), and *Travel Literature and the Evolution of the Novel* (Lexington: UP of Kentucky, 1983); and Charles L. Batten Jr., *Pleasurable Instruction: Form and Convention in Eighteenth-Century Travel Literature* (Berkeley: U of California P, 1978).

9 See Michael McKeon, *Origins of the English Novel 1600–1740* (Baltimore: Johns Hopkins UP, 1987), 103–13.

10 Montagu's joint reference to Knolles and Rycaut makes it likely that she was familiar with the sixth edition of Richard Knolles, *The Turkish History, from the Original of that Nation, to the Growth of the Ottoman Empire* (London, 1687). Sir Paul Rycaut, *The Present State of the Ottoman Empire Containing the Maxims of the Turkish Polity* (London, 1686), was appended to this folio edition. Some other well-known travels to Turkey before Montagu's are Sir Henry Blount, *Voyage into the Levant* (London, 1634), and George Sandys, *A Relation of a Journey begun AD 1610, containing a description of the Turkish Empire* (London, 1615). For a brief description of seventeenth-century travelers to Turkey, see Robin Fedden, *English Travellers in the Near East* (London: Longman, 1958).

11 See Aaron Hill, *A Full and Just Account of the Present State of the Ottoman Empire in all its Branches* (London, 1709), published in a folio edition with massive support from influential subscribers. Hill regales readers with burlesque nationalist accounts, such as that of the hale and hearty Jack Tar who manages to have sex with the women in a harem for ten days before he is discovered and makes his escape, whereas the sexually more sophisticated French ambassador's secretary is apprehended and severely bastinadoed—whipped on the soles of his feet—for attempting a similar libertine escapade (112–15).

12 See Jean Dumont, *A New Voyage to the Levant*, 4th ed. (London, 1705). The same charge is also repeated by Addison in *The Spectator*, ed. Donald F. Bond, 5 vols. (Oxford: Clarendon, 1965), no. 288, 3:22. All subsequent references are to this edition, cited by issue, volume, and page numbers.

13 Montagu is credited by her biographer Robert Halsband with the authorship of a pseudonymous feminist pamphlet. Similar to Astell and Defoe in her advocacy of women, Montagu was also in favor of a female academy. See Montagu, *Woman Not Inferior to Man: By Sophia, A Person of Quality* (1739; London: Brentham, 1975). For the Stoic references, see the feminist theme of the sixth issue of Montagu's short-lived periodical, *The Nonsense of Common-Sense (1736)*, ed. Robert Halsband (Evanston: Northwestern UP, 1947), 27. The periodical achieved greater prominence when it was reprinted in the *London Magazine*. Montagu also anonymously penned a marvelous diatribe against husbands in *The Spectator* no. 573, as a satiric reply to a letter about a club of nine widows in no. 561 by Addison (4:515–18; 4:556–61). Another protofeminist piece, "An Essay on the Mischief of Giving Fortunes with Women in Marriage," published in Curll's *Miscellanea*, is credited to her by Halsband (*Life*, 121).

14 Montagu criticizes Addison's distracting foray into romantic subplot and up-
holds classical Aristotelian notions concerning the unity of action. She finds
Shakespeare's *Julius Caesar* much better in its compression and points out that
Juba and Syphax are too close to Othello in their characterization. She also recommends stronger libertarian rhetoric throughout the play; see "[Critique of
Cato] Wrote at the Desire of Mr. Wortley, suppress'd at the desire of Mr. Adi-
son" (1713), in Halsband and Grundy, *Essays and Poems*, 62–68.

15 Montagu's intellectual profile seems closer to the reassured aristocratic cadences
of Margaret Cavendish than to the precarious improvisations of Aphra Behn.
Astell, who died in 1731, endorses Montagu with a feminist riposte: "I con-
fess I am malicious enough to desire that the World shou'd see to how much
better purpose the LADYS Travel than their LORDS, and that whilst it is sur-
feited with Male Travels, all in the same Tone and stuft with the same Trifles, a
Lady has the skill to strike out a New Path and to embellish a wornout Subject
with variety of fresh and elegant Entertainment . . . in short, let her own Sex at
least do her Justice; . . . Let the Men malign one another" (Halsband, *Complete
Letters* [1:467]. For an account of the admiration the two women had for each
other, see Ruth Perry, *The Celebrated Mary Astell: An Early English Feminist*
(Chicago: U of Chicago P, 1986), 270–71.

16 See Lowe, *Critical Terrains* 51. Montagu's self-validation against male travel
writers is also discussed here (35–52). For a careful historical account of Montagu's authorship, see Isobel Grundy, "The Politics of Female Authorship:
Lady Mary Wortley Montagu's Reaction to the Printing of Her Poems," *The
Book Collector* 31 (1982): 19–37.

17 Montagu, *Nonsense* 25.

18 Despite their empiricist investments, one of the persistent antirealist effects
sought out by seemingly realist travel accounts, both authentic and bogus, was
the possibility of endless decontextualization that rendered the strange familiar,
as does the celebrated example of *Gulliver's Travels* (1726, 1735), or the familiar
strange, as did Montesquieu's satire structured as a collection of pseudo-letters,
The Persian Letters (1721). Pseudo-letters involving foreign topoi would end up
as a dominant eighteenth-century mode, as exemplified by Lord Lyttelton's
Persian Letters (1735), Horace Walpole's *Letter from Xo-Ho* (1757), and Gold-
smith's *Citizen of the World* (1762).

19 *The Spectator* nos. 28, 1:117, and 31, 1:129.

20 See *The Tatler*, ed. Donald F. Bond (Oxford: Clarendon, 1987), no. 18, 1:144–
47; and *The Spectator* no. 28, 1:115–19.

21 Later, Montagu writes in favor of economic nationalism and an anti-Mande-
villean position on luxury, similar to the boycotts that Swift recommends to
the Irish. Englishwomen ought to wear wool for nine months of the year for
reasons of local climate and economics, and the irresponsible mimicry of Con-

tinental fashion has to stop: "[The] regulation of the present Mourning, which is so highly Advantageous to the Woollen Manufacture, the staple Commodity of these Kingdoms, the natural Growth of our own Lands, and the Support of the Poor, [is] reduced now to a very low Ebb, by the Luxury and ill Taste of the Rich, and the fantastick Mimicry of our Ladies, who are so accustomed to shiver in Silks, that they exclaim at the Hardships of Warmth and Decency." Such a reorientation of dress would honor the country and benefit the nation, leading to a sympathetic link between the bodies of the gentry and the tenants, "covered with the warm Produce of our native Sheep" (*Nonsense* 2, 3).

22 A sudden rage for this technique developed subsequently in England, apparently as a result of Montagu's popularization. See Alev Lytle Croutier, *Harems: le monde derrière le voile* (Paris: Editions Belfond, 1989), 53. For an account of eighteenth-century masquerade in terms of the Bakhtinian carnivalesque, see Terry Castle, *Masquerade and Civilization: The Carnivalesque in Eighteenth-Century English Culture and Fiction* (Stanford: Stanford UP, 1986).

23 Montagu may have had the prior benefit of a full-length study of this Turkish code by Du Vignau, Sieur des Joanots, an otherwise obscure French author. She focuses on the great difficulty of deciphering rebuses (mischaracterized by Du Vignau as hieroglyphs). In 1688, Du Vignau published *Le secrétaire turc contenant l'art d'exprimer ses pensées sans se voir, se parler, et sans s'écrire* (Paris, 1688). It was excerpted in English as *The art of making love without speaking, writing or enterview of the lovers* (London, 1688). Montagu had at least some independent knowledge of the selam techniques, given that she describes some symbolic equivalents that do not exist in Du Vignau's text. *Le secrétaire turc* is, nonetheless, a comprehensive dictionary with long narrative examples and hence a useful reference tool to understand the code Montagu encountered. Du Vignau notes that "flowers, fruits, woods, resins, silks, gold, silver, colors, fabrics, and almost anything else that is used in daily commercial transactions, enters into the Turks' transactions concerning Love" (6). He says, "It is reasonable to believe that this [language] derives from the ancient means of communicating through numbers/ciphers [*chiffres*] and figures, as were the hieroglyphs for the Egyptians before the alphabet was invented" (10–11). Alain Grosrichard rightly points out that the selam is closer to the rebus than to the hieroglyph; see *Structures du Sérail* (Paris: Seuil, 1979), 213–20.

24 The secret nature of the selam and its rhyming technique of composition is similar to Cockney slang. Both codes use a two-step rhyming displacement to disguise a concept. For instance, the Cockney term "loaf" stands for "head" through a two-step displacement: "head" rhymes with "bread," then converts to the collective noun for "bread," "loaf." As can be seen in the misogynist examples from *My Fair Lady*, a cant term for wife can be "the Duchess" (via "the Duchess of Fife") or "trouble" (via "trouble and strife"). These designations are

conventional; however, substitutions could also express idiosyncratic desires and private equivalences. See Eric Partridge, *A Dictionary of Slang and Unconventional English,* ed. Paul Beale (London: Routledge, 1984). The classic example from Du Vignau is: "A cube of sugar, known in Turkish as *Cheker,* signifies *seni medem scheker,* which means, *my inside attracts you, my heart yearns passionately for you*" (12). The first syllable associates the color blue (*mevi*) to mean "I'm in love" (*Mefloldum*) (13). The Picardian tradition of the rebus was a significant genre in France and Italy, but not so much in England. See Jean Ceard and Jean-Claude Margolin, *Rébus de la Renaissance: Des Images Qui Parlent* (Paris: Maisonneuve et Larose, 1986). Perhaps the English work that dealt most extensively with the concept was Camden's *Remaines* (1605), which Addison borrows from for a few comments on the rebus. See William Camden, "Name-devises," in *Remaines of a greater work, concerning Britaine, the inhabitants thereof, their languages, names, surnames, impreses, wisespeeches, poesis, and epitaphes* (London, 1614), 164–67; and E. Moore, "An Essay on the Rebus in Art," *The Craftsman* 5 (1903–4): 240. Addison dismisses the rebus as a species of false wit; see *The Spectator* no. 59, 1:250–51. See also the apology for punning by John Birch in *The Guardian,* ed. John Calhoun Stephens (Lexington: UP of Kentucky, 1982), no. 36, 147–50.

25 See Anne-Marie Moulin and Pierre Chuvin, *L'Islam au péril des femmes: une Anglaise en Turquie au XVIIIe siècle* (Paris: La Découverte, 1981), 96. See also Du Vignau: "It must be said that the Turks have no means of indicating gender, and they say the same words to mean 'a handsome man' and 'a beautiful woman,' and the same phrases are used for the (male) lover as for the mistress" (*Le secrétaire turc* 18).

26 For instance, Dervla Murphy argues that Montagu's youthful letters to Anne Wortley were actually coded addresses to her then suitor Edward Wortley; see *The Embassy to Constantinople: The Travels of Lady Mary Wortley Montagu* (London: Century Hutchinson, 1988), 13. For a treatment of Montagu's letters in relation to the techniques of eighteenth-century epistolarity, see Bruce Redford, *The Converse of the Pen: Acts of Intimacy in the Eighteenth-Century Familiar Letter* (Chicago: U of Chicago P, 1986), and Patricia Meyer Spacks, *Gossip* (New York: Knopf, 1985). The manuscript circulation of eighteenth-century letters make them much closer to the cryptic openness of the postcard, deconstructing the public and the private, the fictional and the empirical. In this respect, it is also useful to remember the conceptual pressure put on the philosophical concept of the letter and the postcard by Jacques Derrida, *La Carte Postale: De Socrates a Freud et Au-dela* (Paris: Flammarion, 1980).

27 Victor Turner, "Liminal to Liminoid, in Play, Flow, and Ritual: An Essay in Comparative Symbology," *Rice University Studies* (Summer 1974): 53–92.

28 "Harem," from the opposition in Arabic between *h'alâl* (pure, permitted, legal)

and *h'arâm* (impure, prohibited, illegal), designates female-inhabited spaces in a household that were off-limits to any man other than the husband and his eunuchs, though the same space could be freely visited by women and chil-eunuchs, though the same space could be freely visited by women and children.

29 For two contemporary instances of this oft-repeated charge, see *The Spectator* no. 53, 1:224, and Alexander Pope, *Correspondence,* ed. George Sherburn, 5 vols. (Oxford: Clarendon, 1956), 1:368-69.

30 See Felicity Nussbaum, *Torrid Zones: Maternity, Sexuality, and Empire in Eigh-teenth-Century English Narratives* (Baltimore: Johns Hopkins UP, 1995), 30-41. For Clérambault, see Joan Copjec, "The Sartorial Superego," in *Read My Desire: Lacan against the Historicists* (Cambridge, MA: MIT, 1994), 65-116.

31 The kahya, or steward, was the second most powerful officer of the empire after the vizier. For comments on these meetings, see Moulin and Chuvin, *L'Islam* 18-19. Lowenthal, *Montagu and the Familiar Letter;* Fanny Davis, *The Otto-man Lady: A Social History from 1718 to 1918* (New York: Greenwood, 1986), 117; Deniz Kandiyoti, "End of Empire: Islam, Nationalism, and the State," in *Women, Islam, and the State,* ed. Deniz Kandiyoti (Philadelphia: Temple UP, 1991), 22-47.

32 See Ruth Bernard Yeazell, "Public Baths and Private Harems: Lady Mary Wortley Montagu and the Origins of Ingres's *Bain Turc,*" *Yale Journal of Criti-cism* 7.1 (Spring 1994): 111-38. Ingres copied the bathhouse letter, dated April 1, 1717, into his diary, and worked from it to produce *Le bain turc* (310).

33 Melman, *Women's Orients* 91.

34 This episode is also recounted in Spence's anecdotes, based on an oral account from Montagu that is useful to compare with the written letter: "The first time she was at one of these baths, the ladies invited her to undress, and to bathe with them; and on her not making any haste, one of the prettiest run to her to undress her. You can't imagine her surprise upon lifting my lady's gown, and seeing her stays go all round her. She run back quite frightened, and told her companion, 'That the husbands in England were much worse than in the East, for that they tied up their wives in little boxes, of the shape of their bodies.' She carried 'em to see it. They all agreed that 'twas one of the greatest barbarities of the world, and pitied the poor woman for being such slaves in Europe." See Joseph Spence, *Anecdotes, Observations, and Characters of Books and Men. Col-lected from the Conversation of Mr. Pope and other Eminent Persons of His Time* (London: W. H. Carpenter, 1820), 230-31.

35 Pope, *Correspondence* 1:384. Pope also writes to Montagu about wishing to see her naked: "We shall then see how the Prudes of this world owed all their fine Figure only to their being a little straiter-lac'd, and that they were naturally as arrant Squabs as those that went more loose, nay as those that never girded their loyns at all" (1:353). In another letter, Pope imagines the indolence and voluptuousness of the seraglio that Montagu may be witness to, calling it "a

very mixed kind of enjoyment" (1:422). Three times he mentions that he "detested the Sound of *Honest Woman*, and *Loving Spouse* ever since [he] heard the pretty name of *Odaliche*" (1:364, 441, 496). For analysis of Pope's involvement with Montagu, see Valerie Rumbold, *Women's Place in Pope's World* (New York: Cambridge UP, 1989), 133–43; Cynthia Wall, "Editing Desire: Pope's Correspondence with (and without) Lady Mary," *Philological Quarterly* 71 (1992): 221–37; and Lowenthal, *Montagu and the Familiar Letter* 52–64.

36 See W. S. Lewis, ed., *Horace Walpole's Correspondence*, 48 vols. (New Haven: Yale UP, 1937–83), especially the references to her acquired deformities (30:15), her coarse and unclean clothes (18:306, 22:3), her decay (42:507), her dirt and frugality (34:255), her dirt that ought to put her into quarantine (21:540), her chateau a mere hovel (23:315), her morals (9:392), and especially the references to her as "old, foul, tawdry, painted, plastered" (13:234) and to "the poxed, foul, malicious, black blood of Lady Mary" (30:10). On the other hand, if the constant references by several enemies to Montagu's lack of hygiene are true — even by the relatively rudimentary standards of cleanliness observed by the eighteenth-century English aristocracy — this may also incidentally suggest that she smelled "high" to her much cleaner Turkish counterparts. I thank Moira Ferguson for suggesting this possibility to me.

37 Brant, *Letters* xviii. Lady Mary eloped with Wortley after complex negotiations over her marriage settlement failed between him and her father, the Duke of Pierrepont. However, the stand-off between her father and husband-to-be became public scandal when the details of the financial negotiations made it to the pages of *The Tatler*, a result of Addison's friendship with Wortley. Wortley provided Addison with notes against the conduct of mercenary marriages, material that Addison used to write two essays on the subject. See *The Tatler*, no. 199, 3:65–68, and no. 223, 3:161–65; and Halsband, *Life* 23–28.

38 Montagu's friendship with Robert Walpole's mistress, Maria Skerett, who later became his wife, also undoubtedly contributed to her vilification as Sappho by the Tory opposition. Montagu also briefly entered the pamphlet wars, possibly on Walpole's behalf, by authoring a shortlived periodical (a total of nine issues); see Montagu, *Nonsense* x–xviii. The periodical aimed to counter the charges of corruption by Lord Chesterfield and George Lyttelton against Walpole in *Common Sense*, which began in February 1737.

39 See Jean Thevenot, *Travels into the Levant* (London, 1656). Meanwhile, Rycaut talks at length about the Turkish predilection for homosexuality — calling the Turks "Slaves to this inordinate Passion . . . [that] likewise reigns in the Society of Women" — and of its policing by eunuchs in the dormitories for male youths being trained for high office and by matrons in the women's quarters (13–16). The cloying, voluptuous, and degenerate version of the bathhouse reappears in the accounts of subsequent female travelers, such as Lady Craven, *A Journey through the Crimea to Constantinople* (London: G. Virtue, 1789), 263–

64, and Julia Pardoe, *Beauties of the Bosphorus* (London, 1830), 137. See also the renewed scientific interest in eunuchs and hermaphroditism, fueled by works such as Charles Ancillon, *Traité des eunuques dans lequel on explique toutes les différentes sortes d'eunuques, quel rang ils ont tenu et quel cas on en a fait* (Paris, 1707), translated as *Eunuchism display'd* (London: E. Curll, 1718).

40 "Nothing seems to me a plainer proofe of the irrationality of Mankind (whatever fine claims we pretend to Reason) than the rage with which they contest for a small spot of Ground . . . I am a good deal inclin'd to beleive Mr. Hobbs, that the State of Nature is a State of War" (305).

41 John Milton, *Paradise Lost* 4.304–18. Mary Astell also speaks of the Protestant nunnery as follows: "Happy Retreat! which will be the introducing you into such a *Paradise* as your Mother *Eve* forfeited . . . Here are no serpents to deceive you . . . No provocations are given in this Amicable Society"; see *A Serious Proposal to the Ladies* (London, 1694), 64–67.

42 Harlequin's cultural relativism in Aphra Behn, *The Emperor of the Moon*, in *The Works of Aphra Behn,* ed. Janet Todd, 7 vols. (Columbus: Ohio State UP, 1996), 188–207.

43 See Abdelwahab Bouhdiba, *La Sexualité en Islam* (Paris: Presses Universitaires de France, 1975), 197–213. For Horace Walpole, see n. 37.

44 Ibid., 203.

45 Smollett writes that Montagu's letters were "never equalled by any letter-writer of any sex, age, or nation"; see *Critical Review* 15 (1763): 426.

46 See Bouhdiba, *La sexualité* 199; and Moulin and Chuvin, *L'Islam* 66.

47 See Genevieve Miller, *The Adoption of Inoculation for Smallpox in England and France* (Philadelphia: U of Pennsylvania P, 1957), 45–69; and Robert Halsband, "New Light on Lady Mary Wortley Montagu's Contribution to Inoculation," *Journal of the History of Medicine and Allied Sciences* 8.4 (1953): 390–405. The Royal Society knew about smallpox inoculation as early as 1700 through John Lister's experiments, and Audrey de La Mottraye had observed it in Circassia. However, the technique was considered too dangerous to practice on human subjects until Montagu brought back appropriate methods from Turkey. Montagu includes a brief letter to her husband reporting the inoculation of their son (392). See Montagu's town eclogue, "Saturday: The Small Pox: Flavia," in which she expressed her feelings about the disease (Halsband, *Essays and Poems,* 182). The notorious antifeminist attack on the introduction of the technique was by Wagstaffe: "Posterity perhaps will scarcely be brought to believe, that an Experiment practiced only by a few *Ignorant Women,* amongst an illiterate and unthinking People, shou'd on a sudden, and upon slender Experience, so far obtain in one of the Politest Nations in the World, as to be receiv'd into the *Royal Palace*"; see William Wagstaffe, *A Letter to Dr. Freind Shewing the Danger and Uncertainty of Inoculating the Small Pox* (London, 1722), 5. Montagu wrote

an unsigned letter in *The Tatler* defending the technique and authored a pseud-onymous pamphlet to respond to the attacks made on her. However, she also had her defenders. William Broome wrote a flattering letter saying he would write a poem celebrating her discovery, which she showed to Pope, and Prin-cess Caroline's efforts on her behalf led to the inoculation of orphan children in St. James's Parish. Richard Savage's *Miscellany*, dedicated to her, contained a poem from Aaron Hill's *The Plain Dealer* on smallpox (for a summary, see Halsband, *Life*, 109-11). See also the letter from "Parthenissa" on the ravages of smallpox (*Spectator* 306 [February 20, 1712], 3:100-2).

48 Roland Barthes, *Mythologies*, trans. Annette Lavers (New York: Hill and Wang, 1973), 150.

49 Turner and Turner describe pilgrimage as "an ordered antistructure of patrimo-nial feudal systems" (*Image and Pilgrimage* 254).

50 Michel de Certeau, *The Writing of History*, trans. Tom Conley (New York: Columbia UP, 1988).

51 John Kerslake suggests a Venetian influence in this portrait, perhaps Rosalba's; see *Early Georgian Portraits* (London: Her Majesty's Stationery Office, 1977), 1:190.

52 Du Vignau too has a similar reaction in relation to the fear of losing his fluency in French after so much listening to "a mixture of various Turkish languages, demotic Greek, and Italian" (*Le secrétaire turc*, preface, n.p.).

53 Moulin and Chuvin, in *L'Islam*, speculate that Montagu's religious interlocutor must have belonged to the order of the Bektashi, a secret Janissary syncretist sect. Though Montagu calls them deists, Rycaut interprets the Bektash as athe-ists. See "Arnawutluk" and "Bektashiya" in H. A. R. Gibb and J. H. Kramers, eds., *Encyclopedia of Islam* (Leiden: E. J. Brill, 1974).

54 For a discussion of this passage, see Felicity Nussbaum, *Torrid Zones*, 91-92.

55 Joseph W. Lew, "Lady Mary's Portable Seraglio," *Eighteenth-Century Studies* 24 (1991): 433, claims that Montagu's "description of how Oriental women subverted order anticipated by two hundred fifty years the work of feminists such as Mernissi and Abu-Lughod." Such a claim is dubious and rendered fur-ther problematic by the continuation of transhistorical orientalist approaches in some of the feminist criticisms of Islam. See Fatima Mernissi, *The Veil and the Male Elite: A Feminist Interpretation of Women's Rights in Islam*, trans. Mary J. Lakeland (New York: Addison Wesley, 1991); and Fatna A. Sabbah, *Woman in the Muslim Unconscious* (New York: Pergamon, 1984).

56 As Lisa Lowe argues throughout *Critical Terrains*, heterogeneity and ambiva-lence characterize the diverse orientalisms present at different historical mo-ments.

1 See Terry Eagleton, *The Ideology of the Aesthetic* (Oxford: Blackwell, 1990), 52–61; Frances Ferguson, *Solitude and the Sublime: Romanticism and the Aesthetics of Individuation* (London: Routledge, 1992), 37–54; Gerald Newman, *The Rise of English Nationalism: A Cultural History, 1740–1830* (New York: St. Martin's Press, 1987); and Linda Colley, *Britons, Forging the Nation, 1707–1837* (New Haven: Yale UP, 1992).

2 See Jean-François Lyotard, *The Postmodern Condition: A Report on Knowledge,* trans. Geoff Bennington and Brian Massumi (Minneapolis: U of Minnesota P, 1984), 81; and Martin Jay, *Downcast Eyes: The Denigration of Vision in Twentieth-Century French Thought* (Berkeley: U of California P, 1993).

3 Alain Grosrichard, *Structure du sérail: La fiction du despotisme asiatique dans l'Occident classique* (Paris: Seuil, 1979), 73.

4 All references are to Edmund Burke, *A Philosophical Enquiry into the Origin of Our Ideas of the Sublime and Beautiful,* ed. with an introduction and notes by James T. Boulton (Notre Dame, IN: U of Notre Dame P, 1958). Page numbers are cited parenthetically in the text. See William Cheselden, "An Account of Some Observations made by a young Gentleman, who was born blind," *Philosophical Transactions of the Royal Society* 34 (1728): 447–50. Burke continues, "the boy appears by the account to have been particularly observing and sensible for one of his age: and therefore, it is probable, if the great uneasiness he felt at the first sight of black had arisen from its connexion with any other disagreeable ideas, he would have observed and mentioned it" (145). Burke only slightly modifies Cheselden's description, which runs, "but some Months after, seeing by Accident a Negroe Woman, he was struck with great Horror at the Sight" (448).

5 For a full background of the Molyneux debate and its repercussions, see Michael J. Morgan, *Molyneux's Question: Vision, Touch and the Philosophy of Perception* (Cambridge: Cambridge UP, 1987), and William R. Paulson, *Enlightenment, Romanticism, and the Blind in France* (Princeton, NJ: Princeton UP, 1987), and Jay, *Downcast Eyes,* 83–147. See Locke, *Essay Concerning Human Understanding,* II, ix, §8–9. For a useful summary of the implications of the debate for Enlightenment theories of visual perception, see Michael Baxandall, *Shadows and Enlightenment* (New Haven: Yale UP, 1995), 17–31.

6 Meg Armstrong, "'The Effects of Blackness': Gender, Race, and the Sublime in Aesthetic Theories of Burke and Kant," *Journal of Aesthetics and Art Criticism* 54.3 (summer 1996): 217, 228. Paul Gilroy also cites this passage, as does Sara Suleri (see note 65), but Armstrong's is the first full-scale discussion of the trajectory of this specific tropology. See Paul Gilroy, *The Black Atlantic: Modernity and Double Consciousness* (Cambridge, MA: Harvard UP, 1993), 9–10.

7 For an extended evaluation of Montesquieu's influence on Burke, see C. P. Courtney, *Montesquieu and Burke* (Oxford: Blackwell, 1963).

8   Abacination is a word of Latin origin, to describe punitive blinding, accomplished by searing the eyeballs with a red-hot metal disk or basin.

9   Punitive blinding was practiced in Persia but not in Turkey. See Sir John Chardin, *Le Couronnement de Soliman III, Roi de Perse* (Paris, 1671) and *Voyages de M. le Chevalier Chardin en Perse et autres lieux de l'Orient* (Amsterdam, 1711). Part I of the Voyages was published in London in 1686. False rumors concerning the blinding of Prince Safi are a major theme of the plots following the death of Abbas II in 1666. Safi was crowned king after a faithful eunuch who had seen the prince in the confines of his harem testified to Safi's sight. According to Chardin, Safi was in danger of being passed over for his minor brother by scheming nobles. An earlier king, Abbas I (1587–1629), was renowned for having either killed or blinded all his sons. The punishment preempted the potential usurpation of the throne. See also the discussion in Grosrichard, *Structure du sérail* 71–96.

10 Chardin, *Voyages* 2:214, cited in Grosrichard, *Structure du sérail* 71; my translation.

11 Grosrichard, *Structure du sérail* 73.

12 Ferguson, *Solitude and the Sublime* 40.

13 See Joseph Spence, *An Account of the Life, Character, and Poems of Mr. Blacklock* (London, 1754). Spence says, "some of the greatest Poets that ever were in the World, have been blind; and 'tis very probable, that the Loss of their Sight may have added to the Force of their Imagination . . . our Author speaks of . . . the Flashing, Gleaming, Glowing, Glaring, and Blazing of different Objects; some of these in a literal Way, but more in a profess'd metaphorical one" (36–37).

14 Diderot discusses Saunderson's genius in great detail; see Denis Diderot, *Lettre sur les aveugles à l'usage de ceux qui voient* (Paris: Garnier Flammarion, 1972). See also William Inchclif, *The Life and Character of Dr. Nicholas Saunderson* (Dublin, 1747).

15 Peter de Bolla discusses fruitfully Burke's obsession with power, although not in relation to oriental despotism; see *The Discourse of the Sublime: Readings in History, Aesthetics and the Subject* (Oxford: Blackwell, 1989), 59–72.

16 For a perspicuous treatment of the sublime implications of Job, interpreted in relation to an absorbing collocation of texts, see Jonathan Lamb, *The Rhetoric of Suffering: Reading the Book of Job in the Eighteenth Century* (Oxford: Clarendon, 1995).

17 See *The Spectator* 415 (Thursday, June 26, 1712) in Joseph Addison, *Critical Essays from The Spectator*, ed. Donald F. Bond (New York: Oxford UP, 1970), 186–90, 188.

18 Andrew Ashfield and Peter de Bolla, eds., *The Sublime: A Reader in British Eighteenth-Century Aesthetic Theory* (Cambridge: Cambridge UP, 1996), 6.

19 The black slave woman could be a prime exhibit for Neil Hertz's interpretation of Burke's sublime as a preoedipal casting out of the maternal abject by the

provisional subject, even though I am skeptical of such an interpretation of this episode. Neil Hertz's reading is a useful contrast to that of Thomas Weiskel's, who interprets the Burkean sublime as "negative" and "metaphorical," representing oedipalization and castration anxiety that solidifies the ego as supersensible. See Neil Hertz, *The End of the Line: Essays on Psychoanalysis and the Sublime* (New York: Columbia UP, 1985), 40-60, 217-39; and Thomas Weiskel, *The Romantic Sublime: Studies in the Structure and Psychology of Transcendence* (Baltimore: Johns Hopkins UP, 1976), 28-32; 83-106. Weiskel describes a negative or metaphorical sublime as one in which the subject creates a metaphorical substitution in order to ward off a lack of signification, whereas a "metonymical sublime" consists of an experience of overwhelming meaning that motivates a displacement of signified excess into spatial and temporal contiguity.

20 Hence, Mitchell unconventionally argues for an anti-Romantic strain in Burke. However, this provocative reading of Burke's *Enquiry* retroactively from the response to the French Revolution depends heavily on the homology between sublime aesthetics (Romanticism) and political iconoclasm (the French Revolution). I have tried to show that, on the contrary, the figure of oriental despotism maintains this double structure of discontinuity (lack) and intricacy (excess). Despite this procedural disagreement, I find Mitchell's reading of Burke interestingly provocative, as he is the only recent critic of Burke who accurately identifies the orientalist contexts of Burkean defenses of English idolatry against French iconoclasm. See W. J. T. Mitchell, *Iconology: Image, Text, Ideology* (Chicago: U of Chicago P, 1986), 140.

21 All references are to volume 8 of *The Writings and Speeches of Edmund Burke*, ed. Paul Langford (Oxford: Clarendon, 1978-) and are parenthetical hereafter.

22 *Essay Concerning Human Understanding* II, xi, §2.

23 This section (along with additional later passages that contain yawning precipices) indicates a fear of collapse—in terms of falling asleep or falling off a precipice—which is very close to the metaphorical sublime that Thomas Weiskel describes (*Romantic Sublime* 143, 148).

24 Muhsin Jassim Ali, *Scheherezade in England: A Study of Nineteenth-Century English Criticism of* The Arabian Nights (Washington, DC: Three Continents Press, 1981), 16-17; Robert Heron, preface to *Arabian Tales* (1792) (*Scheherezade in England* 31). According to Robert Halsband, Mary Wortley Montagu owned all ten volumes of Galland's *Mille et une nuits* in 1739. She too, like Pope, was circulating the tales privately as early as 1724. See Robert Halsband, *The Complete Letters of Lady Mary Wortley Montagu* (Oxford: Clarendon, 1965), 1: 385.

25 Gibbon gives little credence to the story or others that circulated about Muhammad's cruelty, including one that reports his disembowelment of fourteen pages to discover which of them had stolen and eaten a melon. However, Gibbon concurs that Muhammad often "spilt a torrent of blood on the slightest provocation." See Edward Gibbon, *The Decline and Fall of the Roman Empire*

(London: Everyman, 1910), 6:472; and L. Thuasne, *Gentile Bellini et Sultan Mohammed II: Notes sure le séjour du peintre vénitien à Constantinople (1479–1480)* (Paris: Ernst Leroux, 1888). See also Voltaire, *Essai sur les moeurs,* (1756; Paris: Garnier Frères, 1963), 817–18.

26 See Jean-François Lyotard, *The Differend: Phrases in Dispute,* trans. George van den Abbeele (Minneapolis: U of Minnesota P, 1988), 168. I am also indebted here to the perspicuous discussion in Jonathan Lamb, "Longinus, the Dialectic, and the Practice of Mastery," *ELH* 60 (Fall 1993): 545–67.

27 See Roger De Piles, *The Art of Painting* (London, 1754), 158.

28 There were several previous attempts to bring the story of Irene to the stage. See Gilbert Swinhoe, *The Tragedy of the Unhappy Fair Irene* (London, 1658); Roger L'Estrange, *Irena* (London, 1664); Charles Goring, *Irene, Or, the Fair Greek* (London, 1708); and George Peele's lost "famous play of Turkish Mahomet and Hyrin the fair Greek." For an account of these antecedents and their relation to Johnson's play, see David Nichol Smith, *Samuel Johnson's* Irene (Oxford: Clarendon, 1929), and Michael R. Booth, ed. Irene *in Eighteenth-Century Tragedy* (London: Oxford UP, 1965), 67–154.

29 See G. B. Hill, ed., *Boswell's Life of Johnson* (Oxford: Clarendon, 1934), 1:197.

30 An anonymous critic addresses this audience desire sarcastically: "I doubt not, but some of our *Conoisseurs* expected, according to the old Story, to have seen her Head taken off by *Mahomet,* at one Stroke of his Scymitar; which, when perform'd to the Height of Expectation, cou'd have been but a Pantomime Trick, and beneath the Dignity of a Tragedy; unless you cou'd suppose, the Hero was bred a Butcher. — As to the Trick, perhaps, some of our tender hearted Countrymen, wou'd have eas'd that Objection, by having her Head cut off in good Earnest, and so have had the Pleasure of a new *Irene* every Night" (*A Criticism on* Mahomet and Irene *in a Letter to the Author* [London, 1749], 16–17).

31 Lamb, *Rhetoric of Suffering* 10.

32 See Gwin J. Kolb, introduction to Samuel Johnson, *Rasselas and Other Tales* (New Haven: Yale UP, 1990), xxxiii. All parenthetical references are to this edition.

33 "The real reason why Ethiopia is called Abassia and the Ethiopians Abyssinians is that that word means a free and independent people (in Arabic, Turkish, and the language of the Ethiopians), who had never recognized a foreign king" (Manoel de Almeida, *The History of High Ethiopia or Abassia,* in *Some Records of Ethiopia 1593–1646,* ed. C. F. Beckingham and G. W. B. Huntingford [London: Hakluyt Society, 1954], 8). The editors amend Almeida's spurious etymology as follows: "This is nonsense, but the old national name Ge'ez which is still applied to the Ethiopic language and which originally meant 'migratory' can also mean 'liberated,' 'manumitted,' and hence 'free'" (8n).

34 In the past, there has been a vibrant debate about specific details in Johnson's source materials. See Ellen Douglas Leyburn, "'No Romantick Absurdities

or Incredible Fictions': The Relation of Johnson's *Rasselas* to Lobo's *Voyage to Abyssinia*," *PMLA* 70.5 (December 1955): 1059–67; and Donald M. Lockhart, "'The Fourth Son of the Mighty Emperor': The Ethiopian Background of Johnson's *Rasselas*," *PMLA* 78.5 (December 1963): 516–28. Lockhart convincingly identifies the original anecdote in Ludolf's *Historica Aethiopia* that lists a fourth son, "N. N.," also referred to as "Rasselach," who "escaped from the Rock of *Amhara*," as well as the name "Imlac" (518). Evaluating a range of Ethiopian histories that Johnson possibly had access to, including narratives by Alvares, Castanhoso, Urreta, Godinho, Telles, Barrati, Ludolf, Poncet, Lobo, and Le Grand, Lockhart debunks Leyburn's derivation of the name Rasselas from the Rassela Christos mentioned in Johnson's translation of Lobo. All this preparatory reading by Johnson—believed to have been developed, according to Lockhart, in the form of notes—casts doubt on the apocryphal anecdote fostered by Boswell that *Rasselas* was conceptualized and executed in a single week.

35 See Samuel Johnson, *A Voyage to Abyssinia by Father Jerome Lobo A Portuguese Jesuit* (London, 1735). Johnson's commitment to a *via negativa* definition of prose realism is obvious in that text. His preface argues that the book presents "no Romantick Absurdities or Incredible Fictions, whatever he [Lobo] relates, whether true or not, is at least probable, and he who tells nothing exceeding the bounds of probability, has a right to demand, that they should believe him, who cannot contradict him . . . he meets with no Basilisks that destroy with their Eyes, his Crocodiles devour their Prey without Tears, and his Cataracts fall from the Rock without Deafening the Neighbouring Inhabitants . . . here are no *Hottentots* without Religion, Polity, or Articulate Language, no *Chinese* perfectly Polite, and completely skilled in all Sciences" (viii). See also the excellent introduction to the Yale Johnson volume 15, in Samuel Johnson, *A Voyage to Abyssinia*, ed. Joel J. Gold (New Haven: Yale UP, 1985), xxiii–lviii.

36 Though there are many such instances of this, it may suffice to mention as an example the description of *Rasselas* as "an educational tale about the nature of aesthetic understanding" (Edward Tomarken, *Johnson,* Rasselas *and the Choice of Criticism* [Lexington: UP of Kentucky, 1989], 6).

37 Gwin J. Kolb, "The Reception of *Rasselas*, 1759–1800," *Rasselas and Other Tales*, xlvi.

38 This is where I disagree with Fredric Bogel's fine reading, "Fables of Knowing: Melodrama and Related Forms," *Genre* 11.1 (spring 1978): 83–108. Bogel asserts that the lack of "concrete particularity" in *Rasselas* makes it "only superficially Eastern . . . Johnson's aim is to nudge the story away from the local and the particular" (84–85). On the contrary, the moral fable and the epistemological fable that Bogel discusses, as Martha Pike Conant's classifications reveal, are most typical of the oriental tale. Paradoxically, the move away from particularity is what resituates the tale back into the orientalist locale from which its fabulism

appears to escape through reference to morality. See Martha Pike Conant, *The Oriental Tale in England in the Eighteenth Century* (New York: Columbia UP, 1908). Similarly, when theorists such as Slavoj Žižek (*The Sublime Object of Ideology* [London: Verso, 1989]) argue that all collectives are based on this rhetorical structure of the false universal, such theorizing is itself based on a spurious universalization of all collectivities. Paradoxical though this may sound, it is important to argue for the particularity of each false generalization that differentiates it from any other false generalization. In an impressive article on "common sense" in *Rasselas* and *Vathek*, Alan Liu also speaks of the collective figment of the false universal, revealed in the two fictions through the trope of the catachrestical synecdoche; see "Toward a Theory of Common Sense: Beckford's *Vathek* and Johnson's *Rasselas*," *Texas Studies in Literature and Language* 26.1 (spring 1984): 183–217. *Rasselas* and *Vathek* are a popular combination for surveys of gothic or orientalia, as they represent what appear to be two extremes of the oriental tale and what is in fact, as Liu provocatively argues, a false polarity. See, for instance, Ernest Baker, "The Oriental Story from *Rasselas* to *Vathek*," in *The History of the English Novel* (London: Witherby, 1934), 55–76; and Harrison R. Steaves, "Oriental Romance," in *Before Jane Austen: The Shaping of the English Novel in the 18th Century* (London: Allen and Unwin, 1966), 226–42.

39 Alvares speaks of a particular instance of an escaped prince, a brother of the Prester John: "everybody said that he would die, or that they would put out his eyes." Succession is described as follows: "as soon as the father should close his eyes, and one of them be made King, the others would go to the mountain like their predecessors." Alvares speaks of being stoned near the mountain gates where "the darkness was like having no eyes," and the punishment for anyone who attempted the gates was "to cut off his feet and hands, and put out his eyes, and leave him lying there." See C. F. Beckingham and G. W. B. Huntingford, eds., *The Prester John of the Indies: A True Relation of the Lands of the Prester John, being the narrative of the Portuguese Embassy to Ethiopia in 1520 written by Father Francisco Alvares*, trans. Lord Stanley of Alderley (London: Hakluyt Society, 1881; rev. Cambridge: Cambridge UP, 1961), 246, 248, 238–39.

40 "I pardon him for leaving the happy valley, though, had he not divested himself of his obedience to his sovereign and father, Sarza and Menas would never have dared to attempt an escape superior to their courage and to their penetration" (Ellis Cornelia Knight, *Dinarbas; A Tale; Being a Continuation of Rasselas, Prince of Abissinia*, ed. Ann Messenger [East Lansing, MI: Colleagues Press, 1993], 61). Many vicissitudes are to follow this return, including reimprisonment in the Happy Valley along with the emperor himself because of the guile of the usurper Menas. Knight ends the sequel with Rasselas's decision to educate his sole surviving younger brother and close the institution of the Happy Valley, as well as with the marriages of Rasselas and Nekayah.

41 Translation modified from Jean Le Rond D'Alembert, *Preliminary Discourse to the Encyclopedia of Diderot* (Indianapolis: Bobbs-Merrill, 1963) 46–47. See Abbé Guillaume-Thomas Raynal, *Histoire philosophique et politique du commerce et des établissemens des européens dans les deux Indes* (Paris, 1781), 1:1–3.

42 A typical reading of this kind is Louis A. Landa's informative article, "Johnson's Feathered Man: 'A Dissertation on the Art of Flying' Considered," in *Essays in Eighteenth-Century English Literature* (Princeton, NJ: Princeton UP, 1980), 160–77. Gwin Kolb also discusses, in his introduction, Johnson's familiarity with John Wilkins's thoughts on flying in his *Mathematical Magick: or the Wonders that may be Performed by Mechanical Geometry* (1648). Another contemporary work on flying that Johnson knew and recommended was Noel Antoine Pluche's *Spectacle de la nature, Or, Nature Displayed* (1733), to which a connection is also made by Landa in the above article. There is also the reference in *The Rambler* 199 (February 11, 1752), to Hermeticus the sage, who says he has "twice dislocated [his] limbs, and once fractured [his] skull, in essaying to fly"; see Samuel Johnson, *The Rambler*, ed. Walter Jackson Bate and Albrecht B. Strauss (New Haven: Yale UP, 1969), 5:271–76.

43 See Johnson, *The Rambler*, nos. 204 and 205, 5:296, 302, 305.

44 The inherent reversibility of Occident and Orient matches the contingent effects of the Longinian sublime in relation to power, in the example of Queen Zenobia as discussed by Lamb, "Longinus, the Dialectic, and the Practice of Mastery," 545–67.

45 See Liu, "Toward a Theory of Common Sense"; and J. C. D. Clark, "Religious Affiliation and Dynastic Allegiance in Eighteenth-Century England: Edmund Burke, Thomas Paine, and Samuel Johnson," *ELH* 64.4 (winter 1997), 1060.

46 See Grosrichard, "Le paradoxe du vizir," in *Structure du sérail* 92–95.

47 See Samuel Johnson, *Journey to the Western Islands*, ed. Mary Lascelles (New Haven: Yale UP, 1971), 164. For a superb rhetorical reading of the implications of this passage, see Martin Wechselblatt, "Finding Mr. Boswell: Rhetorical Authority and National Identity in Johnson's *A Journey to the Western Islands of Scotland*," *ELH* 60.1 (spring 1993): 117–48.

48 See *An Arabian Tale, From an Unpublished Manuscript: With Notes Critical and Explanatory* (London, 1786), 1–2. All references are to this edition, translated from the French by Samuel Henley under Beckford's guidance but published in 1786 without Beckford's permission. Henley's English edition, with its infelicitous punctuation and occasional mistranslation, was the *Vathek* that English readers knew for thirty years until Beckford's so-called third edition of 1816. The novel is available through Roger Lonsdale's revised presentation of the 1816 version in the Oxford World's Classics series. See William Beckford, *Vathek* (London: Oxford UP, 1983).

49 My translation, from D'Herbelot, *Bibliothèque Orientale . . .* (Paris, 1697), 912: "le Khalife Vathek avoit l'œil si terrible, qu'ayant jetté un peu avant sa mort, une

œillade de colere sur un de ses Domestiques qui avoit fait quelque manquement, cet homme en perdit contenance, & se renversa sur un autre qui étoit proche de luy. Et par un accident assez extraordinaire, il arriva que le même étant expiré, & son visage couvert d'un linge, une fouine se glissa par dessous, & luy arracha ce même œil dont les regards étoient si redoutables." Biographers also relate the basilisk stare to Beckford's perception of his father's dreadful gaze. The invaluable reference for all Beckford criticism is the magisterial André Parreaux, *William Beckford, Auteur de* Vathek *(1760-1844)* (Paris: Nizet, 1960).

50 See *Charoba, Queen of Egypt* in *Oriental Tales,* ed. Robert L. Mack (New York: Oxford UP, 1992), 210.

51 The etymology of pismire suggests that the strong smell of formic acid around anthills contributes to the association of ants with "piss"; we might say "sal ammoniac," after the narrator's delightful euphemism for camel urine later in the story.

52 Indeed, *Vathek* represents a moment in the process of externalizing homosexuality as an "Eastern" cultural perversion just when we witness, as Haggerty points out, "the emergence of homosexuality into something like its Victorian configuration" (343). Potkay's reading of Beckford's homosexuality, although sympathetic, tends to replicate the familiarly problematic Freudian developmental narrative. To Potkay, the Palaces of the Five Senses represent "the pancorporal sensuality that precedes the putatively genital-centered sexuality of the adult"; and this results in "Vathek blindly coming under the sway of female ambitions" (80, 82). George Haggerty has associated this trope with the homosexual undertones of male Gothic novelists such as Horace Walpole, "Monk" Lewis, and of course Beckford. Adam Potkay, with the Faustian bargain and its homosexual implications in mind, dubs *Vathek* "the first antibildungsroman." See George E. Haggerty, "Literature and Homosexuality in the Late 18th Century: Walpole, Beckford, Lewis," *Studies in the Novel* 18.4 (winter 1986): 343; and Adam Potkay, "Beckford's Heaven of Boys," *Raritan* 13.1 (summer 1993): 80.

53 The proximity of Piranesi to Beckford is mentioned by Jorge Luis Borges, *Other Inquisitions* (Austin: U of Texas P, 1964), 139; and Mario Praz, introduction to *Three Gothic Novels* (Harmondsworth, UK: Penguin, 1968), 7-34. One critic speculates that Vathek's mistake derives from the occidentalist approach to geography encouraged by Carathis, whereas Beckford wishes to foster an "orientalist perception of the Islamic tolerance, even nurture of repetition." One more indication of this cultural difference in the tale is that, for the Muslim, the "horizontality of the mosque's architecture is an aid rather than an obstacle to spiritualization"; see John Garrett, "Ending in Infinity: William Beckford's Arabian Tale," *Eighteenth-Century Fiction* 5.1 (October 1992): 23, 25-26.

54 See Vijay Mishra, *The Gothic Sublime* (Albany: State U of New York P, 1994), 229-30. Seeing an adjectival sublime as the attempt to contain the sublime

within a descriptive category, Mishra argues that the sublime regressively colonizes the adjective, contaminating its descriptive efficacy. This principle holds true for this chapter's delineation of a broadly oriental sublime as well. Mishra's Lacanian reading describes the Gothic sublime as "the embodiment of a pure negativity" into which the subject inscribes itself as an absence or lack in the structure (17).

55 Ugly eunuchs' names, like "Hyacinth, Narcissus, Rose, Carnation," were names of dried flowers that cannot reproduce; see Grosrichard, *Structure du sérail* 187.

56 There are also errors, such as the missing relative pronoun "who," inserted later by Beckford for the 1816 edition at the point indicated above.

57 Beckford's simultaneous rendition of orientalist parody alongside "serious" orientalism has confused many a critic. This "fringe effect," as Alan Liu calls it, is neither a sign of the lack of stylistic control, as James Rieger has argued, nor is it just the sign of a satire of the genre of the oriental tale, as interpreted by James Folsom. This is why it is never simply a question of sorting out the "oriental" sources from the "nonoriental" ones, as Kenneth Graham attempts to do. See Liu, "Toward a Theory of Common Sense"; James Henry Rieger, "Au Pied de la Lettre: Stylistic Uncertainty in *Vathek*," *Criticism* 4.4 (fall 1962): 302–12; James K. Folsom, "Beckford's *Vathek* and the Tradition of Oriental Satire," *Criticism* 6.1 (winter 1964): 53–69; and Kenneth W. Graham, "Beckford's Adaptation of the Oriental Tale in *Vathek*," *Enlightenment Essays* 5.1 (spring 1974): 24–33.

58 As Garrett says, "the myopic floundering of all characters, good and bad, diminishes them to the status of dwarves" ("Ending in Infinity," 33).

59 Grosrichard, *Structure du sérail* 173.

60 See Nicolas Boulanger, *The Origin and Progress of Despotism in the Oriental and Other Empires of Africa, Europe, and America* (Amsterdam, 1774), 14, 16. Boulanger's opening suggests a Burkean connection: "Even in our times travellers are often spectators of barbarous and tragic scenes, the constant effects of a shocking and detestable constitution, where *one* makes the *whole;* and the *whole* is nothing" (2).

61 See William Beckford, *Biographical Memoirs of Extraordinary Painters* (1780; London, 1834). Given the parodic nature of this instance of Beckford's juvenilia, a camp reading of the illustration could be a fruitful one. Walter Allen describes this as one of the examples of Beckford's grotesque techniques, created by placing an *apparently* inappropriate adjective before a noun. To this we can add the existence of an *apparently* inappropriate frontispiece of decapitation. See Walter Allen, *The English Novel: A Short Critical History* (Harmondsworth, UK: Penguin, 1970), 91.

62 See Tom Furniss, *Edmund Burke's Aesthetic Ideology: Language, Gender, and Political Economy in Revolution* (Cambridge: Cambridge UP, 1993), 1–112; and

Ronald Paulson, *Representations of Revolution (1789–1820)* (London: Yale UP, 1983). Parreaux's suggestion that there was a resurgence of oriental tales from 1787 to 1790 is worthy of investigation in light of the interesting correlation it might have with Revolutionary events (Parreaux, *William Beckford* 311). Beckford, for instance, will always see France as "the land of oriental literature" (312). See Kate Teltscher, *India Inscribed: European and British Writing on India 1600–1800* (New Delhi: Oxford UP, 1995), 166.

63 For Burke's very positive account of Islamic law during the Hastings impeachment, see *Writings and Speeches of Edmund Burke*, ed. Paul Langford; *India: The Launching of the Hastings Impeachment 1786–88* (Volume 6), ed. P. J. Marshall (1991) 353–73. See also *India: Madras and Bengal* (Volume 5), ed. P. J. Marshall (1981); P. J. Marshall, *The Impeachment of Warren Hastings* (Oxford: Clarendon, 1965); and *The Impeachment of Warren Hastings,* ed. Geoffrey Carnall and Colin Nicholson (Edinburgh: Edinburgh UP, 1989). Reaction to the French Revolution, when complicated by the writings on the East India Company and the Hastings impeachment, changes received interpretations of Burke's political reflexes. See especially Burke's brilliant speeches opening the impeachment on February 15, 16, 18, and 19, 1788 (6:264–460).

64 In this context, we should appreciate Frans De Bruyn's perspicuous comment that Burke opted for a "conservative gothic" over "narrow legalism" in his speeches against Hastings, and how his portrait of the governor-general of Bengal resembles Ann Radcliffe's villainous Montoni and Milton's Satan. See Frans De Bruyn, "Edmund Burke's Gothic Romance: The Portrayal of Warren Hastings in Burke's Writings and Speeches in India," *Criticism: A Quarterly Journal of the Arts* 29.4 (fall 1987): 415–38. It is also fascinating to note that Indian and Gothic architecture, both alien forms to eighteenth-century English taste, were equally valued, given their superficial similarities. However, Gothic became the English imperial style for mostly accidental reasons. See Christopher Hussey, *The Picturesque: Studies in a Point of View* (London: G. P. Putnam, 1927).

65 See Sara Suleri, "Burke's Indian Sublime," and "Reading the Trial of Warren Hastings," in *The Rhetoric of English India* (Chicago: U of Chicago P, 1992), 24–48, 49–74.

66 Burke, "Speech on Mr. Fox's East India Bill" *Writings and Speeches* (December 1, 1783), 5:390.

67 Johnson justifies Hastings by saying that a "despotick governour" was best for India on the grounds that one plunderer would still serve the nation better than the existence of many; see *Boswell's Life of Johnson* (4:213).

68 See William Bolts, *Considerations on Indian Affairs* (London, 1772); Alexander Dow, *The History of Hindostan* (Amsterdam, 1774), and the appended *The Origin and Progress of Despotism in the Oriental and Other Empires of Africa, Europe, and America* (1774); and for a discussion, Teltscher, *India Inscribed* 163–64. By

1778, Anquetil-Duperron was already asserting that "a system of despotism was created even though it did not exist anywhere in reality"; see Grosrichard, *Structure du sérail* 44 n 2.

69 J. C. D. Clark revives Conor Cruise O'Brien's influential reading of the *Reflections* which analyzed the Revolution as awakening a "slumbering Jacobite" within the elderly Whig. Burke's Jacobitism, for O'Brien and Clark, consists in an emotional response derived from his Irish roots rather than representing a political position. See Conor Cruise O'Brien, Introduction to Edmund Burke, *Reflections on the Revolution in France*, ed. Conor Cruise O'Brien (Harmondsworth, UK: Penguin Books, 1968) 38, and J. C. D. Clark, "Religious Affiliation and Dynastic Allegiance," 1029-32. Burke, like Swift, was of Anglo-Irish descent (although Burke was only a second-generation Anglican descended from Catholic grandparents). His exceptional humanitarian concern for Indian subjects and his desire for parliamentary oversight of the East India Company's political activities, following from his sympathy for Irish Catholics and American colonists, has led to a debate about his motives. Conor Cruise O'Brien argues the case for his general anticolonial propensities, whereas David Musselwhite asserts that he was motivated principally by venal considerations. See Conor Cruise O'Brien, "Warren Hastings in Burke's Great Melody," in *The Impeachment of Warren Hastings*, ed. Carnall and Nicholson, 58-75; and David Musselwhite, "The Trial of Warren Hastings," in *Literature, Politics, Theory*, ed. Francis Barker et al. (London: Methuen, 1986). The anticolonial profile gives us a Catonic classical parallel here; in addition, Burkean rhetoric has been compared with its Ciceronian counterpart. See Geoffrey Carnall, "Burke as Modern Cicero," in *The Impeachment of Warren Hastings*, ed. Carnall and Nicholson, 76-90.

70 Speech in Reply, 4th day, 5 June 1794; see O'Brien, "Warren Hastings," 72.

71 O'Brien, "Warren Hastings," 73; closing speech, 4th day 294-95.

72 Jonathan Lamb discusses this pun very well in *Rhetoric of Suffering* 198.

73 "Through what variety of untry'd being," *Cato* (5.1.11).

SIX *Equiano and the Politics of Literacy*

1 See Gerald Newman, *The Rise of English Nationalism: A Cultural History* (New York: St. Martin's Press, 1987), 120, and especially 63-120; also Linda Colley, *Britons: Forging the Nation 1707-1837* (New Haven: Yale UP, 1992); Richard D. Altick, *The English Common Reader: A Social History of the Mass Reading Public 1800-1900* (Chicago: U of Chicago P, 1957), 30-66; Benedict Anderson, *Imagined Communities: Reflections on the Origin and Spread of Nationalism* (New York: Verso, 1983; rev. 1991); Ernest Renan, "What Is a Nation?" in *Nation and Narration*, ed. Homi K. Bhabha (New York: Routledge, 1990), 8-22.

2   See Charles H. Nichols, "The Slave Narrators and the Picaresque Mode: Archetypes for Modern Black Personae," in *The Slave's Narrative,* ed. Charles T. Davis and Henry Louis Gates Jr. (Oxford: Oxford UP, 1985), 283–97; and Alden T. Vaughn and Edward W. Clark, eds., *Puritans among the Indians: Accounts of Captivity and Redemption 1676–1724* (Cambridge: Belknap Press of Harvard UP, 1981). Although he is often cited as a precursor to the grand nineteenth-century literary tradition of slave narrative, of which there are around 6,000 examples, Equiano and his contemporaries, such as John Marrant, represent a transition point between it and the older seventeenth-century Puritan literature of Indian captivity and redemption. See Davis and Gates, eds., *The Slave's Narrative,* especially James Olney, "'I was Born': Slave Narratives, Their Status as Autobiography and as Literature," 148–75; William Andrews, *To Tell a Free Story: The First Century of Afro-American Autobiography, 1760–1865* (Urbana: U of Illinois P, 1986); and Henry Louis Gates Jr. *The Signifying Monkey: A Theory of African-American Literary Criticism* (Oxford: Oxford UP, 1988), 152–58. The earliest identified autobiography by an African slave is a straightforward Indian captivity narrative, *Narrative of the Uncommon Sufferings and Surprising Deliverance of Briton Hammon, A Negro Man* (Boston, 1760). Similarly, John Marrant's autobiography, *A Narrative of the Lord's Wonderful Dealings with John Marrant, A Black* (London, 1785), describes a full-scale evangelical mission by the black author among Native Americans.

3   See the insightful discussion in Christopher Miller, *Theories of Africans: Francophone Literature and Anthropology in Africa* (Chicago: U of Chicago P, 1990), 5–6, 31–67. Miller says that "francophone African literature has always practiced some form of anthropological rhetoric" (6). This description can be applied to the early phases of many Anglophone postcolonial "literatures."

4   See Susan M. Warren, "Between Slavery and Freedom: The Transgressive Self in Olaudah Equiano's Autobiography," *PMLA* 108.1 (January 1993): 94–105; and Joseph Fichtelberg, "Word between Worlds: The Economy of Equiano's Narrative," *American Literary History* 5.3 (fall 1993): 459–80. For other important celebrations of Equiano, see Houston Baker, *Blues, Ideology, and Afro-American Literature: A Vernacular Theory* (Chicago: U of Chicago P, 1984); Wilfred D. Samuels, "Disguised Voice in *The Interesting Narrative of Olaudah Equiano, or Gustavus Vassa the African,*" *Black American Literature Forum* 19 (1985): 64–69; Keith Sandiford, *Measuring the Moment: Strategies of Protest in Eighteenth-Century Afro-English Writing* (Selinsgrove, PA: Susquehanna UP, 1988); and Valerie Smith, *Self-Discovery and Authority in Afro-American Narrative* (Cambridge, MA: Harvard UP, 1987). For another qualified criticism of Equiano's "dissident colonialism," see Geraldine Murphy, "Olaudah Equiano, Accidental Tourist," *Eighteenth-Century Studies* 27.4 (summer 1994): 551–68. See also Sonia Hofkosh, "Tradition and *The Interesting Narrative:* Capitalism,

Abolition, and the Romantic Individual," in *Romanticism, Race, and Imperial Culture, 1780–1834*, eds. Alan Richardson and Sonia Hofkosh (Bloomington: Indiana UP, 1996), 330–43.

5 Though I admire Paul Gilroy's transnationalist motivations, I find his analysis too idealized. The black Atlantic, as a public sphere, appears to parody the ideals of Enlightenment cosmopolitanism and socialist internationalism with its frictionless circulation of solidaristic ideas. See Paul Gilroy, *The Black Atlantic: Modernity and Double Consciousness* (Cambridge, MA: Harvard UP, 1993).

6 See C. Lloyd and J. L. S. Coulter, *Medicine and the Navy 1200–1900:* Vol. 3, *1714–1815* (Edinburgh: Edinburgh UP, 1961).

7 [François] Froger, *A Relation of a Voyage Made in the Years 1695, 1696, 1697 on the Coasts of Africa* (London, 1698), 3–4; "Old Dick Grog's Account of Crossing the Line," in *Fairburn's Naval Songster or, Jack Tar's Chest of Conviviality* (London, 1811), 3–5. According to another contemporary definition, ducking is "a penalty which veteran sailors pretend to inflict on those who, for the first time, pass the Equator, if they refuse to pay the usual fine" (Robert Wilson, *The Seaman's Manual* [London, 1788], 36). For a compendium of texts documenting this ceremony, see Harry Miller Lydenberg, ed., *Crossing the Line: Tales of the Ceremony during Four Centuries* (New York: New York Public Library, 1957); and for an exhaustive analysis of the associated practices, see Henning Henningsen, *Crossing the Equator: Sailors' Baptism and Other Initiation Rites* (Copenhagen: Munksgaard, 1961).

8 All references are to the two-volume first edition of 1789 with parenthetical citations to volume and page number. See Adam Potkay and Sandra Burr, eds., *Black Atlantic Writers of the Eighteenth Century: Living the New Exodus in England and the Americas* (New York: St. Martin's Press, 1995), ix. This is not an oversight on the part of the editors. As they explain, their "principle of selection in the present volume serves to exclude 18th-century black writers less centrally concerned with the drama of the Christian life" (18 n. 18). Important figures who are correspondingly excluded are Ignatius Sancho, Briton Hammon, Venture Smith, and the Sierra Leone settlers.

9 Potkay and Burr, on the other hand, are quite sensitive to the question of religious syncretism, suggesting a "proximity between Christian conversion and the West African religious tradition of ecstatic soul possession" (*Black Atlantic Writers* 6). However, the teleology and uneven reciprocity of a sentence such as this one should give us pause: "[S]urely it was evangelicalism that gave these Africans an English voice, but, conversely, these voices gave evangelicalism a new resonance, by making it clear that each Christian self is rooted in cultural pasts that cannot and ought not to be forgotten" (3)! Constructing a "Christian self" as something in the *present* that is, in turn, rooted in a cultural *past* that is "African" makes for an Enlightenment narrative that subsumes more interest-

ing contradictions. Even though Equiano endorses such evolutionism, critics ought to look harder at his *performance* of Christianity for an English audience.

10 See Isabel Rivers, *Reason, Grace, and Sentiment: A Study of the Language of Religion and Ethics in England, 1660–1780: Vol. 1, Whichcote to Wesley* (New York: Cambridge UP, 1991), 206–13.

11 Potkay and Burr, *Black Atlantic Writers* 13.

12 See Margaret Priestley, "Philip Quaque of Cape Coast," in *Africa Remembered: Narratives by West Africans from the Era of the Slave Trade*, ed. Philip D. Curtin (Madison: U of Wisconsin P, 1967), 99–112.

13 Clinging to the third stage, Potkay is forced to interpret the textual subversions and tropicalizations of the genre of spiritual autobiography as Equiano's legacy of "finely honed ethical irony"; see Adam Potkay, "Olaudah Equiano and the Art of Spiritual Autobiography," *Eighteenth-Century Studies* 27.4 (summer 1994): 681, 687, 690.

14 Needless to say, this is the dialectical nature of Equiano's nationalization. See Fredric Jameson, *The Political Unconscious: Narrative as a Socially Symbolic Act* (Ithaca, NY: Cornell UP, 1981), 74. See also Northrop Frye, *The Anatomy of Criticism* (Princeton, NJ: Princeton UP, 1957), 116.

15 The annotations to Carretta's modernization of the 9th edition of 1794 are very useful for tracking changes made by Equiano during his lifetime. See Olaudah Equiano, *The Interesting Narrative and Other Writings*, ed. Vincent Carretta (New York: Penguin, 1995).

16 See Henry Brooke, *Gustavus Vassa, the Deliverer of His Country* (London, 1739).

17 See Walter F. Pitts, *Old Ship of Zion: The Afro-Baptist Ritual in the African Diaspora* (New York: Oxford UP, 1993), 46.

18 The title makes for an interesting ambiguity by printing the first part in unevenly sized capital lines: THE INTERESTING NARRATIVE OF THE LIFE OF OLAUDAH EQUIANO, OR GUSTAVUS VASSA, THE AFRICAN. *WRITTEN BY HIMSELF.* The anomalousness of "GUSTAVUS VASSA, THE AFRICAN" in the title page is one that the caption under the facing-page portrait is probably designed to resolve. The italicized capitals "*WRITTEN BY HIMSELF*" after the period also emphasizes the autobiographical self-reflexivity mirroring book, title, and author.

19 The title page proper has as its epigraph *Isaiah* 12:2, 4.

20 See C. F. Pascoe, *Society for the Propagation of the Gospel in Foreign Parts: An Historical Account* (London: Society for the Propagation of the Gospel, 1901), 256.

21 See Appendix A and Appendix B to Carretta, ed. *The Interesting Narrative*, 309–16.

22 "The work is written with that *naiveté*, I had almost said, that roughness of a man of nature. His manner is that of Daniel De Foe, in his Robinson Crusoe: it is that of Jameira Duval, who from the rank of a cow-keeper to hermits, be-

Notes to Chapter Six

came librarian to Francis the first, and whose unprinted memoirs, so worthy of publication, are in the hands of Ameilhon"; see Abbé Henri Grégoire, *An Enquiry Concerning the Intellectual and Moral Faculties, and Literature of Negroes; Followed with an Account of the Life and Works of Fifteen Negroes, and Mulattoes, distinguished in Science, Literature and the Arts*, trans. D. B. Warden, secretary to the American Legation at Paris (Brooklyn, 1810).

23 Daniel Defoe, *Robinson Crusoe*, ed. Michael Shinagel (New York: Norton, 1994), 113–14.

24 Ibid., 41. "Seeing my Life has been such a Chequer Work of Nature" are the first words of Defoe's Colonel Jack. See Daniel Defoe, *Colonel Jack* (London: Oxford UP, 1989), 3.

25 See *A Narrative of the Lord's Wonderful Dealings with John Marrant, A Black*, 6th ed. (London, 1788), 18; and *A Narrative of the Most remarkable Particulars in the Life of James Albert Ukawsaw Gronniosaw, an African Prince, As related by himself* (Bath, [1772]), 16; and Mary Prince, *The History of Mary Prince* (1831; London: Pandora, 1986), 119.

26 Anna Maria Falconbridge, *Two Voyages to Sierra Leone During the Years 1791–2-3, In a Series of Letters* (London, 1794), iii, 26. Subsequent references are parenthetical in the text.

27 See *Monthly Review* 80 (June 1789): 551–52; and *A Narrative of the Lord's Dealings with John Marrant, A Black* iii.

28 For the conflicts over the changes in production and labor remuneration, see Peter Linebaugh, *The London Hanged: Crime and Civil Society in the Eighteenth Century* (New York: Cambridge UP, 1992).

29 *General Magazine and Impartial Review* (July 1789): 315.

30 William Dodd, *The African Prince, When in England, to Zara at His Father's Court and Zara's Answer* (London, 1755), 6; Thomas Bluett, *Some Memoirs of the Life of Job, the son of Solomon the High Priest of Boonda in Africa* (London, 1734), 11, 22, 38. In *The Image of Africa: British Ideas and Action, 1780–1850* (Madison: U of Wisconsin P, 1964), Philip D. Curtin persuasively argues that Ayuba bin Suleiman Diallo of Bondu was most probably not of royal status, but a merchant. He is yet another royal impostor, like Prince Aniaba, who had been received by the French court of Louis XIV by playing on naïve European expectations of African royalty. Ayuba was received by the British royal family and presented with a gold watch and about £500 in gifts before he was repatriated.

31 For instance, Thomas Thompson, a Guinea Coast missionary, remarks on the captain of his ship who "had a negro youth whom he had brought from *Africa*, for education, a grandson of *Peter*, King of *Cape Monte;* he had caused him to be baptised, and was now carrying him home"; see *Memoirs of an English Missionary to the Coast of Guinea* (London, 1788), 5.

32 See *The Black Prince. A True Story: Being An Account of the Life and Death of*

Naimbana, *An African King's Son, Who arrived in England in the Year 1791, and set sail on his Return in June, 1793* (London, n.d.) For a discussion of this tale, see Moira Ferguson, *Subject to Others: British Women Writers and Colonial Slavery, 1670–1834* (New York: Routledge, 1992), 220–28. For the fullest exposition of the literary history of the trope of the royal slave, see Wylie Sypher, *Guinea's Captive Kings: British Anti-Slavery Literature of XVIIIth Century* (Chapel Hill: U of North Carolina P, 1942).

33 See *A Narrative of the Most Remarkable Particulars in the Life of James Albert Ukawsaw Gronniosaw, an African Prince, as Related by Himself* (Bath, [1772]), 7; Quobna Ottobah Cugoano, *Thoughts and Sentiments on the Evil and Wicked Traffic of the Slavery and Commerce of the Human Species* (London, 1787), 126; and Abbé Grégoire, *Enquiry Concerning the Intellectual and Moral Faculties* 229. The preface to Sancho's letters ascertains the cause for the failed aspiration: "a defective and incorrigible articulation rendered it abortive"; see Ignatius Sancho, *Letters of the Late Ignatius Sancho an African* (London, 1782), x.

34 The closest equivalent to Embrenche is probably Mgburuichi. See Adiele Afigbo, *Ropes of Sand: Studies in Igbo History and Culture* (Ibadan: Oxford UP, 1981), 152.

35 James Ramsay's *An Essay on the Treatment and Conversion of African Slaves in the Sugar Colonies* (London, 1784), 52–62; James Tobin, *Cursory Remarks Upon the Rev. Mr. Ramsay's Essay* (London, 1785), 141–43.

36 See James Tobin, *A Short Rejoinder to the Rev. Mr. Ramsay's Reply* (London, 1787); and Malachy Postlethwayt, *The African Trade, the Great Pillar and Support of the British Plantation Trade in America* (London, 1745), and *The Importance of the African Expedition Considered* (London, 1758).

37 See Henry Smeathman, *Substance of a Plan of Settlement to be made near Sierra Leona on the Grain Coast of Africa . . .* (London, 1786); and C. B. Wadstrom, *Essay on Colonization* (London, 1794), and *Plan for a Free Community at Sierra Leone Upon the Coast of Africa* (London, 1792), iv. The first four Christian churches, according to Swedenborg, were the Adamite, the Noahite, the Israelite, and the Christian.

38 See Granville Sharp, *A Representation of the Injustice and Dangerous Tendency of Tolerating Slavery in England* (London, 1769) 82.

39 See L. E. C. Evans, "An Early Constitution of Sierra Leone," *Sierra Leone Studies* 18 (November 1932), 28; Granville Sharp, *A Short Sketch of Temporary Regulations (until better shall be proposed for the intended settlement on the grain coast of Africa, near Sierra Leona* (London, 1786), vii, xxvii; Granville Sharp, *Free English Territory in Africa* (London, 1791), 6; Prince Hoare, *Memoirs of Granville Sharp, Esq.* (London, 1820), 320. Sharp also says, "every petty planter, who avails himself of the service of Slaves, is an arbitrary monarch, or rather a lawless Basha in his own territories, notwithstanding that the imaginary freedom of the province, whereon he resides, may seem to forbid the observation."

Notes to Chapter Six

40 John Matthews, *A Voyage to the River Sierra-Leone, on the Coast of Africa* (London, 1791), 74.

41 Sharp reports that "all the jealousies and animosities between the Whites and the Blacks had subsided, and that they had been very orderly ever since Mr. Vasa and two or three other discontented persons had been left on shore at Plymouth"; see Prince Hoare, *Memoirs of Granville Sharp* 313. For Equiano's detailed account concerning the peculations of the government agent and the complaints of the settlers, see *Interesting Narrative* 2:230–43.

42 For the best history of the colony, see Christopher Fyfe, *A History of Sierra Leone* (Oxford: Oxford UP, 1962).

43 See Sharp, *Free English Territory*, 3; Philip D. Curtin, *Image of Africa* 60.

44 Quoted from a letter in Prince Hoare, *Memoirs of Granville Sharp* 313, 316.

45 See Curtin, *Image of Africa* 58–87; and *Death by Migration: Europe's Encounter with the Tropical World in the Nineteenth Century* (New York: Cambridge UP, 1989); see also K. G. Davies, "The Living and the Dead: White Mortality in West Africa, 1684–1732," in *Race and Slavery in the Western Hemisphere: Quantitative Studies*, ed. Stanley L. Engerman and Eugene D. Genovese (Princeton, NJ: Princeton UP, 1975), 83–98. For other records of West African epidemics and medical ethnographies, see James Lind, *Essay on the Diseases Incidental to Europeans in Hot Countries* (London, 1768); Benjamin Moseley, *A Treatise on Tropical Diseases* (London, 1787); Johann Peter Schotte, *A Treatise on the Synochus Atrabiliosa, A Contagious Fever* (London, 1782); and Thomas Winterbottom, *Account of the Native Africans in the Neighbourhood of Sierra Leone*, 2 vols. (London, 1803). Curtin's figures of mortality reveal that between 25 and 75 percent of newly arrived Europeans died in the first year. (The same figures should be relevant for nonacclimated settlers of African descent, such as the Nova Scotian blacks.) After the first year, the death rate for the acclimated survivors was a more acceptable (for the time) 10 percent. Military mortality rates show 483/1,000 in West Africa as compared to 78/1,000 for the West Indies. For instance, in 1782, 350 men were sent to the Gold Coast, but by 1785, only 7 were alive and on duty. See *Image of Africa*, 71, 91.

46 *Postscript to the Report of the Court of Directors of the Sierra Leone Company* (October 19, 1791), 4–5.

47 Abbé Grégoire, *Of the Literature of Negroes* 145.

48 *Proceedings of the Sierra Leone Company* (October 19, 1791), 4.

49 For a full account of the 1791 expedition, see James W. St. G. Walker, *The Black Loyalists: The Search for a Promised Land in Nova Scotia and Sierra Leone, 1783–1870* (London: Longmans and Dalhousie UP, 1976).

50 Though Sharp and the settlers believed that Captain Thompson had bought an area of 20 miles square (400 square miles) from King Tom, renewed discussions about the ceded territory continued, with Alexander Falconbridge, King Jimmy, and King Naimbana as the principal negotiators. The initial settlement

was later reduced to a plot of 2¼ miles fronting the sea by 5–6 miles (11–13 square miles), with three-quarters of it barren, rocky, and mountainous. The history of the next few decades shows that there was considerable confusion and misunderstanding about the transactions on either side, which resulted in occasional skirmishes between the colonists and the indigenes.

51 Matthews, *Voyage to the River Sierra-Leone* 4–5.

52 Prince Hoare, *Memoirs of Granville Sharp* 331–33.

53 Brian V. Street, *Literacy: Theory and Practice* (New York: Cambridge UP, 1984); Olivia Smith, *The Politics of Language 1791–1819* (Oxford: Clarendon, 1984), 9.

54 Hoare, *Memoirs of Granville Sharp* 344.

55 Ibid., 345.

56 Ibid., 346.

57 E. P. Thompson, "Patrician Society, Plebeian Culture," *Journal of Social History* 7.4 (1974): 400.

58 See Christopher Fyfe, ed., *"Our Children Free and Happy": Letters from Black Settlers in Africa in the 1790's* (Edinburgh: Edinburgh UP, 1991).

59 It is important for Jones to attest that this is nonstandard English rather than pidgin or advanced pidgin (creolized) or the later development of Krio, one of the current languages of Sierra Leone, that was formed from the interaction of the Nova Scotian settlers with the local languages. However, the settlers' writings, though orthographically and grammatically nonstandard, are illustrative of the working-class Anglophone syntax of the Nova Scotian blacks.

60 Fyfe, *Our Children*, 51.

61 Ibid.

62 Hoare, *Memoirs of Granville Sharp*, 95.

63 Fyfe, *Our Children*, 52.

64 See R[obert] C[harles] Dallas, *The History of the Maroons, from their Origin to the Establishment of their Chief Tribe at Sierra Leone* (London, 1803), 2:285.

65 See Mavis C. Campbell, *Back to Africa: George Ross and the Maroons, from Nova Scotia to Sierra Leone* (Trenton, NJ: Africa World Press, 1993).

66 A few years later, Paul Cuffee's memoirs boast of an African merchant trader "not laden with instruments of cruelty and oppression," commanded by "a free and enlightened African," with a crew of "sable, yet respectable seamen rescued from the galling chain of slavery." Free Africans can prosecute "honourable commerce" on the West African coast. See *Memoir of Captain Paul Cuffee, A Man of Colour* (York, 1811), 22–23.

67 Martin Wight, cited in W. S. Marcus Jones, *Legal Development and Constitutional Change in Sierra Leone, 1787–1971* (Elms Court, UK: Stockwell, 1981), 32.

68 Fyfe, *History of Sierra Leone* 87.

69 Altick, *English Common Reader* 35.

70 See Nini Rodgers, "Equiano in Belfast: A Study of the Anti-Slavery Ethos in a Northern Town," *Slavery and Abolition* 18.2 (August 1997): 75–76; Iain

Notes to Chapter Six

McCalman, *Radical Underworld: Prophets, Revolutionaries, and Pornographers in London, 1795–1840* (Oxford: Clarendon, 1993); and Robert Wedderburn, *The Horrors of Slavery and Other Writings*, ed. Iain McCalman (New York: Markus Wiener, 1991), 72.

71 See Roger Chartier, *The Cultural Uses of Print in Early Modern France* (Princeton, NJ: Princeton UP, 1987); and *Forms and Meanings: Texts, Performances, and Audiences from Codex to Computer* (Philadelphia: U of Pennsylvania P, 1995).

72 See Henry Louis Gates Jr., "The Trope of the Talking Book," in *Signifying Monkey* 127–69, 132.

73 For a searchingly critical approach toward narratives that celebrate literacy as emancipatory of slaves, see Dana Nelson Salvino, "The Word in Black and White: Ideologies of Race and Literacy in Antebellum America," in *Reading in America: Literature and Social History*, ed. Cathy N. Davidson (Baltimore: Johns Hopkins UP, 1989), 140–56.

74 See Walter J. Ong, *Orality and Literacy: The Technologizing of the Word* (London: Routledge, 1982); Tzvetan Todorov, *The Conquest of America: The Question of the Other*, trans. Richard Howard (New York: Harper & Row, 1984).

75 Street, *Literacy: Theory and Practice* 97.

76 See Homi Bhabha, "Signs Taken for Wonders," in *The Location of Culture* (New York: Routledge, 1994), 114–15. Even though Bhabha sees the authority of the book as an instance of colonial hybridity that he opposes to the cancelable nature of the psychoanalytical fetish, in what follows I see the book, for Equiano, as fetish *and* factish in their most (in)authentic colonial sense. My disagreement with Bhabha, as becomes clear, is more a terminological than a substantive one.

77 This ongoing study involves "a study of the history of the idea of the fetish . . . guided by identifying those themes that persist throughout the various discourses and disciplines that have appropriated the term. This method studies the history of the usage of 'fetish' as a field of exemplary instances that exemplify no model or truth prior to or outside this very 'archive' itself; it views the fetish as a radically historical object that is nothing other than the totalized series of its particular usages"; see William Pietz, "The Problem of the Fetish, I," *Res: Anthropology and Aesthetics* 9 (spring 1985): 5, 7, 5–17; "The Problem of the Fetish, II: The Origin of the Fetish," *Res: Anthropology and Aesthetics* 13 (spring 1987): 23–45; "The Problem of the Fetish, IIIa: Bosman's Guinea and the Enlightenment Theory of Fetishism," *Res: Anthropology and Aesthetics* 16 (autumn 1988): 105–23; and "Fetishism and Materialism: The Limits of Theory in Marx," in *Fetishism as Cultural Discourse*, ed. Emily Apter and William Pietz (Ithaca, NY: Cornell UP, 1993), 152–85. The etymology of fetish connects it with the fabricated, fictitious, and factitious, and in this respect it continues a certain medieval perception of witchcraft and idolatry that it nonetheless transforms. The earliest modern cognate, *feitiço*, or *fetisso*, was a Portuguese word

used to describe religious artifacts retrieved from West African cultures and sold as curios. This "original" religious nature of the object involved an untranscendent materiality, contingent upon the metonymic nature of the fetish. The fetish obtains its power by its location upon the living body of the fetishist, a power that was itself dependent on a certain set of social relations, a particular environment, and a radical and contingent historicity. Fetishism, in its sedimented form, is often a nonrational quasi-religious belief, and this is how it is described by a variety of Enlightenment thinkers ranging from Charles De Brosses, who wrote the first full-length book on the subject, *Du culte des dieux fétiches* (1760; Paris: Fayard, 1988), to significant passages on the subject in the work of Voltaire, Kant, and Hegel. This tradition eventually makes its presence felt in the major uses of fetishism by nineteenth- and twentieth-century thinkers such as E. B. Tylor, Emile Durkheim, Auguste Comte, Karl Marx, and Sigmund Freud.

78 By means of this modest cumulative approach, Pietz intends to counteract what he characterizes as the particularist and universalist repudiations of African fetishism by the social sciences. The particularist account has been adopted by various postcolonial anthropologists to describe so-called fetishes within their specific and irreducible cultural contexts with the help of terminology inherent to the culture in question; the universalist account reduces the multiple registers of the fetish to a transcendental psychological truth, such as phallicism, or an analytically inspired philosophical perception of an error of hypostatization. By avoiding the extremes of cultural relativism and universalist rationalist reduction, Pietz hopes to conduct an intellectual history of the fetish in relation to the colonialist discourses that engender its theoretical reduction.

79 See David Hume, *The Natural History of Religion,* ed. H. E. Root (1757; Stanford, CA: Stanford UP, 1957); de Brosses, *Du culte des dieux fétiches;* and J.-F. Lafitau, *Customs of the American Indians Compared with the Customs of Primitive Times,* ed. William N. Fenton and Elizabeth L. Moore (Toronto: Champlain Society, 1974). For the Diderot-Hume-De Brosses correspondence, see Madeleine David, "Lettres inédites de Diderot et de Hume écrites de 1755 à 1763 au président de Brosses," *Revue Philosophiques* 2 (April-June 1966): 135–44.

80 See Bruno Latour, *Petite réflexion sur le culte moderne des dieux faitiches* (Paris: Synthélabo, 1996), 26, 31, 44. See also Alfonso M. Iacono, *Le fétichisme: histoire d'un concept* (Paris: PUF, 1992); and Paul-Laurent Assoun, *Le fétichisme* (Paris: PUF, 1994).

81 Defoe, *Farther Adventures of Robinson Crusoe* (London, 1719) 230, and *Serious Reflections during the life and surprizing adventures of Robinson Crusoe* (London, 1720) 241.

82 Defoe, *Robinson Crusoe,* ed. Michael Shinagel (New York: Norton, 1994) 43.

83 On the other hand, as *bricoleur,* Crusoe fashions utility out of nonexchangeable "uselessness." The modern sense of drug and, for that matter, the notion of lit-

erature itself, is intimately linked to this structure of supplementary uselessness that is appropriated for pleasurable use and/or addiction. See Avital Ronell, *Crack Wars: Literature/Addiction/Mania* (Lincoln: U of Nebraska P, 1991).

84 This veritable tradition of European travel narrative—that regales European audiences with tales of their technological superiority—begins with Portuguese traveler Alvise da Cadamosto. See G. R. Crone, ed., *The Voyages of Cadamosto and Other Documents* (London, 1937). For an excellent discussion of the cultural implications of the facts and fictions concerning Western technological advancement, see Michael Adas, *Machines as the Measure of Men: Science, Technology, and Ideologies of Western Dominance* (Ithaca, NY: Cornell UP, 1989).

85 See Matthews, *Voyage to the River Sierra-Leone* 175. Dogs and slaves are still confused. See Thomas Day, *Sandford and Merton* (London, 1783-89); Dorothy Kilner, *The Rotchfords* (London, 1786); and Maria Edgeworth, *Belinda* (London, 1802). Dogs named Caesar, Pompey, Cato, Syphax, and Juba remind readers of proximate African bodies similarly named.

86 Gates, *Signifying Monkey* 154-55.

87 See Gayatri Chakravorty Spivak, "Subaltern Studies: Deconstructing Historiography," in *In Other Worlds: Essays in Cultural Politics* (New York: Methuen, 1987), 197.

88 Afigbo says that this too might be a free modification on Equiano's part. The term for "loud-voiced" is actually "*Oluda*," whereas "*Ola-udah*" means "resonant ring." See Afigbo, *Ropes of Sand* 154.

89 Davis and Gates, *Slave's Narrative*, xvi; Carretta, ed., *The Interesting Narrative* xxix. For a very useful discussion of the various editions, see James Green, "The Publishing History of Olaudah Equiano's *Interesting Narrative*," *Slavery and Abolition* 16.3 (December 1995) 362-75.

90 See Equiano, *The Interesting Narrative* xv-xvii, 1-28.

91 See Sandiford, *Measuring the Moment* 142.

92 "Let the polished and haughty European recollect that his ancestors were once, like the Africans, uncivilized, and even barbarous. If, when [these Europeans] look round the world, they feel exultation, let it be tempered with benevolence to others, and gratitude to God, 'who hath made of one blood all nations of men for to dwell on all the face of the earth; and whose wisdom is not our wisdom, neither are our ways his ways'" (Acts 17:26).

93 Thompson, *Memoirs of an English Missionary* 13, 27.

94 Bhabha, "Signs Taken for Wonders," 119.

95 See Renée Balibar, "An Example of Literary Work in France: George Sand's 'La Mare au Diable' / 'The Devil's Pool,'" in *1848: The Sociology of Literature*, ed. Francis Barker et al., (Essex, UK: U of Essex, 1978), 27-46.

96 See Wai Chee Dimock, "A Theory of Resonance," *PMLA* 112.5 (October 1997): 1062. Dimock effectively overturns Stephen Greenblatt's earlier validation of a visual "wonder" over an aural "resonance" as a preferable category of cultural

appreciation. See Stephen Greenblatt, "Resonance and Wonder," in *Exhibiting Cultures: The Poetics and Politics of Museum Display,* ed. Ivan Karp and Steven D. Lavine (Washington, DC: Smithsonian Press, 1991), 42–56.

SEVEN *Tropicalizing the Enlightenment*

1 Aimé Césaire, *Toussaint Louverture: La révolution française et le problème coloniale* (Paris: Le club français du livre, 1960), 5; my translation.

2 Hereafter, I refer to the text as *Histoire des deux Indes.* The first edition, dated 1770, was distributed around 1772. A revised and augmented second edition appeared in 1774. The third and most successful edition, significantly reworked by Denis Diderot and dated 1780, was distributed in 1781. There exist two identical but differently paginated third edition texts in the rare book collections of major research libraries: the four-volume quarto and the ten-volume octavo. Page numbers are cited from the ten-volume edition, which is more widely available. For a paperback abridgment of the third edition, see *Histoire philosophique et politique des deux Indes,* ed. Yves Benot (Paris: Maspéro, Éditions de la Découverte, 1981). A critical edition is in progress under the direction of Hans-Jürgen Lüsebrink and Anthony Strugnell.

3 An English translation of the first edition by J. Justamond, entitled *History of the Two Indies,* appeared in 1776, running through at least eighteen editions. The book was at least as popular as the bestsellers in its genre in England during the period, such as Gibbon's *Decline and Fall of the Roman Empire,* Robertson's *History of America,* and Hume's *History of England.* The distribution of 20,000 copies of *Histoire des deux Indes* by the English colonists in America gave Raynal the additional notoriety of having incited the American Revolution. By the early 1780s, there were also editions in German, Italian, Dutch, Russian, and Hungarian. Scholarship on the book's role in the spread of Enlightenment ideas all over Europe is still very much in progress: see the report by Hans-Jürgen Lüsebrink, "L'*Histoire des deux Indes* de Guillaume-Thomas Raynal et ses *Extraits* contemporains," *Studies on Voltaire and the Eighteenth Century* 265 (1989): 1703–6. For an acknowledgment of the shaping role *Histoire des deux Indes* played in antislavery discourse, see Edward D. Seeber, *Anti-Slavery Opinion in France during the Second Half of the Eighteenth Century* (Baltimore: Johns Hopkins UP, 1937). For an appraisal of the book's popularity in England, see D. D. Irvine, "The Abbé Raynal and British Humanitarianism," *Journal of Modern History* 3.4 (December 1931): 564–77. For an account of the reactions of Scottish readers of the *History of the Two Indies,* see Peter France, "Diderot et l'Écosse," in *Diderot: Les dernières années 1770–84,* ed. Peter France (Edinburgh: Edinburgh UP, 1985), 3–14. For its impact on Poland, see Marian Skrzypek, "Diderot, Raynal et le mouvement d'indépendance de la Pologne," in *Diderot* 185–94.

4 In 1938, the same year that James published *The Black Jacobins*, Eric Williams submitted a doctoral dissertation to Oxford University that challenged the then historical consensus that the principal reasons behind the abolition of slavery were humanitarian ones. James's and Williams's scholarship has significantly challenged historians, arguing that political events in the colonies often determined metropolitan democratic politics. Written before the post–World War II wave of Third World liberation movements, both studies have been followed by much historical revision questioning of their specific conclusions. Nevertheless, the trend initiated by James and Williams has helped reverse Eurocentric teleologies in accounts of slavery, emancipation, and decolonization. See C[yril] L[ionel] R[obert] James, *The Black Jacobins: Toussaint L'Ouverture and the San Domingo Revolution*, rev. ed. (New York: Vintage, 1963), and Eric Williams, *Capitalism and Slavery* (London: Capricorn Books, 1966). For subsequent histories that synthesize more recent historical debate concerning the decline of slavery, see David Brion Davis, *The Problem of Slavery in the Age of Revolution 1770–1823* (Ithaca, NY: Cornell UP, 1975), and Robin Blackburn, *The Overthrow of Colonial Slavery 1776–1848* (New York: Verso, 1988).

5 Although the thesis that the Enlightenment was formative of the French Revolution dates back to the German Romantics and Aléxis de Tocqueville, the first attempt to prove this empirically was Daniel Mornet's study of eighteenth-century private libraries. Mornet used quantitative data from testament catalogues; however, this did not fully account for the most popular blacklisted and censored titles, and hence the most politically volatile ones, which never appeared in these catalogues. See Mornet, *Les origines intellectuelles de la révolution française 1715–1787* (1933; Paris: Colin, 1967). The popularity of the authors of the high Enlightenment stemmed from their role as literary entertainers rather than as social and political theorists: Rousseau was famous for *La nouvelle Héloïse*, not *The Social Contract*, and Voltaire was well-known as the author of *Candide*, not *The Philosophical Dictionary*. It comes as a surprise even to eighteenth-century scholars that, along with *Candide* and *La nouvelle Héloïse*, *Histoire des deux Indes* was one of the most widely known, reproduced, excerpted, and pirated Enlightenment texts in France. Feugère's early estimate of a total of seventy editions in the period 1770–89 (including forty pirated editions) is still widely accepted. See Anatole Feugère, *Un précurseur de la révolution: L'Abbé Raynal (1713–1796)* (Angoulême, 1922; Geneva: Slatkine Reprints, 1970); and William R. Womack, "Eighteenth-Century Themes in the *Histoire philosophique et politique des deux Indes* of Guillaume Raynal," *Studies on Voltaire and the Eighteenth Century* 96 (1972): 129–265.

6 In addition to the quantification of a book's popularity, the assessment of reading skills, begun by Daniel Mornet, can lead to crucial theoretical insights about the phenomenology of reading and its causal relation to historical change. If certain books or passages are read aloud or silently, publicly or privately, such

reading practices have a very important role to play in outlining the semantic impact of reading as an activity and its historical and cultural construction. Revising the ideal Kantian-Habermasian picture of a public sphere constituted by the frictionless circulation of print, recent work in the cultural history of the book has emphasized popular publishing techniques, the sociocultural constitution of readerships, and the material effectivity of reading practices themselves in the dissemination of ideas during the pre-Revolutionary period. See especially Keith Michael Baker, *Inventing the French Revolution: Essays on French Political Culture in the Eighteenth Century* (New York: Cambridge UP, 1990); Yves Benot, *Diderot: De l'athéisme à l'anticolonialisme* (Paris: Maspéro, 1970; rev. 1981); Pierre Bourdieu and Roger Chartier, "La lecture: Une pratique culturelle," in *Pratiques de la lecture*, ed. Roger Chartier (Paris: Rivages, 1985); Roger Chartier, "Urban Reading Practices," in *The Cultural Uses of Early Modern Print*, trans. Lydia G. Cochrane (Princeton, NJ: Princeton UP, 1987), 183–239, and *Les origines culturelles de la révolution française* (Paris: Seuil, 1990); Robert Darnton, *The Literary Underground of the Old Regime* (Cambridge, MA: Harvard UP, 1982), and *Édition et sédition: L'univers de la littérature clandestine au XVIIIe siècle* (Paris: Gallimard, 1991); and Daniel Roche, *Les républicains des lettres: Gens de culture et Lumières au XVIIIe siècle* (Paris: Fayard, 1988). For the volume of essays on Raynal, see Hans-Jürgen Lüsebrink and Manfred Tietz, eds., *Lectures de Raynal: L'Histoire des deux Indes en Europe et en Amérique au XVIIIe siècle*, (Oxford: Voltaire Foundation, 1991), and Srinivas Aravamudan, "*Histoire des deux Indes:* Progress Through Violence or From Violence?," in *Progress and Violence in the Enlightenment*, ed. Deidre Dawson and Valérie Cossy (Paris: Champion, 1998).

7 See H[ans]-J[ürgen] Lüsebrink, "Strategies d'Intervention, Identité Sociale et Presentation de Soi d'Un 'Défenseur de l'humanité': La Carrière de l'Abbé Raynal (1713-1796)," in *La rhétorique du discours, objet d'histoire (XVIIIe–XXe siècles)*, ed. Jacques Guilhaumou (Lille: Presse Universitaire de Lille, 1981), 28–64. The three most popular categories of subversive underground literature were political philosophy, pornography, and generally defamatory literature (satires, libels, scandalous chronicles). Often, as in the case of the Marquis de Sade's writings, these categories were not as distinct as they might appear to us now (Chartier, *Origines culturelles de la révolution française* 91). For more around the revolutionary reception of Raynal and the genre of political philosophy in the ancien régime, see Darnton, *Édition et sédition* 13; Feugère, *Précurseur de la révolution* 4, 289; and Lüsebrink and Tietz, *Lectures de Raynal* 3.

8 Michèle Duchet, *Anthropologie et histoire au siècle des lumières* (1971; rev., Paris: Flammarion, 1977), 112; my translation.

9 Ibid., 13; my translation.

10 See ibid., and Michèle Duchet, *Diderot et L'Histoire des deux Indes ou L'écriture fragmentaire* (Paris: Nizet, 1978). The source studies were enabled by the land-

mark publication of Herbert Dieckmann, *Inventaire du fonds Vandeul et inédits de Diderot* (Geneva: Droz, 1951). Diderot wrote an eloquent defense of *Histoire des deux Indes* entitled "Lettre Apologétique de l'Abbé Raynal à Monsieur Grimm," collected in Denis Diderot, *Oeuvres Philosophiques*, ed. Paul Vernière (Paris: Garnier, 1964).

11 Chartier builds on Tocqueville's initial insight that identified rational skepticism as an impetus that "brought into politics all the practices of literature" (*Origines culturelles de la révolution française* 22-23).

12 See Denis Diderot, "Encyclopédie," in *Encyclopédie, ou Dictionnaire raisonné des sciences, des arts et des métiers* (Paris: Briasson, 1751-65), 5:635-49; and Darnton, *Édition* 34. For more on Napoleon and Karsten, see Aravamudan, "Progress Through Violence or From Violence?"

13 Tietz's absorbing analysis of the text's Spanish reception comes closest: "the real victims of the Spanish colonization of the Americas, the *indios,* were far from being able to read the text or shape a revolutionary ideology out of it for themselves; on the other hand, the colonialist conception of the *Histoire* did not correspond to the independence-oriented ideas of the *criollos,* the American ruling class that began distancing itself from Spain" (Lüsebrink and Tietz, *Lectures de Raynal* 130). Roberto Ventura reiterates this conclusion in his essay in the collection on the text's South American reception.

14 Lüsebrink and Tietz, *Lectures de Raynal* 6.

15 See Julia Kristeva, "La musique parlée, ou remarques sur la subjectivité dans la fiction à propos du *Neveu de Rameau,*" in *Langue et langages de Leibniz à l'Encyclopédie,* ed. Michèle Duchet and Michèle Jalley (Paris: Union Générale d'Éditions, 1977), 153-224: "Le contenu ménippéen, polyphonique, sexualisé, transgressif, rieur de ces textes, est précisément la couverture sémantique adéquate de cette économie du sujet traversant l'imposition du sur-moi, engagé comme il est dans une subversion généralisée de sa propre unicité aussi bien que des limites fixées de toute structuration discursive et sociale" (195). See also Homi Bhabha, "Of Mimicry and Man: The Ambivalence of Colonial Discourse," *October* 28 (1984): 125-33, and "Sly Civility," *October* 34 (1985): 71-80; Jacques Derrida, *Spurs: Nietzsche's Styles,* trans. Barbara Harlow (Chicago: U of Chicago P, 1979), 95-101; and Judith Butler, *Gender Trouble: Feminism and the Subversion of Identity* (New York: Routledge, 1990).

16 See Tony Bennett, "Texts in History: The Determinations of Readings and Their Texts," *MMLA* 18.1 (fall 1985): 1-16; Hans-Jürgen Lüsebrink, "Les 14 juillet coloniaux: La Révolution française et sa mémoire dans l'empire colonial français," *Franzosisch Heute* 20.3 (September 1989): 307-19; Hans-Jürgen Lüsebrink and Rolf Reichardt, *The Bastille: A History of a Symbol of Despotism and Freedom* (Durham, NC: Duke UP, 1997); Yves Benot, "Traces de *l'Histoire des deux Indes* chez les anti-esclavagistes sous la Révolution," in *Lectures de Raynal,* ed. Lüsebrink and Tietz, 141-54; Michel Delon, "L'appel au lecteur dans

l'Histoire des deux Indes," in *Lectures de Raynal,* ed. Lüsebrink and Tietz, 53–66; Manfred Tietz, "L'Espagne et *l'Histoire des deux Indes* de l'Abbé Raynal," in *Lectures de Raynal,* ed. Lüsebrink and Tietz, 99–130; and Roberto Ventura, "Lectures de Raynal en Amérique latine aux XVIIIe et XIXe siècle," in *Lectures de Raynal,* ed. Lüsebrink and Tietz, 341–59.

17 Blackburn, *Overthrow of Colonial Slavery* 219, 243. The third edition of *Histoire des deux Indes* suppresses the explicit reference to Spartacus in the passage, a reference retained until the second edition; nonetheless, the passage was renowned as the Spartacus passage. Another significant but very long passage ventriloquizes a slave's anger at his masters, even as it refutes, point by point, pro-slavery arguments. See "Hommes! ou démons! . . ." (6:191–208).

18 See James, *Black Jacobins* 250.

19 See Michel Martin, *Les monuments équestres de Louis XIV: Une grande entreprise de propagande monarchique* (Paris: Picard, 1986).

20 Blackburn, *Overthrow of Colonial Slavery* 243; and Robin Blackburn, "*The Black Jacobins* and New World Slavery," in *C. L. R. James: His Intellectual Legacies,* ed. Selwyn R. Cudjoe and William E. Cain (Amherst: U of Massachusetts P, 1995), 86.

21 Jean-Paul Marat, *Les chaînes de l'esclavage* (1774; Paris: Union Générale d'Éditions, 1972). For the contexts of Robespierre's comment within the Jacobin debates on slavery, see Yves Benot, *La Révolution française et la fin des colonies* (Paris: Éditions La Découverte, 1988), 157–88. One historian suggests that at least four out of ten principal usages of the term *esclavage* in eighteenth-century France were purely metaphorical; see William Doyle, *The Oxford History of the French Revolution* (New York: Oxford UP, 1989), and David P. Geggus, "Racial Equality, Slavery, and Colonial Secession during the Constituent Assembly," *American Historical Review* 94.5 (December 1989): 1291 n. 7. Speaking of the Gramscian collective on South Asian history, Subaltern Studies, Gayatri Spivak sees their work as "an attempt to undo a massive historiographical metalepsis and 'situate' the effect of the subject as subaltern"; see "Subaltern Studies: Deconstructing Historiography," in *In Other Worlds: Essays in Cultural Politics* (New York: Methuen, 1987), 205.

22 A treatise on Saint Domingue, with Raynal as the nominal author, *Essai sur l'administration de Saint-Domingue* (Paris, 1785), was actually Malouet's.

23 See David P. Geggus, *Slavery, War, and Revolution: The British Occupation of Saint Domingue* (Oxford: Oxford UP, 1982), 38; "Racial Equality"; 1290–1308; and "The Haitian Revolution," in *The Modern Caribbean,* ed. Franklin W. Knight and Colin A. Palmer (Chapel Hill: U of North Carolina P, 1989), 21–50; Benot, *La Révolution française*; Alex Dupuy, *Haiti in the World Economy: Class, Race, and Underdevelopment since 1700* (Boulder, CO: Westview Press, 1989); and Carolyn E. Fick, *The Making of Haiti: The Saint Domingue Revolution from Below* (Knoxville: U of Tennessee P, 1990).

24 Blackburn, "*The Black Jacobins* and New World Slavery," 91.

25 James, *The Black Jacobins* x.

26 Dupuy, *Haiti in the World Economy;* and "Toussaint-Louverture and the Haitian Revolution: A Reassessment of C. L. R. James's Interpretation," in *C. L. R. James: His Intellectual Legacies,* ed. Cudjoe and Cain, 106-17.

27 See William Wordsworth, *Poems, in Two Volumes, and other Poems, 1800-1807,* ed. Jared Curtis (Ithaca, NY: Cornell UP, 1983), 160-61. While M. H. Abrams's classic study of Wordsworth's poetry acknowledged that the tropology of mastery and slavery was central to the Romantic tradition, Mary Jacobus's essays on *The Prelude* closely read the significance of Romanticist repressions of the history of the slave trade as a necessary erasure for that poetry's legibility. See M. H. Abrams, *Natural Supernaturalism: Tradition and Revolution in Romantic Literature* (New York: Norton, 1971), 356-72; and Mary Jacobus, "Geometric Science and Romantic History: or Wordsworth, Newton, and the Slave-Trade," in *Romanticism, Writing, and Sexual Difference: Essays on* The Prelude (Oxford: Clarendon, 1989), 93. For Coleridge on Toussaint, see Simon Bainbridge, *Napoleon and English Romanticism* (Cambridge: Cambridge UP, 1995), 26.

28 There exists an interesting variant, listed as 162n:

Meanwhile those eyes retained their tropic fire,

Which, burning independent of the mind,

Joined the lustre of her rich attire

To mock the outcast—O ye Heavens, be kind!

And feel, thou Earth, for this afflicted Race!

29 Kara M. Rabbitt, "C. L. R. James's Figuring of Toussaint-Louverture: *The Black Jacobins* and the Literary Hero," in *C. L. R. James: His Intellectual Legacies,* ed. Cudjoe and Cain, 124.

30 See Gayatri Chakravorty Spivak, "Can the Subaltern Speak?," in *Marxism and the Interpretation of Culture,* ed. Cary Nelson and Lawrence Grossberg (Urbana: U of Illinois P, 1988), 271-313; Mira Kamdar, "Subjectification and Mimesis: Colonizing History," *American Journal of Semiotics* 7.3 (1990): 91-100; and Joan Dayan, *Haiti, History, and the Gods* (Berkeley: U of California P, 1993), 10.

31 Ovid, *Metamorphoses,* trans. Mary M. Innes (New York: Penguin, 1955), 155-66. For Diderot scholars who are tuned in to the classical allusions in the philosopher's writings, this cataclysmic image of "bain de sang" provides one more instance of Diderot's predilection for Lucretius's atomistic materialism. See Jeffrey Mehlman, *Cataract: A Study in Diderot* (Middletown, CT: Wesleyan UP, 1979).

32 For a discussion of Mirabeau's and Domergue's speeches, see Mona Ozouf, "La Révolution française et l'idee de l'homme nouveau," in *The French Revolution and the Creation of Modern Political Culture:* Vol. 2, *The Political Culture of the French Revolution,* ed. Colin Lucas (New York: Pergamon, 1988), 219, 223-24. Gianluigi Goggi has identified Diderot's image of Medea as a bone of conten-

tion in key texts of eighteenth-century political philosophy. The episode is mentioned in chapter 12 of Hobbes's *De Cive*, explained in the section "Rajeunissement" written by Venel for the *Encyclopédie*, and occurs on two other occasions in Diderot's own writings: on the opening page of *Réfutation d'Helvétius* and in a well-known letter to the English radical John Wilkes on November 14, 1771. See Gianluigi Goggi, "Diderot et Médée dépeçant le vieil Éson," in *Colloque International Diderot*, ed. Anne-Marie Chouillet (Paris: Aux Amateurs de Livres, 1985), 173–84; and Denis Diderot, *Correspondance*, ed. Georges Roth and Jean Varloot (Paris: Minuit, 1955–70), 11:223. Medea was also a figure of some importance to the period's literature. The first French tragedy to be published as a book was a version of *Medea* in 1556 by Jean de La Péruse. The best-known dramatic adaptations until then were by Corneille (1635) and Longepierre (1694). Medea was also a popular subject for numerous operatic adaptations in French, Italian, and German, such as the one by Charpentier (1693). See Jean de La Péruse, *Médée*, ed. James Coleman (Exeter: U of Exeter P, 1985).

33 René Girard, *Deceit, Desire, and the Novel: Self and Other in Literary Structure* (Baltimore: Johns Hopkins UP, 1965), 95. Conventional images of oedipality in political discourse imply rivalry between sons and fathers fighting over women, as in Rowlandson's cartoons. In these contexts, political inheritance of democratic liberties, or the country itself, can be allegorized as a woman, unjustly chained by a despotic paternal figure, being wrested from him by a youthful male protagonist. For a detailed investigation of this literature, see Ronald Paulson, *Representations of Revolution (1789–1820)* (New Haven: Yale UP, 1983).

34 Euripides, *Medea*, trans. Philip Vellacott (New York: Penguin, 1963), 24–25; lines 214–70. However, in *Histoire des deux Indes*, women are also credited with inventing the first instance of sociability and civil administration among savages (2:337).

35 See Carolyn E. Fick, "Slave Resistance," and "Appendix A: Interrogation of the Negress Assam," in *Making of Haiti* 46–75, 251–59; Barbara Bush, *Slave Women in Caribbean Society, 1650–1838* (Bloomington: Indiana UP, 1990); Lucille Mathurin, *The Rebel Woman in the British West Indies during Slavery* (Kingston: African-Caribbean Publishers, 1975); Orlando Patterson, *Slavery and Social Death* (Cambridge, MA: Harvard UP, 1982); Rosalyn Terborg Penn, "Black Women in Resistance: A Cross-Cultural Perspective," in *In Resistance: Studies in African, Caribbean, and Afro-American History*, ed. Gary Okihiro (Amherst: U of Massachusetts P, 1986), 188–209; and Gayatri Chakravorty Spivak, "Three Women's Texts and a Critique of Imperialism," *Critical Inquiry* 12.1 (1985): 254. This trope of a self-immolating colonized subject is pervasive in *Histoire des deux Indes*. It is especially dominant in the description of sati ensuing from the Widow of Surat episode (1:110). A topical reference to this portrayal is Antoine Le Mierre's popular play, *La Veuve du Malabar, ou L'Empire des Coutumes*, produced in 1770 and 1780, which depicted a bold French general, Montalban,

saving a young Indian widow from the clutches of Brahminical obscurantism and a fiery death on the funeral pyre of her husband. The widow turns out to be the very woman that the general romantically fancied. *Histoire des deux Indes* also recounts the famous sentimentalist story of Yarico and Inkle, in which an Englishman, whose life is saved by an Amerindian woman while his companions are slaughtered by her menfolk, sells his savior into slavery after eventually escaping with her. The episode was represented graphically as a frontispiece engraving for the third edition, entitled "Un Anglais de la Barbade vend sa maîtresse," by the artist Jean-Marie Moreau le Jeune. First attributed to Richard Steele, the episode surfaces in the section on Barbados (7:359–60). For an analysis of this legend, see Peter Hulme, *Colonial Encounters: Europe and the Native Caribbean, 1492–1797* (New York: Methuen, 1986), 225–63; Hulme also reproduces the *Histoire des deux Indes* engraving (Fig. 14, 224).

36 John Gabriel Stedman, *Narrative of a Five-Years' Expedition against the Negroes of Surinam, 1772–1777* (1796; Amherst: U of Massachusetts P, 1971), 364.

37 See Fick, *Making of Haiti* 57–75; Pierre Pluchon, *Vaudou, sorciers, empoisonneurs: De Saint-Domingue à Haïti* (Paris: Karthala, 1987); Michel Laguerre, *Voodoo and Politics in Haiti* (London: Macmillan, 1989), 65; and Patricia Rooke, "Slavery, Social Death and Imperialism: The Formation of a Christian Black Elite in the West Indies, 1800–1845," in *Making Imperial Mentalities: Socialisation and British Imperialism*, ed. J. A. Mangan (Manchester: Manchester UP, 1990), 23–45.

38 See Jacques Derrida, *Dissemination*, trans. Barbara Johnson (Chicago: U of Chicago P, 1981); Dayan, *Haiti, History, and the Gods* xvii; Duarte Mimoso-Ruiz, *Médée antique et moderne: Aspects rituels et socio-politiques d'un mythe* (Paris: Ophrys, 1982), 173; for an extensive bibliography on the literature surrounding Medea, see 209–31. Mimoso-Ruiz's study is an outstanding piece of comparative myth criticism, synthesizing and situating the rich and varied intertextual representations of Medea over the ages in plays, novels, operas, and paintings. Especially significant is Mimoso-Ruiz's careful appreciation of a vast modern cultural archive, in several languages, that features several anticolonial renditions of Medea. A few of the most significant modern depictions shed light on the way Medea allows artists to analyze the role of gender within antislavery and decolonization. In English, Maxwell Anderson, *Wingless Victory* (1936), and Jim Magnuson, *African Medea* (1968); in Spanish, Alberto Vergel, *Medea* (1971); in Italian, Pasolini's spectacular film starring Maria Callas in the title role of *Medea* (1970); in French, Henri Lenormand, *Médée* (1931). For a suggestive collocation of Spartacus and Medea in the Caribbean, see Benjamin Moseley, *A Treatise on Sugar* (London, 1799), 198. Moseley describes the obeah-practicing Jamaican maroon robber Mansong, or Three-Fingered Jack: "He ascended above SPARTACUS. . . . He would sooner have made a *Medean* cauldron for the whole island, than disturb one lady's happiness."

39 Césaire, *Toussaint Louverture* 263-69; Bernard Dadié, *Îles de tempête: Pièce en sept tableaux* (Paris: Présence Africaine, 1973), 121.

40 See Dayan, *Haiti, History, and the Gods* 31, 17, 4.

41 Ibid., 15.

Conclusion

1 Frantz Fanon, *Black Skin, White Masks*, trans. Charles Lane Markmann (New York: Grove Weidenfeld, 1967), 231.

2 Michel Foucault, "What Is Enlightenment?," in *The Foucault Reader*, ed. Paul Rabinow (New York: Pantheon Books, 1984), 50.

3 Cited in Fanon, *Black Skin, White Masks* 223.

4 See Walter Benjamin, "Theses on the Philosophy of History," in *Illuminations* (New York: Schocken Books, 1969), 262. For a powerful interpretation of Benjamin's modernist antihistoricism, see Fredric Jameson, "Benjamin's Readings," in *Commemorating Walter Benjamin*, ed. Ian Balfour, special issue of *diacritics* 22.3-4 (fall/winter 1992): 19-34.

5 Jacques Derrida, "Archive Fever: A Freudian Impression," *diacritics* 25.2 (summer 1995): 9-63.

6 Foucault, "What Is Enlightenment?," 39.

7 See Tony Bennett, "Texts in History: The Determinations of Readings and Their Texts," in *Post-Structuralism and the Question of History*, ed. Derek Attridge, Geoff Bennington, and Robert Young (New York: Cambridge UP, 1987), 70-71. For earlier versions, see Tony Bennett, "Texts, Readers, Reading Formations," *MMLA* 16.1 (spring 1983): 1-17; and "Texts in History: The Determinations of Readings and Their Texts," *MMLA* 18.1 (fall 1985): 1-16.

8 For two superb renditions of the pluralization of literacy into literacies, see Brian V. Street, *Literacy in Theory and Practice* (Cambridge: Cambridge UP, 1984), and Renée Balibar, "An Example of Literary Work in France: George Sand's 'La Mare au Diable' / 'The Devil's Pool,'" in *1848: The Sociology of Literature*, ed. Francis Barker et al. (Essex, UK: U of Essex, 1978), 27-46.

Index

Abolition(ism), 236–82 passim, 303, 308–9, 312. *See also* Slavery; Slave(s)

Addison, Gulston, 127

Addison, Joseph, 110, 136, 142, 179, 329, 377 n.37; *Cato*, 18, 103–4, 107–26, 135, 138, 143, 148, 156, 165, 361 nn. 18, 23, 362 n.27, 373 n.14; *The Spectator*, 109, 112, 124, 126, 129–31, 166, 197, 363 n.30, 375 n.24; *Whig Examiner*, 127

Addison, Lancelot, 126–27, 363 n.34

Aesop, 3

Aesthetics, 190–229, 233–35

Afigbo, Adiele, 252, 400 n.88

Africa. *See* Ethiopia; Madagascar; North Africa; Sierra Leone; West Africa

African American literature, 235, 247, 271, 286

Agency: and aesthetics, 197; of anti-colonial rebellion, 118–21, 144–45, 261, 264–68, 298, 302–25; and anti-colonial subject position, 140–41, 328; of anticorruption discourse, 103, 127–34, 153; as apparent assimilation, 14, 264; and autobiography, 71–72, 244–45, 278–82; as catachresis, 15, 16, 281, 282, 292, 303; and catechisms (catéchismes politiques), 293, 296–303, 306–8; as colonial mimicry, 15, 286, 300, 314–15; as commercial boycott, 146–53, 369 n.63, 373 n.21;

of concessionary narrative, 75, 77, 124; constraints of, 257, 268; of conversion, 94–102, 242, 266–67; and decolonization, 14, 16; defined, 10–11; and encyclopedic cross-reference (*renvoi*), 297–98; and ethics, 328; as "genealogy," 11, 24, 281–82, 292, 330–31; of hero, 310, 313, 315, 323; and history, 326–27; as levantinization, 21, 160, 188–89; of lingua franca, 15; of linguistic change, 5–6; as literate response, 13–14, 15, 269–72, 279–82, 286–88; and marriage market, 50–57, 343 n.26; and masquerade, 169, 171, 179–80; of metaliteracy, 302; "mistakes" of, 279; and moral fable, 203, 212; mythopoetic potential of, 321–23; as Nachträglichkeit, 11, 73, 283, 307; as nationalization, 21–24, 238; nonhuman, 277; of parody, 32–33, 60–61, 265–66, 300; of phi-losophy, 291; and pirates, 82–86, 87, 93; pragmatics of, 328–30; of read-ing, 11, 14, 15, 19, 23–24, 289–92, 299, 300–303, 330; and revolutionary con-sciousness, 303, 306, 313; and ritual reenactment, 322; and Stoicism, 145, 148; of sublime, 192; and suicide, 31, 122; supernatural, 71–72, 240, 271, 273–78, 280; unburdened by history, 326–27; and violence, 13, 264, 267–68, 275, 303, 320–23; as virtualization,

Agency (*continued*)

16–17, 19, 105–6, 153, 155. *See also* Colonialism; Subject

Alarcón, Daniel Cooper, 31

Aldridge, James, 250

Alexander the Great (Alexander III of Macedon), 133

Alvares, Francisco, 204, 385 n.39

Andrade, Susan, 31

Anne (Queen), 107, 110, 111

Anthropological perspective, 159–89 passim, 236, 262, 273–75, 285, 290, 295–96, 315

Anticolonialism. *See* Agency

Aparicio, Frances, 6

Appleby, Joyce, 105

Architecture, 197, 218, 387 n.53

Aristophanes: *Lysistrata,* 53

Armstrong, Meg, 193–94

Armstrong, Nancy, 95

Ashfield, Andrew, 197

Astell, Mary, 165, 170, 373 n.15, 378 n.41

Athey, Stephanie, 31

Atterbury, Francis, 200, 227

Aurangzeb (Emperor), 88

Australia, 135–36, 255

Autobiography, 71–75, 79–81, 235–85 passim

Avery, John, 78, 88–91, 356 n.30

Baer, Joel, 89, 350 n.14

Bailyn, Bernard, 135

Baker, Polly, 319

Balibar, Renée, 287

Ballaster, Ros, 31

Barthes, Roland, 184

Beautiful, aesthetics of the, 190, 215, 226, 228

Beckford, William (governor of Jamaica), 217

Beckford, William: *Memoirs of Extraordinary Painters,* 221–23; *Vathek,* 20, 191, 195, 214–23, 386 n.48

Behn, Aphra, 14, 29, 50, 111; *Emperor of the Moon,* 180; *Oroonoko,* 15, 17–18, 22, 29–49, 60–70, 75, 99, 121, 123–24, 137–38, 203, 250–52, 284, 303, 314, 329, 336 n.1; and imoindaism, 31–32; and oroonokoism, 29–32

Bellini, Gentile, 201–2

Benjamin, Walter, 327–28, 358 n.4

Bennett, Tony, 300, 329–30

Benot, Yves, 293, 299

Bhabha, Homi, 272, 285–86, 300, 398 n.76

Bible, the, 242, 245–46, 265–91 passim, 400 n.92

Bindon, Francis, 139

Blackburn, Robin, 303, 306

Blacklock, Thomas, 196

Blackness: color of, 30, 193–94, 200, 270

Blake, William, 6–9, 52

Blinding and blindness, 190–215, 381 nn. 9, 13, 385 n.39

Bluett, Thomas, 251

Bolingbroke, Viscount (Henry St. John), 110–11, 367 n.55

Bolla, Peter de, 197

Booth, Barton, 110

Boswell, James, 174, 212, 290

Bouhdiba, Abdelwahab, 181

Boukman (voodoo priest), 313, 323

Boulanger, Nicolas, 221, 388 n.60

Bracegirdle, Anne, 34, 37, 38, 338 n.10

Brant, Clare, 179

Brecht, Bertolt, 330

Brooke, Henry: *Gustavus Vassa,* 115, 244–45, 282

Brown, Laura, 12, 17, 30, 335 n.17, 366 n.49

Brunt, Samuel: *A Voyage to Cacklogal-linia*, 205, 367 n.53
Brutus, Marcus, 121, 133, 142
Bullionism, 145–53
Bunyan, John, 240, 248; *The Pilgrim's Progress*, 2
Burg, B[arry] R[ichard], 96, 355 n.29
Burke, Edmund, 155, 204, 255, 329, 390 n.69; and East India Company, 20, 198, 211, 224–27, 229; *Philosophical Enquiry into the Origins of the Sublime*, 20, 190–202, 209, 214, 218, 221, 222–23, 226; *Reflections on the Revolution*, 198, 200, 222, 223–29, 292, 318
Burnet, Gilbert, 165
Burney, Fanny, 169
Burr, Sandra, 240–42, 392 nn. 8, 9
Byam, William, 31, 42, 46, 47

Cadamosto, Alvise da, 277
Caesar, Julius, 64–66, 108, 110–12, 116–21, 125–26, 133–34, 142, 145, 346 n.41
Capitalism, 79, 86, 100, 101, 105, 130, 217, 236, 333 n.4. *See also* Commodities and Commodification; Mercantilism
Caribbean, 83, 96, 257, 285, 291, 308, 321, 325. *See also* Haiti; Jamaica; Surinam
Caroline (Queen), 184, 187
Carretta, Vincent, 284
Carteret, John (Earl of Granville), 131
Cato the Censor (Marcus Porcius Cato), 108, 124, 147
Cato the Younger (Marcus Porcius Cato Uticensis), 103–35, 138, 142–43, 165. *See also* Addison, Lancelot; Neostoicism; Stoicism; Trenchard, John

Censorship, 132, 293, 317–18
Certeau, Michel de, 185
Césaire, Aimé, 289, 292, 323–24
Chambers, Ephraim, 1, 21
Chapman, George, 121
Chardin, Sir John, 194–95, 220, 381 n.9
Charke, Charlotte, 183
Charles I, 45
Charles II, 34, 46, 111, 126, 364 n.35
Charlotte (Queen), 284, 289
Chartier, Roger, 293, 297, 402 n.6, 403 n.7, 404 n.11
Chávez-Silverman, Susana, 6
Cheselden, William, 193–97, 213, 228
Chodowiecki, Daniel, 175
Christianity. *See* Religion
Chuvin, Pierre, 168–69
Clark, J. C. D., 211, 365 n.46, 390 n.69
Clarkson, John, 258, 262, 266
Clarkson, Thomas, 254, 258
Clérambault, G. G. de, 173
Clothing, 166–67, 171–74, 176–80, 249, 261–62, 264. *See also* Nudity
Cockney slang, 168, 374 n.24
Coffeehouse, 56–57, 175, 182, 343 n.29
Coinage crisis, 145–56
Coleridge, Samuel Taylor, 312
Colley, Linda: *Britons*, 10, 334 n.10
Colonialism: and adventure, 79; and aesthetics, 269, 339 n.12; and anti-conquest, 73–74; and archive, 11, 288, 328; British, 6–8, 14, 126–27, 129–30, 139–41, 192, 224, 242; and capitalism, 101; and democracy, 134–35, 255–56, 259, 261, 264–68; discourse of, 2, 3, 9–10, 30, 32, 134–35, 210–11, 235, 237, 271, 282, 295–300, 306–7, 314, 322 (*see also* Trope[s]); and eighteenth-century studies, 12–16; and encyclopedia, 290–92; French 23, 289–325; and legitimation, 140–41;

Colonialism (*continued*)
and "projectors," 100–102, 237, 250, 256, 260, 329; as sexual acquisition, 37–38; and sublime, 191; trauma of, 11, 47–49, 68–70, 347 n.43; utopian aspects of, 90–91. *See also* Agency; Commodities and Commodification; Mercantilism; Slavery; Slave(s)

Columbus, Christopher, 73, 271

Commerce. *See* Capitalism; Commodities and Commodification; Mercantilism

Commodities and Commodification, 37, 38–39, 40–41, 43–44, 50–55, 56, 67–68, 80–81, 94, 101–2, 124, 128–34, 136, 145–47, 150–51, 170, 181, 182, 248, 270, 271, 276–82, 329, 343 n.29, 366 n.47

Computer literacy, 287–88

Condillac, Étienne Bonnot de, 193

Congreve, William, 57, 63

Constantinople (Istanbul), 159, 171, 177, 185–87, 202

Constitutionalism, 115, 133, 229, 267–68. *See also* Whigs

Conversion narrative, 94–95, 236, 240–46

Cook, James (Captain), 73

Copjec, Joan, 173

Crane, Mary Thomas, 106

Crane, R. S., 109

Crèvecoeur, Michel-Guillaume Jean de, 147

Criminality: literature of, 77–78, 88, 348 n.6, 357 n.32, 358 n.35

Cugoano, Ottobah, 252, 254, 256, 269–70

Dadié, Bernard, 312–13

D'Alembert, Jean le Rond, 205–6, 209, 290

Dallas, R[obert] C[harles], 267

Damiens, Robert-François, 222–23

Dance, 240, 285

Dandridge, Bartholomew, 34

Darnton, Robert, 46, 293

Davis, Fanny, 174

Dayan, Joan, 314, 322, 324–25

De Brosses, Charles, 273–74

Defoe, Benjamin Norton, 132

Defoe, Daniel, 147, 154, 237, 248–50, 329, 354 n.26; "Of Captain Misson," 89–91; *Captain Singleton*, 17, 18, 22, 77–102, 241; *Colonel Jack*, 78, 349 n.11, 394 n.24; *Farther Adventures (Robinson Crusoe 2)*, 83–84, 93, 275, 288; *General History of the Pyrates*, 84–99; *Jonathan Wild*, 78; *King of Pirates*, 78; *Moll Flanders*, 94; *New Voyage Round the World*, 83, 99–100; *Robinson Crusoe*, 15, 17, 18, 22, 71–73, 74–76, 78, 83–84, 93, 144, 249–50, 252, 276–78, 280, 281, 351 n.17; *Roxana*, 173; *Serious Reflections (Robinson Crusoe 3)*, 98, 275; *The True-Born Englishman*, 91, 236, 361 n.23; "A Vision of the Angelic World," 98, 275

Deleuze, Gilles, 15, 17

Delon, Michel, 299

Denis (Saint), 222–23

Dennis, John, 112–13, 114, 120, 124

Denton, William, 247

Derrida, Jacques, 16, 323, 328, 375 n.26

Despotism, 20, 125, 159, 170, 190–229, 329

Dessalines, Jean-Jacques, 310, 314, 324

D'Herbelot, Barthélémy, 214–15, 386 n.49

Diderot, Denis, 23, 193, 274, 290–321 passim

Dieckmann, Herbert, 296

Dimock, Wai Chee, 287, 400 n.96

Dodd, William, 251

Domergue, Urbain, 317

Douglass, Frederick, 247

Dryden, John, 111, 121, 126, 361 n.18, 362 n.23

Duchet, Michèle, 295-96

Dumont, Jean, 165

Dupuy, Alex, 310

Du Vignau (Sieur des Joanots), 374 n.23, 375 nn. 24, 25, 379 n.52

Economics. *See* Capitalism; Commodities and Commodification; Mercantilism

Eighteenth-century studies, 12-16, 329-31, 335 n.17

Elizabeth I, 146

Ellison, Julie, 113-14, 124

English language, 10, 15, 186-87, 234-35, 264-65, 266, 397 n.59

Enlightenment, 23, 134, 140, 190-91, 205, 222-23, 255, 275, 288, 290, 295-99, 307, 313, 318, 326-31, 402 n.5, 403 n.7

Epictetus, 108, 142, 145, 165

Epistolarity, 159-85 passim, 375 n.26

Epstein, William H., 12, 335 n.19

Equiano, Olaudah, 11, 14, 80, 115, 155, 289, 291, 303, 329, 395 n.41; *Interesting Narrative,* 235-88

Erasmus, Desiderius: *Adagia,* 2; *Apothegmata,* 148

Ethiopia, 192, 203-13, 383 n.33, 384 nn. 34, 35, 385 nn. 39, 40

Euripides, 319

Fabricant, Carol, 148

Factish, 269-88. *See also* Agency; Fetish(ism)

Falconbridge, Alexander, 259, 261, 266

Falconbridge, Anna Maria, 238, 249, 258-66

Faller, Lincoln, 355 n.26

Fanon, Frantz, 13, 326-28

Femininity, 162, 166, 168, 190, 319

Ferguson, Frances, 196

Ferguson, Margaret, 30, 31

Ferguson, Moira, 17-18, 30, 31

Ferriar, John: *The Prince of Angola,* 63

Fetish(ism), 22, 32, 38, 141, 173, 177, 215, 234, 236, 238, 245, 271-83, 286-87, 314, 329, 398 nn. 77, 78

Fichtelberg, Joseph, 237

Fielding, Henry, 80

Firth, Charles, 136

Foucault, Michel, 11, 190, 194, 206, 222-23, 326-31

France, 115, 128, 131, 133, 190, 194, 210-11, 233, 291-318 passim. *See also* Revolution: French

Franklin, Benjamin, 106

French language, 292-324 passim

Freud, Sigmund, 11, 274, 275, 278, 328

Froger, François, 239

Frowde, Philip: *The Fall of Saguntum,* 115

Frye, Northrop, 244

Furniss, Tom, 223

Fyfe, Christopher, 266

Gallagher, Catherine, 30, 31

Garrick, David, 63-64, 66

Gates, Henry Louis, Jr., 269-71, 279, 281

Gay, John: *The Beggar's Opera,* 84-85

Gellius, Lucius, 121, 134

Gennari, Benedetto, 34, 36, 37

George I, 111, 129, 145, 149, 151, 152

Germany, 115, 163, 166

Gillray, James, 227-28

Girard, René, 319

Godwin, Francis, 205-7

Gordon, Thomas. *See* Trenchard, John

Gothic themes, 188, 191, 201, 212, 218, 224, 260, 387 n.52, 389 n.64

Grand Tour, 179, 362 n.27

Gray, Thomas, 312

Grégoire, Abbé Henri, 249, 252, 258, 299, 393 n.22

Gronniosaw, Ukawsaw, 249, 252, 269-70

Grosrichard, Alain, 191, 194-95, 221

Guattari, Félix, 15

Gumilla, Joseph, 315

Habermas, Jürgen, 56, 175

Haiti, 289, 292, 302-25 passim, 329. *See also* Revolution: Haitian

Hamilton, Alexander, 134-35

Hammam, 162, 169-84

Hardy, Thomas: as a radical, 268

Harem, 164-65, 170-75, 178, 375 n.28

Harrington, James, 105, 128

Hastings, Warren, 20, 198, 211, 224-27

Hawkesworth, John, 29, 63

Hecht, J. Jean, 41

Henley, Samuel, 220, 386 n.48

Hill, Aaron, 164, 170, 372 n.11

Hill, Christopher, 352 n.20

Hoare, Prince, 264, 266

Hobbes, Thomas, 92, 105, 180, 318, 354 n.26, 378 n.40

Hobsbawm, E. J., 352 n.20

Hoegberg, David, 65

Hogarth, William, 64, 66, 129

Holland (Netherlands), 128, 133, 163, 296

Holland, Peter, 62

Homer, 199

Homoeroticism, 77, 95-98, 355 n.29, 356 n.31, 377 n.39, 387 n.52. *See also* Femininity; Masculinity; Race: and sexuality; Women: and sexuality

Hottentots (Khoi), 296

Hugues, Victor, 309

Hulme, Peter, 75

Hume, David, 273-74, 290

Hume, Robert D., 49

Huntingdon, Countess of (Selina Hastings), 243

Hurd, Richard, 234

Hutcheon, Linda, 344 n.32

Hutner, Heidi, 30

Igbo society, 252, 281, 282, 285

Imperialism, 14, 144-45, 155, 234-35, 237, 268, 295, 300, 307, 320, 323. *See also* Colonialism

India, 20, 88, 127, 128, 224-27

Ingres, Jean-Auguste-Dominique, 175

Inoculation, 162, 183-89

Ireland, 127, 134, 143-56, 268, 369 n.66

Irwin, Joseph, 237, 257

Islam. *See* Religion: Islamic

Jacobins, 155, 156, 192, 227, 268-69, 291, 293-95, 306. *See also* James, C. L. R.

Jacobites, 104, 107, 110, 119, 123, 125, 134, 155, 211, 354 n.24, 363 n.31, 369 n.68, 390 n.69

Jacobus, Mary, 312

Jamaica, 83, 126, 217, 285, 307, 367 n.53

James II, 45, 146

James, C. L. R.: *The Black Jacobins*, 292, 302, 309-10, 313, 324, 401 n.4

Jameson, Fredric, 243-44

Jay, Martin, 191

Jenner, Edward, 184

Jervas, Charles, 171, 175, 177

Job ben Solomon, 251

John the Baptist, Saint, 201

Johnson, Charles: *The Successful Pyrate*, 92, 356 n.31

Johnson, Samuel, 63, 110, 112, 224, 233, 290, 329; *Irene*, 202; *Journey to the Western Islands*, 213-14; *Rasselas*, 15, 20, 191, 202-13, 251; "Seged," 208-9

Jones, Charles, 266
Justus Lipsius, 108, 119-20

Kamdar, Mira, 314
Kant, Immanuel, 193, 197, 274, 328
Kantorowicz, Ernst, 45
Karsten, Franz, 298
Kaul, Suvir, 32, 67
Kendal, Duchess of (Ehrengard Melusina von der Schulenberg), 129, 145
Kidd, William (Captain), 83, 354 n.24
King, William (Archbishop of Dublin), 146
Knight, Ellis Cornelia: *Dinarbas*, 204-5, 385 n.40
Knight, Robert, 129
Kolb, Gwin J., 202-3
Kréyole (Haitian), 309, 322, 324
Kristeva, Julia, 299, 404 n.15

Lafitau, Joseph-François, 274
Lamb, Jonathan, 73, 202
Landry, Donna, 13, 335 n.19
Laplanche, Jean, 160
Las Casas, Bartolomé de, 290-91
Latour, Bruno, 274
Law, John, 128
Leclerc, Victor-Emmanuel, 310
Lee, Nathaniel: *Lucius Junius Brutus*, 113
Lely, Peter, 37
Lennox, Charlotte, 165
Levantinization, 159-229; defined, 19-21, 159-61
Lillo, George, 109
Liminality and reaggregation, 161-62, 169-70, 181-82, 184-87, 237, 239-41, 262
Linebaugh, Peter, 87, 352 n.19
Lipking, Joanna, 40-41

Literacy: 10, 16, 17, 214, 233-35, 238, 263-68, 269-90, 293, 298-300, 302-3, 309, 314, 329. *See also* Literature; Nationalization
Literature, 170, 182, 233-36, 238, 246, 253, 263-88 passim, 317-18, 330-31
Liu, Alan, 212, 385 n.38, 388 n.57
Livy (Titus Livius), 122
Lloyd, David, 344 n.31
Lobo, Jeronimo, 203, 384 n.35
Lock, F. P., 136
Locke, John, 105, 125, 128, 146, 193, 194, 199
Longinus, Dionysius, 198, 386 n.44
Louis XIV, 38, 363 n.34
Louis XVI, 267, 317
Louis Napoleon (Napoleon III), 314
Louverture, Toussaint. *See* Toussaint Louverture
Lowe, Lisa, 159, 165
Lowenthal, Cynthia, 161, 174
Lowndes, William, 146
Lucan (Marcus Annaeus Lucanus), 108
Lüsebrink, Hans-Jürgen, 293, 294-95, 299, 300
Lyotard, Jean-François, 191, 201-2

Machiavellianism, 105, 117, 118, 128
Madagascar, 85, 88, 90-91, 96
Makandal, François, 322
Mallet, David: *Mustapha*, 115-16
Mandeville, Bernard, 109, 126, 147
Marat, Jean-Paul: *Les chaines de l'esclavage*, 4, 106, 306
Marie-Antoinette, 227-28
Maritime culture, 76-77, 86, 93, 239-41, 253, 265. *See also* Piracy
Markley, Robert, 100
Marlborough, Duke and Duchess of (John and Sarah Churchill), 110, 111
Marrant, John, 249, 250, 269-70

Martin George, 43

Marx, Karl, 272, 274, 275, 277, 297, 314, 327, 333 n.4

Mary II, 45

Mary of Modena (James II's queen), 45

Masculinity, 39, 43, 114, 163, 170, 175–76, 179, 182–83, 190, 315, 319, 327–28. *See also* Femininity; Homoeroticism

Masquerade and carnival, 162, 166–71, 177–80, 183, 227, 239–41

Matthews, John, 256, 262, 278

May, Thomas, 108, 119

Mazarin, Duchess of (Hortense Mancini), 34, 36, 37, 38, 46

McCalman, Iain, 268

McKeon, Michael, 2, 163–64

McMahon, Marie, 128

Melman, Billie, 159

Mercantilism, 18, 23, 79, 81–82, 86–87, 91–93, 101, 102, 103–5, 107, 109, 114, 124–27, 140–41, 154, 237, 246, 247–48, 251, 256, 258, 273, 290–92, 295. *See also* Commodities and Commodification

Mercier, Louis-Sébastien, 134, 300–302

Metaliteracy, 271, 273, 281, 289–92, 300–325. *See also* Literacy; Nationalization

Mignard, Pierre, 34–35, 37, 338 n.10

Miller, Christopher, 391 n.3

Milton, John, 112, 159, 180, 253

Mimoso-Ruiz, Duarte, 322, 408 n.38

Minority literature, 235, 236, 238, 269–88

Mirabeau, Count (Honoré-Gabriel-Riqueti), 317

Mishra, Vijay, 218, 387 n.54

Mitchell, W. J. T., 197–98, 382 n.20

Moïse, 310, 311

Molesworth, Viscount Robert, 131, 153, 369 n.68

Molyneux, William, 152, 193

Monboddo, Lord (James Burnett), 188

Montagu, Lady Mary Wortley, 14, 19, 109, 192, 259, 262, 329; *Letters from the Levant (Turkish Embassy Letters)*, 19, 159–89; *The Nonsense of Common Sense*, 165

Montesquieu, Baron (Charles-Louis de Secondat), 190, 191, 194–95, 221

Montgolfier brothers (Joseph-Michel and Jacques-Étienne), 210–11

Moore, J. R., 86, 351 n.18, 354 n.26

Morgan, Henry, 83

Morrison, Toni, 114

Moulin, Anne-Marie, 168–69

Mountfort Verbruggen, Susanna, 57

Muhammad II (Emperor), 201–2, 222

Murray, David: *Sophonisba*, 124

Murry, Middleton, 154

Naimbanna, King, 261–62

Naimbanna, Prince (Henry Granville), 262, 272

Napoleon Bonaparte (Napoleon I), 298, 300–314

Nationalism: British, 10, 13, 114–16, 140–41, 190, 233–35, 238, 242, 244, 283–85, 288, 372 n.11; French, 292–300; Haitian, 292, 300–315; and national allegory, 114–26, 315–17; and national regeneration, 315–18, 324, 325

Nationalization, 233–325; defined, 21–24, 233–35, 244, 282–83, 286, 289, 292, 315

Neal, Larry, 128–29

Neoclassicism, 103–56 passim, 165, 187–89, 190, 204, 321–22

Neocolonialism, 16, 237, 287, 325

Neostoicism, 17, 18, 103–56. *See also* Addison, Joseph; Stoicism; Swift, Jonathan; Trenchard, John

Newman, Gerald, 233

Nichols, Arthur, 63
Nietzsche, Friedrich, 11
North Africa, 104, 113–27, 162, 163, 173, 187–88, 203
Novak, Maximillian E., 354 n.26, 356 n.30
Nudity, 169, 171, 175–76, 180–82. *See also* Clothing
Nussbaum, Felicity, 12, 173, 335 n.17

O'Brien, Conor Cruise, 390 n.69
O'Connor, Arthur, 155–56
Olney, James, 250
Orality, 150, 270, 287, 369 n.66. *See also* Literacy; Metaliteracy
Oriental despotism. *See* Despotism
Orientalism, 10, 19, 159–60, 163, 168, 173, 189, 192, 204, 218. *See also* Despotism; Levantinization
Orme, Daniel, 247
Ottoman Empire, 19, 126–27, 131, 159–89, 192, 194, 201–2, 363 n.34
Otway, Thomas: *The Orphan*, 113
Ovid (Publius Ovidius Naso), 317
Oxford, Earl of (Robert Harley), 111, 128
Ozouf, Mona, 317–18

Parody, 59–61, 62, 64–65, 98–99, 141–42, 240, 261–62, 264, 265–66, 307, 344 nn. 32, 33, 388 n.57
Pascoe, C[harles] F[rederick], 246
Paterson, William: *Arminius*, 115
Patterson, Orlando, 66
Paulson, Ronald, 223
Pepys, Samuel, 174, 338 n.9
Performance, 81, 160–61, 169, 174, 175–79, 191, 193, 198, 201–2, 204, 213, 217, 219–21, 279–84; of Addison's *Cato*, 110–11, 121; of Southerne's *Oroonoko*, 62–64

Persia, 194–95
Peters, Hugh, 222
Peters, Thomas, 258
Pethood, 32–49, 55–56, 61–62, 66, 69–70, 75, 125, 277, 278, 329, 339 nn. 13, 14, 340 n.18, 347 n.43, 400 n.85
Philips, Ambrose: *The Briton*, 115
Philips, William: *Hibernia Freed*, 115
Phillipson, Nicholas, 364 n.36
Picart, (and) Bernard, 198–99, 317–18
Pietz, William, 273, 398 n.77, 399 n.78
Piracy, 17, 18, 77, 81–93, 100, 101–2, 126, 133, 140–41, 143, 239, 350 n.13, 355 n.29, 367 n.53. *See also* Maritime culture
Piranesi, Giambattista, 191, 218
Pitts, Walter, 245
Plutarch, 65
Pocock, J. G. A., 105, 125, 128, 352 n.20, 364 n.36
Pompey the Great (Gnaeus Pompeius Magnus), 64, 108, 122
Pontalis, Jean-Baptiste, 160
Pope, Alexander, 64–65, 110, 114, 154, 160, 178–79, 187, 200, 227, 376 n.35
Portsmouth, Duchess of (Louise Renée Penancoët de Kéroualle), 34–35, 37, 38, 46, 338 n.10
Postcolonialism: as identity, 22; as methodology, 12–16, 24, 235, 292, 315, 326–31
Postlethwayt, Malachy, 254
Potkay, Adam, 240, 241–44, 387 n.52, 392 nn. 8, 9, 393 n.13
Pratt, Mary Louise, 6, 18, 73
Prester John, 203, 204, 385 n.39
Pretender, Old (James Stuart), 123
Pretender, Young (Charles Edward Stuart), 104, 116
Price, Richard, 222
Prince, Mary, 249
Print culture, 10, 150, 233–35, 244–45,

Print culture (*continued*)
270–73, 308–9, 402 n.6, 403 n.7. *See also* Literacy
Prior, Matthew, 111

Quaque, Philip, 242, 246
Quin, James, 64, 66, 110

Rabbitt, Kara, 313
Race: and aesthetics, 193–94; and atavistic fantasies, 162, 188; and "color" of narrative, 250; and debasement, 2–4, 270; and deformity, 188, 218–21; as epistemology for Gulliver, 137–39, 141–43, 155; in Haitian politics, 308–9, 324–25; hybridity of, 270; as metaphoric principle, 59; as metonymic principle, 59, 114; and passing, 116, 161, 184, 239–41, 285; polymorphousness of, 76; and purification, 1–4, 254; and racialism vs. racism, 2, 10, 333 n.1; and religious exclusion, 246–47 (*see also* Religion); and sentimentalism, 113–14, 312, 315; and sexuality, 31, 38–40, 43–44, 52, 57–59, 64, 66, 260, 284, 341 n.21; as transitive, 116, 124; typing of African Americans vs. Afro-Britons, 247. *See also* Blackness
Ramsay, James, 253–54
Rapin-Thoyras, Paul de, 115
Rawson, Claude, 136, 138–39
Raynal, Abbé Guillaume-Thomas de, 291, 293–95, 299, 302; *Adresse à l'Assemblée Nationale*, 293–94; *Histoire des deux Indes*, 23, 88, 206, 289–325, 401 n.3
Rediker, Marcus, 86, 88, 350 n.13
Reeve, Clara: *Charoba*, 215
Religion: African, 245, 273; Amerindian, 198, 200; Anglican, 133, 240, 242, 246–47, 256; Armenian,

188; Arminian, 241, 244; Arnount, 187; Bektash, 379 n.53; Calvinist, 112, 241, 244, 252; Catholic, 115, 129, 134, 155, 163, 285; of Cham-Chi-Thaungu, 275; Chinese, 163; Christian (in general), 170, 180, 187, 203, 241, 245, 247, 280, 284, 285, 286, 311, 321–22; Deist, 187; Dissenting, 104; Druidical, 198, 200; Evangelical, 236, 240–47; Greek, 218; Hindu, 198, 256; Huntingdonian, 241; Igbo, 241–42, 245; Islamic, 159, 163, 170, 182, 187, 203, 224–25; Jewish, 129, 241–42, 285; Methodist, 240, 242, 269; Millenarian, 268, 269; Monophysite, 203; and origins of fetish, 273–74; Pagan, 122, 275; polytheist, 273; Protestant, 217, 237, 256; Puritan, 129, 238, 277; Quaker, 94, 247, 248; Satanic, 72, 275, 277; voodoo, 292, 313, 315, 321–23
Renan, Ernest, 233
Republicanism, 103–25 passim, 137, 163, 255–56, 297–98, 306
Revolution: American, 103, 104, 106, 134–35, 156, 253, 258, 291, 401 n.3; English, 104, 222; French, 22, 23, 155–56, 198, 200, 222, 223–29, 267, 291–300, 306, 308–10, 312–13, 324; Glorious, 30, 107, 110, 112, 152; Gutenberg, 272; Haitian, 14, 23, 134, 292, 299–325, 329; perpetual, 329; socialist, 16, 327
Richardson, Jonathan, 185–86
Richardson, Samuel: *Clarissa*, 3
Rivers, Isabel, 241
Rivière, Joan, 162, 189
Roach, Joseph, 338 n.10
Robbins, Caroline, 135
Robespierre, Maximilien, 294–95, 306, 324
Roche, Daniel, 293, 297

Rodowick, David N., 17

Rome, 92, 104–35 passim, 255, 285, 354 n.26

Rose, Margaret, 59, 344 n.32

Rosenthal, Laura, 67–68

Ross, George, 267

Rousseau, Jean-Jacques, 303

Rowe, Nicholas, 108, 113; *Jane Shore,* 117

Rushdie, Salman, 5, 11, 15

Rycaut, Sir Paul, 164, 377 n.39

Said, Edward, 136; *Orientalism,* 13

Saint-Domingue. *See* Haiti

Sams, Henry, 109, 359 n.7

Sancho, Ignatius, 252, 263–64, 395 n.33

Sartre, Jean-Paul, 327

Saunderson, Nicholas, 196

Scot, William, 43

Sedgwick, Eve Kosofsky, 54–55

Selam (secret language), 168–69, 179, 185, 374 nn. 23, 24

Seneca, Lucius Annaeus, 112, 122, 319

Sentimentalism, 32, 61, 62, 70, 113, 126, 251, 307, 347 n.43. *See also* Race: and sentimentalism

Sessarakoo, William Ansah, 251

Sexuality. *See* Colonialism: as sexual acquisition; Homoeroticism; Race: and sexuality; Women: and sexuality

Shaftesbury, Earl of (Anthony Ashley Cooper), 126, 197

Shakespeare, William: *Henry VIII,* 117; *Julius Caesar,* 373 n.14; *King Lear,* 117; *The Merchant of Venice,* 117; *Othello,* 49, 64, 66, 117, 142, 250–52, 373 n.14; *Richard II,* 45; *Richard III,* 117; *The Tempest,* 6

Sharp, Granville, 255–59, 264–67, 395 nn. 39, 41

Sherman, Sandra, 100

Sierra Leone (and Resettlement Proj-

ect), 22, 236–37, 249, 251, 253–68, 286–87, 396 n.50. *See also* West Africa

Sierra Leonean settlers: Jamaican maroons as, 267–68; mortality of, 239–40, 257–60, 396 n.45; Nova Scotian blacks as, 258–59, 267–68; resistance of, 260, 264–68, 302; treatment of, 254–58, 260; writings of, 237–38, 264–67, 269, 275, 289

Sill, Geoffrey, 74

Slavery: and Defoe, 74–76; and emancipation, 115, 242, 254–58, 283, 285, 308–10, 397 n.66; etymology of, 5; French, 253–54; and illiteracy, 269–72; institution of, 236, 246, 247, 279, 284, 291; and marronage, 70, 226, 322; and patriarchy, 346 n.42; and rebellion against, 31, 43–48, 70, 90, 121, 138, 226, 254, 292, 300–315, 329, 341 n.20, 367 n.53; and slave narrative genre, 235, 247, 282, 323; and slave trade, 6–9, 34–38, 43, 52, 54, 60, 69–70, 90, 237, 262–64, 265, 284, 291, 306; as trope, 306, 308, 319, 329, 405 n.21. *See also* Abolition(ism); Slave(s)

Slave(s): and body, 311–12; and currency, 38–39, 43, 68, 268, 278, 339 n.11, 342 n.24, 343 n.29; European women as, 50–55, 179; former, 247, 268; Greeks mistaken as, 165; as pets, 34–49; punishment of, 45–49, 69, 201–2, 253; renaming of, 64–66, 244–45, 284; runaway, 345 n.40; and sacrifice, 320–24; Turkish women mistaken as, 170. *See also* Abolition(ism); Slavery

Smallpox, 183–84, 378 n.47. *See also* Inoculation

Smeathman, Henry, 255

Smith, Adam, 248, 274

Smith, Olivia, 264

Smollett, Tobias, 183, 239, 378 n.45

Sonthonax, Léger-Félicite, 309

Soulouque Faustin (Faustin I), 314

Southerne, Thomas, 18, 49; *Oroonoko*, 38, 49-59, 68-69, 121, 329, 341 n.22, 343 n.30

South Sea Bubble, 18, 104, 127-35, 367 n.53. *See also* Mercantilism

Spain, 290-91, 309, 404 n.13

Spartacus, 121, 134; "black Spartacus," 292, 300-316, 323, 324, 405 n.17, 408 n.38

Spence, Joseph, 196, 376 n.34, 381 n.13

Spengemann, William, 30, 31

Spivak, Gayatri Chakravorty, 5, 13, 33, 281, 314, 320, 334 n.9, 405 n.21

Stedman, John Gabriel, 6-9, 47, 52

Steele, Richard, 34, 109, 110

St. John, J. A., 159

Stoicism, 103-4, 106, 108-9, 112, 141-43, 145, 165, 311-12, 372 n.13. *See also* Neostoicism

Street, Brian, 264, 272

Subaltern: history, 281; identity, 282, 314; as projection, 6, 14. *See also* Agency; Tropicopolitan(s)

Subject: aesthetic, 190-94, 200-202; becoming, 272, 278-80, 284; black, 270-71, 273, 282; blind, 191-96; bourgeois, 95, 244, 333 n.4; Britain as collective, 234, 273; colonialist, 314; democratic, 296-98, 306; early modern, 95; "eccentric," 299; emancipated, 327; and fantasy, 160; female, 164, 166, 169, 171, 179-80 (*see also* Femininity; Women); Friday as, 74-76, 277, 278; Gulliver as split, 137-39; historically constructed, 327-28; honorary, 44, 161; infantile, 219; Juba as, 116; Levantine, 181; literate, 269-88; medieval, 244; modern, 101, 244; political, 191; postcolonial,

283; rationalist, 297, 299; Robinson Crusoe as, 72-73, 275-78; virtual, 33, 39, 44-45, 55-56, 116, 124, 277, 307. *See also* Agency; Pethood

Sublime, aesthetics of the, 20, 48, 159, 190-229, 312, 329, 381 n.19

Suleri, Sara, 224

Surinam, 41, 42, 47. *See also* Caribbean

Sussman, Charlotte, 31, 366 n.47

Swedenborg, Emanuel, 255, 395 n.37

Swift, Jonathan, 14, 22, 110, 126, 156, 329, 367 n.55; *The Drapier's Letters*, 18, 104, 111, 136, 143, 145-55, 369 n.68; *Gulliver's Travels*, 18, 40, 61, 99, 104, 135-45, 154, 373 n.18; *A Modest Proposal*, 155; *The Tatler*, 142

Swinburne, Algernon, 49

Tacitus, Gaius Cornelius, 122; *Germania*, 115

Technology: colonialism and, 205-8, 400 n.84; of literacy, 269-88

Teltscher, Kate, 224

Tennenhouse, Leonard, 95

Theobald, Lewis, 108

Thomas, Keith, 33, 39

Thompson, E. P., 99, 266, 357 n.32

Thompson, James, 101

Thompson, Thomas, 286, 394 n.31

Thomson, James, 115; *Sophonisba*, 113, 114, 123-25, 362 n.28

Tiebout, Cornelius, 247

Tietz, Manfred, 293, 299, 404 n.13

Tindal, Nicholas, 115

Tobacco, 47, 69, 277, 340 n.19, 343 n.29

Tobin, James, 254

Tocqueville, Aléxis de, 297

Todd, Janet, 29, 46

Tories, 103-35 passim. *See also* Whigs

Tourism, 170, 172, 187-88. *See also* Travel narrative

Toussaint Louverture, 11, 14, 23–24, 134, 155, 291–92, 299–315

Trade. *See* Capitalism; Commodities and Commodification; Mercantilism

Travel narrative, 40, 159, 163–70, 184–85, 189, 239, 295–96, 371 n.8, 373 n.15. *See also* Tourism

Trenchard, John, and Thomas Gordon: *Cato's Letters*, 104, 127–35, 148, 156. *See also* South Sea Bubble

Trope(s): of accounting, 73, 76, 77–102, 160; apostrophe as, 297–99, 307; as attitudinal shift, 2, 32; Biblical, 241–45; of blackamoor, 1–4, 185; of black surrogacy, 114, 325; of blinding, 20, 204; of cannibalism, 76, 131, 190, 226, 236, 252–53, 265, 324, 349 n.8; catachresis as, 5, 281; and Cato, 103, 106, 127, 134–35; of checker-work, 249–50; of Christomimesis, 45, 47–48, 243; counterallegory as, 136; of deafness, 213–14, 218–21; of decapitation, 201–2; defined by Chambers, 1–3; diasparagmos as, 322; disciplinary opportunity of, 3; of emasculation, 327; of euhemerism, 282, 284, 310, 312–13; of eunuch, 219, 221, 245, 256; and Faust, 217; of flight, 205–8, 209–11; of footprint, 71–73, 74; and Jews, 126; and Juba, 116; of Levant (East), 159, 187–89; of levant (wager), 160, 170, 183, 189; of Levanter (wind), 159, 226; of materialist metamorphosis, 142; and Medea, 23–24, 292, 315–25, 406 n.32, 408 n.38; metalepsis as, 4; metaphor as, 1–3, 59, 272, 310–12; metonymy as, 59, 272, 280; of Moor, 114; of mulatto, 114; national allegory as, 116, 119, 315–17; and Oroonoko, 99; of passions, 124; of piracy, 91–92, 100, 358 n.34; and polemic vs. meta-

polemic, 133; of rape, 327–28; rebus as, 168–69, 245, 322; of royal slave, 33, 42, 44–49, 65–66, 121, 125, 250–52, 303, 311–12, 323; of shibboleth, 324; of soulouquerie, 314; of Stoic, 156; of talking book, 236, 269–91, 314, 329; of tropical baptism, 238–40, 253, 392 n.7; as vehicle for agency, 11. *See also* Tropicalization; Tropicopolitan(s)

Tropicalization: defined, 5–6; as goal, 330; as open-ended, 15–16; as retroactive change, 10, 292; as revision of discourse, 15, 24, 281, 290; and trope as reversible, 24. *See also* Levantinization; Nationalization; Trope(s); Tropicopolitan(s); Virtualization

Tropicopolitan(s): as colonial pawn, 313; as constituting aesthetics, 192; defined, 4–5; as factish, 283; and new contexts, 329–31; as unintended addressee of discourse of colonialism, 307. *See also* Agency; Subject; Trope(s); Tropicalization

Tropology. *See* Trope(s)

Trotskyism, 292, 302, 310

Tryon, Thomas, 39, 67, 347 n.43

Turkey, 159–89 passim. *See also* Ottoman Empire

Turkish women. *See* Women: Turkish

Turley, Hans, 95

Turner, J[oseph] M[allord] W[illiam], 191

Turner, Victor, 169–70, 181, 379 n.49

Universalism, 203–4, 234, 241, 281, 285, 290

Van Dyck, Anthony, 34

Vanmour, Jean-Baptiste, 171–73, 185

Vassa, Gustavus. *See* Brooke, Henry; Equiano, Olaudah

Vegetarianism, 347 n.43
Vico, Giambattista, 292
Virtualization, 29–102; defined, 16–
19, 60, 67, 106, 292, 315. *See also*
Pethood; Subject: virtual
Virtue. *See* Neostoicism; Stoicism
Vision, 190–219, 291, 329
Voltaire (François-Marie Arouet), 201,
219, 221, 290

Wadstrom, Charles, 255
Wagstaffe, William, 378 n.47
Walker, Ellis, 367 n.54
Waller, Edmund, 111
Wallerstein, Immanuel, 237
Walpole, Horace, 179, 183, 377 n.36
Walpole, Robert, 84–85, 129, 132, 134,
146–47, 152–53, 154, 351 n.17, 377 n.38
Wanley, Nathaniel, 119–20
Warren, Susan, 237
Washington, George, 116, 135, 365 n.45
Webster, Noah, 106
Wedderburn, Robert, 269
Wedgwood, Josiah, 5
Wehrung, Maurice, 79
Wesley, John, 241, 257, 269
West Africa, 236, 242, 252–64, 276–86,
313. *See also* Sierra Leone
West Indies. *See* Caribbean
Wharton, Thomas, 127
Wheatley, Phillis, 263–64
Wheeler, Roxann, 76
Whigs, 12, 103–35 passim, 154, 163, 189
Whitefield, George, 240, 241, 243
Wilberforce, William, 268, 269
William III, 38, 45, 51, 111, 126, 339 n.11
Williams, Eric, 401 n.4
Williams, Francis, 263–64
Williams, Raymond, 13
Willoughby of Parham, Francis, 41, 42,
46
Wollstonecraft, Mary, 285
Women: and agency, 14, 50–57, 160–
61, 166, 292, 321, 323; Amazonian,
323; and authorship, 29, 160, 162–
69, 180, 182–83; black, 31–32, 57–
59, 193–96, 200, 201, 219, 228, 382
n.19; and colonial democracy, 259;
as crypto-lesbian, 168–69, 179; as
female Quixotes, 165; and gender
anxiety, 43, 130, 165; German, 166,
171; as infanticides, 319, 321; and
male oppression, 319; and metaliteracy, 315–24; as mimics, 167; and
monstrosity, 322–23; and Orient,
159; of Orinoco, 315, 319–21; and
pets, 34–41, 66, 185; of Prague, 166;
and prostitution, 260; and public
sphere, 56–57, 175; and sacrifice, 292,
323; and sexuality, 168–69, 181–82,
284, 319–20; and Stoicism, 122–24,
165, 312; Turkish, 160–61, 162, 164–
65, 170–74, 329; Viennese, 166; and
violence, 315–23; and voodoo, 321–
23. *See also* Femininity; Masculinity;
Subject
Wood, William, 145, 146–50, 151, 154
Wordsworth, William, 220, 292, 310–
12, 406 nn. 27, 28
World history, 290–92, 327, 331
Wortley, Edward, 19, 159, 165, 178, 179,
362 n.27, 375 n.26, 377 n.37
Wortley Montagu, Edward, 172
Wycherley, William: *The Country Wife*,
54–55, 343 n.27

Xenophobia, 10

Yeats, William Butler, 154, 328, 370
n.69
Yeazell, Ruth Bernard, 175
Young, Edward: *Busiris*, 114

Zionism, 21
Žižek, Slavoj, 385 n.38

*Srinivas Aravamudan is Associate Professor of English
and Comparative Literature at the University
of Washington.*

Library of Congress Cataloging-in-Publication Data
Aravamudan, Srinivas.
Tropicopolitans : colonialism and agency, 1688–1804 /
Srinivas Aravamudan.
p.   cm. — (Post-contemporary interventions)
Includes index.
ISBN 0-8223-2283-8 (cloth : alk. paper). —
ISBN 0-8223-2315-X (pbk. : alk. paper)
1. English literature—18th century—History and criticism.
2. Colonies in literature.   3. Nationalism and literature—
Great Britain—Colonies—History.   4. French literature—
18th century—History and criticism.   5. Nationalism and
literature—France—Colonies—History.   6. Imperialism in
literature.   7. Slavery in literature.   8. Blacks in literature.
9. Colonies—History.   I. Title.   II. Series.
PR448.C64A73   1999
820.9'358—DC21   98-23374
CIP